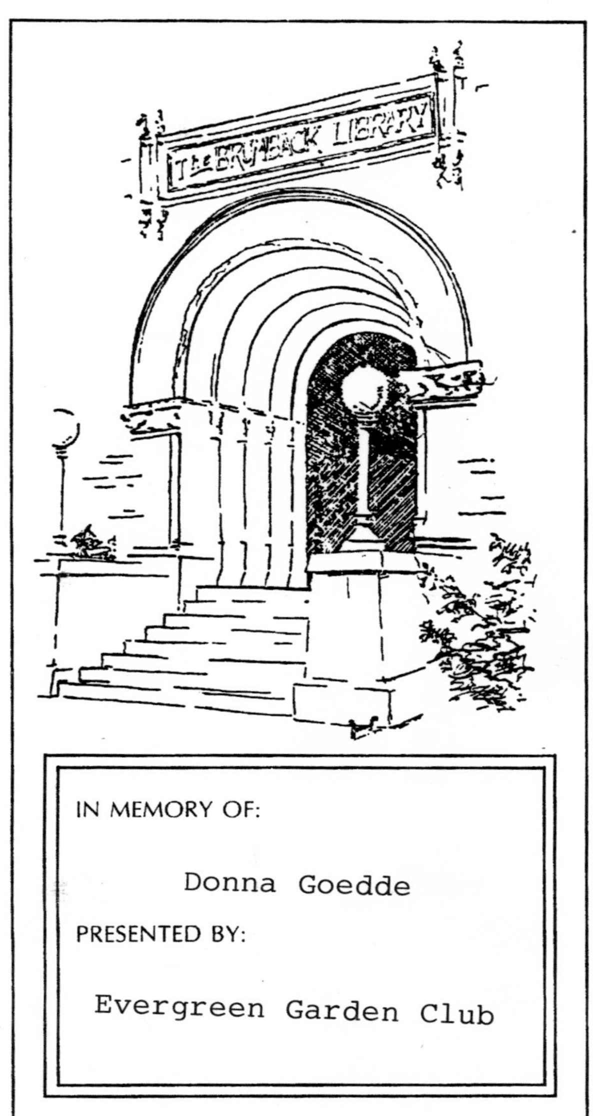

IN MEMORY OF:

Donna Goedde

PRESENTED BY:

Evergreen Garden Club

PERENNIALS

The Gardener's Reference

SUSAN CARTER

CARRIE BECKER

BOB LILLY

Foreword by Ann Lovejoy

Photographs by Lynne Harrison

Timber Press

635.932
CAR

Frontispiece: A summer border, *Agapanthus* 'Prolific Blue', with the New Zealand grass *Anemanthele lessoniana*, *Crocosmia ×crocosmiiflora* 'Solfatare', *C.* 'Jenny Bloom', *Rudbeckia fulgida* var. *sullivantii* 'Goldsturm', and *Cornus sericea* 'Sunshine'; foreground, *Lysimachia nummularia* 'Aurea' and *Ophiopogon planiscapus* 'Nigrescens'.

To Mousemilk, Bullslops, and Treacleberries

Text copyright © 2007 by Susan Carter, Carrie Becker, and Bob Lilly.
Photographs © 2007 by Lynne Harrison.
All rights reserved.

Published in 2007 by

Timber Press, Inc.
The Haseltine Building
133 S.W. Second Avenue, Suite 450
Portland, Oregon 97204-3527, U.S.A.

www.timberpress.com

For contact information regarding editorial, marketing, sales, and distribution in the United Kingdom, see www.timberpress.co.uk.

Printed in China

Library of Congress Cataloging-in-Publication Data

Carter, Susan, 1944-
Perennials : the gardener's reference / Susan Carter, Carrie Becker, and Bob Lilly ; photographs by Lynne Harrison.
p. cm.
Includes bibliographical references and index.
ISBN 978-0-88192-820-4
1. Perennials. I. Becker, Carrie. II. Lilly, Bob, 1947- III. Title.
SB434.C37 2007
635.9′32--dc22 2006033224

A catalog record for this book is also available from the British Library.

CONTENTS

FOREWORD

If you love flowers in general and are perfectly content to make do with the seasonal offerings found at the grocery or hardware store or at a big box garden center, you don't really need this book (though it will vastly improve your gardening techniques and broaden your horticultural horizons in an astonishing manner). If, however, you lust after the rare and covet the unusual, desire choice collector's plants, or simply want to know how to care for a full range of perennial plants, this book is the one you have been longing for in vain, because it didn't previously exist.

Indeed, while browsing through these pages, you may find yourself rejoicing out loud. Here at last are the answers to questions that very few garden books address at all, let alone in depth. Where else will you find out how to site and plant or when and whether to pinch back or deadhead lovely creatures like *Armoracia rusticana* 'Variegata', *Meum athamanticum*, or *Telekia speciosa*?

Plant care is treated less generically here than is usual, and the voice of experience sings through very clearly. The overview of appropriate gardening practices may lift a few eyebrows, since some of the authors' recommendations contradict the simplistic and often soil damaging weed-and-feed approach taken by many generalists. The focus is on successful and sustainable techniques that steadily improve soil tilth and quality, reducing the need to feed and water your plants. As a walk in any natural environment demonstrates, healthy soil can support healthy plants very well without human inputs. When a bit of help is needed for a particular plant, you'll find specific suggestions for such assistance, along with timing tips.

The book in your hand is a genuine labor of love and the fruit of several lifetimes of hands-on experience, bolstered by sound theory. Those who have contributed to this volume represent hundreds of years of direct, practical, and daily practice of what is preached herein. Rather than saying "achilleas run," the authors spell out the habits and proclivities of as many achilleas as they find garden-worthy, explaining precisely how each varies from the other and where the runners might best be used.

Striking and culturally compatible combinations are liberally offered with the plant profiles, helping you to partner each plant pleasingly. You'll also find ideas for extending the season of interest for various vignettes, perhaps by prolonging a color story with appropriate companions, or by screening fading foliage with fresh.

I have watched with great interest as this book has gradually grown over the years. Most garden books offer the experience of one person, delivered in a single voice. Here, the three main authors (all with distinctive voices) are joined by guest gardeners who offer pithy and detailed observations of their own. A true collaboration, it is yet a coherent and tightly conceived guidebook that is easy to use and full of telling details. Welcome to one of the most enchanting aspects of the natural world—the magical kingdom of perennials. Perennials are indeed the lifeblood of the border, and there is to date no better introduction to that delightful company than this.

Ann Lovejoy
Bainbridge Island

Late spring in the shade, a north-facing bed under an old apple tree, with *Clematis montana* working its way up the trunk. In the foregound is *Omphalodes cappadocica*, *Pulmonaria longifolia* subsp. *cevennensis*, and the shiny foliage of *Colchicum autumnale*. Foliage repetition in the midground is courtesy of *Podophyllum pleianthum* and *Macleaya cordata*; the large central shrub in flower is *Viburnum lantana* 'Variefolium'.

PREFACE

This book is a collection of information gathered in collaboration. We, the ones who wrote it, have nearly two hundred years of collective gardening experience. Some of us garden on heavy clay, some on sandy soil; and a variety of experiences in growing plants have been had by all. Often we've had the pleasure of acquiring a plant new to us—and then the frustration of not being able to locate cultural information on the plant. We have read a great deal and have trialed (and errored) a lot of plants, figuring out how to grow them well. It became clear to us that there was a need for this information, in one place and easy to use. This prompted us to put it all in writing, and that is how this book came about. Now we will tell you how to use it—what's here, what's not, and why.

Sections concerning plant families and characteristics; plants for specific types of gardens and certain times of the year; and general garden maintenance follow. At the back of the book, you will find, among other things, a glossary of terms, some recommended reading (books we find useful), a list of nurseries and other sources for the plants, and a list of common names followed by their scientific counterparts for those of you who (like us) originally knew these plants by their charming colloquial and historical names. Speaking of books we find useful, the *RHS Plant Finder*, which is compiled and updated annually, is our final authority on plant nomenclature. Names are always in flux, but the *RHS Plant Finder* represents the most current information available on the subject.

Most importantly, in between, you will find an A-to-Z section—the bulk of the book—that tells genus by genus all the information we consider relevant for successful cultivation of the plants themselves. To convey these methods of maintenance for herbaceous perennials is the primary objective of this book. That is our focus. Each genus includes a chart of specific plants and their characteristics, to help with plant selection and siting. Also included are some subshrubs that are indispensable to the mixed herbaceous border. These small, hardy shrubs usually have perennial relatives and are often evergreen (*Convolvulus cneorum*, for example); if they die back part way in cold-winter conditions, they will regrow the following spring.

That covers what's here. What's not here is information on annuals, trees, most biennials, and most bulbs and shrubs. This book is not a complete plant dictionary by design. Why? This book concerns perennials that can be acquired and grown well in many parts of North America. Although our experience with gardening has been in the maritime region of the Pacific Northwest, the information we include about perennials is general and should be helpful to all those who grow herbaceous perennials.

ACKNOWLEDGMENTS

Our special thanks go to Ann Bucher and Susan Buckles for always being available to help us with this project. We appreciate the years of meeting in one or the other's home, their valuable editorial contributions, and their commitment to help us compile the most accurate information on perennials.

We also want to thank Susan Latter, Linda Longmire, Lee Neff, Linda Orantes, Darby Ringer, Luke Senior, and Sara Gerhart Snell, who gave us assistance with research and editing; Janet Endsley, who worked on format; and Cheryl Peterson, who helped with data entry.

We all began gardening at different times and were influenced by many people. From the early days of the Northwest Perennial Alliance: Kevin Nicolay, Jerry Sedenko, Roy Davidson, Jerry Flintoff, Pam Snow, Eleanor Carnwath, and, of course, Ann Lovejoy. From the lecture circuit, our mentors from Great Britain: Penelope Hobhouse, Rosemary Verey, Dilys Davies, Christopher Lloyd, and Graham Rice. From the Seattle area, our garden friends, whose gardens we actually had time to sit in: Susan and Barry Latter, Darlene and Dan Huntington, Mark Henry, Steve Antonow, Rosemary and Cliff Bailey, Barbara Flynn, the Severences, the Mulligans, Margaret Lockett, Pat and John Bender, Elfi and Bill Rahr, Loie Benedict, Marian Raitz, and Judy Prindle.

Where would we be without our grandparents, especially in those families where gardening skipped a generation? Our appetite for perennials would never have been met without all the wonderful growers we found through the years, either at the specialty plant sales or through the many retail nurseries who found plants for us, even the ones we didn't know we wanted or needed.

Finally, the Perennial Borders created by the Northwest Perennial Alliance (NPA) at the Bellevue Botanical Garden have been an inspiration and a laboratory for us all. Without that project, we would have learned less and might never have seen the need for this book.

PLANT FAMILIES AND CHARACTERISTICS

Plants are typically grouped into families based on similarities in their structures. Here we list the family names, both scientific and common (parenthetically), of the genera we chose as main entries in the A-to-Z portion of the book; a listing of those genera; and the dominating characteristics of each family.

Acanthaceae (acanthus family): acanthus, strobilanthes. Flowers in spikes, sometimes with brightly colored bracts.

Acoraceae (sweetflag family): acorus. Rhizomatous. Flowers are insignificant, in a spadix. Monocots.

Aizoaceae (fig marigold family): delosperma. Ice plants, fleshy leaves.

Alliaceae (onion family): agapanthus, allium, nectaroscordum. Flowers in umbels; members need sharp drainage, full sun; heavy feeders. All *Allium* species are true bulbs and edible. Monocots.

Alstroemeriaceae (Peruvian lily family): alstroemeria. Formerly part of the Liliaceae. Rhizomes and tubers. Invasive; exploding seed capsules. Monocots.

Apiaceae (carrot family): aegopodium, astrantia, chaerophyllum, cryptotaenia, eryngium, ferula, foeniculum, meum, myrrhis, oenanthe, pimpinella. Flowers in umbels; leaves divided and carrotlike. Taproots, and therefore difficult to divide, transplant, or move. Self-sows, some aggressively.

Apocynaceae (dogbane family): amsonia. Blue, starlike flowers.

Araceae (arum family): arisaema, arisarum, arum, dracunculus, pinellia, zantedeschia. Corms or rhizomes. Typically, flowers have a spathe and spadix, with the spathe enclosing the spadix. Prefers shade and moist, rich, well-drained soil. Best in an open woodland or high shade. Monocots.

Aristolochiaceae (birthwort family): asarum. Flowers are hidden under the foliage; cordate leaves. Grow in part shade to full shade; some are evergreen; drought tolerant once established; some like humus-rich soil.

Asclepiadaceae (milkweed family): asclepias. Leaves are simple. Milky sap; may have interesting seed capsules; sun lovers.

Asphodelaceae (asphodel family): asphodeline, eremurus, kniphofia. Formerly part of the Liliaceae. Flowers in spikes. Full sun, sharp drainage; prairie and steppe plants. Monocots.

Asteraceae (daisy family): achillea, anaphalis, anthemis, artemisia, aster, bidens, boltonia, buphthalmum, centaurea, chrysanthemum, chrysogonum, cirsium, coreopsis, cosmos, cynara, doronicum, echinacea, echinops, erigeron, eupatorium, helenium, helianthus, heliopsis, inula, kalimeris, leucanthemum, liatris, ligularia, petasites, rudbeckia, silphium, silybum, solidago, ×solidaster, stokesia, syneilesis, tanacetum, telekia, vernonia. The only thing the genera have in common is the flower. It consists of disk flowers and ray flowers arranged in a capitulum. This family (formerly the Compositae) has in the past been divided into tribes that happen to require similar culture. There is a

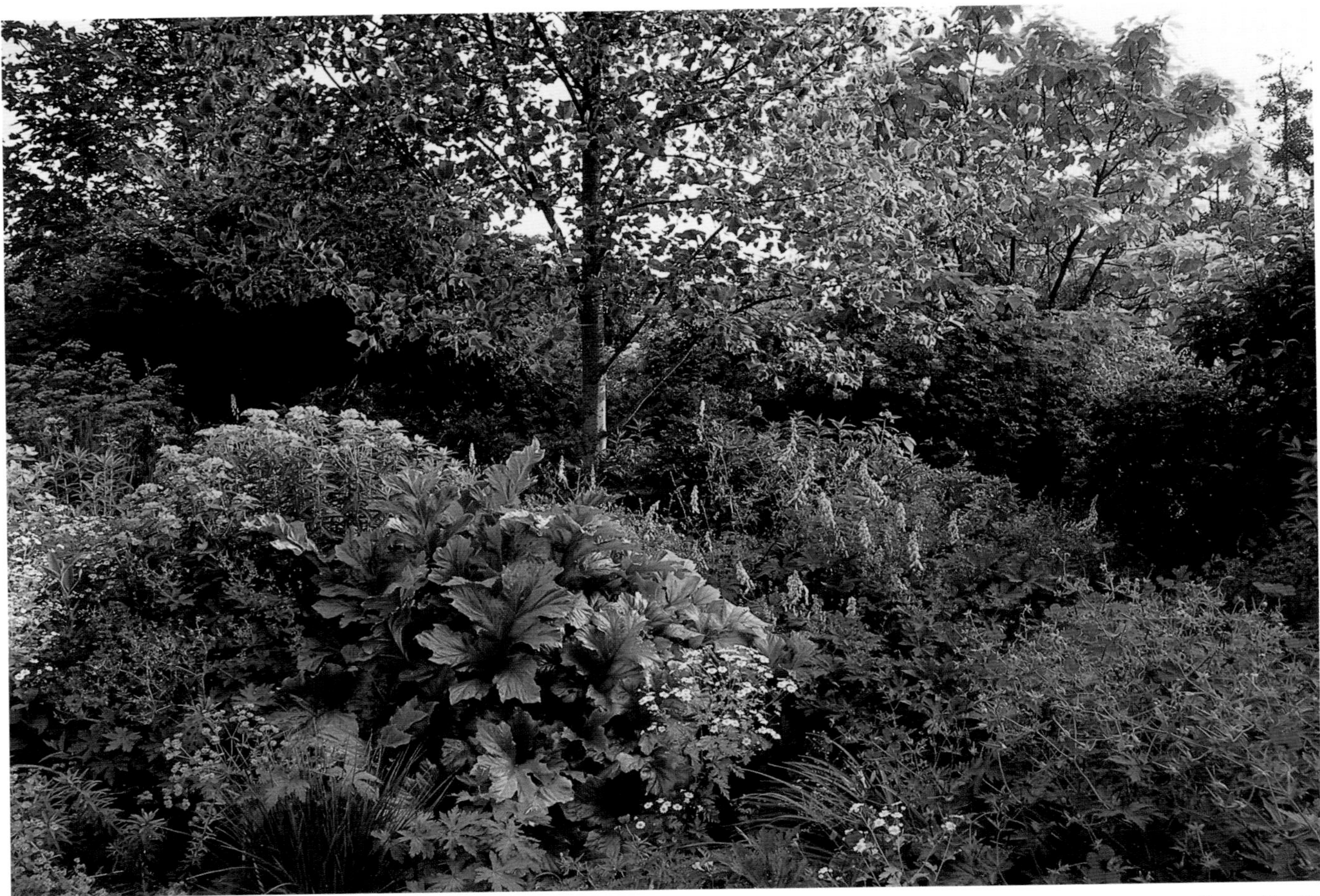

An early summer border with morning sun and dappled afternoon shade lets us grow *Acanthus mollis* 'Hollard's Gold' and *Geranium psilostemon*, with *Tanacetum parthenium* 'Aureum', *Euphorbia schillingii*, and *Aconitum lycoctonum* subsp. *vulparia*. Breaking up that afternoon sun is *Liriodendron tulipifera* 'Aureomarginatum', with *Rosa* 'Henri Martin' to the right and *Catalpa bignonioides* 'Aurea' above.

member in this family for every situation. Most make good cut flowers.

Begoniaceae (begonia family): begonia. The garden-worthy begonias are herbaceous; they have fleshy stems and male and female flowers on the same plant. They do best in part shade.

Berberidaceae (barberry family): epimedium, jeffersonia, podophyllum, vancouveria. This handsome group of plants is rhizomatous except for jeffersonia. They form large colonies over time and are shade and woodland plants.

Bignoniaceae (bignonia family): incarvillea. Lime-loving plants with taproots and large, tubular, fluted flowers.

Boraginaceae (borage family): anchusa, brunnera, mertensia, myosotis, omphalodes, pulmonaria, symphytum. This family has mostly blue flowers, curled inflorescence in bud, and hairy leaves. They like winter and spring sun. The forget-me-nots (myosotis) are the only prolific self-sower among them.

Brassicaceae (mustard family): armoracia, cardamine, crambe, erysimum, hesperis, iberis, lunaria. Formerly the Cruciferae. Flowers are cross-shaped with four petals. Mostly sun lovers, with a wide range of cultural requirements. Beloved of the cabbage moth.

Campanulaceae (bellflower family): adenophora, campanula, jasione, lobelia, platycodon. Flowers are mostly bell-shaped; lots of blue flowers. A wide range of cultural requirements.

Cannaceae (canna family): canna. Require sun, heat, and moisture; all are tender except *Canna indica*.

Do you have wet ground? The round, bronze leaves of *Ligularia dentata* 'Desdemona' make a striking contrast to the vertical foliage of *Iris pseudacorus* 'Variegata', *I. sibirica*, and the starry blue flowers of *Camassia leitchlini* subsp. *suksdorfii* 'Blauwe Donau'. Two golden-foliage plants frame this composition: on the left is *Physocarpus opulifolius* 'Dart's Gold' and on the right, *Cornus alba* 'Gouchaultii'.

They have massive woody roots that must not freeze. Monocots.

Caryophyllaceae (pink family): dianthus, gypsophila, lychnis, saponaria, silene. Mostly pink flowers. Like limy soil, sun, and sharp drainage, and are generally short-lived.

Commelinaceae (spiderwort family): tradescantia. Three-petaled flowers with prominent stamens. Monocots.

Convallariaceae (lily of the valley family): convallaria, disporum, liriope, ophiopogon, polygonatum, smilacina, tricyrtis, uvularia. Small bell-like flowers, not necessarily pendent; the leaves clasp the stems. Formerly part of the Liliaceae, this is a diverse family with a wide range of cultural requirements. Monocots.

Convolvulaceae (morning glory family): convolvulus. Calyx and corollas in fives; flowers are trumpet-shaped and clasped by a calyx, and last only one day or one night; milky sap. They always twine (if they twine) to the right.

Crassulaceae (stonecrop family): sedum. Succulent herbaceous perennials with fleshy leaves. All are drought tolerant.

Dipsacaceae (teasel family): cephalaria, knautia, scabiosa. Flowers and seedheads resemble pincushions. The seed is food for songbirds.

Euphorbiaceae (spurge family): euphorbia. Milky toxic sap. Unusual inflorescence; the showy parts are colored bracts, mostly yellow. Ropey roots.

Your grandmother's pink: *Rosa* 'Cerise Bouquet', backed by an exuberant *Robinia pseudoacacia* 'Frisia', is enlivened by a complementary foreground of *Iris sibirica* and *Salvia* ×*sylvestris*. *Geranium psilostemon* adds its bright magenta flowers to this demonstration of the color wheel.

Gentianaceae (gentian family): gentiana. Some of the best blues among garden plants. Flowers tubular; leaves opposite.

Geraniaceae (cranesbill family): geranium. Five-petaled flowers, mostly pink or blue. Seedhead looks like a cranesbill; they toss their seed.

Gunneraceae (gunnera family): gunnera. Grown for the foliage; a wide range of foliage forms and sizes.

Hemerocallidaceae (daylily family): hemerocallis. Formerly part of the Liliaceae. Straplike foliage; flower parts in threes or multiples of three. Monocots.

Hostaceae (hosta family): hosta. Formerly part of the Liliaceae. Mostly blue to violet flowers in racemes above the foliage; ornamental leaves on strong petioles. Monocots.

Hyacinthaceae (hyacinth family): camassia, eucomis, galtonia. Flowers in racemes above straplike foliage. Monocots.

Hydrangeaceae (hydrangea family): kirengeshoma. Yellow shuttlecock flowers.

Iridaceae (iris family): belamcanda, crocosmia, dierama, iris, libertia, schizostylis, sisyrinchium. Flower parts in threes or multiples of three; narrow leaves with parallel veins. Seed in capsules. Monocots.

Lamiaceae (mint family): agastache, ajuga, calamintha, dracocephalum, lamium, marrubium, melissa, monarda, nepeta, origanum, perovskia, phlomis, physostegia, salvia, stachys. Formerly the Labiatae. Many are aromatic, many are invasive; all have square stems and two-lipped flowers.

Startling simplicity—every garden has a perfect photograph. Here, a luminescent *Eryngium giganteum* shows up against *Geranium* 'Ann Folkard', *Knautia macedonica*, and *Astilbe chinensis*. Design by Sharon Nyenhuis.

Linaceae (flax family): linum. The flower parts are organized in fives; flowers are mostly blue.

Loganiaceae (strychnine family): spigelia. Poisonous plants, with flowers that are small and star-shaped.

Malvaceae (mallow family): alcea, callirhoe, malva, sidalcea. Five-petaled hollyhocklike flowers; each petal has a conspicuous notch. Seeds in a wheel like cheese inside a papery calyx. Does best in sun and heat.

Morinaceae (mulberry family): morina. Formerly part of the Dipsacaceae. Short-lived; spiny foliage.

Onagraceae (evening primrose family): epilobium, gaura, oenothera. Four-part stigma, flower parts in fours. A weedy group of plants.

Orchidaceae (orchid family): bletilla. Ground or terrestrial orchids. Monocots.

Paeoniaceae (peony family): paeonia. Fleshy-rooted, herbaceous perennials.

Papaveraceae (poppy family): corydalis, dicentra, eomecon, glaucium, macleaya, meconopsis, papaver, romneya, sanguinaria, stylophorum. A diverse family (soon to be divided). Colored or white milky sap; distinctive seedpods.

Papilionaceae (pea family): baptisia, galega, lathyrus, lupinus, thermopsis, trifolium. Formerly the Leguminosae and for fifteen minutes the family Fabiaceae—what next? After the grass family, this is the most important food source for man. Nitrogen fixing.

Phytolaccaceae (pokeweed family): phytolacca. Large, fleshy-rooted herbaceous perennials.

Plantaginaceae (plantain family): plantago. Parallel-veined leaves, somewhat weedy plants. Monocots.

Plumbaginaceae (plumbago family): armeria, ceratostigma. Flowers have five petals, five stamens, and five sepals, which are often thin and papery.

Polemoniaceae (phlox family): phlox, polemonium. Flowers have five petals that join in a narrow tube. Tough plants, slowly increasing.

Polygonaceae (knotweed family): fallopia, persicaria, rheum, rumex. Showy, long-lasting in flower and in seed; flowers in tight spikes. Aggressive plants.

Primulaceae (primrose family): dodecatheon, lysimachia, primula. Flower parts in fives.

Ranunculaceae (buttercup family): aconitum, actaea, anemone, anemonella, aquilegia, caltha, cimicifuga, clematis, delphinium, helleborus, hepatica, pulsatilla, ranunculus, semiaquilegia, thalictrum, trollius. Numerous stamens; no fusion of floral parts. Majority love moisture; many are poisonous.

Rosaceae (rose family): acaena, alchemilla, aruncus, filipendula, fragaria, geum, gillenia, potentilla, sanguisorba. Flower parts in fives. A large family with many woody plant members.

Rubiaceae (madder family): phuopsis. Leaves in whorls, distinctive odor.

Rutaceae (rue family): dictamnus. Distinctive seed capsules.

Saururaceae (lizard's-tail family): houttuynia. Moisture-loving plants.

Saxifragaceae (saxifrage family): astilbe, astilboides, bergenia, darmera, francoa, heuchera, ×heucherella, mukdenia, peltoboykinia, rodgersia, saxifraga, tellima, tiarella, tolmiea. Flowers have five petals, five sepals, and ten stamens; most are fairly small, in airy racemes. Leaves are mostly basal; many plants are grown for their ornamental leaves.

Scrophulariaceae (snapdragon family): chelone, cymbalaria, diascia, digitalis, linaria, mimulus, parahebe, penstemon, phygelius, rehmannia, scrophularia, verbascum, veronica, veronicastrum. Flowers are mostly two-lipped, tubular, with podlike seed capsules.

Solanaceae (nightshade family): physalis. Family with great economic value (potatoes, tomatoes); all seem to have both edible and poisonous parts. The perennials have decorative seedpods.

Trilliaceae (trillium family): paris, trillium. All plant parts in threes or multiples of three. Never pick the flowers, as this may severely set the plant back. Monocots.

Tropaeolaceae (nasturtium family): tropaeolum. Tubers. Palmately lobed leaves.

Valerianaceae (valerian family): centranthus, patrinia, valeriana. Small flowers, aromatic plants.

Verbenaceae (verbena family): verbena. Flowers are small, funnel-shaped, and in clusters; leaves are dark green, rough, toothed.

Violaceae (violet family): viola. Flowers are pansylike and irregular, with five petals often with a facelike pattern; all are edible.

Zingiberaceae (ginger family): hedychium, roscoea. Tuberous roots. Monocots.

PLANTS FOR SPECIAL GARDENS

THE EARLY SPRING BORDER

The very early spring border color is dominated by chionodoxa, muscari, narcissus, primula (Group 1), and *Ranunculus ficaria* cultivars. These are often layered under shrubs and trees, and the more vigorous of the summer perennials, such as *Geranium psilostemon* and persicaria. This spring border also includes *Lathyrus vernus*, omphalodes, *Pulmonaria angustifolia*, and *Veronica peduncularis* 'Georgia Blue'.

SPRING EPHEMERALS

These are a group of plants that bloom heavily in early spring and die down entirely by summer. Most can stand some summer drought. Clean up when ratty, or leave alone and let other plants grow over the dying foliage. *Anemone nemorosa*, *A. blanda*, anemonella, *Geranium tuberosum*, *G. malviflorum*, *Dicentra spectabilis*, and *Ranunculus ficaria* fall into this category.

THE SUMMER BORDER

Perennials that bloom in summer (late June through August, for us) in full sun include achillea, alstroemeria, anchusa, baptisia, campanula, centranthus, *Coreopsis verticillata*, crocosmia, delphinium, *Euphorbia schillingii*, *E. sikkimensis*, hemerocallis, inula, penstemon, pimpinella, salvia, stachys, geraniums by the score, and geums that repeat bloom.

THE COTTAGE GARDEN

The cottage garden is usually less under control than most perennial gardens and borders. More than half of this list are either thugs or self-sowers, and some are biennials: alcea, alchemilla, anthemis, aquilegia, artemisia, *Campanula persicifolia*, centaurea, *Coreopsis grandiflora*, delphinium, dianthus, *Digitalis purpurea*, *Eryngium giganteum*, *Geranium ×magnificum*, gypsophila, leucanthemum, nepeta, physostegia, polemonium, potentilla, primula, *Saponaria officinalis*, *Saxifraga ×urbium*, scabiosa, *Tanacetum parthenium*, thalictrum, tradescantia, veronica, and viola.

In this shade border, repetition of one kind of variegation ties together a group of plants. The creamy variegation on the foreground plants of *Polygonatum* ×*hybridum* 'Striatum' is repeated in the shrubs *Philadelphus coronarius* 'Variegatus' and *Cornus kousa* 'Snowboy'. The composition is enriched by *Hydrangea macrophylla*, the foliage of *Hosta* 'Halcyon', and astilbe in bloom, on the right.

THE LATE SUMMER BORDER

This group includes late-flowering perennials, most of tall stature and many of which are in the daisy family: agapanthus, aster, chelone, cimicifuga, echinacea, echinops, eryngium, eupatorium, filipendula, helenium, helianthus, heliopsis, kniphofia, ligularia, lobelia, miscanthus and other grasses, monarda, penstemon, persicaria, *Phlox paniculata*, phygelius, rudbeckia, salvia (taller forms), solidago, and ×solidaster. Of all these, only the asters should be pinched back in the Pacific Northwest.

THE AUTUMN BORDER

This group includes late asters, chrysanthemum, hardy fuchsias, *Helianthus salicifolius*, *H. maximiliani*, *Miscanthus sinensis* cultivars, *Persicaria microcephala*, *Salvia guaranitica*, *S. uliginosa*, *Sedum spectabile* and hybrids, and schizostylus.

THE SHADE BORDER AND THE WOODLAND GARDEN

Plants that do best in part shade (half a day) with an emphasis on foliage: arisaema, arum, asarum, astilbe, brunnera, darmera, *Dicentra eximia*, *D. formosa*, disporum, *Gentiana asclepiadea*, *Helleborus orientalis*, heuchera, ×heucherella, hosta, kirengeshoma, paris, peltoboykinia, podophyllum, polygonatum, pulmonaria, rodgersia, smilacina, stylophorum, tolmiea, tricyrtis, trillium, uvularia, and viola.

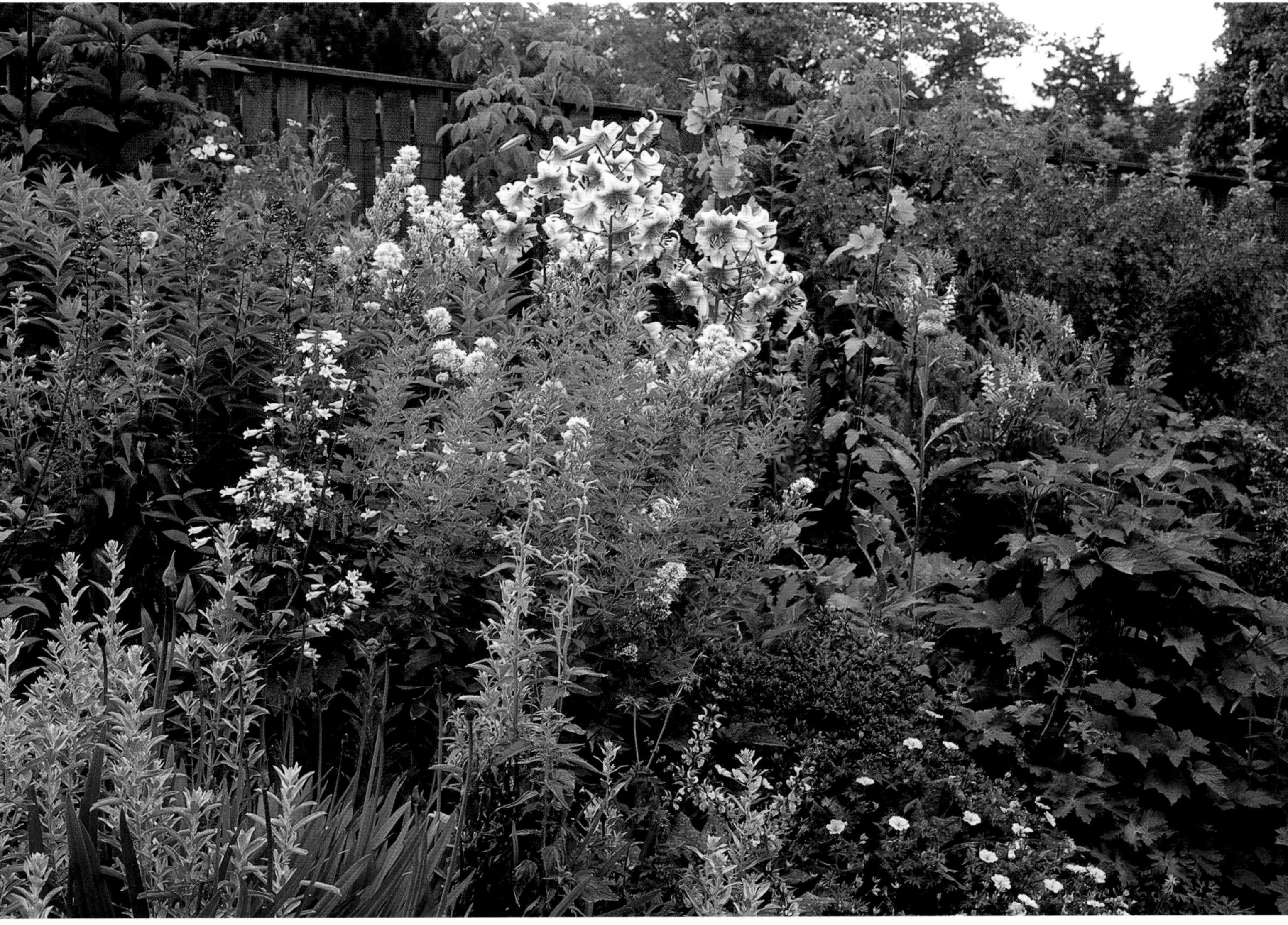

Summer hits its stride in this home border using the best of the immense herbaceous summer perennials: *Phlox paniculata* just barely coming into flower, *Penstemon digitalis* 'Husker Red', and *Phygelius* ×*rectus* on the left. A large clump of *Lilium* 'Tiger Babies' is flanked on the right by *Lavatera olbia* and *Campanula lactiflora*. Even the foreground plants, *Artemisia ludoviciana* and *Dictamnus albus* var. *purpureus*, are large in scale.

THE BACK OF THE BORDER, THE ALLEY, AND TOO TALL FOR WORDS

Aconitum 'Spark's Variety', alcea, the taller asters, boltonia, *Eupatorium cannabinum*, *E. purpureum*, fallopia, ferula, galega, *Helianthus* 'Lemon Queen', *H. maximiliani*, macleaya, *Phytolacca americana*, rheum (in flower), *Rumex hydrolapathum*, silphium, *Thalictrum flavum* subsp. *glaucum*, *T. lucidum*, verbascum, and vernonia.

THE MEADOW GARDEN

Plants that look stunning with a forest or evergreen background in an open sunny to part shade location are actaea, amsonia, *Anaphalis triplinervis*, the taller astilbes, cimicifuga, digitalis, disporum, hesperis, kirengeshoma, patrinia, polygonatum, rodgersia, smilacina, and thalictrum.

Hot borders have become very popular, and flowers with such warm hues are best sited in full sun. In the background, *Berberis thunbergii* f. *atropurpurea* and its selections 'Helmond Pillar' (left) and 'Rose Glow' (right) offset the intensity of *Phygelius* ×*rectus* 'Devil's Tears' and *Euphorbia griffithii* 'Fireglow'; the green foliage of *Iris sibirica* and crocosmia is the perfect complement. Planted to great effect in the foreground are *Heuchera cylindrica* 'Greenfinch' and in the upper right, *Delphinium* 'Alice Artindale', a grand old double.

MAINTENANCE GUIDELINES

Although the bulk of this book will tell how to maintain specific herbaceous perennials, we have some general maintenance observations to pass along first. In the A-to-Z, where we get specific, the sections are arranged roughly in the order in which you would deal with your garden plants, from purchase to putting to bed for the winter ("propagation" is an ongoing process, depending on the ripening of seed, weather, and so forth, so that follows "management"; next up is "pests and diseases"—a never-ending battle in time . . .). Each genus entry will refer to these techniques or concerns briefly. This section amplifies what we say in shorthand for the rest of the book, and can be used to check up on what to do and most importantly, how. We hope this simple, concise, and clear set of guidelines will ensure as much success as possible—they work quite well for us.

SOIL AND AMENDMENTS

Soils (which figure strongly under "preferred conditions" in the A-to-Z) vary throughout the country. In the Pacific Northwest, for example, we have a range of soil conditions: sandy loam, loam, clay, rocky clay, and variations thereof. Understanding what your soil structure is, assessing your site and your plant requirements, will save you a lot of moving and rearranging down the line. If you know what deficiencies your garden soil has, you will be able to make the correct improvements and plan and plant accordingly.

That said, most of us have never sent for a soil analysis, and we don't really know what the pH of our garden is. But we do know that the soil here is generally more acidic, and most of our plants want the Holy Five: a moderately fertile, well-drained, humus-rich, moist, and moisture-retentive soil. Making good garden soil should be the first thing on your list, as it's the foundation for all the plants we long to grow. The first two words on any improvement list should be compost and manure. Organic material promotes soil structure and sets the scene for healthy plants.

We recommend thorough preparation of your site before planting. This may require lots of digging and the addition of amendments. After the garden has been prepared and planted, it will then require an annual application of manure or compost to keep the soil healthy and your garden weed-free.

If your soil passes the reasonable texture test (squeeze a handful, open your palm, and if the lump falls apart, the soil is passable), you only need to add greensand, rock phosphate, and an all-purpose organic fertilizer. Then till to about eight inches to mix it all together and further loosen your topsoil (or dig it in yourself).

Larger plants with deeper roots can be planted in areas prepared in this manner with the soil mixed in the hole, 1:1 with the subsoil. Don't plant in areas where the subsoil does not drain. Water that remains in a test hole eighteen inches deep for more than twenty-four hours indicates a drainage problem.

EXPOSURE

First, there is light. By **sun**, we mean full, all-day sun. That is, the south side of a house and any location fully exposed to the south. Some areas with a lot of reflected heat from walls or pavement will qualify even if not in sun all day.

Tarting-up a hot border with short-lived but sweet perennials (left to right), *Geranium pratense*, *Salvia nemorosa*, dwarf bedding dahlias, *Dianthus barbatus*, *Knautia macedonica*, and *Lychnis chalcedonica*. The background is filled in with more permanent plantings of *Cornus controversa* 'Variegata', *Fuchsia magellanica*, *Berberis thunbergii*, *Trochodendron aralioides*, and a good dark-foliaged red rose. Design by Rick Kyper.

Part sun can mean afternoon sun (the warmer areas of your garden with sun after eleven in the morning) or morning sun, that is, sun until eleven o'clock in the morning (even though these areas can have as much sun as afternoon sun, they will still be cooler).

Part shade means dappled sun in summer, or only late afternoon or early morning sun. In our climate zone, this is the best place for natives from the eastern part of the United States, which need the heat as much as the shade. Another way to think of part shade is spring sun, summer shade.

Shade means areas with no sun in summer. They may get winter sun if shaded by deciduous trees or shrubs during the growing season.

With these four light recommendations, our hope is that plants will get the right location the first time. In the Pacific Northwest, many shade and part shade plants will be able to take more sun than they are listed for. There will also occasionally be notes to protect plants from wind, drying and otherwise (winter wind from the north is our coldest weather pattern). The north side of fences and buildings will be death to tender perennials. Also be aware of wind that funnels between houses.

Consider too that some areas are exposed to the east in winter, when a frozen morning on sunny days can cause damage. Also look for pockets in the garden that will hold cold air. You can improve these with a frost drain: cold air behaves like a liquid and will flow down hill.

PLANTING

Most perennials should be planted at crown level with the roots in the ground and the stem and leaf structures above soil level. The precise term for this is crown specific, and for certain plants (strawberries, for instance) this procedure must be followed. If an entry in the A-to-Z doesn't have any specific planting instructions, this is the default advice! Peonies, on the other hand, do rate special planting instructions; if planted too deep, they will not flower; the tips of the pointed red pips should be visible by midwinter. You can mulch around peonies, but not over the crown. Over time this would make them too deep in the mulch and they would not bloom.

Perennials that form a green winter crown are not as fussy as peonies but still should not be heavily mulched. A lightweight covering of maple or oak leaves or evergreen branches will offer some winter protection but needs to be removed by late winter.

Some plants can be mulched over heavily each year with no adverse effects: acanthus, aconitum, arisaema, arum, crocosmia, dicentra, hemerocallis, hosta, lysimachia, macleaya, paris, phytolacca, pinellia, polygonatum, smilacina, trillium, zantedeschia, and all bulbs and tuberous-rooted plants.

Herbaceous perennials that form a crown composed of a cluster of tiny rosettes—such as anthemis, aquilegia (often solitary rosettes), chaerophyllum, chrysanthemum, lobelia, meconopsis, and sedum—should be planted and maintained with these at the surface level, if not slightly above. Sedums benefit from the latter a great deal.

Evergreen perennials such as dianthus, dierama, heuchera, ×heucherella, *Stachys byzantina*, tellima, and tiarella should never have their foliage buried at planting time or be mulched over.

MULCHING

The most important thing you can do for your garden is an annual application of mulch. Mulch does several things for a garden: it adds organic matter, conditions the soil, suppresses weeds, conserves moisture, and provides winter protection.

There are a number of choices of material to use for mulch, and where you live plus what kind of gardening you are doing will affect your choices. We have lots of bark here, small, medium, and large; we have composted bark in bags, and composted bark with dairy cow manure and chicken manure ("chicken and chips"). Horse manure and bark is another combination, and there's even mushroom compost; a city program where clean green yard waste from the county is made into mulch and sold to the public; and last but not least, Zoo Doo, from the herbivores at our local zoo. The bagged manures from local stores can have a lot of bark or sawdust in them. We also have (but usually in bulk only) sawdust mixed with urea and composted to a nice dark brown. We also drink a lot of coffee here, so coffee hulls are available. Out and about in the rural areas or at feed stores, we can find hay or straw. Even if we don't make compost per se, we can make leaf mold by shredding and piling leaves and allowing them to age. In short, if you have plenty of deciduous trees around, as well as green garden waste, you have the means for making your own compost at home.

Generally speaking, an annual mulch of manure or compost works well for the mixed herbaceous border. The best time for application is from late fall until late winter because most of the plants have been cut back, and the garden is at its most open and accessible. This allows you to find places for your feet and readily avoid manuring over the crowns of the plants. The freezing and thawing and rain help break down the mulch, beginning the process whereby it becomes a part of the soil itself. Usually two to four inches is plenty. Never mulch against the trunks of shrubs or trees, but get close. This blanket of mulch will suppress winter weeds and provide a bit of insulation.

Years of experience have taught us to always keep a pile of mulch around. In summer as we clean up leaves or as spring ephemerals go dormant, bare ground becomes visible and we apply supplemental mulch as needed. In the fall, when we plant bulbs, we immediately mulch over them, and then we remember where they are and where else we can plant.

If you use uncomposted barks, either leave them on the surface or, if you dig them into the soil, add some nitrogen (manure, blood meal, ammonium nitrate) to help the process of decomposition. Bark incorporated into soil will take nitrogen out naturally in order to break down, and your plants will have to compete with the bark for available nitrogen.

We have found that a fall/winter application of dairy cow manure (our preferred mulch) will, by the following fall, have decomposed from four inches down to one inch, just in time for a new application.

COMPOST

The best product for your garden—either as a soil amendment, to fill holes or low spots where plants have been removed, or as a mulch—is homemade compost. You can produce good useable compost in six months by layering a good-sized bin (three square feet or more) with the

You *can* use red and pink together, especially en masse. Here, toned down with a creamy orange *Achillea* 'Hoffnung', are *Crocosmia* ×*crocosmiiflora* 'Emberglow' and a bright pink *Buddleja davidii*; *B. d.* 'Harlequin' and *B. d.* 'Black Knight' fill the background, with a wisp of *Canna indica*, also in pale orange.

following material, about four to six inches for each layer (except the soil, which is two to three inches).

1) Soil from the garden or last year's compost.
2) Green plant parts, leaves, or stems (nothing from conifers or evergreen shrubs).
3) Autumn leaves (except for walnut and liquidambar).
4) Old potting soil (even from houseplants).
5) Worm castings from your worm bin.
6) Choppings—leaves and stems of perennials and annuals cut into four- to six-inch lengths.

Each layer can be chopped in the bin before the soil layer is added. This will speed up the process. If you turn these layers, your compost will form more quickly, but as this is very difficult with materials from perennial gardens, go for the passive method—it takes longer, but the product is just as good. You can also speed up the process a bit with a commercial "compost maker" or bacteria (summer only). The presence of soil is important, as it inoculates your pile with bacteria and microorganisms, which do all the work. Compost piles should be watered in summer.

Do not compost the following material. Dispose of them some other way.

1) Peony and lily leaves and stems (too much potential disease).
2) Grass clippings if not well mixed (makes compost too gooey and dense).
3) Perennial grasses (take too long to compost).
4) Iris foliage (too long to compost and has disease problems).
5) Hellebore and tulip foliage (disease).

High tide in the garden with waves of summer color rolling down the slope. The top wave has *Rudbeckia laciniata* 'Herbstsonne', *Delphinium elatum*, and *Miscanthus sinensis* 'Zebrinus'. In the central billows are *R. fulgida* var. *sullivantii* 'Goldsturm', *Patrinia scabiosifolia* 'Nagoya', and *Agapanthus* 'Prolific Blue'. In the foreground are *Phygelius* ×*rectus* 'Salmon Leap', *Hypericum* ×*inodorum* 'Elstead' in fruit and a variegated hypericum, and *Berberis thunbergii* f. *atropurpurea* 'Golden Ring'.

FERTILIZING

A well-established perennial garden needs no additional fertilizing if it is mulched with compost (homemade) or manure. Keep in mind, you are feeding the soil as well as the plants. A soil with a loose texture and lots of organic matter will produce a better garden than heavy applications of commercial fertilizers. The one exception to this rule: spring bulbs should be fed in early spring, when the narcissus bulbs are up about one and a half to two inches tall; this will help them produce a good bulb for the following year.

New plants can be fertilized at planting time. A small amount of a transplanter, an all-purpose plant food, or a similar organic plant food mixed in the planting hole will increase survivability and promote a good "take" that first year.

General overall fertilizing of perennials should be with an all-purpose type of granular fertilizer, organic or not. You can also use vegetable fertilizer, which is usually a similar balance of N-P-K (nitrogen, phosphorus, potassium) like 5-10-10 or 4-8-8. This should be done in early spring.

Slow-release fertilizers can be used, but the expensive encapsulated ones need to be incorporated into the soil to work best. If granular or encapsulated products are used on the surface, they can flush all at once in hot weather; early, cooler-season applications are better.

WATERING

If you don't want to stake your perennials, don't overhead water. When flowers get laden with water and weighed down, plants flop. Install a leaky pipe system like Aquapore or Netafin, and keep water off the foliage and flowers. This will also reduce disease.

A good heavy application, once a week, of an inch of water is usually sufficient, except for newly planted areas, where watering individual plants is still necessary until well established. Perennials do very well with a heavily water-retentive soil under the more prepared humus-rich soil in your planting beds.

If you can, you should always water in the morning, so your foliage can go through the night as dry as possible. A loose mulch that acts as insulation will conserve water and keep your soil moist and reduce water loss by evaporation from the soil surface through capillary action.

THE DRY-GARDEN, DROUGHT-TOLERANT MYTH

Some perennials can take less watering once established but will need to be watered or watched now and then (every seven to ten days). The bulk of good garden plants come from areas that receive summer rain—the United States east of the Mississippi, wetter areas of Europe, China, and New Zealand. Nothing looks worse than a perennial border in England in a severe drought year; they are very strict on watering, and most gardens have little supplemental water and rarely an irrigation system. Our climate is unusual in that we can have very dry (but not hot) summers and very wet falls, winters, and springs.

In a dry year, let your lawn fend for itself, and save your water for the perennials and shrubs. Lawns usually come back but a bone-dry delphinium is a dead delphinium.

Some plants that can be grown in drier soil *once established* are adenophora, allium, anaphalis, artemisia, camassia, centranthus, delosperma, dierama, euphorbia (most of them), ferula (but it will be shorter), glaucium, kniphofia (fleshy roots and deep rooting), *Papaver atlanticum*, *P. orientale* (usually goes summer dormant), perovskia, romneya, salvia (some), sedum, tellima, tolmiea, tradescantia (fleshy roots and a large root system), *Viola adunca*, *V. labradorica*, and vancouveria.

WET FEET

A few perennials can take wet feet most of the time, although the winter water level cannot rise above the level of the crown. These plants can be used at the edge of a stream, pond, or lake if planted above the high-water mark. If they wish to be closer, most will grow in that direction. *Iris ensata*, *I. laevigata*, and *I. pseudacorus* will grow in water. See the A-to-Z for specifics about these plants ("planting" will tell how far above the high-water mark they should be): acorus, darmera, gunnera, houttuynia, *Primula beesiana*, *P.* ×*bulleesiana*, *P. bulleyana*, *P. japonica*, trollius.

PINCHING

This is the term for the practice of removing the tip growth on each stem of an herbaceous plant. The purpose is to keep the plant more compact so that staking will not be required and so that the plant will "fit" its allotted space. This practice is not a universal one—some plants respond well, others don't, and it is important to know who likes what before pinching back or pinching out. Examples of a positive outcome would be chrysanthemum, aster, and boltonia; plants that do not respond well to this treatment are sedum, *Campanula lactiflora*, and *Phlox paniculata*. What is less than satisfactory is the effect on the flower heads themselves, which are usually much smaller than they would be if left alone. Pinching changes the character of the inflorescences. Often a short, cool summer does not give enough time for a good-sized flower head to form.

STAKING

This is the process of propping up plants that have a tendency to fall over, flop, or splay. Plants should be staked in early spring as they emerge from dormancy for two reasons: you can get into the garden to do it; and it is much better to do it in advance—if you wait until the need is obvious, it is usually too late to do it well. Staking should be as unobtrusive as possible once the plants have grown up into the supports.

With many herbaceous plants, support is lent by what we call pea sticks. These are bits of brushy wood with sturdy, thin twigs—hazelnut, birch, or maple twigs, for example—with their single, broader stem end forced into the ground around the plants they're meant to support. Taller plants like delphinium will need straighter, taller supports and some tying-in. Paeonia and *Helleborus argutifolius* are examples of plants that can benefit from those circular wire hoops (which you've put in early, for them to grow up through).

GROOMING

Herbaceous plants need grooming throughout the year. Many have their flower stems completely removed after flowering. In some cases, this will result in rebloom, depending on the type of plant. Some plants simply

Scrim plants, the delicious *Helianthus salicifolius* (willow-leaved sunflower) and *Verbena bonariensis*, fronting a mass of *Cortaderia selloana* 'Sunstripe' backed by *Sambucus nigra* 'Guincho Purple' and a bit of *Arundo donax* (top right).

have the spent flowers removed to the next leaf or pair of leaves, and this stimulates further flower production in response to this removal of any possible seed production. If you are interested in saving seed, you can select a couple of stems that look really good to leave for seed production. If you like the appearance of the seedheads, you can leave them until you want to remove them; the latest they should remain is into the following spring, when growth recommences.

Other grooming, carried out as needed, involves removing dying, damaged, or diseased foliage as it occurs. Daylilies often need their bad leaves removed—in this case, it's leaf by leaf. There are more serious kinds of grooming as well. For example, *Alchemilla mollis* is groomed (cut) to the ground after all the flowers turn brown. All the leaves and flower stems are removed. The plant will releaf within a couple of weeks with a heavy watering; the result is a handsome plant for the rest of the season. This process also reduces self-sowing. Be sure to water well any plant you subject to this extreme treatment.

Many plants have the occasional bad-looking leaf or two; just remove as needed. The plants will usually show you what to do.

DEADHEADING

Deadheading is a lot like grooming but specific to the flower heads. Again it is important to know whether and when to do this. For example, most peonies benefit from having their spent flowers removed—they look better, and it reduces the chance of disease forming on the old petals and jumping to the leaves. A few peonies, however, have beautiful seedheads, and some can be seed-grown. You can either admire for a while, before deadheading, or leave any species to form seeds (hybrid peonies rarely form seed).

Delphiniums are often deadheaded to the leaves below the flower structure, but we now know that the plants will be more robust if you forgo the funny little second flowers and just cut them to the ground after flowering. You may in fact get a great reboom in late summer or fall. Do not do this to young plants.

Never deadhead by simply removing the flowers and leaving the stems. This looks dreadful, and as the flower stems die back, the plant will either look even worse or may become diseased along the stem (pansies, for example, are prone to this).

CUTTING BACK

A specific form of grooming, this is the process of taking plants nearly to the ground. There are several occasions where this might be the appropriate course of action.

1) Many herbaceous plants are cut back during the fall and winter months. Usually this is based on both the appearance of the plants and the gardener's need for access. Especially following the first serious frost, a lot of plants begin to go into dormancy, and the upper growth deteriorates—sometimes overnight. Some plants will have a basal structure that is visible and green below the decaying stems. If so, cut only to this new growth, leaving an inch or two of old stem to mark the place where the plant is and to protect it from your big feet. Other plants will have nothing visible except their dead stems, and these should also be cut down to one to two inches, for the same reasons.
2) Many plants are dormant at times other than autumn. Spring bloomers can go dormant by summer; some don't leave a trace, and others need a bit of cutting back. It will be obvious.
3) Some perennials should not be cut back until spring. Maybe they're valuable for interest in the winter garden, or because they protect their crowns during the cold months. Another reason you might wait is to provide food and shelter to the other garden dwellers. Plants to leave up might include helianthus, foeniculum, rudbeckia, and phytolacca.

SHEARING

Shearing is for lambs and lavender. This is not an appropriate term for the care of most herbaceous plants since we do not use shears on them.

WINTER CARE

Put your garden to bed for the long dormancy of winter. It is best to let your perennials go fully dormant before cutting them back for winter. Allow the iris to turn yellow and nut-brown, and let your peonies go through their nice reds, oranges, and golds. Cut lilies back after all leaves have turned; your cut should be at a sharp angle so some water will run off. Do not compost peonies and lily leaves—too much disease present.

Plants with a visible winter crown like sedums and asters can be cut close and do not get covered with mulch. Hostas and daylilies can be cut quite close and covered with mulch. If you need to walk in your beds, leave a few stems up high enough so your plants show above the mulch. Try not to step on the crown of any plant.

Clean up your crowns, and check for slugs and weeds in the center of the clump or just at the edge, hiding under foliage. Don't worry about accidentally removing some soil or mulch at this point, as this is the best time to put fresh mulch on. Plant your bulbs as you clean up so they can have a good mulch too. Put the waste in your compost, and layer with leaves, soil, and chopped green stems.

Many perennials and grasses can be left for winter interest, but this can be a bit messy. You'll need to decide what is best for your garden.

1) Perennials that have good fall color but no strong, upright stems (hostas and daylilies) should be cleaned up first and checked for slugs, which can still do a lot of damage throughout the winter.
2) If protected, leave the plant up for the chance of hoarfrost and a stunningly beautiful, if fleeting effect.
3) If windy, we recommend cutting grasses down just before they begin to fall apart.
4) Woody and semi-woody flower stems can be left until they break off easily (astilbe, eryngium, rudbeckia).

This is the time to put limestone chips (marble chips) on the crowns of your hellebores and peonies. These chips are normally used for terrazzo floors. They slough molecules constantly and will change the pH around and on the crown they cover, but not the overall pH of the soil. This slightly less acid "mulch" will interfere with the overwintering of the botrytis organisms, so the plants don't pick up this disease when emerging in the spring. This technique also makes the crowns easy to locate when mulching as both of these plants should not be mulched over.

In this single color scheme, *Phlox paniculata* 'Bright Eyes' is framed by a mass of centaureas in the foreground and backed by *Viburnum carlesii* and *Macleaya cordata*.

WINTER MULCH

In addition to normal mulching, some plants will benefit from specific winter mulches. If you are planning to plant a new area in spring that is currently either in lawn or weeds, you can reduce your work by mowing or weeding the area (weedwhacker, blow torch, goats) and then covering it with thick piles of newspaper, overlapping for complete coverage. Then apply ten to twelve inches of straw, hay, manure, or leaves. If using leaves, top-dress with compost or something heavy enough to keep the leaves in place. By spring you should be able to turn in the mulch and plant without having to remove the lawn, as it will be dead and the paper will have rotted away.

Another winter mulch would be the application of fir boughs or other coniferous blow-downs or pruning as an insulation over tender plants; newly planted and not-established plants; plants that might frost-heave in your garden; and plants you didn't get planted (still in their containers). This blanket of covering keeps things under it from freezing. Do not use hemlock, as it will just drop its needles and you'll have a mess to clean up. We even cut up our holiday trees (afterward) and use those boughs in the garden.

Some plants benefit from a mulch of their own big leaves in winter for cold protection, for instance, *Gunnera manicata* and hedychium. Cut off leaves in fall and cover the plants for the winter; remove them in spring, as the buds swell and weather warms up.

Much of the mulching material for winter can be incorporated in the soil if sufficiently decomposed, or it can be chopped up and added to the compost heap come spring. The exception would be the conifer branches, which should be disposed of in another manner.

CUT FLOWERS

We all know that the best time to cut flowers for arranging is early in the morning. That said, do it when you can, and avoid the hottest part of the day. The further you can get from noon, in either direction, the better.

Flowers should immediately be placed in water as you cut them. This is not always practical but get them in water as soon as possible. The best florists condition cut flowers overnight by immersing them up to their necks, with the flowers above the tepid water; they arrange the stems the following day. If any cut stem spends time between being cut and being in water, recut the stems before conditioning.

Some plants have milky or liquid saps that run out the cut end. These (poppies, macleaya, euphorbia) and those plants with hairy stems should be singed with a match or other flame before going into water. If you do not do this, they won't be able to draw water up and will go limp in the vase.

Hellebores are a special case. Cut them, then take a pin or the like and poke holes up and down the stems. Fill a sink or tub with water, and float the hellebores in it overnight. Arrange the next day, and you'll have two weeks of flowers.

Plants with woody stems should be cut at an angle, split at the bottom with your pruners, and hammered (smashed) at the base before putting in water.

There are some good floral products to add to the water that will prolong the vase life of flowers. Change the water every few days to help keep the flowers as long as possible.

PROPAGATION

As gardeners most of us are involved in some method of plant propagation. If you are seriously interested in collecting seed or taking cuttings, we recommend that you do further reading on these subjects; there are good books that cover this in great detail. Division, however, is a technique that benefits many plants, whether you are planning on having additional plants or simply dividing a congested one, so your plant will bloom better and look better. We have noted the best time to divide, if appropriate, for each individual plant throughout the A-to-Z. The standard rules are these: plants that bloom in spring and early summer are divided in autumn; plants that bloom in late summer and autumn are divided in the spring. But some plants, such as astrantia or plantago, can be divided in spring or autumn without any noticeable set back. Pulmonaria can be divided in early spring at flowering time.

Some of the perennials that really benefit from division also have features that make it a challenge. *Iris sibirica* forms very large, dense clumps; a sharp axe may be the only way to split it up. Others are tap-rooted (aquilegia, eryngium), and another means of propagation may be the best, in this case by seed.

Seed collection in perennial gardens occurs throughout the summer into fall. Many of our common plants will come true from seed, especially the species. Some cultivars, such as *Eupatorium purpureum* subsp. *maculatum* 'Gateway' and *Tanacetum parthenium* 'Aureum', can also be grown from seed.

Collect seed when capsules are open or have turned brown, black, or tan. Collect it in open paper bags and dry as quickly as possible—the back seat of a car is the perfect location. Never collect seed on a wet day, as they are often too soggy to dry before mildew sets in. Remove as much chaff as possible before storing in paper envelopes (never plastic). Long-term storage of envelopes of seeds (except for tropical and subtropical plants) can be in sealed plastic boxes in your refrigerator. Do not open these chilled boxes until they reach room temperature (to avoid condensation on the seeds).

If you want to try to grow from seed, try mail order or look for local groups that offer seed exchanges for nominal cost like the Northwest Perennial Alliance or the Hardy Plant Society of Oregon. Often this is the only way to find rare perennials like *Delphinium elatum* or *Lathyrus vernus*. Also, look for annuals and biennials to seed about in your garden.

PESTS

Slugs are a most problematic pest. Add their introduced shelled cousins, the snails, and you have in many places of our country a year-round problem. Only in the hottest part of August can we be fairly certain of no slug activity, unless it rains. There are several kinds of slugs: little gray ones that feed all winter and most of the spring; the bigger brown slugs that hibernate in winter if it's cold but otherwise seem to eat all year; and the native banana slugs (these are okay—don't kill them, in other words). If you find slug eggs—little translucent balls, usually found in dark places—you could squish them or just uncover them. We use two different baits: iron-based pelletized safe baits, which we broadcast throughout the year (read the instructions on the container, it doesn't take much); and the liquid bait (metaldehyde) with which you can draw dotted lines around vulnerable plants. There is also a pelletized version of the liquid bait; both are toxic, so should be used with care. It's actually possible to put the

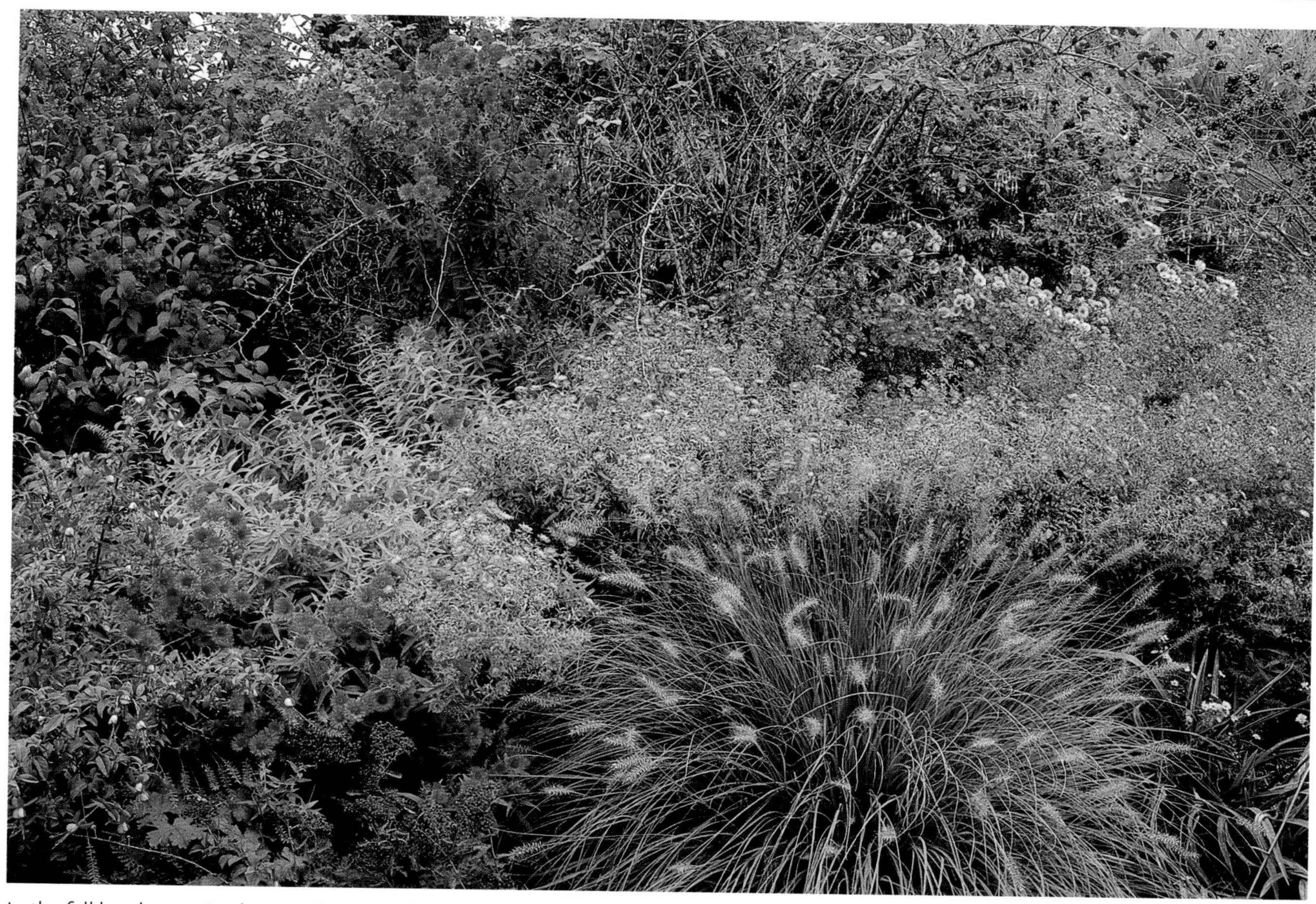

In the fall border, a mixed array of asters is balanced by a soft clump of dwarf *Pennisetum alopecuroides* 'Hameln' and 'Pat's Dream' fuchsia. At top, a sprinkling of the bright orange hips of *Rosa rubiginosa* (top) gives a taste of the winter to come.

liquid bait in an open-sided container in the garden, and then only slugs and snails will have access to it. This keeps it off the soil and away from other life forms. Whenever it is damp and especially after heavy rains, baits have to be reapplied.

Cutworms are another pesky issue. Two remedies: pick them out and squash them (they are often in the crowns of larger-leaved plants and will fall to the ground if they sense your presence); or make birds welcome in your garden (some will eat the cutworms). Cutworms do an enormous amount of damage to foliage, leaving plants unsightly for the entire growing season.

Sawfly larvae eat columbine foliage among other things. They lie along the edges of the leaves and munch their way to the midribs. If you don't catch them early you will have skeletonized leaves. If this happens, cut the columbine to the ground and water it well; it will almost always come right back. Unfortunately, sometimes sawflies will have moved through their life cycle and will attack a second time.

We have trouble with both the larval and adult forms of root weevils. The larvae (white to beige C-shaped grubs) live in the ground and dine on the roots of bergenia, corydalis (except *C. lutea* and *C. ochroleuca*), heuchera, ×heucherella, mukdenia, primula (*P. polyanthus* and *P. vulgaris* types), saxifrage, tellima, tiarella, tolmiea, and sedum, especially plants in containers, over the winter. If you notice one of these plants looking limp and dull, lift it, and you will likely find no roots and half a dozen or more grubs. The adults prey principally on rhododendrons and other ericaceous plants and are night feeders above ground; the adult damage is notching (noshing) on the edges of the leaves. The safest control is to go out at night with a flashlight and drop them in a can of alcohol. Beneficial nematodes can be applied to the soil to kill the weevil grubs—a slow but sure solution.

Aphids—or, to English gardeners, plant lice. A creepy but apt common name. There are all kinds of aphids, in an array of colors. Many are specific pests on specific plants. Usually they are worst when a plant is either in stress or rapidly growing new foliage in spring. The remedies range from squishing them to blasting them off with a forceful spray of water. You can help by relieving the stress on the plant (more food, more water?), making the plant less vulnerable. Birds who eat insects will clean up a lot of aphids given half a chance. Ladybug larvae eat lots of them, too. You could, of course, spray something like insecticidal soap, but then there would be little for the birds to eat and you'd kill the ladybugs, too. So don't, is our advice.

SHORT-LIVED PERENNIALS

Even perennials, alas, may be short-lived for several reasons, and not just because they've been decimated by slugs or root weevils.

1) Some do not get enough heat. Try to place them in a warm and sunny location in soil on the dry side, so there is less winter wet and cold feet. Most American prairie plants fall in this category—achillea, asclepias, *Aster* ×*frikartii*, callirhoe, echinacea, lupinus, silphium, *Tanacetum coccineum*, and the verbascums with flower color other than white or yellow.

2) Some grow too well, exhausting themselves in one to three years (and often like a leaner soil). Examples are anthemis, centranthus, *Coreopsis grandiflora*, erysimum, gaura, nepeta, *Oenothera versicolor* 'Sunset Boulevard', and penstemon.

3) Some tender perennials will not survive an exceptionally cold winter: *Agapanthus africanus* (and cultivars with *A. africanus* genes), agastache (except *A. foeniculum*), begonia, canna, convolvulus, cosmos, delosperma, diascia (most), *Geranium* ×*riversleaianum*, glaucium, origanum (some), *Physalis peruviana*, salvia (except *S. nemorosa*, *S.* ×*superba*, *S.* ×*sylvestris*, and *S. uliginosa*), and zantedeschia (except *Z. aethiopica*, *Z. albomaculata*, and *Z. elliottiana*).

Perennials A-to-Z

Plant your garden for backlighting, it's brief and it's lovely. Here, sunlight streams into *Eupatorium purpureum* subsp. *maculatum* 'Gateway' and *Molinia caerulea* 'Variegata', and strikes the top of *Pleioblastus viridistriatus* f. *variegatus*.

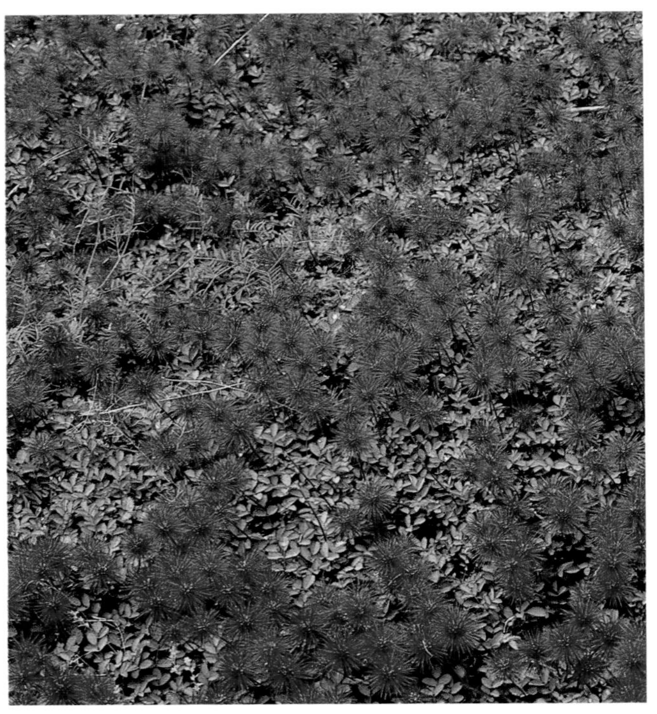

Acaena microphylla.

ACAENA Rosaceae

A compact, creeping, and usually evergreen perennial genus valued for its mat-forming foliage and colorful round seedheads. The flowers are insignificant, but the seedheads, which form soft burrs, are wonderful. The burrs appear spiny, prickly, and threatening but are actually soft to the touch, although they may be a nuisance and attach themselves to pets or socks (hence the common name northwest sock-burr). The small bluish gray to copper-colored leaves grow on prostrate stems, which root where they touch the soil. Typically, plants grow clustered together, forming large mats, and will grow in virtually any soil except one that is heavy and wet. ~ *Susan Carter*

Scientific Name: From the Greek *akaina* ("thorn," "spine").
Common Name: Sheepsburr, New Zealand burr, redspine sheep's burr.
Origin: New Zealand, southeastern Australia.
Preferred Conditions: Any average to poor, well-drained soil. Plants are drought tolerant once established.
Light: Sun to part shade.
Management: You can cut plants back in autumn (to control spread) and remove dead, spent flower heads and stems, but this is optional, not necessary. When the mats become bare and open, remove the central portions in spring or fall; lift and replant from the fuller sections.
Propagation: Division or cuttings and seed.
Pests and Diseases: Powdery mildew.
Companions: Sedges, *Plantago major* 'Rubrifolia', and paving stones.
Notes: Use acaena to knit borders and paths together—a gray-green to bronze carpet for the edges of your garden.

Species and Cultivars	Height/ Spread	USDA Hardiness Zone	Flowers (bloom time)	Foliage	Comments
caesiiglauca	2–4in × 2ft	6–8	Reddish burrs (M)	Pinnate, silky bluish gray	Silver-leafed New Zealand burr
inermis	2–3in × 2ft+	6–8	Brown-red burrs (M)	Pinnate, bronze-green	
microphylla	2–4in × 2ft	6–8	Copper-reddish burrs (M)	Small, pinnate, coppery-bronzy green	Vigorous, RHS Award
m. 'Kupferteppich' (syn. 'Copper Carpet')	1½–3in × 2ft+	6–8	Bright red burrs (M)	Pinnate, bronze to red-brown	Smallest in stature
saccaticupula 'Blue Haze'	3–4in × 2ft+	6–8	Dark brownish red burrs (M)	Pinnate, blue-gray edged in bronze, reddish pink stems	Vigorous, foliage is larger than *A. microphylla*

ACANTHUS Acanthaceae

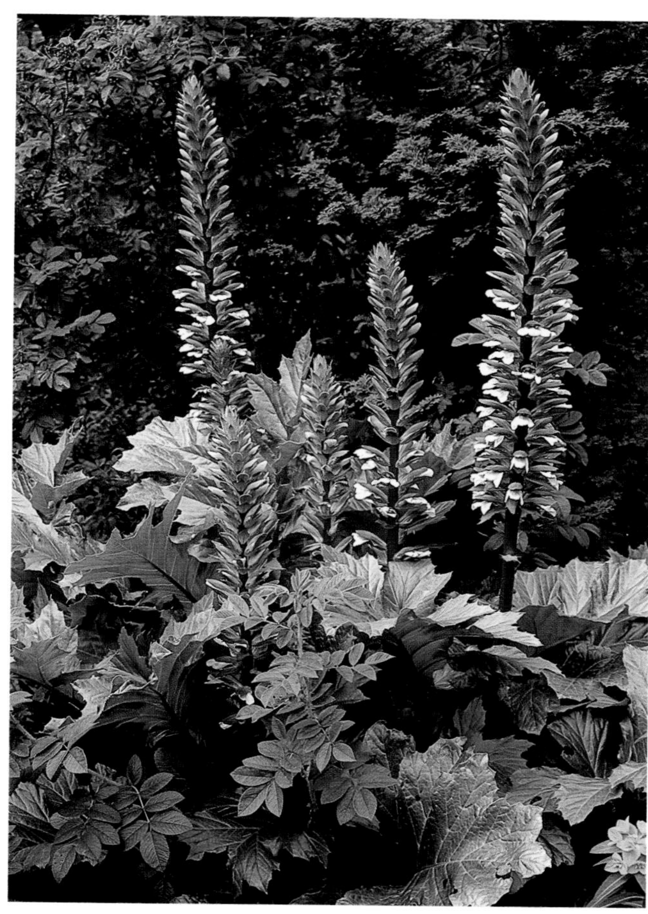
Acanthus mollis 'Hollard's Gold'.

We fear that we cannot be objective in our description of these plants, having fought them for years. They are fast colonizers of anything that looks like earth, from shiny blue clay to glacial till (Dan Hinkley's Heronswood catalog suggested "disgustingly bad soil"). Graham Stuart Thomas (1990) describes acanthus as "statuesque plants of classical dignity," but this is not so in winter after a hard frost, when they can look like wilted lettuce rescued from the back of the refrigerator. Fear not, they will arise as good as new the next day. Let us be fair, *A. spinosus* and *A. mollis* do look handsome for many months, either standing alone as majestic specimens or filling large spaces with their big, deeply divided arching leaves and spiky flowers. *Acanthus mollis* inspired a favorite decoration in classical sculpture, the Corinthian column capital.

All acanthus are easily propagated from root cuttings, even unintentionally. Removal is usually unsuccessful, especially from rockeries. If you get close up and look inside the flower, you will see a tiny green frog, armed with a vicious spine, sitting there looking out at you. So, go ahead, I dare you to plant one. ~ *Susan Buckles*

Scientific Name: From the Greek *akanthos* ("thorn," "prickle").
Common Name: Bear's breeches.
Origin: Asia, Africa, southern Europe.
Preferred Conditions: Tolerant of most any well-drained, fertile soil. Somewhat drought tolerant once established.
Light: Sun to part shade. Will grow in shade but flowers better in sun.

Species and Cultivars	Height/ Spread	USDA Hardiness Zone	Flowers (bloom time)	Foliage	Comments
caroli-alexandri	1ft × 2ft	7–9	White and pink (M)	Finely divided, green	Very floriferous
hungaricus (syn. balcanicus, longifolius)	2½–3ft × 3ft	6–9	White to pale pink with purple bracts (M)	Deeply divided, glossy olive-green	Very hardy, runs somewhat
mollis	3–5ft × 4ft	7–9	White with purplish bracts (M)	Glossy dark green, deeply cut	May need winter protection, semi-evergreen in mild winters
m. 'Hollard's Gold'	3ft × 4ft	7–9	Smoky purple (M)	Glossy golden green, lobed	Part shade to sun, may need winter protection, semi-evergreen in mild winters

Species and Cultivars	Height/ Spread	USDA Hardiness Zone	Flowers (bloom time)	Foliage	Comments
m. Latifolius Group	3–4ft × 3ft	7–9	White with purplish bracts (M)	Rounded, lobed, veined, dark green	More floriferous than the species; runs severely, may need winter protection, semi-evergreen in mild winters
spinosus	4–5ft × 2ft+	5–9	Pink and white with purple hood and gray-green bracts (M)	Glossy dark green, deeply divided, spiny	Runs severely, very hardy
s. Spinosissimus Group	3–4ft × 2ft	6–9	Muted purples, pinks, and greens (M)	Long, narrow, more finely divided, with silvery points, very spiny and sharp	Runs slowly, very hardy

Management: Bait for slugs, especially with the new young growth. Proper watering in dry weather may help prevent mildew. Protect plants by mulching in the first winter or until thoroughly established. Top-dress with organic material, preferably in late fall. Declining foliage can be cut back at any time. Digging around plants can be problematic, as cut roots may turn into new plants.

Propagation: Division in late spring; two- to three-inch root cuttings in late winter.

Pests and Diseases: Slugs, mildew.

Companions: Large-scale grasses, *Geranium psilostemon, Iris pseudacorus*, aconitum, cars. Excellent where a dramatic effect is desired and particularly expressive when planted en masse.

Notes: The best location for acanthus is where there are natural barriers. This plant supports the old adage, "If it's hard to establish, there's a good chance it's a thug." On the bright side, it makes a good cut flower. If this plant freezes and disappears completely above ground, it will come back from the roots, though it can take a year or more to do so.

ACHILLEA Asteraceae

Achilleas, with few exceptions, are fairly capricious plants, unreliable both in terms of survivability and performance. When they do perform well, they are desirable for their platelike, almost flat flower heads and, in some species and cultivars, for the feathery gray foliage.

Achillea filipendulina and its cultivars are short-lived at best. *Achillea* 'Taygetea' and *A.* 'Moonshine' prefer a dry, lime-rich location but even then live only several years and ultimately give up. *Achillea millefolium* is invasive, and its selections can revert to the wild type, leaving you with a multicolored mass (or mess). *Achillea ageratum* 'W. B. Childs' is a beautiful plant with serrated leaves and white flowers in the typical inflorescence; it needs division to prosper but is worth the effort. Personally we could live without them all, except maybe *A.* 'Terracotta': when it dies, we'll buy more and replace it. It blooms repeatedly from mid to late summer with upright flower stems and heads that go through several color changes, eventually becoming pale orange.

We have noticed that the gray-foliaged forms do not do well with competition. They want their own space, the perfect alley cat. ~ *Carrie Becker*

Scientific Name: After Achilles, of Greek mythology, who is said to have used it medicinally.

Common Name: Yarrow, sneezewort.

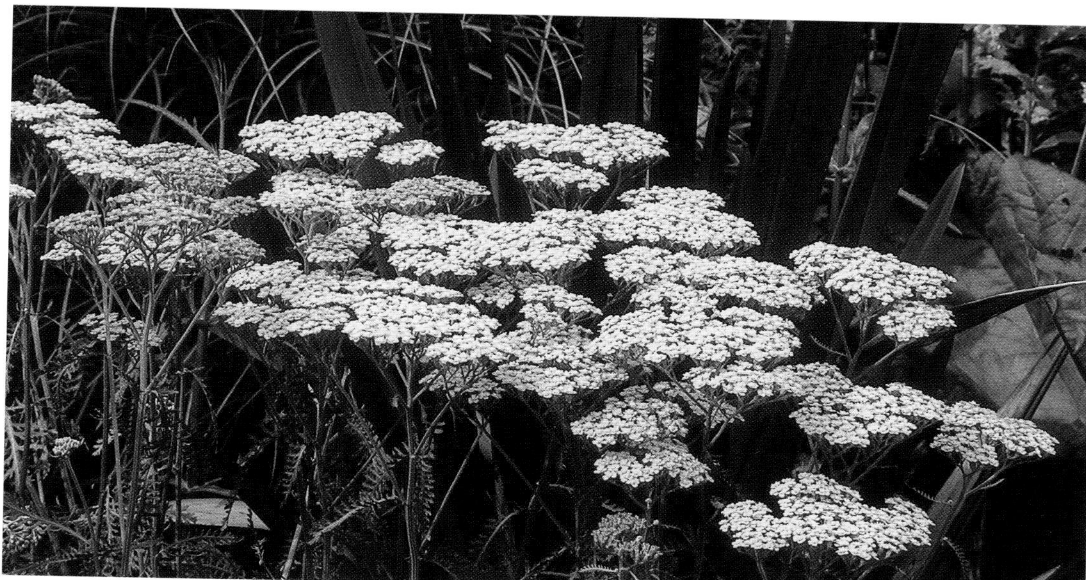

Achillea 'Terracotta'.

Origin: Southeastern Europe, Mediterranean, Asia.

Preferred Conditions: Light, well-drained, and not-too-rich soil. A poor soil is best to avoid flopping. Drought tolerant once established. Plants may show distress in severe drought but should recover.

Light: Sun.

Management: Achilleas benefit from division every three to four years when the center of the plant begins to die out. Cut to new basal foliage once flowering is completed. Cut old growth back to ground in winter when new growth begins. Some cultivars may need staking.

Propagation: Division in spring; semi-mature cuttings in summer and fall; sow seed in April or May in a warm location.

Pests and Diseases: Some will suffer from mildew if allowed to dry out.

Companions: Asiatic lilies, eryngium, salvia, ornamental grasses, rudbeckia, phlox, phygelius, dahlia, hemerocallis.

Notes: Flowers are excellent in fresh or dried arrangements. To dry, cut and hang upside down in a dark area with good ventilation. Most cultivars will grow to very large clumps if given the room and sun. In the chart, "fernlike" is shorthand for pinnate leaves that are composed of pinnate leaflets; the epithet millefolium is apt. The symbol ∞ = infinite spread.

Species and Cultivars	Height/ Spread	USDA Hardiness Zone	Flowers (bloom time)	Foliage	Comments
ageratum 'W. B. Childs'	1½–2ft × 2ft	3–8	White with dark green eye (M)	Bright green, fernlike	Long bloomer, good cut flower, not invasive, RHS Award
'Anthea'	2–2½ft × 1½ft	3–8	Light yellow, fading to cream (E–L)	Cut leaf, silvery-gray	Vigorous, not invasive, bushy, rebloom is common
'Apfelblüte' (syn. 'Appleblossom')	2–3ft × 2ft	3–8	Pinkish peach (M–L)	Fernlike, muted grayish green, compact	Vigorous
'Coronation Gold'	2½–3½ft × 2½ft	3–8	Large, golden yellow (M–L)	Fernlike, green with a bit of gray	Wide-spreading, great for drying, hard to propagate, RHS Award

Species and Cultivars	Height/ Spread	USDA Hardiness Zone	Flowers (bloom time)	Foliage	Comments
'Credo'	3–4ft × 2ft	3–8	Light yellow, fading to cream on strong green stems (M–L)	Fernlike, green	Strong grower, RHS Award
'Debutante'	2ft × 2ft	3–8	Large flower with a full range in the pink shades (M–L)	Thick mats of dissected leaves	Resembles millefolium
'Feuerland' (syn. 'Fireland')	2–3ft × 2ft	3–8	Strong red fading to deep pink, salmon, and soft gold, with golden center (M–L)	Fernlike, green	Self-supporting, multicolored effect
filipendulina	3–5ft × 3ft	3–8	Golden yellow clusters (M–L)	As above	Good en masse, dries well
f. 'Gold Plate'	4–5ft × 3ft	3–8	Deep yellow-gold, huge flat plates of flowers (M–L)	Fernlike, ash-gray	Usually needs staking, RHS Award
f. 'Parker's Variety'	2–3ft × 2ft	3–8	Large, golden yellow (M)	Fernlike, green	RHS Award
'Heidi'	1½–2½ft × 2ft	3–8	Carmine-pink fading to clear pink then to blush (M–L)	As above	Holds its color well, good cut, RHS Award
'Hoffnung' (syn. 'Great Expectations')	1½–2ft × 2ft	3–8	Sulphur-yellow tinged with pink (M–L)	Fernlike, gray-green	Compact habit
×kellereri	8–12in × 1–1½ft+	3–8	Large, pure white with yellow center (M–L)	Finely divided, gray	Good in the rock garden
'Lachsschönheit' (syn. 'Salmon Beauty')	2–3ft × 2ft	3–8	Coral-pink fading to cream (M–L)	Fernlike, green	RHS Award
millefolium	2–3ft × ∞	3–8	Red, white, and pink with yellow center (M–L)	Fernlike, aromatic, pale dark green	Common yarrow, best used where its invasiveness is an asset, not a nuisance
m. 'Cerise Queen'	2–3ft × ∞	3–8	Cherry-red (M–L)	Feathery, deep blue-green	Good cut, fresh or dried
m. 'Fire King'	2–2½ft × ∞	3–8	Crimson (M–L)	Delicate, grayish green	
m. 'Lilac Beauty' (syn. 'Lavender Beauty')	2ft × 2ft	3–8	Lavender-pink (M–L)	Fine, feathery, green	An older lavender cultivar
m. 'Paprika'	1½–2½ft × ∞	3–8	Bright orange-red with tiny yellow center (M–L)	Green, fernlike	A very good variety
m. 'Red Beauty'	1½–2ft × ∞	3–8	Large crimson-red (M–L)	Fernlike, dark green	The best deep red
'Moonshine'	1½ft × 2ft	3–8	Lemony-yellow (M–L)	Silvery-gray	Good foliage, doesn't spread, RHS Award
ptarmica	14in × 24in	3–8	Pure white (E)	Green	Prolific flowering, resembles baby's breath

Species and Cultivars	Height/ Spread	USDA Hardiness Zone	Flowers (bloom time)	Foliage	Comments
p. The Pearl Group	1½–2ft × 2ft	3–8	Double white, pearl-shaped (M–L)	Lanceolate, bright green, not divided	Vigorous spreader, self-sows
Summer Pastels Group	2–3ft × 2ft+	3–8	Blend of ivory, yellow, orange, pink, lavender, purple, red, and white (M–L)	Gray-green, finely laced, compact habit	
'Summerwine'	1½–2½ft × 2ft+	3–8	Rich burgundy-red aging to purple (M–L)	Fernlike, green	RHS Award
'Taygetea'	1½ft × 2½ft	3–8	Wide heads, yellow fading to cream (E–M)	Grayish green	Resembles *A.* 'Coronation Gold', long-flowering
'Terracotta'	2½–3½ft × 2½ft	3–8	Multicolored, bright peach aging to orange tones (M–L)	Silvery, fernlike	A superior plant
tomentosa	8–12in × 12in	3–8	Creamy-yellow (E)	Fernlike, gray-green	Dwarf yarrow
t. 'Aurea' (syn. 'Maynard's Gold')	8–12in × 12in	3–8	Bright yellow (E–M)	As above	Low rock rock garden plant
t. 'King George'	8in × 12in	3–8	Creamy-yellow (E–M)	As above	Dwarf
'Walther Funcke'	2–2½ft × 2ft	3–8	Bright red-orange with a yellow eye (M–L)	Fine, feathery, grayish green	Stems don't flop
'Wesersandstein' (syn. 'Weser River Sandstone')	1½–2½ft × 2ft	3–8	Deep pinkish red with white center on strong stems (M–L)	Fernlike, grayish green	Self-supporting

ACONITUM Ranunculaceae

Aconitums resemble delphiniums (both genera are poisonous) but are sturdier. Perennial clumps of bright green foliage are visible at ground level in January. *Aconitum* 'Ivorine' is earliest to bloom, in late spring, when columbines and early peonies are in flower; with small ivory flowers and dissected palmate leaves; it is a lovely, tall plant to light up a shaded area. Next to flower is *A. lycoctonum* subsp. *vulparia* with pale yellow flowers on even taller arching plants. Most others are shades of blue or purple, much more like delphiniums in appearance but with a hooded flower. A wide range of bloom times means that it is possible to have aconitum in bloom from spring through late fall.

These are good plants for woodland conditions. The darker-flowered forms are a bit lost in low light, however; try the paler blues or whites with blue edges instead, and plant the darkest forms in sun. ~ *Bob Lilly*

Scientific Name: From the Greek *akoniton* ("dart"), referring to the fact that this plant once provided poison for the arrows of warriors. Others believe the name is derived from *aconae*, its supposed place of origin; still others suggest it derives from the word *akone* ("cliffy," "rocky"), for one of the plant's favorite habitats.
Common Name: Monkshood, wolfsbane.

Aconitum 'Ivorine' with *Knautia macedonica.*

Origin: Russia, China, Europe.

Preferred Conditions: Well-drained soil, moist but not too wet. Will suffer in full sun if too dry.

Light: Sun to part shade.

Management: Resents root disturbance but can be divided in spring every five or six years when clumps become congested and flower production diminishes. Plants can be pinched back in spring to control height (be sure to wash your hands if you do this manually); this will produce smaller, more numerous flowers, and plants may bloom later. We do not recommend pinching in the Pacific Northwest. Deadhead after flowering to lateral bud for small, second bloom. Cut stems to ground in winter before new growth begins. Staking may be necessary. An annual feeding of organic material is beneficial.

Propagation: Division in spring or sow seeds as soon as ripe, generally late summer or autumn. Seeds take many months to germinate.

Pests and Diseases: Crown rot, verticillium wilt, powdery mildew, aphids.

Companions: Grasses, astrantia, astilbe, cimicifuga (actaea), eupatorium.

Notes: Roots of aconitum were used to poison wolves. The root has been mistaken for a horseradish root; do not plant near edibles. Makes a good cut flower for fresh arrangements. Wash your hands after planting or working with aconitum: the entire plant is poisonous.

Species and Cultivars	Height/ Spread	USDA Hardiness Zone	Flowers (bloom time)	Foliage	Comments
'Bressingham Spire'	3ft × 2ft	4–8	Deep violet-blue (M–L)	Glossy, divided, dark green	Doesn't need staking, RHS Award
×cammarum 'Bicolor'	3–4ft × 1½ft	4–8	White with violet-blue edges (M–L)	Finely toothed, mid-green	Susceptible to verticillium wilt, RHS Award
carmichaelii (syn. fischeri)	1½–2½ft × 2ft+	3–8	Rich blue (M–L)	Thick, leathery, glossy, lighter green	
c. 'Arendsii'	3½–4ft × 2ft	3–9	Large dark blue on thick stems (M–L)	Dark green, glossy	May need staking, RHS Award
'Eleonara'	3–3½ft × 1½ft	4–8	Off-white with blue edge (M–L)	Deep green, glossy, divided	Improved *A. ×cammarum* 'Bicolor'
'Ivorine' (syn. septentrional 'Ivorine')	2–3ft × 2ft+	4–8	Ivory-white and narrow, flushed green (E–M)	Deep green, deeply cut	Very upright and stiff
'Late Crop'	3½ft × 2ft+	2–9	Royal-blue (L)	Deep green, bold	Very late to flower
lycoctonum subsp. neapolitanum (syn. lamarkii)	2½–4ft × 2ft+	4–8	Pale sulphur-yellow (M)	Mid-green, deeply cut	Lax stems, tends to flop
l. subsp. vulparia	3–5ft × 3ft+	4–8	Creamy-yellow (M)	Dark green, deeply cut, dark stems	Tends to flop, has more branching stems than other aconitums
napellus	3–5ft × 2½ft+	4–8	Deep blue (L)	Dark green, glossy, deeply divided	Common monkshood, very vigorous, self-sows
n. subsp. vulgare 'Albidum'	2½–3ft × 2ft	4–8	White (L)	As above	Weaker than the species
n. subsp. vulgare 'Carneum'	3ft × 1½ft	4–8	Pale rose-pink (L)	Dark green	Flowers may fade in too much heat
'Newry Blue'	3–5ft × 2ft	5–8	Rich deep blue (M)	As above	Very dark blue
'Spark's Variety'	3–4ft × 2ft	4–8	Deep purplish blue (M–L)	Dark green, deeply lobed	RHS Award
'Stainless Steel'	3–3½ft × 1½ft	4–8	Metallic blue, creamy-white inside (M)	Dark grayish green, deeply divided	Striking color

Acorus gramineus 'Ogon' with hellebores.

ACORUS Acoraceae

Most aroids are grown for their flowers—not this one. Acorus is a quietly intriguing foliage plant. The most interesting in spring is *A. calamus* 'Argenteostriatus', which comes out of dormancy with strongly pink-tinged new blades for the first several weeks. This is a quality worth exploiting: use it as an echo of other foliage and flower colors; for example, pair it with *Geum rivale*, whose flower buds and centers are of a color similar to the emerging acorus. *Acorus calamus* (sweet flag) is a very vertical plant, growing best in continually moist soil. Some measures have to be taken before the swordlike leaves emerge or slugs will devour them. Graham Stuart Thomas (1990) relates that the cinnamon-scented (when crushed) leaves of *A. calamus* were strewn about floors in an attempt to counteract household odors (pre–vacuum cleaners).

All forms of *A. gramineus* are best sited at the edges of plantings, as they are relatively short and most appreciated where they can be seen en masse. These plants grow out radially from the center, and the foliage, which is straplike, plaits itself in one direction from the center (rather like hair). All perform best in wet to moist soil. If grown drier, full sun will likely burn or discolor them. ~ *Carrie Becker*

Scientific Name: From an ancient word of Latin origin, *akoron* ("aromatic plant").
Common Name: Japanese sweet flag, sweet flag.
Origin: Asia, North America.
Preferred Conditions: Fertile, acid soil that is constantly moist. Tolerates a wide range of conditions as long as moisture is available. Resents drying out; if subjected, will produce brown tips and burnt foliage.
Light: Sun to part shade.

Planting: Place one foot from high-water mark, if siting near water.
Management: May benefit from division every three to four years; divide the rhizomes and replant them. The center of the clumps will become sparse, and it will be obvious that it's time to divide. Other than cutting out dead or bad-looking foliage and keeping it moist, acorus doesn't require much maintenance.
Propagation: Division in spring.
Pests and Diseases: Prone to slug damage.
Companions: Canna, yellow daylilies, *Euphorbia palustris*, trollius, ligularia, rodgersia, *Ranunculus ficaria*.
Notes: *Acorus calamus* rhizomes grow back and forth across each other and can become quite dense.

Species and Cultivars	Height/ Spread	USDA Hardiness Zone	Flowers (bloom time)	Foliage	Comments
calamus 'Argenteostriatus' (syn. 'Variegatus')	3–4ft × 2ft+	4–10	Greenish, insignificant (E–M)	Vertical creamy-yellow and white stripes, pink-tinged at the base in spring, sword-shaped	Evergreen, may die back in cooler climates, spreads slowly by underground rhizomes
gramineus	1ft × 2ft+	4–10	As above	Mid-green, fragrant, small, grasslike	Evergreen, slow to increase but makes a good clump
g. 'Licorice'	8–12in × 2ft+	4–10	Small, white, insignificant (E–M)	Straplike, solid green, fragrant—aptly named	Slow to increase, a bit tender
g. 'Ogon'	10–12in × 2ft+	4–10	As above	Straplike, gold and green variegation	As above
g. var. pusillus	2–5in × 1ft	4–10	As above	Straplike, dark green	A bit tender, dwarf, also comes in a gold form
g. 'Variegatus'	8–12in × 2ft+	4–10	As above	Straplike, white and green variegation	Striking with black mondo grass, a bit tender

ACTAEA Ranunculaceae

The baneberry has another common name, doll's eyes, because the berries, which can be either red or white, have a dark dot on them that resembles the iris of a doll's eye. As the berries are very poisonous (hence baneberry), the charming name doll's eyes seems a bit misleading. This woodlander from the North American forest bears white flowers in spring in short racemes, similar to a bottlebrush; the leaves are trifoliate and finely divided. Plants like a bit of early spring sun but prefer summer shade. They are very long-lived but slow to increase. ~ *Bob Lilly*

Scientific Name: From the Greek *aktea* ("elder"), whose leaves this genus resembles.
Common Name: Baneberry, doll's eye.
Origin: North America.
Preferred Conditions: Moderately fertile, humus-rich soil.
Light: Part shade to shade.

Actaea rubra.

Management: Mulch in summer to keep cool and moist. Cut down after the autumn fruit falls. Water well in summer. Wilting during the growing season will destroy the flower buds.

Propagation: Division in spring or seed. For seed collection, dry the fruit capsule and then break it open.

Pests and Diseases: Slugs in the spring.

Companions: Ferns, arisaema, asarum, epimedium, pulmonaria, brunnera, helleborus, hosta, *Gillenia trifoliata*, jeffersonia, polygonatum, *Smilacina racemosa*, *Disporum sessile* 'Variegatum'.

Notes: The fruit lasts late into the season.

Species and Cultivars	Height/ Spread	USDA Hardiness Zone	Flowers (bloom time)	Foliage	Comments
alba (syn. pachypoda, rubra f. neglecta)	2–3ft × 2ft	4–9	White on stiff, slender red stalks (E)	Coarse, green, fernlike	White baneberry, clump-forming, RHS Award
rubra	1½–3ft × 2ft	4–9	White on thin green stalks (E)	As above	Scarlet berries, clump-forming, more vigorous than *A. alba*, RHS Award

ADENOPHORA Campanulaceae

The ladybells are a genus of graceful, hardy border perennials, very similar in habit and flower shape to the campanula. Adenophora generally differs from campanula in having vertical stalks with the bell-shaped flowers hanging down and packed a little tighter. Basal crowns grow in the spring followed by tall leafy stems, rising to a fairly pointed end; the nodding flowers bloom on these from the bottom up, with flowers tending to be smaller at the top. Unfortunately ladybells are invasive, running underground by small, thin rhizomes that grow into new plants if broken. They are difficult plants to control once established and are best used in a controlled area, like a narrow bed along a driveway. ~ *Carrie Becker*

Scientific Name: From the Greek *aden* ("gland") and *phorea* ("to bear"), referring to the glandular disk at the base of the flower style.
Common Name: Ladybells.
Origin: North Asia, Europe.
Preferred Conditions: Deep, rich, moisture-retentive, well-drained, alkaline soil, but will grow in most garden conditions. Tolerates quite dry conditions once established.
Light: Sun to shade.
Planting: Should be grouped for best effect.
Management: Cut spent flower stems to ground. It's best not to let it go to seed. Cut dead foliage to ground in winter. Roots do not like to be disturbed (how odd for an invasive plant).
Propagation: Division in spring, seed in July and August, and February to April.
Pests and Diseases: Slugs.
Companions: Ferns, *Iris germanica*, hosta, astilbe, hakonechloa, astrantia, geranium.
Notes: This plant is inappropriately used among perennials like peonies that have a woody crown; you will never get the adenophora roots out of them. In the chart, the symbol ∞ = infinite spread.

Species and Cultivars	Height/ Spread	USDA Hardiness Zone	Flowers (bloom time)	Foliage	Comments
'Amethyst'	2ft × ∞	4–8	Spires of long, down-facing bells of smoky lilac-pink (M–L)	Green, heart-shaped basal leaves, toothed edges	More of a "color" than the types below
bulleyana	3–4ft × ∞	4–8	Large, lavender (M)	Oblong and ovate, broad and hairy	Somewhat invasive
confusa	2–3ft × ∞	4–8	Deep blue, nodding, bell-shaped, 1in long, on upright branched stems (M)	Heart-shaped basal leaves, 3in long, finely toothed	Drought tolerant once established
liliifolia	2–4ft × ∞	4–8	Light blue, slightly fragrant, bell-shaped (M–L)	Light green, pointed, on dark stems	Likes a moist site, the common old garden variety

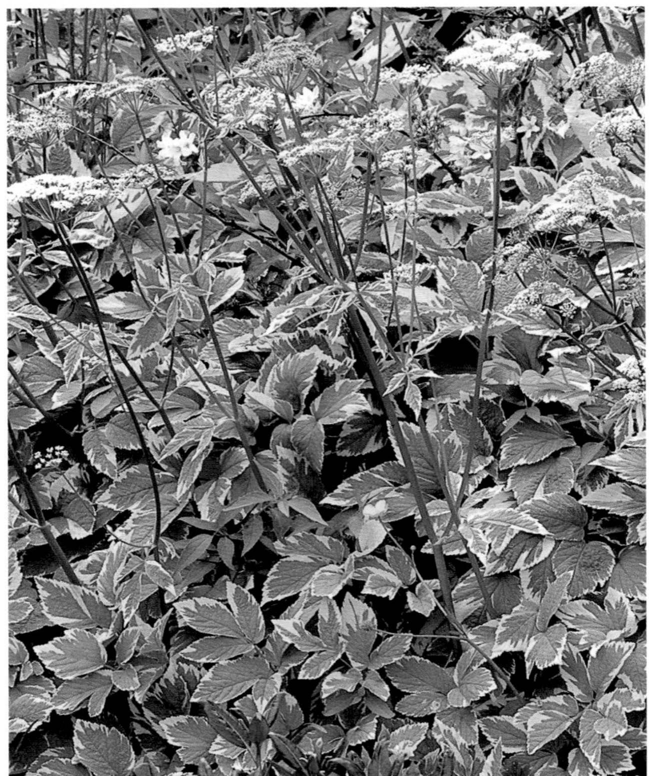

Aegopodium podagraria 'Variegatum'.

AEGOPODIUM Apiaceae

Bishop's weed makes a good groundcover. The variegated leaves are very attractive. It is tough and hardy. But praise pales before the incontestable fact—it is very, very invasive, especially the plain green form. Watch closely for reversions in the variegated form. Even a propensity to spider mites poses no threat. If rigidly controlled, it can enhance shady places, and it does combine well with our West Coast natives. I'm trying to be nice, but it's no good. I have seen what it can do in England, where it is comfortably in control in all wild areas. It is great in difficult areas, maybe in the Sahara, or the Arctic perhaps? Danger, Will Robinson. ~ *Susan Buckles*

Scientific Name: From the Greek *aix* ("goat") and *podion* ("little foot"); plants were once thought to be a cure for gout.
Common Name: Bishop's weed, goatweed, goutweed, ground elder.
Origin: Europe, Asia.
Preferred Conditions: Thrives in most soils.
Light: Sun to shade.
Management: You can remove flowers in summer, as they are not very attractive.
Propagation: Division anytime if well watered.
Pests and Diseases: Mildew and spider mites in some conditions (drought).
Companions: A great groundcover for moist to dry shade in large-scale areas under trees.
Notes: Not evergreen in the Pacific Northwest. In the chart, the symbol ∞ = infinite spread.

Species and Cultivars	Height/ Spread	USDA Hardiness Zone	Flowers (bloom time)	Foliage	Comments
podagraria	12in × ∞	3–8	White, insignificant (M)	Plain green	Bishop's weed, slightly more vigorous than *A. podagraria* 'Variegatum'
p. 'Variegatum'	10in × ∞	3–8	As above	Broadly variegated, creamy white and green	Striking in mass plantings

AGAPANTHUS Alliaceae

Commonly called lily of the Nile, these fleshy-rooted perennials are spectacular in summer. The large globular heads of many tubular flowers are all attached at the same point on a strong green stem. Best known for the intense blue flowers and striking seedheads, which turn a golden brown late in the season, agapanthus are almost the last seed to ripen for us.

Agapanthus 'Peter Pan' is the hardiest africanus type and like all cultivars involving *A. africanus* is usually evergreen. The campanulatus cultivars are what we use here in the Pacific Northwest; unlike the africanus cultivars, these are completely deciduous and hardy. They are heavy feeders but should not be mulched over the top of the crown. In an extremely cold winter, a cover of fir boughs will help protect them.

Agapanthus is a full-sun perennial, and plants are very long-lived. They resent competition and should not be located where other foliage will grow over them. This is an excellent cut flower and good container plant. They like to be pot-bound; even the africanus types can be used in pots but do not allow them to freeze. ~ *Bob Lilly*

Species and Cultivars	Height/ Spread	USDA Hardiness Zone	Flowers (bloom time)	Foliage	Comments
africanus (syn. 'Umbellatus')	3ft × 2ft	9–10	Rich blue (M)	Green, wide, straplike	Evergreen, not truly hardy in the northwest, RHS Award
a. 'Albus'	2–3ft × 2ft	9–10	White (M)	As above	Evergreen, RHS Award
'Blue Baby'	1½ft × 2ft	7–9	Amethyst (M)	As above	Deciduous
'Blue Triumphator'	2–2½ft × 2ft	7–9	Blue (M)	As above	As above
'Bressingham Blue'	3–3½ft × 2ft	7–9	Deep blue (M)	As above	Best dark blue for the garden, deciduous
'Bressingham White'	3ft × 2ft	7–9	Pure white (M)	Mid-green, narrow	Not a heavy flower producer, deciduous
campanulatus	3–3½ft × 1¼ft	7–9	Blue (M)	Narrow, grayish green	Good cut, hardiest, deciduous
c. 'Isis'	1–2ft × 1½ft	7–9	Deep blue (M)	Mid-green, narrow	Deciduous
c. 'Profusion'	1–2ft × 1½ft	7–9	Light and dark blue (M)	As above	As above
Headbourne Hybrids	3–4ft × 1½ft	7–9	Varying shades of blue and white (M)	As above	As above
inapertus	3–5ft × 2ft	7–9	Deep violet-blue, nodding (L)	Rich green, straplike	As above
'Kingston Blue'	1½–2ft × 1½ft	7–9	Indigo-blue (M)	As above	As above
'Lilliput'	1½ft × 1ft	7–9	Dark blue (M–L)	Light green, very narrow	Dwarf, compact, deciduous
'Loch Hope'	4ft × 2ft	7–9	Violet-blue (M)	Mid-green, narrow	Deciduous, RHS Award
'Midnight Blue'	3–4ft × 2ft	7–9	Dark blue (M)	As above	Deciduous
'Mood Indigo'	3–4ft × 2ft	7–9	Deep violet (M)	Large, bright green	As above
'Peter Pan'	1½ft × 1½ft	8–10	Deep blue (E–M)	Mid-green, straplike, narrow	Hardiest africanus type, dwarf, evergreen
'Pinocchio'	1½–2ft × 1ft	7–9	Cobalt-blue (M–L)	Straplike, deep green	Dwarf, deciduous
'Storm Cloud'	2–3ft × 2ft	7–9	Large, deep blue, in large heads (M)	Mid-green, wide, straplike	Deciduous, vigorous
'Tinkerbell'	2ft × 1ft	7–9	Soft blue (E–M)	Variegated with creamy white and green linear stripes	May need winter protection, evergreen
'White Superior'	1–2½ft × 1½ft	7–9	White (M–L)	Light green, straplike	Deciduous, vigorous

Agapanthus 'Loch Hope'.

Scientific Name: From the Greek *agape* ("love") and *anthos* ("flower").
Common Name: Lily of the Nile.
Origin: South Africa.
Preferred Conditions: Well-drained, rich soil. Keep well watered during growing season. Drought tolerant once established.
Light: Sun.
Planting: Plant with crown just at the surface.
Management: Divide when flower production slows down. Plants will benefit from an annual feeding in spring and organic mulch in the fall. Avoid digging near, as roots are brittle and resent being disturbed. They grow toward the light so will look their best in a south-facing border. Remove stems and cut to the ground as they die back in fall. Remove stressed leaves anytime.
Propagation: Division, although it is a major job to untangle all the heavy, fleshy roots. This can be done in spring, just as new growth begins. Seeds germinate easily in soil temperatures of 59–77F, March through May.
Pests and Diseases: Snails, slugs.
Companions: Contrasts well with yellow flowers. Easily combined with kniphofia, crocosmia, phygelius, potentilla, iris, and tropical foliage.
Notes: Blooms its best once established and a bit crowded in the crown.

Agastache rupestris.

AGASTACHE Lamiaceae

Here is a plant that belongs in an herb garden, a cottage garden, or a garden that has semi-wild areas. It's also a good border plant, depending on which species or cultivar you select. Agastache needs hot, dry conditions to do well; it then combines well with other herbs with its dark, rough-textured leaves, flower spikes in blending colors, and, in some species, pleasing fragrance (anise or root beer, depending on your sense of smell). Find plants just the right spot to grow in, and you will enjoy their presence for several years. Agastaches bloom at a time when the summer colors of most other plants are over and will stay in flower until frost. They also do very well in containers and make a good cut flower for fresh arrangements. Flowers are edible (do avoid the bitter calyx) and make a good addition to green salads; enjoy the butterflies, bees, and hummingbirds that will be attracted to them in late summer. ~ *Susan Buckles*

Scientific Name: From the Greek *agan* ("very much") and *stachys* ("ear of wheat").
Common Name: Giant hyssop, anise hyssop.
Origin: North America, Mexico, China, Japan.
Preferred Conditions: Fertile, evenly moist, well-drained soil. Will thrive in most conditions but does not like cold, wet feet. Drought tolerant once established.
Light: Sun.
Management: Erect and self-reliant so does not require a lot of maintenance. Seedheads can be left on for winter interest, but if you deadhead them plants will reflower in response. Leave stems on through the winter and cut them to new growth in the spring.

Propagation: Basal cuttings, especially for prized cultivars, to ensure replacements in case of severe winter weather; seed.

Pests and Diseases: Will get mildew if allowed to get too dry.

Companions: Monarda, helenium, knautia, geranium, nepeta, origanum.

Notes: In zones 4–6, agastaches may be an annual or self-sow. Most cultivars do not appear to be very hardy in the maritime Northwest—probably due to wet ground in the winter. Try one or two and see if they grow well for you before relying on them as part of a planned design.

Species and Cultivars	Height/ Spread	USDA Hardiness Zone	Flowers (bloom time)	Foliage	Comments
'Apricot Sunrise'	18–24in × 12in	4–10	Fragrant apricot-orange (M–L)	Gray-green	Heat and drought tolerant
'Blue Fortune'	30in × 12in	4–10	Dense cluster of rich blue (M–L)	Green, strong and stiff upright growth	RHS Award
foeniculum	30in × 12in	4–10	Soft-looking clusters of blue flowers inside violet bracts (M–L)	Green, very stiff upright growth	Anise hyssop, self-sows, very aromatic, good cut
f. 'Alba'	24in × 12in	4–10	White (M–L)	Light green, very stiff upright growth	Aromatic (anise)
f. 'Aureum'	30in × 12in	4–10	Pale violet (M–L)	Gold	Comes true from seed
'Pink Panther'	18–24in × 18in	4–10	Bright rose-pink (M–L)	Dark green, lanceolate	Aromatic foliage
rupestris	24in × 24in	4–10	Coral-orange (M)	Gray-green	Very aromatic foliage

AJUGA Lamiaceae

Ajugas are popular low-spreading or clump-forming groundcovers—resilient and adaptable plants that will take almost any condition. The flowers are borne on spikes in whorls in late spring to early summer in shades of blue and pink. The attractive leaves vary in shape from obovate and coarsely toothed to ovate and crinkled. Leaf color ranges from light green to bronze-purple or even variegated. Many of the variegated forms will revert to green, are shorter-lived, and suffer from slug predation. Ajuga is visually lost against dark mulch or soil; it looks its best planted next to something lighter and brighter, such as *Lysimachia nummularia* 'Aurea'. Most forms of *A. reptans* spread very quickly and can be invasive under good conditions. ~ *Susan Carter*

Scientific Name: Obscure.

Common Name: Bugleweed, carpet bugle.

Origin: Europe.

Preferred Conditions: Heavy, humus-rich soil. Moist conditions are preferred except for the variegated forms. Most will need supplemental watering only during the worst dry spells.

Light: Sun to shade.

Planting: In colder areas, plant the young plants in spring.

Management: Cut off spent flower stems. If prone to mildew, cut flowering stems off immediately after flowering. Can become invasive if not kept in check, but easy to control. Cut off the stoloniferous roots to control spread. Tidy up by removing dead leaves and stems.

Propagation: Division anytime but preferably in spring or fall. Take cuttings from April through June.

Pests and Diseases: Aphids, mildew, crown rot.

Ajuga reptans 'Pink Elf'.

Companions: A good edge-softener for polygonatum, *Coreopsis verticillata* 'Moonbeam', *Hosta* 'Sum and Substance', bronze fennel, grasses, iris, *Lysimachia nummularia* 'Aurea', and like plants; also works well under fruit trees and bulbs.

Notes: Ground-covering plants act as a living mulch. Don't worry about growing ajuga around larger perennials or shrubs, as it will not harm them; just don't let the ajuga overgrow anything else. Listed in most books as a shade plant, in the Pacific Northwest ajuga does just as well in full sun and heavy soil. In the chart, when foliage is described as toothed, the teeth are typical of the mint family: rounded, with scalloping of various sizes.

Species and Cultivars	Height/ Spread	USDA Hardiness Zone	Flowers (bloom time)	Foliage	Comments
genevensis	8–10in × 24in	3–10	Pink spikes (E–M)	Coarsely toothed, green, glossy, clump-forming	Rock garden variety, more restrained, prefers drier soil
g. 'Pink Beauty'	6–8in × 24in	5–10	Soft pink on upright spikes (E)	Large-toothed, green, glossy, clump-forming	Not as hardy as the species
pyramidalis	2–10in × 18in	3–10	Violet-blue (E–M)	Roundish, glossy, slightly toothed, very dense	Slow to spread
p. 'Metallica Crispa'	6in × 12in	3–10	Deep blue (E–M)	Reddish brown with a metallic glint, crinkled and very dense	Tidy, clumping habit, slow to spread, beautiful
reptans	4–8in × 24in+	3–10	Violet-blue (E)	Dark green, bronze, or mottled	Spreads by runners, invasive, will tolerate dry shade
r. 'Alba'	6–8in × 24in	3–10	White with a hint of yellow (E)	Light green	Spreads slowly
r. 'Atropurpurea' (syn. 'Bronze Beauty')	6–8in × 30in+	3–10	Deep blue (E)	Bronze-purple, rounded and flat	Spreads rapidly, RHS Award

Species and Cultivars	Height/ Spread	USDA Hardiness Zone	Flowers (bloom time)	Foliage	Comments
r. 'Braunherz' (syn. 'Bronze Heart')	6–8in × 24in+	3–10	As above	Glossy deep-purple	Good introduction, RHS Award
r. 'Burgundy Glow'	4–6in × 24in+	3–10	Blue (E)	Reddish purple, variegated with white and pink	Tricolor with good fall color, spreads fast, doesn't like to be dry, RHS Award
r. 'Catlin's Giant'	8–12in × 36in+	4–10	Dark blue (E)	Very large, fluted purple leaves, glossy	Vigorous, a bit less hardy, RHS Award
r. 'Jungle Beauty'	10–15in × 36in+	4–10	Blue (E)	Very large, mahogany-purple, glossy	Vigorous, a bit less hardy
r. 'Multicolor' (syn. 'Rainbow')	8–10in × 24in+	3–10	Deep blue (E)	Pink, white, and yellow variegated, shiny	Slow to grow
r. 'Pink Delight'	8–10in × 24in+	3–10	Clear pink (E)	Crinkled, green	Best if given adequate moisture and bright light
r. 'Pink Elf'	4in × 12in	3–10	Deep pink (E)	Dark green-bronze, small	A little thing
r. 'Purple Brocade'	6–8in × 24in+	3–10	Sky-blue (E)	Deep purple, glossy, brocaded	
r. 'Purple Torch'	12in × 24in+	3–10	Lavender-pink (E)	Green, turning bronze in winter	
r. 'Silver Beauty'	4–6in × 12in	3–10	Light blue (E)	Silver-green and white variegation	Good contrast plant, not as vigorous
r. 'Variegata'	4–6in × 12in	3–10	As above	Gray-green leaves edged and splotched with creamy yellow	Needs part shade for best variegation, not as vigorous

Alcea ficifolia hybrid.

ALCEA Malvaceae

Hollyhocks have long been associated with cottage gardens and the far reaches of herbaceous borders. In nature, they are plants of dry hills and steppes and rocky areas. It should come as no surprise, then, that the best-looking and healthiest hollyhocks are found in cement cracks and baking neighborhood back alleys, where—because the climate overall is not that of Turkey, Iran, and southern Russia—they don't live long, especially here in the Pacific Northwest. There is nothing quite like them though, and if you've had problems with the common hollyhock (*A. rosea*), then you will appreciate *A. ficifolia* for its rust resistance and large yellow flowers. ~ *Carrie Becker*

Scientific Name: From *alkaia*, the Greek name for a kind of mallow.
Common Name: Hollyhock.
Origin: Siberia.
Preferred Conditions: Well-drained and moderate to poor and drier soil.

Light: Sun.
Management: Cut to new basal growth in fall or late winter. May require staking.
Propagation: Seed.
Pests and Diseases: Slugs may damage new growth in spring.
Companions: Delphinium, larger campanulas, large grasses, picket fences.
Notes: New hybrids between *A. ficifolia* and *A. rosea* give us more color choices and are also rust resistant. *Alcea rosea* is considered to be biennial here in the Pacific Northwest: perhaps they die; perhaps one just wishes they would, as they are so afflicted with rust.

Species and Cultivars	Height/ Spread	USDA Hardiness Zone	Flowers (bloom time)	Foliage	Comments
ficifolia	3–8ft × 2ft+	3–9	Pale, clear yellow (M–L)	Green, figleaf-shaped	

ALCHEMILLA Rosaceae

Above all, let us consider *A. mollis*, which is the species most often grown and the lady's mantle with the largest leaves, gray-green and softly fuzzy. Every morning you can observe one of its well-known characteristics, guttation (or perking of water) on the edges of the foliage—it looks like a string of clear pearls on each leaf. As the morning progresses, dew (another process) collects in the center of the leaves. When *A. mollis* flowers, the entire display is lovely. The flowers give the impression of little clouds of chartreuse sitting atop and about the foliage.

The other alchemillas are of smaller stature and some are shiny green. None of the smaller forms self-sows as wildly as *A. mollis*. All are great groundcovers or edge-softeners and look good near water. All make good cut flowers, both fresh and dried. To dry, pick just as it comes into full flower and hang upside down in a dark room with good air circulation; they turn a wonderful golden tan. ~ *Carrie Becker*

Alchemilla mollis.

Alchemilla mollis with *Iris ensata* and *Lysimachia punctata*. Design by Michael Schultz.

Scientific Name: From the Arabic *alkemeluch* ("alchemy").
Common Name: Lady's mantle.
Origin: Europe.
Preferred Conditions: This is a tough plant, and any conditions are good except for boggy areas. It's drought tolerant once established. Self-sows and pops up in almost any nook and cranny.
Light: Sun to shade.
Management: Cut flowering stems back to basal growth before going to seed and remove dead leaves as needed. Alternatively for the larger forms, cut the entire plant to the ground as soon as blooms begin to fade and water well; it will quickly leaf out again and produce mounds of fresh foliage. In late fall or early winter, leaves will turn brown and mushy; cut foliage back to ground.
Propagation: Divides very well in early spring before the leaves are fully formed; seed.
Pests and Diseases: Spider mites can sometimes be a problem.

Companions: Works well with most blue, purple, red, burgundy, and red-violet flowers; try it with early dark red astilbe, or for high contrast, plant with 'Magic Carpet' spiraea, which has red-orange new foliage. Other companions would be grasses, white foxgloves, golden marjoram, geranium, and campanula; often planted under roses as a groundcover.
Notes: Seedlings are easy to remove; get them while they're young!

Species and Cultivars	Height/ Spread	USDA Hardiness Zone	Flowers (bloom time)	Foliage	Comments
alpina	6–8in × 18in	5–10	Loose clusters of green-yellow, somewhat insignificant (E–M)	Kidney-shaped, lobed, with a fine silver edge, silky-hairy and silver beneath	Good for the rock garden
ellenbeckii	6–8in × 24in+	5–10	Insignificant (E–M)	Green, pleated, on wiry red stems	Good rock garden and groundcover plant, runs
erythropoda	4–6in × 18in	5–10	Chartreuse, foamy (E–M)	Blue-green pleated, densely and softly hairy on both sides	Compact, low mounds, smaller version of *A. mollis*, RHS Award
mollis	18–24in × 24in	5–10	Chartreuse, in delicate airy sprays, long-blooming (E–L)	Gray-green, pleated, downy, fan-shaped	Self-sows, RHS Award
m. 'Auslese'	18–24in × 24in	5–10	Airy, frothy mounds of chartreuse (E–L)	Pleated, green, somewhat evergreen	Self-sows
m. 'Thriller'	18in × 24in	5–10	Yellowish, airy, frothy (E–L)	Gray-green	Very similar to *A. mollis* 'Auslese', self-sows

ALLIUM Alliaceae

Onions are the best example of a true bulb. Many layers surround a growth point from which arises a single flower stem. The flowers are at the top of the strong stems in tight or loose clusters (umbels) in a full range of colors, from white through to pink, blue, and purple and even yellow. Alliums are good cut flowers for fresh arrangements and also make an excellent decorative element when dried. Seedheads can be left in the garden for a show both after bloom and in the winter, or cut for fall arrangements.

Most of the larger-flowered forms do not increase for us and need to be treated as annuals; the best perennial alliums are *A. cristophii* and *A. sphaerocephalon*. We list only the forms we consider to be hardy. Even so, they are best used in full sun so their leaves can cure well for next year's flower production. Leaves can be a bit iffy or messy by flowering time, so it is a compromise: how to hide the foliage and still allow enough sun for it to cure. ~ *Bob Lilly*

Scientific Name: Greek name for garlic.
Common Name: Flowering onion.
Origin: Europe, Asia, North America.
Preferred Conditions: Deep, fertile, rich, well-drained soil. Don't overwater during the summer months, as the bulbs should be allowed to cure.
Light: Sun.

Allium moly.

Management: Divide if clumps become too congested. Some are very invasive (see the chart). Most large-flowering forms cure their leaves at flowering time. Cut foliage down when dead. Watch for slugs and rabbits in early spring, and don't let the invasive ones go to seed.

Propagation: Division if congested or flower production is reduced; seed (may take three or more years to flower); and bulbs in the fall.

Pests and Diseases: Slugs, rabbits, mildew, rust.

Companions: Roses, penstemon, iris, early salvia, knautia, astrantia, euphorbia, kniphofia, grasses, hosta. Looks good in groupings, coming up through shrubs or perennials.

Notes: Dried seedheads have an even wider range of companions. Plant alliums in groups, not singly. All alliums are entirely edible—foliage, bulb, and flower. In the chart, the symbol ∞ = infinite spread.

Species and Cultivars	Height/ Spread	USDA Hardiness Zone	Flowers (bloom time)	Foliage	Comments
aflatunense	3ft × 1ft	4–9	Purple (E)	Green, turns brown by flowering time	Needs summer drought (bulbous)
cernuum	1–2ft × 1ft	4–8	Pink to purple, nodding (M–L)	Glaucous to dark green, narrow, straplike, clump-forming	North American native, very adaptable, vigorous, bulbous
cristophii	1–2ft × 1½ft	4–8	Huge, airy lilac globes of star-shaped blooms with a metallic cast (M)	Straplike, gray-green, dies back before flowers bloom	Star of Persia, bulbous, self-sows, RHS Award
giganteum	4–6ft × 1ft	4–8	Purplish, with prominent stamens (M)	Large, straplike, glaucous	Giant allium, glaucous stems, bulbous, RHS Award

Species and Cultivars	Height/ Spread	USDA Hardiness Zone	Flowers (bloom time)	Foliage	Comments
hollandicum 'Purple Sensation'	18–24in × 10in	4–9	Violet, spherical umbel (E)	Green, straplike	Very perennial, increases slowly in the garden
moly	6in × 6in	4–9	Yellow (E)	Gray-green	Invasive, prolific, bulbous
schoenoprasum	9–12in × 18in	4–9	Round umbels of tiny bell-shaped pale purple blooms (E–M)	Green, hollow, cylindrical, clump-forming	Chives, self-sows, edible, may flower better in lighter, drier soil
s. 'Forescate'	9–12in × 18in	4–9	Round umbels, deep purplish pink (E–M)	As above	Grown for its flower color, vigorous
senescens	10–12in × 12in	4–9	Lilac to rose-pink, cup-shaped, in umbels (M–L)	Straplike, green to silver-gray, tends to twist	Clump-forming, circle allium, vigorous
s. subsp. montanum var. glaucum (syn. glaucum)	6–12in × 12in	4–9	Pinky-mauve globes (M–L)	Glaucous, turns orange in fall, often twisted	Clump-forming, doesn't like competition
sphaerocephalon	2–3ft × 4in	4–10	Wine-purple, in egg-shaped umbels(M)	Mid-green, hollow, cylindrical	Drumstick allium, bulbous
unifolium	8in × ∞	4–9	Pink up-facing florets (M)	Grasslike, green, flops to ground at flowering time then cures	Invasive, prolific, self-sows, bulbous, RHS Award

ALSTROEMERIA Alstroemeriaceae

If you haven't grown the Peruvian lilies, you've probably had them in a fresh floral arrangement; but these long-lasting flowers deserve a place in both a vase and the garden. The foliage is arranged in whorls up the wiry stems and topped off by a cluster of exotic lilylike blooms. These striking flowers appear in a large range of colors, from shades of bright orange to softer combinations of pink and white, yellow streaked with red, and even a red and green one. Most have beautiful markings and show off their stuff in the height of the summer.

Alstroemerias spread by fleshy roots that form new tubers. In the case of *A. aurea*, the hardiest species, these roots can become very invasive. They will also seed in the Pacific Northwest. With so many new hybrids that behave quite well, we wouldn't encourage you to grow this species in your mixed border, but rather in a place where its spread could be controlled or appreciated. *Alstroemeria ligtu* hybrids can also become invasive over time.

The seedheads of alstroemeria are very attractive and can be left on until fall cleanup if they haven't already been cut for the vase. If you do use them for fresh arrangements, instead of cutting the flower off of the stem, give the entire stem a good quick tug, pulling it from the crown. This will signal the plant to produce new stems, prolonging the flowering season. Cut flower growers use this system on their field crops. ~ *Susan Carter*

Scientific Name: After Baron Claus Alstroemer (1736–1794).
Common Name: Peruvian lily.
Origin: Chile, Brazil, Peru.

Alstroemeria ligtu hybrids.

Alstroemeria ligtu with *Lychnis coronaria*, *Verbascum chaixii* 'Album', and various white lilies mixed in for accent.

Preferred Conditions: Rich, fertile, well-drained soil with average water. Tolerates a heavier and poorer soil once established.

Light: Sun to part shade. Provide shade from intense heat.

Planting: Plant deep, approximately nine inches, although they will find their own depth.

Management: Plants resent being moved. Very young plants should be protected for the first and second winter with mulch. Some support is often needed; try pea sticks or grow them through shrubs.

Propagation: Careful division in March. Seed requires stratification.

Pests and Diseases: Slugs are a problem, particularly early in the season.

Companions: Caryopteris, hypericum (shrubby forms), hemerocallis, baptisia, spiraea.

Notes: The series bred for pot culture or cut flower culture may not be as hardy. In the chart, the symbol ∞ = infinite spread.

Species and Cultivars	Height/ Spread	USDA Hardiness Zone	Flowers (bloom time)	Foliage	Comments
aurea (syn. aurantiaca)	2½–3ft × ∞	6–10	Golden orange, spotted with red, multibranched umbels (M)	Limp, lanceolate, gray-green, roots go down deep (to Chile)	Invasive, hardiest species
hookeri	8–12in × 12in	6–10	Pink, on very short stems (M)	Gray-green	Dwarf, needs lots of heat
ligtu hybrids	2–4ft × ∞	6–10	White, cream, orange, red, pink, salmon, or yellow, streaked with red, in loose clusters of 15 or more on wiry stems (M)	As above	Self-sows, invasive, RHS Award
Princess Series	2–2½ft × 2ft+	6–10	Wide range of colors, both pastel and bright (M–L)	Mid-green	Bred for cut flower trade, runs, some have RHS Awards
psittacina	2–3ft × 3ft+	6–10	Red and green, exotic-looking, in clusters of 4 or more (M–L)	Mid-green, evergreen in mild zones	Parrot flower, mulch for winter protection, runs
p. 'Royal Star' (syn. p. variegated)	2–3ft × 3ft+	6–10	As above	White-edged, otherwise as above	Doesn't run as much, but will revert

Amsonia tabernaemontana.

AMSONIA Apocynaceae

Amsonia is a small genus of eastern U.S. woodlanders with a great deal of charm. These slow-growers are hard to find but worth pursuing (*A. tabernaemontana* is most widely available); they make good cut flowers, but you might want to wait for plants to get well established before cutting. ~ *Bob Lilly*

Scientific Name: After Charles Amson, eighteenth-century Virginia physician and botanist.
Common Name: Blue star.
Origin: Eastern United States, west to Texas.
Preferred Conditions: Deep, well-drained, moisture-retentive, fertile soil. Likes heat and plenty of moisture.
Light: Full sun to part shade.
Management: This is a low-maintenance plant. Mulch lightly in early spring. Plants can be cut back during the season to prevent their becoming too tall after flowering; they will then produce feathery new shoots. Doesn't need frequent division, and doesn't like to be disturbed. In late fall, cut woody stems to the ground. Watch for slugs in early spring.
Propagation: Division in spring; seed in spring.
Pests and Diseases: Slugs.
Companions: Narcissus, paeonia, achillea, euphorbia, iris; good as a specimen or in groups, and works well as a late-spring filler plant.
Notes: Grows well on the verge of woodlands, where the shade of trees gives way to sun. Sun enhances their striking fall color.

Species and Cultivars	Height/ Spread	USDA Hardiness Zone	Flowers (bloom time)	Foliage	Comments
ciliata	3ft × 1½ft	4–9	Bright blue (M)	Feathery, turns bright gold in fall	Spreads by underground runners
hubrichtii	3–4ft × 1½ft	4–9	Light blue, starlike (E–M)	Needlelike, turns orange-gold in fall	
orientalis (syn. *Rhazya orientalis*)	1ft × 1½ft	4–9	Pale gray-blue, darker in bud (E)	Dull green	RHS Award
tabernaemontana	2½–3½ft × 1½ft	4–9	Light blue, starlike, funnel-shaped, in clusters (E–M)	Dull green turning golden yellow in fall, willowlike, clump-forming	Best form for maritime Northwest
t. var. salicifolia	2½ft × 1½ft	4–9	Light blue with a white throat and small beard within (E–M)	Narrow, good gold to orange fall color	A wonderful willowy look

Anaphalis triplinervis.

ANAPHALIS Asteraceae

Only two species of these daisy family members are used as border perennials. The native *A. margaritacea* is found throughout the Pacific Northwest, and since our weather tends toward wet winters and springs and drier summers and falls, it's safe to assume that these conditions suit this species. Both have grayish leaves, indicating their fondness for poorer soils, and quietly charming little gray-white flowers. The more attractive species is *A. triplinervis,* which has broader leaves (perhaps half an inch across) with three prominent veins; it's one of the few gray-foliaged plants that actually thrives in the shade. ~ *Carrie Becker*

Scientific Name: Greek name for another everlasting.
Common Name: Pearly everlasting.
Origin: Himalayas, Cascades, widespread in temperate subalpine zone.
Preferred Conditions: Average and well-drained soil. Doesn't like to dry out. Tolerates strong sun and poor soil.
Light: Sun to part shade.
Management: Top-dress lightly with a mulch in spring. Cut back old stems and dead leaves in fall.
Propagation: Division in fall; seed.
Pests and Diseases: Mildew can be a problem with dry soil.
Companions: Sedum, verbascum, carex, hosta, low fall asters, salvia, *Lychnis coronaria, Scabiosa ochroleuca.*
Notes: Good for drying but must be cut in tight bud.

Species and Cultivars	Height/ Spread	USDA Hardiness Zone	Flowers (bloom time)	Foliage	Comments
margaritacea	18in × 24in+	4–8	Grayish white with tiny yellow center (M–L)	Narrow, gray	Northwest native, pearly everlasting, runs
triplinervis	12in × 12in	4–8	As above	Silver gray-green and felted underneath with 3 distinct veins	Clump-forming, gray foliage for the shade! RHS Award
t. 'Sommerschnee'	12in × 12in	4–8	As above	Narrow, gray	Great cultivar and gray foliage for the shade, RHS Award

Anchusa azurea 'Loddon Royalist'.

ANCHUSA Boraginaceae

We all need a bit of bugloss in the garden! *Anchusa azurea* is a good perennial for the middle of the border; its selections are strong performers but should be kept from too much feeding, as this can make them a bit lanky. Only this one species and its cultivars are commonly available. Their colors are wonderful in the garden, but as with many fast-growing perennials, they are short-lived. ~ *Bob Lilly*

Scientific Name: Greek name denoting a pigment obtained from the roots of some species and used as a cosmetic.
Common Name: Bugloss, alkanet.
Origin: Europe, Africa.
Preferred Conditions: Deep and well-drained, moist soil. Will not tolerate wet conditions, especially winter wet, but don't allow it to dry out.
Light: Sun to part shade.
Management: Cut back stems after flowering; this encourages basal growth and further bloom and discourages self-sowing. Cut back again in fall cleanup. So short-lived in heavy soils, we suggest using new plants each year. They may become invasive in too rich of a soil. Do not overfertilize.
Propagation: Root cuttings in early spring for cultivars; seed in spring for species.
Pests and Diseases: Root rot.
Companions: Lupinus, nepeta; useful as a filler plant. In early summer, pair *A. azurea* 'Loddon Royalist' with the coarse hairy stems and leaves of *Papaver orientale* (the strong orange forms)—the two are a perfect counterpoint as well as a perfect complement in color. Add some orange geums and deep blue siberian iris, with a little *Euphorbia griffithii* 'Fireglow' nearby—an eye-popping combination.

Species and Cultivars	Height/ Spread	USDA Hardiness Zone	Flowers (bloom time)	Foliage	Comments
azurea	3–5ft × 2ft	3–8	Purplish blue (M)	Coarse, dark green, hairy leaves and stems	Superseded by its cultivars
a. 'Dropmore'	3–4ft × 2ft	3–8	Gentian-blue (M)	Coarse, hairy	
a. 'Little John'	1½ft × 2ft	3–8	Deep blue, small (M–L)	As above	Dwarf alkanet
a. 'Loddon Royalist'	3ft × 2ft	3–8	Deep blue, large (M)	Coarse, hairy, on heavy branching spikes	Bushy and well branched, RHS Award

ANEMONE Ranunculaceae

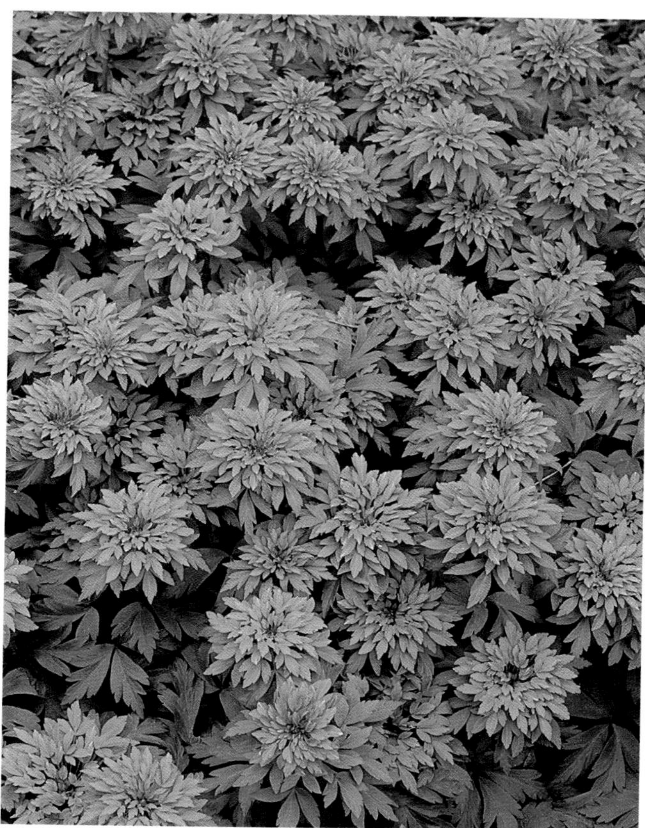
Anemone nemorosa 'Viridiflora'.

The genus *Anemone* is large and diverse, with species occurring in a wide range of habitats, from woodland to open meadowlands; gardeners everywhere will therefore be able to grow many of them. We deal with the herbaceous perennial forms, with their nodding, often fragrant, single and semi-double pastel flowers. The lovely common name windflower, originally applied to *A. blanda* from Greece, is now applied to all anemones. Windflowers that are truly perennial are generally best in the wild garden or the front edge of an understory. Various species provide interesting foliage, colorful flowers, and unusual seedheads; even the flower buds can be striking, some being shiny, translucent, and pearl-like.

Every garden needs a windflower; I think it should be possible to have an anemone in flower somewhere in your garden from early spring to fall. The Japanese anemones will want to take over the autumn border, however, and need to be strictly controlled. Fall division is not recommended: these are *spring division* plants!

A word of caution: the entire plant is poisonous. ~ *Susan Buckles*

Scientific Name: From the Greek *anemos* ("wind").
Common Name: Windflower.
Origin: China, Europe, northwestern Asia, Japan.
Preferred Conditions / Light / Management:
Group 1. Woodland anemone (blanda, ×lesseri, multifida, nemorosa, sylvestris). Sun to part shade in well-drained, humus-rich soil that doesn't dry out. Doesn't need division except for propagation. Spring- or summer-flowering; goes dormant after blooming.
Group 2. Japanese anemone (hupehensis, ×hybrida, rivularis, tomentosa). Sun to part shade in well-drained, fertile, humus-rich soil. Some may be invasive once established. They will benefit from a winter mulch. Dig around the plants (root prune) every year to help control spread, although without removal of the extra roots you may be propagating these anemones! Cut foliage down when dead in winter. Fall-flowering.
Propagation: Division in spring as new growth appears. Japanese anemones can also be propagated from root cuttings in spring.
Pests and Diseases: Slugs.
Companions: For spring bloomers—bulbs, aquilegia, dicentra, helleborus, omphalodes, *Ranunculus ficaria*, trillium, primula. For late summer and fall bloomers—grasses, hardy fuchsias, aster, dahlia, eupatorium, phlox, astrantia.
Notes: Watch for flop on *A. hupehensis* and *A. h.* var. *japonica*; try pea sticks or contain with shrubs. In our gardens, all Japanese anemones run and can cover much more ground than noted in the chart.

Species and Cultivars	Height/ Spread	USDA Hardiness Zone	Flowers (bloom time)	Foliage	Comments
blanda	3–4in × 4in	4–8	Blue, white, or pink (many cultivars) (E)	Deeply divided, green and very short, dies down by summer	Grecian windflower, tuberous, RHS Award
hupehensis (syn. japonica)	2–3ft × 2ft+	5–8	Pink inside, maroon on reverse, 5–6 rounded segments (M–L)	3-lobed, oval to rounded, dark green, toothed and divided	Chinese anemone, extremely invasive
h. 'Hadspen Abundance'	2–3ft × 2ft+	5–8	Single to semi-double, deep rose-pink, golden yellow center (M–L)	Deep green, 3-lobed, oval to rounded, toothed and divided	RHS Award
h. var. japonica	2–3ft × 2ft+	5–8	Variable, creamy pink to magenta, appears double (M–L)	Deep green, maple-leaf shape	Japanese anemone, invasive, self-sows
h. var. japonica 'Bressingham Glow'	2–3ft × 2ft+	5–8	Darker rose-pink with a white sheen, semi-double to double (M–L)	Dark green	A bit better behaved
h. var. japonica 'Pamina'	2–4ft × 2ft+	5–8	Deep rose-red, semi-double (M–L)	As above	RHS Award
h. var. japonica 'Prinz Heinrich' (syn. 'Prince Henry')	2–4ft × 2ft+	5–8	Deep pink with yellow center, semi-double (M–L)	As above	Clump-forming, aggressive, RHS Award
h. 'Praecox'	2–3ft × 2ft+	4–8	Carmine-pink (M)	As above	
h. 'Splendens'	2–3ft × 2ft+	5–8	Deep red (L)	Dark green, deeply divided	Aggressive
×hybrida (syn. japonica)	3–5ft × 2ft+	5–8	Pale rose-pink, golden yellow center, single to double (M–L)	Dark green, 3-lobed, ovate, toothed, slightly hairy	Japanese anemone, aggressive, may need staking
×h. 'Alice'	3–4ft × 2ft+	5–8	Light pink, semi-double (M–L)	Dark green, deeply cut	Clump-forming, spreads slowly
×h. 'Andrea Atkinson'	3ft × 2ft+	6–10	White with chartreuse center, single (M–L)	Deep green, maple-leaf shape	Seedheads turn a rich brown, vigorous
×h. 'Elegans' (syn. 'Max Vogel')	3ft × 2ft+	4–8	Pink, silvery reverse, single (M–L)	Deep green	Wiry stems, vigorous, RHS Award
×h. 'Honorine Jobert' (syn. 'Alba')	3–4ft × 3ft+	4–8	White with yellow stamens, single (M–L)	Mid-green, deeply cut	Strong plant once established, can be invasive, RHS Award
×h. 'Königin Charlotte' (syn. 'Queen Charlotte')	3ft × 2ft+	5–8	Soft silvery-pink, pale purple on reverse, semi-double (M–L)	Dark green	Vigorous, RHS Award
×h. 'Kriemhilde'	3–4ft × 2ft+	4–8	Light pink with deep pink reverse, semi-double (M–L)	As above	Vigorous
×h. 'Margarete'	3–4ft × 2ft+	4–8	Deep rosy-pink, golden center, semi-double (M–L)	Slightly hairy	A bit better behaved
×h. 'Richard Ahrens'	3–4ft × 2ft+	4–8	Dark pink, bright gold center, single (M–L)	Lobed, coarse, slightly hairy	As above

Species and Cultivars	Height/ Spread	USDA Hardiness Zone	Flowers (bloom time)	Foliage	Comments
×h. 'Robustissima'	2–4ft × 3ft+	5–8	Light pink-mauve, single (M–L)	Deep green, grape-leaved	Vigorous, spreading
×h. 'September Charm'	2–3ft × 3ft+	4–8	Rich silvery-pink, darker reverse (M–L)	Dark green, deeply divided	Clump-forming, strong plant, RHS Award
×h. 'Whirlwind'	2–4ft × 3ft+	4–8	Large, white, gold center, semi-double (M–L)	Mid-green	Strong plant once established, can be invasive
×lesseri	1–1½ft × 1ft	5–8	Small, deep rose-red, white center (E–L)	Fernlike, mid-green, toothed, lobed, hairy	Erect, clump-forming, not long-lived
multifida	8–10in × 8in	4–8	Small, white to creamy-yellow (M)	Deeply divided, hairy, mid-green	North American native, vigorous
nemorosa	6–12in × 12in+	4–8	White to bluish white to pink and blue, single (E)	Dark green, 3- to 5-part, deeply cut and toothed	Wood anemone, aggressive, summer dormant, long-lived once established, RHS Award
n. 'Allenii'	6–10in × 12in+	4–8	Deep rich lavender-blue inside, paler blue outside, large (E)	Mid-green	Strong grower, summer dormant, RHS Award
n. 'Blue Eyes'	6–10in × 12in+	4–8	White aging to blue in center, double to nearly single (E)	As above	Summer dormant
n. 'Flore Pleno	6–10in × 12in+	4–8	White, double to semi-double (E)	As above	As above
n. 'Robinsoniana'	6–12in × 18in+	4–8	Lavender-blue inside, pale creamy-gray outside (E)	As above	Dark maroon stem, summer dormant, RHS Award
n. 'Vestal'	6in × 12in+	4–8	White, extremely double, tufted center (E)	As above	Clump-forming, summer dormant, RHS Award
n. 'Viridiflora'	6in × 12in+	4–8	Green bracts and petals, very double (E)	As above	Summer dormant, charming curiosity
rivularis	2–3ft × 1ft+	6–8	White with blue-gray reverse, blue center (M)	Green, divided	Clump-forming
sylvestris	1–1½ft × 1½ft+	4–8	White, yellow stamens, nodding, cup-shaped, fragrant (E–M)	Deeply cut, light green	Snowdrop anemone, repeat bloom in fall, vigorous, runs
s. 'Elise Fellmann'	10–15in × 18in+	3–8	White, double (E–M)	Deeply cut, mid-green	May repeat bloom in fall, runs
s. 'Macrantha'	1–1½ft × 1½ft+	4–9	White with yellow stamens, double, nodding, fragrant (E–M)	Deeply cut, hairy	White seedheads, runs
tomentosa	3–4ft × 2ft+	4–9	Soft pink or white, darker reverse (M–L)	Divided, deeply veined, mid-green, 3-part oval, toothed, hairy	Clump-forming, aggressive spreader, can be invasive

Anemonella thalictroides f. *rosea* 'Oscar Schoaf'.

ANEMONELLA Ranunculaceae

Anemonella thalictroides is a native wildflower of the central and eastern American woodland. The white or pink flower has five to ten petal-like sepals surrounding a cluster of stamens and pistils. In the case of the doubles, the stamens become petal-like. The flowers are arranged in loose umbels. The leaves, which emerge after the flowers, are reminiscent of thalictrum. True to their origins, anemonellas enjoy rich, moist but well-drained soil. They colonize very slowly from tuberous roots and need to be protected from competition in the root zone. Double forms last longer in flower and multiply more rapidly. Plants disappear by midsummer (summer dormant), earlier if they don't get enough moisture. ~ *Ann Bucher*

Scientific Name: Diminutive of anemone.
Common Name: Rue anemone.
Origin: Eastern North America.
Preferred Conditions: Humus-rich, moist, and moderately fertile.
Light: Part shade.
Management: They resent disturbance. Remove dead foliage and mark location of plants; even when dormant, they need to be kept moist.
Propagation: Carefully separate small outer portions of the tuberlike root clusters in late winter; each piece needs a tiny pip or growth point; seed as soon as ripe.
Pests and Diseases: Slugs, powdery mildew, rust.
Companions: Small ferns, bulbs, viola, hosta, *Anemone nemorosa* (but give them their own spot).
Notes: All forms increase slowly by forming a cluster of tuberous roots; they do not run.

Species and Cultivars	Height/ Spread	USDA Hardiness Zone	Flowers (bloom time)	Foliage	Comments
thalictroides	6–10in × 6in	4–8	White to pale pink, single and double (E)	Similar to thalictrum, deeply divided but on a smaller scale	
t. 'Big Green Picture'	6–8in × 6in	4–8	Green with white congested petals in center, large (E)	As above	
t. 'Cameo'	6–8in × 6in	4–8	Soft pink (E)	As above	
t. 'Jade Feather'	6–8in × 6in	4–8	Green (E)	As above	
t. f. rosea 'Oscar Schoaf'	6–8in × 6in	4–8	Pink, double (E)	As above	Elegant double flower
t. semi-double white	6–8in × 6in	4–8	White, semi-double (E)	As above	
t. 'Stephanie Feeney'	6–8in × 6in	4–8	Pink, single, large (E)	As above	

ANTHEMIS Asteraceae

The flowers of these daisylike perennials consist of a yellow center surrounded by yellow, orange, or white ray flowers. All "daisies" have these ray flowers surrounding a center of disk flowers. (Please don't quibble about the double ones.) The foliage is aromatic, deeply cut, and fernlike. Anthemis are easy to grow in full sun and are valuable filler plants in a border setting. They make a good cut flower for floral arrangements, both fresh and dried. The plant habit (floppy, messy, gawky, sloppy) is a bit annoying in our dim summers and wet soils. A hard cut after flowering can kill them. ~ *Susan Carter*

Anthemis tinctoria 'Sauce Hollandaise'.

Scientific Name: Greek name for this plant.
Common Name: Golden marguerite.
Origin: Mediterranean.
Preferred Conditions: Lean, alkaline, well-drained soil. Doesn't require a lot of water. Drought tolerant once established.
Light: Sun.
Management: Keep plant deadheaded and the spent flower stems cut down. This will encourage new basal growth. Pinch back in spring for a bushier growth habit. Try pea sticks to help control the flop. Do not let plants dry out as growth begins.
Propagation: Replace every two or three years in spring. Stem cuttings. Seed indoors in winter or outside in spring.
Pests and Diseases: Slugs, aphids, occasional mildew.
Companions: Solidago, grasses, sages, geranium, monarda, patrinia.
Notes: Even though this is a very short-lived plant, it's very handsome and a long bloomer while alive.

Species and Cultivars	Height/ Spread	USDA Hardiness Zone	Flowers (bloom time)	Foliage	Comments
sancti-johannis	18–24in × 2ft	4–9	Orange rays around a yellow center (M)	Gray-green, divided	
'Tetworth'	18–24in × 2ft	3–7	White, semi-double (M–L)	Gray-green, feathery	Long flowering season
tinctoria	18–36in × 2ft	3–7	Rich yellow with yellow center (M–L)	Mid-green, gray-green below, finely cut	Short-lived, used as a dye
t. 'E. C. Buxton'	18–28in × 2ft	3–8	Lemon-yellow with yellow center (M–L)	Dark green, ferny	Bushy
t. 'Kelwayi'	18–24in × 2ft	3–8	Clear golden yellow (M–L)	Dark green, feathery	Old-fashioned marguerite
t. 'Sauce Hollandaise'	18–24in × 2ft	4–9	Pale cream, white (M–L)	Dark green, finely divided	
t. 'Wargrave Variety'	24–36in × 2ft	3–7	Lemon-yellow, palest of all *A. tinctoria* (M)	Deep green, finely divided	Short-lived

AQUILEGIA Ranunculaceae

What would spring be like without columbines? I would not refuse space to any columbine in my garden—the deep blue flowers of *A. alpina,* blooming with narcissus, dogtooth violets, pulmonaria, and the sharp green foliage of *Milium effusum* 'Aureum', is just one vignette that comes to mind. There is a columbine for every color scheme, from the strangely hued *A. vulgaris* 'William Guiness' (deep maroon and ivory flowers and gray-green foliage) or the fabulous *A. v.* 'Adelaide Addison' (double granny's-bonnet flowers in purple and white) to the frilly *A. v.* var. *stellata* 'Nora Barlow', with densely doubled petals of green, pink, and cream. They're good as cut flowers, but don't last very long. Typical of the buttercup family, all aquilegias are poisonous. They seed about easily and cross among themselves, producing surprises throughout the garden. Isolate the special one to conserve the color or type. ~ *Carrie Becker*

Scientific Name: From the Latin *aquila* ("eagle"), referring to the shape of the petals.
Common Name: Columbine.

Aquilegia vulgaris var. *stellata* 'Black Barlow'.

Origin: Northern hemisphere.

Preferred Conditions: Well-drained, moisture-retentive, and don't let the soil dry out. Taller varieties may need protection (staking) from wind.

Light: Sun to part shade. Alpine forms need full sun.

Planting: Transplant as young as possible from containers or sow in place.

Management: Resents disturbance (deep taproot). Not demanding in culture. Staking is not usually necessary. Cut hard after flowering to help control leaf miners and mildew, if present. Many are short-lived and should be replaced every four or five years. Some will give a repeat bloom if deadheaded.

Propagation: Fresh seed is easiest; sow when ripe in summer. Seed needs light to germinate so don't cover with much soil.

Pests and Diseases: Mildew, leaf miners, aphids. Snip off leaves at first sign of leaf miner infestation (usually affects only the appearance of the plant). Sawfly larvae are a new pest that can skeletonize the entire plant; pick off the green larvae, and cut back foliage if damage is severe—plants usually recover.

Companions: Viola, *Alchemilla mollis*, geranium, hemerocallis, paeonia, digitalis, hosta, euphorbia, pulmonaria.

Notes: Aquilegias are a must for the hummingbird garden.

Species and Cultivars	Height/ Spread	USDA Hardiness Zone	Flowers (bloom time)	Foliage	Comments
alpina	12–18in × 12in	3–9	Blue or white, short spurs, nodding (E)	Green, finely divided, compact	Good for rock gardens
Biedermeier Group	8–18in × 10in	3–9	Yellow, blue, white, pink, red, white-tipped, single and double, out-facing (E–M)	Gray-green, compact	Nosegay columbine, dwarf, dainty
caerulea	2–2½ft × 18in	3–9	Blue and white, on erect stems, long spurs (E–M)	Green, 3-parted	Rocky Mountain columbine, likes it cool, RHS Award

Species and Cultivars	Height/ Spread	USDA Hardiness Zone	Flowers (bloom time)	Foliage	Comments
canadensis	2–3ft × 1ft	3–9	Bicolored, red and yellow, up-facing (E–M)	Dark green	Native, long-lived, less susceptible to leaf miner, self-sows, RHS Award
chrysantha	2½–4ft × 1ft	3–9	Yellow, long spurs, fragrant (E)	Rich green, thin, divided	Golden spur columbine, shade tolerant, good rebloomer if deadheaded
c. 'Yellow Queen'	2½–3½ft × 18in	3–9	Golden yellow with long spurs, large 3in flowers (E–M)	Green, thin, divided	
'Crimson Star'	18–30in × 18in	3–9	Crimson and white with long spurs (E–M)	Green, sparse, open	Good cut
'Dragonfly'	18–24in × 18in	3–9	Rose, blue, yellow, white, pink, red, and pastels, long spurs (E–M)	As above	Good cut
flabellata	10–12in × 12in	3–9	Blue or white-lilac, yellow-tipped, nodding, short spurs (E–M)	Glaucous, fanlike, broad	Dwarf, RHS Award
f. 'Ministar'	6in × 8in	3–9	White with blue spurs (E–M)	As above	Dwarf
formosa	2–3ft × 18in	3–9	Red and yellow, nodding (E)	Airy stems, bluish green, finely divided	Western columbine, native
fragrans	30in × 18in	3–9	Milky-white or pale blue, fragrant (M)	Green	
'Hensol Harebell'	3ft × 18in	3–9	Deep blue, short spurs (E)	Green, sparse, open	Strong grower, RHS Award
'Irish Elegance'	2ft × 18in	3–9	White with greenish tint on tips, double, no spurs (E)	Dark blue-green	
McKana Group (syn. 'McKana Giants')	2–3ft × 18in	3–9	Yellow, pink, red, white, large, long spurs, lightly fragrant (E–M)	Blue-green	Good cut
Music Series	16–18in × 18in	3–9	Bicolored with outer petals of blue, pink, or red with white or gold center, large, long spurs (E–M)	Green, compact	Uniform, strong plant, good cut, full range of colors, RHS Award
Songbird Series	16–24in × 18in	3–9	Blend of colors, large (E–M)	As above	As above
viridiflora	12in × 12in	3–9	Dark olive with short spurs, bell-shaped, scented (E)	Green, lightweight	Flowers are easy to miss
vulgaris	18–30in × 18–24in	3–9	White, yellow, purple, red, small, short spurs (E–M)	Gray-green, divided, erect clumps	Granny's bonnet, common columbine, self-sows freely

Species and Cultivars	Height/ Spread	USDA Hardiness Zone	Flowers (bloom time)	Foliage	Comments
v. 'Adelaide Addison'	24–36in × 18in	3–9	Blue-purple with white center, double, nodding (E–M)	Green, erect clumps	Self-sows
v. var. flore-pleno	12–24in × 18in	3–9	Violet, rose, and white, double, spurless (E–M)	As above	As above
v. var. stellata (syn. clematiflora)	30–36in × 18in	3–9	Rose, white, blue, violet, flat, nodding, spurless (E)	As above	Flowers are charming but shatter easily
v. var. stellata 'Black Barlow'	30in × 18in	3–9	Black and deep violet shades, double (E)	As above	Good cut
v. var. stellata 'Nora Barlow'	30–36in × 18in	3–9	Shades of pink, white, and soft green in the same flower, double (E–M)	Green, compact, erect clumps	A distinctive look, RHS Award
v. Vervaeneana Group	18–24in × 18in	3–9	Off-white, pale blue, pale pink (E–M)	Splashed with golden variegations	Grown mostly for foliage
v. Vervaeneana Group 'Woodside Blue'	18–24in × 18in	3–9	Pale blue (E–M)	As above	As above
v. 'William Guiness' (syn. 'Magpie')	24–30in × 18in	3–9	Dark maroon with ivory corolla (E)	Gray-green, open, some maroon	Superb flower, good cut

ARISAEMA Araceae

Not all of these relative newcomers to the gardening scene have yet been named, let alone discovered. Even so, gardeners are already presented with good choices. We are drawn to these unusual plants because they lend an aura of mystery to the shadier parts of the garden; every aspect of their development is fascinating to watch.

Arisaemas grow from underground tubers of various shapes; these provide clues to identification. The foliage is attractive, emerging from papery sheaths around the pseudostem, and often the leaves are held above the inflorescence like an umbrella. The leaf stem itself is often attractively mottled and the leaves, sometimes variegated, can produce five to twenty leaflets, though only one to three leaves are produced from the tuber. The inflorescence is the crowning glory. It is constructed of an ornamental bract called a spathe, within which is a tubelike spadix carrying the reproductive parts. The spathe can taper to a threadlike appendage, which can wave above the plant or arch over to the ground; it is thought that this may be connected with pollination. Lastly, from the female flowers, come attractive bright red or orange fruit in fall. Arisaemas protect themselves by being very poisonous. It is doubtful that the garden designer would choose to include a drift of arisaemas, but hidden under trees, in pockets of part shade, nothing equals the arisaema in its ability to cause astonishment, smiles, or quizzical second glances.

Arisaemas do well in woodland gardens. The main problem is protecting their location after they go dormant; we use a small tripod of thin green stakes, which also helps to support the plant as it grows up the next year. It doesn't hurt to enrich the soil regularly, and after the tubers have been planted out in late January, the anticipation begins and increases from then on. What fun.
~ *Susan Buckles*

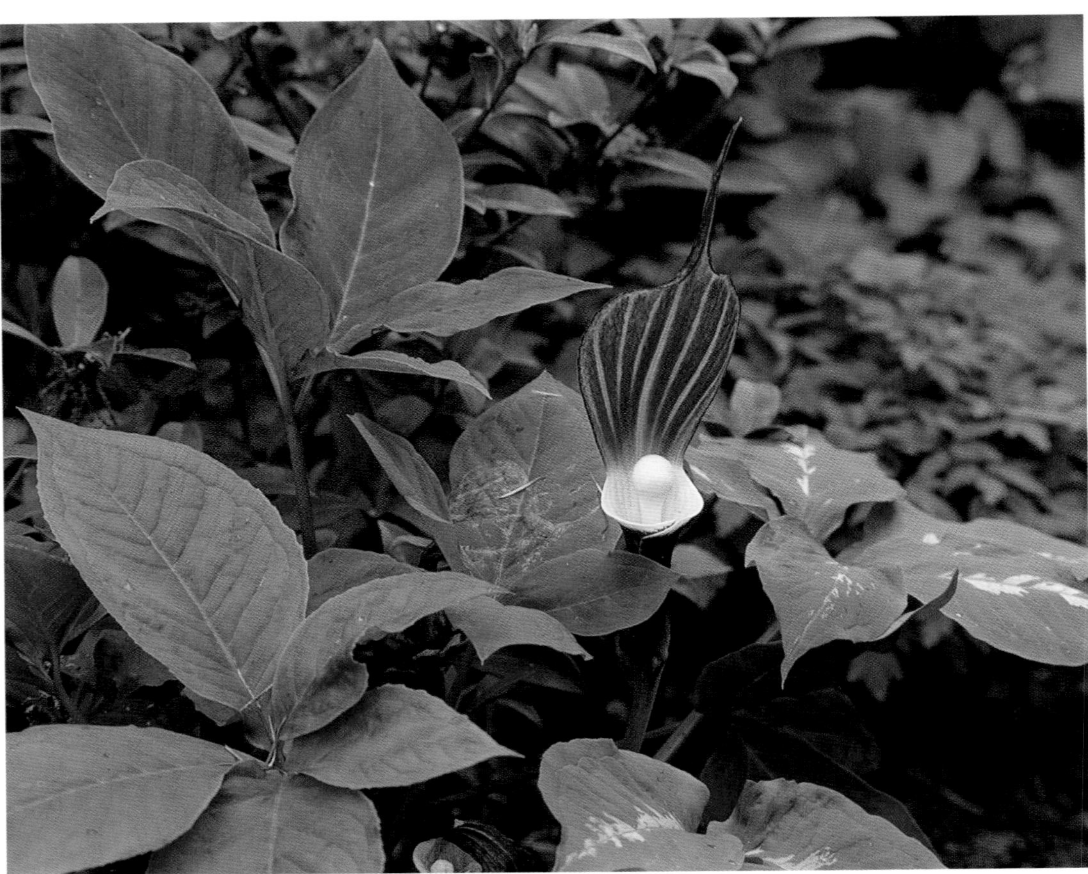

Arisaema sikokianum.

Scientific Name: Greek *aron* ("arum") and *haema* ("blood"), referring to the red-blotched leaves.

Common Name: Cobra lily, Jack-in-the-pulpit.

Origin: China, Japan, North America, Korea, Himalayas.

Preferred Conditions: Cool, fertile, humus-rich, well-drained soil. Plants need moisture-retentive soil in spring, but tolerate drought after they go dormant. Avoid boggy or waterlogged conditions.

Light: Part shade to shade.

Management: Plants are late emerging, especially *A. candidissimum* (late June), and go dormant in late summer, especially during drought or with excessive heat. Protect leaves of early flowering forms from late frosts. Remove spent seedheads, clear away old foliage as it dies back, and mark location. May benefit from a winter mulch.

Propagation: Divide offsets in autumn when dormant (*A. sikokianum* may take two to four years to flower, but *A. candidissimum* multiplies well from offsets). Seed from types that don't provide offsets.

Pests and Diseases: Slugs, snails. Some varieties may be victims of predation by voles.

Companions: Ferns, helleborus, hosta, primula, polygonatum, smilacina, disporum, disporopsis.

Notes: Be sure to mark their location and don't step on the dormant tubers.

Species and Cultivars	Height/ Spread	USDA Hardiness Zone	Flowers (bloom time)	Foliage	Comments
candidissimum	12–16in × 24in	6–9	Hooded white spathe with pink stripes, white spadix, fragrant (M)	Green, broad, 3-lobed, glossy	Late to emerge, orange seeds, RHS Award
consanguineum	2½–4ft × 2ft	7–9	Green spathe with a long tail (E)	Large, green, peltate	Red fruit
flavum	12in × 8in	6–9	Variable small green flower, yellow canopy, tightly hooded green and white spathe spotted purple inside, short spadix (M)	Green, tripartite	Small in stature
griffithii	2ft × 2ft	7–9	Dark purple, striped white, rolled, cobralike spathe (E–M)	Green, trifoliate, deeply corrugated, often with a sheen	Spathe up to 3in wide, spadix has a whip 2ft long
jacquemontii	12–18in × 18in	6–9	Narrow green spathe, light green inside, white stripes, base is dark purple, purple spadix (M)	1–2 green palmate leaves with 3–9 leaflets	
ringens	2½–3ft × 2ft	6–9	Hooded green spathe, purple stripes and white tips, green spadix (M)	Green, glossy, coarse 3-lobed leaves with ovate leaflets	Japanese cobra lily
sikokianum	12–24in × 18in	5–9	Hooded purple, maroon, and white spathe, striped green and brown, spadix is white (E)	Green, 2 leaves, 5-lobed, bordered in pink, may age with silvery markings	Japanese cobra lily, red fruit, spathe is pure white inside
speciosum	2ft × 2ft	7–9	Large hooded spathe, maroon inside, green-striped outside, creamy-white spadix (M)	Rich green edged in red-brown, 3-lobed 18in-wide	
taiwanense	3ft × 2ft	6–9	Hooded purple spathe with long white spadix (E)	Green, peltate, long, narrow, deeply divided	Stems are mottled like snakeskin, maroon and green
tortuosum	4–5ft × 2ft	6–9	Hooded green spathe, long purple spadix (sometimes green) (E–M)	Green, 2 leaves, 3-lobed, divided into 5–17 elliptic leaflets	Snakeskinlike stems
triphyllum	12–24in × 18in	4–9	Hooded, green spathe, purple striped inside, greenish brown spadix (E–M)	Green, 2 leaves, 3-lobed, narrow-oblong to ovate leaflets	Jack in the pulpit, orange to red berries, U.S. native

Arisarum proboscideum.

ARISARUM Araceae

You will know the mouse plant by its tail. Extending beyond the shiny green leaves is a long, black, narrow protuberance that looks for all the world like a tail. Given a clump, which is the usual situation, it looks like a mouse convention. If you look closely you will see that the tail is the termination of a quite lovely maroon and white spathe. Come summer they disappear, to reappear next spring in greater numbers and in new spaces. Children of all ages enjoy this plant. ~ *Ann Bucher*

Scientific Name: From *arisaron*, the Greek name for *Arisarum vulgare* (now *Dracunculus vulgaris*), a tuberous herb mentioned by Dioscorides.
Common Name: Mouse plant.
Origin: Italy, Spain.
Preferred Conditions: Moist, cool, humus-rich, moisture-retentive soil.
Light: Part shade.
Management: Remove dead foliage and tidy up in winter. May suffer in a severe winter; mulch will help.
Propagation: Division of clumps in autumn and winter or during summer dormancy.
Pests and Diseases: Slugs.
Companions: Ferns, primula, *Polygonatum humile*, small cyclamen, *Viola cornuta*.

Species and Cultivars	Height/ Spread	USDA Hardiness Zone	Flowers (bloom time)	Foliage	Comments
proboscideum	4–6in × 8–10in	7–9	Hooded spathe, dark purplish brown above, gray-green beneath with a long, thin, black curled tip (E)	Small, shiny, dark green, arrow-shaped	Mouse plant, clump-forming

Armeria alliacea.

ARMERIA Plumbaginaceae

Thrift is a common evergreen perennial along the coastlines of Portugal, Spain, and North America. Looking like tufts of grass with round clusters of small pink flowers on thin straight stems, these are clumping and very hardy. There are two main groups: the rock garden types and the larger forms, which actually make good cut flowers. The smaller types can form large, almost woody mats that, like dianthus, may get a bit bald in the center and will need to be repropagated or replaced. Divisions in the usual manner are not practical, because they do not always root down as they spread. Tuck them among rocks in locations with full sun and even poor soil, and they will bloom heavily.

The larger forms (*A. alliacea*, *A.* 'Bee's Ruby', *A. pseudarmeria*, *A.* 'Ornament') are the more standard herbaceous perennials. The large-leaved armerias, as with kniphofia, are best left alone over the winter and only cleaned up a bit in spring. *Never cut back hard. ~ Bob Lilly*

Scientific Name: Latin for a cluster-headed dianthus.
Common Name: Thrift, sea pink.
Origin: Europe, Asia, North America.
Preferred Conditions: Well-drained soil, not too rich. Will not tolerate wet feet.
Light: Sun to part shade.

Species and Cultivars	Height/ Spread	USDA Hardiness Zone	Flowers (bloom time)	Foliage	Comments
alliacea (syn. plantaginea)	1–1½ft × 1½ft	3–9	White to pale pink to deep rose (E–M)	Broad, grassy, may turn reddish in winter	Plantain thrift
'Bee's Ruby'	1–2ft × 1½ft+	4–9	Bright pink to reddish purple (E)	Narrow, lanceolate, dark green	Clump-forming, good cut, RHS Award

Species and Cultivars	Height/ Spread	USDA Hardiness Zone	Flowers (bloom time)	Foliage	Comments
juniperifolia	2–4in × 4–24in	4–8	Tiny, soft pink to white (E–M)	Tight rosettes, gray-green, hairy, stiff	Spanish thrift, mat-forming, RHS Award
j. 'Bevan's Variety'	2–3in × 4–24in	5–8	Deep rose-pink (E–M)	Grassy, dark green, tight rosettes	Alpine thrift, RHS Award
maritima	6–12in × 12in+	3–9	Rose-pink (E–M)	Narrow, stiff, dark green	Common thrift, sea thrift, long-blooming
m. 'Alba'	6–10in × 10in+	3–9	White (E–M)	Dark bluish green	Long-blooming
m. 'Bloodstone'	6–10in × 10in+	3–9	Dark rose-red (E–M)	As above	Long-blooming
m. 'Cottontail'	8in+ × 12in	3–9	White (M)	Dark green, glossy	
m. 'Düsseldorfer Stolz'	8–10in × 10in+	3–9	Bright rose-red (E–M)	Dark bluish green	Good rebloomer
m. 'Rubrifolia'	8–10in × 8in+	3–9	Deep rosy-pink (E–M)	Reddish purple or burgundy, grassy	Will rebloom
m. 'Splendens'	6–10in × 10in	3–9	Bright reddish pink (E–M)	Narrow, bluish green	Good cut
'Ornament'	1–1½ft × 18in	4–9	White to dark pink to red, large (E–M)	Narrow, straplike, dark bluish green	As above
pseudarmeria hybrids	1–2ft × 18in	4–9	White, pale pink, and lilac to red (E–M)	Mid-green, toothed, veined, lanceolate	Pinball thrift, good cut

Management: Cut off flowers and stems immediately after the flowers fade, and they will rebloom. Replace plants after they become loose and straggly. In the spring, poke pieces of stem into soil, where they will root. Long, straggly stems can either be layered or removed from the plant and poked.

Propagation: Seed and layering.

Pests and Diseases: Slugs, rust.

Companions: Santolina, thymus, sempervivum, sedum, Pacific Coast iris, saxifraga, lavandula, *Ceratostigma plumbaginoides*, *Eryngium maritimum*. Use as an edging plant or groundcover.

Notes: Height in chart is flower stem length.

ARMORACIA Brassicaceae

This horseradish is for the lover of variegation who has everything. Irregular patches of cream on upright, coarse green leaves! It does have a presence in the garden. Perhaps an ornament for the vegetable patch, or grow it with the variegated Alaska Series nasturtium and scarlet runner beans. This plant is a chimera; the cells that determine its variegation are at the root/top growth junction. Root cuttings will not be variegated, nor is the variegation stable. Still, it is worth growing. ~ *Carrie Becker*

Scientific Name: The classical Latin name of a related plant.

Common Name: Horseradish.

Origin: Southeastern Europe.

Armoracia rusticana 'Variegata'.

Preferred Conditions: Rich, fertile, moist soil. It survives in dry, not-so-fertile soil but will not produce as much root mass.
Light: Sun.
Planting: Grows best if soil is loosened to a depth of at least two feet. This is a deep, aggressive rooter!
Management: Can be an aggressive spreader. Keep plant contained, or dig up entire plant every year or so. Be sure to remove all the roots. Replant only a few roots or crown divisions. Cut foliage down when dormant.
Propagation: Division when dormant; tissue culture.
Pests and Diseases: Slugs really can make this plant very unattractive.
Companions: Grasses, crambe, *Campanula glomerata* var. *alba, Iris foetidissima, Nicotiana alata*, and sushi.
Notes: Be patient, they are often not variegated very much for the first two years.

Species and Cultivars	Height/ Spread	USDA Hardiness Zone	Flowers (bloom time)	Foliage	Comments
rusticana 'Variegata'	3ft × 2½ft	5–8	Probably won't flower, but don't let it	Broad, wavy, splashed with irregular bright green and white markings	Forms a dense, rounded mound

Artemisia ludoviciana 'Valerie Finnis'.

ARTEMISIA Asteraceae

Jelitto and Schacht's *Hardy Herbaceous Perennials* (1990) lists twenty-seven species of artemisias, including annuals, biennials, and perennials. Graham Stuart Thomas (1990) describes eleven gardenworthy perennial artemisias, most having the recognizable qualities of silver or gray aromatic foliage with soft hairs on one or both sides of the leaves and small yellow composite flowers. Artemisias have long been cultivated for other qualities too, particularly for their medicinal or herbal properties. They are more suited to the herb garden than the perennial border, but some are handsome, erect semi-woody small shrubs that deserve a place as an ornamental, growing best in hot, dry situations in sandy soil. The best ones to incorporate in the border are *A.* 'Powis Castle', *A.* 'Huntington', and *A. lactiflora* Guizhou Group. Almost all the others we list are invasive and require control to maintain their place in the society of plants.

You can always find a spot for artemisias. Combine *A. ludoviciana* 'Silver Queen' with alstroemeria in a parking strip and throw in a bit of crocosmia. Some work wonders in a fresh or dried floral arrangement. ~ *Susan Buckles*

Scientific Name: After the Greek goddess Artemis.
Common Name: Wormwood, mugwort.
Origin: Europe, North America, North Africa, Asia.
Preferred Conditions: Poor to average, well-drained, light soil. Drought tolerant once established. Tolerant of rocky, dry exposure or cool, foggy coastal climates. Adaptable to many garden environments. Doesn't do well in wet, soggy areas.
Light: Sun.
Planting: A handful of soft rock phosphate will boost root growth. Compost or sand can be added to heavy clay soils to improve the tilth.
Management: Large shrubby artemisias should be cut back to six to twelve inches from ground level in spring, and the dwarf forms just given a trim to tidy up. You can cut some back to prevent blooming (e.g., *A. ludoviciana* 'Valerie Finnis', *A.* 'Powis Castle', *A. alba* 'Canescens'). Some cultivars can be helped with gravel or crushed rock mulch. Herbaceous forms should be cut down completely when foliage is dead. All except *A. lactiflora* have inconspicuous flowers at best. At worst, flowers are ugly and detract from the foliage; flowering stems are best removed as soon as they appear.
Propagation: Division in spring. Most are easily divided (exceptions are *A. absinthium* 'Lambrook Silver' and *A.* 'Powis Castle'). Take cuttings in spring; and for the woody forms, cuttings only.
Pests and Diseases: Mildew, rust (*A. lactiflora*), aphids (*A. absinthium* 'Lambrook Silver', *A.* 'Powis Castle').
Companions: Ornamental grasses, lilies, white flowers, allium, aster, sedum, nepeta.
Notes: Don't fertilize, and artemisias will live longer in the garden. This includes manure mulch. A hard prune in the fall can kill most of the shrubby forms.

Artemisia 'Huntington' with *Agastache* 'Apricot Sunrise', ×*Solidaster luteus*, *Ruta graveolens*, a helianthus cultivar in flower and *Helianthus maximiliani* (above).

Species and Cultivars	Height/ Spread	USDA Hardiness Zone	Flowers (bloom time)	Foliage	Comments
abrotanum	3–4ft × 2ft	5–10	Yellowish, insignificant (M–L)	Woody, multibranched, gray-green, fernlike, aromatic subshrub	Southernwood, prune in spring, may benefit from a midsummer clip, RHS Award
absinthium	2–4ft × 2ft	5–10	Yellow-gray (M–L)	Silvery gray-green, coarse, feathery, aromatic	Common wormwood, keep pruned for best shape, evergreen
a. 'Lambrook Silver'	2½–3ft × 3ft	5–10	Grayish white sprays (M)	Delicate and airy clumps of silky-gray divided leaves	Cut back flower shoots, evergreen, RHS Award
alba 'Canescens'	10in × 18in	5–10	Small, yellow (M)	Silver, threadlike, and lacy on woody stems	Good groundcover, needs good drainage, remove flowers, RHS Award

Species and Cultivars	Height/ Spread	USDA Hardiness Zone	Flowers (bloom time)	Foliage	Comments
'Beth Chatto'	15–18in × 18in+	5–9	Insignificant (M)	Silvery, low, dense	Good groundcover, needs good drainage
'Huntington'	3–4ft × 3ft+	6–10	Tiny, insignificant (L)	Lacy, loose, silver leaves, upright, bushy, woody plant	Well-drained, cut back to 6in in spring as new growth starts
lactiflora	4–6ft × 2ft	5–10	Creamy-white plumes on sturdy erect stems, fragrant (M–L)	Dark green, ferny, paler beneath	White mugwort, looks like a tall astilbe, prefers heavier moisture-retentive soil, herbaceous perennial, RHS Award
l. Guizhou Group	4–6ft × 2ft	5–10	Ivory-white on dark purple stems, fragrant, astilbelike plumes (M–L)	Blackish green, dissected, coarse, on black stems	Likes a richer, moist soil, tolerates part shade, herbaceous perennial
ludoviciana	4ft × 3ft	5–10	Yellow-white, insignificant (M)	Silver-gray, willowy, aromatic, bushy on slender erect stems	Western mugwort, this and its selections are best artemisias for cutting, all are herbaceous perennials
l. 'Silver King'	2–3ft × 2ft	5–10	Silver-white, insignificant (M–L)	Long, narrow, silver-white	Spreading habit, cut to ground in fall
l. 'Silver Queen'	2½–3ft × 2ft	5–10	Insignificant, seldom produced (M–L)	Low mound, silver-white	Best of the ludovicianas for cut flowers, RHS Award
l. 'Valerie Finnis'	1½–2ft × 2ft	5–10	Tiny, insignificant (M)	Large, silver-white, felty, jagged	Cut mature plants to ground midsummer, will reappear at lower height, RHS Award
'Powis Castle'	2–3ft × 2ft+	6–10	As above	Finely cut, silver-gray, shrubby woody plant	Responds well to pruning in late winter to 1ft. May be short-lived in rich soils and hard winters, RHS Award
schmidtiana 'Silver Mound'	1ft × 1ft	5–10	White, insignificant (M)	Silver, velvety, fernlike, aromatic, compact	May need cutting back in midsummer, short-lived, likes good drainage, herbaceous perennial
stelleriana	1½–2½ft × 2ft+	5–10	Tiny, yellowish on gray stems (M)	Grayish white, felty, chrysanthemumlike, evergreen in mild climates	Beach wormwood, rock garden plant, sensitive to winter wet, semi-herbaceous perennial, cut back in spring
s. 'Boughton Silver' (syn. 'Silver Brocade')	6–10in × 2ft+	5–10	White, insignificant (M–L)	Silver with a hint of green, felty, evergreen in mild climates	Groundcover or edging plant, like it dry, compact
versicolor	1ft × 3ft	5–10	Insignificant (M)	Pale, gray, curly with a blue-green cast, woody at base	Dwarf, foliage dries well for arrangements

ARUM — Araceae

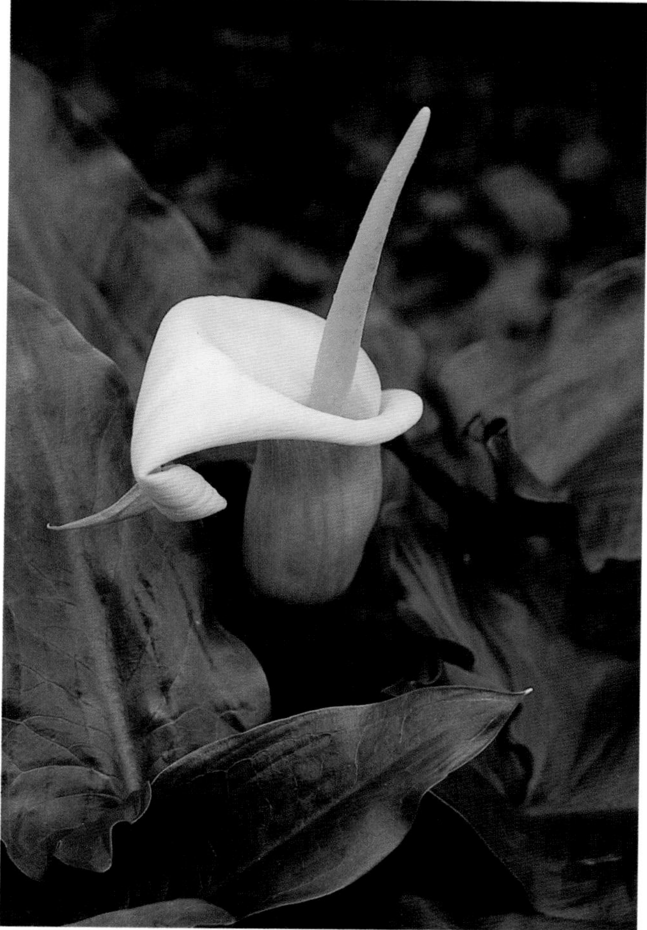
Arum creticum.

Arums are indispensable winter plants. In early winter one or two leaves appear and remain attractive all through the season. Once established, the clumps can become very dense and leafy. The arrow-shaped leaves are narrow or wide, veined in silver or mottled with yellow; some have black spots. They cover the ground when we need it and last well in floral arrangements. The inflorescence—which consists of a yellowish or greenish white shaft (or spadix) surrounded by a greenish white hood (or spathe)—appears in spring. In fall, the spadix stands alone (the leaves having gone dormant), covered with red-orange berries. A dramatic sight! In a perfect year, the combination of new leaves and bright fruit is a delight in late fall and early winter.

Arums take some time to establish but will colonize summer-dry spaces in either sun or shade over time. Beware, all parts of the plant are poisonous. ~ *Ann Bucher*

Scientific Name: From the Greek *aron*, the name for these poisonous plants.
Common Name: Lords and ladies, cuckoo pint.
Origin: Britain, Europe, Crete, Italy, North Africa, Turkey.
Preferred Conditions: Deep, well-drained, humus-rich soil. Keep them moist but don't overwater during summer dormancy.
Light: Part shade to shade, sun in winter. Will take sun in summer with adequate water.
Management: Arums are a low-maintenance plant. Organic mulch may be applied in autumn. Clumps eventually become large and begin to spread, and an aggressive spading program only aggravates this problem. To control some spreading, harvest seed when stems collapse. Remove dead foliage and leave fruiting stems.
Propagation: Division in early fall during dormancy. In early spring, separate offsets and replant. Needs to form a good-sized tuber to produce seed, and seed can take a year to germinate.
Pests and Diseases: Slugs, snails.
Companions: Astilbe, epimedium, hosta, ferns, snowdrops and other early bulbs, *Helleborus orientalis*, *H. foetidus*, *Vancouveria planipetala*, xanthorhiza, disporum, *Smilacina racemosa*.
Notes: *Arum italicum* can get quite dry in late summer with no harmful effects.

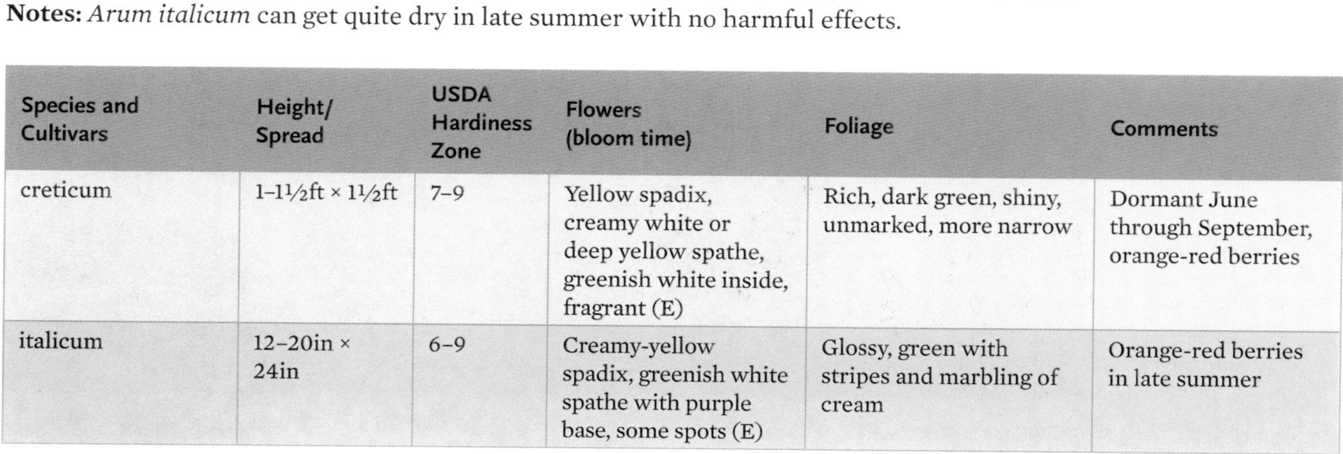

Species and Cultivars	Height/ Spread	USDA Hardiness Zone	Flowers (bloom time)	Foliage	Comments
creticum	1–1½ft × 1½ft	7–9	Yellow spadix, creamy white or deep yellow spathe, greenish white inside, fragrant (E)	Rich, dark green, shiny, unmarked, more narrow	Dormant June through September, orange-red berries
italicum	12–20in × 24in	6–9	Creamy-yellow spadix, greenish white spathe with purple base, some spots (E)	Glossy, green with stripes and marbling of cream	Orange-red berries in late summer

Species and Cultivars	Height/ Spread	USDA Hardiness Zone	Flowers (bloom time)	Foliage	Comments
i. subsp. italicum 'Marmoratum' (syn. 'Pictum')	1–1½ft × 1½ft	6–9	Bright yellow spadix, pale green and white spathe (E)	Broad, rich dark green with gray marbling and veining	Red-orange berries, RHS Award
i. subsp. italicum 'Spotted Jack' (syn. 'Jack Sprat')	1–1½ft × 1½ft+	6–9	As above	Wider, dark green with marbling and veining	Heavy orange-red fruit
i. subsp. italicum 'Tiny'	<8in × 8in	6–9	As above	Small dark green leaves	Orange fruit
i. subsp. italicum 'White Winter'	<1ft × 1ft	6–9	As above	Very slender, with bold markings, more white than green	Orange fruit, best foliage cultivar
maculatum	1–1½ft × 1ft	6–9	Yellow spadix, whitish green spathe with red spots (E)	Glossy, dark green, spotted purple, much larger than *A. italicum*	Lords and ladies, coral-red berries, aggressive

ARUNCUS Rosaceae

The two species of aruncus have in common their deeply cut foliage and terminal plumes of creamy white flowers in summer. They differ in size. *Aruncus dioicus* is a very tall plant that grows slowly at first but eventually reaches a spread of four feet—and it's not easy to divide! The plant is dioecious, and the male flowers are more attractive. Seedheads of female plants reach their peak in the fall. *Aruncus aethusifolius* is very similar to a dwarf astilbe in both form and flower, with a less pronounced difference between males and females; it will seed about in some locations. ~ *Ann Bucher*

Aruncus dioicus 'Kneiffii'.

Aruncus dioicus with *Geranium psilostemon* and *Rosa glauca* (background, top right). Design by Ann Lovejoy.

Species and Cultivars	Height/ Spread	USDA Hardiness Zone	Flowers (bloom time)	Foliage	Comments
aethusifolius	8–12in × 12in+	3–9	Clusters of tiny white spikes (M)	Deeply cut, olive-green, good fall color	Clump-forming, good container, groundcover, and rock garden plant, self-sows, RHS Award
dioicus	4–7ft × 3–4ft	3–9	Cream (M)	Light green	West Coast wild astilbe, tallest form, RHS Award
d. 'Glasnevin'	2–3ft × 2ft	3–9	Creamy-white plumes (M)	Light green, finer than species	
d. 'Kneiffii'	2½–3ft × 2ft	3–9	Creamy-white plumes (E)	Extremely finely divided	Grown for the foliage
d. 'Zweiweltenkind'	4–6ft × 3–3½ft	3–9	White, drooping plumes (M)	Light green, finely divided, dense, bushy	Clump-forming

Scientific Name: From the Latin *aruncus* ("beard of a goat").
Common Name: Goatsbeard.
Origin: Europe, Asia, North America.
Preferred Conditions: Tolerates any soil that retains moisture. Drought tolerant once established.
Light: Part shade to shade for *A. dioicus*. Sun for *A. aethusifolius* (better fall color).
Planting: Plants are dioecious; select for the males.
Management: Cut to the ground in autumn when it dies back. If leaf scorch develops, remove leaves.
Propagation: Division in early spring and fall when dormant. Roots are tough and hard to cut. Seed.
Pests and Diseases: None of consequence.
Companions: *Campanula latiloba*, shrub roses; it's good as a specimen plant, for the more wild parts of the garden, or the back of the perennial border.
Notes: Tolerates root competition from other plants if soil is moist. Seedheads make a nice fall display.

ASARUM Aristolochiaceae

Asarums are ideal groundcovers for shaded areas in the garden. The heart-shaped leaves may be deciduous, semi-deciduous, or evergreen, depending on the species and your climate; some have handsome markings. The small cup-shaped flowers are mostly hidden under the leaves but are worth searching for and last well when picked. Plants spread by seed and rhizomes, slowly at first. Crush the plant, and you will smell the sweet ginger scent that gives it its common name. ~ *Ann Bucher*

Scientific Name: From *asaron*, the name Dioscorides used for this genus.
Common Name: Hardy ginger.
Origin: Europe, East Asia, North America.
Preferred Conditions: Deep, rich, well-drained, moisture-retentive soil that is slightly acid. Tolerates dry shade once established.
Light: Part shade to shade.
Planting: Slow growers; will take several years to establish and form a good clump. Don't plant too deep.
Management: Asarum needs little care, except for slug patrol. They never require division but can be divided for propagation purposes. Groom as needed. In summer, cutting back for regeneration needs to be followed by a heavy fertilization and watering.
Propagation: Divide in spring or fall (especially the native species).
Pests and Diseases: Slugs, snails. This plant is a slug magnet, which explains why they are difficult to establish. There may be some forms the slugs do not like as much as others.
Companions: Ferns, rhododendron, trillium, hosta, ajuga, vancouveria, astilbe, polygonatum.
Notes: All but *A. canadense* are evergreen for us, and *A. shuttleworthii* seems to object to our cooler summers. New species and varieties, including a rare white-flowering clone of *A. caudatum*, are appearing from Japan, China and North America.

Asarum caudatum.

Species and Cultivars	Height/ Spread	USDA Hardiness Zone	Flowers (bloom time)	Foliage	Comments
canadense	6–8in × 30in+	3–9	Brownish purple (E)	Light, dull green, cordate, velvety	Snakeroot, drought tolerant, vigorous
caudatum	7–10in × 30in+	3–9	Brownish purple, bell-shaped (E)	Semi-glossy, gray, cordate, hairy stems	Canadian wild ginger, spreads
europaeum	6–8in × 10in+	3–9	Greenish purple (E)	Glossy, deep rich green, cordate, leathery, clumps	European wild ginger, spreads slowly
hartwegii	1ft × 1ft	6–10	Brownish red, fragrant (E)	Cordate, shiny, dark green with silver markings, clumps	Very slow-growing, slug magnet
shuttleworthii	4–9in × 9in	6–9	Brown to blood-red, spotted (E)	Cordate, mottled with silver, semi-glossy, clumps	Hexastylis wild ginger, very shade tolerant
splendens	8in × 12in+	6–9	Dark purple (E)	Large, dark green with silver mottling	Chinese wild ginger, vigorous, easy to grow

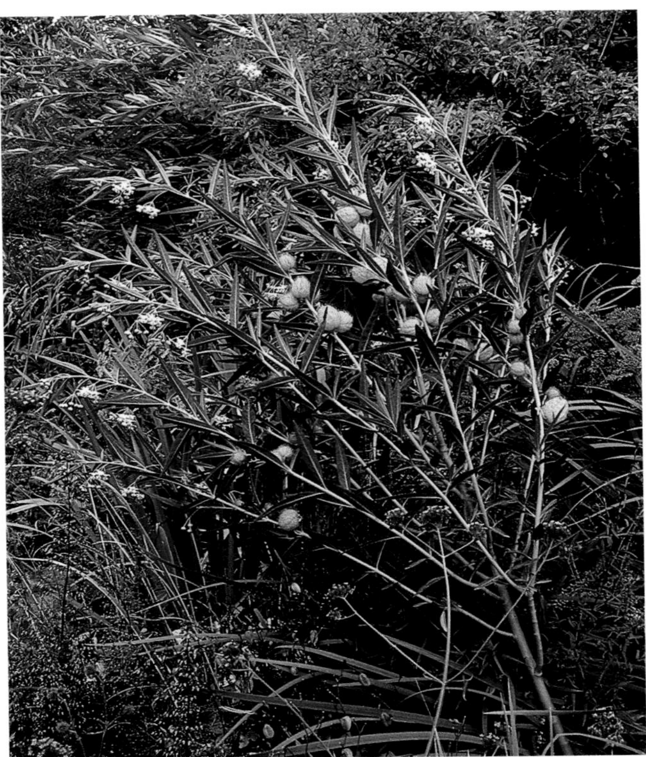

Asclepias physocarpa.

ASCLEPIAS Asclepiadaceae

All the milkweeds we discuss are host to monarch butterfly larvae (*A. speciosa*, which typically grows east of the Cascade Mountains, is their primary food). Most garden asclepias, grown for their flower color, are *A. incarnata* or *A. tuberosa*. The inflorescence is a dense cluster of small star-shaped flowers, in pink, white, orange, or red. They bloom for a long time and make good cut flowers. The long narrow seedpods, filled with silky winged seeds, are also attractive. But beware, the stiff, narrow-leaved foliage contains latex, which can be a skin irritant. ~ *Ann Bucher*

Scientific Name: After the Greek god of medicine, Asklepios.
Common Name: Milkweed, butterfly weed.
Origin: North and South America, central and southern Africa.
Preferred Conditions: Well-drained, average to poor soil. These plants need heat, plant them in your warmest spot.
Light: Sun. Tolerates part shade.
Planting: Heavy shade or rich conditions will lead to floppy stems. The thick roots can be damaged during transplanting; it's best to transplant young plants and handle them very carefully. They can be difficult to establish.
Management: Late to emerge in spring, so good labeling (or leaving their stalks on) will help to remind you where they are. They don't like to be disturbed. If you don't want to collect seed or to dry the seedpods, deadheading will encourage new bloom. Cut down in late fall after foliage dies back.
Propagation: Cuttings or seed. Set out young plants in spring.
Pests and Diseases: Aphids, slugs in early spring. Butterfly larvae are not considered pests on this plant!
Companions: Salvia, aster, echinacea, kniphofia, other prairie plants.

Species and Cultivars	Height/ Spread	USDA Hardiness Zone	Flowers (bloom time)	Foliage	Comments
'Cinderella'	3ft × 1½ft	3–9	Pink (M)	Green	
incarnata	4–5ft × 2ft	3–9	Dusty pink, sweet scent (M)	Green, densely branched thick stems	Swamp milkweed, grows in varying sites from boggy to dry
i. 'Ice Ballet'	3ft × 2ft	3–9	Tiny white clusters (M)	Rich green	Long-lasting cut, tolerates dry site
i. 'Soulmate'	3ft × 2ft	3–9	Deep rose (M)	As above	As above
physocarpa (syn. *Gomphocarpus physocarpa*)	4–5ft × 2ft	5–9	White (M–L)	Green	Fuzzy inflated seedpods, a bit tender
speciosa	3ft × 2ft	3–9	Pink (M–L)	Green, heavy, very milky when broken	Big seedpods
tuberosa	2–3ft × 2ft	3–9	Large orange clusters (L)	Green, fuzzy, narrow	Butterfly weed, most common variety
t. 'Gay Butterflies'	2ft × 2ft	3–9	Mix of red, orange, and yellow (M)	Fuzzy, green	

ASPHODELINE Asphodelaceae

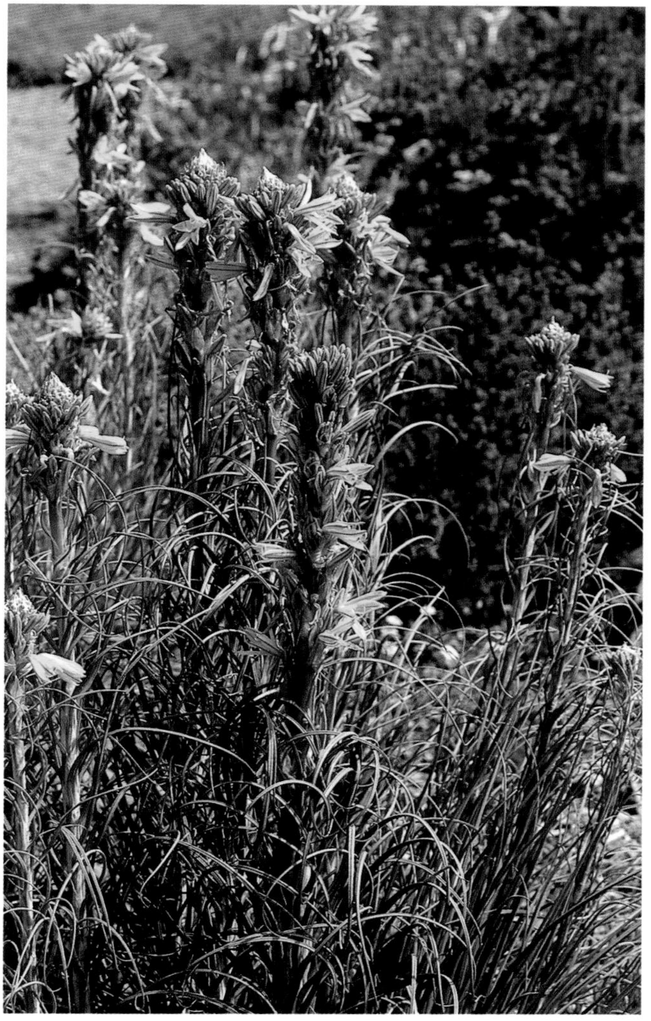
Asphodeline lutea.

King's spear is indeed an apt common name for *A. lutea.* The starlike gold flowers are evenly distributed on a two- to three-foot spike above the foliage. I particularly like the foliage, which is evergreen—or in this case everblue, narrow, curly, and low-arching. I also appreciate the fact that this plant thrives in my dry, sandy soil; when grown in heavy, rich soil, the flower spikes get quite tall and can lean over a bit too much—giving us the king's spear. The seed spikes are nice in dried arrangements. ~ *Ann Bucher*

Scientific Name: Sometimes associated with Homer's Elysian Fields and the Greek plant *Asphodel.*
Common Name: Jacob's rod, yellow asphodel, king's spear.
Origin: Mediterranean region.
Preferred Conditions: Poor, well-drained, lightweight soil.
Light: Sun.
Planting: Plant in spring or fall in a sunny position.
Management: Leave the stems on after flowering for globular seedpods. Remove ragged leaves as necessary. This species is evergreen and cannot be cut back. Plants need frequent division to stay attractive; this will keep them vigorous, tidy, and flowering. Very slow to increase. Will self-sow but is not a nuisance.
Propagation: Division in spring.
Pests and Diseases: Slugs in early spring.
Companions: Ceanothus, euphorbia, thermopsis, *Alchemilla mollis,* baptisia, salvia (tall forms).

Species and Cultivars	Height/ Spread	USDA Hardiness Zone	Flowers (bloom time)	Foliage	Comments
lutea	3–4ft × 2ft	6–10	Star-shaped, yellow, emerging from buff-colored bracts (E–M)	Bluish gray-green, very narrow, arching	Stiff upright stems, clump-forming

Aster novi-belgii cultivars with *Verbena bonariensis*, *Berberis jamesiana* in fall color, and *Rosa rubiginosa* with its hips just visible behind.

ASTER Asteraceae

One thing is certain, the impossibility of having just one aster. A collection of asters, in all colors and varied heights, is a joy to behold, though the similarity of their small leaves, which are not particularly attractive, is a minor drawback to the display. Most asters flower together, at a time of year when we look for any color to dispel the coming of late fall and winter. We think of them as close to being wild plants, usually found in meadows or waste ground. The species are tough colonizers and survivors. Even the modern hybrids look uneasy in a strictly regulated border, and go better with thistly things, in cottage gardens.

On the whole asters are sun-loving and require good drainage. Most are not good for cutting as they are short-lived in the vase, but the larger single flowers of such a plant as *A.* ×*frikartii* will last several days. Clumps of asters can be left to go dormant gracefully, their seedheads forming clouds of small, fluffy balls that look good after a hard frost. We like best the dark stems and leaves of *A. laevis* 'Calliope' or *A. lateriflorus* 'Prince' and, as for the flowers, the good clear pink *A. novi-belgii* 'Fellowship' cannot be bettered. We would not be without any of our asters, tamed or wild. ~ *Susan Buckles*

Scientific Name: From the Greek *aster* ("star"), a reference to the starlike flowers.
Common Name: Michaelmas daisy.

Aster sedifolius 'Nanus'.

Origin: Africa, Eurasia, northeastern United States, Canada, South America.

Preferred Conditions: Average, well-drained, humus-rich soil in south-facing beds. Tolerates sand or clay. *Aster ×frikartii* and *A. amellus* prefer alkaline soil; others do best in neutral soil. All need prairie conditions with summer water and good air circulation to prevent mildew.

Light: Sun. Tolerates some high canopy shade.

Planting: Lift and divide asters frequently and replant directly in refreshed soil mix to keep plants young and vigorous.

Management: For more dense, compact plants, asters (*A. novi-belgii*, *A. novae-angliae*) should be pinched back on 1 July (earlier for *A. ×frikartii*). Do not let them dry out! Novi-belgii asters in particular are very susceptible to mildew if allowed to dry out. Cut back completely in fall when new growth shows at base. Bait crown for slugs in winter and early spring.

Propagation: Division in spring and soft tip cuttings, or seed (rarely).

Pests and Diseases: Mildew, slugs, rabbits. None are slug or rabbit proof.

Companions: Grasses, old roses, Japanese anemones, *Phlox paniculata*, sedum, fennel, solidago, coreopsis, rudbeckia, monarda, aconitum, late kniphofias, hardy fuchsias, salvia. Asters look best in large groups; there is nothing like an aster border for that autumn show.

Notes: A wilt from lack of water when in full growth will trigger a bad case of mildew. Be vigilant with summer water. *Aster novae-angliae* (New England aster) is the most mildew resistant for us. If given space almost all asters will cover a larger area than we show on the chart, except for *A. ×frikartii* and cultivars.

Species and Cultivars	Height/ Spread	USDA Hardiness Zone	Flowers (bloom time)	Foliage	Comments
amellus	2ft × 1½ft	4–7	Violet-blue, pale to deep purplish pink, yellow disk (L)	Green, lanceolate to obovate	Needs lime in the Northwest
a. 'King George'	1½–2ft × 1½ft	4–7	Rich purple-blue, large, orange disk (M–L)	Gray-green, well-branched lax stems	RHS Award

Species and Cultivars	Height/ Spread	USDA Hardiness Zone	Flowers (bloom time)	Foliage	Comments
a. 'Veilchenkönigin' (syn. 'Violet Queen')	2½ft × 1½ft	4–7	Deep violet, yellow disk (M–L)	Deep green, small, narrow, on short bushy branches	RHS Award
'Cape Cod'	2½ft × 2ft	4–7	Tiny white sprays (L)	Green	One of latest to bloom, mildew resistant, good cut, no staking
'Climax'	4½–6ft × 2ft	4–7	Lavender-blue, pale yellow disk (L)	Broad, rich green, purple stems	Mildew resistant, good cut
'Coombe Fishacre'	4ft × 2ft	4–7	Pale purple-pink, turning red, darker eye (M)	Green	Mildew resistant
cordifolius	4ft × 2ft	4–7	Lavender-blue, sometimes almost white, yellow disk turning red (M–L)	Dull green, thin, slightly hairy	Tolerant of some shade
divaricatus	1½–2½ft × 2ft	4–7	White rays, yellow disk turning brown (M–L)	Dark green, cordate, coarsely serrated, dark stems	White wood aster, tolerates shade and dry soil, flops but nicely
ericoides	3ft × 1ft	4–7	White sprays, sometimes tinged pink, yellow center (M–L)	Slender, green, on bushy branched sprays	Heath aster
e. 'Blue Star'	2–3ft × 1ft	4–7	Light lavender-blue, yellow center (M–L)	Tiny, green, bushy mounding habit	RHS Award
e. 'Pink Cloud'	3ft × 1ft	4–7	Pastel pink, yellow center (M–L)	As above	RHS Award
e. f. prostratus 'Snow Flurry'	6in × 10in	4–9	White with tiny green gold center (M–L)	Tiny green, on bright green stems	Floriferous carpet, RHS Award
×frikartii	2–3ft × 1½ft	4–9	Lavender-blue, yellow center (M–L)	Dark green	A summer bloomer
×f. 'Flora's Delight'	1½ft × 1½ft	4–9	Lilac, paling with age, yellow center (M–L)	As above	More compact
×f. 'Jungfrau'	2ft × 1½ft	4–9	Violet, gold center (M–L)	Deep green, reddish stems	
×f. 'Mönch'	2–3ft × 1½ft	4–9	Lavender-blue, golden center (M–L)	Fuzzy, green	RHS Award
×f. 'Wunder von Stäfa'	2–3ft × 1½ft	4–9	Large, violet-blue with gold center (M–L)	Green	Least desirable of *A. ×frikartii* cultivars, RHS Award
'Kylie'	2ft × 1½ft	4–7	Small, pale pink on wiry tall spires (L)	As above	Strong clumps, RHS Award
laevis	2–4ft × 1½ft	3–8	Lavender to violet, yellow center (M–L)	Blue-green, smooth, mostly toothless	Smooth aster, clump-forming

Species and Cultivars	Height/ Spread	USDA Hardiness Zone	Flowers (bloom time)	Foliage	Comments
l. 'Calliope'	5–6ft × 1½ft	4–7	Single lilac-purple in an open spire, yellow center (M–L)	Purple-tinted shoots, rich dark green, thick and waxy	Clump-forming, mildew resistant
lateriflorus	3–3½ft × 1½ft	4–8	White to pale purple with a maroon and yellow center (M–L)	Tiny, toothed, lanceolate to elliptical	Sturdy, compact, slender stems
l. var. horizontalis	2–3ft × 2ft+	4–8	White reflexed rays, pink center turning deep reddish purple (M–L)	Small, toothed, lanceolate to elliptical, purple-tinted in spring	Wide-spreading, RHS Award
l. 'Lady in Black'	3–4½ft × 1½ft+	4–8	White, star-shaped, rays tinted pink, deep rose-pink center (M–L)	Tiny, black-purple, bronze in spring	Compact clumps with open sprays, upright
l. 'Prince'	2–3ft × 1½ft+	4–8	White, reflexed rays, pink center (M–L)	Rich purple-black, toothed, dark stems	Compact clumps, upright
'Little Carlow' (cordifolius hybrid)	3–4ft × 2ft+	4–9	Bright lavender-blue, yellow center (M–L)	Deep green, broader	Strong clumps, RHS Award
'Little Dorrit' (cordifolius hybrid)	4ft × 1½ft+	4–9	Light pink (L)	Deep green, lanceolate	Vigorous clumps, RHS Award
novae-angliae	3–6ft × 2ft	4–8	Range from pink to purple and blue, gold center (M–L)	Narrow, rough, dull pale green, hairy	New England aster, mildew resistant
n. 'Andenken an Alma Pötschke'	3–4ft × 2ft	4–8	Red-violet rays, gold center (M–L)	Bright green, broad, linear or lanceolate, hairy	Distinctive color, RHS Award
n. 'Harrington's Pink'	4ft × 2ft	4–8	Light rose-pink (M–L)	Green, linear or lanceolate, hairy	A true pink, RHS Award
n. 'Hella Lacy'	2–3ft × 2ft	4–8	Deep violet-purple, yellow-gold center (M–L)	Dark green, lanceolate, hairy	Strong clumps
n. 'Septemberrubin'	4–5ft × 2ft	4–8	Rich purple-red, large, gold center (M–L)	As above	Compact clumps
n. 'Treasure'	4½ft × 2ft	4–8	Light violet, large (M–L)	Green	
novi-belgii	1–1½ft × 3ft	4–8	Purple, pink, blue, red, or white, gold center (M–L)	Green, lanceolate, toothed	New York aster, mildew is a problem, clump-forming
n. 'Alert'	1–1½ft × 3ft	4–8	Rich purple-red, yellow center, semi-double (M–L)	Green	
n. 'Coombe Violet'	4ft × 3ft	4–8	Deep violet-blue (L)	Small, narrow, mid to dark green	May need staking

Species and Cultivars	Height/ Spread	USDA Hardiness Zone	Flowers (bloom time)	Foliage	Comments
n. 'Fellowship'	3ft+ × 3ft	4–8	Pale pink, double, large (M–L)	Green	Requires more water than most, may need staking
n. 'Lady in Blue'	1ft × 3ft	4–8	Lavender-blue (M–L)	Fine, green	Good dwarf cultivar, strong tight clumps
n. 'Patricia Ballard'	3ft × 3ft	4–8	Bright mauve-pink, large, double (L)	Green	Vigorous clumps, open sprays
n. 'Peter Harrison'	2½ft × 3ft	4–8	Pale mauve-pink, small, single (L)	As above	
n. 'Priory Blush'	3½ft × 3ft	4–8	White, tinted pink, small (L)	As above	
n. 'Professor Anton Kippenberg'	1–2ft × 2ft	4–8	Lavender-blue, prominent gold center (L)	Dark green	
n. 'Purple Dome'	1½–2ft × 2ft	4–8	Deep heather-purple, semi-double (M–L)	As above	Strong sprays, bushy branches
n. 'Schneekissen' (syn. 'Snow Cushion')	1ft × 1ft	4–8	Small white rays, good clean white (L)	Green	
n. 'Winston S. Churchill'	1½ft × 1ft	4–8	Unusual purple-red, single, yellow center (M)	As above	
'Photograph'	3ft+ × 2ft	4–9	Lavender-blue, airy (M–L)	As above	RHS Award
pilosus var. pringlei 'Monte Cassino'	3–4ft × 3ft	4–9	Starry white (M–L)	Very fine, narrow, asparagus fern–like	Largely grown for florists, RHS Award
'Ringdove' (ericoides hybrid)	3½ft × 3ft	4–9	Pale lavender rays, prominent creamy yellow center (L)	Long, narrow, green	Strong sprays, RHS Award
sedifolius	2–4ft × 2ft+	4–7	Lavender-blue, pale purple-pink or white rays, small pale yellow center (M–L)	Divided, gray-green, narrow, linear	Mildew resistant, dense-growing, may flop
s. 'Nanus'	1–1½ft × 1ft	4–7	Lavender-blue (M–L)	Tiny, divided, gray-green	Very floriferous, dense-growing
tataricus 'Jindai'	4–5ft × 2ft+	4–9	Light lavender-blue, prominent yellow center (L)	Very large, coarse, pale green, on hairy stems	Very floriferous, long-blooming
thomsonii 'Nanus'	10in × 20in	4–9	Lavender-blue, yellow center (M)	Pale green, ovate to elliptic, coarse	Clump-forming
tongolensis	1–1½ft × 1ft	4–9	Lavender-blue, orange center (M)	Green, oblong-lanceolate, hairy	Spreading
t. 'Wartburgstern' (syn. 'Wartburg Star')	1–1½ft × 1ft	4–9	Violet-blue, yellow center (M–L)	Verdant green on reddish stems	Short-lived in the Pacific Northwest
'White Climax'	3–5ft × 2ft	4–9	Large, white (M–L)	Dark green on black-purple stems	Doesn't need staking

Astilbe 'Snowdrift'.

ASTILBE Saxifragaceae

The graceful plumelike panicles of this genus adorn the garden in a variety of colors over a long season. There are early, midseason, and late astilbes, with blooms in shades of red, white, purple, and pink rising above their ferny foliage. The foliage is almost as much of an attribute as the flowers are. Most have dark green, ferny or feathery foliage that sometimes emerges with beautiful reddish hues. Others have bronze, reddish brown, or purplish foliage, while a few are light green. Astilbes range in size from four inches to five feet and are very adaptable to many conditions except summer drought.

Although astilbes are tough plants and thrive in the moist weather of the Northwest, they are the wrong plants for dry shade, under large fir trees. They will just sit and sulk, have little growth or bloom and eventually dry up and die, although the low ones seem more tolerant.

There are several large groups with specific characteristics. *Astilbe chinensis* is vigorous with dense plumes, a late-season bloomer in shades of horticultural original sin (mauve-magenta); it and its kin can be short or tall with hairy foliage. *Astilbe japonica* has large, wide panicles in the full color range, blooming in midseason or earlier. *Astilbe* ×*arendsii* from Georg Arends in Germany blooms in midseason or earlier in a wide color range; fernlike foliage emerges dark, with some cultivars keeping the dark or bronze coloring throughout the season. *Astilbe simplicifolia* is smaller, with finely divided, shiny foliage and a shorter inflorescence. *Astilbe thunbergii* has taller, arching plumes.

Astilbes make an excellent cut flower if harvested when half open. Many are also cut and air-dried then used in dried floral arrangements. The dried rust-colored seedheads can also be left on to extend the interest into winter and then removed before new growth begins in the spring.
~ *Susan Carter*

Scientific Name: Greek for "without brilliance."
Common Name: False spirea.
Origin: Eastern Europe, China, Japan.
Preferred Conditions: Acid, humus-rich, moisture-retentive. Doesn't like it too dry.
Light: Sun to part shade.
Management: Little is required during the growing season except to make sure plants don't dry out. They can be mulched but not with fresh manure. When clumps become worn out or bare and woody in the middle, they can be rejuvenated by lifting the clumps, discarding the center, and replanting the vigorous pieces from the edge of the clumps. Spent flower heads can be removed anytime after flowering.
Propagation: Division in late winter to spring. Best to divide when completely dormant. Seed in February and March—usually takes two years to flower.
Pests and Diseases: Root weevil, especially the chinensis varieties over time. A heavy infestation of weevils can severely damage the semi-woody crowns of astilbes.
Companions: Hosta, pulmonaria, helleborus, epimedium, ferns, polygonatum, Japanese iris; particularly effective in groups.
Notes: Do not mulch over the crowns with fresh manure as it can burn the pips and the newly emerging growth. Astilbes prefer a high-humidity location.

Species and Cultivars	Height/ Spread	USDA Hardiness Zone	Flowers (bloom time)	Foliage	Comments
'Amethyst' (×arendsii)	2–2½ft × 2ft	5–8	Clear lilac-pink (M)	Dark green, lacy, fernlike	Good cut flower
'Anita Pfeifer' (×arendsii)	2–2½ft × 2ft	5–8	Salmon-pink (M)	Dark green	
'Aphrodite' (simplicifolia hybrid)	1½ft × 1½ft	5–8	Salmon-red (M–L)	Dark bronze	Good foliage
×arendsii	2–4ft × 1½ft	5–8	Various (M–L)	Semi-glossy, feathery, green	Rarely grown from seed
'Betsy Cuperus' (thunbergii hybrid)	4ft × 2ft	5–8	Pale pink on large, gracefully arching stems (M)	Green	Spreading habit, good cut
'Bonn' (japonica hybrid)	1½–2ft × 1½ft	5–8	Deep carmine-rose (E)	Fernlike, green	
'Brautschleier' (×arendsii) (syn. 'Bridal Veil')	2½ft × 1½ft	5–8	White to creamy-yellow, open sprays (M)	Dense, fernlike, green, glossy	Profuse bloomer, RHS Award
'Bremen' (japonica hybrid)	2ft × 1½ft	5–8	Crimson-rose (E–M)	Green	
'Bressingham Beauty' (×arendsii)	3–3½ft × 1½ft	5–8	Clear pink (M)	Mid-green, fernlike	Expansive habit
'Bronze Elegans' (simplicifolia hybrid)	12–15in × 12in	5–8	Clear pink with a salmon tinge (M–L)	Bronze-green, shiny	Vigorous for a simplicifolia hybrid, RHS Award
'Bumalda' (×arendsii)	2ft × 1½ft	5–8	White plumes with a soft pink tinge (E–M)	Green	
'Cattleya' (×arendsii)	3ft × 1½ft	5–8	Rose-pink on open spikes (M–L)	Leafy, dark green, stems have bronze tint when young	Vigorous

Species and Cultivars	Height/ Spread	USDA Hardiness Zone	Flowers (bloom time)	Foliage	Comments
chinensis	2–3ft × 2ft+	5–8	Mauve-pink (M–L)	Dense with hairy leaflets, fernlike	Vigorous, spreading roots, esp. in fertile soil
c. var. davidii	4–5ft × 3ft	5–8	Rose-purple on erect spikes (M–L)	Green, divided, fernlike, in basal rosettes	A very tall plant, needs full sun
c. 'Finale'	20–24in × 2ft	5–8	Soft pink (M–L)	Green, fernlike	Vigorous spreading roots, more drought tolerant
c. 'Intermezzo'	1–2ft × 2ft	5–8	Salmon-pink (M–L)	As above	
c. var. pumila	8–12in × 10in+	5–8	Mauve-pink turning brown while upper portion is still in bloom (M–L)	As above	Tolerant of full sun, short and stout, good edge plant, RHS Award
c. var. taquetii 'Purpurlanze'	4ft × 2ft	5–8	Rosy-purple (M–L)	Shiny, dark bronze, ferny	Striking inflorescence
c. var. taquetii 'Superba'	4ft × 2ft	5–8	Lilac (M–L)	Crinkled, red-tinged green, fernlike	Tall open inflorescence, RHS Award
c. 'Veronica Klose'	1–2ft × 1½ft	5–8	Dark pink (M–L)	Emerges deep green, ages to clear green, coarse	Vigorous, compact growth
c. 'Visions'	15in × 18in	5–8	Mauve-pink (M)	Bronze-green, ferny	Sun tolerant, compact grower
×crispa 'Lilliput'	8in × 8in	5–8	Salmon-pink (M–L)	Dense, glossy, dark green	Very compact, slow
×c. 'Perkeo'	8–10in × 8in	5–8	Dark pink on short stiff stems (M)	Delicate, jagged, dark green	Very compact, slow, RHS Award
'Darwin's Margot'	20in × 12in	5–8	Rosy-red (E)	Green	Compact
'Deutschland' (japonica hybrid)	20–24in × 12in	5–8	White, fragrant (E–M)	Deep green, glossy	Vigorous, full, and large
'Diamant' (×arendsii)	2–3ft × 1½ft	5–8	Clear white in narrow plumes (M)	Deep green	
'Dunkellachs' (simplicifolia hybrid)	1–1½ft × 1ft	5–8	Rich salmon-pink (M–L)	Coppery, fernlike, shiny	Red stems
'Düsseldorf' (japonica hybrid)	20–24in × 12in	5–8	Light crimson-red (M)	Green	
'Elisabeth' (japonica hybrid)	2–2½ft × 1½ft	5–8	Raspberry (M)	As above	
'Elizabeth Bloom' (×arendsii)	2–2½ft × 1½ft	5–8	Pure pink (M)	Deep, glossy green	
'Erica' (×arendsii)	2–2½ft × 1½ft	5–8	Clear bright pink in long, narrow plumes (M)	Bronze-red aging to deep green	
'Etna' (japonica hybrid)	2ft × 1½ft	5–8	Dark red (E)	Reddish aging to mid-green	
'Europa' (japonica hybrid)	2ft × 1½ft	5–8	Pale pink in heavy spikes (E)	Mid-green	Very floriferous, good cut

Species and Cultivars	Height/ Spread	USDA Hardiness Zone	Flowers (bloom time)	Foliage	Comments
'Fanal' (×arendsii)	2ft × 1½ft	5–8	Dark crimson-red in dense short spikes, best landscape red (E)	Dark reddish brown aging to green, deeply cut	Best for red foliage, RHS Award
'Federsee' (×arendsii)	2–2½ft × 1½ft	5–8	Carmine-rose, large full plumes (M)	Green	Adapts well to dry conditions
glaberrima var. saxatilis	4–8in × 8in	5–8	Shell-pink (M)	Glossy, dark green	Nice for rock gardens, RHS Award
'Gloria' (×arendsii)	1½–2ft × 1½ft	5–8	Lavender-pink (E–M)	Fernlike, green	
'Glut' (×arendsii) (syn. 'Glow')	2½–3ft × 1½ft	5–8	Deep ruby-red, narrow feathery spikes (M–L)	Bronze-red aging to mid-green	
'Granat' (×arendsii)	3ft × 1½ft	5–8	Garnet-red fading to pink	Purplish bronze aging to green	
'Grete Püngel' (×arendsii)	2–3ft × 1½ft	5–8	Vivid pink (E–M)	Purplish aging to green	
'Hennie Graafland' (simplicifolia hybrid)	4–8in × 8in	5–8	Shell-pink (M)	Glossy, dark green	Dwarf astilbe, easy to grow, increases well
'Hyazinth' (×arendsii)	3ft × 1½ft	5–8	Dark lavender-pink (E–M)	Green, fernlike	
'Inshriach Pink' (simplicifolia hybrid)	8–12in × 10in	5–8	Light pink, airy plumes (L)	Dark bronze, crinkled	Slow
'Irrlicht' (×arendsii)	2ft × 1½ft	5–8	White with rose tinge (E–M)	Dark green	
'Maggie Daley'	2½ft × 1½ft	5–8	Purplish rose (M)	Dark green, shiny	
'Mainz' (japonica hybrid)	2ft × 1½ft	5–8	Violet (E–M)	Dark green	
'Moerheimii' (thunbergii hybrid)	5ft × 2ft	5–8	White, large arching plumes (M)	Green	
'Montgomery' (japonica hybrid)	2½ft × 1½ft	5–8	Dark red (M)	Bronze-red aging to dark green	
'Obergärtner Jürgens' (×arendsii)	1½–2ft × 2ft	5–8	Crimson (E)	Dark green	
'Professor van der Wielen' (thunbergii hybrid)	3–4ft × 2ft+	5–8	White, long stems of gracefully arching sprays (M)	Green, open, on strong stems	Good cut, a different look for an astilbe
'Queen of Holland' (japonica hybrid)	2ft × 2ft	5–8	White (E)	Green	
'Red Sentinel' (japonica hybrid)	2–3ft × 1½ft	5–8	Deep crimson-red (E–M)	Dark green, glossy, bronze tinge, red stems	
'Rheinland' (japonica hybrid)	1½–2ft × 1½ft	5–8	Clear bright pink, intense (E–M)	Dense, green, fernlike	RHS Award
×rosea 'Peach Blossom'	2ft × 1½ft	5–8	Pink (M)	Light green, glossy, fernlike	A very soft look
simplicifolia	6–12in × 8in	5–8	White (E–M)	Dark green, somewhat glossy	Dwarf, slow, RHS Award
s. 'Darwin's Snow Sprite'	1ft × 1ft	5–8	White (M–L)	Dark green, delicately cut	More robust than A. 'Sprite'

Species and Cultivars	Height/ Spread	USDA Hardiness Zone	Flowers (bloom time)	Foliage	Comments
'Snowdrift' (×arendsii)	2ft × 1½ft	5–8	Pure white (M)	Bright green	Good cut
'Spinell' (×arendsii)	3ft × 1½ft	5–8	Carmine-red, long plumes (M)	Deep red aging to reddish green	
'Sprite' (simplicifolia hybrid)	8–12in × 10in	5–8	Light pink (L)	Rich dark green, bronze in spring, glossy, delicately cut	Slow, 1994 PPA Award, RHS Award
'Straussenfeder' (thunbergii hybrid) (syn. 'Ostrich Plume')	3–3½ft × 2ft	5–8	Coral-pink in large, open, arching plumes (M)	Bronze aging to green	Vigorous, RHS Award
'Vesuvius' (japonica hybrid)	2ft × 1½ft	5–8	Carmine-red (M)	Bronze-green	
'Washington' (japonica hybrid)	1½–2ft × 1½ft	5–8	Strong white (E)	Green	
'Weisse Gloria' (×arendsii)	2–2½ft × 1½ft	5–8	Creamy-white on erect spikes (M)	Dark-green, fernlike, shiny	Strong growth
'William Buchanan' (simplicifolia hybrid)	8–18in × 12in	5–8	Light pink (L)	Green, tinged red, shiny	More vigorous than *A.* 'Sprite'

ASTILBOIDES Saxifragaceae

Astilboides tabularis provides an exotic touch to the garden with its umbrellalike (peltate) leaves and flowers similar to rodgersia or astilbe. The round, scalloped leaves are more interesting than the flowers. This plant used to be classified as a species of rodgersia but now has been placed in a

The large leaves of *Astilboides tabularis*.

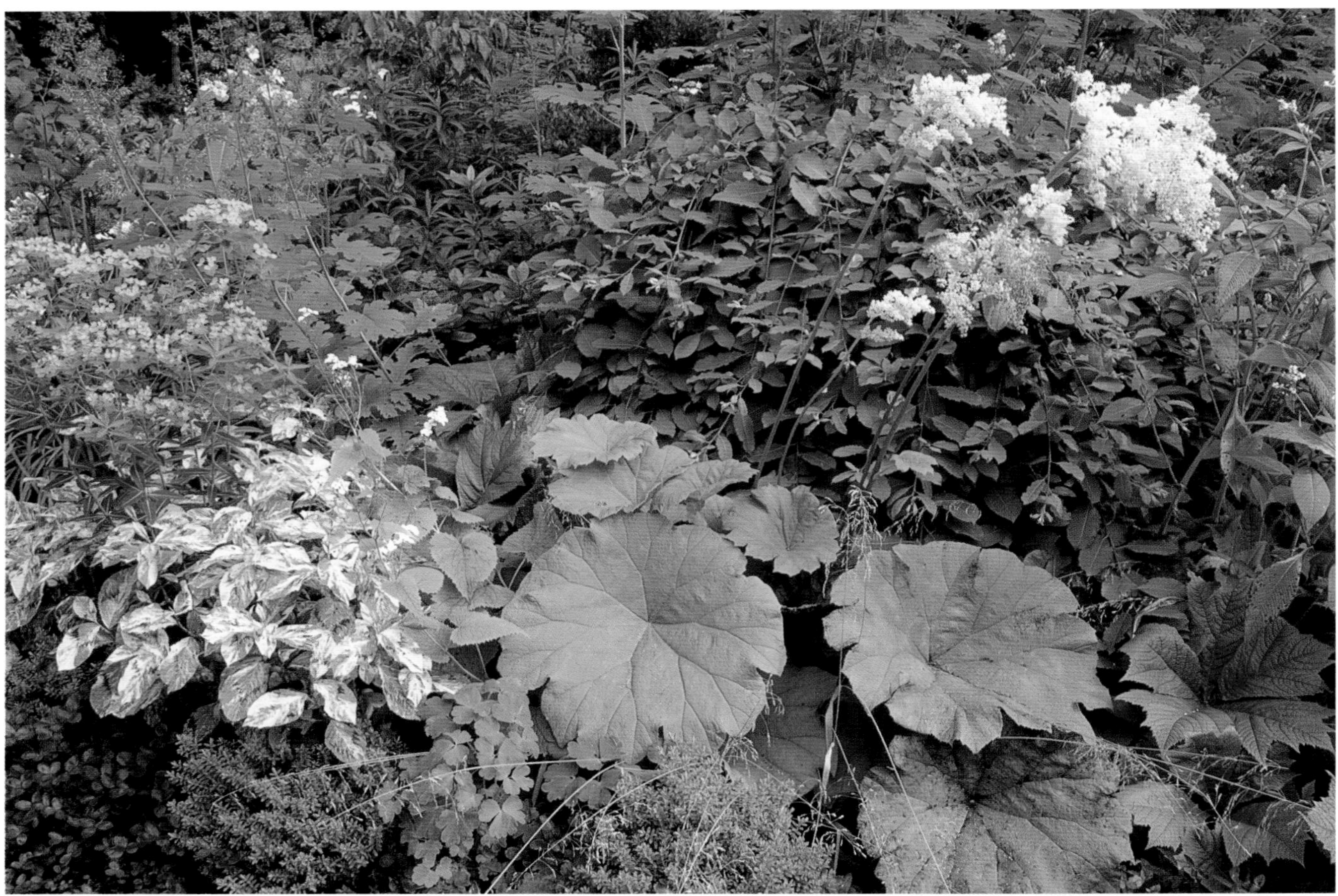

Astilboides tabularis in flower, with *Macleaya cordata*, *Persicaria virginiana* Variegata Group 'Painter's Palette', and *Euphorbia schillingii*. Design by Ann Lovejoy.

genus all its own. It is happiest in moist, boggy conditions in part shade and is extremely slow to increase. Do not step on the crowns. ~ *Susan Carter*

Scientific Name: Greek name for a plant resembling the astilbe or rodgersia flowers.
Common Name: Shieldleaf rodgersia.
Origin: China.
Preferred Conditions: Rich, humus-rich, moist soil.
Light: Shade to part shade. Tolerates part sun with adequate water.
Planting: Likes to be under deep-rooted trees or alongside water.
Management: Cut down in autumn to tidy up. Leaves are usually shed by this time. It would appreciate a mulch over the winter.
Propagation: Divide roots in spring, or seed in July and August.
Pests and Diseases: Slugs, slugs, slugs, and big feet.
Companions: Large-scale ferns, hosta, astilbe, aruncus, filipendula, helleborus, ligularia, telekia, *Primula japonica*.

Species and Cultivars	Height/ Spread	USDA Hardiness Zone	Flowers (bloom time)	Foliage	Comments
tabularis	3–5ft × 3ft	4–9	White plumes (M)	Pale olive-green, rounded, big (2ft across), shiny, smoother on top	Clump-forming, very slow to increase

Astrantia major 'Roma' with *Anthriscus sylvestris.*

ASTRANTIA **Apiaceae**

Astrantia major is a variable species, with differences in plant size, flower size, and flower color. Its flowers consist of a whorl of bracts surrounding a pincushionlike mound (umbel) of small flowers in shades of white, red, pink, or green. This floral arrangement has a long period of looking showy. It's a good idea to buy the plant in bloom if you can; many of the unnamed reds are not very graceful, and the flower fades to white shortly after bloom. Avoid placing its white-flowering forms with other white flowers, as they tend to make the astrantias look dirty. The handsome basal leaves are lobed and coarsely toothed. *Astrantia major* subsp. *involucrata* 'Shaggy' has the largest flowers, of green flushed with white; the foliage is less full and slower to increase, and its overall form less attractive than the species. *Astrantia major* 'Sunningdale Variegated' has a good clean variegation to its foliage in early spring; this fades away very near to the time of bloom.

Astrantia major is not difficult to grow. You must watch for self-sown seedlings; many will rebloom if deadheaded, so remember this maintenance advice and you'll prolong its flowering season plus save yourself time and effort pulling out seedlings later. This species will not survive in a hot, dry climate; plants are slow to establish but very long-lived and successful once established.

Astrantia maxima is somewhat more demanding. It needs good soil and room to spread its rhizomes. The flower, which has larger bracts, is a lovely chalky pink on a shorter stem. This makes it somewhat less useful for cutting, and it does have a shorter bloom season. *Astrantia* 'Buckland' (a hybrid of *A. major* and *A. maxima*), with a similar flower, is a much more graceful plant. ~ *Ann Bucher*

Scientific Name: From the Latin *aster* ("star"), referring to the starlike flowers.
Common Name: Masterwort.
Origin: Central and southern Europe, western Asia.
Preferred Conditions: Humus-rich, fertile, heavy soil. Tolerates drier soil but will not thrive.
Light: Sun to part shade.
Management: Deadheading will prevent self-sowing (this is especially important if you are growing cultivars) and extend flowering season. Keep moist in the summer. Cut back when foliage is dead in late fall.
Pests and Diseases: Aphids (on young plants), slugs, especially in spring.
Propagation: Divide in spring or fall. Sow seed as soon as ripe, and give planted seed a two-month warm period followed by cold.
Companions: *Lilium martagon*, *Iris sibirica*, *Milium effusum* 'Aureum', hosta, pulmonaria, chaerophyllum, pimpinella, campanula, *Phlox paniculata*, adenophora, geranium.
Notes: Makes a great cut flower, both fresh and dried.

Species and Cultivars	Height/ Spread	USDA Hardiness Zone	Flowers (bloom time)	Foliage	Comments
'Buckland'	2ft × 2ft	4–9	Tiny, dusty pink, with silvery-pink and green bracts (M)	Palmate, green	A very good form
carniolica	1–1½ft × 1½ft	4–9	White, tinged pink, with shorter white, green-tipped bracts (M)	More divided than *A. major*, green, deeply lobed, toothed	Smaller than *A. major*
'Hadspen Blood'	2½ft × 2ft	4–9	Rich dark red bracts (M)	New foliage tinted purple, aging to green	Thought to be a hybrid with *A. maxima*
major	2–3ft × 2ft	4–9	Wide range—red, pink, white, some green-tipped, some with more or less color in bracts or in central flowers (M–L)	Mid-green, palmately lobed, coarsely toothed	Masterwort, self-sows
m. alba	2–2½ft × 2ft	4–9	White, with white bracts (M)	Palmate, mid-green	
m. subsp. biebersteinii	1ft × 1ft	4–9	Smaller, white, tinted pale pink (M)	Green, smaller, more divided	
m. subsp. involucrata	2–3ft × 2ft	4–9	White tinted green or pink, white bracts with green tips (M)	Green, larger	Very large bracts
m. subsp. involucrata 'Orlando'	2–3ft × 2ft	4–9	White and green bracts (M)	As above	Improved form of *A. major* subsp. *involucrata* 'Shaggy'

Species and Cultivars	Height/ Spread	USDA Hardiness Zone	Flowers (bloom time)	Foliage	Comments
m. subsp. involucrata 'Shaggy' (syn. 'Margery Fish')	2–2½ft × 2ft	4–9	White, long white bracts with green tips and pink undersides (M)	Green, deeply divided, larger than most	RHS Award
m. 'Lars'	2½ft × 1½ft	4–9	Red with dark red bracts (M)	Dark green	
m. 'Pat Bender's Form'	2ft × 2ft	4–9	Red with dark wine-red bracts (M)	Dark green, emerges even darker	Keeps its color well, earliest red to bloom
m. 'Primadonna'	2½ft × 2ft	4–9	Dark maroon bracts (M)	Deep green, palmate	Vigorous, similar to *A. major* 'Rosensinfonie'
m. 'Roma'	2½–3ft × 2ft	4–9	Clear rich pink (M)	Mid-green	Free-flowering, may be a hybrid with *A. maxima*
m. var. rosea	2½ft × 2ft	4–9	Pale pink, dark pink in bud, bright pink bracts (M)	Deeply lobed, green, lush	
m. 'Rosensinfonie'	2½ft × 2½ft	4–9	Rose-pink, bracts and flowers fade to white (M)	Palmate, green	Fades to white quickly, seeds to mixed colors
m. 'Rubra' (syn. carniolica var. rubra)	1–2½ft × 2ft	4–9	Bracts vary, shades of red, maroon, and pink (M)	Lacy, green	
m. 'Ruby Cloud'	2½ft × 2ft	4–9	Red-purple with red bracts, red stems (M)	Light green, shiny	A very good red
m. 'Ruby Wedding'	2½ft × 2ft	4–9	Dark red with dark red bracts and maroon-black stems (M)	Dark green tinged with purple	Doesn't come true from seed
m. 'Sunningdale Variegated' (syn. major 'Variegata')	2ft × 2ft	4–9	Greenish white, barely tinged pink (M)	Irregularly splashed with cream and yellow, fades back to green in summer, deeply lobed	Needs full sun for best leaf color, RHS Award
maxima	2ft × 2ft+	4–9	Pink, with large, sharply pointed pink bracts (M)	Green, deeply divided, 3-lobed	Prefers sun, bracts age to green when dried, spreads by fine runners, sets little viable seed, RHS Award
m. 'Mark Fenwick'	2½ft × 2ft	4–9	Deeper pink (M)	As above	

Baptisia australis.

BAPTISIA Papilionaceae

Baptisia gives us everything we could ask from a plant, beginning with asparaguslike stalks in early spring (which are late to emerge). Typical pea family flowers appear in late spring to early summer in shades of deep violet-blue, creamy-yellow or white, bright yellow, and smoky purple. The handsome foliage is bluish green and on a mature shrubby plant really makes a statement in the border. By autumn, the flowers have turned into very interesting swollen black seedpods that rattle. False indigo loves sun and a warm spot, and may not perform at its best without it. It's quite slow to establish (and may take several years to bloom) and responds very well to a layer of mulch. Baptisia is good as a cut flower if picked just as the first flowers open (unfortunately, the buds will not open). The seedpods are used in dried arrangements. ~ *Susan Carter*

Species and Cultivars	Height/ Spread	USDA Hardiness Zone	Flowers (bloom time)	Foliage	Comments
alba	2–4ft × 2ft	4–9	White (E–M)	Blue-green, palmate, obovate to lanceolate, charcoal-gray stems	
a. var. macrophylla (syn. lactea, leucantha)	3–5ft × 2½ft	4–9	Creamy-white, sometimes tinged purple (M)	Blue-gray, purple-tinged, waxy, glaucous stems	Olive-green pods, turning black
australis	3–4ft × 3ft	3–9	Indigo or deep violet-blue (E–M)	Blue-green, waxy, obovate to oval, grayish green stems	Blue false indigo, gray-black seedpods, long-blooming, RHS Award
bracteata (syn. leucophaea)	2ft × 2ft	4–9	Creamy-yellow (E–M)	Grayish, bristly, hairy	
'Purple Smoke'	3–4ft × 2ft	3–9	Smoky purple with purple eye (E–M)	Blue-gray green, velvety, stems are dark charcoal-green	Vigorous, black seedpods
tinctoria	2–4ft × 2ft	4–9	Bright yellow (M)	Blue-green	Indigo, rattleweed, used in dye

Scientific Name: From the Greek *bapto* ("to dye"); plants were used as a substitute for indigo.
Common Name: False indigo.
Origin: East coast of North America.
Preferred Conditions: Deep, well-drained, acidic to neutral and poor to average soil. Prefers moist conditions but tolerates drought once established.
Light: Sun. Tolerates part shade.
Management: Low-maintenance plant. Taproots don't like to be disturbed. Cut foliage down in fall cleanup or in spring before new shoots appear. The plants are sturdy and erect, but taller forms may need staking, especially in exposed areas. Top-dress with organic material in winter.
Propagation: Division in early spring (plants have taproots); root cuttings; seed takes three years to bloom.
Pests and Diseases: Powdery mildew, rust, fungal leaf spot.
Companions: *Salvia guaranitica*, euphorbia, helictotrichon, rudbeckia.
Notes: Baptisias are late to emerge in the spring.

BEGONIA Begoniaceae

The two hardy species of begonia are grown for their tropical foliage and profusion of small flowers. *Begonia grandis* has exceptionally attractive leaves—backlit, the red underside of the large leaf shines through. Since this is not a very tall plant, it is seen to best advantage in a container (which needs winter protection), or elevated so that it is closer to eye level. The flowers, very similar to the annual fibrous begonia, are welcome in late summer and last throughout the fall. *Begonia sutherlandii* has smaller orange flowers and is more lax in habit. It too does well in containers but is probably less hardy than *B. grandis* so it will need winter protection whether

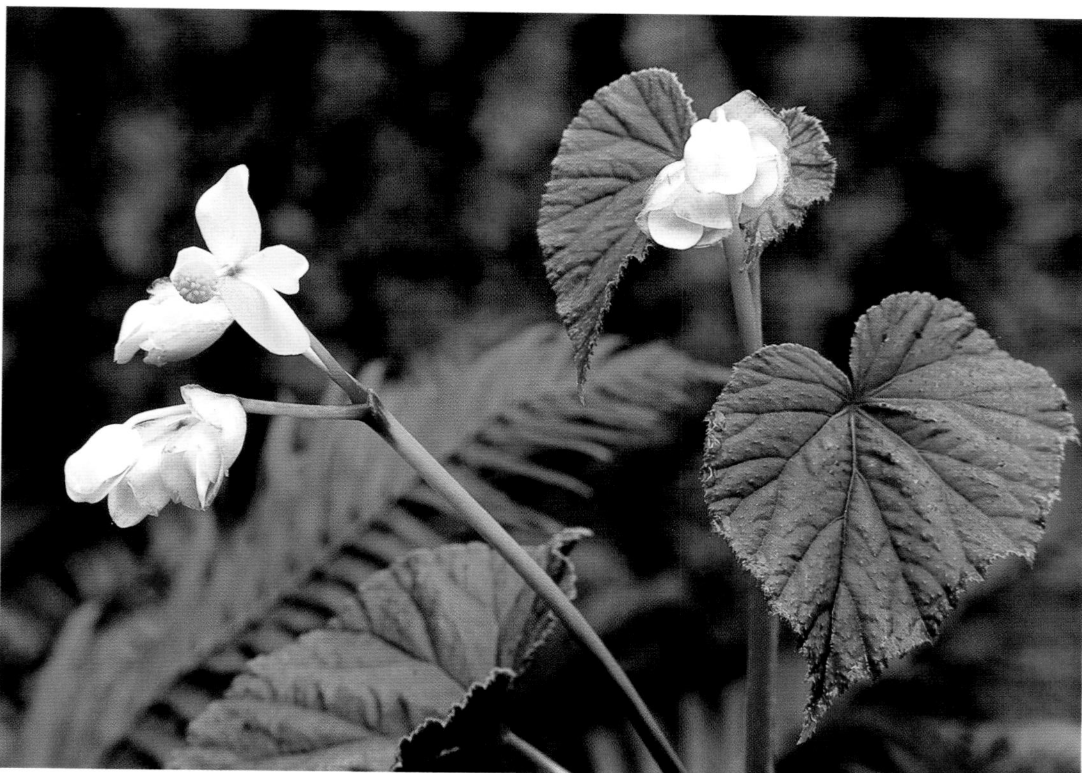

Begonia grandis subsp. *evansiana* var. *alba*.

Begonia grandis subsp. *evansiana* with *Peltoboykinia watanabei*, *Lamium maculatum* 'White Nancy', *Iris foetidissima* 'Variegata', and a hydrangea that has aged to purple.

grown in the ground or in containers. Small bulbils in the leaf axils in both of these species assure an abundant supply of plants. These begonias, while very prolific, are not a nuisance. They grow from small tubers and are easy to remove. ~ *Carrie Becker*

Scientific Name: After Michael Begon, governor of French Canada.
Common Name: Hardy begonia.
Origin: China, Japan.
Preferred Conditions: Humus-rich, moist soil in a warm, sheltered place.
Light: Part shade to part sun.
Management: Cut the dead foliage back in the fall (leaves are usually shed by this time). Light mulching will help the plants overwinter. As long as the tubers don't freeze the plants will sprout again in the spring. You can also just bring pots of begonias indoors to a frost-free space and take them back out next late spring. They will die back but will return with proper watering and outdoor conditions.
Propagation: Small bulbils form in the leaf axils; divisions can be dug up and moved in the spring; cuttings.
Pests and Diseases: Powdery mildew, root weevils.
Companions: Ferns, hosta, dicentra, fuchsia, hakonechloa, abutilon.

Species and Cultivars	Height/ Spread	USDA Hardiness Zone	Flowers (bloom time)	Foliage	Comments
grandis subsp. evansiana	10–24in × 12in	7–10	Drooping, pink, on red stems (M–L)	Wing-shaped with hairy texture, red veins underneath	Tuberous and spreading (not invasive), RHS Award
g. subsp. evansiana var. alba	10–24in × 12in	7–10	Drooping, white (M–L)	As above	Tuberous
sutherlandii	12–18in × 18in+	7–10	Tangerine-orange, small but abundant (E–L)	Small, triangular, bright green, red-veined	Very small tubers, RHS Award

BELAMCANDA Iridaceae

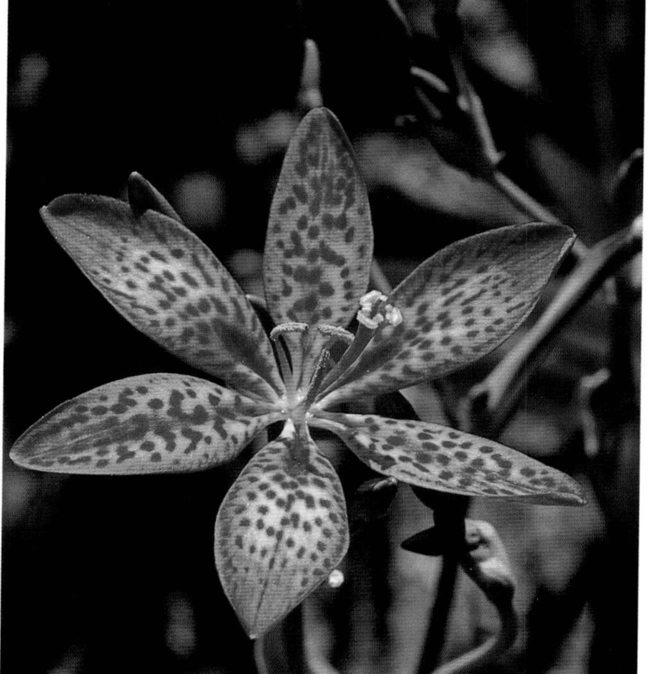

Belamcanda chinensis.

I grew *B. chinensis* last year for the first time—a nice plant with pale orange flowers and red spots increasing in density toward the flower center. Multiple flowers open each day over a fairly long period of time; the fans of foliage slowly expand in size and number. Do not deadhead, as the bonus with this plant is clusters of black fruits that look for all the world like ripe blackberries. My plant came through a hard winter in good condition, even in a pot. Belamcandas are extremely vulnerable to early spring slug shredding. ~ *Carrie Becker*

Scientific Name: Latinized common name from East Asia.
Common Name: Blackberry lily, leopard flower.
Origin: China, Himalayas, Southeast Asia, Japan.
Preferred Conditions: Will grow well in any type of moisture-retentive, well-drained soil. Don't allow to dry out.
Light: Sun. Tolerates part shade.
Planting: Plant rhizomes about one inch deep in spring (three inches deep in colder areas).
Management: Cut stems and leaves down in fall cleanup. They will benefit from a mulch in winter, especially in colder areas. Staking is a must, or a friend to lean on, particularly in rich, moist soil. Remove dead or dying leaves any time.
Propagation: Easy from seed in spring; division in spring.
Pests and Diseases: Iris borer, slugs, snails.
Companions: Artemisia, grasses, perovskia, agapanthus, helenium, salpiglossis, crocosmia, dark-foliaged dahlias; it would be nice with late daylilies in similar color tones.
Notes: Good for fresh flower arrangements; the dried seed capsules are also great in arrangements. This plant likes a lot of heat; best to site in a warm, protected spot in the maritime Northwest.

Species and Cultivars	Height/ Spread	USDA Hardiness Zone	Flowers (bloom time)	Foliage	Comments
chinensis	2–3ft × 1ft	5–9	Orange, spotted with maroon (M–L)	Irislike, sword-shaped, rich green	Shining black seedheads, resembling clusters of blackberries
c. 'Hello Yellow'	2ft × 1ft+	5–9	Yellow (unspotted) (M–L)	Broad, sword-shaped rich green	Dwarf cultivar

Bergenia emeiensis.

BERGENIA Saxifragaceae

We've come a long way since the megasea of Gertrude Jekyll's day. This genus includes some of the best broad-leaved evergreen perennials for the winter garden as well as stalwarts of the spring garden. Not all are wonderful winter plants though. Some get pretty beaten up through the course of a year; continuous dead-leafing helps with this problem. Others, however, are just excellent for winter color alone; *B.* 'Rotblum', *B.* 'Baby Doll', and *B. cordifolia* 'Winterglut', for example, all have leaves ranging from burgundy and scarlet to liver-colored throughout the winter.

Bergenias are best planted at the edges of beds or borders. There is a fair range of sizes and an excellent range of color, from the loud *B.* 'Ballawley' with carmine stems and red-violet flowers to the soft pink of *B.* 'Baby Doll' or the white, aging to pink flowers of *B.* 'Silberlicht'. The deciduous *B. ciliata* and the evergreen *B. purpurascens* are worth seeking out.

Mulching will help keep soil moist and cool in hot weather, but bergenias do not like manure on their above-ground rhizomes. ~ *Carrie Becker*

Scientific Name: For university professor Karl August von Bergen.
Common Name: Pigsqueak, megasea.
Origin: Asia.
Preferred Conditions: Rich, well-drained, moist soil. Tolerates a wide range of conditions.
Light: Shade to sun.
Planting: Fertilize moderately at planting time and each spring with a low-nitrogen, high-phosphorus and -potassium fertilizer.
Management: Deadhead spent flowers as necessary and cut back any damaged leaves after winter, or anytime during the growing season. Cut flower stems out after flowering. Susceptible to damage by root weevils, which can notch the leaves as on rhododendrons; night patrols are the most effective control from mid April through summer. Damaged by late frosts in mild winters.
Propagation: Division in spring using a good section of the rhizome; stem cuttings.
Pests and Diseases: Root weevils.
Companions: Omphalodes, *Brunnera macrophylla*, hamamelis, primula, helleborus, ophiopogon, chaerophyllum, larger-scale bulbs; good for edges and at their best when mass planted.
Notes: Bergenias like to expand their clumps, so remove the oldest pieces to keep them neat and not too congested. Look for 'Tubby Andrews', a new variegated selection of *B. cordifolia*.

Species and Cultivars	Height/ Spread	USDA Hardiness Zone	Flowers (bloom time)	Foliage	Comments
'Abendglut' (syn. 'Evening Glow')	10–12in × 12in+	4–8	Dark red, double (E)	Broad, reddish, ovate, bronze-brown in autumn	Smaller leaves than *B. cordifolia*
'Baby Doll'	12in × 12in+	4–8	Soft pink, darkening with age (E)	Green, rounded, toothed, turns maroon with crimson undersides in winter	As above, slow to expand
'Ballawley'	12–18in × 18in+	4–8	Red-violet (E)	Glossy, large, green, vivid red stems	RHS Award
'Bressingham Ruby'	15–18in × 18in	4–8	Strong pink (E)	Bronze-green, aging to maroon in winter	Compact clumps
'Bressingham Salmon'	12in × 18in+	4–8	Salmon-pink on compact spikes (E)	Long leaves (9–12in), green, tinged pink or purple in winter	Late flowering, doesn't like wet ground
'Bressingham White'	18–24in × 24in+	4–8	White, turning pink with age (E)	Green, leathery	As above, RHS Award
ciliata	12–18in × 18in	4–8	Pink or white, large (E)	Large, green, rounded, hairy	Deciduous
cordifolia	18–24in × 24in+	4–8	Pink or white (E)	Dark green, bronze-tinged, round to cordate, toothed	Heart-shaped bergenia, evergreen, the most common form grown from seed, expands to large clumps
c. 'Redstart'	18in × 18in	4–8	Vibrant red (E)	Green, turning red in winter	Compact clumps
c. 'Winterglut'	12–18in × 18in	4–8	Ruby-red clusters (E)	As above	As above
emeiensis	12in × 12in	6–9	White or pink clusters with reddish throat and flower stem, more nodding (E)	Green with reddish tones in winter, more narrow leaf	Mounding, evergreen, not reliably hardy
'Morgenröte' (syn. 'Morning Red')	15in × 15in	4–8	Bright carmine-pink (E)	Green	Reblooms in fall, RHS Award
purpurascens	15in × 12in	4–8	Bright pink on magenta stems (E)	Dark green, turning red in winter	RHS Award
'Rotblum'	12–18in × 18in	4–8	Deep reddish purple (E)	Green, shiny, red-tinged in winter	Excellent winter color, dense clumps
'Silberlicht'	12–18in × 24in+	4–8	White turning pink with age, red center (E)	Large, green	Strong grower, RHS Award
'Sunningdale'	18in × 18in	4–8	Carmine-lilac (E)	Green aging to magenta in winter	Tolerates full sun
'Wintermärchen'	15in × 15in+	4–8	Dark rose (E)	Leathery, green, turning reddish in fall	

Bidens heterophylla.

BIDENS Asteraceae

These North American natives grow best in full sun and usually need little more care than staking. In our gardens they can be quite vigorous, which may make them flop a bit, so the less nitrogen they get the better; avoid overhead watering as well. The small, up-facing daisy flowers are usually in the yellow range (although a new deep pink one has been introduced from Lotus Land in California). The obsessive among us deadhead to increase flower production. ~ *Bob Lilly*

Scientific Name: Latin *bis* ("twice") and *dens* ("tooth"), referring to two teeth on the seed.
Common Name: Tickseed.
Origin: North America.
Preferred Conditions: Well-drained, rich soil with lots of light. Needs to be well watered during the growing season.
Light: Sun. Tolerates part shade.
Planting: Give them lots of room, as they can run.
Management: Deadhead after flowering. Cut back to ground in winter cleanup. Bait crown for slugs in winter.
Propagation: Division in spring when new growth begins.
Pests and Diseases: Slugs.
Companions: Solidago, helianthus, anthemis, perovskia, agapanthus, *Salvia guaranitica*, *S. patens*, *S. discolor*, grasses.
Notes: Self-sowing in the Pacific Northwest does not seem to be a problem.

Species and Cultivars	Height/ Spread	USDA Hardiness Zone	Flowers (bloom time)	Foliage	Comments
heterophylla	3–4ft × 3ft+	5–8	Pale yellow, daisylike on strong upright stems (E–L)	Green, deeply cut, willowy	Needs staking even if planted in full sun, runs
'Madame Ganna Walska'	3–4ft × 4ft+	5–8	Rose-pink with yellow center (M–L)	Green	Vigorous and clumping
triplinervia	6ft × 2ft+	5–8	Yellow (M)	Green, divided, 3-part	North American native, needs summer water, runs

BLETILLA Orchidaceae

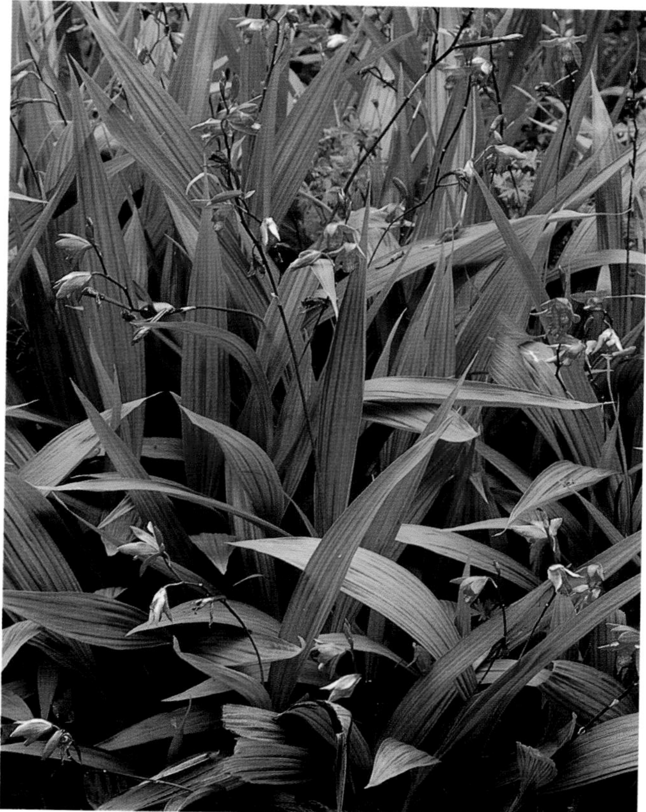

Bletilla striata.

I planted my first bletilla the year a famous person from England spoke to our Hardy Plant Study Weekend. He said bletilla was difficult to bloom. Mine was in full bloom, and I felt very smug. That was probably fifteen years ago. I remember it blooming only once since then—that was the year I moved it to a sunnier location. This year I'm experimenting: some I divided and replanted shallowly, some I put in pots, some I left alone. We'll see. They had, somehow, in three years, gotten deeper and more crowded.

The pleated leaves are attractive in themselves, but the lovely flowers are worth some effort. Once properly sited they will bloom and spread well, but they may need more heat than we have in the Pacific Northwest. A certain backyard picket fence in View Ridge, Seattle, may be the answer.
~ *Ann Bucher*

Scientific Name: After eighteenth-century Spanish apothecary Louis Blet.
Common Name: Hardy Chinese orchid.
Origin: China, Japan.
Preferred Conditions: Humus-rich, moisture-retentive, well-drained soil. Likes it moist, so don't allow them to dry out.
Light: Sun to part shade.
Planting: Don't plant too deep; one inch is ideal.
Management: Leave undisturbed to make large drifts, but divide when colonies become too crowded to bloom. Mulch heavily in cold areas. Late frosts can be a problem. Cut dead foliage down in autumn.
Propagation: Divide in spring.
Pests and Diseases: Slugs, especially as they first emerge in spring.
Companions: Heuchera, hakonechloa, primula, polygonatum, corydalis.
Notes: All forms will spread to more than three feet over time.

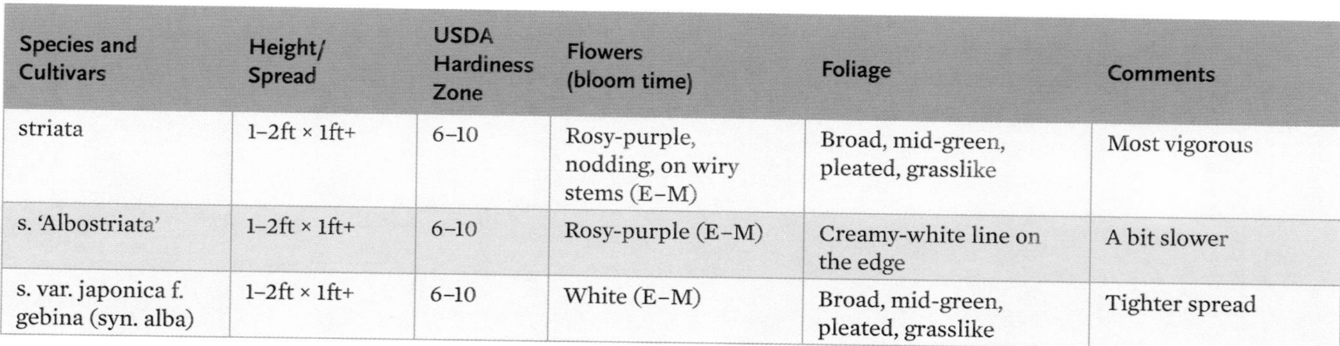

Species and Cultivars	Height/ Spread	USDA Hardiness Zone	Flowers (bloom time)	Foliage	Comments
striata	1–2ft × 1ft+	6–10	Rosy-purple, nodding, on wiry stems (E–M)	Broad, mid-green, pleated, grasslike	Most vigorous
s. 'Albostriata'	1–2ft × 1ft+	6–10	Rosy-purple (E–M)	Creamy-white line on the edge	A bit slower
s. var. japonica f. gebina (syn. alba)	1–2ft × 1ft+	6–10	White (E–M)	Broad, mid-green, pleated, grasslike	Tighter spread

Boltonia asteroides var. *latisquama*.

BOLTONIA Asteraceae

All boltonias are North American natives. All have glabrous stems and foliage. They are appealing plants, with gray leaves, upright habit, and finely rayed daisy flowers. They have a fresh appearance; when they bloom in late summer to fall, they have that new, bright, generous quality of spring bloomers. The best performer is *B. asteroides*, which has white flowers and stands up well on its own in full sun. The forms with colored flowers, especially *B. a.* 'Pink Beauty', are lax in habit, shyer to bloom, and not nearly as good garden plants.

Plants increase rapidly, and it's not necessary to buy one larger than a four-inch pot since it will be more than adequate size by bloom time in the first year. ~ *Carrie Becker*

Scientific Name: In honor of British botanist James Bolton.
Common Name: Thousand-flowered aster.
Origin: North America.
Preferred Conditions: Moist, fertile, well-drained soil. Plants grown in dry soil may be smaller than normal. Drought tolerant once established.
Light: Sun. Tolerates part shade.
Management: You can pinch back by half on 1 June to make for a more compact plant and heavier bloom. Plants grown in shade or very rich soil may need support. Bait crown for slugs in winter.
Propagation: Divide in spring, or take tip cuttings in summer. Seeds of cultivars will not come true.
Pests and Diseases: Slugs; does not suffer from powdery mildew like asters.
Companions: Boltonias are beautiful in combination with yellow phygelius, solidago, and late white-flowering phlox. Try them with *Sedum* 'Herbstfreude', *Eupatorium purpureum*, perovskia, miscanthus, aconitum, *Molinia caerulea* 'Variegata'.

Species and Cultivars	Height/ Spread	USDA Hardiness Zone	Flowers (bloom time)	Foliage	Comments
asteroides	4–7ft × 2½ft	3–9	White with yellow center (L)	Narrow, lancelike, gray-green, on stiffly erect stems	Stake at 4ft
a. var. latisquama	6ft × 2½ft	3–9	Small, violet-blue in dense clusters (L)	Gray-green	Needs staking
a. var. latisquama 'Nana'	2–3ft × 2½ft	3–9	Lilac with yellow center (L)	As above	Good for cutting, dwarf variety
a. var. latisquama 'Snowbank'	3–5ft × 2½ft	3–9	Pure white with yellow center, dense (L)	Gray-green on branching stems, lower stem may be bare	North American native, large-scale plant
a. 'Pink Beauty'	2–4ft × 2½ft	3–9	Pale pink (L)	Gray-green, very open habit, lower stems may be bare	Good cut flower, weak stems

BRUNNERA Boraginaceae

One of the loveliest sights in late winter, early spring is the emerging foliage of *B. macrophylla* 'Hadspen Cream'. This plant has large cordate (heart-shaped) leaves edged in cream and (when completely unfolded) spotted faintly with silver. The small airy flowers are an intense cobalt-blue with yellow center. They are lovely with early bulbs and *Ranunculus ficaria* 'Double Mud' or *R. f.* 'Randall's White'. Newer in cultivation and an absolutely outstanding foliage plant is *B. macrophylla* 'Jack Frost'. Large (four inches or more) leaves covered in silver with a netting of green veins make this plant shine in the shade.

Brunneras are best in spring sun and summer shade, or shady woodland conditions. In this situation, *B. macrophylla* 'Jack Frost' is beaconlike, with excellent foliage from spring through fall, a first-rate plant.

Eventually, brunneras form large clumps, especially the greener leaf forms. Division in fall will help solve this problem. Cut foliage back hard in summer if it looks bad. *Brunnera macrophylla* 'Langtrees' can self-sow plain green, and these seedlings should be promptly removed.

Brunnera macrophylla 'Hadspen Cream' and *B. m.* 'Jack Frost' are best not cut back until fall; the former is less vigorous and needs its leaves to photosynthesize and build up its crown, while *B. m.* 'Jack Frost' does not seem to look bad until after the first frost. Keep moist and remove individual leaves as necessary on these two cultivars. ~ *Carrie Becker*

Scientific Name: After Swiss botanist Samuel Brunner (1790–1844).
Common Name: Siberian bugloss.
Origin: Siberia, Caucasus.
Preferred Conditions: Average, cool, well-drained, humus-rich, moisture-retentive soil. Prefers to be moist but will tolerate drought. May go dormant if too dry.
Light: Part shade to shade. Sun in cooler climates. Will bloom less in full shade.
Management: Mulch to keep cool and moist, although the plain-leaved forms are drought tolerant once established. If the foliage looks bad in midsummer, cut it back to the ground and water deeply. New foliage will soon appear. Cut the dead foliage down in fall cleanup. Brunnera tolerates neglect but is handsome only if healthy.

Brunnera macrophylla 'Hadspen Cream'.

Propagation: Division in late fall or early winter; root cuttings; seed is often difficult to germinate although they can self-sow in some conditions.

Pests and Diseases: Slugs, some mildew if allowed to dry out.

Companions: Thalictrum, dicentra, epimedium, trollius, muscari, narcissus, *Ranunculus ficaria*, hyacinthoides, trillium, omphalodes; good under deciduous trees and shrubs (spring sun, summer shade).

Notes: There's a new cultivar (of course), *B. macrophylla* 'Looking Glass', a sport of *B. m.* 'Jack Frost' and apparently very similar.

Species and Cultivars	Height/ Spread	USDA Hardiness Zone	Flowers (bloom time)	Foliage	Comments
macrophylla	1–1½ft × 2ft	3–9	Tiny bright blue with yellow center (E–M)	Large, dark green, cordate, hairy	Clump-forming, self-sows, RHS Award
m. 'Dawson's White' (syn. 'Variegata')	1–1½ft × 1½ft	3–9	Bright blue (E–M)	Dark green, cordate, creamy-white border and marbling, browns easily in full sun	Keep out of sun, leaves may revert to green, keep moist
m. 'Hadspen Cream'	1–1½ft × 1½ft	3–9	Blue, starry (E–M)	Green, cream borders, broad, cordate, fuzzy	Prefers part shade and steady moisture, may revert, RHS Award
m. 'Jack Frost'	1–1½ft × 1½ft	3–9	As above	Silver with green veins	Best new form for vigor, takes more sun
m. 'Langtrees' (syn. 'Aluminum Spot')	1–1½ft × 2ft	3–9	As above	Dark green with silvery-gray spots and borders, large, cordate, hairy	Seedlings vary in prominence of the spots, select the best ones

Buphthalmum salicifolium.

BUPHTHALMUM Asteraceae

The oxeye daisy is an easy plant to have. It is often staked, but it is more beautiful when allowed to flop among other stronger-stemmed perennials. Divide your clumps in spring when they have spread too far. Long-lasting as a cut flower, "but it's just another yellow daisy." - *Bob Lilly*

Scientific Name: From the Greek *bous* ("ox") and *ophthalmos* ("eye"), referring to the flowers.
Common Name: Oxeye daisy.
Origin: Europe, western Asia.
Preferred Conditions: Humus-rich, moisture-retentive, moist soil.
Light: Sun to part shade.
Management: Deadhead after flowering for a cleaner look. Cut dead foliage down in autumn. Weak plants may require staking.
Propagation: Seed is best; divide in spring.
Pests and Diseases: Slugs in spring.
Companions: Ligularia, larger ferns, *Lysimachia ciliata* 'Firecracker', *Carex elata*, oxen.

Species and Cultivars	Height/ Spread	USDA Hardiness Zone	Flowers (bloom time)	Foliage	Comments
salicifolium (syn. *Inula* 'Golden Beauty')	3ft+ × 2ft+	3–7	Deep yellow, daisylike, on slender stems, fragrant, long-blooming (M–L)	Narrow, dark green	Spreads slowly, but not invasive

CALAMINTHA Lamiaceae

Calamintha is another diminutive member of the mint family. Some calaminthas have the invasive habit of mints; a few are clump-forming. Several years ago I planted *C. grandiflora* in a pot with other perennials—an experiment. I thought it would be a good perennial trailer to hang down the sides of the pot. It did this very well! Now the plant owns the pot, having forced out everyone else. If you grow the spreading forms you will need to be watchful and carry a trowel to ensure the survival of smaller or less aggressive neighbors.

All the calaminthas are lovely later-season plants, making little clouds of aromatic flowers and foliage. Trimmings of the more enthusiastic forms can be used in sachet and potpourri. Think of them as filler in the front of the border. ~ *Carrie Becker*

Scientific Name: From the Greek *kallos* ("beautiful") and *minthe* ("mint").
Common Name: Calamint.
Origin: Southern Europe, northwest Africa, northern Turkey, Russia.
Preferred Conditions: Average and well-drained soil. *Calamintha grandiflora* can take light shade and is drought tolerant once established.
Light: Sun.
Management: Though really not necessary due to their naturally short stature, you can cut back as needed to keep full and dense. Cut dead foliage down in autumn.
Propagation: Division in early spring, sow seed in cold frame in early spring, or take cuttings. Seed is best.
Pests and Diseases: Powdery mildew, but normally pest- and disease-free.
Companions: Sedum, aster, perovskia, ×solidaster, solidago, coreopsis, scabiosa.

Calamintha grandiflora 'Variegata'.

Species and Cultivars	Height/ Spread	USDA Hardiness Zone	Flowers (bloom time)	Foliage	Comments
grandiflora	12–18in × 18in	5–9	Pink, sagelike on erect stems, long-lasting (M)	Fuzzy, dark green, aromatic, strongly toothed, on a dense bushy plant	Rhizomatous, plant inside a root barrier
g. 'Variegata'	15–24in × 18in	5–9	Small, pink (M)	Fuzzy, dark green, variegated, speckled in mint-green and white, aromatic	Sun for best leaf color; will revert, pinch out green leaves
nepeta	18–20in × 12in	5–9	White or lilac, thymelike, long-flowering (M–L)	Aromatic, light green	Short-lived esp. in wet winters and heavy soils, bees love this plant
n. subsp. glandulosa 'White Cloud'	12in × 12in	5–9	Tiny, white, and lots of them (M–L)	Aromatic, green	Cut back mature plants to encourage a succession of flowers
n. subsp. nepeta (syn. nepetoides)	12–18in × 12in	5–9	Tiny, lilac and white, turning blue with age (M–L)	Aromatic, green, wiry little bushlets	Long flowering season, bees love it, noninvasive

CALLIRHOE Malvaceae

Poppy mallow is another American prairie plant that needs full sun and few neighbors. This species forms a thick, fleshy root that, in deep soil, can get up to three feet long. Flowers are sparsely held but are an incredible bright color. Plant in a sunny location, where it can flop about and live out its short life. ~ *Bob Lilly*

Callirhoe involucrata.

Scientific Name: For a character in Greek mythology.
Common Name: Poppy mallow.
Origin: United States, Mexico.
Preferred Conditions: Dry, hot sites in well-drained, light soil. Tolerant of poor soil.
Light: Sun.
Planting: Avoid damage to taproot when planting.
Management: Given its long taproot, doesn't like being moved. Cut back dead stems in autumn. Protect from winter wet.
Propagation: Seed in early spring.
Pests and Diseases: Powdery mildew, rust, aphids, spider mites.
Companions: Yucca, sedum, stachys, echinacea, festuca, helictotrichon.
Notes: Grow this once in your life—the color must be seen to be believed!

Species and Cultivars	Height/ Spread	USDA Hardiness Zone	Flowers (bloom time)	Foliage	Comments
involucrata	6–12in × 3ft+	4–8	Red-violet, white at base, 5-petaled, deep-cupped (M–L)	Roundish, deeply cut, green, on hairy, sprawling stems	

CALTHA Ranunculaceae

This is no ordinary buttercup. Bright yellow or white flowers appear in late spring on these slowly spreading, moisture-loving plants. Full sun and constant moisture is preferred, but drier soil in summer, when the plant is dormant, is tolerated in part shade. They will accept root restriction in aquatic containers. Slugs are usually the reason these plants fail. ~ *Ann Bucher*

Caltha palustris.

Scientific Name: Latin for a yellow-flowered plant.
Common Name: Marsh marigold, kingcup, Molly blob.
Origin: Northern hemisphere.
Preferred Conditions: Rich, organic, moist to boggy soil. Tolerant of drier areas if shaded from full sun. Can tolerate standing water in spring.
Light: Sun in the spring, part shade in the summer.
Management: Tidy up after it goes dormant.
Propagation: Division in late spring after flowering; sow ripe seed on damp soil mix in partially shaded cold frame.
Pests and Diseases: Slugs.
Companions: Waterside and aquatic plants—*Iris pseudacorus*, *Acorus gramineus*, ferns, *Primula japonica*, *P. florindae*, *P. bulleyana*, *P. beesiana*, juncus.
Notes: Keep the crown above water level.

Species and Cultivars	Height/ Spread	USDA Hardiness Zone	Flowers (bloom time)	Foliage	Comments
palustris	1–2ft × 2ft	4–8	Bright yellow, single, with rich yellow stamens in loose clusters (E)	Shiny, rounded, green	Molly blob, goes dormant in mid to late summer, RHS Award
p. 'Flore Pleno'	1–1½ft × 1½ft	4–8	Double, bright yellow (E)	Compact, lush, glossy, green, rounded	Blooms longer than species, goes dormant early, clump-forming, RHS Award
p. var. palustris 'Plena'	1–1½ft × 1½ft	4–8	Double, golden yellow (E)	Shiny, rounded, green	Shallow water or very moist soil, goes dormant early, clump-forming

CAMASSIA Hyacinthaceae

A genus of bulbous perennials growing in the fertile, moist spring meadows of western North America. They resemble a tall scilla with starry, slender-petaled blossoms. Color range includes blue, purple, white, and cream. *Camassia quamash* is low-growing with narrow foliage, more suitable for naturalizing. *Camassia cusickii* and *C. leichtlinii* are quite suitable for the border, appearing between the early bloomers and the bulbs of later summer. They all make good cut flowers. The bulbs were a staple food of Northwest native peoples. They are at home here. ~ *Ann Bucher*

Scientific Name: From North American Indian name, quamash or camas.
Common Name: Camas, Indian hyacinth, quamash.
Origin: Western North America.
Preferred Conditions: Rich in organic material, moisture-retentive soil. Moist meadows in spring but not standing water, especially in winter. Will not tolerate spring drought and prefers spring wet then summer dry. In nature they get exactly this.
Light: Sun. Tolerates part shade.
Planting: Plant in the fall after weather cools, three to six inches deep depending on bulb size, in groups of a dozen or more.

Camassia leichtlinii subsp. *suksdorfii* 'Blauwe Donau'.

Management: Cut scruffy-looking flower stems to ground, or leave on for the seedpods. May need to lift and divide when showing signs of congestion. Leave foliage on to ripen as with other spring-flowering bulbs, after which they can be lifted and divided.

Propagation: Division of bulbs in fall; seed into cold frame in late summer when seed is ripe.

Pests and Diseases: Slugs on spring foliage.

Companions: Filipendula, *Carex elata*, ligularia foliage, *Iris sibirica*, *I. pseudacorus* 'Variegata', late-season tulips, late narcissus.

Notes: *Camassia leichtlinii* can get quite large and form massive clumps; useful in the large-scale border. Plant these in clumps of five to seven bulbs for best effect.

Species and Cultivars	Height/ Spread	USDA Hardiness Zone	Flowers (bloom time)	Foliage	Comments
cusickii	2–3ft × 1ft	3–8	Pale blue, narrow-petaled, starlike (E–M)	Long, waxy, green, grassy	Good cut flower, bulbs are large and can weigh ½ pound
leichtlinii subsp. leichtlinii (syn. 'Alba')	3–4ft × 1ft	3–8	Cream-colored, waxen, on long stems, may be double (M)	Straplike, green	Seeds itself in rich damp soil, seldom needs support, RHS Award
l. subsp. suksdorfii	1½–2ft × 1ft	3–8	Deep blue with yellow stamens (E)	Broad, upright green blades	
l. subsp. suksdorfii 'Blauwe Donau'	3–4ft × 1ft	3–8	Dark blue (E)	Wide, green blade	Very strong plant, will make immense dense clumps
quamash (syn. esculenta)	1½ft × 1ft	3–8	Violet blue-white (E–M)	Narrow, grasslike, green	Good cut, vigorous

Campanula lactiflora.

CAMPANULA Campanulaceae

You know it's a campanula when you see a cup- or bell-shaped corolla made up of five petals fused at the base. The petals will usually be blue, but some are purple, white, lilac, rarely red or yellow. There is a campanula for almost any niche, and there are campanulas determined to fill every niche!

Campanula is a very complex genus; we have divided its members into three groups and have noted in the chart to which group each species or cultivar belongs. Some of them do well in the alpine or rock garden, many suit the border, and a few have unique characteristics. *Campanula carpatica* and its many cultivars are good plants for the front of the border, large rockery, or containers. *Campanula persicifolia*, which also has many forms, is an excellent cut flower. *Campanula glomerata, C. latifolia, C. lactiflora,* and *C. latiloba* are also suitable for cutting. ~ *Ann Bucher*

Scientific Name: From the Latin *campana* ("bell"), referring to the shape of the flowers.
Common Name: Bellflower.
Origin: Northern hemisphere.
Preferred Conditions / Light:

Group 1. Most taller species and cultivars. Prefer fertile soil that is neutral to alkaline. Moist, well-drained but will tolerate heavy moist soil. The taller ones may need staking. Cut them back after flowering to prevent self-sowing and to encourage a second bloom. Sun to part shade.

Group 2. Alpine, rock garden conditions. Likes moist, well-drained soil. Open sunny area to part shade. Drought tolerant once established.

Group 3. Those that don't fall in Group 1 or 2. *Campanula carpatica* falls between Groups 1 and 2; *C. primulifolia* prefers moist, humus-rich, well-drained soil, and shade; *C. rapunculoides* spreads quickly in light soil and tolerates a wide range of conditions.

Campanula persicifolia, *Geum* 'Mrs. J. Bradshaw', *Achillea* 'Moonshine', *Phygelius aequalis* 'Yellow Trumpet' (top left), *Lonicera nitida* 'Baggesen's Gold' (top center), *Alstroemeria ligtu* hybrid (top right). Design by Rick Kyper.

Management: Many can be deadheaded or cut back for a second bloom, which is often not as robust as the first flowering. Cut dead foliage down in autumn (or raise rabbits). The taller ones may need staking. Some may become congested and should be lifted, divided, and replanted.

Propagation: Division in spring or fall; seed; cuttings.

Pests and Diseases: Slugs, snails, leaf spot, spider mites, powdery mildew, rust.

Companions: Polygonatum, hosta, coreopsis, eryngium, roses, achillea, verbascum, papaver, dicentra, geranium. If you have a lonely perennial, there is probably a campanula for it.

Notes: *Campanula persicifolia*, *C. poscharskyana*, and *C. portenschlagiana* are all very sun tolerant if they can root deeply under rocks. The forms of *C. carpatica* that are noted as short-lived are often grown as pot plants, for a brief life as a houseplant. Some campanulas are infinite spreaders (∞) so site them accordingly or mix with other strong, invasive plants or thugs.

Species and Cultivars	Height/ Spread	USDA Hardiness Zone	Flowers (bloom time)	Foliage	Comments
alliariifolia	1½–3ft × 1½ft	3–8	White or cream, bell-shaped, nodding, long-blooming (M–L)	Ovate to cordate, toothed, gray-green, hairy	Group 1, clumping, self-sows, vigorous
alpestris (syn. allionii)	5in × 10in	3–8	Lilac or whitish purple bells, large (E–M)	Narrow, green rosettes	Group 2, rhizomatous, long-lived
'Birch Hybrid'	4–8in × 12in+	4–8	Violet-blue or purple, bell-shaped, nodding, large (M–L)	Ovate to cordate, toothed, bright green, evergreen	Group 2, vigorous, prostrate, RHS Award
carpatica	6–12in × 12in	3–9	White to dark violet or blue, open, up-turned large bells, long-blooming, all forms have flowers above the foliage (M–L)	Bright green, toothed, triangular to rounded or cordate, glossy	Group 3, Carpathian harebell, mounding, RHS Award
c. f. alba 'Weisse Clips' (syn. 'White Clips')	6–12in × 12in	4–9	White bells (M–L)	Green, toothed, triangular to rounded or cordate, glossy	Group 3, clumping, spreading, short-lived
c. 'Blaue Clips'	6–12in × 12in	4–9	Lavender-blue, up-facing bells, large, long-blooming (M–L)	Bright green, toothed, triangular to rounded or cordate, glossy	Group 3, compact, short-lived
c. 'Chewton Joy'	6–8in × 12in	4–9	Pale blue with a darker edge (M)	As above	Group 3
c. 'Deep Blue Clips'	6–10in × 12in	4–9	Deep blue, bell-shaped, long-blooming (M–L)	Dark green, toothed, triangular to rounded or cordate, glossy	Group 3, clumping, short-lived
c. 'Light Blue Clips'	6–8in × 10in	3–9	Light blue, long-blooming (M–L)	Bright green, toothed, triangular to rounded or cordate, glossy	Group 3, clumping, short-lived
c. var. turbinata	3–6in × 6in	4–9	Upright, pale blue bells (M)	Dark green	Group 3, dwarf
cochleariifolia (syn. pusilla)	3–6in × 8in+	4–8	White to pale blue or lavender, pendent, bell-shaped, all forms have flowers above the foliage (M)	Rosette-forming, toothed, ovate to cordate or lanceolate, bright green, shiny	Group 2, fairy thimbles, spreading, RHS Award
c. var. alba	3–4in × 6in+	4–8	White, nodding, bell-shaped (M)	As above	Group 2, spreading
c. 'Elizabeth Oliver'	3–6in × 6in+	5–8	Double, pale lavender-blue bells (M)	As above	Group 2, slowly spreading
garganica	2–6in × 12in	5–8	Bright violet-blue to lilac, white throat, star-shaped clusters (M)	Gray-green, cordate to kidney-shaped, glossy, toothed	Group 2, Adriatic bellflower, spreading, RHS Award

Species and Cultivars	Height/ Spread	USDA Hardiness Zone	Flowers (bloom time)	Foliage	Comments
g. 'Dickson's Gold' (syn. 'Aurea')	4–6in × 10in	4–9	Bright blue, star-shaped (M)	Golden yellowish green, cordate	Group 2
glomerata	1–2ft × 1ft+	3–9	Clusters of dark violet-blue up-facing bells (E–M)	Hairy, wavy, toothed, ovate to lanceolate, dark green	Group 1, long-lasting, good cut, invasive spreader
g. var. alba	1–2ft × 1ft+	3–9	White, bell-shaped (M)	Green	Group 1, cut back for repeat bloom, vigorous
g. var. alba 'Schneekrone' (syn. 'Crown of Snow')	16–20in × 18in+	3–8	Dense cluster of white bells (M)	Deep rich green	Group 1, good cut
g. 'Joan Elliott'	16–18in × 18in	3–8	Deep violet-blue, bell-shaped, up-facing, large long-blooming (E–M)	As above	Group 1, good cut, invasive
g. 'Superba'	1–2ft × 1½ft	3–8	Deep violet-blue clusters, bell-shaped, large (M)	Dark green	Group 1, good cut, aggressive, RHS Award
kemulariae	1ft × 1ft+	4–9	Bright, purplish blue, broad bell-shaped (E–M)	Shiny, green, cordate to oval, toothed	Group 2, clump-forming, spreading
'Kent Belle'	2–3ft × 2ft+	5–9	Deep violet-blue, glossy bells, large, very rich color (M–L)	Glossy, green	Group 1, good cut, vigorous, spreading, RHS Award
lactiflora	4–5ft × 2ft	4–8	Light blue to milky white, up-facing (M–L)	Rosettes of mid-green, toothed, oval to lanceolate, clump-forming	Group 1, milky bellflower, may need support, self-sows, its cultivars do not come true from seed
l. 'Loddon Anna'	3–5ft × 2ft	4–8	Soft pink to lilac, nodding (M–L)	As above	Group 1, may need support, doesn't come true from seed, RHS Award
l. 'Pouffe'	10–18in × 18in	4–8	Pale lavender-blue, long-blooming (M–L)	As above	Group 1, shorter variety, mounding
l. 'Prichard's Variety'	3–4ft × 2ft	4–8	Dark violet-blue, white center, bell-shaped, large (M–L)	As above	Group 1, clump-forming, RHS Award
l. 'White Pouffe'	10–18in × 18in	4–8	White (M–L)	As above	Group 1, same as *C. lactiflora* 'Pouffe' but white
latifolia	3–4ft × 2ft	4–8	Violet-blue, tubular bells (M)	Ovate to oblong, toothed, coarse, mid-green, nettlelike	Group 1, great bell flower, self-sows, vigorous
l. var. macrantha	3–4ft × 2ft	3–10	Dark purplish blue (M)	Sparse	Group 1, good cut

Species and Cultivars	Height/ Spread	USDA Hardiness Zone	Flowers (bloom time)	Foliage	Comments
latiloba	2½–3ft × 2ft	4–8	Rich lavender-blue on stiff erect stems, cup-shaped (M)	Mid-green rosettes, long, narrow, toothed	Group 1, good cut, evergreen
l. 'Alba'	2½–3ft × 2ft	4–8	White, creamy chartreuse buds (M)	Deep green rosettes	Group 1, evergreen, good cut, RHS Award
l. 'Hidcote Amethyst'	2–3ft × 2ft	4–8	Light lilac-pink with deeper purple shading (M)	Deep green rosettes, a bit scruffy after flowering	Group 1, evergreen, RHS Award
persicifolia	2–3ft × 2ft+	3–8	Lilac-blue or white, nodding, cup-shaped, long-blooming (M)	Narrow, bright green, toothed, glossy	Group 1, evergreen, self-sows, good cut
p. var. alba	2–3ft × 2ft+	3–8	White, open cup-shaped (M)	As above	As above
p. 'Boule de Neige'	2–3ft × 2ft+	3–8	Double white (M)	As above	As above
p. 'Chettle Charm' (syn. 'George Chiswell')	2–3ft × 2ft+	3–9	Cream-white, edged in pale lavender, bell-shaped (E–M)	Deep green, willowy	As above
p. 'Grandiflora Alba'	2½–4ft × 1½ft+	3–7	Pure white with purplish hue, large (M)	Green, willowy	As above
p. 'Kelly's Gold'	2–3ft × 2ft+	3–8	Blue (M)	Golden yellow	Group 1, good cut, grown for its foliage, evergreen
p. 'Telham Beauty'	2–3ft × 2ft+	3–9	Pale china-blue, cup-shaped, large (M)	Deep green	Group 1, good cut, evergreen
portenschlagiana (syn. muralis)	6–9in × 1½ft+	4–9	Pale lavender, bell-shaped, white center (E–L)	Mid-green rosettes, glossy, toothed, wavy, cordate	Group 2, evergreen, Dalmatian bellflower, RHS Award
p. 'Resholdt's Variety'	4–8in × 8in+	4–9	Deep vivid violet-blue, bell-shaped, large (M)	Cordate, scalloped, mid-green	Group 2, not hard to control, trailing
poscharskyana	6–24in × 12in+	3–9	Pale lavender, white center (E–L)	Mid-green, toothed, round to ovate	Group 2, Siberian bellflower, self-sows, vigorous, invasive
p. 'E. H. Frost'	4–6in × 12in+	3–9	Milky white with pale blue eye (E–M)	Mid-green	Group 2
p. 'Stella'	6–15in × 12in+	3–8	Dark violet-blue, white center, star-shaped (M–L)	Deep green, cordate	Group 2, not as aggressive, RHS Award
primulifolia	3ft × 1½ft	4–9	Purple-blue with paler base, wide up-facing (M)	Green, coarse, hairy, in basal rosettes	Group 3, short-lived, self-sows
punctata	1–2ft × ∞	4–9	Creamy-white or mauve, flushed pink, dotted red inside, large pendent bells (M)	Dark green rosettes, ovate, toothed, slightly hairy, cordate at base	Group 1, invasive, conditions determine its spreading

Species and Cultivars	Height/ Spread	USDA Hardiness Zone	Flowers (bloom time)	Foliage	Comments
p. f. rubriflora	1–2ft × ∞	5–9	Cream to rosy-purple with crimson spots, large pendent bells (M)	Rich green	Group 1, vigorous
p. f. rubriflora 'Cherry Bells'	1–2ft × ∞	5–9	Cherry-red, edged in white, large pendent bells (M)	Mid-green	Group 1, erect, vigorous, good cut
p. 'Wedding Bells'	1½–2ft × ∞	5–9	Double white (hose in hose), flushed pink, spotted deep red inside, large pendent bells (M)	Deep green	Group 1, spreading
pyramidalis	4–6ft × 1½ft	8–10	Light blue or white, starry cups, fragrant, flowers last longer if not pollinated (E–M)	Light to mid-green rosettes, ovate to lanceolate, toothed, glossy	Group 1, chimney bellflower, often treated as a biennial, self-sows, short-lived, needs support
p. alba	4–6ft × 1½ft	8–10	White, cup-shaped, fragrant, flowers last longer if not pollinated (M)	As above	As above
rapunculoides	2–4ft × ∞	3–10	Violet-blue, starry bells (M–L)	Green, nettlelike, toothed, ovate to cordate, veined	Group 3, self-sows, creeping, thug
rotundifolia	1–1½ft × 1ft	3–9	Dark blue to light lavender-blue to white, bell-shaped, nodding, above foliage (M–L)	Rounded rosettes, upper leaves narrow, grasslike, toothed, light green	Group 2, harebells, vigorous, long-blooming
r. 'Olympica'	9–12in × 12in	3–9	Dark blue, nodding, bell-shaped, above foliage (M)	Dark green, toothed	Group 2, good cut, compact
takesimana	1½–2ft × ∞	5–8	Pale lilac and white, spotted maroon inside, tubular bells (M–L)	Basal rosettes, cordate, toothed, mid-green with reddish tinge, glossy	Group 1, Korean bellflower, colonizes, rhizomatous
t. 'Beautiful Trust'	2–3ft × 2ft	5–8	White, like a giant vancouveria, many petals (M–L)	Mid-green, divided, toothed and laced	Group 1, vigorous
t. 'Elizabeth'	1½–2ft × ∞	5–8	Rose-pink, spotted deep red inside, pendent, bell-shaped (M)	Rosettes, heart-shaped, toothed, mid-green	Group 1, vigorous, rhizomatous
trachelium	2–3ft × ∞	4–8	Mid-blue to lilac, purple or white, tubular bells (M)	Mid-green, sometimes red-tinged, toothed, ovate	Group 1, nettle-leaved bellflower, spreading
t. 'Bernice'	1½–2ft × ∞	4–8	Double, lilac-blue, starry bells (M)	As above	Group 1, slow-growing, good cut, clumping and spreading

CANNA   Cannaceae

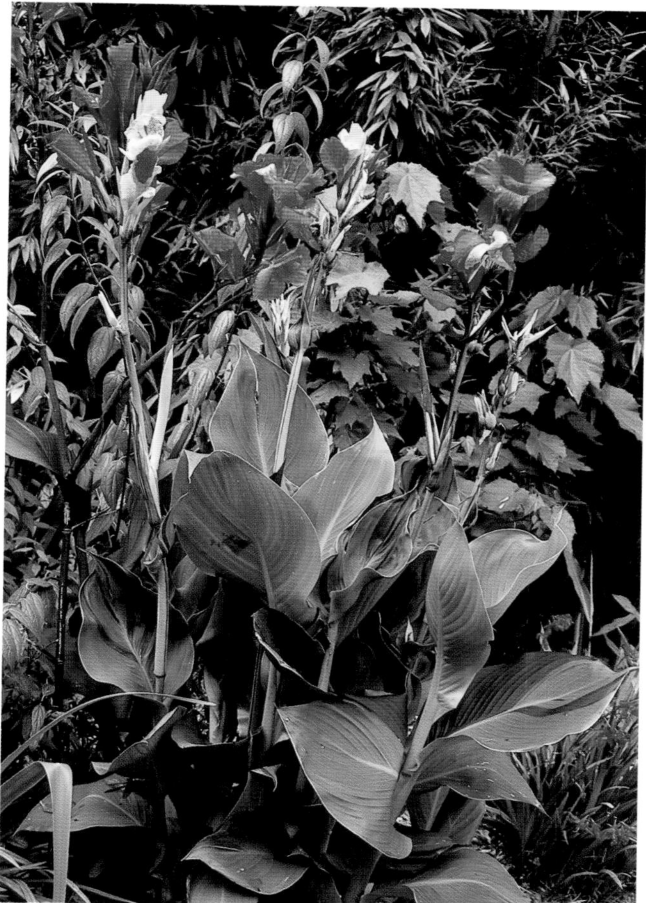
Canna 'Cleopatra'.

Cannas are among the easiest and most popular bold-foliaged subtropical plants for non-subtropical climates, and new cultivars are appearing in nurseries every year. Most are tender and must either be dug and stored or left to dry in the pots and kept from freezing. Once growth has begun, you will get better results with a program of regular feeding and plenty of water. If you let them go to seed, you will find out why they are called Indian shot, although spent-flower removal will increase your flower production.

We have found we can mulch the hardier forms with a mound of their own dead leaves; this protects the crown from a hard freeze. The only problem with this is they will not grow until the ground warms up, which can delay leaf and flower production. As cannas are mostly used for their bold foliage, they are often best in pots, where you can watch for slugs; the soil heats up earlier in a container, and you can feed plants more often and locate them so that the wind does not damage the leaves. ~ *Bob Lilly*

Scientific Name: From the Greek *kanna* ("reed").
Common Name: Indian shot.
Origin: Central and South America, West Indies, Asia.
Preferred Conditions: Fertile, moisture-retentive soil, rich in organic material. Tolerates a wide range of soil.
Light: Sun. Tolerates part shade but will not bloom as much.
Planting: Plant rootstock in spring after all danger of frost is past, five inches deep.
Management: They're heavy feeders during the growing season. Top-dress with compost or manure in winter. Cannas will need a protective winter mulch, or dig them up and overwinter. They need plenty of water during growing time. Remove faded flowers after bloom to promote continued flowering. Cut just below the lowest flower on the stalk and a secondary stalk will form, or if foliage is the main attraction, cut stalks back into the foliage. The tuberous rootstock can be dug up in the fall and stored in a frost-free place and then started into growth again the next spring, six to eight weeks before the last anticipated frost. After the foliage has turned black, cut the stems back to about six inches. Lift the clumps, retaining as much soil as possible, and place in a container or a box. Store them in a dry place with temperatures between 40 and 50F. You may need to sprinkle them with a bit of water to keep the roots from drying out. In early spring, remove the soil and cut rootstock into sections two to four inches long, making sure each section has an eye. Let the cut rhizomes air-dry overnight. Pot up each rhizome and place in a greenhouse or sunny window. Water lightly until first signs of growth.
Propagation: Division of fleshy rootstock in spring after winter storage.
Pests and Diseases: Slugs, snails.
Companions: Ornamental grasses and bananas, hedychium, solenostemon (syn. coleus), dahlia, tropaeolum, crocosmia.

Notes: The common name Indian shot comes from its seed, which is the size of a large pea. The cut flowers do not keep well. The cultivars in our list are primarily ×*generalis* hybrids and can be grown in water and damp sites; an undivided clump can get wider than the chart shows by the second year.

Species and Cultivars	Height/ Spread	USDA Hardiness Zone	Flowers (bloom time)	Foliage	Comments
'Cleopatra'	4½ft × 1½ft	8–10	Red and yellow (M)	Green with large purple blotches	
'Durban'	4½ft × 1½ft	8–10	Scarlet (E–M)	Reddish purple with yellow veins	
edulis	4ft × 2ft	8–10	Small, orange (E–L)	Gray-green, smallish	Will spread slowly
glauca	4ft × 2ft	8–10	Nectarine-orange, small (M)	Narrow, blue-green	Erect, can grow in standing water
indica	4–6ft × 2ft	8–10	Rich red on burnished dull red stems (E–L)	Bronze-flushed, 1½ft long	
iridiflora	5ft × 2ft	8–10	Deep pink, trumpet-shaped, pendent (L)	Blue-green, 2–3ft, handsome	
'Panache'	5–6ft × 1½ft	8–10	Salmon-pink at base to pale yellow at tip (M–L)	Gray-green, narrow	Can grow in standing water
'Phasion' (syn. 'Tropicanna')	5–6ft × 1½ft	8–10	Bright orange (M–L)	Emerge purple, become striped with red, yellow, green, and pink	RHS Award
'President'	3–4ft × 1½ft	8–10	Large, bright red (M–L)	Dark green, glossy	
'Striata' (syn. 'Pretoria', 'Bengal Tiger')	6–7ft × 1½ft	8–10	Bright orange and yellow (M)	Bold, densely striped green and yellow with maroon edge	Likes it wet, RHS Award
'Striped Beauty' (syn. 'Minerva', 'Nirvana')	4½ft × 1½ft	8–10	Red buds open to a burnt yellow (M–L)	Variegated white, green, and yellow on green background	
'Stuttgart'	6–7ft × 1½ft	8–10	Soft apricot-pink (M–L)	Bold, green and white irregular stripes, will burn in full sun but needs the heat	
'Wyoming'	6ft × 1½ft	8–10	Apricot-orange, frilled (M–L)	Purple, tinged green	RHS Award

Cardamine pratensis 'Flore Pleno'.

CARDAMINE Brassicaceae

For many years the ordinary lady's smock or cuckooflower was the only cardamine we had for our enjoyment. Looking just like common shotweed or bittercress when not in flower, *C. pratensis* is often inadvertently weeded out in spring, but don't panic—it transplants well. Look for its lovely double pink form. We now have many newer cardamines thanks to the late, lamented Heronswood and other mail-order nurseries. As with *C. pratensis*, the flowers are brief but sweet. Grow in a woodland or part shade location; cardamines, especially the larger forms, respond well to a mulching of leaf mold. They can run a bit by very brittle rhizomes, so share with friends. ~ *Bob Lilly*

Scientific Name: From the Greek for a related plant, *kardamon* ("watercress").
Common Name: Bittercress, cuckooflower.
Origin: Northern hemisphere.
Preferred Conditions: Humus-rich, moisture-retentive, moist soil.
Light: Shade to part shade. Tolerates sun if kept moist.
Management: Top-dress with leaf mold or other organic material. Cut back as foliage begins to fade. Some go into dormancy early.
Propagation: Divide in spring or after flowering. May also form offsets or plantlets that can be replanted. Sow seed in cold frame in autumn or spring.

Pests and Diseases: Powdery mildew, slugs, rust.

Companions: Corydalis, Pacific Coast iris, primula, pulmonaria, viola, brunnera, helleborus, narcissus.

Notes: Graham Stuart Thomas (1990) uses this as an alternative to the usual swear words, "Cardamine! Damnacanthus!" *Cardamine pratensis* is a sweet plant, but the foliage looks just like common shotweed.

Species and Cultivars	Height/ Spread	USDA Hardiness Zone	Flowers (bloom time)	Foliage	Comments
diphylla	6–9in × 2ft+	5–8	White (E)	Dark green, 3 leaflets	Stoloniferous, eastern North America, summer dormant
dissecta	10–12in × 24in	5–8	Pink, bell-shaped (E)	Green, ferny, deeply dissected	Eastern North America, goes dormant by midsummer
enneaphylla	8–12in × 18in	5–8	Creamy yellow, nodding (E)	Purplish, aging to dark green	Eastern Europe
heptaphylla	12–20in × 24in	5–8	White, large (E)	Dark green, pinnate, 5–7 leaflets	Eastern Europe
laciniata	8–15in × 24in	6–8	Pinkish white (E)	Green, deeply dissected	Eastern North America, cut-leaved toothwort; goes dormant after bloom
macrophylla	18–24in × 24in	5–8	Lilac-pink (M)	Green with bronze tinge, large-leaved, pinnate	Eastern Nepal, winter and summer dormant in drought
maxima	6–16in × 16in	5–8	Large white or pale purple (E)	Bold, 3-parted, green	Eastern North America
pentaphylla	12in × 12in+	5–8	White buds opening to a soft lilac-pink (E)	Mid-green, pinnate	Eastern Europe, RHS Award
pratensis	12–18in × 10in+	5–8	Lilac or white (E)	Ferny, dark green, in clumps	Happy in bog conditions, tends to run and needs to be thinned out.
p. 'Edith'	6–9in × 10in+	5–8	Double, pink in bud, opening to white (E)	Ferny, dark green	As above
p. 'Flore Pleno'	8–12in × 10in+	5–8	Double, lilac-pink (E)	Small, cresslike, in a flat rosette	Longer lasting flowers, runs, RHS Award
quinquefolia	4in × 12in+	6–8	Light lavender (E)	Glossy, green	Eastern Europe, evergreen
rhaphanifolia (syn. latifolia)	15in × 15in+	5–8	Purple, lilac, or white (E–M)	Dark green, evergreen	
trifolia	6in × 6–24in	5–8	White, sometimes pink (E)	Dark green, purple reverse, 3-parted, evergreen	Italy, Croatia, makes a dense low clump
waldsteinii	10in × 12in	5–8	White, largest flowers (E)	Dark green	Large mats, winter dormant

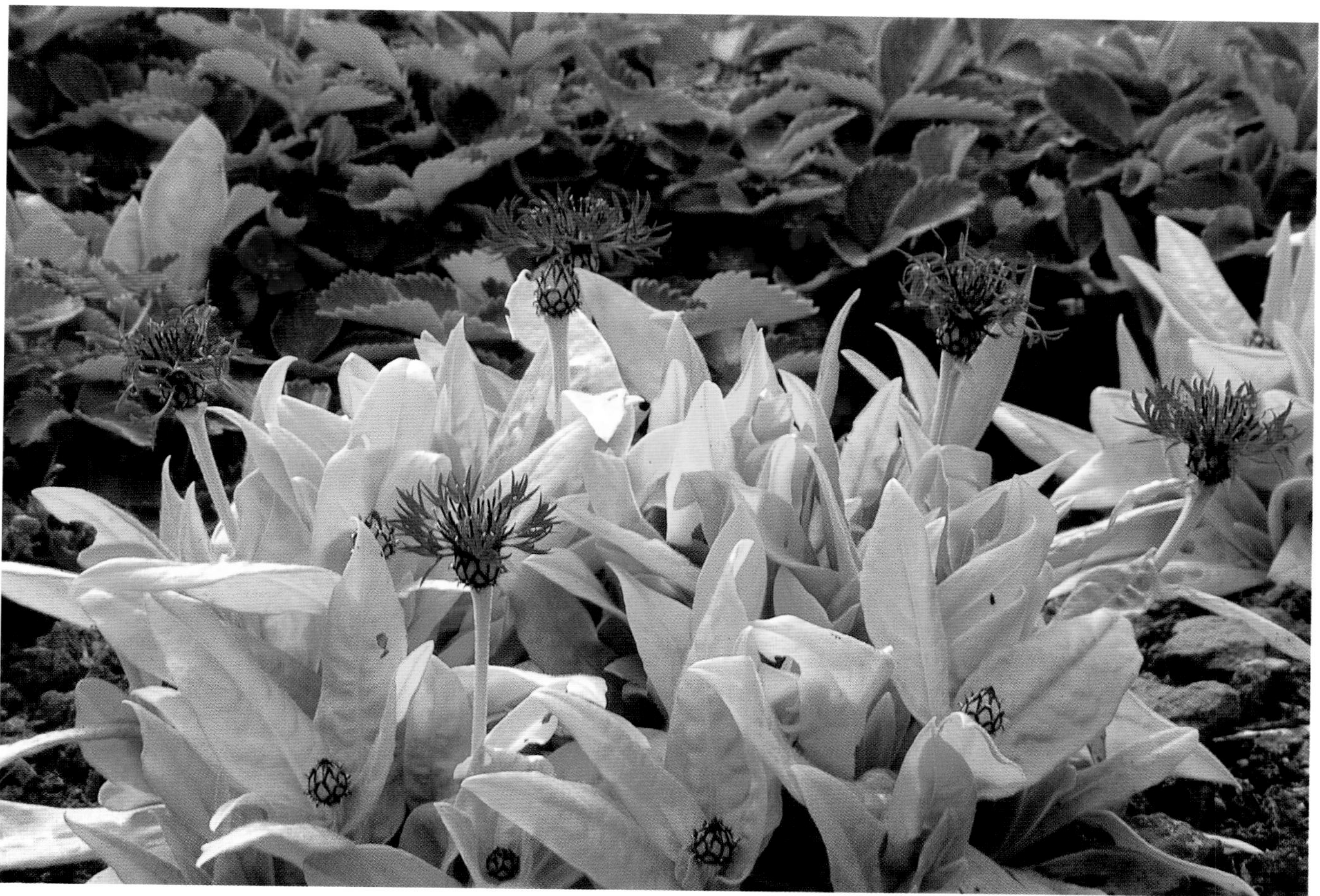

Centaurea montana 'Gold Bullion'.

CENTAUREA Asteraceae

The bachelor's buttons are a colorful group of flowers perfectly suited for an informal, old-fashioned cottage garden. The fringed and ruffled flowers bloom in shades of pink, yellow, purple, white, and deep blue; they are long-blooming, from late spring to midsummer. The foliage varies from species to species, in texture, color, and shape.

Centaurea macrocephala is a standout, not only for its stately size but for its incredible flower buds, which open to golden yellow thistlelike blooms. You can find this species on some state noxious weed lists. Although it's not a problem in western Washington, be cautious and do not let it escape your garden. *Centaurea montana* is everyone's first plant and is still popular with its early blue flowers. Unfortunately, mildew can make them unsightly, but cutting them back after the first bloom will produce a fresh crop of leaves and a second bloom. Under the right conditions, it will self-sow with a vengeance.

Many centaureas are good for cut flowers, both in fresh and dried arrangements. ~ *Susan Carter*

Scientific Name: From the Greek *kentauras* (centaur); centaurs are said to have used it medicinally.
Common Name: Bachelor's button, cornflower.
Origin: Asia Minor, Europe, Mediterranean.

Preferred Conditions: Average, well-drained (especially in winter) soil. Tolerates drought in summer. Becomes lanky and flops in the shade.

Light: Sun to part shade.

Planting: Set out for planting anytime the weather is mild enough, but best in spring or fall.

Management: Deadhead for second bloom and to avoid self-sowing. Cut back flower stems in summer after bloom. Cut to the ground after frost when foliage becomes black and mushy. *Centaurea montana* will get the flops plus mildew (this can be limited by cutting back hard after the spring flush of bloom); it also benefits from division every three years.

Propagation: Division in spring; seed.

Pests and Diseases: Powdery mildew, rust.

Companions: Campanula, *Iris sibirica*, *I. germanica*, delphinium, alchemilla, tradescantia, low grasses; the spring cottage garden.

Notes: Cornflowers are a group of wildflowers that were common (especially the annual *C. cyanus*) to wheat fields in Europe and England in the Middle Ages (corn was the original term for wheat).

Species and Cultivars	Height/ Spread	USDA Hardiness Zone	Flowers (bloom time)	Foliage	Comments
dealbata	2–3ft × 2ft	4–8	Lilac, pink, and purple with white inside (M–L)	Light green, finely cut to deeply lobed, gray reverse	Persian cornflower, good cut, may need staking
d. 'Rosea'	1½–2½ft × 2ft	4–8	Soft rose-pink (M)	Gray-green, finely cut	May need support
hypoleuca 'John Coutts'	1½–2½ft × 2ft	4–8	Deep rose, long-blooming (E–M)	Green, deeply lobed, bluish white underneath	Good seedheads
macrocephala	3½–4ft × 2–2½ft	4–8	Golden yellow, very thistlelike (M)	Light green, bold	Incredible flower buds, on noxious weed list in some states
montana	1½ft × 2ft	4–8	Deep blue, star-shaped, with reddish thistlelike center (E–M)	Narrow, grayish green	Floppy, self-sows
m. 'Gold Bullion'	1½–2ft × 2ft	4–8	As above	Pale golden yellow	From Blooms of Bressingham
ruthenica	3–4½ft × 2–2½ft	6–8	Lemon-yellow with thistlelike center (M)	Dark green, ferny, toothed, green undersides	

Centranthus ruber with *Sisyrinchium striatum*, *Hesperis matronalis*, *Linaria triornithophora*, *Lysimachia punctata*, columbines, roses, and ripening euphorbia foliage.

CENTRANTHUS Valerianaceae

Centranthus is a monotypic (one-species) genus. Plants are used as fillers or knitters rather than as specimens and are best planted in groups of the same color (or repeated in close proximity). In flower, they have a rather frothy appearance; the white form looks lovely with pale-flowered bearded iris and early roses. Short-lived (two to three years), they ensure their survival by sowing about. Remove older plants in favor of youthful seedlings and remove most seedlings to prevent being overrun with centranthus; they are very easy to remove. Centranthus has pleasant, smooth grayish leaves that are a nice foil to the spurred flowers. They are good cut flowers and attract butterflies—think cottage garden. ~ *Carrie Becker*

Scientific Name: From the Greek *kentron* ("spur") and *anthos* ("flower").
Common Name: Red valerian, Jupiter's beard.
Origin: Mediterranean.

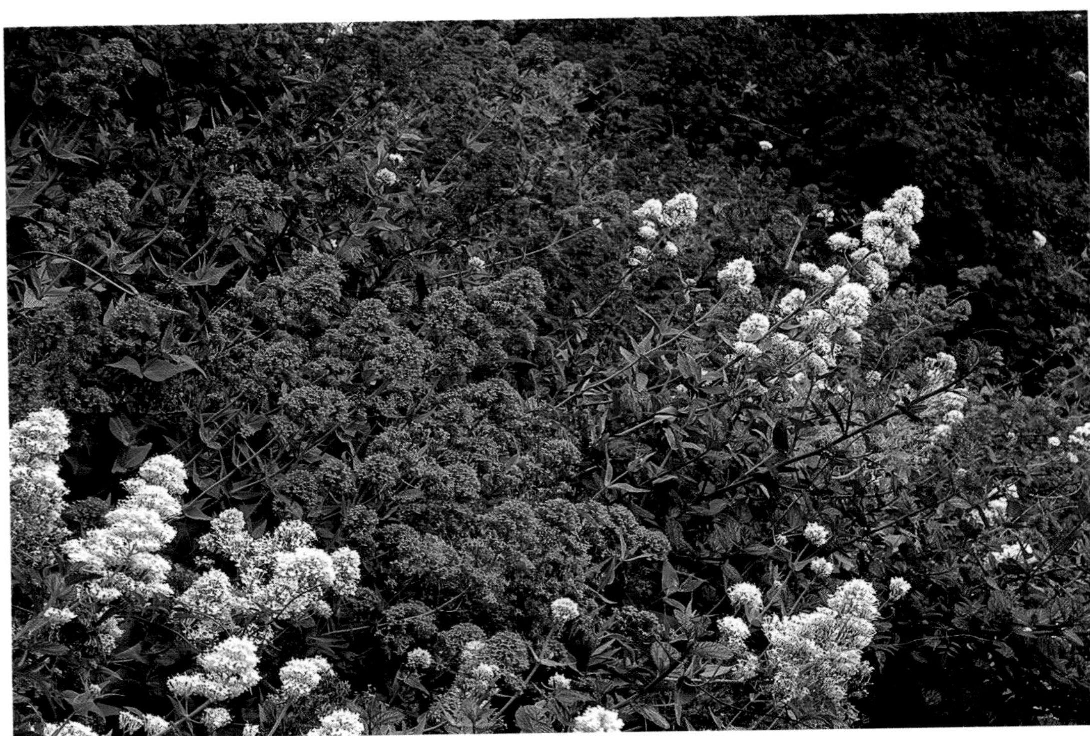

Centranthus ruber mixed.

Preferred Conditions: Average, well-drained soil. Thrives in infertile, chalky soil (i.e., White Cliffs of Dover and Seattle back alleys) and may flop in soils that are too rich. Drought tolerant even in full sun.

Light: Sun to part shade.

Management: Cut back flowering heads every time they finish to stimulate continued bloom all summer. Deadheading before they go to seed helps prevent their taking over. This is a tap-rooted plant and does not like to be disturbed. Clean up in autumn.

Propagation: Seed or basal cuttings in spring or summer.

Pests and Diseases: Resistant to most all problems.

Companions: Echinacea, cosmos, nepeta, bearded irises, geranium, *Papaver orientale*, *Iris sibirica*; the wild seashore garden; often colonizes abandoned lots and old rockeries.

Species and Cultivars	Height/ Spread	USDA Hardiness Zone	Flowers (bloom time)	Foliage	Comments
ruber	2–3ft × 2ft	5–8	Tiny, deep rosy-pink, in compact sprays, fragrant (M–L)	Fleshy, glaucous	Often naturalized in cracks in walls, self-sows
r. 'Albus'	2–3ft × 2ft	5–8	Clean white, fragrant (M–L)	As above	Good cut, less seen naturalized in cracks in walls
r. var. coccineus	2–3ft × 2ft	5–8	Deep coppery-red, fragrant (M–L)	As above	Good cut, often naturalized in cracks in walls
r. 'Roseus'	2–3ft × 2ft	5–8	Rose-pink, fragrant (M–L)	As above	As above

Cephalaria gigantea.

CEPHALARIA Dipsacaceae

We deal with two good garden plants here, both having flowers just like a scabiosa and both pale yellow. They would benefit from staking but do not look good tied up; pea sticks would be the better method, although the plants don't hide them well. They are large-scale background plants for the mixed border; try to give them full sun. As with all teasels, these make good cut flowers and have interesting seedheads. ~ *Bob Lilly*

Scientific Name: From the Greek *kephale* ("head"), referring to the flowers, which are borne in heads.
Common Name: Giant scabious.
Origin: Siberia, Central Alps.
Preferred Conditions: Average soil with organic material. Likes it moist.
Light: Sun. Tolerates part shade.
Planting: Deep rooted so plant out when young. It's best to start with new plants rather than trying to transplant or divide. Plant in autumn or spring.

Species and Cultivars	Height/ Spread	USDA Hardiness Zone	Flowers (bloom time)	Foliage	Comments
gigantea (syn. tatarica)	5–8ft × 3ft+	3–8	Pale primrose-yellow, green center on wiry stems (M)	Dark green, divided, hairy undersides	May need staking in exposed areas, not long-lived, self-sows
leucantha	5–8ft × 3ft+	3–8	Paler yellow than above on nearly rounded stems (M)	Dark green, a bit less coarse than above	Round seedheads

Management: You can pinch the stems of *C. gigantea* in late spring to keep them below six feet and increase width. Deadhead *C. gigantea* to prevent self-sowing. May need staking in exposed areas. Top-dress with manure or compost in winter. Carefully divide or start new plants every five years or when vigor declines. If allowed to dry out, leaf margins turn black and the foliage quickly deteriorates. Cut back in fall when dormant.
Propagation: Division in spring; seed in cold frame early spring or fall.
Pests and Diseases: Slugs on new growth can be a problem in early spring.
Companions: Ligularia, miscanthus, *Campanula lactiflora*, *Crambe cordifolia*, phygelius (yellow forms); mixes well with the herbaceous shrub background of a mixed border, especially yellow-variegated shrubs.
Notes: Both form the most wonderful pale cream seedheads.

CERATOSTIGMA Plumbaginaceae

Ceratostigma plumbaginoides is a very good groundcover with terminal heads of blue flowers blooming from August through October. Plants form attractive colonies of new growth in spring; the foliage is green throughout the growing season until fall, when the onset of cool weather turns the foliage scarlet. Then the plant is at its own form of perfection: blue flowers atop red foliage. Best in sun, these would be lovely with red-foliaged barberries, and I have used them to good effect as a carpet under white-flowering roses. ~ *Carrie Becker*

Scientific Name: From the Greek *keras* ("horn"), referring to the hornlike growth on the stigma.
Common Name: Leadwort, blue plumbago.
Origin: China, Africa.
Preferred Conditions: Average, well-drained, light, humus-rich soil. Adapts to a wide range of conditions, even poor, stony soil. Likes it moist but will not tolerate soggy conditions.
Light: Sun to part shade.
Planting: Plant out before midsummer, best in the spring.
Management: Breaks dormancy late and may be damaged by late frost or gardeners with clumsy feet. Cut to the ground in winter when dormant. Older plants die out in the center, so dig out dead area and fill in gap with fresh soil. Appreciates a winter mulch in colder areas.
Propagation: Division, tip cuttings, or seed in spring.
Pests and Diseases: Powdery mildew.
Companions: Grow as a groundcover under late-season colored foliage such as grasses, *Berberis thunbergii*, *Acer palmatum*, *Hydrangea quercifolia*, disanthus, fuchsia.
Notes: Slow in the Pacific Northwest, where a close planting of four-inch pots is recommended for *C. plumbaginoides*.

Ceratostigma plumbaginoides, fall color.

Species and Cultivars	Height/ Spread	USDA Hardiness Zone	Flowers (bloom time)	Foliage	Comments
griffithii	2ft × 2ft	8–10	Bright blue (L)	Gray-green with bronze tints in autumn	Subshrub, full sun, winter protection, cut to ground in spring
plumbaginoides	8–12in × 18in	6–9	Intense gentian-blue, 5-petaled (M–L)	Dark green, rounded, smooth, turning red in fall	Compact, low-spreading, RHS Award
willmottianum	1½ft × 2ft	7–10	Cobalt-blue (M–L)	Green with red tints in leaves and stems in autumn	Subshrub, cut to ground in spring, put in a protected location

Chaerophyllum hirsutum 'Roseum'.

CHAEROPHYLLUM Apiaceae

Impossible to pronounce, impossible to resist! This perennial has finely divided foliage like Queen Anne's lace but softer, with similar flowers on shorter stems. But the final step toward perfection: the flowers are pink. *Chaerophyllum hirsutum* 'Roseum' is fairly tolerant of a sunny location if in heavy soil. We have discovered that this plant does not like fall division. It also has stolonlike structures, which often lie over the crown; these will root if broken off in early spring—a simple method of propagation. ~ *Bob Lilly*

Scientific Name: From the Greek *chairo* ("to please") and *phyllon* ("leaf").
Common Name: Chervil.
Origin: Southern Europe.
Preferred Conditions: Average, moist soil.
Light: Sun to part shade.
Management: Cut down in fall after foliage dies back. Don't allow it to be overgrown by other plants.
Propagation: Sow seed in cold frame in spring or as soon as ripe; divide in spring just before growth begins.
Pests and Diseases: Aphids, slugs, snails, powdery mildew (if too dry).
Companions: Primula, paeonia (early forms), geranium, *Stachys byzantina*, white narcissus, tulips, shorter grasses, hyacinth, viola.

Species and Cultivars	Height/ Spread	USDA Hardiness Zone	Flowers (bloom time)	Foliage	Comments
hirsutum 'Roseum'	2ft × 2ft+	6–8	Soft pink flat-topped umbels (E)	Bright green, finely cut	Entire plant is slightly aromatic

CHELONE Scrophulariaceae

Chelone lyonii 'Hot Lips'.

A perennial requiring very little care. Cut down in winter; don't let them dry out; divide if necessary (when they take up more space than you want, or are not flowering because they need "freshening"). That's it! Plants are erect and about three feet tall, maximum, standing up with no staking. Very nice dark green leaves are topped by tubular flowers in pink or white, looking like upright turtles' heads with their mouths agape. Very good for the late-summer border, and a good cut flower. ~ *Carrie Becker*

Scientific Name: From the Greek *chelone* ("turtle"); the corolla is shaped like a turtle's head.
Common Name: Turtlehead.
Origin: North America.
Preferred Conditions: Deep, moisture-retentive, fertile soil. Likes it moist, near streams and ponds. Tolerant of dry soil in the summer as long as spring conditions are moist. Heavy clay and boggy is okay, too.
Light: Sun to part shade.
Management: These are easily maintained plants. Cut to one inch when dormant. You can pinch to reduce height, but this may alter the natural form of the plant, reduce the flower size, and delay bloom time. Mulch in early spring with manure or compost. Divide when clumps become too large in spring or late autumn. Plants are strong enough on their own and won't need staking. Bait crown for slugs.
Propagation: Seed in cold frame in early spring or outdoors when ripe; division in the spring; soft-tip cuttings in spring or early summer.
Pests and Diseases: Powdery mildew (if too dry), rust, slugs, snails.
Companions: *Astilbe chinensis*, *Cimicifuga simplex*, ferns, sedges, Japanese anemones, eupatorium, persicaria, aster.
Notes: For cut flowers, remove all the large leaves. In the maritime Northwest, plants are best in full sun.

Species and Cultivars	Height/ Spread	USDA Hardiness Zone	Flowers (bloom time)	Foliage	Comments
glabra	2–3ft × 2ft	5–8	White flushed with pink, long-blooming, 3–4 weeks (M–L)	Narrow, dark green	White turtlehead, vigorous, likes cool, moist conditions
lyonii	2–3ft × 3ft	5–8	Rosy-pink with a yellow beard, long-blooming, 4 weeks (M–L)	Dark green, broader	Pink turtlehead, good cut
l. 'Hot Lips'	2–3ft × 2ft	5–8	Rosy-pink with a spot of white at base, red stems (M–L)	Emerge purplish bronze and age to deep green, toothed	Long-blooming
obliqua	2–3ft × 2ft	5–8	Rosy-purple (M–L)	Stiff, dark green	Long-blooming, most heat tolerant

Chrysanthemum 'Apricot'.

CHRYSANTHEMUM Asteraceae

Few of what were called chrysanthemums are still classified as such. These hardy perennials are most useful: they flower very late in the season and make large clumps by slow-spreading, short stolons. The few cultivars we list here are mostly in the rubellum "class," whose members produce a tremendous show of flowers; our grandmothers had a better selection of these "true mums," which have in large part disappeared from commerce. Please note, autumn chrysanthemums offered in the current market are bred as a pot-crop and are not reliably hardy; they bloom earlier the following season in the garden and are prone to slug problems.

Related genera are *Dendranthema*, *Leucanthemum*, and *Tanacetum*. ~ *Bob Lilly*

Scientific Name: From the Greek *chrysos* ("gold") and *anthos* ("flower").
Common Name: Mum.
Origin: Worldwide.
Preferred Conditions: Well-drained, moist, and humusy but not overly rich soil.
Light: Sun.
Management: Pinch twice after 1 May (one month apart) until mid July to achieve the best performance. Water freely in dry weather. Cut stems back in fall cleanup after flowering to six inches (or wait until spring to cut back, the stems will help protect the crown). Apply a mulch for winter protection and remove in spring, before the slugs dine on the new shoots. Slugs gravitate toward early crown shoots and can set your plants back a great deal. Watch for them in early spring.
Propagation: Division in spring every two or three years to maintain vigor.
Pests and Diseases: Slugs, snails.
Companions: Grasses, perovskia, hardy fuchsias, sedum, aster, solidago, salvia.
Notes: The old mums, from pompoms to football mums, were often pinched, disbudded, and forced into flower in glass greenhouses. Their relations are now available as clusters of small flowers on long stems in almost any color, even green, at florists and flower stalls. In the garden these true mums bloomed so late they often had to be covered to protect them from frost, one of the reasons they have fallen out of fashion.

Species and Cultivars	Height/ Spread	USDA Hardiness Zone	Flowers (bloom time)	Foliage	Comments
'Apricot' (rubellum)	3–4ft × 2ft	5–9	Single, soft apricot, spidery, open (L)	Gray-green	Good cut
'Bronze Elegans' (early pompom)	2–3ft × 2ft	5–9	Bronze, buttonlike (L)	Pale green	Sport of *C.* 'Mei-kyo'
'Clara Curtis' (rubellum)	2–3ft × 2ft	3–9	Single rose-pink with yellow center, fragrant (M–L)	Dark blue-green, divided, bushy clumps	Good cut, long-lasting
'Emperor of China' (rubellum)	4ft × 2ft	5–9	Rose-pink, semi-double, long-blooming (L)	Green turning crimson in autumn	May need support
'Innocence' (rubellum)	2–2½ft × 2ft	3–9	Single pale pink with white eye (L)	Green	Good cut
'Mary Stoker' (rubellum)	2–2½ft × 2ft	3–9	Large pale apricot turning peach, single (M)	As above	As above
'Mei-kyo' (early pompom)	2–3ft × 2ft	5–9	Small, double lavender-pink (L)	As above	A charming buttonlike flower
weyrichii 'Pink Bomb'	8–10in × 12in	3–8	Large rosy-pink (L)	Shiny, dark green	Spreads by stolons, rock garden plant
w. 'White Bomb'	1ft × 1ft	3–8	Single white, aging to pink, yellow eye (L)	As above	Free-blooming, good cut, spreads by stolons

CHRYSOGONUM Asteraceae

With a lot of these daisy family genera, we deal with only one species and its cultivars. This one has two good modern selections that are not too different from the straight species. These are

Chrysogonum virginianum.

small plants for us, and not very perennial; they appear to like more heat than we have during our normal summers. Watch for slugs at all times. Often used as a groundcover in a sunny location. ~ *Bob Lilly*

Scientific Name: From the Greek *chrysos* ("golden") and *gonu* ("knee"), referring to the yellow flowers and jointed stems.
Common Name: Goldenstar.
Origin: Eastern North America.
Preferred Conditions: Average, moisture-retentive, humus-rich, well-drained soil.
Light: Part shade. Tolerates sun if kept moist.
Management: Tidy up in fall cleanup
Propagation: Division in spring or fall, or separate runners and replant; seed as soon as ripe.
Pests and Diseases: Slugs, snails.
Companions: Ferns, hosta, polemonium, geranium.

Species and Cultivars	Height/ Spread	USDA Hardiness Zone	Flowers (bloom time)	Foliage	Comments
virginianum	6–12in × 12in	4–9	Solitary, bright yellow, starry, 5-petaled, on long hairy stems (E–L)	Dark green, slightly toothed and hairy	Long bloomer, groundcover, may be evergreen in mild winters
v. 'Allen Bush'	10in × 12in	4–9	Small, star-shaped, yellow, 5-petaled (E)	Green	Long bloomer
v. 'Pierre'	6in × 12in	4–9	Small yellow daisy (E)	Soft green, clump-forming	As above

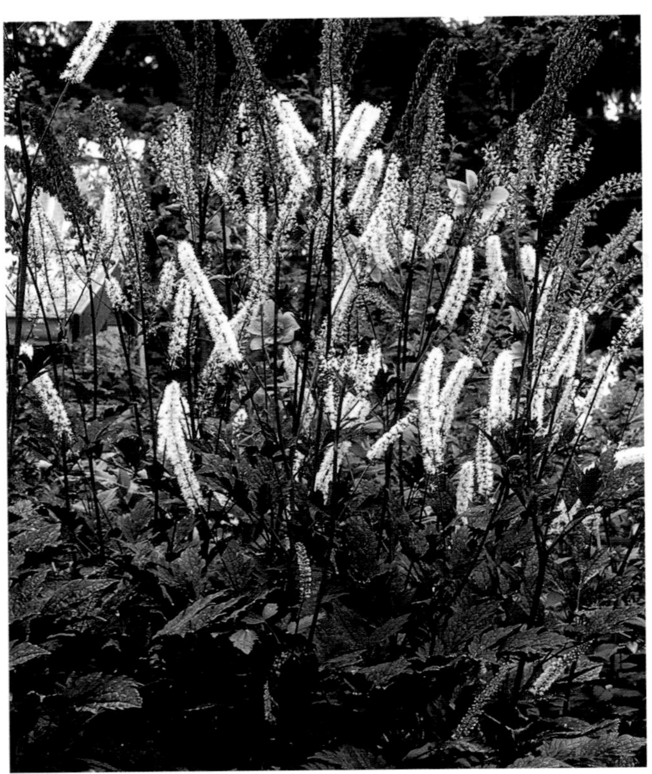

Cimicifuga simplex Atropurpurea Group 'Brunette'.

CIMICIFUGA — Ranunculaceae

Cimicifuga (syn. *Actaea*) is a genus of woodland plants with deeply divided foliage and a tall, spikelike inflorescence of usually white flowers made up mostly of stamens. Bugbanes are striking perennials, with welcome late flowers; they are almost the last of the woodland perennials to bloom and the very last to ripen their seeds. The clusters of seedpods are very decorative in a dried arrangement. We have found that most do better in more sun rather than less, and the dark-foliage forms are actually better colored with a good half-day of sun. Watch for slugs in early spring and mark the crowns, as the emerging new growth is very brittle and very late, so can easily be damaged. Moisture is a requirement for cimicifugas, and they are slow-growing.

We have left the cimicifugas separate from the actaeas: we consider them to be different enough to warrant their own place, even though taxonomists may disagree. ~ *Bob Lilly*

Scientific Name: From the Latin *cimex* ("bug") and *fugo* ("to repel").
Common Name: Bugbane, snakeroot, black cohosh.
Origin: Siberia, Japan, North America, China, Korea, Russia.

Preferred Conditions: Very adaptable but prefers humus-rich, cool, deep soil. Drought tolerant once established.

Light: Shade to sun.

Management: Easy to care for. Cut down in fall after frost. Mulch to keep cool and moist. They usually don't need staking, and they don't like being disturbed. They are late to emerge, so mark the location and leave several inches of stems so you know where they are and don't accidentally step on the crowns.

Propagation: Division in spring; seed.

Pests and Diseases: Rust and slugs.

Companions: Hakonechloa, boltonia, geranium, hosta, heuchera, aconitum, ferns, *Anemone japonica*, miscanthus, rodgersia (or other shade lovers with bold foliage), lilies.

Notes: A wilt in growth will severely affect flower quality. Bloom time order is *C. racemosa, C. dahurica, C. simplex*, and *C. matsumurae*.

Species and Cultivars	Height/ Spread	USDA Hardiness Zone	Flowers (bloom time)	Foliage	Comments
dahurica	5–6ft × 3ft	4–9	Creamy-white fluffy sprays, fragrant (M)	Green tripartite leaflets, ovate to heart-shaped, divided, toothed	Clump-forming
japonica (syn. acerina)	2–4ft × 2ft	4–8	Pure white, pink-blushed, dense, starry (M–L)	Dark green, shiny, divided, toothed, maplelike leaflets	Ground-hugging foliage, purplish black stems
matsumurae 'Elstead Variety'	3–4ft × 2ft	4–9	Purplish brown buds open to pure white, fragrant (L)	Dark green, finely divided	Purplish black stems, RHS Award
m. 'White Pearl'	3–4ft × 2ft	4–9	Pale green buds open to creamy-white, fragrant (L)	Light green, finely cut, tripartite	Pale green seedpods ripen to light brown, latest to flower
racemosa	6–8ft × 2ft+	3–9	Creamy-white, narrow bottlebrushes, fragrant (M)	Dark green, divided, toothed	Black snakeroot, clumping, RHS Award
simplex	3–6ft × 2ft	4–8	White, fragrant (M–L)	Light green, smooth, divided	Leaves scorch in sun
s. Atropurpurea Group	4–8ft × 2ft+	4–9	Creamy-white, purple in bud, fragrant (M–L)	Dark coppery-purple; color may vary if grown from seed	Reddish purple stems, too much heat may drain color
s. Atropurpurea Group 'Brunette'	4–6ft × 2ft+	4–9	Creamy-white with pink-purple tinge, fragrant (M–L)	Glossy, lacy, bronze-purple-black, black-purple stems	Purple seedpods, too much heat may drain color from leaves, RHS Award
s. Atropurpurea Group 'Hillside Black Beauty'	4–7ft × 2ft+	4–8	White with pink tinge, fragrant (M–L)	Dark purplish black, retains color throughout the season	Darkest leaf color so far
s. Atropurpurea Group 'James Compton'	3–4ft × 2ft+	4–9	Creamy-white, fragrant (M–L)	Dark purple, very stable color	Flowers are above the foliage
s. 'Pritchard's Giant' (syn. ramosa)	5–7ft × 2ft+	4–9	As above	Grayish green, divided, reddish stems	Amazingly tall

Cirsium rivulare 'Atropurpureum'.

CIRSIUM Asteraceae

A good plant with a thistlelike appearance. The fact that it vaguely resembles a common thistle in flower may frighten some people, but in the case of *C. rivulare* 'Atropurpureum' nothing is to be feared. This plant has a slowly spreading, groundlevel rosette–forming habit. When it flowers, the stems rise to approximately four feet. These lax stems could be staked, but how? There are usually half a dozen on a well-established plant, carrying flowers in an appealing shade of garnet, which must be why many of us grow this somewhat ungainly beauty. Full sun and poor soil might help with the habit. There is an uncommon rose-pink form. ~ *Carrie Becker*

Scientific Name: From the Greek *kirsion,* a kind of thistle.
Common Name: Plume thistle.
Origin: Europe, Russia.
Preferred Conditions: Average, moisture-retentive, well-drained, humus-rich, lime-free soil. Tolerant of poor soil.
Light: Sun.
Management: Water well during the growing season. Deadhead to prevent self-sowing. Cut back in the fall when foliage dies down. May rebloom if you cut flower stems down after plant is finished blooming. Flower stems may require some support to prevent them from flopping.
Propagation: Division in spring; seed in spring or as soon as ripe.
Pests and Diseases: Powdery mildew, rust.
Companions: Hardy fuchsias, penstemon, bergenia, *Molinia caerulea* 'Variegata', *Stachys macrantha*; a plant for the summer border.

Species and Cultivars	Height/ Spread	USDA Hardiness Zone	Flowers (bloom time)	Foliage	Comments
rivulare 'Atropurpureum'	4ft × 2ft	4–8	Deep maroon, pincushionlike, on erect stems (M)	Dark green, narrow, prickly-looking	Clump-forming; spreads but not invasive

Clematis ×durandii.

CLEMATIS Ranunculaceae

Hardy herbaceous clematis are not the vines that most people associate clematis with, but instead are deciduous, shrubby or scrambling short-climbing perennials that are often left to ramble through shrubs and other perennials in the border. The flowers of each vary in size and color; *C. recta* 'Purpurea', for instance, has dark burgundy foliage and fragrant creamy-white flowers on erect but floppy stems. It looks fabulous at the end of the season with its silvery seedheads, but it must be supported, or it will flop on the ground. Support it early or regret it.

None of the herbaceous clematis, in fact, have clasping petioles that wrap and support themselves around the nearest twig or trellis. Some weave, sprawl, and flop through any nearby foliage of perennials, grasses, or shrubs and may need help with support; others have strong stems and form good shrubby clumps, but even these may need support. All are long-lived and bear flowers on the current year's shoots. Some, such as *C. recta*, *C. heracleifolia*, and *C. ×durandii*, make good cut flowers. ~ *Susan Carter*

Scientific Name: From the Greek *klematis*, a climbing plant.
Common Name: Clematis.
Origin: China, Europe, Asia, North America.
Preferred Conditions: Fertile, well-drained, moisture-retentive, humus-rich soil with a cool root run. They prefer lime but will do fine in neutral to slightly acid soil.
Light: Sun.
Management: Will appreciate monthly feedings throughout the growing season. Staking is usually needed. Mulch in the winter with organic material. *Clematis recta* can be cut back by half after

flowering. Cut *C. recta* and *C. ×durandii* to the ground in fall cleanup. *Clematis heracleifolia* and *C. integrifolia* should be pruned hard in late winter, back to a pair of strong buds near the ground. *Clematis ×jouiniana* is pruned back hard once it becomes woody at the base.

Propagation: Division in spring when clumps are big enough (three years old or more), seed, and cuttings.

Pests and Diseases: Slugs, snails, powdery mildew.

Companions: *Clematis ×durandii* with *Cornus alba* (variegated forms) and *Salvia guaranitica*; *C. recta* 'Purpurea' with bronze fennel, *Phlox paniculata*, miscanthus, *Physocarpus opulifolius* 'Diabolo', *Dahlia* 'Bishop of Llandaff'.

Notes: The standard method can be used for all herbaceous clematis: cut old growth to the ground in spring when new growth is beginning. The woodier species should be pruned back to the lowest pair of buds in early spring. If unsupported, the clematis in the chart will sometimes reach twice the listed spread.

Species and Cultivars	Height/ Spread	USDA Hardiness Zone	Flowers (bloom time)	Foliage	Comments
×durandii	3–6ft × 3ft	5–9	Indigo-blue, 4-petaled, yellowish stamens, ribbed, semi-nodding at end (M–L)	Dark green, ovate with a pointed tip, herbaceous	Support needed, good cut, RHS Award
heracleifolia	3–5ft × 5ft	3–9	Light blue, small, hyacinthlike tubular clusters, fragrant (M–L)	Broad, divided, dark green, toothed, woody	Strong stems, good cut, silvery fluffy seedheads
integrifolia	2–3ft × 3ft	3–9	Violet-blue, cream anthers, nodding, urn- or bell-shaped (M–L)	Dark green, ovate-lanceolate to elliptic, herbaceous	Floppy, sprawling, light support, fluffy silvery-brown seedheads
i. 'Rosea'	2ft × 3ft	4–9	Bright pink, scented (M–L)	Dark green, ovate-lanceolate to elliptic, herbaceous	RHS Award
×jouiniana	10–12ft × 12ft+	4–9	Milky-blue with cream stamens, small, fragrant (M–L)	Mid-green, 3–5 palmate leaflets, woody	Vigorous, sprawling
'Mrs. Robert Brydon'	5–10ft × 12ft+	4–9	Starry, pale bluish white, fragrant (M–L)	As above	Upright, vigorous
'Praecox'	10–12ft × 12ft+	3–9	Bluish white and mauve, creamy-white anthers (M–L)	Dark green, large, trifoliate, serrated, woody	Needs support, or let it sprawl, RHS Award
recta	4–5ft × 3ft+	3–9	Star-shaped, creamy-white with creamy anthers, fragrant (M)	Bluish green, pinnate with 5–9 ovate leaflets, herbaceous	Erect but leans, needs support, fluffy silvery seedheads
r. 'Purpurea'	4–5ft × 3ft+	3–9	White with creamy-white anthers, purple-red stems, fragrant (M)	Copper-purple turning to dark green by flowering time, herbaceous	Silvery seedheads, good cut
tubulosa (syn. heracleifolia var. davidiana)	3–4ft × 3ft+	3–9	Tubular clusters, hyacinthlike, indigo-blue, fragrant (M–L)	Deep green, toothed, deeply lobed, woody	Needs support, sprawling, silky, hairy seedpods, vigorous
t. 'Wyevale'	3–4ft × 3ft+	3–9	Deep blue, prominent yellow stamens, fragrant (M–L)	As above	Needs support, RHS Award

Convallaria majalis 'Variegata'.

CONVALLARIA Convallariaceae

In my own garden I have a patch of lily of the valley that came to me thirty years ago from my great-grandmother's garden. This is worth mentioning because my great-grandmother had the reputation of having a black thumb—she couldn't grow much, but this plant did well for her. Virtually industrial-strength once established, *C. majalis* comes up in spring and makes a weed-excluding carpet, especially useful and attractive under shrubs and trees in drier, more "natural" parts of the garden. The little, white, down-facing bells are lovely on the type plant. They are fragrant and wonderful for little bouquets, and are often followed with fruit that turns red in fall. The fruit is very poisonous. The cultivated forms have some good features, too; *C. majalis* 'Variegata' is my favorite of the group for its striped leaves and sweetly fragrant flowers.

Convallaria does not play well with other perennials. As it ages it forms colonies that nothing else will or can grow in. The roots on an old mass are so dense, you'll only be able to divide them by cutting it up into square sections. ~ *Carrie Becker*

Scientific Name: From the Latin *convallis* ("valley"); plants often grow in valleys in the wild.
Common Name: Lily of the valley.
Origin: Europe.
Preferred Conditions: Thrives in a variety of soils but prefers well-drained, moisture-retentive, and humus-rich, with plenty of water in the spring. Tolerant of poor, dry soil. Leaves will look poor in dry conditions.
Light: Part shade to sun. Tolerates deep shade. Leaves will be lighter green in sun.
Planting: Plant clumps one to two feet apart, or single pips four to five inches apart and one to one and a half inches deep. Lay roots horizontally, cover, and water well.
Management: Cut foliage to the ground when it dies back. This plant may need to be contained. Where spreading is not wanted, a bit of root pruning and removal with a spade is a quick remedy. Top-dress with leaf mold in autumn. Divide to increase stock, or when they flower poorly due to overcrowding.

Propagation: Divide roots in fall or February and March, or indeed anytime, as long as proper attention is given until plants are reestablished.
Pests and Diseases: None.
Companions: Ferns, oxalis, epimedium, asarum, *Iris foetidissima*, *Brunnera macrophylla*, *Arum italicum*.
Notes: Dead foliage must always be cut off—this plant just won't let go! In the chart, the symbol ∞ = infinite spread.

Species and Cultivars	Height/ Spread	USDA Hardiness Zone	Flowers (bloom time)	Foliage	Comments
majalis	6–9in × ∞	1–9	White, nodding, bell-shaped, fragrant (E)	Dark rich green, broad, often glossy	Rampant groundcover, can be a pest, sometimes red berries in fall, RHS Award
m. 'Fortin's Giant'	12–15in × ∞	1–9	Large, showier white bells, fragrant (E)	As above	Vigorous, blooms a little later than species
m. var. rosea	6–8in × ∞	1–9	Small pinkish, dainty sprays, fragrant (E)	As above	Less vigorous a spreader
m. 'Variegata'	6in × 1ft+	1–9	Single white, fragrant (E)	Rich green striped with creamy yellow	May revert to green if grown in shade, less vigorous

CONVOLVULUS Convolvulaceae

Within this family are invasive thugs and ten-foot shrubs. Here we will deal only with two perennial herbaceous forms and one shrubby form in common use. *Convolvulus cneorum* is lovely in foliage and flower; *C. althaeoides*, with finely filigreed foliage, is more a trailer than climber. Keep it in containers and grow on the dry side. The noninvasive *C. sabatius*, with lovely trumpet-shaped sky-blue flowers throughout the summer, is also a great container plant. These plants are not the stars of the show but are lovely accessories to showier plants. All are marginally hardy here, with *C. cneorum* being the most persistent. ~ *Carrie Becker*

Scientific Name: From the Latin *convolva* ("to twine").
Common Name: Morning glory.
Origin: Southern Europe.
Preferred Conditions: Light, well-drained soil.
Light: Sun.
Management: An occasional light haircut may improve the shape and encourage new growth. They may be cut back by frost. They need winter protection and are best kept in a cold greenhouse during wet winters.
Propagation: Sow seed in late spring; root softwood cuttings in late spring and greenwood cuttings in summer; division in spring except *C. cneorum* (cuttings).

Convolvulus sabatius.

Pests and Diseases: Rust, spider mites, aphids.

Companions: Lavender and other gray-leaved plants, low-growing grasses, artemisia, tall sedums, salvia.

Notes: All convolvulus climbers twine to the right, a totally irrelevant but interesting fact.

Species and Cultivars	Height/ Spread	USDA Hardiness Zone	Flowers (bloom time)	Foliage	Comments
althaeoides subsp. tenuissimus (syn. elegantissimus)	3–4ft × 3–4ft	6–8	Pale pink, funnel-shaped, on trailing stems (M)	Green in spring, changes to silvery gray-green, finely cut, hairy	Has a running root and can be invasive
cneorum	2–3ft × 2½ft	6–8	Twisted pink buds opening to white (M–L)	Silver, softly hairy, evergreen	Shrubby, RHS Award
sabatius (syn. mauritanicus)	1ft × 1½ft	6–8	Pale to mid blue (M–L)	Light green, ovate, slightly hairy	Mound-forming, RHS Award

Coreopsis verticillata 'Golden Gain'.

COREOPSIS Asteraceae

Coreopsis is a tough, versatile, varied, high-performance perennial with pale to bright yellow, yellow-orange, red-violet, or pink flowers. Plants are long-blooming, some performing from spring through fall. They are not long-lived, however—probably only three to four years before the show begins to dwindle; regenerate from divisions at the outer edge of the clump to help extend their life. The *C. verticillata* types have threadlike, airy, bright green foliage rising to two feet; the *C. grandiflora* types have dark green, hairy, lanceolate leaves on plants only six to twelve inches tall.

The modern breeding directions in pink coreopsis have apparently drifted away from perennialhood, as in *C.* 'Limerock Ruby' and *C.* 'Limerock Passion', but these plants are worth the trouble of replacing every year. *Coreopsis verticillata* is low-maintenance and a good filler plant for gaps. Seed-eating birds, such as goldfinches, are attracted to *C. grandiflora*. ~ *Susan Carter*

Scientific Name: From the Greek *koris* ("bug") and *opsis* ("like"), a reference to the seeds, which look like ticks.

Common Name: Tickseed.

Origin: North America.

Preferred Conditions: Thrives in most soils but prefers fertile, well-drained, and not too wet. Overly rich soil promotes flopping, especially in *C. grandiflora*. Drought tolerant once established.

Light: Sun to part shade.

Planting: Bare-root planting is best done in the spring. Potted plants almost anytime except near a hard frost.

Management: Deadhead to keep flowering. Top-dress with manure in fall. Cut back hard after frost. Dig up and divide every three years or longer, discarding the oldest sections of the plants. Before replanting, rejuvenate the soil; this will promote a longer flowering season.

Allow some youngsters in the *C. grandiflora* group to go to seed. Watch and bait for slugs on all *C. verticillata* types in early spring when growth begins to emerge.

Propagation: Division in spring or fall; seed (except *C. verticillata* 'Moonbeam', which is almost sterile).

Pests and Diseases: Slugs, snails, mildew, and root rot if left in standing water.

Companions: Echinacea, campanula, penstemon, santolina, salvia, solidago, grasses, aster, lavandula, perovskia; try *C. verticillata* 'Moonbeam' with hakonechloa.

Notes: The *C. grandiflora* types are not long-lived for us; apparently they do not like wet winters.

Species and Cultivars	Height/ Spread	USDA Hardiness Zone	Flowers (bloom time)	Foliage	Comments
auriculata	1–2ft × 2ft+	3–9	Golden yellow single (E–L)	Dark green, ovate	Long-blooming, stoloniferous but seldom invasive
a. 'Nana'	6–12in × 12in	3–9	Bright orange-yellow, long-blooming (E–L)	As above	Mouse-ear coreopsis, low-spreading, dwarf
'Goldfink' (syn. 'Goldfinch')	8–12in × 12in	3–9	Single yellow with orange center on stiff stems (M–L)	As above	True dwarf
grandiflora	1–2ft × 1½ft	3–9	Bright yellow, orange center, semi-double (E–L)	Dark green, hairy, lanceolate	Self-sows, good cut, short-lived, may bloom itself to death
g. 'Domino'	15in × 15in	3–9	Golden yellow, black center, large, single (E–L)	As above	Dwarf
g. 'Double Sunburst'	2–3ft × 1½ft	3–9	Double golden yellow, buttonlike center (E–L)	As above	Good cut
g. 'Early Sunrise'	1½–2ft × 1½ft	3–9	Large, single golden yellow, dark center (E–L)	As above	Disease resistant, good cut
lanceolata	1–2½ft × 1½ft	3–9	Single yellow on pale green stems, brown center (M–L)	Mid-green, narrow, mostly basal, hairy	Lanceleaf coreopsis, similar to *C. grandiflora*, longer-lived
l. 'Sterntaler'	1–2½ft × 1½ft	3–9	Golden yellow with brownish center (E–L)	Fine, airy, green	
'Limerock Passion'	1–1½ft × 1½ft	6–9	Lavender-pink, yellow center (M–L)	Dark green, threadlike	Short-lived in Pacific Northwest
'Limerock Ruby'	1–1½ft × 1½ft	6–9	Ruby-red, yellow center (M–L)	As above	As above
rosea	1–2ft × 2ft+	3–9	Small, rose-pink with yellow center (M–L)	Bright green, finely textured (needlelike), low mounds	Moisture-loving, short-lived, can tolerate more shade
r. 'American Dream'	1–1½ft × 1½ft	3–9	Light rose-pink, better color than *C. rosea* (M–L)	Green, finely textured, low mounds	Vigorous spreader, use with caution in the border

Species and Cultivars	Height/ Spread	USDA Hardiness Zone	Flowers (bloom time)	Foliage	Comments
'Sonnenkind' (syn. 'Baby Sun')	1–2ft × 1ft	3–9	Golden yellow with reddish center, single (M–L)	Mid-green	Good cut, short and compact
'Sunray'	1½–3ft × 1ft	3–9	Semi-double and double, large, golden yellow (M)	As above	Good cut, compact
'Tequila Sunrise'	14–16in × 12in	3–9	Single yellow-orange with reddish center (E–L)	Olive-green with a cream edge and pinkish tinge, dark purple in fall	A weaker plant
tripteris	6–8ft × 2½ft	3–9	Light yellow disk florets, turns purplish, fragrant (M–L)	Mid-green, lanceolate	Tall tickseed, thrives in part shade, no staking, long-blooming
verticillata	1½–3ft × 2ft+	3–9	Bright yellow, single (M–L)	Green, threadlike	Thread-leaf coreopsis, slow to emerge in spring
v. 'Golden Gain'	16–24in × 2ft+	3–9	Golden yellow (M)	Dark green, needlelike	Compact
v. 'Grandiflora' (syn. 'Golden Shower')	24–30in × 2ft+	3–9	Large, golden yellow, star-shaped (M–L)	Green, needlelike, dense	Vigorous, good cut, RHS Award
v. 'Moonbeam'	1–2ft × 2ft+	3–9	Pale lemon-yellow (E–L)	Dark green, needlelike	Late to emerge, 1992 PPA Award, RHS Award
v. 'Zagreb'	1–2ft × 2ft+	3–9	Brassy yellow (M–L)	As above	A strong color, vigorous, late to emerge, RHS Award

CORYDALIS Papaveraceae

Corydalis is a very popular and interesting genus of plants in the poppy family. The four-petaled, two-lipped flowers have long spurs and look somewhat like a small snapdragon. Colors range from bright to pale yellow and on through pink and red to, of course, the blues. The delicate foliage is often grayish green and finely divided (resembling dicentra foliage, only smaller). Plants that have been through the "must have" phase include *C. flexuosa* 'Blue Panda', *C. f.* 'China Blue', and *C. f.* 'Père David'—the flexuosa group has wonderful blue flowers. All have a serious problem with slugs and must be watched carefully to protect them from being eaten up.

These perennials have a range of growing conditions that we have separated into three groups. Please see the plant chart and note the group each one is associated with. Even though they will leave an open space when they go summer dormant, don't let their site get totally overcome by the summer perennials if you want them to return. ~ *Susan Carter*

Scientific Name: From the Greek for "crested lark," referring to the spur of the flower, which resembles the crest of a lark.
Common Name: Fumewort, fumitory.
Origin: China, Europe, North America, Britain.
Preferred Conditions / Light:
Group 1. Full sun or part shade in fertile, well-drained soil. Self-sows. Evergreen.

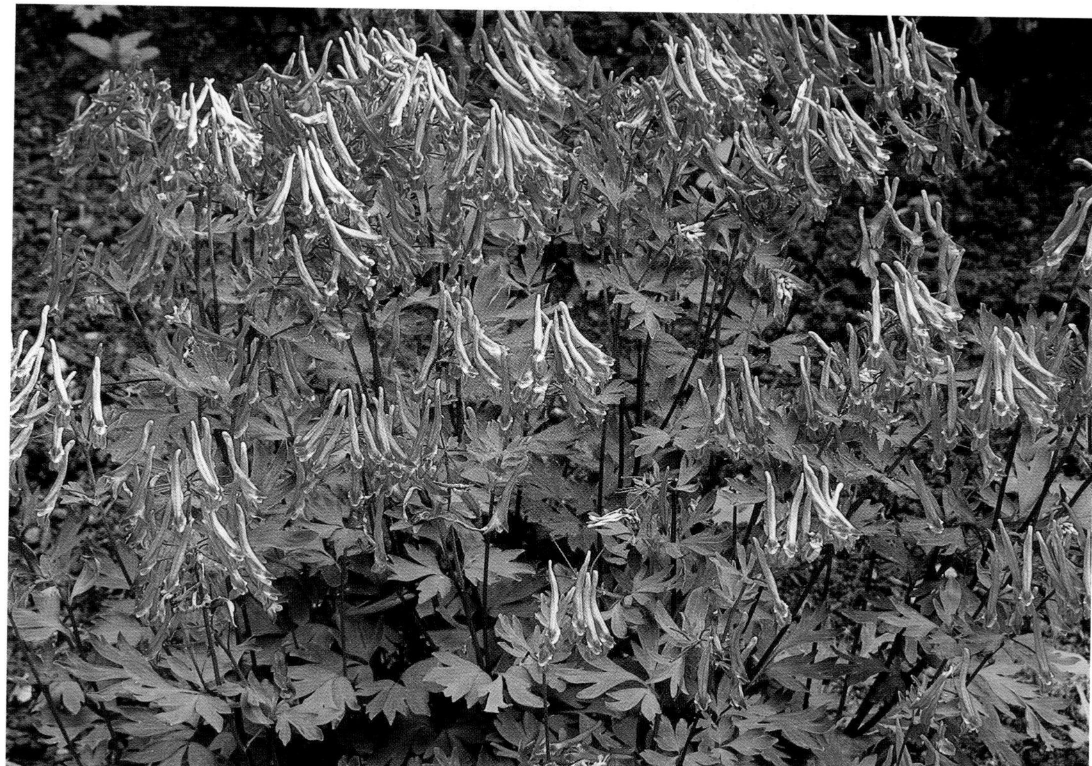

Corydalis flexuosa 'China Blue'.

Group 2. Full sun in sharply drained, moderately fertile soil. Tolerates part shade.
Group 3. Part shade in moderately fertile, humus-rich, moist, well-drained soil. May go dormant in the summer, especially in full sun. May rebloom if cut back.

Management: Deadhead to keep self-sowing under control. Cut *C. flexuosa* to nearly the ground after flowering; this may stimulate another round of blooming. Dormancy is usually obvious and can be triggered by heat or drought.

Propagation: *Corydalis flexuosa* and *C. elata* can be divided when dormant; seedlings of *C. lutea*, *C. ochroleuca*, *C. cheilanthifolia*, *C. scouleri*, and *C. solida*.

Pests and Diseases: Mildew, rust, slugs, and snails (slugs are a serious problem on *C. flexuosa*).

Companions: Ferns, primula, epimedium, hosta, *Ranunculus ficaria*, pulmonaria, brunnera, omphalodes.

Notes: *Corydalis flexuosa* types do better in heavy soils; loss is almost always due to slug grazing.

Species and Cultivars	Height/ Spread	USDA Hardiness Zone	Flowers (bloom time)	Foliage	Comments
'Blackberry Wine'	8–15in × 15in+	4–9	Deep purple over a base of whitish blue, fragrant (E–L)	Glaucous, divided, lacy	Group 1, sprawling, summer dormant if dry
cheilanthifolia	8–15in × 15in+	5–8	Clusters of bright yellow with a tint of green (E–M)	Fernlike, soft olive-green, bronze-tinted	Group 1, not long-lived

Species and Cultivars	Height/ Spread	USDA Hardiness Zone	Flowers (bloom time)	Foliage	Comments
elata	10–15in × 15in+	5–8	Cobalt-blue on reddish stems, fragrant (E–M)	Chartreuse-green, ferny	Group 3, clump-forming, erect, likes heat, easier than *C. flexuosa*
flexuosa	12–16in × 12in+	6–9	Bright blue, sometimes purplish, white throat (E–M)	Glaucous, may be marked with purple, fernlike	Group 3, may go dormant if dry, RHS Award
f. Award of Merit Form	12in × 12in+	5–9	Electric blue (E–M)	Glaucous, fernlike	Group 3, reblooms in fall if cut back
f. 'Blue Panda'	12–15in × 12in+	5–9	Bright sky-blue, fragrant (E–M)	Glaucous, divided	Group 3, less prone to going dormant
f. 'China Blue'	10–15in × 12in+	5–9	Sky-blue, fragrant (E–M)	Glaucous, finely divided, small reddish blotches	Group 3, may rebloom in fall, vigorous
f. 'Golden Panda'	8–12in × 10in+	5–9	Cobalt-blue (E–M)	Emerge green, become infused with yellow	Group 3, weaker plant
f. 'Père David'	8–12in × 12in+	5–9	Bright blue, fragrant (E–M)	Glaucous, marked purple, divided, willowy reddish stems	Group 3, may rebloom if cut back, vigorous
f. 'Purple Leaf'	8–12in × 12in+	5–9	Bright-blue (E–M)	Purplish blue, especially in spring	Group 3
lutea	8–15in × 18in+	4–8	Golden yellow, tiny (E–L)	Gray-green, divided, glossy	Group 1
ochroleuca	12–15in × 18in+	5–9	Pale yellow and white, long spurs (E–M)	Glaucous	Group 1, semi-evergreen
scouleri	24–36in × 24in+ slowly	6–7	Pinkish purple or white, long spurs (E–M)	Green, finely divided	Group 2, fumewort, West Coast native, vigorous
sempervirens	2ft × 2ft	6–9	Tubular, pink and yellow (E–L)	Pale green with whitish bloom, finely divided	Group 2, rock harlequin
s. 'Alba'	2ft × 2ft	6–9	Creamy-yellow (E–L)	As above	Group 2
solida (syn. bulbosa)	8in × 10in	5–8	Small, tubular, mauve to rich lilac and white (E)	Bluish gray-green, deeply divided	Group 2, dislikes extreme cold or heat, bulbous
s. subsp. solida 'George Baker'	8in × 8in	5–8	Red (E)	As above	Group 2, summer dormant, bulbous, RHS Award

COSMOS Asteraceae

Cosmos atrosanguineus.

Most of you are probably familiar with the common annual *C. bipinnatus*. *Cosmos atrosanguineus*, commonly called the chocolate cosmos because it smells good enough to eat, is the only species grown as a perennial. This is a long-blooming plant with flowers reminiscent of a single dahlia—a rich, velvety, dark maroon with an even darker center, held on reddish brown stems; they make a good cut flower. Watch out, though: *C. atrosanguineus* is often lost to slugs, who can devour this slow-emerging plant. ~ *Susan Carter*

Scientific Name: From the Greek *kosmos* ("beautiful").
Common Name: Chocolate cosmos.
Origin: Mexico.
Preferred Conditions: Moisture-retentive, deep, well-drained, fertile, moist soil. Winter wet and frost will kill it. Doesn't like to be crowded.
Light: Sun.
Management: Very late to emerge; mark it appropriately so it won't be dug up or planted over accidentally. Deadhead flowers as needed. Some light brush staking (pea sticks) is recommended. Tubers can be lifted and stored like dahlias, or left in the ground and mulched. Tubers must have one visible eye to survive. Cut down after frost and mulch.
Propagation: Cuttings in fall, basal cuttings in spring; overwinter in a greenhouse. If you divide this plant, you must leave each tuber with a visible pip.
Pests and Diseases: Slugs, powdery mildew (especially if allowed to dry out).
Companions: Artemisia, aster, 'Goldflame' spiraea, dark-foliaged dahlias, second flush of foliage on *Geranium phaeum* var. *phaeum* 'Samobor', late perennials like *Helianthus salicifolius*, *Rudbeckia fulgida* var. *sullivantii* 'Goldsturm'.
Notes: Look for a new, large-flowered, pink perennial cosmos.

Species and Cultivars	Height/ Spread	USDA Hardiness Zone	Flowers (bloom time)	Foliage	Comments
atrosanguineus	18–30in × 18in	7–10	Dark maroon with darker center, velvety, on wiry stems (M–L)	Rich green, bushy clumps, coarsely cut	Chocolate-scented flowers, leaves do not appear until late spring

Crambe maritima.

CRAMBE Brassicaceae

The crambes are handsome, bold, and dramatic architectural contributions to the garden. *Crambe cordifolia* has very large, crinkled, heart-shaped leaves, some measuring up to two feet, forming a mound of two to three feet. A huge fragrant cloud of small white flowers forms high above the foliage. It's an incredible sight when in flower, somewhat like a giant baby's breath.

Crambe maritima has floppy mounds of fleshy, light blue-green foliage that is fringed or curled at the edge. This plant smells just like rotting cabbage, but we really don't notice this until we cut back the mushy leaves. The young foliage is purple, turning glaucous with age. Sweetly scented white flowers rise above the leaves in late spring. The seedheads are wonderful—angular, gray-green stems with green pearls along them.

Both species are somewhat particular about their growing conditions and do best in full sun and well-drained soil. *Crambe maritima* will grow in nearly pure sand or pea gravel, as it is a seaside plant; *C. cordifolia* will need lots of water during the growing season. ~ *Susan Carter*

Scientific Name: From the Greek for "cabbage."
Common Name: Sea kale, colewort.
Origin: Caucasus, Iran, Afghanistan, Europe.
Preferred Conditions: Deep, fertile, well-drained, coarse soil that is moderately alkaline. Tolerant of light shade and poor conditions but does not do well with roots in standing water. High winds can damage *C. cordifolia* flower heads.
Light: Sun.
Planting: Plant out as young plants. In heavier soil, add grit or sharp sand to help with drainage.
Management: These are deep-rooted plants and do not like to be moved. *Crambe cordifolia* may need staking. You can cut back the flower heads as they go over, but they may produce nice seedheads and remain presentable for a while. The bright green leaves continue to

make an impressive effect even after the flowers have faded; cut off disfigured leaves. This species needs time to reach flowering stage (two to three years in some cases). *Crambe maritima* can be cut to the ground after flowering, or remove mushy-looking leaves and new leaves will emerge. Cut to the ground in winter cleanup.

Propagation: Seed, root cuttings in winter; spring division.

Pests and Diseases: Cabbage caterpillars, snails. Slugs are a big problem, especially on emerging growth.

Companions: For *C. cordifolia*, delphinium, baptisia, papaver, nepeta, lavatera, cardoon, phlox; the large-scale cottage garden. For *C. maritima*, sedum, gray grasses, *Parahebe perfoliata*, *Salvia officinalis*.

Notes: *Crambe cordifolia* can take some shade but may then take even longer to reach flowering stage. *Crambe maritima* really must have sun to shine. In spring *C. maritima* is forced (blanched) like rhubarb and eaten as a vegetable (sea kale). Look for *C. filiformis*, a charming airy annual.

Species and Cultivars	Height/ Spread	USDA Hardiness Zone	Flowers (bloom time)	Foliage	Comments
cordifolia	6–7ft × 4ft	6–9	Tiny, white, on pale green stems, slightly scented (E–M)	Large (up to 2ft), heart-shaped, on long stalks, forming a loose, low mound	Very long-lived, RHS Award
maritima	2–3ft × 4ft	6–9	Creamy-white in domes above the foliage, sweetly scented (E)	Floppy mound of glaucous, fleshy basal leaves	Blue sea kale, grows well in a xeriscape, RHS Award

CROCOSMIA Iridaceae

Crocosmias bloom from early summer until early fall, depending upon which cultivars you grow. The larger forms add an element of erect exclamatory foliage; they are physically able to stand up to some of the larger grasses, which they mimic in habit. Bronze-foliaged forms like *C.* ×*crocosmiiflora* 'Solfatare' are complemented by such plants as *Carex buchananii*, *Anthriscus sylvestris* 'Ravenswing', or *Dahlia* 'Yellow Hammer'. One of the latest forms to bloom is the beautiful *C.* ×*crocosmiiflora* 'Emily McKenzie'. Em has very large flowers (for a crocosmia); they are flatter than most and are iridescent orange, marked in the middle with deep burgundy. She looks nice with phygelius and *Achillea* 'Terracotta'. All are easy to grow. The larger-flowered forms are tender, requiring protection in winter and replanting from time to time. They respond well to heavy mulching. Hummingbirds adore them. ~ *Carrie Becker*

Scientific Name: From the Greek *krokos* ("saffron") and *osme* ("smell"); the dried flowers smell like saffron.

Common Name: Montbretia.

Origin: South Africa.

Preferred Conditions: Thrives in most fertile, moisture-retentive, well-drained, humus-rich soil but doesn't like excessive clay, especially cultivars.

Light: Sun to part shade. Shade may contribute to a sprawling habit.

Crocosmia ×crocosmiiflora 'Queen Alexandra'.

Management: Divide, lift, and replant corms when they become congested. The top corms are the most vigorous. Divide every three or more years for best blooming. Mulch in winter to protect corms that have grown close to the surface. Cut back in fall when the leaves turn brown.

Propagation: Division of corms in spring; seed as soon as ripe.

Pests and Diseases: Red spider mites in hot, dry weather; slugs; thrips (banded streaks and brown tips).

Companions: Hemerocallis, agapanthus, berberis, *Euphorbia griffithii*, miscanthus, carex, dahlia, phygelius, *Physocarpus opulifolius* 'Diabolo', *Anemanthele lessoniana*.

Notes: Large-flowered forms tend to run about and seem to be less hardy. In the chart, the symbol ∞ = infinite spread. We have listed only those cultivars that are most commonly available; there are many more.

Species and Cultivars	Height/ Spread	USDA Hardiness Zone	Flowers (bloom time)	Foliage	Comments
Bressingham Beacon	2–3ft × 3ft	6–9	Bicolor, orange and yellow, on purple stems (M–L)	Swordlike, mid-green	Vigorous, long arching spikes
×crocosmiiflora	2–4ft × ∞	5–9	Orange-red, yellow inside with reddish brown throat (M–L)	As above	Common montbretia, vigorous, can be invasive
×c. 'Citronella'	2–3ft × 3ft	6–9	Soft lemon-yellow, long-blooming (M–L)	Narrow, bright green	Needs frequent replanting, vigorous
×c. 'Emberglow'	2–3ft × 3ft+	6–9	Red-orange with red throat, upward-arching (M)	Mid-green, swordlike	Similar in color to C. 'Lucifer', but smaller and blooms later

Species and Cultivars	Height/ Spread	USDA Hardiness Zone	Flowers (bloom time)	Foliage	Comments
×c. 'Emily McKenzie'	2–3ft × 2½ft	7–9	Dark orange, dark maroon markings, yellow and orange banding, large (M–L)	As above	Purple stems, good cut, does not clump
×c. 'George Davison'	2–2½ft × 2½ft	6–9	Nodding, soft yellow (M–L)	As above	Mixed up in the trade with *C. ×crocosmiiflora* 'Citronella'
×c. 'James Coey'	2ft × 2ft	6–9	Dark orange-red, paler inside, yellow throat (M)	As above	
×c. 'Lady Hamilton'	3ft × 2½ft	7–9	Apricot-orange with magenta center, a bit larger (M–L)	As above	Vigorous, good cut
×c. 'Norwich Canary' (syn. 'Lady Wilson')	2–2½ft × 2¼ft	6–9	Canary-yellow (M–L)	As above	Good clumper
×c. 'Plaisir'	2–2½ft × 2½ft	7–9	Salmon (M)	As above	
×c. 'Queen Alexandra'	2ft × 2ft	6–9	Orange outside, flushed maroon on the tube, light orange inside with maroon blotches (M)	As above	
×c. 'Solfatare'	1½–2ft × 2ft	7–9	Apricot-yellow (M–L)	Smoky bronze tinted green, swordlike	Smaller clumps, RHS Award
×c. 'Star of the East'	2½–3ft × 2½ft	8–9	Soft apricot-yellow, paler orange throat, large (M–L)	Mid-green, swordlike	Spreads slowly, vigorous, seems to overwinter best in lighter soil, doesn't clump, RHS Award
×c. 'Venus'	1½–2ft × 2ft	6–9	Peach-yellow with maroon markings at throat (M–L)	As above	
'Jenny Bloom'	2–2½ft × 2½ft+	6–9	Intense yellow (M)	As above, a bit narrower	Open clumps, tolerant of most weather conditions
'Jupiter'	2½–3ft × 3ft	6–9	Pale orange, yellow highlights, out-facing (M–L)	Bronze-green, narrower	
'Lucifer'	2–4ft × 4ft+	5–9	Deep vivid red, up-facing (M)	Broad, swordlike, pleated, mid-green	May need support, vigorous, good seedheads, very large corms
masoniorum	2–4ft × ∞	7–9	Reddish orange to bright yellow-orange, up-facing (M)	Broad, pleated, dark green	Good cut, invasive, coarse, very robust
pottsii	2ft × 2ft	8–9	Orange with yellow throat M)	Shorter, broader, green	Erect, vigorous, tender, large corms

Cryptotaenia japonica f. atropurpurea.

CRYPTOTAENIA Apiaceae

We deal only with the purple (or bronze) leaf form here, which is very useful as a contrast color in a border. A broad, toothed, and three-lobed leaf is surmounted by thin, fingerlike stems and clusters of small white flowers. This is one of the last seeds to ripen in summer and can seed about some. It seems not to mind competition from other plants. Young spring leaves are edible and used as a leafy vegetable. ~ *Bob Lilly*

Scientific Name: From the Latin *cryptos* ("hidden") and *taenia* ("bands," "ribbons"), reference obscure.
Common Name: Japanese honewort, Japanese parsley.
Origin: Asia.
Preferred Conditions: Thrives in most types of soil.
Light: Sun to part shade.
Management: This plant runs a bit but is not considered a problem to control.
Propagation: Sow seed when ripe; spreads by short runners to make good-sized clumps.
Pests and Diseases: Aphids; plants can be grazed on in early spring by slugs, and in summer may get a few spittlebugs.
Companions: *Crocosmia* ×*crocosmiiflora* 'Solfatare', *Erysimum* 'Bowles' Mauve', *E.* 'Julian Orchard', *E.* 'Wenlock Beauty', *Hemerocallis* 'Golden Chimes', *H.* 'Corky', *Sedum telephium* 'Mohrchen', *S. t.* subsp. *ruprechtii*, *Plantago major* 'Rubrifolia', bronze-leaved grasses, carex, *Anthriscus sylvestris* 'Ravenswing'.

Species and Cultivars	Height/ Spread	USDA Hardiness Zone	Flowers (bloom time)	Foliage	Comments
japonica f. atropurpurea (syn. 'Atropurpurea')	30in × 18in	6–8	Small, white, like airy baby's breath (L)	Bronzy, dark purplish, 3-lobed	Tight and sturdy mounds, will seed about

Cymbalaria muralis.

CYMBALARIA Scrophulariaceae

Cymbalaria muralis (Kenilworth ivy) is a semi-evergreen perennial in the Pacific Northwest, often found in older gardens or the ubiquitous, irregular "basalt rockery" of Seattle. It will come and go, depending on the harshness of the winter, but always manages to return for us, if only from a few seedlings. The more ornamental dwarf forms of cymbalaria are charming when covered with their small, snapdragonlike flowers but must be kept free of slugs, or they'll disappear quickly. ~ *Bob Lilly*

Scientific Name: From the Greek *kymbalon* ("cymbal"), referring to the shape of the leaves.
Common Name: Kenilworth ivy, ivy-leaved toadflax.
Origin: Europe, northern Italy, northern Adriatic.
Preferred Conditions: Average, moisture-retentive, well-drained soils.
Light: Part shade.
Management: No fall cleanup required; save this work for spring. It is best to leave the entire plant alone so some small piece survives the winter.
Propagation: Division in spring; seed and stem cuttings in summer.
Pests and Diseases: Slugs.
Companions: *Erigeron karvinskianus*, rock crevices, stonewalls. This is a niche plant, and it goes where it wishes.

Species and Cultivars	Height/ Spread	USDA Hardiness Zone	Flowers (bloom time)	Foliage	Comments
aequitriloba	2in × 24in	3–10	Violet, snapdragonlike (M)	Green, small, ivylike, 3-lobed	Groundcover
a. 'Alba'	2in × 12in	3–10	White (M)	Pale green, ivylike, 3-lobed	Groundcover
muralis	1ft × 3ft	3–10	Small, violet with a yellow-speckled lip, dark purple stems (M–L)	Green, ivylike	Kenilworth ivy, can grow very long stems in one season
m. 'Nana Alba'	3in or less × 6in	3–10	White with yellow throat (M–L)	Apple-green, ivylike	Compact, short-lived

Cynara carduncululus.

CYNARA Asteraceae

Both the cardoon (*C. cardunculus*) and the globe artichoke (*C. cardunculus* Scolymus Group) can be grown for their ornamental foliage. Cardoon is bolder, with more vertical foliage, and is grayer in appearance than the edible artichoke cultivars. Both will be completely herbaceous in a hard winter, even to the point of death. Both also need to be in full sun and well watered in the summer. We let cardoons flower, as they are a beautiful blue-violet and attract a lot of bees.

The best results with cynara for us are achieved by leaving the plants alone until spring, with a nice mulch of leaves, hay, or straw and a surrounding of manure (not over the crown). All parts of the plant are very ornamental; leaves and flowers can be cut for arrangements, and the flower heads can also be dried. ~ *Bob Lilly*

Scientific Name: From the Greek *kyon* ("dog"); the spines on the involucre (ring of bracts around the flower) resemble a dog's teeth.
Common Name: Cardoon, globe artichoke.
Origin: Southwestern Europe, Mediterranean.

Species and Cultivars	Height/ Spread	USDA Hardiness Zone	Flowers (bloom time)	Foliage	Comments
carduncululus	6–8ft × 4–5ft	6–10	Violet-blue or white thistlelike heads bursting from a prickly bud (M–L)	Silvery-gray, pointed, deeply divided, with strong spines	Cardoon, RHS Award
c. Scolymus Group	5–6ft × 4–5ft	6–10	Larger flower heads, purplish blue, from buds 3–6in wide (M)	Gray-green, spineless	Globe artichoke, more vigorous, grown mainly as a vegetable

Preferred Conditions: Tolerant of most garden soils but thrives in one that is deep, humus-rich, and well-drained. Takes some drought but will be smaller. Plants will die out in a wet cold winter.
Light: Sun.
Planting: Divide and plant up basal sprouts after flowering. Plant out seedlings in late April.
Management: Resents disturbance of deep roots. For best foliage effects, remove flowering stems as they emerge. Apply regular topdressing of fertilizer in spring and summer. Protect rootstock with mulch in colder temperatures. Remove the dead leaves and litter as new growth starts, and bait for slugs! Stems may need support. Keep leaves and flower stems on in winter unless unsightly.
Propagation: Seed or division in spring.
Pests and Diseases: Aphids, cutworms, caterpillars. Watch for slugs and snails in spring.
Companions: Rhubarb, large-scale grasses, *Artemisia* 'Huntington'; most effective as a specimen plant.
Notes: The early spring leaf stems are the "vegetable" part of *C. cardunculus* and are usually blanched like celery.

DARMERA Saxifragaceae

This northwest California and Oregon native had to go to Europe and return for us to have it available in numbers. The large leaves are like a small version of *Petasites japonicus*, with more disease and slug resistance. Giant rhizomes, right at the soil surface, creep slowly outward and can even be a bright green. In spring, flowers appear on strong, tall (eighteen-inch-plus) stems; flowers are pink and starlike, an obvious characteristic of their membership in the saxifrage family.

Darmera peltata

Darmeras will grow in very wet soil, but not standing water, and are wonderful bold plants for the garden that doesn't have room for a gunnera. They can be aggressive, but divisions with a sharp poaching shovel and an axe make them easy to control. ~ *Bob Lilly*

Scientific Name: In honor of nineteenth-century horticulturist Karl Darmer of Berlin.
Common Name: Umbrella plant, Indian rhubarb.
Origin: Northwestern California to Oregon.
Preferred Conditions: Moist, cool, organic-rich, boggy conditions in heavy soil.
Light: Shade. Tolerates sun if kept moist.
Planting: Place one foot from high-water mark, if siting near water.
Management: Easy maintenance. Likes an annual mulch of organic material. Protect from late frosts. Woody creeping rhizomes are aggressive, leading one to shovel prune. The leaves are shed naturally in the fall.
Propagation: Division in early spring or fall; dig out chunks of rhizomes and replant; seed.
Pests and Diseases: Slugs are a problem.
Companions: Grasses, *Cimicifuga racemosa*, *Primula japonica*, polygonatum, large ferns; good for erosion control on muddy banks.
Notes: Rhizomes can become tightly packed together; lift and divide, replanting the largest and healthiest pieces. *Darmera peltata* 'Nana' may merely be a young plant not up to size yet.

Species and Cultivars	Height/ Spread	USDA Hardiness Zone	Flowers (bloom time)	Foliage	Comments
peltata	2–4ft × 4ft+	5–9	Pink aging to white (E–M)	Dark green, coarsely toothed, peltate, veined, copper-red fall colors, 1–2ft across	Hairy, reddish stems, RHS Award
p. 'Nana'	1–2½ft × 3ft+	5–9	As above	Dark green, coarsely toothed, peltate, veined, 8–10in across	Dwarf form

DELOSPERMA Aizoaceae

The hardy ice plants need full sun and benefit from a mulch of crushed rock or pea gravel, which helps prevent crown rot. Like other succulents, they can be brought through a cold winter with a layer of evergreen branches (fir or pine; never use hemlock, as it sheds early on) over them for a bit of insulation; when you use this method, be sure to remove the branches before the needles fall off. ~ *Bob Lilly*

Scientific Name: From the Greek *delos* ("evident") and *sperma* ("seed"); the seeds are exposed in an open capsule.
Common Name: Ice plant.
Origin: South Africa.
Preferred Conditions: Well-drained, average soil, but not too fertile. Drought tolerant.
Light: Sun.
Management: Intolerant of wet soil, so stop watering in mid-fall to prepare for winter. Leaves are easily damaged by winter wet or hail. A light covering of conifer branches will help them survive to Zone 5. Not a heavy cover, as they don't want to be "in the dark." Deadhead as needed.

Delosperma cooperi.

Propagation: Cuttings in spring or summer, or seed.
Pests and Diseases: Crown rot, mealy bugs. Watch for aphids; if they appear, remove them as soon as possible.
Companions: Smaller sedums, sempervivum, jovibarba, *Phlox subulata*; the edge of the dry border.
Notes: Plants do very well for us as long as they have sharp drainage for the winter.

Species and Cultivars	Height/ Spread	USDA Hardiness Zone	Flowers (bloom time)	Foliage	Comments
cooperi	3–4in × 12in	5–10	Purple-carmine with white center (M–L)	Mid-green turning red in fall, long, thin, succulent	Semi-evergreen, vigorous spreader
floribundum 'Starburst'	4in × 12in	5–10	Bright pink with white center, shimmering iridescent petals (M–L)	Long, thin, succulent, green	Evergreen, clumping
nubigenum	1–3in × 18in	5–10	Bright yellow (E–M)	Small, fleshy, green, turning reddish in fall and winter	More tolerant of wet soils and cold, creeping mat-forming, will trail over a pot's edge

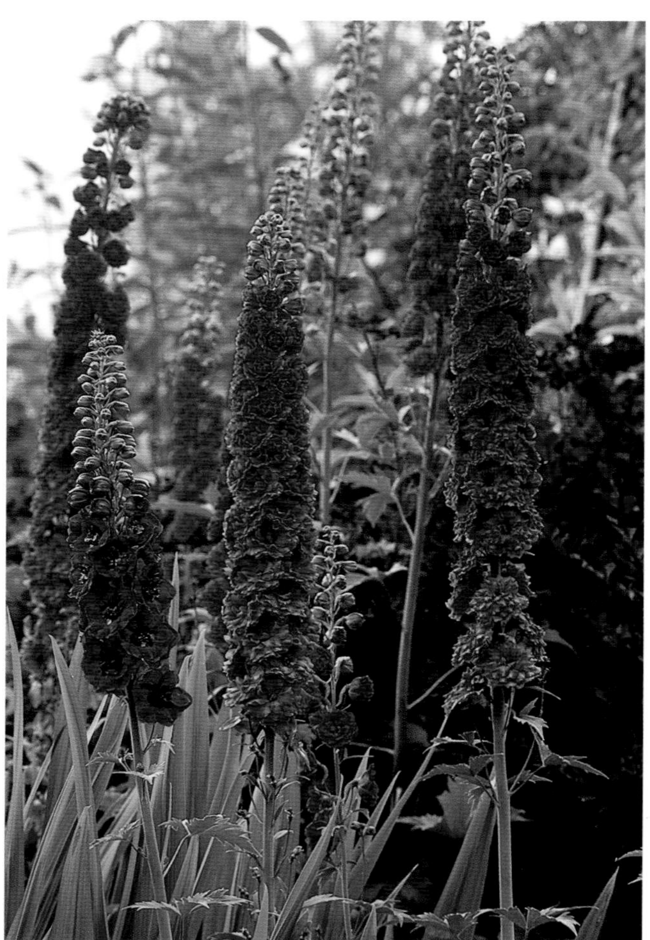

Delphinium 'Alice Artindale'.

DELPHINIUM Ranunculaceae

Delphiniums are the classic cottage garden plant, grown for their tall, stately spires of densely clustered flowers. True blue was the traditional and most common color, but the range has broadened to include indigo-blue, pale blue, pink, purple, white, and red, with a new black one soon to hit the market. Popular also are the semi-double and double flowers, some multicolored.

Delphiniums have been much hybridized; the best known of the several resulting groups are the Pacific Hybrids named for characters from King Arthur's court. Most of these grow to a height of four to six feet. There are also dwarf types, one to three feet high, which are very versatile growing among lower perennials.

As Queen of the Border, the delphinium is a high-maintenance perennial, demanding constant attention: disease control, slug baiting, pinching, early staking, tweaking, poking, feeding, and praying. Nevertheless, its presence is such that many of us continue to value it in our gardens, even though we may treat it as an annual or short-lived perennial. All parts of this plant are poisonous. It makes a good cut flower, if briefly. ~ *Susan Carter*

Scientific Name: From the Greek *delphis* ("dolphin"), referring to the shape of the flowers.

Common Name: Larkspur.

Origin: North America, Europe, Siberia, China, Caucasus.

Preferred Conditions: Delphiniums are lime lovers, requiring well-drained, fertile, humus-rich soil. Keep them evenly moist especially during the growth time. Shelter the taller ones from strong winds.

Light: Sun to part shade. The taller ones are most sensitive to high heat over an extended period.

Planting: Don't bury the crown; it may rot. Fall is not a good time to divide, as plants are usually dormant.

Management: High maintenance. These are heavy feeders, apply a balanced fertilizer every two to three weeks for show flowers. Bait for slugs and snails before the new growth appears, or they will graze off the new growth at ground level and set your plants back considerably. Thin new shoots when they reach three inches in length; leave a minimum of two or three shoots on young plants and five to seven strong shoots on well-established ones. Most need secure staking. Cut back after flowering to small flowering side shoots, and they may flower again after a short rest period. For a rebloom in late summer, cut back to base all the stems that have flowered.

Propagation: Fresh seed (mainly for the Belladonna Group and *D. elatum*), basal cuttings in spring; division for cultivars.

Pests and Diseases: Slugs, snails, powdery mildew, crown and root rot, botrytis, leaf miners, caterpillars, spider mites, stem borers, leaf spot, and rust—the hypochondriac of the perennial border.

Delphiniums in the border, with roses, *Achillea* 'Taygetea', *Eryngium giganteum*, and clouds of *Clematis recta* 'Purpurea' and euphorbia.

Companions: Campanula, geranium, lilac, shrub roses, lupinus, lunaria, taller baptisias, thalictrum, aquilegia; the back of the border.

Notes: The newer cultivars *D. elatum* 'New Heights' and *D. e.* 'New Millennium' are stronger and have more closely spaced flowers. Look for more new cultivars to appear.

Species and Cultivars	Height/ Spread	USDA Hardiness Zone	Flowers (bloom time)	Foliage	Comments
'Alice Artindale'	3½–4ft × 2ft	4–8	Double blue and mauve, narrow spikes (M)	Large, green, stiff and uniform	A very old cultivar
Astolat Group (Pacific Hybrids)	4–8ft × 2ft	3–8	Semi-double, shades of lilac and pink with darker eye (E)	Light green	Needs support

Species and Cultivars	Height/ Spread	USDA Hardiness Zone	Flowers (bloom time)	Foliage	Comments
Belladonna Group	3–4ft × 1½ft	3–8	Single light blue to pink and white on wiry stems, open inflorescence (M–L)	Mid-green, smaller, more cut	Bushy, seldom needs support, likes summer heat
B. 'Casa Blanca'	3–4ft × 1½ft	3–8	Pure white, open inflorescence (M–L)	As above	Well-branched
×bellemosum	3–4ft × 1½ft	3–8	Deep gentian-blue, single with spurs, large (M–L)	Light to mid-green, finely lobed	Seldom needs staking
Black Knight Group (Pacific Hybrids)	4–6ft × 2ft	3–8	Dark violet-blue with black eye, semi-double (M)	Light green	Darkest of the Pacific Hybrids
Blue Bird Group (Pacific Hybrids)	4–6ft × 2ft	3–8	Shades of mid-blue with white eye, double (M)	As above	
Blue Fountains Group (Belladonna)	2½–3ft × 1½ft	3–8	Single, shades of blue and white (M)	Green, finely divided	Compact
'Blue Jay' (Pacific Hybrids)	4–5ft × 2ft	3–8	Semi-double, mid-blue with dark eye (M)	Light green	
'Blue Mirror'	1–2ft × 2ft	3–8	Bright gentian-blue, spurless, single, open inflorescence (M–L)	Deep green, finely cut	Treat as a biennial
cardinale	2–4ft × 1½ft	7–9	Single red with yellowish inner petals, spurs (E–M)	Green, appears in autumn, large, finely divided	Scarlet larkspur, California native, keep dry in the summer, short-lived
Connecticut Yankees Group	2–3ft × 1½ft	4–9	Shades of blue (E–L)	Light green, smaller	Bushy, free-branching, no staking needed, tolerant of heat
elatum	4–7ft × 1ft	3–8	Single to semi-double, blue to dull purple, spurs, white eye (E–M)	A darker mid-green, smaller, dark stems	Very tall and narrow, flowers widely spaced
e. 'New Heights'	6–8ft × 1½ft	3–8	White, cream, pink, lavender, maroon (E–L)	Mid-green	Vigorous, more tolerant of heat and humidity, needs no staking
e. 'New Millennium'	3½–4ft × 1½ft	3–8	Blue, violet, turquoise, pink, mauve, white (E–L)	As above	Dwarf
Galahad Group (Pacific Hybrids)	4–6ft × 1½ft	3–8	Semi-double, pure white with white eye	Light green	A bit weak
grandiflorum (syn. chinense)	1–2ft × 1½ft	3–8	Single, gentian-blue, spurs and lower petals often red-violet, open inflorescence (M)	Dark green, palmate, free-branching	Often grown as an annual, long-blooming

Species and Cultivars	Height/ Spread	USDA Hardiness Zone	Flowers (bloom time)	Foliage	Comments
g. 'Blauer Zwerg' (syn. 'Blue Dwarf', 'Blue Elf')	10–16in × 12in	2–9	Gentian-blue, large, inflorescence (M–L)	Mid-green	Bushy dwarf, may self-sow, grown as an annual
g. 'Blue Butterfly'	10–18in × 12in	3–9	Bright blue, single, open inflorescence (M–L)	Deep green, finely cut	Treat as a biennial or annual
Guinevere Group (Pacific Hybrids)	4–5ft × 1½ft	3–8	Light rosy-lavender-pink with white eye, semi-double (M–L)	Light green	Let's hope breeding gives us a good pink
King Arthur Group (Pacific Hybrids)	4–5ft × 2ft	3–8	Royal violet with white eye, double (E–M)	Mid-green	
Magic Fountains Series	2–3ft × 1½ft	3–8	Range of blue, lavender, rose, and white with or without eye, double, large (M–L)	Green, deeply lobed	Dwarf, open inflorescence
nudicaule	1–2ft × 1ft	6–9	Soft orange-red, long spurs, single, red to yellow throat (M)	Green, rounded, lobed	Goes mostly dormant after flowering, keep dry in summer, often grown as an annual, California native
Summer Skies Group (Pacific Hybrids)	4–5ft × 2ft	3–8	Light sky-blue tones with white eye, semi-double (E–M)	Light green	One of the most popular colors

DIANTHUS Caryophyllaceae

If you can provide an environment with sharp drainage, sandy soil, full sun, and somewhat alkaline soil, by all means try the larger-flowered, taller, grayer forms of dianthus—most folks are drawn to these big ones, which do not like acidic soil or cold, wet winters. These taller forms may need support and look floppy to sloppy, since it is hard to stake them discreetly; you might try growing them in containers. Otherwise, grow the lovely, subtle small forms. Best used as short-lived perennials allowed to flop and crawl about at the edge of a border or over a wall.
~ *Carrie Becker*

Scientific Name: From the Greek *di* ("two"; also the name for Zeus or Jove) and *anthos* ("flower").

Common Name: Carnation, pink.

Origin: Europe, Asia, Great Britain.

Preferred Conditions: Slightly alkaline but will do fine in neutral or mildly acidic. Well-drained, moisture-retentive, sandy or gritty soil. Drought tolerant. Does not like heavy soil, especially in winter wet. Keep away from soggy soil, rabbits, and drying wind especially in the spring.

Light: Sun.

Dianthus gratianopolitanus 'Firewitch'.

Management: Likes a dressing of bonemeal in early spring. Add limestone to raise the alkalinity. Deadhead for neatness and to keep the modern cultivars blooming through summer and into fall. Some may need support. Propagate every two or three years to replace losses.

Propagation: Seed, stem cuttings in the summer after blooming. Stems lie on the ground and can be layered to form roots for division.

Pests and Diseases: Slugs, snails, crown root, rust, fungal diseases, squirrels, rabbits, deer, cutworms, aphids, spider mites. Watch for slugs hiding under the foliage.

Companions: *Stachys byzantina*, roses, *Erigeron karvinskianus*, diascia, and other over-the-wall floppers.

Notes: Most dianthus will spread more than we list over time, but the centers may go bare. The best dianthus forms for the Northwest are smaller in habit, usually green (sometimes gray-foliaged), and smaller flowered.

Species and Cultivars	Height/ Spread	USDA Hardiness Zone	Flowers (bloom time)	Foliage	Comments
'Allspice'	12in × 12in	4–9	Single, raspberry-red fading to purple, white margins, fringed, fragrant (E–L)	Blue-green, in low dense mats, evergreen	Border pink, prolific bloomer
alpinus	3–8in × 8in	3–8	Single, deep pink to crimson with darker spots, large, no fragrance (E–L)	Dark green, evergreen	Alpine pink, short-lived
'Aqua'	10–12in × 12in	3–9	Double white, frilly, clove-scented (E–M)	Bluish green, dense, blue-gray stems, evergreen	Border pink

Species and Cultivars	Height/ Spread	USDA Hardiness Zone	Flowers (bloom time)	Foliage	Comments
'Bath's Pink'	6–12in × 12in	3–9	Single, soft pink with darker eye, clove-scented (E–M)	Silvery blue-green, narrow, grassy, evergreen	Cheddar pink, rock garden plant, doesn't rebloom
'Bat's Double Red'	7–12in × 12in	4–8	Semi-double, red-wine with darker eye, fringed, scented (M)	Blue-green, grassy, evergreen	Border pink, repeats in autumn, vigorous
'Bourbon'	3in × 12in	2–9	Single, dark pink (E–M)	Mid-green, grassy tufts, evergreen	Compact
'Candy Dish'	10–12in × 12in	4–8	Double, frilly pink with red streaks (E–M)	Bluish green, evergreen	As above
caryophyllus	12in × 12in	7–10	Double and semi-double, pink, scented (M–L)	Grayish to blue-green, evergreen	Wild carnation, its cultivars are grown for the cut flower trade, short-lived
'Dad's Favourite'	12–18in × 12in	4–8	Semi-double white with maroon markings and maroon-purple center (M)	Gray-green, grassy, evergreen	Border pink, very old cultivar
'Danielle Marie'	10–12in × 12in	4–10	Double, salmon-orange to coral-red, toothed, fragrant (M)	Gray-green, evergreen	Modern border pink
deltoides	8in × 18in+	3–9	Single, starry, colors range from purple through reds and pinks to white with darker eye, no scent (M)	Mid to dark green, grasslike, broad-leafed, evergreen	Maiden pink, self-sows, long-blooming, mat-forming, RHS Award
d. 'Albus'	6–8in × 18in+	2–9	Single, white with pink eye (M)	Pale green, evergreen	Mat-forming, spreading, self-sows
d. 'Arctic Fire'	6–8in × 18in+	3–9	Single, white with red eye, fringed, fragrant (M)	Dense, dark green, evergreen	Spreading, mat-forming, cut back after first bloom
d. 'Brilliant'	6–12in × 18in+	3–9	Single, bright dark red (M)	Deep green, evergreen	Spreading, mat-forming
d. 'Flashing Light'	6–8in × 18in+	2–9	Single, deep ruby-red (M)	Dark bronzy-green, evergreen	Mat-forming
d. 'Zing Rose'	6–8in × 18in+	3–9	Single, bright rose-red with darker ring around eye, fragrant (M)	Green, dense, evergreen	Mat-forming, will repeat if cut back after first bloom
'Doris'	10in × 12in	3–10	Semi-double, bright salmon-pink with red patch, fragrant (M)	Gray-green, evergreen	Modern pink, vigorous, long-lived, RHS Award
'Essex Witch'	5–8in × 12in+	4–9	Semi-double, rose-pink with darker zones, fringed, fragrant (E–L)	Gray, evergreen	Rock garden pink, one of the best, not tolerant of high temperatures

Species and Cultivars	Height/ Spread	USDA Hardiness Zone	Flowers (bloom time)	Foliage	Comments
'Frosty Fire'	4–8in × 8in	3–9	Semi-double, deep ruby-red, fragrant (E–M)	Bluish green, evergreen	Long-blooming
gratianopolitanus	6–12in × 12in	3–9	Single, rose-pink, red, or white, toothed, fragrant (E–L)	Glaucous, grassy, evergreen	Cheddar pink, mat-forming, long-lived, RHS Award
g. 'Dottie'	4–5in × 10in	3–8	Single, frilled white with maroon eye (E–M)	Mid-green, evergreen	Rock garden pink, dwarf, compact
g. 'Firewitch'	6in × 10in	3–8	Single, bright carmine-magenta, fragrant (E–M)	Glaucous, grassy, evergreen	Rock garden pink, spreading
g. 'Tiny Rubies'	3in × 10in+	3–9	Double, rose-pink, tiny, fragrant (E–M)	Grayish green, grassy, evergreen	Rock garden pink, long-blooming
'Helen'	10–12in × 12in	4–8	Double, salmon-pink (M–L)	Blue-green, evergreen	Modern pink, a very good cultivar
'Her Majesty'	8–10in × 12in	4–9	Double white, fringed (M)	Gray, dense, evergreen	Antique border pink
'Hoffman's Red'	12in × 12in	4–9	Single, bright red (E–L)	Green, evergreen	Rock garden pink
'Horatio'	6–8in × 10in	4–9	Semi-double, bright rose-pink, maroon eye, fragrant (E–L)	Blue-green, evergreen	Rock garden pink, a very good cultivar
'Inchmery'	10–12in × 12in	4–9	Double, pale pink, fringed, fragrant (M)	Silvery blue-green, evergreen	Antique border pink, mat-forming, vigorous
'ItSaul White'	8–12in × 12in+	3–8	Frilly, pure white, fragrant (E–M)	As above	Modern border pink
knappii	12–18in × 8in	3–9	Single, pale yellow, toothed, no scent (E–M)	Gray-green, grassy, lax stems, semi-evergreen	Short-lived, self-sows, clumps
'Laced Hero'	10–12in × 12in	3–8	Double white, laced with dark reddish purple, fragrant (E–L)	Blue-gray, evergreen	Modern border pink, long-blooming
'Little Jock'	6in × 6in	5–9	Semi-double, pink with maroon eye, fringed, fragrant (M)	Silvery-blue, compact cushions, evergreen	Rock garden pink
'Mrs. Sinkins'	6–12in × 12in	5–9	Double white, fringed, light green eye, very fragrant (M)	Blue-green, evergreen	Antique pink, shaggy and untidy
'Musgrave's Pink' (syn. 'Charles Musgrave')	10–12in × 12in	5–9	Single, white with green eye, fragrant (M–L)	Mid-green, evergreen	Antique pink, good cut
'Oakington' (syn. 'Oakington Rose')	6–8in × 12in	5–9	Double, deep rose, fringed, fragrant (M)	Bluish green, evergreen	
'Paisley Gem'	12in × 12in	5–9	Double, maroon with white splashes and edges, fragrant (M)	Evergreen	

Species and Cultivars	Height/ Spread	USDA Hardiness Zone	Flowers (bloom time)	Foliage	Comments
'Pheasant's Eye'	12–15in × 12in	4–8	Semi-double white with deep maroon center, fringed, fragrant (M)	As above	Antique pink
plumarius	10–18in × 12in+	4–10	Single, pink, fringed, fragrant (E–M)	Glaucous, grassy, veined, evergreen	Cottage pink, long-blooming, mat-forming
'Rose de Mai'	12–18in × 18in+	4–9	Double, mauve-pink with slightly darker zones, fragrant (M–L)	Blue-gray, evergreen	Antique border pink, long-blooming
'Snowfire'	15–18in × 18in	5–9	Fringed, white with red eye (M)	Evergreen	Modern pink, 1978 All-America Selection
'Sops-in-Wine'	8in × 12in	5–9	Double, velvety wine-red with white spot on each petal, fragrant (M)	As above	Old-fashioned pink
'Spotty'	6–8in × 8in+	3–9	Single, rose-red, edged and spotted silvery-white, fragrant (E–M)	Gray-green, evergreen	Rock garden pink
superbus	12–24in × 12in	3–9	Single, pale lilac, pink, or white, fringed, large, fragrant (M–L)	Mid-green, grassy, evergreen	Fringed pink, often treated as a biennial, very floriferous
'Waithman's Beauty'	6–8in × 8in	4–8	Single, raspberry-red splashed pink with 2 irregular white eyes, fragrant (M)	Evergreen	Rock garden pink
'War Bonnet'	6–10in × 12in	4–9	Double, deep purplish red, white edges, fragrant (M)	Green, grassy, evergreen	Border carnation

DIASCIA Scrophulariaceae

The sweet little twinspurs have just that on the back of every flower. Many cultivars are available, some taller, and some larger flowered, and some more perennial. All look quite similar to each other. Low-growing, they look best in the foreground or at the edges of planting areas, or as a container plant spilling over the sides of a pot. Once they begin to bloom in summer they will bloom until frost if you shear them over after the first flush of flowers. These short-lived perennials perform so well and for so long that when they die they should just be replaced. ~ *Carrie Becker*

Scientific Name: From the Greek *di* ("two") and *askos* ("sac"), referring to the two spurs on the flower.
Common Name: Twinspur.
Origin: South Africa.

Diascia 'Emma'.

Preferred Conditions: Moist, well-drained, rich loam. Tolerant of average garden soil as long as they don't dry out and are not crowded out by other plants.

Light: Sun to shade.

Management: Cut back or shear flower stems into foliage after the first flush of bloom, as they look unkempt and rangy; they will rebloom in several weeks. Take cuttings of the more tender cultivars in case they don't survive the winter. Usually need to be replaced after two or three years; better managed as an annual.

Propagation: Tip cuttings in spring and summer; often lost when divided.

Pests and Diseases: Snails, spider mites if grown too dry or with poor air circulation. Watch for slugs in early spring.

Companions: Silver-foliaged plants such as artemisia (less aggressive forms), lavender and blue campanulas, *Viola cornuta* and other violas, gaura, geranium. Try them with *Scabiosa* 'Butterfly Blue' for all-summer flowers.

Species and Cultivars	Height/ Spread	USDA Hardiness Zone	Flowers (bloom time)	Foliage	Comments
barberae	12in × 18in	8–11	Rose-pink, large, on erect stems (E–L)	Green with bluish cast	More tender than most
b. 'Blackthorn Apricot'	12in × 18in	8–10	Large, apricot-pink with broad lip and long spurs (M)	Pale green, small, in a loose mat	Good weaver, RHS Award
b. 'Ruby Field'	8in × 10in	7–9	Deep pink with bluish tint (E–M)	As above	Rock garden plant, RHS Award
'Emma'	18in × 18in	7–9	Rich deep rose on tall stems (M–L)	Shiny olive-green to deep green	Vigorous, can take a wide range of conditions, long-lived
fetcaniensis	18in × 18in	7–9	Salmon-pink, more upright (E–L)	Lush dark green, broadly ovate and toothed	Good weaver, long-lived

Species and Cultivars	Height/ Spread	USDA Hardiness Zone	Flowers (bloom time)	Foliage	Comments
integerrima	18–20in × 18in	7–9	Rose-pink, small, sharply curved spurs (M–L)	Gray-green, narrow, pointed slightly, toothed at base	Runs underground, tolerates drier conditions, RHS Award
i. 'Blush'	12–24in × 18in	7–9	Pale pink to white (M–L)	Gray-green, small, narrow	Good weaver
'Lady Valerie'	10–12in × 12in	7–9	Pale apricot-pink (M–L)	Gray-green, arrow-shaped, serrated	Bushy habit, refined and delicate, RHS Award
'Lilac Mist'	8–12in × 12in	7–9	Pale lavender-pink with darker center, sharply curved spurs (M)	Green, large, toothed	Spreading, RHS Award
rigescens	18in+ × 18in+	7–9	Clear deep pink (M–L)	Gray-green, coarsely toothed	Robust and vigorous, RHS Award
'Salmon Supreme' (syn. 'Hector Harrison')	8–12in × 12in	7–9	Salmon fading with age (M–L)	Light green, small, trailing	Long-blooming
vigilis	12in × 24in	7–9	Delicate clear pink (M–L)	Bright green, ovate	RHS Award

DICENTRA Papaveraceae

I have never met a dicentra I didn't like. Some are more appealing than others, but all are winners. The best have foliage that is an asset when the plant is not blooming; this is particularly true of

Dicentra 'Adrian Bloom'.

D. formosa and *D. eximia*. Their varying shades of gray-green to blue-gray are perfect complements to many other broader-leaved woodland plants. Generally, formosa hybrids run, and eximia hybrids are more clumping.

Dicentra spectabilis is the queen of the tribe, earliest to bloom and of a much larger stature. Many of us have had our hearts melted by the beautiful, delicate gray-green leaves and larger pink and white hearts of this species. The white-flowered forms are lovely in low light. Personally, I like *D.* 'Stuart Boothman' best for its extremely finely dissected pewter-colored leaves and rosy hearts; it and other more dwarf forms bloom on through midsummer, while *D. spectabilis* may go dormant about that time. The only solution is to grow them all! ~ *Carrie Becker*

Scientific Name: From the Greek *di* ("two") and *kentron* ("spur").
Common Name: Bleeding heart, Dutchman's breeches (*D. cucullaria*).
Origin: North America, Japan, China.
Preferred Conditions: Fertile, humus-rich, moisture-retentive, free-draining soil. Don't allow them to get too dry during the summer months.
Light: Sun to part shade.
Management: Keep soil moist and cool in order to have the foliage last longer, particularly the taller ones. Otherwise the foliage will yellow and should be cut back. Many of the smaller forms are rhizomatous and spread, occasionally becoming invasive. Not the easiest plant to divide—a knife is usually needed. Split clump in such a way as to produce pieces that have both a bud (eye) and roots. *Dicentra spectabilis* will survive many years without division; *D. s.* 'Alba' may seed about on its own (this is a good thing).
Propagation: Root cuttings in spring; division in spring (carefully); seed.
Pests and Diseases: Mildew, slugs, snails.
Companions: Narcissus, hosta, asarum, epimedium, astilbe, brunnera, ferns, pulmonaria, primula, helleborus, tiarella; the woodland garden.
Notes: Turn the flower (heart) of *D. spectabilis* upside-down, open the petals, and you will see, sitting, the little white shape that suggests the other common name, lady in the bath. Dicentras, if left to their own devices, will spread further than we show, especially the rhizomatous ones, but rarely swamp other perennials.

Species and Cultivars	Height/ Spread	USDA Hardiness Zone	Flowers (bloom time)	Foliage	Comments
'Adrian Bloom' (formosa hybrid)	10–18in × 12–24in+	3–8	Raspberry-red (E–M)	Dark gray-green, fernlike	May rebloom, vigorous, rhizomatous
'Bacchanal'	12–18in × 18in+	6–9	Very dark wine-red (M)	Blue-green, fernlike	Long-blooming, rhizomatous, RHS Award
'Bountiful' (formosa hybrid)	12in × 24in+	6–9	Purplish red (M)	Blue-green, cut leaf, red-tinged stems	May rebloom, rhizomatous
eximia	12–18in × 18in	3–9	Deep rosy-pink, heart-shaped (E–M)	Pale gray-green, dense mounds, fernlike	Fringed bleeding heart, clumps, may rebloom, rhizomatous
e. 'Snowdrift' (syn. 'Alba')	12–15in × 12–18in	3–9	White (E–L)	Pale gray-green, fernlike	Rhizomatous, clumps
formosa	12–18in × 24in	3–9	Rose-pink, heart-shaped (E–M)	Pewter-gray, tinged with maroon, fernlike	Western bleeding heart, self-sows, rhizomatous

Species and Cultivars	Height/ Spread	USDA Hardiness Zone	Flowers (bloom time)	Foliage	Comments
f. 'Aurora'	12in × 24in	3–9	White (E–L)	Grayish blue	Vigorous, rhizomatous
f. 'Margery Fish'	12–18in × 24in	3–9	Pure white (E–L)	Lacy blue	As above
f. 'Tuolumne Rose'	12in × 24in	3–9	Large, rose-pink (E–M)	Large, bright blue-green	
'Langtrees' (formosa hybrid)	12in × 24in	3–9	Creamy-white, pink-tinged (E–L)	Glaucous	Rhizomatous but not invasive, RHS Award
'Luxuriant' (formosa hybrid)	12–18in × 24in	3–9	Dark pink, long-blooming (E–M)	Blue-green, fernlike	Foliage persists throughout summer, good cut, rhizomatous, RHS Award
scandens	6–12ft × 2ft	7–9	Dangling, narrow yellow lockets, aging to amber (M–L)	Mid-green, divided	Climbing, vining, forms a big woody root
'Snowflakes' (eximia hybrid)	12in × 18in	3–8	White (E–M)	Lacy, light green	Clumps
spectabilis	2–3ft × 2ft	3–9	Rose-red with white tip, pink in bud, heart-shaped (E–M)	Gray-green, divided, go dormant in summer	Common bleeding heart, good cut, long-lived
s. 'Alba'	2–3ft × 2ft	3–9	Creamy-white (E–M)	Light green, with almost transparent green stems	Less vigorous, good cut, RHS Award
s. 'Gold Heart'	24–36in × 18in	3–9	Pink, heart-shaped (E–M)	Brilliant gold	Burns in full sun, a bit weak, RHS Award
'Stuart Boothman' (formosa hybrid)	12in × 18in+	3–9	Light pinkish red (E–M)	Glaucous, very narrowly divided	Slowly spreading, self-sows, rhizomatous, RHS Award
'Zestful' (formosa hybrid)	12in × 24in	3–9	Deep rose (E–M)	Fernlike, pale grayish green	Clumping, rhizomatous

DICTAMNUS Rutaceae

The gas plant! Slow to establish and late to emerge in the spring, this showy, handsome plant requires little care once it takes hold and in fact is extremely long-lived, so choose its location carefully. Plants have shiny, erect, pinnate foliage topped by spikes of white or pink flowers in summer. Their seedpods are good in the garden and in dried floral arrangements. Aromatic oil gives the plants a strong citrus fragrance; this volatilized oil can be lit with a match on warm, still summer evenings. Don't expect much—it's a brief flash and does not affect the plant (unless you hold the match too close). Entertain your friends! ~ *Carrie Becker*

Scientific Name: From the herb *Origanum dictamnus* (dittany of Crete).
Common Name: Gas plant.
Origin: Asia, southern Europe.

Dictamnus albus.

Preferred Conditions: Fertile, well-drained, deeply cultivated, alkaline (needs dolomite lime).
Light: Sun.
Management: This plant resents disturbance because it has deep, fine roots. It appears late in the spring, so mark the spot to avoid damaging roots and crowns. Cut down dead stems in autumn.
Propagation: Seed, as soon as ripe (four or five years to flower initially); divide with care.
Pests and Diseases: Slugs, snails.
Companions: Geranium, campanula, monarda, hemerocallis, grasses, paeonia, aconitum, delphinium, *Sisyrinchium striatum*, pimpinella, Bic lighter.
Notes: Plant is poisonous. The seed capsules open explosively, ejecting round, smooth, shiny black seeds. Here in the Northwest, dictamnus needs a very warm location to amount to much.

Species and Cultivars	Height/ Spread	USDA Hardiness Zone	Flowers (bloom time)	Foliage	Comments
albus	2–3ft × 2ft	3–8	White, purple, or pinkish, long stamens (E–M)	Rich green, deeply divided, leathery, glossy	Star-shaped seedpods, black seeds, lemony fragrance
a. var. purpureus	2–3ft × 2ft	3–8	Soft mauve-purple with darker veins (E–M)	As above	As above, RHS Award

Dierama pauciflorum.

DIERAMA Iridaceae

From a vertical series of underground corms (a new one is produced each year) grow grassy green leaves; in summer, flowers in shades of pink, red, mauve, and deep maroon (depending on the species or cultivar) hang down from wiry stems. *Dierama pulcherrimum*, *D. pendulum*, and *D. pauciflorum* are tall and very graceful. *Dierama dracomontanum*, while also graceful, is much lower and denser. The leaves are evergreen. New growth does not appear until late spring, so take care when removing unsightly older leaves. All dieramas come from the summer-moist regions of South Africa and will need adequate moisture with good drainage to thrive (they need perfect drainage in our wet winters). I grow *D. cooperi*, a short, spreading plant, as a pot plant; it seems to need more moisture in winter but otherwise thrives during that season in a dry, sunny spot. Spring division should be done with care, as roots are extremely brittle. ~ *Ann Bucher*

Scientific Name: From the Greek for "funnel," referring to the shape of the flower.
Common Name: Angel's fishing rod, fairy wand.
Origin: South Africa.
Preferred Conditions: Deep, well-drained, moisture-retentive, acid soil, rich in organic material. Keep it moist but not too wet. Graceful, arching inflorescences are highly decorative when hanging over the garden pond but are probably more successful cultivated on a slope with good drainage.
Light: Sun.
Planting: Plant no deeper than they are when purchased.
Management: Resent being moved. If they look ratty in winter do not shear them back, but remove the dead leaves, in spring only, by giving a sharp tug or cutting off as low as possible. No support is needed. Do not move in autumn. Do not plant at all in autumn, even if container grown.
Propagation: Seed as soon as ripe, April to May (harvest seed by shaking); division in April and May (include several corms in each clump).

Pests and Diseases: Rust, red spider mites.
Companions: A nice big rock—dierama makes a good focal point on its own.
Notes: Clumps over time do get quite large. It's best not to transplant, divide, or groom in the fall.

Species and Cultivars	Height/ Spread	USDA Hardiness Zone	Flowers (bloom time)	Foliage	Comments
cooperi	2½ft × 1½ft	7–9	Peachy-pink, a smaller flower, floriferous (M)	Green, narrow, grassy	Seems to grow faster than *D. pulcherrimum*, but likes it hot, sunny, and dry
dracomontanum	18–24in × 24in	7–9	Satiny rose-pink, light pink, coral, red, purple, or mauve, wider open flowers (M)	Green, grassy, evergreen	Vigorous, clump-forming, happiest in moist soil
pauciflorum	3–6ft × 2ft	7–9	Light to reddish pink on arching stems (M)	Green, grassy	May be the hardiest
pendulum	3–6ft × 2ft	7–9	Pale pink-purple, bell-shaped, on tall branched spikes (M)	Green, stiff, narrow	Needs winter protection
pulcherrimum	4–6ft × 2½ft	7–9	Pale to deep magenta to pink, occasionally purple (M)	Green, long, grassy, leathery, evergreen	Can take a year or so to establish, attractive silvery seedheads

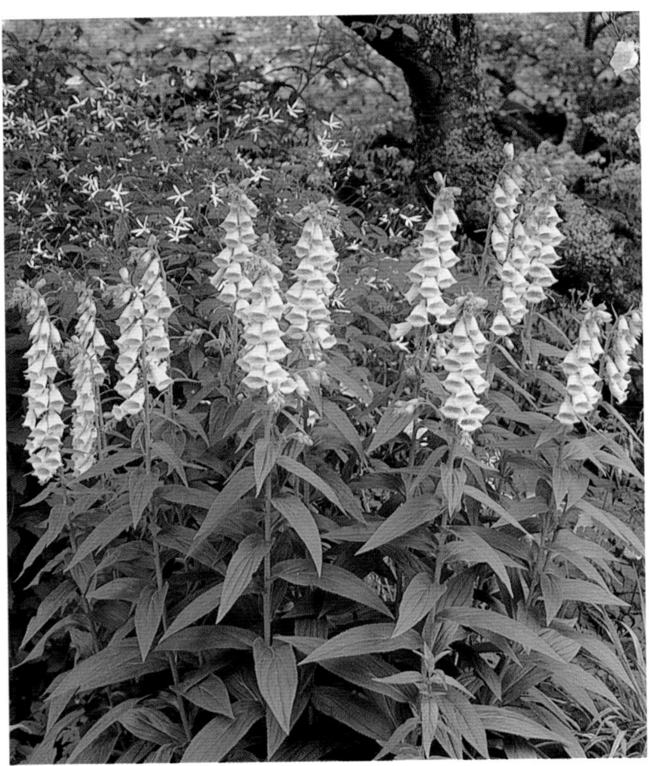

Digitalis grandiflora.

DIGITALIS Scrophulariaceae

Foxgloves come in two versions, the strong and the weak, and unfortunately the strong are annuals or biennials, and the weak are perennials. *Digitalis purpurea*, the common foxglove introduced from Europe by the settlers and westward expansion, is common throughout the West. White-flowering forms have long been popular, and it's easy to get them in the garden: simply pull all the rest as soon as the flower color is apparent, and let the whites seed about. More recent color selections have brought digitalis back into our gardens in creams and apricots, including some with dramatically marked throats.

The perennial foxgloves all form a semi-evergreen leafy crown, which has a tendency to rot in wetter winters (a rain-protected location is about the only defense we have). Try to keep spent flower stems completely removed to help form stronger basal growth for next year. ~ *Bob Lilly*

Scientific Name: From the Latin *digitus* ("finger"), referring to the fingerlike flowers.
Common Name: Foxglove.

Origin: Central Asia, Europe, northwestern Africa.

Preferred Conditions: Rich in organic material, well-drained, moist but not waterlogged. Tolerant of a wide range of soils, *D. purpurea* will colonize in very poor soil.

Light: Sun to shade. May not bloom as well in heavy shade.

Management: Early removal of the entire spent stalk usually stimulates some autumn flowering from basal shoots. This method is most successful for keeping the plants perennial. Some species self-sow profusely, so deadhead after flowering. Clean up bad leaves any time. Support is seldom needed.

Propagation: Division in spring or fall; seed is best (but only on the biennials).

Pests and Diseases: Snails, mildew, leaf spot. Bait for slugs regularly. Cutworms in early spring are also a problem and have increased in recent years; the only good method of control is hand-picking and squishing.

Companions: Dicentra, hosta, ferns, aruncus, cimicifuga, iris, astilbe, paeonia, aquilegia.

Notes: The drug digitalis, used to treat heart disease, is extracted from the leaves of *D. purpurea*. All parts of all foxgloves are poisonous. Contact with the foliage may irritate skin. Bees and hummingbirds love this plant.

Species and Cultivars	Height/ Spread	USDA Hardiness Zone	Flowers (bloom time)	Foliage	Comments
ferruginea	3–4ft × 1½ft	4–7	Yellowish brown, dark red veins (E–M)	Dark green, lanceolate, deeply veined, rosettes	Rusty foxglove, clump-forming, short-lived, RHS Award
f. 'Gelber Harold' (syn. 'Yellow Harold')	3–4ft × 1½ft	4–7	Rusty golden yellow (M)	As above	Short-lived, clump-forming
grandiflora (syn. ambigua)	2–3ft × 1½ft	3–8	Pale yellow, tubular (E–M)	Mid-green, broad, hairy, lanceolate	Yellow foxglove, long-lived, self-sows, good cut, RHS Award
g. 'Carillon'	1–2ft × 1ft	3–8	Soft yellow with brown markings (E–M)	As above	Shorter cultivar
laevigata	3ft × 1½ft	7–9	Creamy yellow, veined with reddish brown (E–M)	Mid-green, lanceolate	Clump-forming
lanata	2ft × 1½ft	4–9	Pale yellow to almost white with purple netting inside (E–M)	Matte gray-green, lanceolate, evergreen	Grecian foxglove, RHS Award
lutea	2–3ft × 1½ft	3–8	Creamy-yellow with small brown spots (E–M)	Dark green, glossy, lanceolate to oval	Clump-forming, self-sows, longer lived
×mertonensis	24–36in × 20in	3–8	Rosy-pink, spotted in shades of rose, pink, and white (E–M)	Dark green, velvety, hairy, oval to lanceolate	Strawberry foxglove, short-lived, true from seed, RHS Award
obscura	1–2ft × 1ft	4–8	Rusty-brown to orange-yellow with red veins and spotting (E–M)	Gray-green, lanceolate-oblong	Shrubby

Species and Cultivars	Height/ Spread	USDA Hardiness Zone	Flowers (bloom time)	Foliage	Comments
parviflora	2–3ft × 1½ft	4–8	Orange-brownish with purple-brown lip and violet veins (E–M)	Dark gray-green, oblong to lanceolate	Clumping, looks dingy from a distance
purpurea	3–4ft × 2ft	4–8	White, pink to purple with markings in the throat (E–M)	Gray-green, large, basal	Very adaptable, self-sows
p. 'Pam's Choice'	3–4ft × 2ft	4–8	White with maroon spots in throat	As above	

DISPORUM Convallariaceae

Disporum smithii is worth waiting for. It takes a long time, but the shiny dark green leaves eventually emerge on burgundy stems to form a tight shrublike clump. There it stands until it turns yellow in the fall. Terminal clusters of bell-shaped white flowers hang from the tip of the stems and appear in late spring; they are followed by fleshy orange-red fruit. *Disporum hookeri* is similar but less robust. Identifying features include shorter tepals that allow the stamens to be seen and the very narrow taper (hook) at the end of the leaf. These two Northwest natives are said to need moist soil, but I have found they will grow, albeit slowly, in drier soil; they surely need shade. *Disporum sessile* 'Variegatum' is the one that you may have to curb, as it runs quickly. ~ *Ann Bucher*

Scientific Name: From the Greek *di* ("two") and *spora* ("seed"); each ovary chamber contains two seeds.
Common Name: Fairy bells.
Origin: East and Southeast Asia, North America.
Preferred Conditions: Humus-rich, well-drained, moist soil.
Light: Part shade.
Management: Top-dress with leaf mold in summer. Root barriers may be necessary under certain conditions to prevent spreading. Clean up when dormant. Divide when they start spreading or become crowded.
Propagation: Division in fall or spring when dormant; sow fresh seed outdoors in summer; germination may take one or two years.
Pests and Diseases: Slugs, root weevils, fungal leaf spot.
Companions: Hosta, astilbe, ferns, trillium, astrantia, paris, *Helleborus orientalis*; *H. argutifolius* 'Janet Starnes' with *D. sessile* 'Variegatum'.
Notes: Look for new forms from China, Japan, and Korea from mail-order nurseries that specialize in woodland plants. For an evergreen version of the look of this genus, choose *Disporopsis pernyi*.

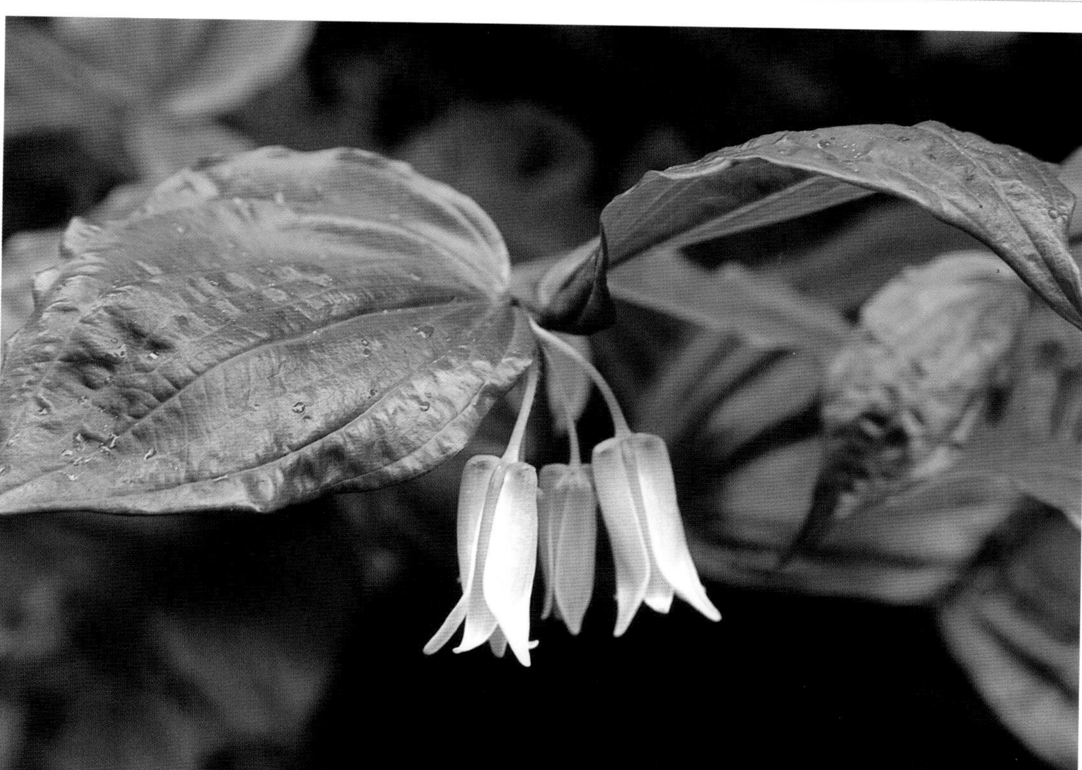

Disporum smithii.

Species and Cultivars	Height/ Spread	USDA Hardiness Zone	Flowers (bloom time)	Foliage	Comments
flavens	2–2½ft × 1½ft	4–9	Soft yellow, tubular, nodding (E)	Green, glossy, lanceolate	Clump-forming, rhizomatous, black berries in fall
hookeri	2–3ft × 2ft	4–9	Greenish cream, bell-shaped (E–M)	Green, glossy, ovate-lanceolate, cordate bases	Clump-forming, NW native, rhizomatous, orange-red berries
h. var. oreganum	3ft × 2ft	4–9	Creamy-white bells (E)	As above	NW native, orange-red berries in late summer
sessile 'Variegatum'	1–1½ft × 3ft+	4–9	Creamy-white with green tips, narrow bells (E)	Light green with bright white variegation, lanceolate	Rhizomatous, black berries in fall, can become rampant in light soil
smithii	1ft × 1ft	4–9	Greenish white to creamy-yellow, narrow bells (E–M)	Shiny dark green, lanceolate	NW native, bushy clumps, pale orange berries, rhizomatous, slow to increase

Dodecatheon dentatum.

DODECATHEON Primulaceae

We have several native shooting stars on the West Coast, and they are a delight and a surprise to find in the wild. They usually grow in open areas that are spring-damp and often very dry in summer, among smaller grasses and other perennials that do not completely swamp them. Use this as a guide for siting them in your garden. They go dormant by midsummer, so be sure to mark where they are. Dormancy can also be triggered by transplanting or almost any other stress—try to locate them in an area that gets little disturbance. The roots, which form a seastar shape, can be very close to the surface. All make good cut flowers, especially *D. meadia*, which has a relatively tall-flowering form. ~ *Bob Lilly*

Scientific Name: From the Greek *dodeka* ("twelve") and *thios* ("god"), implying that this was a powerful medicinal plant under the care of the twelve leading gods.
Common Name: Shooting star.

Species and Cultivars	Height/ Spread	USDA Hardiness Zone	Flowers (bloom time)	Foliage	Comments
dentatum	6in × 4–6in	2–9	White with purple anthers (E)	Pale to mid-green, jagged edge, dormant in summer	Washington, Oregon, and California native, spreads, RHS Award
hendersonii	6–12in × 3in	2–9	Violet with yellow and white bases (E)	Green, round, fleshy, dormant in summer	West Coast native, RHS Award
meadia	12in × 6in	2–9	Pale pink to white at base (E–M)	Mid-green, frequently red at base, dormant in summer	RHS Award
m. f. album	18in × 6in	2–9	Creamy-white with dark center (E)	As above	RHS Award

Origin: North America.
Preferred Conditions: Well-drained and humus-rich. Keep them damp in the spring and dry the rest of the year.
Light: Part shade to sun.
Planting: Best in spring, before dormancy breaks.
Management: Clean up when dormant.
Propagation: Sow seed when ripe in spring (slow from seed); division of multicrowned plants at planting time in spring.
Pests and Diseases: Rust. Watch for slugs and snails in very early spring and bait accordingly; they devour these little guys, eating the growth tip, which will damage the plant for the entire season.
Companions: Primula, epimedium, aquilegia, smaller ferns, jeffersonia, omphalodes.
Notes: Height shown in the chart is for the flower stem; foliage is all at the base.

DORONICUM Asteraceae

The garden forms of leopard's bane are spring ephemerals; they go dormant after flowering. They like heavy soil, and if happy will run about by short rhizomes that usually start with one small leaf, leading to the mistake of thinking they are seedlings. The flowers are borne on tall, straight stems even in shade, their favorite habitat. The golden daisies, with very thin ray petals, make a good cut flower. ~ *Bob Lilly*

Scientific Name: Obscure.
Common Name: Leopard's bane.
Origin: Southeastern Europe, Asia, Turkey.
Preferred Conditions: Fertile, humus-rich, moist, well-drained.
Light: Sun to part shade.

Doronicum orientale 'Magnificum' with *Narcissus* 'Pipit'.

Management: Plants go dormant by midsummer. May need to be cleaned up at this time. Deadhead after flowering to encourage a sporadic second flowering; this also helps the foliage to remain more attractive. Cut down flowering stems when they start to look bad. Soil moisture is important; they are tolerant of a somewhat drier soil in late summer, when they are dormant, but they must have moisture in spring and during flowering.
Propagation: Division in autumn; seed in spring.
Pests and Diseases: Leaf spot, root rot, powdery mildew. Doronicum is prone to early, often very severe damage by slugs and snails.
Companions: Spring bulbs, primula, brunnera, pulmonaria, hosta, viola, myosotis, dicentra, *Milium effusum* 'Aureum'.

Species and Cultivars	Height/ Spread	USDA Hardiness Zone	Flowers (bloom time)	Foliage	Comments
'Little Leo'	12–15in × 15in	5–9	Bright yellow, semi-double, daisy flowers (E–M)	Bright green	Compact and clumping
orientale (syn. caucasicum)	12–24in × 24in	5–9	Yellow, single, on stout stems (E)	Dark green, cordate with toothed and scalloped edges	Rhizomatous
o. 'Magnificum'	12–30in × 24in+	5–9	Bright yellow, single, larger daisy flowers (E)	Dark green, cordate	As above

DRACOCEPHALUM Lamiaceae

"May be invasive if site is too welcoming." Well, as someone who has grown *D. grandiflorum* in very dry conditions, edged by gravel, and had it invade mightily, I think the caution is too kind. *Watch out* for this one: it has the habit of a mint (same family) and territorial inclinations. The flowers are pretty enough, but the plant reeks. Stems are very lax and would benefit from pea sticks or other plants to lean against. So, let's see—we've got a stinky thug with floppy stems that is not easy to remove. I think not. ~ *Carrie Becker*

Scientific Name: From the Greek *drakon* ("dragon") and *kephale* ("head'), referring to the flower shape.
Common Name: Dragonhead.
Origin: Siberia, North Africa, North America, Europe.
Preferred Conditions: Well-drained, moderately fertile, moist. It is an understatement to say it may become invasive in these conditions.
Light: Sun to part shade.
Management: Yes, we do advise pinching early and border patrol. Cut down when dormant in autumn or sooner if messy.

Dracocephalum grandiflorum.

Propagation: Seed, basal cuttings in spring; careful division in spring or autumn.
Pests and Diseases: A trouble-free plant.
Companions: Alchemilla, aquilegia, filipendula.

Species and Cultivars	Height/ Spread	USDA Hardiness Zone	Flowers (bloom time)	Foliage	Comments
grandiflorum (syn. rupestre)	1–2ft × 2ft+	3–8	Large, dark violet-blue in whorls on spikes, hooded with darker spots on the lower lip (M)	A good strong green	Upright, clump-forming but also rhizomatous, may be invasive

Dracunculus vulgaris.

DRACUNCULUS Araceae

I have fond childhood memories of this peculiar plant. We had a big one in the side yard next to the house. When it bloomed I'd invite my friends to come over to see it, and particularly to smell it. The maroon "flowers" are huge, with a deep burgundy-black spadix in each one. The floral structure had an odor that made you think something had died nearby. As kids, we always thought it was carnivorous. ("Feed me, Seymour!") This very dramatic species has earned its place in our more "tropical" plantings. Especially fine planted as a "surprise" in the landscape, combined with other bold-foliaged companions. Be careful not to let it dry out in the summer, or it will die back early. ~ *Carrie Becker*

Scientific Name: From the Greek for "little dragon."
Common Name: Dragon arum, dragon plant.
Origin: Mediterranean.
Preferred Conditions: Humus-rich, well-drained, moist but dry in the summer.
Light: Sun. Tolerates shade but will take longer to reach blooming size.
Planting: Plant tubers six inches deep.
Management: Protect with a loose winter mulch. Separate tubers every few years, so they can gather enough strength to flower. The plant dissolves naturally post-bloom.
Propagation: Separate offsets and replant immediately in spring or autumn.
Pests and Diseases: Slugs, a bit.
Companions: Podophyllum, rodgersia, thalictrum, *Epipactis gigantea* 'Serpentine Night', a fan to blow the odor away!

Species and Cultivars	Height/ Spread	USDA Hardiness Zone	Flowers (bloom time)	Foliage	Comments
vulgaris	3–5ft × 2ft	8–10	Maroon-purple spathe (2–2½ft across), with erect near-black spadix (M)	Dark green, fan-shaped, marked purple-brown on mottled stems, new shoots are pale green with purple spots	May develop heavy heads of scarlet fruit, a bit tender

Echinacea purpurea 'Magnus'.

ECHINACEA Asteraceae

There are only about five species of perennials in the genus *Echinacea*, and all share common characteristics (summed up by such adjectives as "sharp," "stiff," "rough," "dry," "tough," "bold," even "harsh-textured"), which indicates these plants are not for the unforgiving gardener. Most species are native to the prairies of central Canada and the midwestern United States. They all have recognizable cone-shaped flower heads, with ray florets in various colors—pinks, purples, crimson-red, dark red, and creamy-white. In the perennial border, their erect, coarse stems are a good contrast to soft, floppy plants.

Echinaceas are much valued as a cut flower. The central cone (disk) is also used in fresh and dried arrangements and can be left standing over winter for the birds. The dried root is used in modern herbal medicines, skin creams, and shampoos.

Coneflowers grow best in lots of heat and without competition from close neighboring plants. They are short-lived even in the best conditions and worth replacing shortly after the funeral.
~ *Susan Buckles*

Scientific Name: From the Greek *echinos* ("hedgehog"), referring to the prickly "cones."
Common Name: Purple coneflower, coneflower.
Origin: North America.
Preferred Conditions: Well-drained, average, loamy soil with steady moisture. They are tolerant of poorer soil and somewhat drought tolerant once established. Spring-moist, summer-dry.
Light: Sun.

Management: Cut back stems to base as blooms fade to encourage further flower production, or leave seedheads on for winter interest. They will occasionally self-sow. Divide every three to five years.

Propagation: Division in spring or fall; root cuttings; seed as soon as ripe (stratification is required).

Pests and Diseases: Mildew, leaf miner. Watch out for snails and slugs, especially as new growth emerges.

Companions: Phlox, geranium, grasses, solidago, monarda, achillea, hemerocallis, delphinium, echinops, coreopsis and other prairie flowers.

Notes: Some have purple stems; choose the best ones when shopping. Echinaceas generally like hot, full-sun situations in the Pacific Northwest; in particular, *E. paradoxa* and its cultivars (the newer orange ones) need heat to flower. Watch for new color forms (orange, gold, yellow) bred in the Midwest by the Chicago Botanic Garden and others, although their paradoxa blood may make them less hardy for us.

Species and Cultivars	Height/ Spread	USDA Hardiness Zone	Flowers (bloom time)	Foliage	Comments
angustifolia	1–2ft × 1ft	3–8	Rose, purplish pink, and sometimes white, with orange-brown central cone, ray petals very narrow (E–M)	Narrow, dark green, lanceolate, hairy	Long-blooming, drought tolerant, used in herbal medicine
pallida	3–5ft × 1ft	3–8	Creamy-white, pink, or pale purple, orange-brown central cone (M–L)	Dark green, lanceolate, coarse	Taller plants are weak-stemmed, may flop and need support
paradoxa	2–4ft × 1ft	3–8	Golden yellow with dark brown cone, ray petals very narrow (E–M)	Dark green, narrow, lanceolate	Needs maximum heat
purpurea	2–5ft × 1½ft	3–9	Purplish rose-pink drooping rays with bronze-brown cone (M–L)	Dark green, lanceolate, coarse, red-tinted stems	Long bloomer, drought and heat tolerant, gardenworthy group
p. 'Bravado'	2–3ft × 1½ft	3–9	Big, rosy-pink, brown cone (M–L)	As above	Large flower
p. 'Bright Star'	2–3ft × 1½ft	3–9	Bright rose-pink, maroon cone (M–L)	As above	
p. 'Green Edge'	3ft × 1½ft	3–9	White with green tips, petals are horizontal (M)	Dark green, lanceolate	
p. 'Kim's Knee High'	1–2ft × 1ft	3–9	Bright pink, bronze-brown cone (M–L)	Leathery, green	A nice compact plant
p. 'Magnus'	2½–4ft × 1½ft	3–9	Purplish pink, horizontal petals, dark orange cone (M–L)	Heavy, dark green	1998 PPA Award, RHS Award
p. 'White Swan'	2–4ft × 1½ft	3–9	Creamy-white, lime-green cone turns orange-brown, fragrant (M–L)	Mid-green	Honey-scented, a little less perennial

ECHINOPS Asteraceae

Echinops ritro.

Globe thistles make wonderful background plants for more dramatic and attractive neighbors. Their finely cut foliage and globular heads of blue or white flowers blend nicely into the whole. All they ask for is sun and good drainage—poor soil is a plus. *Echinops ritro* self-sows for me, which is appropriate to its supportive role. It can find spots I never could. *Echinops ritro* subsp. *ruthenicus* might be a better choice, as it's not disfigured by spittlebugs like *E. ritro* is.

Echinops is good as a dried flower if cut right before the florets begin to open—good as a fresh cut at any time. As with all members of the daisy family, this plant is the "bee's knees" to bees. ~ *Ann Bucher*

Scientific Name: From the Greek *echinos* ("hedgehog") and *ops* ("like").
Common Name: Globe thistle.
Origin: Europe, India.
Preferred Conditions: Well-drained, poor to average soil. Drought tolerant once established.
Light: Sun to part shade.
Management: The first flowers on young plants should be cut for the vase, as the plant may not be strong enough to support the flower stalk. Established plants are hard to move, so start with new ones. Staking is not usually needed except for some of the taller species. Post-flowering foliage is often ratty-looking, so cut back once the flowers begin to fade. If mildew is a problem after flowering, cut to the ground.
Propagation: Division in spring or fall; root cuttings; easy from seed in spring; dig out and transplant offsets that form at the base of older plants.
Pests and Diseases: Mildew, aphids, spittlebugs.
Companions: Rudbeckia, helenium, hemerocallis, campanula, echinacea, monarda, smaller miscanthus, phlox, allium, nepeta, santolina, perovskia.

Species and Cultivars	Height/ Spread	USDA Hardiness Zone	Flowers (bloom time)	Foliage	Comments
bannaticus	4–6ft × 1½–2ft	4–9	Large (1–2in), gray-blue, with thick, woolly gray stems (M–L)	Gray-green, hairy	Clump-forming, doesn't flop, reblooms if cut back
b. 'Blue Globe' (syn. 'Blue Glow')	2–4ft × 1½ft	4–9	Large (2½in), dark blue (M)	Grayish green	Reblooms if cut back
b. 'Taplow Blue'	2–4ft × 1–2ft	4–9	Large (2–3in), steel-blue with silvery cast (M)	Grayish green, divided	Vigorous, RHS Award
exaltatus	4–6ft × 2ft	3–8	Large (2in), steel-blue with white woolly stems (M)	Gray-green, whitish and hairy beneath, coarse, prickly, deeply cut	Russian globe thistle, vigorous, clump-forming

Species and Cultivars	Height/ Spread	USDA Hardiness Zone	Flowers (bloom time)	Foliage	Comments
ritro	24–60in × 20in	4–9	Large (1½in), steel-blue, maturing to a lighter blue with white woolly stems (M–L)	Grayish green, silvery beneath, stiff and leathery	Long-lasting, compact, spittlebugs a problem, RHS Award
r. subsp. ruthenicus	36–52in × 20in	4–9	Large (2½in), bright steel-blue on gray stems (M)	Shiny, dark green, jagged, narowly divided	Spittlebugs not a problem, RHS Award
r. 'Veitch's Blue'	2–4ft × 2ft	4–9	Large (1½in), dark blue in bud, light steel-blue when open (M)	Gray-green	
sphaerocephalus	4–8ft × 1–2ft	4–9	Large (1½–2½in), gray-white to gray-blue (M)	Gray-green, hairy beneath	Great globe thistle, vigorous, clump-forming
s. 'Arctic Glow'	2–4ft × 1–2ft	4–9	Large (1½in), silvery-white (M)	As above	White globe thistle

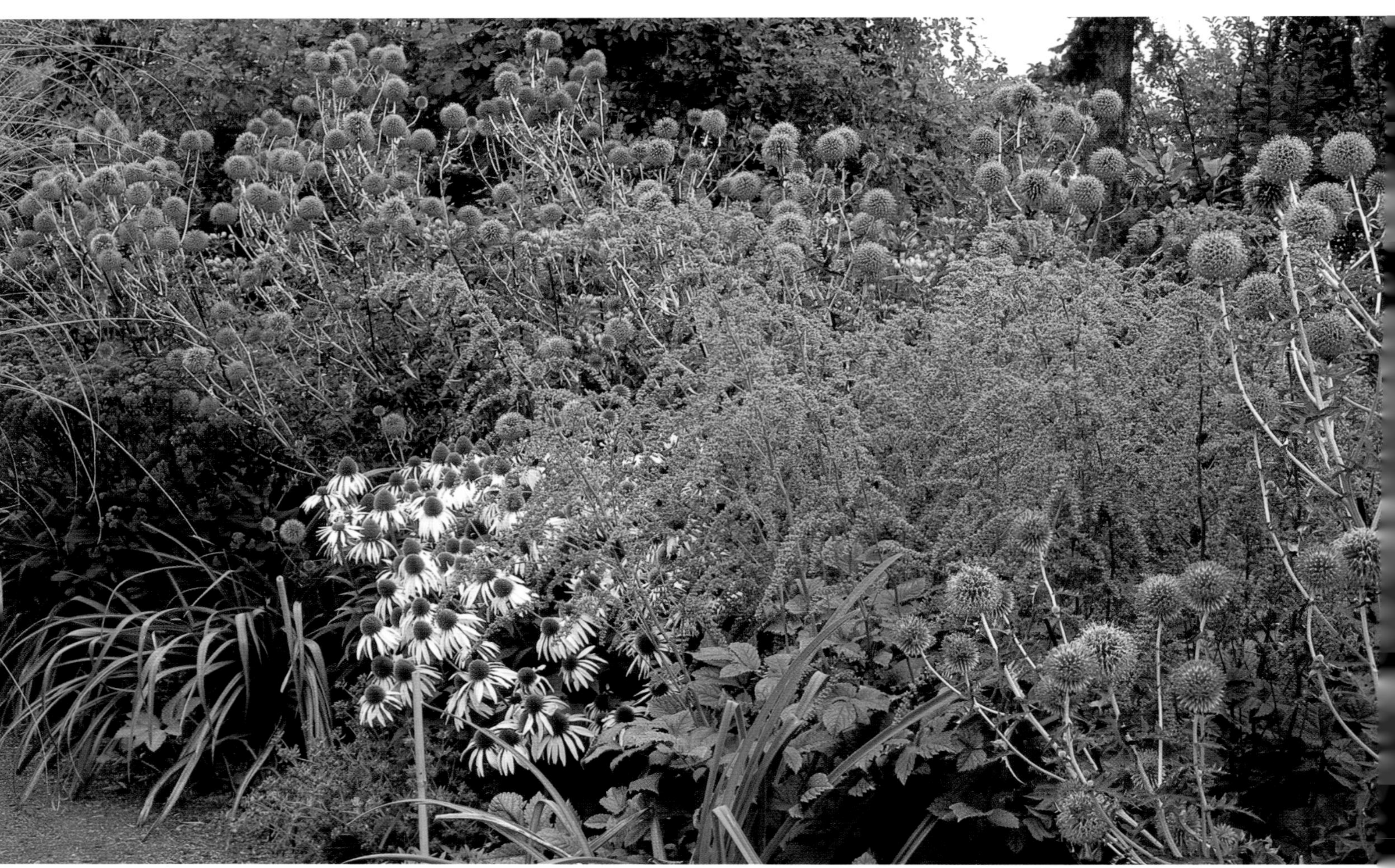

Echinops ritro subsp. *ruthenicus* with *Sedum telephium* subsp. *maximum* 'Atropurpureum', *Astilbe* 'Professor van der Wielen' seedheads, and *Echinacea purpurea* 'White Swan'.

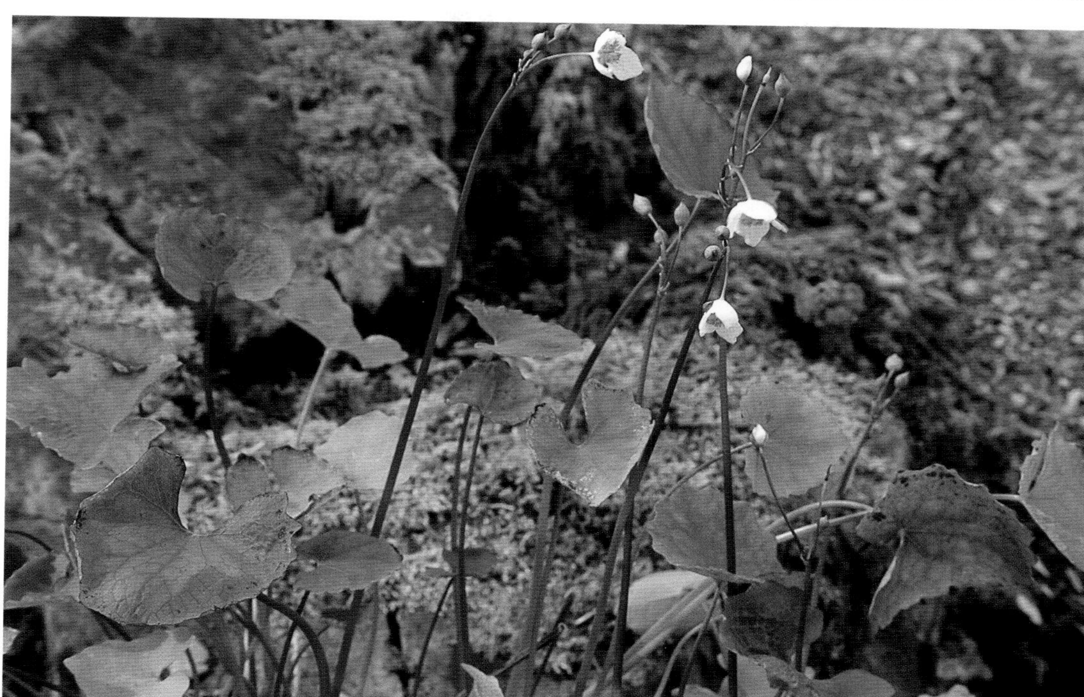

Eomecon chionantha.

EOMECON Papaveraceae

Another poppy family member, the genus *Eomecon* has only one species, *E. chionantha.* Rarely found in nurseries, it is usually at the smaller plant sales or traded among friends. When it finds a spot it likes, it can be quite aggressive. Even so, it is not hard to control, and it can be perfect for that contained yet impossible site. Isn't it curious that there are so many poppy relatives that do well in shade: meconopsis, chelidonium, stylophorum—and eomecon, which stands out with its small, white, nodding flowers? ~ *Bob Lilly*

Scientific Name: From the Greek *mecon* ("poppy").
Common Name: Snow poppy.
Origin: China.
Preferred Conditions: Humus-rich, moist, well-drained. Dislikes drought or cold and heavy soil.
Light: Part shade.
Management: Will appreciate an annual mulch of leaf mold. Cut back foliage when it becomes poor-looking, probably early autumn. It may be necessary to keep under control by constantly digging around it (spade pruning) and removing runners. It does wander but is not a pest.
Propagation: Divide and separate rooted runners in spring.
Pests and Diseases: Watch for slugs and snails at all times of the year.
Companions: Ferns, hosta, dicentra, brunnera, mertensia, pulmonaria.
Notes: "Where nothing else will grow, and no one can escape."

Species and Cultivars	Height/ Spread	USDA Hardiness Zone	Flowers (bloom time)	Foliage	Comments
chionantha	1ft × 2ft+	7–9	Glistening white, nodding, with yellow-gold stamens (E–M)	Large, dull gray-green, cordate, leathery, slightly crinkle-edged and veined	Vigorous, orange-red sap

Epilobium angustifolium var. *album*.

EPILOBIUM Onagraceae

Fireweed is a pest! It has a deep root and runs in almost any soil. Willow herb, the English common name, sounds so much better; in northern England and Scotland the species is shorter, and the flowers seem closer together. *Epilobium angustifolium* var. *album* is a pure white form, with new growth a clear light green. For best effect let it run about in a section of the border with other summer perennials to hold its stems up (or use pea sticks if your clump is dense enough); it does not appear to set viable seed. ~ *Bob Lilly*

Scientific Name: From the Greek *epi* ("upon") and *lobos* ("pod").
Common Name: Fireweed, willow herb.
Origin: Northern Europe, North America, Asia, Japan.
Preferred Conditions: Well-drained, humus-rich—any reasonable soil that is not too dry.
Light: Sun to part shade.
Management: Deadhead after flowering to reduce self-seeding and encourage some repeat bloom. Clean up in fall dormancy. Can be an elusive wanderer and really doesn't need fertilizer. For best results, don't cut back in the first three years.
Propagation: Divide in autumn or spring; cuttings from basal side shoots in spring; or sow seed in containers in cold frames.
Pests and Diseases: Mildew, rust, snails. Watch for slugs when plants first emerge in the spring—but how can a pest have a pest?
Companions: *Helleborus foetidus*, smilacina, ferns, acanthus, *Aruncus dioicus*; at the edge of a wood or shrub border.
Notes: *Epilobium angustifolium* has been known to throw slight color variations in the wild; some named clones of it have been sighted, but they will be just as vigorous. In the chart, the symbol ∞ = infinite spread.

Species and Cultivars	Height/ Spread	USDA Hardiness Zone	Flowers (bloom time)	Foliage	Comments
angustifolium	5–6ft × ∞	2–9	Rose-pink (M–L)	Narrow, dark green, undersides gray-green	Invasive
a. var. album (syn. leucanthum)	4–5ft × ∞	2–9	White, saucer-shaped with silky seedheads (M–L)	Very narrow, pale green	Less invasive but can still be a nuisance

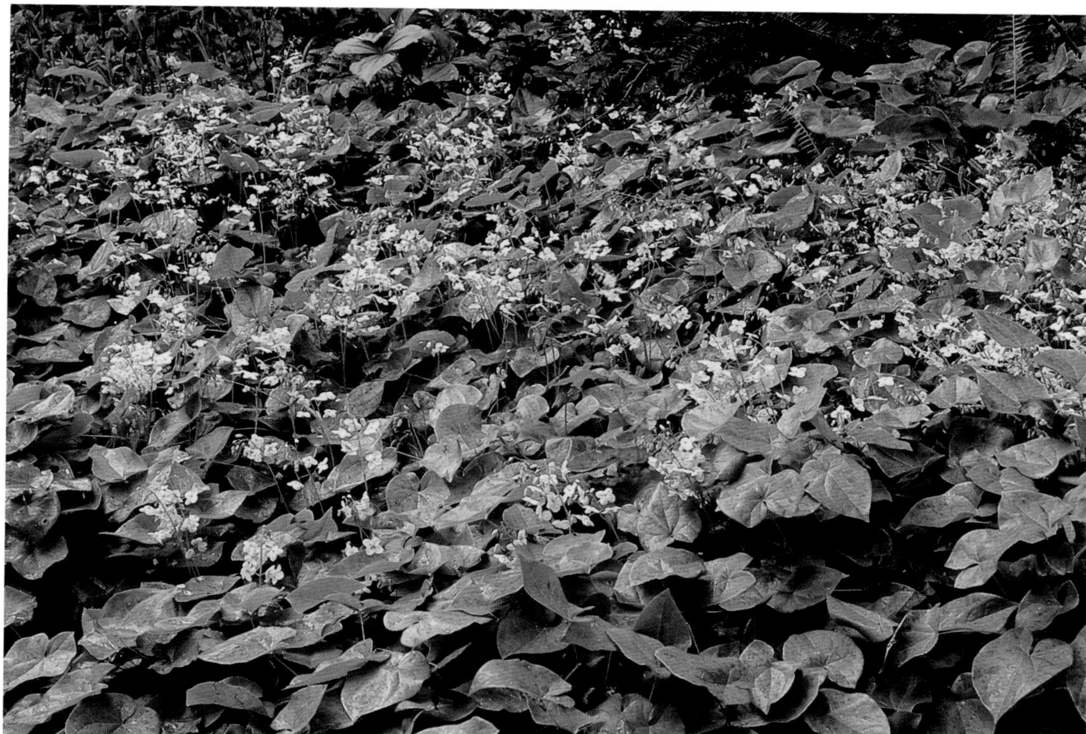

Epimedium perralderianum.

EPIMEDIUM Berberidaceae

An underused and underappreciated genus of wonderful woodland plants. Epimediums are among the best plants for dry shade. Their foliage is variable in size, from less than one inch to up to ten inches long. The new growth often has beautiful tints, variously edged and mottled with maroon, and many forms have equally lovely leaves in fall and winter. Flowers too are variable in color, ranging from white, light yellow, and bright yellow to reddish orange and rosy purple; they are borne in spring on tender stems. Most are held facing downward; often they have prominent spurs. Several plants are evergreen, but all receive the same treatment from us: once they are established, their leaves are removed to the ground in winter before the flower stems rise anew. Their stems become wiry over the course of a year, but the new stems are easily broken; so—in order to see the flowers, which are often hidden in the old foliage, and to enjoy the beautiful new leaves as they emerge—we trim back the old foliage in winter.

Epimediums begin to bloom when the narcissus are blooming, making lovely color combinations possible: *Narcissus* 'Pipit' with any pale yellow–flowering epimedium; *N.* 'Waterperry' with *E.* ×*warleyense*; *N.* 'Thalia' and *E.* ×*youngianum* 'Niveum' are just a few examples. ~ *Carrie Becker*

Scientific Name: From the Greek *epi* ("upon") and *media*, the country of the Medes.
Common Name: Bishop's hat, barrenwort, bishop's mitre, fairy wings.
Origin: Southeastern Europe, Asia Minor, East Asia, Algeria.
Preferred Conditions: Well-drained, moderately moist, humus-rich. Some will tolerate dry shade and competition from tree roots. Most will flourish under more moist conditions.
Light: Sun to shade.
Management: This is a low-maintenance plant. Remember to trim back foliage in winter, before the new flower stems appear. Give plants an annual top dressing of leaf mold or other organic material (no deeper than two inches). Many are slow to establish; for best results leave all varieties alone for the first two years, then begin the winter cutback for flower show.

Propagation: Division in early spring as new growth begins, or in autumn. Division is easiest if clumps are washed first so you can see the roots. The older the clump, the harder to divide.

Pests and Diseases: Slugs, snails, aphids. Root weevils can be a big problem.

Companions: *Anemone blanda*, narcissus, muscari, hyacinthoides, arisarum, hosta, astilbe, ferns, pulmonaria, brunnera, helleborus, primula; under trees and shrubs.

Notes: Plant *E.* ×*youngianum* and cultivars where you want clumping rather than spreading plants. The flowers and the leaves are a good choice for arrangements. There are many wonderful species and cultivars, but those available at retail seem to be dwindling—try mail order. The parents of *E.* ×*perralchicum* are *E. perralderianum* and *E. pinnatum* subsp. *colchicum*, and this is important to know because these are often confused in the trade.

Species and Cultivars	Height/ Spread	USDA Hardiness Zone	Flowers (bloom time)	Foliage	Comments
acuminatum	12in × 18in	5–9	Large, rosy-purple and white, long spurs, arching sprays (E–M)	Marbled reddish brown when young aging to green, glossy, spiny margins, leathery, ovate to lanceolate	Evergreen, variable in the wild
alpinum	6–12in × 12in	5–9	Small, creamy yellow with red sepals (E)	Green turning reddish in fall, spiny margins, cordate	Alpine barrenwort, herbaceous, tolerant of dry soil
brachyrrhizum	8–12in × 12in	5–8	Rose-pink (E)	Pink to rose-purple when young, ages to dark green, leathery	Evergreen
×cantabrigiense	8–18in × 24in	5–9	Small, light yellow with reddish edges, spurless (E)	Mid-green with ovate leaflets, leathery, good autumn tones	Evergreen, vigorous, tolerant of dry soil
davidii	12–20in × 18in+	5–9	Yellow or yellow and purplish red, spurred (E–M)	Coppery when young, aging to green, ovate to ovate-lanceolate, glossy, jagged-edged	Evergreen, long-blooming
'Enchantress'	16in × 12in	5–9	Small, pale lilac-pink, long spurs, floriferous (E)	Dark green, glossy	Evergreen, vigorous
epsteinii	6–10in × 12in+	5–9	White with reddish purple spurs, floriferous (E)	Green, glossy	As above
franchetii	8–24in × 18in+	6–9	Light yellow with pale yellow or greenish inner petals, long spurs (E–M)	Long green pointed leaflets, coppery in spring	Evergreen
grandiflorum (syn. macranthum)	8–15in × 12in	5–9	Large, crimson and white or pink and white, pendent, long spurs (E)	Bronze-tinted when young aging to green, ovate-cordate, prominent veins	Herbaceous, good autumn color, RHS Award
g. 'Album'	6–12in × 12in	5–9	Large, white, long spurs (E)	Bright green, dark edges, on wiry stems	Herbaceous, smaller plant
g. 'Lilafee'	8–12in × 12in	5–9	Large, violet-purple, long spurs (E)	Tinted purplish bronze when young aging to green	Floriferous, vigorous, herbaceous

Species and Cultivars	Height/ Spread	USDA Hardiness Zone	Flowers (bloom time)	Foliage	Comments
g. 'Nanum'	6–10in × 12in	5–9	White (E)	Green, edged with red	Dwarf, herbaceous, RHS Award
g. 'Rose Queen'	12–15in × 12in	5–9	Large, deep rose-pink, white-tipped spurs (E)	Reddish in spring, dark bronze in fall, small	Herbaceous, RHS Award
g. f. violaceum	7–10in × 12in	5–9	Large rosy-pink with white tips (E)	Light reddish with purple tints in spring, aging to green	Herbaceous
g. 'White Queen'	8–15in × 12in	5–9	Large, white (E)	Small, reddish in spring aging to dark green	Herbaceous, RHS Award
×perralchicum	12–18in × 18in+	5–9	Large, bright yellow, pendent, short spurs (E)	Large, bronze in spring aging to green, glossy, toothed, leathery, rounded	Evergreen, runs over time, vigorous, best in full sun, tolerant of dry soil, RHS Award
×p. 'Frohnleiten'	8–16in × 18in+	5–9	Bright yellow, pendent, short spurs (E)	Reddish tints in spring and fall, aging to dark green, shiny, toothed, veined, leathery	Evergreen, tolerant of dry soil, vigorous, spreads
perralderianum	12–15in × 24in	5–9	Tiny, bright yellow, flattish, brown spurs (E)	Bronze in spring marbled with light green, aging to dark green, glossy, toothed, cordate-ovate	Evergreen, tolerant of dry soil, vigorous
pinnatum	8–15in × 18in	4–9	Bright yellow with brownish purple spurs (E–M)	Dark green, bronze margins in spring, oval-cordate, leathery	As above
p. subsp. colchicum	10–18in × 18in	5–9	Large, bright yellow, brown or yellowish spurs (E)	Deep green, rounded leaflets, glossy, burgundy tints in fall and winter	As above, RHS Award
p. subsp. colchicum 'Black Sea'	10–18in × 18in	5–9	Small, bronzy-yellow (E)	Blue-green, red stems, purple tints in fall	Evergreen, tolerant of dry soil
pubigerum	18in × 12in	5–9	Tiny, creamy white, pink or yellow, tall sprays above the leaves (E)	Soft green, ovate-rounded, leathery, glossy	As above
×rubrum	9–12in × 12in	4–9	Small, crimson and creamy-white (E)	Bronze-red when young aging to green, bronze in fall, spiny edges, cordate	Semi-evergreen, tolerates dry soil, floriferous, clump-forming, RHS Award
×versicolor	12–16in × 18in	5–9	Pale yellow and pink with red-tinted spurs (E)	Coppery-red and brown aging to mid-green, cordate, toothed	Evergreen to semi-evergreen, slow spreader
×v. 'Neosulphureum'	8–12in × 12in	5–9	Soft yellow clusters, short spurs (E)	Emerge bronze, age to green	Evergreen, clump-forming
×v. 'Sulphureum'	10–16in × 16in+	5–9	Pale sulphur-yellow with yellow and white spurs (E)	Mid-green, speckled red and brown, cordate, leathery, great fall color	Evergreen, vigorous, spreads, RHS Award
×v. 'Versicolor'	12–14in × 16in+	5–9	Small, yellow with deep reddish pink sepals (E)	Coppery-red in spring, aging to green, coppery-red in fall	Semi-evergreen, tolerant of dry soil, spreads

Species and Cultivars	Height/ Spread	USDA Hardiness Zone	Flowers (bloom time)	Foliage	Comments
×warleyense	12–20in × 18in+	5–9	Small, reddish orange inner sepals, bright yellow petals with brown tips (E)	Tinted red in spring and fall, ages to light green, ovate-cordate, toothed	Evergreen, tolerant of dry soil, spreads
×w. 'Orangekönigin'	18–20in × 18in+	5–9	Light orange (E)	Bright green, tinted red in fall, ovate-cordate	Evergreen, slow to establish, clump-forming
×youngianum	8–12in × 12–14in	5–9	Small, white, nodding, spurred or spurless (E)	Marked red in spring aging to green, deep red in fall, toothed	Herbaceous, one of the last to bloom, clump-forming
×y. 'Niveum'	6–12in × 12–14in	5–9	Small, white, sometimes spurred (E)	Small, pale brownish fading to light green, toothed, reddish tints in fall	Herbaceous, clump-forming, slow-growing, RHS Award
×y. 'Roseum' (syn. 'Lilacinum')	6–12in × 12in+	4–9	Rose-pink tinted shades of purple (E)	Variable, red in spring, ages to green then red in fall, often mottled burgundy, cordate	Herbaceous, slow-growing

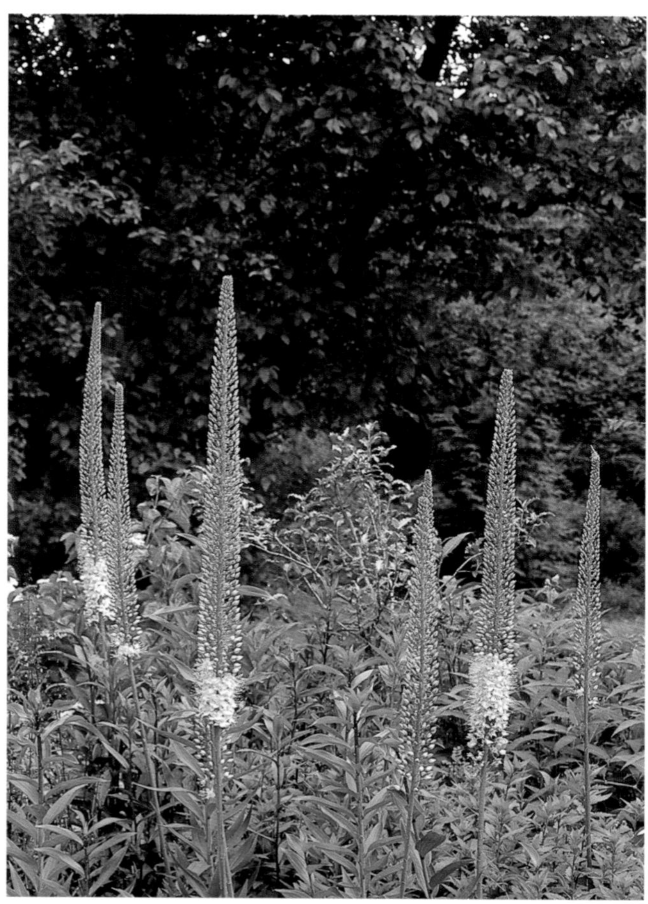

Eremurus ×isabellinus 'Cleopatra'.

EREMURUS Asphodelaceae

Foxtail lilies have an interesting character right from the beginning. Often listed as bulbs, these perennials form a starfish-shaped crown of long, fleshy roots. Drainage is critical, and they like a summer bake. Give them your warmest site for the best performance. Well-grown plants can exceed six feet in height. Just imagine a group of eight or so *E. ×isabellinus* 'Cleopatra', towering stems with the upper third in coppery orange flowers that collectively resemble a bushed-out foxtail. Plant in front of shrubs with maroon- to copper-colored foliage for a beautiful combination. If you can bear to cut them, they make good cut flowers. ~ *Carrie Becker*

Scientific Name: From the Greek *eremia* ("desert") and *oura* ("tail").

Common Name: Foxtail lily, desert candle.

Origin: West and Central Asia.

Preferred Conditions: Well-drained, fertile, sandy. Moist during the growing season, but dry during dormancy. Doesn't like winter-wet. Shelter from wind (stems are stronger in the wild, where they grow in lean soils in the open).

Light: Sun.

Planting: Usually planted in the fall. Be sure not to plant them too deep or where foot traffic might compromise their brittle roots. Don't plant too close together; the roots become quite extensive, and competition can shade the foliage, in which case your eremurus will decline rapidly and go away. Don't let the roots dry out when transplanting.

Management: Remove dead leaves as they die back in summer. Taller ones may need staking. Crowns and fleshy roots are easily damaged, so noting their location before dormancy would be a good idea. New young growth can be damaged by a late frost, so protect with a mulch and remove when frost danger is past. Cut back flower stem if you like. The old stems are pretty interesting and could be left until they're not.

Propagation: Seed—sow fresh right after harvest (slow to germinate); division of established clumps in midsummer after blooming; it's best to buy new crowns.

Pests and Diseases: Slugs in early spring.

Companions: Verbascum, kniphofia, euphorbia, miscanthus, 'Goldflame' spiraea, *Crambe cordifolia, Cotinus coggygria* 'Royal Purple'; good at the back of the border, where they can appear above or in between other plants and then die back into obscurity.

Notes: The spread given in the chart is the width of the crown of basal foliage, which dies back by midsummer.

Species and Cultivars	Height/ Spread	USDA Hardiness Zone	Flowers (bloom time)	Foliage	Comments
himalaicus	3–6ft × 3ft	5–9	White (M)	Green, straplike	Elegant
×isabellinus 'Cleopatra'	4–6ft × 4ft	5–9	Deep burnt-orange (M)	As above	Striking color
×i. Ruiter Hybrids	4–6ft × 4ft	5–9	Mixed pastels and bright yellow, orange, and white (M)	As above	Usually mixed colors
robustus	8–10ft × 4ft	5–9	Pink (M)	Long, broad, coarse, with rough edges	Very large form, RHS Award
stenophyllus	3–5ft × 4ft	5–9	Dark yellow fading to orange-brown (M)	Narrow, gray-green, straplike	RHS Award
s. subsp. stenophyllus (syn. bungei)	3–6ft × 3ft	5–9	Deep yellow (M)	As above	Compact, doesn't resent having dormant crowns shaded as long as not damp

ERIGERON Asteraceae

Fleabanes must work—there are no fleas nearby. Nor have I seen leopards. Generally short-lived but such good performers you can just accept replanting them from time to time. They are easy to grow and very long-blooming, especially if deadheaded regularly. Variable habits among the species mean that you can have taller, large-flowering plants in mixed herbaceous borders, some that bloom for months, or you can grow the diminutive forms. One of the best of these is *E. karvinskianus*, which self-sows if happy (well-drained soil, sun, some winter protection) and blooms from late spring until late fall. The individual flowers on this plant are less than one inch across, opening white and gradually changing to deep pink, with all colors present on the plant at the same time. It is wonderful in paving or trailing out of containers, and also works well as a rockery plant—plant it at the top, and over time it will seed into the wall and cascade down the face to the ground. ~ *Carrie Becker*

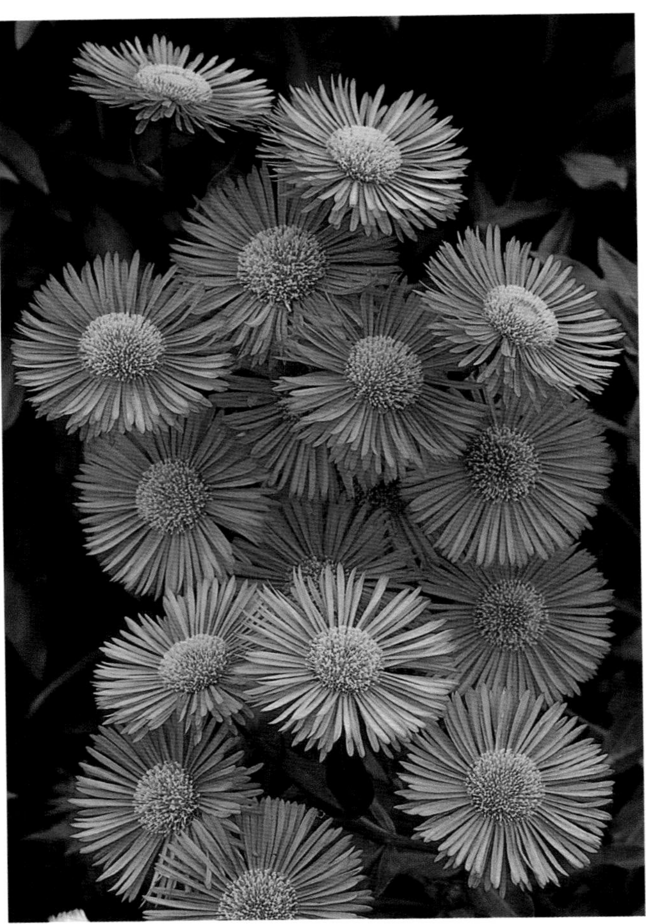

Erigeron 'Prosperity'.

Scientific Name: From the Greek *eri* ("early") and *geron* ("old man").

Common Name: Fleabane.

Origin: North and South America, eastern Europe.

Preferred Conditions: Any well-drained, fertile soil. Takes average moisture but tolerates drought.

Light: Sun.

Management: The taller ones may need staking, especially if grown in fertile soil. Deadhead for repeat bloom. Cut back large-flowering forms after blooming to basal leaves. *Erigeron karvinskianus* can be cut back by half in spring if too leggy. Divide every two or three years or when the middle part of the plant wears out. Trim to control, and clean up in the fall.

Propagation: Seed is best; root basal cuttings February through May; division in spring.

Pests and Diseases: Powdery mildew, aphids, rust, leaf spot, slugs.

Companions: Lavandula, coreopsis, iris, rudbeckia, stachys, *Anaphalis triplinervis*, heuchera, oenothera, phlox, smaller grasses, eryngium, sedum, artemisia, kniphofia.

Notes: Full sun is best in the maritime Northwest. Butterflies love the flowers. Some make a good cut flower if picked when fully open.

Species and Cultivars	Height/ Spread	USDA Hardiness Zone	Flowers (bloom time)	Foliage	Comments
aurantiacus	10–15in × 12in	6–8	Bright orange, semi-double (M)	Velvety, green, spoon-shaped, on thick stems	Clump-forming, not reliably winter hardy
'Dunkelste Aller' (syn. 'Darkest of All')	18–24in × 12in	5–8	Deep violet-blue with yellow center, semi-double (M)	Gray-green, lanceolate, hairy	Short-lived, RHS Award
glaucus	12–18in × 12in	5–8	Lavender-pink to pink (M–L)	Blue-green	Semi-evergreen
karvinskianus (syn. 'Profusion')	6–8in × 8in	8–10	Small, daisylike, opens white and ages to pink-purple, with a yellow center (E–L)	Dark green, lanceolate, on trailing stems	Very airy, not reliably winter hardy, self-sows in warmer climates, RHS Award
'Prosperity'	12–24in × 12in	5–8	Lavender-blue, yellow center, single to semi-double (M)	Lanceolate	Erect, clump-forming
'Rosa Juwel' (syn. 'Pink Jewel')	12–30in × 12in	5–8	Bright to pale pink, yellow center, semi-double (M–L)	As above	

Eryngium alpinum.

ERYNGIUM Apiaceae

There is nothing like an eryngium for that bold, exotic look. Hard to believe these teasel-like flower heads belong to the carrot family! The seeds all have little barbs on them—Miss Willmott must have worn leather gloves, or had bloody fingers (it is actually best to let *E. giganteum* seed about). Some like heavy soil; all do best with the soil a bit lean and not too much competition from aggressive neighbors. Most have a crown of large basal leaves that need to get a good day of sun; the strong stems that come up from the crown rarely need staking. Flower heads are cone-shaped and made up of very small florets that bloom from the base upward; they are loved by bees and butterflies. These heads usually have prominent bracts, which are sharp and spiny, or even soft. All dry well; *E. giganteum* in particular dries to a ghostly almost-white. For beautifully marked foliage, look for *E. variifolium* and *E. bourgatii*. ~ *Bob Lilly*

Scientific Name: From the Greek for a thistle with spiny-toothed leaves.
Common Name: Sea holly, eryngo.
Origin: West and Central Asia, Mediterranean, Europe, North and South America.
Preferred Conditions / Light: Most will adapt to a wide range of conditions from fertile, average soil to some really dreadful conditions. All bloom best in sun but tolerate part shade.
Group 1. Blue or white flowers. Likes dry, well-drained, poor to moderately fertile soil in sun. No winter wet.
Group 2. Tends to have green flowers. Likes moist, well-drained, more fertile soil in sun. Cool nights produce the best color.
Management: Has deep taproots and does not like to be disturbed. Will benefit from a gravel or crushed rock mulch around the crown, out to about six inches and two inches deep; this will keep winter-wet off the crowns, a situation that we have found kills the broader-leaved forms (*E. agavifolium*, *E. yuccifolium*). If grown in overly rich soil or with too much fertilizer, some of the larger species can flop and may need staking. Cut back when no longer attractive to you, or by spring at the latest.

Eryngium ×*tripartitum* and *Penstemon heterophyllus* 'Catherine de la Mare' share a border with *Alcea rosea*, a good red hemerocallis, Asiatic and Oriental lilies in bud and bloom, and 'Japanese Bishop' dahlia.

Propagation: Seed when ripe in late summer but can be a challenge to germinate; root cuttings in late winter; division in spring—remove the pups that form at the base.

Pests and Diseases: Powdery mildew, root rot. Watch for slugs and snails in early spring.

Companions: Ornamental grasses, late alliums, helenium, artemisia, echinacea, brodiaea, anthemis, achillea, *Alchemilla mollis*, hardy fuchsias, *Phlox paniculata*, aster, galtonia; the summer border.

Notes: These are long-lasting blooms and eventually dried flower heads in the garden. With their strong stems, they can even be left up for winter interest. Great for drying—pick before all the florets are finished opening and hang them to dry. Also good for fresh cut arrangements. The spread in chart is the width of the basal foliage; leaves are basal unless otherwise noted.

Species and Cultivars	Height/ Spread	USDA Hardiness Zone	Flowers (bloom time)	Foliage	Comments
agavifolium (syn. bromeliifolium)	3–5ft × 2ft	5–8	Greenish white, thimble-shaped, small bracts (M)	Broad, sword-shaped, rich green, glossy, sharp-toothed	Group 2, evergreen
alpinum	1½–2½ft × 1½ft	5–8	Emerge white, aging to steel-blue, then to tan, blue bracts (M–L)	Oval to heart-shaped, mid-green with upper leaves tinged blue, glossy	Group 1, blue stems, RHS Award
a. 'Blue Star'	1½–2½ft × 1½ft	5–8	Deep metallic blue (M)	As above	Group 1
a. 'Slieve Donard'	1½–2½ft × 1½ft	5–8	Large, deep blue, with soft bracts (M)	As above	Group 1
a. 'Superbum'	2½ft × 1½ft	5–8	Large, intense steel-blue with soft, spiny bracts (M)	As above	Group 1
amethystinum	1½–2½ft × 1½ft	5–8	Small, amethyst-blue with long, steel-blue bracts (M–L)	Green, upper leaves blue, leathery, narrow and divided	Group 1, best in a hot summer garden
bourgatii	1½–2ft × 1½ft	5–8	Spiny, blue-green with steel-blue bracts (M)	Gray-green with white veins, prickly and deeply cut	Group 1, hot sun, evergreen, clumping
eburneum (syn. paniculatum)	3–5ft × 2ft	5–8	Tiny, green with white stamens, whitish green bracts (M)	Mid-green, arching, grassy, with thin spines, sword-shaped	Group 2, evergreen, clumping
giganteum (syn. 'Miss Willmott's Ghost')	2–4ft × 1ft	5–8	Silvery-gray, bluish tint when young, with silver bracts (M–L)	Mid-green, heart-shaped, dries to stiff, very sharp	Group 1, biennial, RHS Award
maritimum	1–2ft × 2ft	5–8	Pale bluish green, a few broad, spiny, silvery bracts (M–L)	Glaucous, stiff, leathery	Group 1, sea holly, needs perfect drainage
×oliveranum	2–3ft × 2ft	5–8	Large, blue with brilliant blue bracts (M–L)	Dark green, spiny, toothed	Group 1, clumping, RHS Award
planum	2–3ft × 1½ft	5–8	Small, steel-blue with spiky blue-green bracts (M–L)	Dark green, heart-shaped, spineless, scalloped	Group 1, evergreen, may need staking if grown in rich soil
p. 'Blaukappe'	2–2½ft × 1½ft	5–8	Intense blue, spiky blue bracts (M–L)	Dark green, heart-shaped	Group 1, evergreen basal growth
×tripartitum	2–3ft × 1½ft	5–8	Steel-blue with spiky dark blue bracts (M–L)	Dark green rosettes, white veins, toothed	Group 1, evergreen, RHS Award
variifolium	18–24in × 10in	5–8	Gray-blue with wide spiny bracts (M–L)	Dark green, small, rounder, white veins	Group 1, evergreen, clumping
yuccifolium	3–4ft × 2ft	5–8	Small, whitish green with gray-green bracts (M–L)	Blue-gray, straplike, spiny margins	Group 2, rattlesnake master, semi-evergreen
×zabelii	1½–2½ft × 1½ft	5–8	Large, intense blue, green-tipped blue bracts (M–L)	Dark-green, heart-shaped, spiny-toothed	Group 1, semi-evergreen
×z. 'Donard Variety'	2½–3ft × 1½ft	5–8	Steel-blue heads and bracts (M–L)	Green, white-veined, large-toothed, leathery	Group 1, good summer foliage

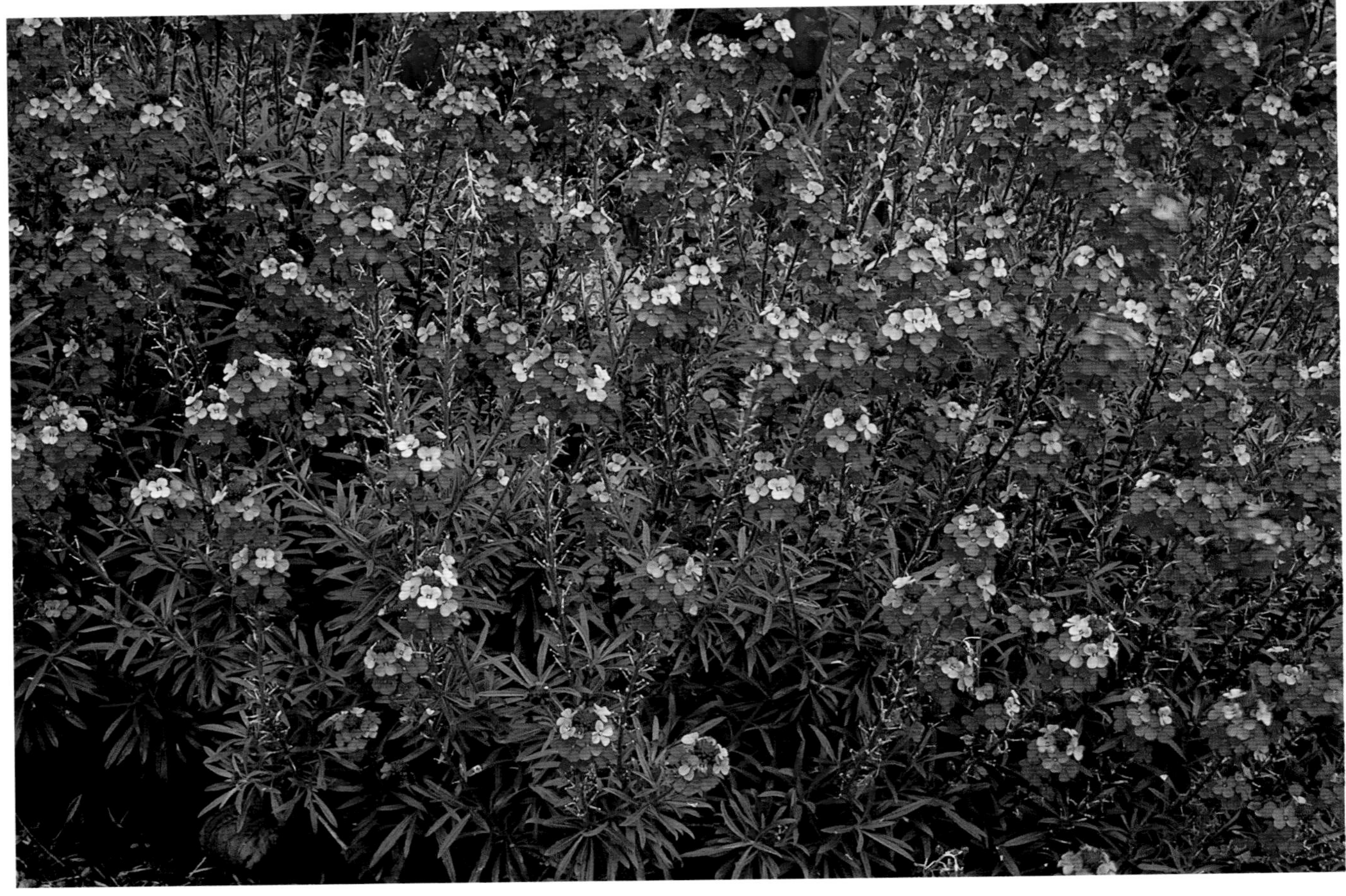

Erysimum 'Bowles' Mauve'.

ERYSIMUM Brassicaceae

These stalwart late winter and early spring bloomers have long been relied upon for their early performance. The smallish four-petaled flowers in tall racemes provide masses of color and make good plants for bedding out. Erysimums are subshrubby and short-lived (my approach is to start cuttings to replace the current plants); but every rule has its exception, and my *E.* 'Bowles' Mauve' has made a four-foot hedge—in the front of the border, of course. Meanwhile its replacements are dying in the pots.

We have listed here the perennial erysimums we consider the hardiest. Most wallflowers in the trade are *Cheiranthus cheiri* (bedding wallflower) and are extremely fragrant—and biennial. - *Ann Bucher*

Scientific Name: From the Greek *erysimon,* which word was applied to biennial and perennial herbs.

Common Name: Wallflower.

Origin: North America, Europe, Asia.

Preferred Conditions: Poor to moderately fertile, neutral to alkaline soil that is well-drained. Winter hardiness is more of a problem with wet and soggy conditions. Protect from strong winds.

Light: Sun to part shade.

Management: Remove flower stems as they finish; snip off down a few leaves into the foliage, and you will be rewarded with a more compact and uniform plant. Take cuttings annually to ensure against winter losses. Shape plants after they bloom to stimulate new growth. Put a light mulch around them in winter, but not over the crown. Deadhead as necessary. They might benefit from lime as they prefer an alkaline soil.

Propagation: Seed in summer; cuttings in summer.

Pests and Diseases: Clubroot, downy mildew, fungal leaf spot, snails, slugs, cabbage moth.

Companions: Aquilegia, dicentra, viola, primula, scabiosa, knautia, tulips, narcissus, hyacinth, nassella.

Notes: Take the plunge and cut the flower stems off *E.* 'Bowles' Mauve' before they finish flowering. It is nearly never out of bloom, which makes taking our advice difficult. Actually, every time you deadhead, it goes right back into bloom, so you can hardly go wrong.

Species and Cultivars	Height/ Spread	USDA Hardiness Zone	Flowers (bloom time)	Foliage	Comments
'Bowles' Mauve'	2–3ft × 3ft+	6–9	Rich mauve-purple on long racemes (E–L)	Silvery grayish green flushed purple underneath, narrow, lanceolate	Upright, long-blooming, evergreen, short-lived, RHS Award
cheiri 'Harpur Crewe'	10–12in × 12in	6–9	Double, deep yellow, fragrant (E–L)	Dark green, narrow, pointed	Bushy, short-lived, evergreen
'John Codrington'	8–12in × 12in	6–9	Red-bronze buds open to smoky burgundy, fade to pale yellow, fragrant (E–M)	Deep green, narrow, lanceolate	Small, shrublike, evergreen
'Julian Orchard'	15–20in × 12in	6–9	Deep reddish purple with red flush, fades to purple slightly fragrant (E–M)	Deep blue-green	Compact, evergreen
linifolium 'Variegatum'	1–2ft × 1½ft	6–9	Deep purple and brown aging to mauve-purple and copper (E–L)	Green, edged in white and cream, narrow	Very short-lived, evergreen
'Margaret Lockett'	2ft × 2ft	6–9	Mauve-purple (E–L)	Silvery grayish green	More compact than 'Bowles' Mauve' but very similar otherwise, evergreen
'Orange Flame'	3–6in × 10in	4–9	Orange, fragrant (E–L)	Light green, toothed	Prostrate, evergreen
'Wenlock Beauty'	1–1½ft × 1½ft	6–9	Variable, mauve-purple, bronze, and pink with peach overtones, slightly fragrant (E–L)	Dark green, lanceolate	Compact, evergreen

Eucomis comosa.

EUCOMIS Hyacinthaceae

This very hardy perennial bulb from South Africa does very well for us in the Pacific Northwest. They do like it a bit dry during dormancy and look good in pots, but don't leave them unprotected in a wet, cold winter in those pots. You can divide when the clumps get large, or propagate from leaf cuttings—a rare feature in the hyacinth family. This is a good cut flower and can't be beat for late interest in the summer border or as a container plant. ~ *Bob Lilly*

Scientific Name: From the Greek *eu* ("good") and *kome* ("hair")—a beautiful head, in other words.
Common Name: Pineapple flower, pineapple lily.
Origin: South Africa.
Preferred Conditions: Well-drained, rich soil with lots of humus; moisture-retentive during growing season, but dry during dormancy.
Light: Sun to part shade.
Management: A good winter mulch of straw or fir boughs will help protect from the cold. Divide when plant becomes too crowded and flower production is reduced. Allow the leaves to cure before removal.
Propagation: Seed, but plants take three to four years to reach flowering size; division when necessary in spring; offsets can be detached and replanted in spring; leaf cuttings in the fall.
Pests and Diseases: Watch for snails and slugs at all times.
Companions: Kniphofia, angelica, nepeta, hosta, short grasses, carex; excellent in pots alone or in combination with other summer perennials and grasses.

Species and Cultivars	Height/ Spread	USDA Hardiness Zone	Flowers (bloom time)	Foliage	Comments
bicolor	1–2ft × 1½ft	8–10	Nodding, starry green, margined with purple (M)	Light green with wavy edges, straplike, stems mottled with brownish red	Variegated pineapple lily, RHS Award
comosa (syn. punctata)	1½–2ft × 2ft	8–10	White to pink (M)	Light green with purple spotting beneath, stems spotted purple at base	Wine eucomis, purple seed capsule
c. 'Sparkling Burgundy'	15–20in × 2ft	8–10	Green blushed purple with purple bracts (M)	Deep burgundy-purple	Will propagate from leaf cuttings

Eupatorium purpureum subsp. *maculatum* 'Gateway'.

EUPATORIUM Asteraceae

"If you have nothing nice to say..." The intrigue of these plants has definitely waned for some of us. All it took was a few years of growing *E. purpureum* subsp. *maculatum* 'Gateway' and having it self-sow into the crowns of everything else. The standard maintenance advice is to just deadhead it at the end of bloom time. The problem is, how does a six-foot plant with no head look in the garden? The foliage is coarse and has no redeeming value except for that of *E. rugosum* 'Chocolate', which has become our favorite. In full sun, it has lovely brownish purple leaves and then in fall, flat corymbs of fluffy white flowers. And it doesn't seem to self-sow. (If you like ageratum, you'll understand from its flowers why *E. rugosum* is called hardy ageratum.)

We should mention another one or two eupatorium "qualities." One, the difficulty of dividing mature plants—get out your pry bar; and two, the color of the flowers—dingy mauve at best. ~ *Carrie Becker*

Scientific Name: Greek name, from Mithridates Eupator, king of Portus.
Common Name: Joe-Pye weed, hardy ageratum, boneset.
Origin: Europe, North Africa, Central Asia, eastern North America.
Preferred Conditions: Fertile, moisture-retentive soil. Tolerates a variety of conditions, but plant size may be affected. Keep them moist until established, then they're fairly drought tolerant.
Light: Sun to part shade; sun only for *E. rugosum* 'Chocolate' for best color.
Management: They can be pinched back in May or June for a shorter plant and later bloom. They also can be cut back to as short as six inches in June (this doesn't work very well in the Pacific Northwest). Frequent division slows the rampant instincts of some, and rejuvenates failing clumps in others. Cut back after flowering or during the fall/winter cleanup when dormant. In exposed areas, some may need staking (with three- to four-foot pea sticks). Fluffy seedheads left on during the winter extend the season of interest, but plants do become fertile with age and will self-sow profusely.

Propagation: Division in winter and spring; some forms self-sow.

Pests and Diseases: Mildew, leaf spot, leaf miners.

Companions: Grasses, *Sedum* 'Herbstfreude', *Hydrangea paniculata, Echinacea purpurea, Helenium autumnale,* aster, cimicifuga, solidago, *Rudbeckia fulgida* var. *sullivantii* 'Goldsturm'.

Notes: Attractive to butterflies and bees. Flowers are good for both fresh and dried arrangements. Large, established clumps of *E. purpureum* subsp. *maculatum* 'Gateway' should not be allowed to get bone dry.

Species and Cultivars	Height/ Spread	USDA Hardiness Zone	Flowers (bloom time)	Foliage	Comments
album	3ft × 2ft	3–8	White (M)	Green, serrated, hairy stems	Eastern U.S. native, slugs love this plant
cannabinum	4ft × 3ft	3–8	Pink to coppery-red, sometimes white (M)	Light green	Self-sows, considered a weed in Britain
c. 'Flore Pleno'	4ft × 3ft	3–8	Soft-pink, double (M)	As above	Sterile, doesn't self-sow
fistulosum	6–14ft × 3ft	3–8	Purple-mauve, flower heads 1ft wide (M–L)	Dark green, serrated, in whorls, purple stalks are bamboolike and hollow	Joe-Pye weed
f. 'Selection'	5–6ft × 3ft+	3–8	Lilac-mauve, in clusters, 1–1½ft wide (M–L)	As above	
purpureum	7–10ft × 3ft	3–8	Pale pink to purple or white, 1–1½ft wide (M–L)	Green, whorled, with a vanilla scent, green stems are hollow	Vigorous
p. 'Bartered Bride'	4–8ft × 3ft	3–8	White, in large clusters on stiff stems (L)	Pale green	Long-flowering
p. subsp. maculatum	5–8ft × 3ft	3–8	Reddish purple, dense (L)	Pale green, purple speckled and mottled stems	More cold hardy, RHS Award
p. subsp. maculatum 'Atropurpureum'	4–7ft × 3ft+	3–8	Reddish purple, 1½ft wide (L)	Green, textured, in whorls, purplish black stems	
p. subsp. maculatum 'Gateway'	6ft × 3ft+	3–8	Rose-mauve, very large flower heads (L)	Green, large, textured, in whorls, purplish black stems	Bold, comes true from seed
rugosum	3–4ft × 2½ft	4–9	White, ageratumlike, loose (L)	Green, pointed, ovate and sharply toothed	White snakeroot, may need staking
r. 'Chocolate'	3–4ft × 2½ft	4–9	White (L)	Chocolate-purple with shiny purple stems	Striking foliage, RHS Award

Euphorbia griffithii 'Fireglow' with Siberian iris.

EUPHORBIA Euphorbiaceae

One of the most dramatic plants for your garden, spurge offers diversity of height, form, color and habit. The genus includes many tender species, such as poinsettias, which are grown in tropical and subtropical zones. Fortunately for us, however, there are spurges that put on quite a show and increase very well in a variety of conditions throughout the United States. Showy bracts surround small flowers in shades that will satisfy one's lust for almost any color, from lime-green to the orange-red of *E. griffithii* 'Fireglow'. Spurges are also valued for their (usually whorled) leaves, with everything from glaucous or variegated greens through to the dark bronze-purple of *E. dulcis* 'Chameleon'.

Are euphorbias too good to be true? Well, shameless propagators (*E. schillingii*, *E. characias*) seed about, and others (*E. amygdaloides* var. *robbiae*, *E. cyparissias*) spread assertively by runners. Many keep their shape and form for months, some even the entire year. Some are deciduous and will need to be cut down in winter. *Euphorbia characias*, one of our most valuable garden plants, has a specific care regimen: it and all its forms flower off the previous year's growth, which

Euphorbia characias 'Portuguese Velvet'.

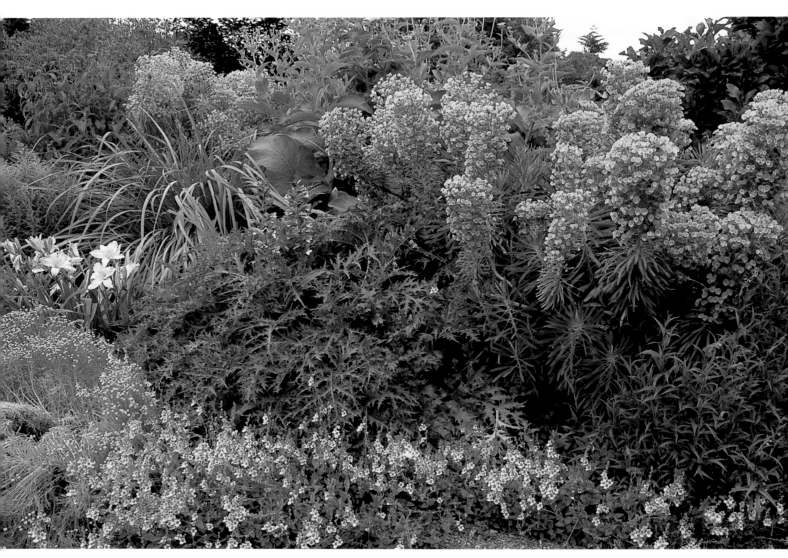

Euphorbia characias subsp. *wulfenii*, its seedheads just going over, with *Acanthus spinosus* in a border edged by a good pink diascia.

is removed either at the end of flowering, or after seed sets, or after the bracts no longer look showy. The first option gives you a more controlled compact plant (and no seedlings!). Its blue-gray foliage is a wonderful look in winter.

Euphorbias exude a caustic, milky sap from the roots and stems that may cause skin rashes and burns. If you get any of this juice on your skin, wash it off immediately and on no account get it anywhere near your eyes. Skin irritation can be worse if exposed to direct sunlight (phototoxicity).

Spurges associate well with other plants, offering their companions a dramatic edge, architectural stature, and vivid yellows and golds. Place *E. characias* subsp. *characias* 'Humpty Dumpty' in front of dark evergreen shrubs, with spring bulbs in the foreground, and you'll really appreciate this beauty. They deserve all the attention they get! ~ *Susan Carter*

Scientific Name: For Euphorbus, physician to the king of Mauritania.
Common Name: Spurge, mousemilk.
Origin: Southwestern Asia, Britain, Europe, Mediterranean.
Preferred Conditions / Light:
Group 1. Well-drained, light soil in full sun.
Group 2. Moist, humus-rich soil in part shade.
Group 3. Permanently moist soil and full sun.
Planting: Move seedlings when small; large plants do not transplant easily. The fleshy roots don't hold soil well.
Management: Resents disturbance. After blooming, cut spent flower stems to new basal growth, and new growth will quickly appear. It is best to wait for the basal growth to begin before cutting back.
Propagation: Division in spring for named varieties (*E. characias* is not dividable—seed only); seed as soon as ripe; basal or small branchlet cuttings in spring and early summer.
Pests and Diseases: Collar rot at soil level and on the roots when grown in too-wet soil. Powdery mildew, especially on *E. dulcis* (particularly on *E. dulcis* 'Chameleon'), *E. ×martini*, and *E. amygdaloides* 'Purpurea'.
Companions: *Euphorbia characias* stands alone or with large grasses and *Helleborus argutifolius*; *E. schillingii*, with helianthus, taller vernonicas, *Geranium psilostemon*, and *G.* 'Ann Folkard'; *E. griffithii*, with *Geum* 'Borisii', *Geranium phaeum*, hemerocallis, carex, and *Iris sibirica*. Pair smaller varieties with heuchera and plantago and use as foreground plants in rockeries.
Notes: *Euphorbia characias* is short-lived, which is why it self-sows (self-preservation); after a few years leave a few seedlings or say good-bye. Look for its new variegated selection, 'Tasmanian Tiger'. In the chart, the symbol ∞ = infinite spread.

Species and Cultivars	Height/ Spread	USDA Hardiness Zone	Flowers (bloom time)	Foliage	Comments
amygdaloides	1–1½ft × 1½ft	4–9	Greenish yellow bracts (E–M)	Green with reddish stems, evergreen	Group 2, wood spurge, self-sows
a. 'Purpurea' (syn. 'Rubra')	1–1½ft × 1½ft	5–9	Yellow-green bracts (E–M)	Burgundy aging to green, stems tinted with purplish red, evergreen	Group 2, redwood spurge, mildew prone, self-sows
a. var. robbiae	1–2ft × 2ft+	5–9	Yellowish bracts (E–M)	Dark green rosettes, glossy, leathery evergreen	Group 2 or 3, good for dry shade, spreads by runners and seed, RHS Award

Species and Cultivars	Height/ Spread	USDA Hardiness Zone	Flowers (bloom time)	Foliage	Comments
a. 'Variegata'	16in × 16in	5–9	Cream bracts (E–M)	Green with cream margins, evergreen	Group 2
characias	2½–3ft × 3–3½ft	7–9	Lime-green to yellow green bracts with purple nectaries (E–M)	Bluish green, evergreen	Group 1, self-sows, drought tolerant
c. 'Canyon Creek'	1½–2ft × 3–3½ft	7–9	Golden yellow bracts (E–M)	Deep green, tinted red, evergreen	Group 1, drought tolerant
c. subsp. characias	2½–3ft × 3–3½ft	7–9	Acid-yellow bracts (E)	Bluish gray, evergreen	Group 1, RHS Award
c. subsp. characias 'Humpty Dumpty'	2½–3ft × 3ft	7–9	Lime-green with red nectaries (E)	Bluish gray, evergreen	Group 1, bushy, compact
c. 'Portuguese Velvet'	2–2½ft × 3ft+	7–9	Large, yellow-green bracts (E–M)	Bluish gray with velvety downy hairs, evergreen	Group 1, RHS Award
c. subsp. wulfenii	3–4ft × 3–4ft	7–9	Yellow-green bracts (E–M)	Bluish green, leathery, evergreen	Group 1, RHS Award
c. subsp. wulfenii 'Emmer Green'	2–2½ft × 2ft	7–9	Cream variegated bracts (E–M)	Edged in creamy white, evergreen	Group 1
c. subsp. wulfenii 'John Tomlinson'	3ft × 3ft+	7–9	Bright yellow-green (E–M)	Bluish green, evergreen	Group 1, RHS Award
c. subsp. wulfenii 'Lambrook Gold'	2½–3ft × 3ft+	7–9	Golden yellow bracts (E–M)	Grayish to pale green, evergreen	Group 1, bushy, compact, RHS Award
corallioides	2–2½ft × 2½ft	6–9	Lime-green with long yellow bracts (E–M)	Gray-green, pink-tinged turning rusty red in autumn, deciduous	Group 1, coral spurge, self-sows, short-lived or biennial
cyparissias	8–12in × ∞	3–8	Yellow-green (E–M)	Feathery, needlelike, bluish green, deciduous	Group 1, cypress spurge, very aggressive
c. 'Fens Ruby' (syn. 'Purpurea', 'Clarice Howard')	8–12in × ∞	3–8	Yellow-green fading to orange (E–M)	Emerging dark purplish red turning bluish green, needlelike, deciduous	Group 1, aggressive, stoloniferous
c. 'Orange Man'	10–15in × ∞	3–8	Bright yellow turning orange (E–M)	Soft green, feathery, deciduous	As above
dulcis	10–20in × 20in	4–9	Yellowish (E–M)	Green, deciduous	Group 2, self-sows, good autumn color
d. 'Chameleon'	1½–2ft × 1½ft+	4–9	Bright yellow with a purple tinge (E–M)	Dark bronze-purple with green tint, deciduous	Group 2, self-sows, mildew prone
griffithii	2½–3ft × 3ft+	6–9	Orange-red (E–M)	Green with pale pink midrib, reddish stems, deciduous	Group 1, Griffith's spurge, good fall color
g. 'Dixter'	2–3ft × 3ft+	6–9	Orange (E–M)	Dark green with red flush, grayish pink beneath, deciduous	Group 1, spreads quickly, RHS Award
g. 'Fern Cottage'	2–3ft × 3ft+	5–9	As above	Green with reddish margins, bronzy-pink tips, reddish stems, deciduous	Group 1, good fall color

Species and Cultivars	Height/ Spread	USDA Hardiness Zone	Flowers (bloom time)	Foliage	Comments
g. 'Fireglow'	3ft × 3ft+	5–9	Orange-red (M)	Soft green, new growth tinged red, red stems, deciduous	Group 1, red fall color
'Jade Dragon'	3–4ft × 3ft+	6–9	Large, greenish yellow bracts (E–M)	Green, purple tint to new growth, evergreen	Group 1
×martinii	2–3ft × 2–3ft	6–9	Large, greenish yellow, red stems (E–M)	Grayish green with bronze-red tints, evergreen	Group 2, RHS Award
×m. 'Red Martin'	1½–2ft × 2ft	6–9	Yellow-green (E–M)	Green with purplish red tints, velvety new growth, evergreen	Group 2
myrsinites	8–10in × 10in	5–9	Bright yellowish to lime-green (E–M)	Trailing, bluish green, evergreen	Group 1, donkeytail spurge, short-lived, self-sows, RHS Award
nicaeensis	1½ft × 1½ft	6–9	Yellow-green (M)	Grayish green with pinkish red stems, evergreen	Group 1, Nice (as in France) spurge
palustris	3ft × 3ft	5–8	Dark yellow (E–M)	Green, willowlike, turns red in fall, deciduous	Group 3, swamp spurge, for bogs and water gardens, RHS Award
polychroma (syn. epithymoides)	1–1½ft × 1½ft	4–8	Bright yellow (E–M)	Pale green, good autumn color, deciduous	Group 1 or 2, cushion spurge, short-lived in Pacific Northwest, RHS Award
p. 'Candy' (syn. 'Purpurea')	1–1½ft × 1½ft	4–9	Sulphur-yellow bracts (E–M)	Green with purple flushed tips in spring, narrow, curvy edges with bluish tint, deciduous	Group 1 or 2, tidy low mound
p. 'Midas'	12–15in × 1½ft	4–9	Bright golden yellow (E)	Bright green, good fall color, deciduous	Group 1 or 2, early bloomer
rigida (syn. biglandulosa)	1–2ft × 2ft	7–10	Bright yellow aging to orange (E–M)	Fleshy blue-green, pointed, evergreen	Group 1, semi-prostrate, early bloomer
schillingii	3–4½ft × 3ft+	7–9	Greenish yellow (M–L)	Soft green with pale green or white midribs, narrow, deciduous	Group 2 or 3, clump-forming, erect, RHS Award
seguieriana	20in × 24in	8–10	As above	Bluish green, semi-evergreen	Group 1, spreading
s. subsp. niciciana	20in × 24in	8–10	As above	Bluish green, narrow, lanceolate, semi-evergreen	As above
sikkimensis	3–4ft × 3ft+	6–9	As above	Deep green fading to soft green, pinkish midrib and veining, deciduous	Group 2 or 3, spreading but easy to manage, erect, RHS Award
wallichii	2ft × 2ft	6–9	Greenish yellow (M)	Dark green with white and reddish veins, deciduous	Group 1, erect

Fallopia japonica var. *compacta* 'Milk Boy'.

FALLOPIA Polygonaceae

Personally, I would avoid the running forms of fallopia except for *F. japonica* var. *compacta* 'Milk Boy', which is not as invasive as the others if grown in heavier soil (and which—never mind its name—is not very compact). Its variegated foliage is lovely in low light (it is sure to burn in sun), and the way the strange coral new growth comes out of the ground in spring is quite entertaining. *Fallopia japonica* 'Crimson Beauty', which also dies to the ground for the winter, is well worth having if you can find the room: it easily reaches twelve feet at maturity. ~ *Carrie Becker*

Scientific Name: For Italian anatomist Gabriele Fallopio, for whom fallopian tubes are also named.
Common Name: Japanese knotweed.
Origin: Japan, Korea, Taiwan, China.

Species and Cultivars	Height/ Spread	USDA Hardiness Zone	Flowers (bloom time)	Foliage	Comments
japonica (syn. *Polygonum cuspidatum*)	4–8ft × 5ft	5–9	Small, white (L)	Heart-shaped	Running rootstock, listed as a weed of concern
j. var. compacta (syn. *Polygonum reynoutria*)	2–3ft × 3ft+	5–9	White turning deep pink (M–L)	Leathery green, good fall color, beet-red stems	Crimson seedheads, running rootstock
j. var. compacta 'Milk Boy' (syn. 'Variegata')	3–4ft × 4ft+	5–9	White (M–L)	White-splashed green, pink stems	Can burn even in shade and may revert, running rootstock, not a dense spreader
j. 'Crimson Beauty'	8–12ft × 5–6ft	5–9	White turning dark crimson (M–L)	Green, celadon-green stems	Spreads slowly outward on all sides

Preferred Conditions: Moist, average to poor soil.
Light: Sun to part shade.
Management: May require regular thinning-out and reduction of clump size to control invasive habit. Cut to ground during the fall/winter cleanup. Control the spread by removal!
Propagation: Division in spring; seed and cuttings.
Pests and Diseases: Leaf miner.
Companions: Eupatorium, dahlia, miscanthus, shrub roses, *Hydrangea quercifolia*, actaea; use *F. japonica* var. *compacta* 'Milk Boy' as a variegated color echo.
Notes: Fallopia, persicaria, tovara, reynoutria, bistorta, and polygonum are confused in the trade.

FERULA Apiaceae

Ferula communis (giant fennel) is one of the most dramatic species in the carrot family. Its foliage is similar to common fennel or dill, but on a much larger scale. It takes several years to develop a crown and root system of sufficient size to send up a flowering stalk. Size will be affected by the soil—in poor soil they will be shorter than the ten feet they can attain in ideal conditions. The stalks can be used fresh, for the special effect of their rounded heads of greenish yellow flowers, or in large dried flower arrangements. Plants can be monocarpic or perennial through side shoots off the central crown. Seedheads are a dark nut-brown and persist well into fall for an attractive autumn look in the border. ~ *Bob Lilly*

Scientific Name: The classical Latin word for a carrier or vehicle.
Common Name: Giant fennel, hog fennel.
Origin: Mediterranean, Central Asia.
Preferred Conditions: Well-drained, moisture-retentive, and well-cultivated with organic material.
Light: Sun.
Planting: Only young plants; they have taproots.

Ferula communis.

Management: To enhance the foliage, remove the flowering stems as soon as they show or right after blooming. Cut to ground in fall/winter cleanup. The crown may require protection from winter cold and wet. Always leave any green leaves to turn color (yellow) in the fall. This plant needs every bit of food to form a large-enough clump.
Propagation: Seed as soon as ripe.
Pests and Diseases: Aphids, snails, slugs, mildew.
Companions: Phormium, crocosmia, euphorbia, miscanthus, cortaderia.
Notes: This is a stand-alone plant for the back of the border.

Species and Cultivars	Height/ Spread	USDA Hardiness Zone	Flowers (bloom time)	Foliage	Comments
communis (syn. 'Gigantea')	6–10ft × 2½–3ft	6–9	Tiny, purple when young aging to yellow, in umbels on a thick flower stalk (E–M)	Large, shiny, rich green, finely cut, in a mound 2ft wide and tall	Size depends on location and summer heat

FILIPENDULA Rosaceae

Meadowsweet offers showy clusters of tiny flowers in shades of red, pink, or white; these are borne in dense plumes at the end of strong, upright flower stems over a long season, beginning in late spring for some forms. Foliage is light to dark green and pinnately compound with a palmate terminal leaflet; it may start looking dreadful in the summer, with dried-up leaves, so cut it back to the ground and a new crop of leaves will form, as long as plants are kept moist. All but *F. vulgaris* prefer moist or even boggy conditions. *Filipendula rubra* and *F. r.* 'Venusta' run about a foot a year in every direction. *Filipendula vulgaris* is even more of a spreader and can be a nuisance: it flops a bit and may need support. You can solve this problem by growing it lean, in lighter soil and more sun.

Filipendula palmata.

Filipendulas make a great cut for floral arrangements. Cut before the flowers have fully opened. During the middle ages, *F. vulgaris* was scattered on the floors to alleviate bad odors, and *F. ulmaria* is still used for its many medicinal qualities. ~ *Susan Carter*

Scientific Name: From the Latin *filum* ("thread") and *pendulus* ("hanging").
Common Name: Meadowsweet, dropwort.
Origin: North America, Europe, Asia.
Preferred Conditions: Moisture-retentive, well-drained, moderately fertile conditions (except *F. vulgaris*).
Light: Sun to part shade.
Management: Mulch to keep roots cool. Keep well watered in dry conditions. If foliage starts to look ratty, cut to the ground and new leaves will emerge as long as soil is moist. New clumps spread rapidly and need frequent division to keep them from crowding out other plants. Control spread by regular removal of runners.
Propagation: Division in spring, use the youngest pieces; seed in autumn outdoors, or root cuttings.
Pests and Diseases: Powdery mildew.
Companions: Miscanthus, hardy lobelia, geranium, astilbe, astrantia, *Iris sibirica*, shrub roses, persicaria; phlox for *F. rubra* 'Venusta'.
Notes: In the chart, the symbol ∞ = infinite spread.

Filipendula ulmaria 'Aurea' with a bright *Geranium psilostemon* and hemerocallis in bloom.

Species and Cultivars	Height/ Spread	USDA Hardiness Zone	Flowers (bloom time)	Foliage	Comments
'Kakome'	6–12in × 8in	4–9	Dark rose buds, opening to pink (M)	Dark green, deeply divided, maplelike	Dwarf pink meadowsweet, long-lasting
palmata	3–4ft × 3ft	3–9	Tiny, deep pink in bud, opening to pale pink, fading to white (M)	Light green with woolly white hairs beneath	Siberian meadowsweet, clump-forming, no staking needed
purpurea	3–4ft × 2ft	4–9	Deep pink, paler with age, purple-red stems, fragrant (M–L)	Large, bright green, deeply divided, forms big clumps	Japanese meadowsweet, no staking needed, RHS Award
p. 'Elegans' (syn. palmata 'Elegantissima')	3–4ft × 2ft	4–9	Large, white with red stamens, fragrant (M)	Green, finely cut	Bronze-red seedheads, more compact
rubra	4–8ft × ∞	3–9	Large, peach-pink plumes on branching red stems, fragrant (M)	Dark green, jagged, hairy beneath	Long bloomer, needs no support, runs
r. 'Venusta' (syn. 'Venusta Magnifica')	4–6ft × ∞	3–9	Deep rose to almost carmine-red, becomes paler as it ages, fragrant (M–L)	Large, green, toothed	Martha Washington plume, needs no support, runs, RHS Award
ulmaria	3–6ft × 2ft	3–9	Creamy-white, fragrant (E–L)	Green, fernlike, rough on top and felty-white beneath	Self-sows, thrives in boggy areas
u. 'Aurea'	2–3ft × 2ft	3–9	As above	Emerge golden yellow, turning pale green in summer, divided	Does best in shade, cut down in midsummer for fresh autumn growth, seeds don't come true
u. 'Variegata' (syn. alnifolia 'Variegata')	2½–4ft × 2ft	3–9	As above	Green and creamy yellow, may revert to green	Prone to mildew, may scorch in full sun
vulgaris (syn. hexapetala)	1–3ft × 2ft	4–9	Creamy-white, pink in bud, may be red-tinged on outside (E–M)	Dark green, lanceolate, finely divided	Dropwort, likes drier alkaline soil, full sun, may need support, spreads
v. 'Multiplex' (syn. 'Plena', 'Flore Pleno')	1½–2ft × 2ft	4–9	Small, double white, bronze buds (E–M)	Deep green, finely divided, fernlike	Somewhat weedy, may need support, long-lasting, prone to mildew

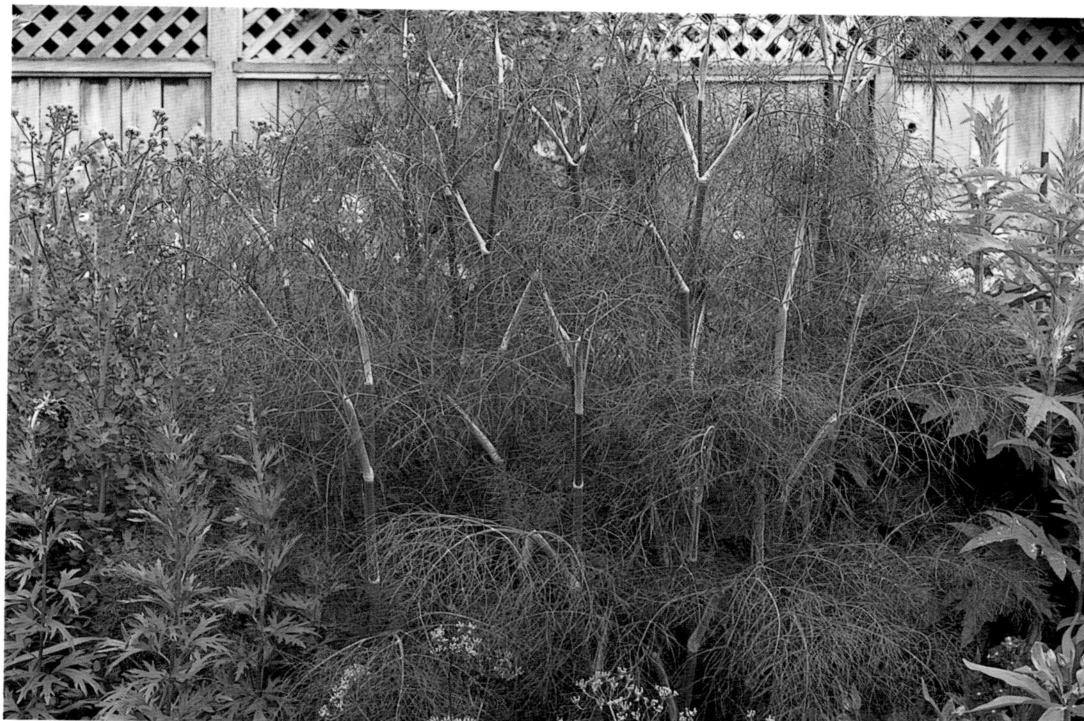

Foeniculum vulgare 'Purpureum'.

FOENICULUM Apiaceae

Foeniculum vulgare 'Purpureum' (bronze fennel) is a noticeable presence in the border, providing an attractive color and foliage contrast. Its coppery-purple leaves are finely divided and thread-like; its tiny acid-yellow flowers are arranged in large flat umbels atop six-foot stems. Both are aromatic. It is an herb with the same culinary and garden uses as the green type, *F. vulgare*, and will self-sow just as enthusiastically.

Don't confuse this plant with the annual vegetable, *F. vulgare* var. *azoricum*, grown for its edible bulbous stem, although they do share a similar mildly sweet licorice flavor. Bronze fennel can be used wherever dill is called for; both seeds and leaves are edible. Its chopped leaves are excellent in soups, salads, and stews, and it even makes its way into breads, cakes, and scones. Makes a nice garnish, too. Very attractive to bees and butterflies, and birds will eat the seeds in the fall—but never enough of them. ~ *Susan Carter*

Scientific Name: From the Latin *foenum* ("hay"), a reference to the sweet smell.
Common Name: Bronze fennel, copper fennel.
Origin: Europe, Mediterranean.
Preferred Conditions: Any moist, well-drained soil. Tolerates drought because its roots run deep.
Light: Sun.
Management: Cut back before seed ripens to prevent self-sowing; a new tuft of fresh foliage will be produced before the end of the season.
Propagation: Seed when ripe; the best-colored seedlings must be chosen. Do not plant candied fennel seeds; it's a waste of a good snack.
Pests and Diseases: Aphids, snails, slugs.

Companions: Crocosmia, phlox, allium, nepeta, salvia, hemerocallis, phormium, canna, dahlia (bronze-foliage forms), *Miscanthus sinensis*, *Physocarpus opulifolius* 'Diabolo', purple-leaf barberries, euphorbia.

Notes: Medieval peasants hung fennel over doorways to ward off evil spirits. Don't compost the seedheads (which means don't put the seedheads in your compost), and don't plant the green form in your garden: it self-sows infinitely.

Species and Cultivars	Height/ Spread	USDA Hardiness Zone	Flowers (bloom time)	Foliage	Comments
vulgare 'Purpureum' (syn. 'Bronze')	3–6ft × 3ft	4–10	Yellow-green from yellow buds (M–L)	Purple-mahogany on young foliage, aging to bronze, and then green, finely cut	Self-sows

FRAGARIA Rosaceae

Beware of these pretty little flowers! Some strawberries that are introduced into the garden are there to stay, regardless of efforts to keep them under control. In my garden I treat them as weeds. Although the strawberry makes an excellent groundcover, it's not normally associated with perennial borders. But even *F. ×ananassa*, the one cultivated for eating, has some ornamental forms. The popular hybrids *F. ×ananassa* 'Pink Panda' and *F.* 'Lipstick' have numerous bright pink flowers that bloom over a long period; their foliage is also quite nice, deep green, glossy, and evergreen. *Fragaria vesca* (alpine strawberry), highly prized in Europe, has a brighter green leaf, white flowers, and smaller, usually red fruit. Soak them in chenin blanc and weed until dark.

Strawberries are the classic crown specific plant. They must be planted with the soil level at crown level; plant too deep or too shallow, and they will not bloom or bear fruit. One of the most successful uses of strawberries is planted under blueberries or rhododendrons among lily of the valley—thugs with thugs. ~ *Susan Carter*

Scientific Name: From the Latin *fragans* ("fragrance"), referring to the scent of the fruit.
Common Name: Strawberry, wild strawberry.
Origin: Europe, Asia, North America, Chile.
Preferred Conditions: Fertile, humus-rich, well-drained, not too wet or dry. Tolerates acidic soils, but thrives in alkaline.
Light: Sun to part shade (except *F. vesca*, which will take shade).
Planting: Plant six to twelve inches apart and direct runners to fill in gaps, or plant a foot apart (staggered).
Management: Pinching off runners in the first year promotes fruit production and helps create larger, sturdier mother plants that will fill in quicker. Leaves may look ratty in the spring and can be trimmed (or mowed) back; this also helps control disease. Cut down to the crown to clean up (with *F. vesca*, cutting down to an inch or two is fine). Leave the healthy leaves of *F. ×ananassa* on over the winter.
Propagation: Seeds or division of youngest plantlets or offsets (runners root and produce plantlets wherever they touch ground).
Pests and Diseases: Crown rot (especially in overly wet soil), powdery mildew, spider mites, root weevils.
Companions: Hosta, astilbe, spring bulbs, heuchera, pulmonaria, bergenia.
Notes: *Fragaria ×ananassa* appreciates a mulch to help keep the fruit drier.

Fragaria ×ananassa 'Pink Panda'.

Species and Cultivars	Height/ Spread	USDA Hardiness Zone	Flowers (bloom time)	Foliage	Comments
×ananassa 'Pink Panda'	4–6in × 10in+	5–8	Bright rose-pink with yellow eye (E–L)	Deep green, glossy	Seldom fruits, stoloniferous, vigorous
×a. 'Red Ruby'	4–6in × 10in+	5–8	Deep rose, yellow eye (E–L)	As above	Semi-evergreen, seldom fruits
×a. 'Variegata'	6–8in × 10in+	5–8	White with yellow center (M)	Creamy-white margin, dark green center	Good fruit, stoloniferous
'Lipstick'	4–8in × 10in+	4–8	Deep red to fuchsia with yellow eye (E–L)	Deep green, glossy	Small red fruits, everbearing
vesca	6–12in × 12in	4–8	White, yellow eye (E–L)	Bright green, prominent veins, compound with 3 leaflets	Alpine strawberry, small red fruit
v. 'Alexandra'	6–12in × 12in	4–8	White (E–L)	Bright green	Everbearing
v. 'Aurea'	6–12in × 12in	4–8	As above	Chartreuse	Small red fruit
v. 'Fructu Albo'	6–12in × 12in	4–8	As above	Bright green	Small white fruit
v. 'Rügen'	6–12in × 12in	4–8	As above	As above	Small red fruit

Francoa sonchifolia.

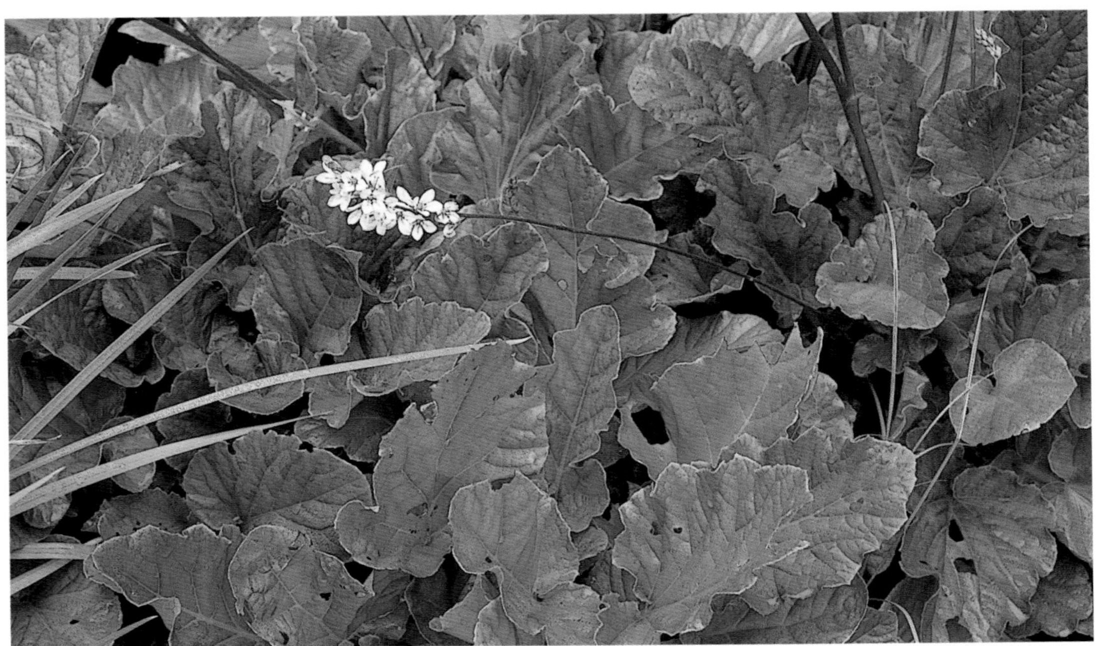

FRANCOA Saxifragaceae

Bridal wreath, as it's commonly called, is a tender, short-lived evergreen perennial with broadly lanceolate, deeply lobed leaves that form large basal rosettes; the delicate flowers are pale pink or white with darker pink markings and borne on unbranched stems. The ratio of foliage vs. flowers is a bit imbalanced in favor of the foliage. Still, plants are long-blooming and often cultivated for the cut flower business. ~ *Susan Carter*

Scientific Name: After sixteenth-century Spanish physician Francisco Franco.
Common Name: Bridal wreath.
Origin: Chile.
Preferred Conditions: Any good humus-rich, well-drained soil. Best in a warm, sheltered location. Keep moist during the growing season. Drought tolerant once established.
Light: Sun to part shade.
Management: Cut off spent flowering stems (sets tons of very fine seed but rarely seeds about in the garden). Remove leaves as they become unattractive and clean up the crowns in spring.
Pests and Diseases: The usual root weevil problem of the saxifrage family, as well as slugs, snails, and cutworms.
Propagation: Divide in spring; seed in the spring.
Companions: Fuchsia, astilbe, hosta.
Notes: Doesn't like wet winters or competition; if overgrown by its companions this plant will surely disappear. In the maritime Northwest, it may be best used as a container plant.

Species and Cultivars	Height/ Spread	USDA Hardiness Zone	Flowers (bloom time)	Foliage	Comments
ramosa	2½ft × 2½ft	7–9	Starry white, pink stripe on each petal (M)	Pale green, shiny	Graceful
sonchifolia	2–2½ft × 2½ft	7–9	Pale pink with deep pink spots at base, long-lasting (M)	Dark green, hairy, wavy-edged, stiff	Clumping and spreading

Galega ×hartlandii 'Lady Wilson'.

GALEGA Papilionaceae

In many places, *G. officinalis* (common goat's rue) is considered a noxious weed. *Galega ×hartlandii*, the species we are concerned with here, is not a problem: it is a short-lived, strong-growing bushy perennial with pea flowers, usually blue, white, mauve, or bicolored, borne in racemes. Its soft green leaves are pinnate, and some have a blue tinge. This long-flowering, heavy-blooming plant will thrive almost anywhere there is sun. ~ *Susan Carter*

Scientific Name: From the Greek *gala* ("milk"); it was thought that if it was fed to goats, it would improve their milk flow.
Common Name: Goat's rue.
Origin: Europe, western Asia, East Africa.
Preferred Conditions: Moist and deeply tilled with organic matter, but will tolerate a wide range, including poor soil.
Light: Sun.
Planting: Plant out when young.
Management: Does not like to be moved when mature. Cut to the ground once flowering is complete to prevent self-seeding, if it is a problem. May need support. Cut back in the fall. Rich soil might cause it to rapidly increase. Resents competition and overcrowding and needs plenty of space; do not let it be overcome by other perennials.
Propagation: Seed (of species); crown division between autumn and spring.
Pests and Diseases: Aphids, cutworms, mildew.
Companions: Paeonia, campanula, early aconitums, miscanthus, linum, *Papaver rhoeas*, linaria.

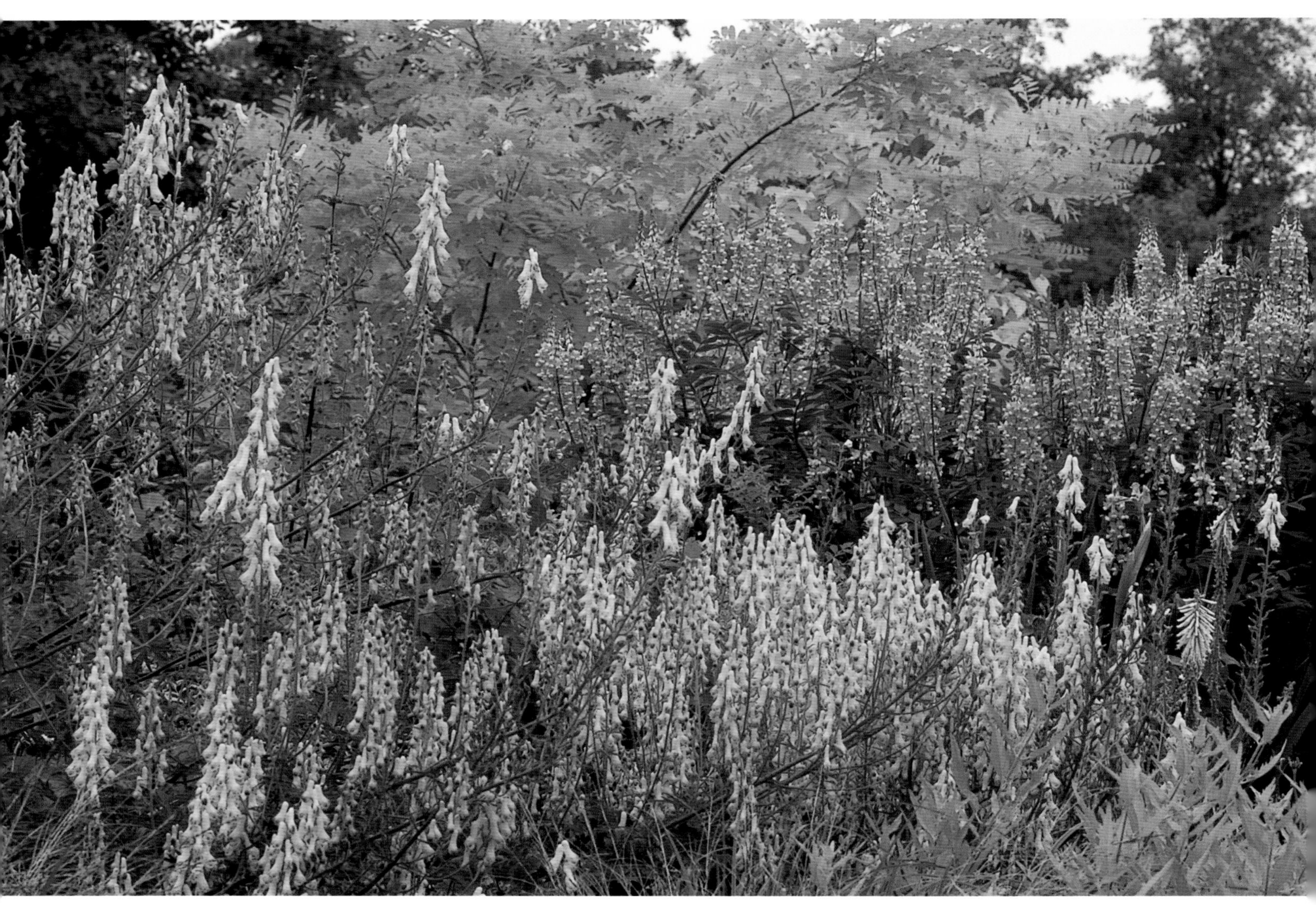

Galega ×*hartlandii* 'Lady Wilson' holding its own between *Robinia pseudoacacia* 'Frisia' and *Aconitum lycoctonum* subsp. *vulparia*.

Species and Cultivars	Height/ Spread	USDA Hardiness Zone	Flowers (bloom time)	Foliage	Comments
×hartlandii	3½–5ft × 3ft	3–9	Bicolored, blue-violet and white (M)	Soft green	Good cut
×h. 'Alba'	3½–5ft × 3ft	3–9	Pure white (M)	Green	Long racemes, RHS Award
×h. 'His Majesty'	4–5ft × 3ft	3–9	Bicolored, mauve-pink and white, scented (M–L)	Soft green	Erect, clump-forming
×h. 'Lady Wilson'	4–5ft × 3ft	3–9	Bicolored, mauve-pink and white, tinged with rose (M–L)	As above	Clump-forming, RHS Award

Galtonia viridiflora.

GALTONIA Hyacinthaceae

Summer hyacinths are, as their name implies, large summer-blooming bulbous perennials that look to some people like stretched hyacinths. Plants have large racemes of drooping or pendulous, bell-shaped flowers, widely spaced on sturdy stems. The flowers also have a pleasant fragrance, although scent, like color, can be very subjective. Galtonia is not a fussy plant: just plant it, feed it, and enjoy it. ~ *Susan Carter*

Scientific Name: After British explorer and polymath Sir Francis Galton.
Common Name: Summer hyacinth.
Origin: South Africa.
Preferred Conditions: Fertile, moist, well-drained soil, deeply cultivated with organic material.
Light: Sun.
Planting: Plant six to nine inches deep and at least four inches apart in groups of a dozen or more.
Management: Does not like to be disturbed. Cut flower spikes after flowering to prevent self-sowing. Don't let it dry out in the growing season. Needs to be well fed to give its best flower show. Staking should not be needed if planted in proper site. Use a heavy mulch in severe winters but remove it in spring as soon as new growth begins and bait for slugs and snails. Galtonia will deteriorate if closed in by neighboring plants. Cut to the ground when foliage has cured.
Propagation: Seed as soon as ripe (keep seedlings frost-free for first two years). Detach small bulbs in spring and replant.
Pests and Diseases: Slugs, snails.
Companions: *Rudbeckia occidentalis* 'Green Wizard', helianthus, monarda, ornamental grasses, iris, *Nicotiana langsdorfii*, *N.* 'Lime Green', *Pelargonium sidoides*; the summer border.

Species and Cultivars	Height/ Spread	USDA Hardiness Zone	Flowers (bloom time)	Foliage	Comments
candicans	2–4ft × 1ft	7–10	Pure creamy-white, drooping bells with dark stamens, fragrant (M)	Gray-green, lanceolate, fleshy, 2–2½ft long	Good seedheads, RHS Award
viridiflora	2–3ft × 1ft	7–10	Pale lime-green, nodding, bell-shaped, petals more pointed, scented (M)	Gray-green, lanceolate, 2ft long	A beefier-looking plant

Gaura lindheimeri 'Siskiyou Pink'.

GAURA Onagraceae

This is a native North American genus of charming and graceful perennials. Plants are vase-shaped and multistemmed, growing up to four feet by the end of the summer. The long-blooming delicate flowers have reflexed petals and prominent stamens and are held directly on the stems. The flowers of *G. lindheimeri* open white and fade to pale pink; the bright pink flowers of its selection, 'Siskiyou Pink', were brought to us courtesy of the Siskiyou Rare Plant Nursery. Other selections and hybrids, some more compact, have since appeared on the market.~ *Susan Carter*

Scientific Name: From the Greek *gauros* ("superb"), a reference to the flowers.

Common Name: Beeblossom.

Origin: Southern and southwestern United States, Mexico, Central and South America.

Preferred Conditions: Well-drained, moist (not too wet or too heavy) soil, preferably lean. Can take neglect. Tolerates drought once established.

Light: Sun.

Management: Remove spent flowering spikes, and flowering will continue. Cut back to eight inches midseason of the second year to encourage a fuller growth. Cut back during the fall/winter cleanup, but not too hard. May need winter protection such as a mulch, but not against the crown.

Propagation: Seed—sow early; softwood cuttings in spring or late summer; semi-ripe heel cuttings; division is not recommended.

Pests and Diseases: Rust, snails, slugs.

Companions: Tuck in among stronger plants; plant in front of a dark background, sedums, grasses, nepeta, iris, oenothera, oregano; admirably used in full-sun parking strips here in the Pacific Northwest.

Notes: Short-lived in heavy soil in the maritime Northwest, but it will give you everything it's got for its brief life. We often use it as an annual; it is worth replanting on a regular basis. Dark spots on foliage are probably an inherent aspect (perhaps a virus); they are not a problem but rather an additional attractive foliar component.

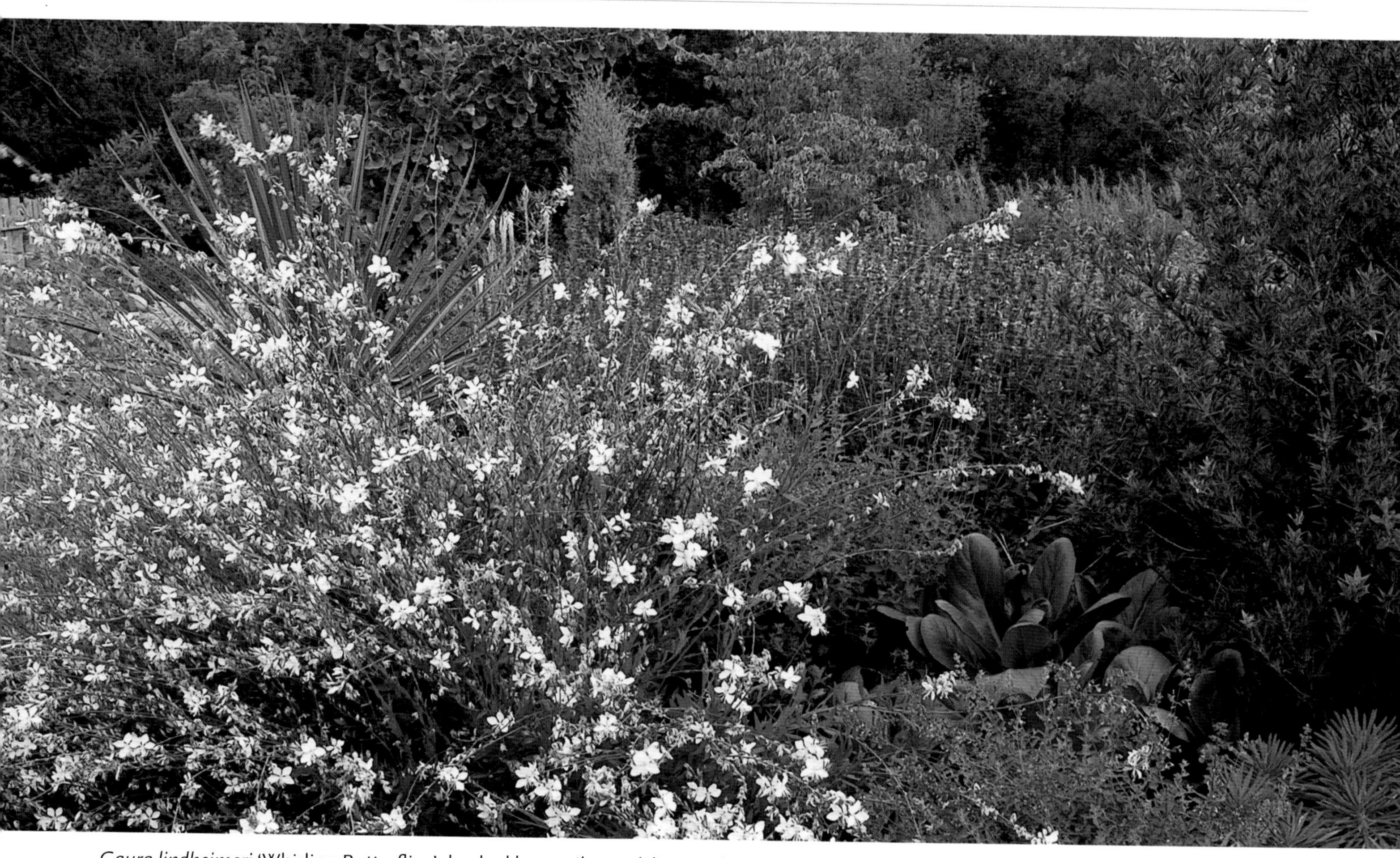

Gaura lindheimeri 'Whirling Butterflies', backed by a spiky cordyline, with *Nepeta sibirica*, 'Tutti-frutti' agastache, and the foliage of euphorbia and bergenia. Design by Withey/Price.

Species and Cultivars	Height/ Spread	USDA Hardiness Zone	Flowers (bloom time)	Foliage	Comments
lindheimeri	3–4ft × 2ft	4–9	Pinkish white buds, opening to white, fading to pale pink, long stamens (M–L)	Gray-green, hairy, spoon-shaped to lanceolate	Bushy, erect stems, graceful, RHS Award
l. 'Corrie's Gold'	2–3ft × 2ft	5–9	White, from pink buds (M–L)	Green, cream- and gold-margined	Less hardy than species
l. 'Crimson Butterflies'	2–4ft × 2ft	4–9	Hot pink on red stems (M–L)	Dark crimson	Very compact
l. 'Franz Valley'	1½–2ft × 1½ft	4–9	White, very small, fragrant (M–L)	Gray-green, smaller and finer	Compact, spreading
l. 'Passionate Pink'	2½ft × 1½ft	4–9	Pink (M–L)	Red-green	More compact and upright
l. 'Siskiyou Pink'	2–4ft × 2ft	4–9	Maroon buds, opening bright pink, changing to deep rich rose (M–L)	Dark green, mottled maroon	From Siskiyou Rare Plant Nursery
l. 'Whirling Butterflies'	2–3ft × 2ft	4–9	Larger, pure white with pinkish tinge, fading to rosy-pink, red stems (M–L)	Gray-green, willowy	Much like the species but may be more compact

Gentiana lutea.

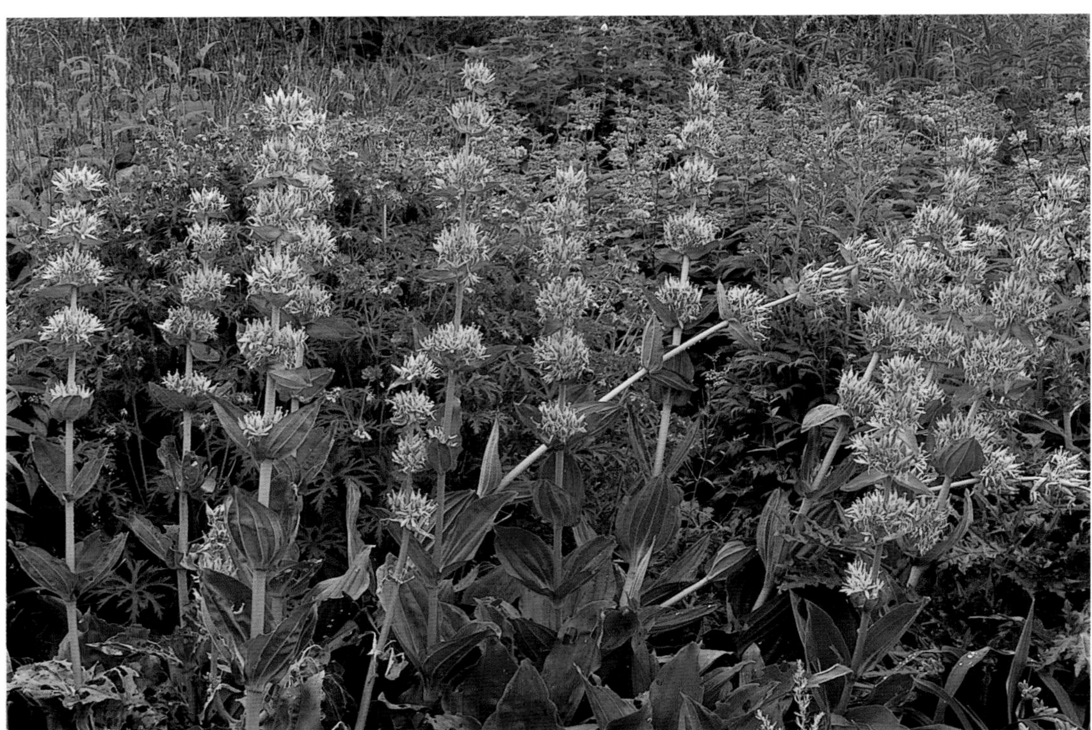

GENTIANA Gentianaceae

A large genus of annual, biennial, and perennial plants, many suitable for the rock garden. We include here only the three species of gentians that work well for us in the border; *G. asclepiadea* in particular, with its willowlike leaves and arching stems holding deep to light blue and white blossoms, is one of the finest flowers for the fall shade border. Gentians are long-lived once established and make a good cut flower for large floral arrangements, if you can stand to cut them. Although these plants are poisonous to cattle, their fleshy roots are used in distilling liquor. ~ *Susan Carter*

Species and Cultivars	Height/ Spread	USDA Hardiness Zone	Flowers (bloom time)	Foliage	Comments
asclepiadea	1½–3ft × 3ft	6–9	Variable, dark blue, white, pink, light blue, some with white throat, out-facing, trumpet-shaped (M–L)	Green, willow-shaped, on long, arching stems	Willow gentian, clump-forming, long-blooming, RHS Award
a. var. alba	1–2ft × 3ft	6–9	White with green-tinge in throat (M–L)	As above	White willow gentian
lutea	3–5ft × 2ft	6–9	Pale yellow, enclosed in a cupped green bract, starry, tubular (M)	Blue-green, smooth, pleated	Felwort, bitterwort, upright, good cut, attractive seedheads
triflora	1½ft × 1ft	5–8	Deep blue to purple-blue, streaked white outside, narrow, bell-shaped (L)	Mid-green, narrow, lanceolate, glossy, on erect stems	

Scientific Name: After Gentius, king of Illyria.
Common Name: Gentian.
Origin: Central Europe, North America, China, Japan.
Preferred Conditions: Well-drained, humus-rich, moist, cool, and (except *G. lutea*) lime-free.
Light: Part shade for *G. asclepiadea* and *G. triflora*; sun for *G. lutea*.
Management: Don't allow gentians to dry out during the growing season. Cut back in fall/winter cleanup or when the foliage turns brown, although dead stems can be attractive throughout winter. If left on in winter, remove stems before new growth in spring. Top-dress with organic matter in winter or early spring. Resents disturbance.
Pests and Diseases: Snails, slugs, especially on emerging growth.
Propagation: Seed of species in containers in a cold frame when ripe; plant offsets in the spring; dislikes division.
Companions: Ferns, hosta, hakonechloa, pulmonaria, astrantia, geranium, hydrangea, rodgersia.
Notes: Usually available as little plants; don't hesitate to try them.

GERANIUM Geraniaceae

How many hardy geraniums do you need to have? We have found it difficult to limit our choices, as so many of these praiseworthy plants can be used throughout the garden, in a variety of conditions and microclimates. It's no wonder they are considered the perfect plant—somewhere, they are! Diversity of flower color and leaf shape and ease of care are only some of their qualities. Many geraniums work well in the border as filler plants, while others do great in rockeries or as edgers, groundcovers, or focal points. They are great companions to such plants as old roses, grasses, iris, and spring bulbs.

Geraniums bloom in shades of white, pink, blue, violet, purple, and magenta. Some, such as the *G. himalayense* cultivars, bloom over a long season from spring through autumn. Many are grown as much for their foliage as for their flowers. The large, deeply cut dark green leaves of *G. ×magnificum* look fresh and bold among other plants. The chartreuse leaves of *G.* 'Ann Folkard' are quite exceptional against its magenta flowers. *Geranium phaeum* var. *phaeum* 'Samobor', a striking foliage plant, has large, green leaves with a prominent purplish brown zone.

Most will grow in any fertile soil, in full sun to part shade. Some will benefit from being cut back after the first bloom and then will produce a fresh crop of leaves (see chart). Cutting back will also help to reduce the self-sowing of the more prolific ones: three of these, *G. endressii*, *G. ×oxonianum*, and *G. ×oxonianum* f. *thurstonianum*, can be floppy and also seed about very aggressively; some authorities recommend not including them in the garden at all.

Geraniums rank at the top in our pursuit of the perfect plant. There are many to experiment with, and new ones appear on the market every day. Bet you can't have just one! ~ *Susan Carter*

Scientific Name: From the Greek *geranos* ("crane"); the fruit of the plant resembles the head and beak of a crane.
Common Name: Hardy geranium, cranesbill.
Origin: Temperate regions, mostly Europe and Asia.
Preferred Conditions: Adaptable to a wide range. Most enjoy well-drained, acid to alkaline soil that is not too wet. Drought tolerant once established.
Light: Sun to part shade. Some varieties (*G. macrorrhizum*, *G. maculatum*, *G. phaeum*, to name a few) take shade well.
Management: Cut back certain forms (see chart) after flowering to give a second crop of flowers. Given the invasive nature of some species, careful attention must be given to

Geranium ×*magnificum* and *G.* ×*oxonianum* with *Alchemilla mollis*, *Epilobium angustifolium* var. *album*, and a scrim of purple penstemon.

Geranium pyrenaicum 'Bill Wallis'.

controlling self-seeding: if you wait until flowering slows with *G. endressii*, *G. ×oxonianum*, and their kin, it will be too late—they will already have self-sowed and still be in flower.

Propagation: Divide in spring, cuttings from side shoots; seed is hard to collect but many will come true from seed; sterile forms can be propagated by root cuttings.

Pests and Diseases: *Geranium pratense* and its varieties are subject to mildew and cutworms, but most geraniums are trouble-free plants.

Companions: Depends on the specific geranium. The larger ones are a good cover for spring bulb foliage as it cures; the smaller varieties can be used in the rock garden or foreground of the perennial border. *Geranium phaeum*, *G. wlassovianum*, *G. pratense*, and *G.* 'Nimbus' do well in the summer border; pair them with hemerocallis, geum, crocosmia, euphorbia, delphinium, anthriscus, helenium, heliopsis. *Geranium ×cantabrigiense* grows well over stone to soften edges; pair with dicentra and cyclamen. Pair *G. ×riversleaianum* 'Mavis Simpson' with astilbe, *Lathyrus vernus*, chaerophyllum, and *Euphorbia characias* 'Portuguese Velvet'. Try *G. psilostemon* with acanthus, helianthus, paeonia, aconitum, and taller astilbes.

Notes: In the chart, CBAF = cut back after flowering.

Species and Cultivars	Height/ Spread	USDA Hardiness Zone	Flowers (bloom time)	Foliage	Comments
'Anne Thomson'	18–24in × 24in	5–9	Gentler magenta with black eye and purple veins (M–L)	Green	More compact than but similar to 'Ann Folkard, difficult to propagate, sun to part shade
'Ann Folkard'	18–48in × 36in	5–9	Rich magenta with black eye and black veins, saucer-shaped (M–L)	Chartreuse in spring, greener in summer, toothed lobes	Sterile, difficult to propagate, heavy bloomer, sun to part shade, scrambling, RHS Award
×antipodeum 'Stanhoe'	8–10in × 12in	7–9	Pale pink (M–L)	Light gray-green to pinkish brown, roundish	Trailing, sun to part shade, edge plant
'Brookside'	12–24in × 24in	5–7	Deep blue, paler at center, fine violet-blue veins (E–M)	Green, finely cut, roundish form	Vigorous, sun, propagate by division
×cantabrigiense	8–12in × 24in	4–9	Bright pink (E–M)	Green, glossy, good fall color (red), lobed, aromatic, evergreen	Sterile, sun, floriferous
×c. 'Biokovo'	8–12in × 24in+	4–9	White with pink tinge, pink in bud (E–L)	Mid-green, glossy, aromatic, good fall color, evergreen	Less vigorous, sun to part shade
×c. 'Cambridge'	8–10in × 24in+	4–9	Light blue-pink (E–L)	Glossy green, evergreen	Sun to part shade, drought tolerant
×c. 'Karmina'	6–8in × 24in	4–9	Dark magenta-pink (E–L)	Dark green, aromatic, evergreen	Sun to part shade
×c. 'St. Ola'	6in × 24in	4–9	Creamy-white, fades to a pale pink (E–L)	Green, glossy, evergreen	Sterile, sun to part shade, vigorous
cinereum 'Ballerina'	6–8in × 12in	4–9	Lavender-pink with darker center and veins (E–L)	Grayish green, scalloped edge	Rock garden plant, sun, RHS Award

Species and Cultivars	Height/ Spread	USDA Hardiness Zone	Flowers (bloom time)	Foliage	Comments
c. 'Laurence Flatman'	6–8in × 12in	5–9	Rose-purple with dark purple veins and blotches (E–L)	As above	Rock garden plant, sun
clarkei 'Kashmir Purple'	12–24in × 24in+	4–9	Deep violet-purple with pink veins, large (M)	Mid-green, deeply cut	Rhizomatous, part sun, CBAF
c. 'Kashmir White'	12–18in × 24in+	4–9	Large, white with pale lilac veins, saucer-shaped (E–M)	As above	Rhizomatous, part sun, CBAF, RHS Award
dalmaticum	4–6in × 20in	4–9	Clear shell-pink (E–M)	Green, glossy, deeply lobed, serrated edge, aromatic, red in fall	Dwarf cranesbill, evergreen, sun, RHS Award
d. 'Album'	5in × 18in	4–9	White with pink flush (E)	Green, glossy, aromatic	Rare, evergreen, lacks vigor, sun
'Dilys'	9in × 24in	4–9	Light magenta with red veins and darker eye (M–L)	Green, deeply dissected	Sun to part shade, trailing
endressii	12–18in × 18in	3–9	Warm pink, notched petals, funnel-shaped (E–L)	Mid-green, deeply cut, toothed, semi-evergreen	Vigorous, self-sows, CBAF, rhizomatous, sun to shade, RHS Award
e. 'Wargrave Pink'	12–18in × 18in	3–9	Soft salmon-pink, constant bloomer (E–L)	Mid-green, deeply cut, toothed	As above, RHS Award
'Francis Grate'	18–24in × 24in	7–9	Pale mauve (M)	Gray-green, silver beneath, deeply cut	Hardy, sun, similar to *G. incanum*, spreads
himalayense	12–18in × 18in+	5–9	Deep violet-blue with red veins, red-blue center, saucer-shaped (M–L)	Mid-green, finely cut, large, rounded, good fall reddish color	Rhizomatous, part sun to shade, CBAF
h. 'Gravetye'	15in × 15in	5–9	Purplish blue with red eye, large (M–L)	Mid-green, deeply cut, good fall color	Long-blooming, part sun to shade, spreading but more compact, RHS Award
h. 'Irish Blue'	15in × 15in	5–9	Pale blue to pinkish with darker veins and central red zone, large (M)	Mid-green, finely cut, good fall color	Vigorous, free-flowering over a long period, part sun to shade
h. 'Plenum' (syn. 'Birch Double')	12–18in × 18in+	5–9	Double violet, tinged pink (M)	Mid-green, small, rounded, deeply divided, good fall color	Sterile, sun, shy and slow, smaller but heavier leaves
incanum 'Sugar Plum'	8in × 12in+	8–9	Ruby-red (E–L)	Gray-green, gray beneath, very dissected, aromatic	Short-lived, sun, crowns tend to rot out in wet soil
'Ivan'	24in × 24in	5–6	Magenta with black veins and eye (M–L)	Mid-green, large, lobed	Sun

Species and Cultivars	Height/ Spread	USDA Hardiness Zone	Flowers (bloom time)	Foliage	Comments
'Johnson's Blue'	12–18in × 18in+	5–9	Lavender-blue with reddish veins (E–L)	Mid-green, slight gray tinge, finely cut, reddish at base	Sterile, spreads, rhizomatous, sun, several forms are sold, RHS Award
'Kashmir Blue'	12–30in × 24in+	5–9	Soft pale blue (M)	Green, deeply cut	Rhizomatous but slow about it, sun to part shade, CBAF
macrorrhizum	8–10in × 24in+	4–9	Light magenta to pink, reddish brown sepals (E–L)	Light green, slightly hairy, rounded, broad, sticky, aromatic, red in fall, semi-evergreen	Bigroot geranium, sun to shade, dry conditions
m. 'Album'	8–10in × 24in	4–9	White, flushed pale pink with rose-red stamens and pink calyx, pink buds (M–L)	As above	Sun to shade, dry conditions, RHS Award
m. 'Bevan's Variety'	8–10in × 24in	4–9	Deep magenta with deep red sepals (E–L)	Mid-green, aromatic, good fall color, semi-evergreen	Sun to shade
m. 'Ingwersen's Variety'	8–10in × 24in	4–9	Soft pink (E–L)	Large, light green, rounded and lobed, sticky, aromatic, good fall color, semi-evergreen	Sun to shade, RHS Award
m. 'Pindus'	8–10in × 12in	4–9	Bright magenta (M–L)	Green, no scent, smaller leaf	Spreads well, sun to shade
m. 'Spessart'	12in × 24in	4–9	White with pink stamens (E–M)	Mid-green, rounded, lobed, slightly hairy, scented, semi-evergreen	Sun to shade
m. 'Variegatum'	12in × 12in	4–9	Bright magenta (E–M)	Grayish green, splashed with cream and pinkish tints, aromatic	Very slow to increase, needs sun and moisture
maculatum	15–26in × 18in	3–8	Pale to deep pink or blue-pink, clusters (E–M)	Mid-green, lobed, toothed, shiny	East Coast woodland native, shade to sun, moist, CBAF
m. f. albiflorum	18–24in × 18in	3–8	White (E–M)	Good dark green for a white-flowering plant	Shade, CBAF
m. 'Chatto'	18–24in × 18in	3–8	Large pale violet-blue with purple veins (E–M)	Dark green, deeply divided, quilted	As above
m. 'Elizabeth Ann'	18–24in × 18in	3–8	Lilac-pink (E–M)	Dark greenish brown, green veins	Stunning leaf color, shade, CBAF
×magnificum	18–24in × 24in	5–9	Large violet-blue with dark veins (E–M)	Dark green, rounded, hairy, deeply cut	Sterile, a bold plant, spreads, sun, CBAF, RHS Award
malviflorum	12–18in × 18in+	7–8	Violet-blue with dark veins, large (E)	Green, deeply divided	Summer dormant, tuberous, sun

Species and Cultivars	Height/ Spread	USDA Hardiness Zone	Flowers (bloom time)	Foliage	Comments
×monacense	18–24in × 24in	4–9	Purplish pink with central white zone, petals reflexed (E–M)	Green, blotched with reddish brown	Good for shade
×m. var. monacense 'Muldoon'	15in × 20in	4–9	Maroon fading to violet, reflexed (E–L)	Green with purplish brown blotches	Sun to shade, drought tolerant
'Nimbus'	10–24in × 24in	5–9	Lavender-blue, light center and dark veins (E–M)	Very finely cut, green with golden tinge when young	CBAF, vigorous, self-sows, sun, RHS Award
nodosum	8–10in × 12in	4–8	Pink to lavender and its shades, variable from seed (M)	Dark green, glossy, 3-lobed	Shade, spreads by seed and rhizomes, aggressive
orientalitibeticum	8–12in × 12in+	5–9	Deep pink with pale central zone (M)	Light green, marbled yellow-green, small	Sun to part shade, tuberous, spreads
×oxonianum	24–30in × 24in	4–9	Various pink shades with dark veins (E–L)	Mid-green, glossy, faintly blotched	Vigorous, sun to shade, CBAF, all forms, to prevent self-sowing
×o. 'A. T. Johnson'	15–18in × 24in	5–8	Light silvery-pink, translucent (E–L)	Mid-green, finely toothed	Sun to shade, compact, CBAF, RHS Award
×o. 'Bressingham's Delight'	16in × 24in	5–8	Soft pink, darker pink veins (E–L)	Light green, finely toothed	Sun to shade, CBAF
×o. 'Claridge Druce'	18–24in × 24in	4–8	Deep rosy-pink with darker veins (E–L)	Grayish green, glossy, divided, semi-evergreen	Vigorous, sun to shade, self-sows, CBAF
×o. 'Katherine Adele'	15–20in × 24in	5–9	Pale silvery-pink with purple veins (E–L)	Mid-green with brownish central zone	Varies greatly in seedlings, sun to shade, CBAF
×o. 'Phoebe Noble'	18in × 24in	5–9	Dark pink with darker veins, notched petals (E–L)	As above	Sun to shade, CBAF
×o. 'Rose Clair'	15–18in × 24in	5–9	Rosy-pink aging to deep pink (E–L)	As above	Long-blooming, sun to shade, CBAF
×o. f. thurstonianum	18–24in × 24in+	5–9	Bright reddish purple with white base, magenta veins (E–L)	Mid to dark green, blotched purplish brown	Sun to shade, self-sows, CBAF
×o. f. thurstonianum 'Southcombe Double'	12–15in × 24in	5–9	Deep salmon-pink, often with petaloid stamens that make flowers appear double (E–M)	Mid-green with brownish central zone	Less vigorous, sun to shade, CBAF
×o. f. thurstonianum 'Southcombe Star'	15–18in × 24in	5–9	Bluish pink magenta veins, narrow petals (E–L)	As above	Sun to shade, CBAF
×o. 'Walter's Gift'	15–24in × 24in	5–9	Pale pink with dark lavender veins (E–M)	Green, zoned in bronze and purple	As above
'Patricia'	24–30in × 18–24in	4–8	Magenta, with dark eye (M–L)	Mid-green, deeply cut, large	Sun to part shade

Species and Cultivars	Height/ Spread	USDA Hardiness Zone	Flowers (bloom time)	Foliage	Comments
phaeum	18–30in × 18in	3–9	Dark purple-maroon, reflexed petals, nodding (E–L)	Mid-green, finely toothed, often spotted or banded purplish or brown	Mourning widow, shade to sun, clump-forming, CBAF
p. 'Album'	18–24in × 18in	3–9	White, reflexed, nodding (E–L)	As above but more subtly spotted or banded	Needs a bit more moisture, less clump-forming, CBAF, shade to part sun
p. 'Lily Lovell'	18–24in × 18in	3–9	Purplish with purple veins and white eye, nodding, reflexed, large (E–L)	Light green, no blotches	CBAF, shade to part sun
p. var. lividum 'Joan Baker'	18–36in × 18in	3–9	Pale lavender with darker ring near the center, nodding, reflexed (E–L)	Mid-green, finely toothed, often spotted or banded purplish or brown	As above
p. var. phaeum	15–18in × 18in	3–9	Lighter maroon, with brown veins, maroon stems, white eye (E–L)	Light green, no blotches	As above
p. var. phaeum 'Samobor'	15–18in × 18in	3–9	Dark maroon, reflexed, nodding (E–L)	Large, deep green, with purplish brown zone	Sun to part shade, comes true from seed, CBAF
p. 'Taff's Jester'	15–18in × 12in	3–9	Dark purple-maroon (E–L)	Green splashed with yellow-green and blotched dull purple in leaf notches	Variegation tones are less in summer, best in shade CBAF
p. 'Variegatum'	18–24in × 12in	3–9	Dark purple-maroon, reflexed, white eye (E–L)	Green splashed with sage-green and cream, red blotches	Variegation improves in summer shade, CBAF
'Philippe Vapelle'	10–15in × 12in	4–8	Large bluish purple with dark veins (E)	Soft blue-gray, quilted, deeply notched	Sun, *G. renardii* hybrid
pratense	2–3ft × 2ft	3–8	Large bluish purple, veined (E–M)	Mid-green, serrated	Meadow cranesbill, sun, CBAF, dwindles with competition
p. 'Mrs. Kendall Clark'	2–3ft × 2ft	3–8	Light violet-blue with white veins (E–M)	Green, deeply cut	May rebloom in fall, sun to part shade, CBAF, RHS Award
p. 'Plenum Caeruleum'	18–24in × 24in	3–8	Double light lavender-blue, flushed pink (M)	Dark green, finely cut	Sun, moist, doubles are not cut back
p. 'Plenum Violaceum'	18–24in × 24in	3–8	Double, rich violet pompoms, perfectly formed (M)	As above	Sun, doubles are not cut back, RHS Award
p. 'Striatum' (syn. 'Splish Splash')	12–20in × 18in	3–8	White, blue-speckled and -splashed (M)	Green	Sun to part shade, CBAF, good foliage plant

Species and Cultivars	Height/ Spread	USDA Hardiness Zone	Flowers (bloom time)	Foliage	Comments
p. 'Victor Reiter'	15in × 15in	5–9	Rich deep blue-violet (E–M)	Purple fading to purplish green, deeply cut	May be short-lived and resents competition, CBAF, sun
psilostemon	2–4ft × 3ft	4–9	Magenta with black eye and veins (M)	Mid-green, large, deeply cut, sharply toothed, good fall color	Variable from seed, CBAF, sun, RHS Award
p. 'Bressingham Flair'	2–3ft × 3ft	4–9	Softer magenta with maroon veins and blotch (M)	As above	Very similar to species, more compact, sun, CBAF
pyrenaicum 'Bill Wallis'	12–16in × 12in	5–9	Intense violet-purple, dark red stems (E–L)	Small, green, round, deeply cut	Sun, self-sows politely, short-lived, CBAF
renardii	10–12in × 12in	5–8	White with purple veins, hint of pale lavender (E)	Soft sage-green, corrugated, velvety, round	Sun, evergreen, RHS Award
×riversleaianum 'Mavis Simpson'	10–15in × 36in	8–9	Shell-pink with silver sheen, darker veins, trailing stems (E–L)	Soft gray-green	Sun, short-lived, wide-spreading, long bloomer
×r. 'Russell Prichard'	10–15in × 36in	8–9	Rich magenta-pink with black eye and veins (E–L)	Gray-green, broadly lobed	Long bloomer, spreads, sun, short-lived, RHS Award
robustum	2–3ft × 2ft	8+	Pale purple (M)	Gray-green, silvery backed, dissected	Tender, tall, and ungainly, sun
'Salome'	10–12in × 36in	5–9	Light violet-lavender, maroon veins and dark central zone, large (M–L)	Chartreuse, marbled very slightly	Clump-forming but rambles, long-blooming, sun
sanguineum	10–12in × 12in	3–8	Magenta, saucer-shaped (E–L)	Small, green, deeply divided, good fall color	Bloody cranesbill, self-sows, sun
s. 'Alan Bloom'	10–12in × 12in	3–9	Bright pink (E–L)	Green, deeply divided, good fall color	Long-blooming, sun
s. 'Album'	12–18in × 12in	4–8	White with pink veins (E–L)	As above	Sun, sprawling, RHS Award
s. 'Alpenglow'	12–18in × 12in	4–9	Rose-red magenta (E–M)	Dark green, deeply lobed	More compact, sun
s. 'Ankum's Pride'	6–15in × 15in	4–9	Bright pink with dark veins (E–M)	Mid-green, divided	Sun
s. 'Cedric Morris'	18–24in × 12in	4–9	Magenta-pink, red veins (E–L)	Dark green, divided	As above
s. 'John Elsley'	12–18in × 15in	4–9	Purplish blue, darker veins (E–L)	Rich green	Trailing growth habit, long season, sun
s. 'Max Frei'	6–10in × 12in	4–9	Magenta, saucer-shaped (E–M)	Dark green, deeply lobed, fall color	Sun to part shade, compact
s. 'New Hampshire Purple'	12–24in × 15in	4–9	Reddish purple, magenta veins (E–L)	Mid-green, reddish tints in fall	Long-blooming, sun

Species and Cultivars	Height/ Spread	USDA Hardiness Zone	Flowers (bloom time)	Foliage	Comments
s. 'Shephard's Warning'	8–10in × 12in	4–9	Dark reddish pink, notched (E–M)	Dark green	Slow to increase, difficult to propagate, sun, RHS Award
s. var. striatum (syn. var. lancastriense)	6–10in × 12in	4–9	Light pink, deep pink veins (E–L)	Deep green, deeply cut, good fall color	Sun to part shade, drought tolerant, RHS Award
subcaulescens	6–9in × 8in	4–10	Magenta-red with black center and veins, black stigma and anthers (E–M)	Gray-green, small, scalloped edge	Sun, RHS Award
s. 'Giuseppii'	8–10in × 12in	5–9	Magenta with dark veins (E–L)	Grayish green	Vigorous, sun
s. 'Splendens'	4–6in × 6in	5–9	Bright magenta, dark center (E–L)	Grayish green, shallowly lobed	Not as robust as the species, more compact, sun, RHS Award
sylvaticum	18–28in × 24in	5–9	White, pink, or purple with white center, saucer-shaped (E–M)	Mid-green, divided	Wood cranesbill, part shade to sun, moist
s. 'Album'	18–28in × 24in	5–9	Large, white with translucent veins (E–M)	As above	Comes true from seed, shade to sun, RHS Award
s. 'Amy Doncaster'	18–28in × 24in	5–9	Deep violet-blue with white eye (E–M)	As above	Shade to sun
s. 'Mayflower'	18–28in × 24in	5–9	Large rich violet-blue with white center (E–M)	Mid-green, lobed, broadly divided	Shade lover, RHS Award
s. 'Silva'	18in × 18in	5–9	Bluish purple with white eye (E–M)	Dark green, sharply divided	Sun to shade
tuberosum	9in × 12in	7–9	Rosy-lilac fading to cool lilac with darker veins (E–M)	Green, finely cut, feathery	Summer dormant, tuberous, sun in spring
versicolor	15in × 18in	5–9	White with magenta veins, trumpet-shaped, notched petals (E–L)	Pale green, hairy, toothed	Self-sows, sun
wallichianum	10–12in × 24in+	5–8	Purple, white eye and deep purple veins (E–M)	Dusky mid-green, trailing stems	Drought tolerant, spreads, sun
w. 'Buxton's Variety'	10–12in × 24in+	5–8	Violet-blue with pink center, later flowers clear blue and white eye (M–L)	Dusky mid-green, deeply cut	Collect seed all season as heads brown, sun to part shade, RHS Award
wlassovianum	18–24in × 24in	4–9	Purplish violet, darker veins (M–L)	Velvety green with brown band, variably good fall color	Sun to part shade

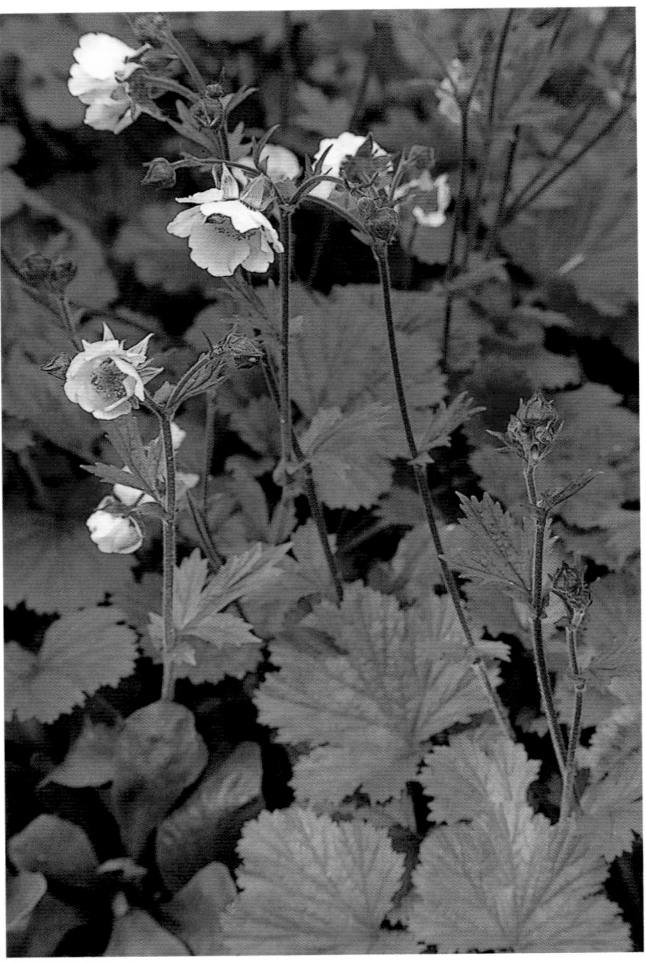

Geum 'Coppertone'.

GEUM Rosaceae

Looking for something bright? Try one of the geums. These long-blooming members of the rose family will reward you with flowers in shades of orange, yellow, scarlet, copper, or pink. They are single, semi-double or double, cup- or bell-shaped; some are up-facing while others nod. *Geum rivale* and *G. triflorum* have interesting fluffy seedheads. Foliage varies from dark to bright green or gray-green, and is usually hairy and wrinkled; leaves are pinnate with a terminal leaflet usually larger, scalloped and toothed, and sometimes actually divided into three. Plants form a low, basal mound. Geums hate cold, wet winters and will die in winter in waterlogged soil. To use cut, pick when flowers are just half open. ~ *Susan Carter*

Scientific Name: The classical Latin name for this plant.
Common Name: Avens.
Origin: Temperate regions of Europe, Asia, North and South America, South Africa, New Zealand.
Preferred Conditions: Fertile, well-drained, average soil. Doesn't like to dry out.
Light: Sun. Tolerates part shade.
Management: The seed-grown varieties and most of the newer cultivars will repeat bloom if old flower stems are regularly removed. Remove dead lower leaves regularly as well. Taller cultivars may need support. Geums can become congested and do best when divided every two or three years; late spring is a good time for this. Throw away the old woody growth and replant the fresh young growth.
Propagation: Seed (species) when ripe, or division in spring.
Pests and Diseases: Downy mildew, fungal leaf spot, powdery mildew, spider mites, some problem with root weevil.
Companions: *Alchemilla mollis*, *Geranium* 'Johnson's Blue', *Oenothera fruticosa* 'Fyrverkeri', *Iris sibirica*, salvia (blue or purple cultivars), smaller grasses, heuchera, potentilla, achillea, carex.

Species and Cultivars	Height/ Spread	USDA Hardiness Zone	Flowers (bloom time)	Foliage	Comments
'Borisii'	10–12in × 12in	5–9	Orange, up-facing, cup-shaped (E–M)	Mid-green, hairy, rounded, pinnate	Clump-forming
chiloense (syn. coccineum, quellyon)	16–24in × 18in	5–9	Scarlet, single or double, up-facing (E–M)	Pale green, hairy, pinnate	Clump-forming, repeats in fall, needs annual division
'Coppertone'	10–12in × 10in	5–9	Copper-apricot, wavy petals, reddish brown sepals, brown stems, slightly pendent (E–M)	Mid-green, toothed, pinnate	A very charming color, a *G. rivale* hybrid but stays smaller
'Fire Opal'	12–30in × 12in	5–9	Reddish orange, single, semi-double, dark purple stems (E–M)	As above	RHS Award
'Georgenburg'	10–12in × 10in	5–9	Light yellow-orange, single, red stems (E–M)	Bright green, pinnate	Pinkish buff seedheads
'Lady Stratheden' (syn. 'Goldball')	24in × 24in	5–9	Soft, rich yellow, semi-double, cup-shaped (E–M)	Mid-green, hairy, pinnate to ovate	Comes true from seed, short-lived, RHS Award
'Lemon Drops'	12–14in × 12in	5–9	Pale yellow, pendent, orange stamens (E–M)	Bright green, pinnate	*G. rivale* hybrid
'Lionel Cox'	12in × 12in+	5–9	Pale yellow, pendent, dark stems (M)	As above	As above
'Mrs. J. Bradshaw' (syn. 'Feuerball')	16–24in × 24in	5–9	Scarlet, semi-double to double (E–M)	Bright green, hairy, pinnate	Comes true from seed, clump-forming, short-lived, RHS Award
'Red Wings'	16–24in × 12in	5–9	Scarlet-orange, semi-double (E–M)	As above	
rivale	12–24in × 18–24in	5–9	Dusky pink, red-brown sepals, nodding, bell-shaped (E–M)	Dark green, dense, hairy, toothed, pinnate, leaflets very small	Water avens, Indian chocolate, likes it cool and moist
r. 'Leonard's Variety'	12–18in × 18in	5–9	Pale apricot, double, bell-shaped, mahogany stems, nodding (M)	Dark green, pinnate	
'Starker's Magnificum'	15–18in × 18in	5–9	Apricot, double (E–M)	Mid-green, pinnate	Long-blooming, short-lived
triflorum	10–16in × 12in	3–9	Light maroon to almost yellow, nodding, bell-shaped (E–M)	Gray-green, silky, pinnate, hairy, many leaflets	Prairie smoke, clump-forming, North American native

Gillenia trifoliata.

GILLENIA Rosaceae

One of the best native North American perennials, this time from the eastern woodlands, *G. trifoliata* is usually a surprise the first time you see it, with starlike white flowers borne on the end of very fine, wiry branches over light and airy foliage. A good cut flower but hard to sacrifice. Buy this long-lived species whenever it is offered. ~ *Bob Lilly*

Scientific Name: After seventeenth-century German botanist Arnold Gille.
Common Name: Bowman's root, Indian physic.
Origin: North America.
Preferred Conditions: Fertile, well-drained, moisture-retentive, humus-rich, acidic to neutral soil.
Light: Sun to part shade.
Management: Very easy to grow. Needs summer water but no staking. Cut back in winter. Resents competition.
Propagation: Seed in spring but slow to germinate; division is not recommended.
Pests and Diseases: Watch for slugs as plants first emerge in spring.
Companions: Ferns, meconopsis, dicentra, polygonatum, hosta, hardy cyclamen, hardy fuchsias, brunnera.

Species and Cultivars	Height/ Spread	USDA Hardiness Zone	Flowers (bloom time)	Foliage	Comments
trifoliata	3–4ft × 2½ft	5–9	Small, white to pinkish white, star-shaped, narrow petals, reddish stems (E–M)	Bronze-green, coarsely toothed, turns red in fall	North American native, good fall color, RHS Award

Glaucium flavum.

GLAUCIUM Papaveraceae

In its native range, including Greece, the horned poppy actually grows in pure beach sand. In most of our soils and locations, however, it is a short-lived perennial or even biennial. The two species we list are similar plants but very different in flower color. If you keep them from setting seed, they may bloom longer than they normally would. Glaucium was named for its glaucous leaves and follows the gray-leaf rule: "full sun and lean soil." ~ *Bob Lilly*

Scientific Name: From the Greek *glaukos* ("gray-green"), referring to the leaves.
Common Name: Horned poppy.
Origin: Europe, North Africa, Central and Southwest Asia.
Preferred Conditions: Lean to moderately fertile, well-drained soil. Minimal water needs.
Light: Sun.
Management: Resents root disturbance. Cut back to new basal leaves in fall after they collapse.
Propagation: Seed, collect when ripe and sow in situ in spring or autumn, division is not recommended.
Pests and Diseases: Free of problems except a bit of slug damage in early spring.
Companions: Yucca, artemisia, helictotrichon, *Salvia patens*, *Euphorbia rigida*, *Ruta graveolens*; the dry border.
Notes: Really cool seedpods—something like an eschscholzia (California poppy) seedhead but much bigger.

Species and Cultivars	Height/ Spread	USDA Hardiness Zone	Flowers (bloom time)	Foliage	Comments
corniculatum	24–30in × 18in	6–9	Crimson-red to orange with a black spot at base of each petal (M–L)	Silver-gray, slightly hairy	Red horned poppy
flavum	24–36in × 18in	6–9	Golden yellow or orange, gray stems (M)	Glaucous, rough, lobed or finely cut	Yellow horned poppy, unruly, seedpods 10–12in long

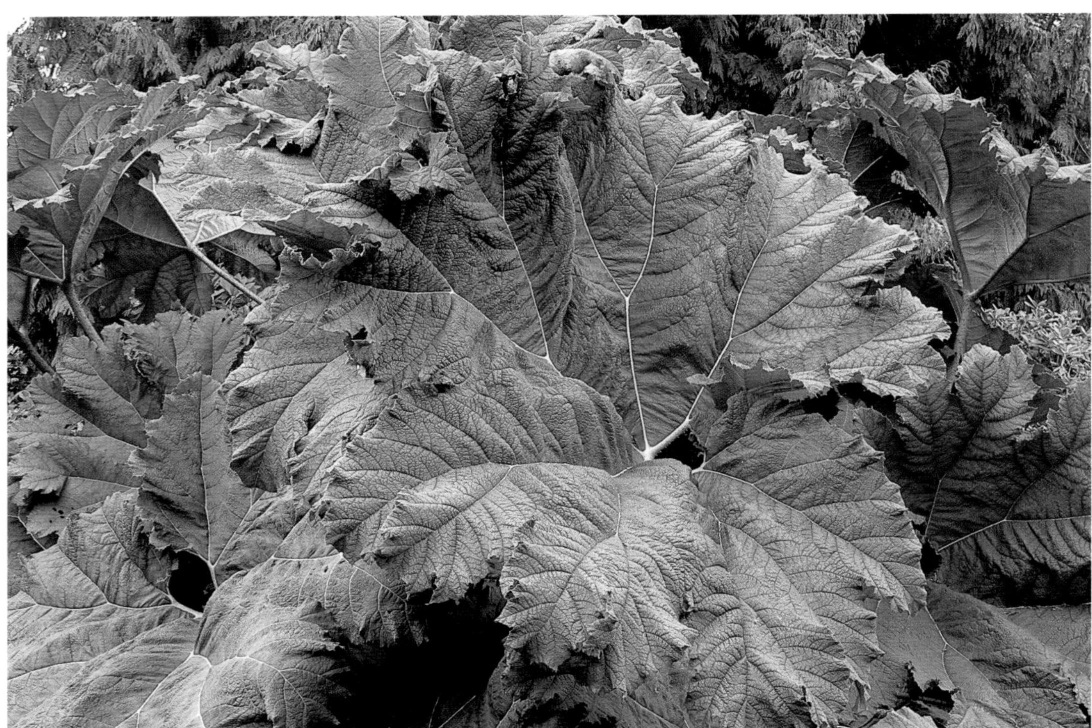
Gunnera manicata.

GUNNERA Gunneraceae

This is not a rhubarb. Most gunneras are from subtropical areas but are quite hardy. Most of the spectacular ornamental gunneras are extremely large and are best seen in botanical gardens like Van Dusen in Vancouver, British Columbia, and Strybing in San Francisco; few are in small city gardens. The large clump-forming species, *G. tinctoria* and *G. manicata*, particularly appreciate a deep mulch of manure; this will create their wonderful huge leaves. The two groundcover forms seem to be less hardy and have quite curious leaves. ~ *Bob Lilly*

Scientific Name: After Ernst Gunnerus, Norwegian bishop and botanist.
Common Name: Prickly rhubarb, giant rhubarb.

Species and Cultivars	Height/ Spread	USDA Hardiness Zone	Flowers (bloom time)	Foliage	Comments
magellanica	6–10in × 24in+	8–10	Tiny, green, with orange-red fruit (M)	Bright to dark green, glossy, scalloped, cupped kidney-shaped, 2–3in	Mat-forming, stoloniferous
manicata	8–10ft × 12ft	8–10	Tiny, greenish to pinkish on thick thorny stalks (E–M)	Deep green, round to kidney-shaped, pleated, 8ft long, 4–6ft wide	Clump-forming, RHS Award
prorepens	4in × 24in	8–10	Greenish white, insignificant (M)	Bronze-green to brownish, ovate, scalloped, short-stalked	Dense, mat-forming groundcover, mulberrylike clusters of dark red fruit
tinctoria (syn. chilensis)	6–10ft × 8ft+	8–10	Tiny, rust-red, reddish stem, thick cone-shaped stalk (M)	Deep green, heart-shaped to round, deeply lobed and toothed, puckered, 3–6ft long, 4–5ft wide	The smaller of the giant gunneras

Origin: South Africa, South America, Hawaii, New Zealand, Tasmania.

Preferred Conditions: Deep, humus-rich, moisture-retentive soil; don't let it dry out. Gunneras tolerate wet ground but not flooded areas. The large species need shelter from cold and drying winds.

Light: Sun to part shade. Takes full sun in the Northwest.

Planting: Place gunnera one to two feet above the high-water mark, if siting near water.

Management: Protect the massive crowns of large species in winter with a heavy insulating mulch. Cover crowns with their own leaves, cut and placed upside down, then straw or manure. They are heavy feeders, so dress generously with manure every spring. Remove flowers on the large species to increase size of the leaves. As the plant spreads outward, it may become bald in the center. This is the time to start a new colony, or try and reestablish growth in the center.

Propagation: Seed in containers as soon as ripe; keep containers cool and frost-free through the winter, germination is slow; division in spring.

Pests and Diseases: Slugs and snails, slugs and slugs, and slugs, odd as it is for a plant with so many spines. Bait and hunt early to help leaves stay good-looking.

Companions: Large species are best grown as focal points, with lower-growing perennials in mass plantings (petasites, darmera, rodgersia, primula), or with a big group of Japanese iris, ligularia, and ferns; the damp garden.

Notes: South American native people eat the leaf stalks of *G. manicata* and *G. tinctoria*. Watch for concrete casts of gunnera leaves as garden decorations.

GYPSOPHILA Caryophyllaceae

A great blender for the border, gypsophila produces masses of small, white or almost pink flowers on nearly invisible stems. Pick when in full bloom for use as a fresh or dried cut flower. This is a good plant to grow over those areas where you have spring bulbs or oriental poppies; it will hide their foliage as it cures, or fill in their space once they are gone. ~ *Bob Lilly*

Scientific Name: From the Greek *gypsos* ("gypsum") and *philos* ("loving").

Common Name: Baby's breath, chalk plant.

Origin: Mediterranean, Central Asia, northwestern China, Caucasus.

Preferred Conditions: Deep, moderately fertile, well-drained, limy soil that warms up quickly in the spring. Average water conditions; will not tolerate wet or damp conditions. Protect from strong winds and too much competition.

Gypsophila paniculata.

Light: Sun.

Planting: Plant out in spring when plants are young; grafted forms—plant graft just below soil level.

Management: Dislikes disturbance of taproots. Large flower sprays cause plants to become top-heavy. Install wire rings when growth is only a few inches high, or pea sticks or bamboo for later support. Cut back after flowering and before seed clusters form to encourage a second bloom. May also benefit from a bit of lime or limestone chips. Cut back in fall when foliage has cured.

Propagation: Seed; basal root cuttings (species only) in late winter; division in spring.

Pests and Diseases: Crown gall, crown and stem rot are uncommon (lime will reduce these problems), snails, slugs.

Companions: Sweet peas, allium, dianthus; use with large-flowered, coarse-textured plants (yucca, delphinium) for contrast.

Notes: It's the slugs, stupid! Baby's breath failure in the Pacific Northwest is ninety percent due to slug and snail grazing on the tiny new growth tips as they first appear in spring. Nor do the crowns like our wet winters. We wish they grew here!

Species and Cultivars	Height/ Spread	USDA Hardiness Zone	Flowers (bloom time)	Foliage	Comments
fastigiata 'Festival' (Festival Series)	2–3ft × 3ft	4–8	Double and semi-double white, sometimes pink-blushed (M–L)	Bluish green, lanceolate	Vigorous, erect, compact, bred in Israel for cut flower trade
f. 'Festival Pink'	2–4ft × 3ft	4–8	Pink (M)	As above	As above
f. Happy Festival = 'Danghappy'	2–2½ft × 2ft	4–8	Larger, white, double and semi-double (M)	As above	More compact, may rebloom in fall
paniculata	2–4ft × 3ft	4–8	Single to double white, trumpet-shaped (M–L)	Glaucous, lanceolate, somewhat sparse	May need support, good cut
p. 'Bristol Fairy'	2–4ft × 3ft	4–8	Double white, large (M)	As above	Best cultivar, may need support, RHS Award
p. 'Flamingo'	2½–3ft × 2½ft	4–8	Double, pale lilac-pink (M)	As above	Bushy, may need staking
p. 'Perfekta'	3–4ft × 3ft	4–8	Double white, large (M)	Gray-green, lanceolate	A favorite with florists, may need support
p. 'Pink Fairy'	1½–2ft × 2ft	4–8	Double, light pink, large	As above	Semi-dwarf, dense
p. 'Schneeflocke' (syn. 'Snowflake')	3ft × 3ft	4–8	Double white (M)	Gray-green, narrow	Blooms earlier than most
repens	4–6in × 12in+	4–8	Rose-pink (M)	Gray-green, lanceolate, smooth, tiny	Creeping, a sweet groundcover or rockery plant, short-lived for us, RHS Award
'Rosenschleier' (syn. 'Rosy Veil')	1½ft × 1½ft	4–8	Semi-double, pale rose-pink, opening white (M)	Green, small, lanceolate	Can take moist soil, RHS Award
'Viette's Dwarf'	1–1½ft × 1½ft	4–8	Double, pink fading to white (M)	Bluish green, narrow, lanceolate	Compact, dense

HEDYCHIUM Zingiberaceae

The hardy ginger lilies are very nice, upright, late-season bloomers for us; depending on the summer heat, they begin to flower in late August if it's a warmer summer, mid September if it's a mild summer. The hardiest and showiest seems to be *H. coccineum* 'Tara', and *H. densiflorum* 'Stephen' blooms just as reliably for us. Hedychium leaves are nearly as fine as the flowers—erect, glaucous, and exotic-looking. All are best planted in the spring, as soon as plants are available, so they can get established for their first winter. ~ *Carrie Becker*

Scientific Name: From the Greek *hedys* ("sweet") and *chion* ("snow").
Common Name: Garland lily, ginger lily.
Origin: Asia, China, Nepal.
Preferred Conditions: Humus-rich, well-drained, moisture-retentive, acidic soil. Don't allow to dry out during the growing season. Shelter from wind.
Light: Sun.
Management: Can be late emerging in spring. Don't move during dormant period. Best time is just when they begin growth in spring. Cut off spent stems in late autumn, down to the ground after frost damage. Mulch in winter.

Hedychium coccineum 'Tara'.

Hedychium coccineum 'Tara' with *Hakonechloa macra* 'Aureola', *Hydrangea macrophylla* 'Hamburg', and *Magnolia sieboldii* in fruit.

Propagation: Seed as soon as ripe; divide rhizomes in spring.
Pests and Diseases: Aphids, root rot, leaf spot.
Companions: Hydrangea, cimicifuga, rodgersia, oriental lilies (to extend bloom time in the garden).
Notes: Best results if heavily mulched. This is one of the plants you run around and cover with fir boughs when a cold snap is due. Plant in the warmest part of your garden for the best bloom.

Species and Cultivars	Height/ Spread	USDA Hardiness Zone	Flowers (bloom time)	Foliage	Comments
coccineum	6–8ft × 3ft	8–10	Deep red, orange, pink and white with prominent red stamens, fragrant (M)	Mid-green, narrow, sharply pointed, lanceolate, 2ft × 2in	Hardy but needs heat, RHS Award
c. 'Tara'	3–5ft × 3ft	8–10	Light orange spikes with long red stamens, fragrant (M)	Dark green, broadly lanceolate, 2ft × 2in	Hardier than species, a very strong element in the garden, RHS Award
densiflorum 'Stephen'	3–5ft × 3ft+	8–10	Orange-red spikes, fragrant (M)	Dark green, broadly lanceolate, ribbed, shiny	Hardy
greenii	3–4ft × 2ft	9–10	Red-orange spikes (L)	Dark green, maroon reverse, glossy	Prefers some shade, tender

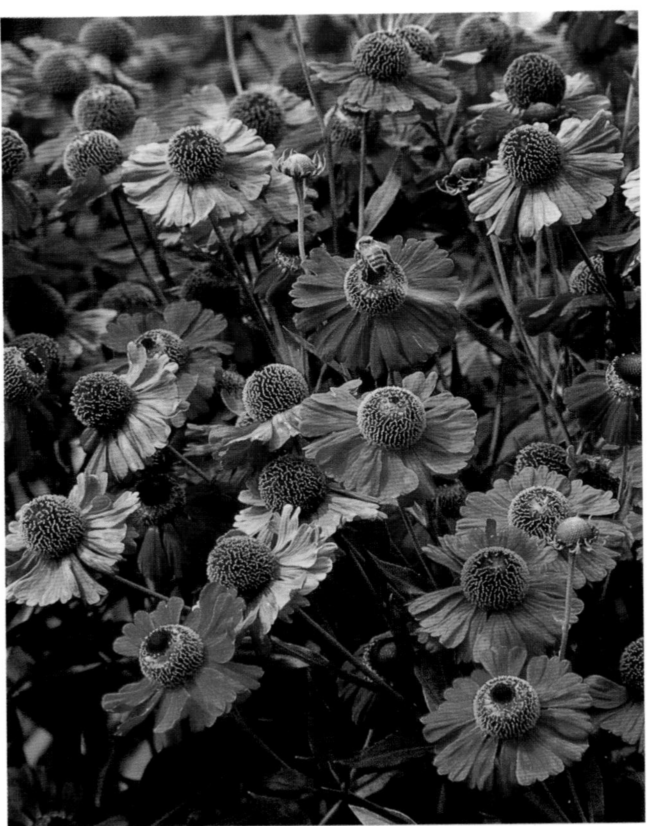

Helenium 'Moerheim Beauty'.

HELENIUM Asteraceae

North American natives, the sneezeweeds have beautiful daisylike flower heads with raised central disk flowers surrounded by prominent ray flowers in shades of yellow, red, and copper. They produce dense clumps of branching stems with lanceolate, toothed leaves. Heleniums are indispensable in the midsummer and early fall garden, providing an abundance of flowers over a long season. They are a good cut flower for fresh arrangements. It is definitely worth waiting for these reliable plants to get established. ~ *Susan Carter*

Scientific Name: From the Greek *helonion*, a name for another plant that was possibly named after Helen of Troy.
Common Name: Sneezeweed.
Origin: North America, South America, Central America.
Preferred Conditions: Moisture-retentive, well-drained, with cool roots in a hot, sunny location. Tolerates wet soil. Easy to grow in any fertile soil, but too-rich soil will produce more foliage.
Light: Sun.

Management: While not necessary, timely pinching when stems are six to eight inches tall can delay flowering and modify height, but this is not an advantage worth taking just to get a shorter plant (especially in our usually cool summers). Deadhead to promote rebloom (remove down to the next bud). Don't allow to dry out; leaves will droop and drop if short of water. Top-dress with organic material and mulch to keep roots cool. Taller forms may need support, especially with wind or heavy rain. Cut back to crown in winter. Bait for slugs and snails in early spring to protect young shoots.

Propagation: Division in spring or autumn every two or three years.

Pests and Diseases: Slugs, snails, powdery mildew, rust.

Companions: Crocosmia, rudbeckia, achillea, artemisia, monarda, solidago, tall grasses, phlox, anthemis.

Notes: All parts of the plant may cause severe discomfort if ingested, and contact with the foliage may aggravate skin allergies. *Helenium hoopesii* (recently transferred to the genus *Hymenoxys*) is poisonous to animals, especially sheep.

Species and Cultivars	Height/ Spread	USDA Hardiness Zone	Flowers (bloom time)	Foliage	Comments
autumnale	3–6ft × 2ft	3–9	Golden yellow, red and copper, brownish yellow center, 2–2½in (M–L)	Green, lanceolate	Clump-forming, will suffer if too dry
bigelovii	2–3ft × 1½ft	3–9	Deep yellow, brownish yellow center, 2½–3in (M)	Green, shiny, lanceolate	Clump-forming, good cut
'Bruno'	2–4ft × 2ft	3–9	Mahogany-red, brown center, 2–3in (M–L)	Dark green, lanceolate	Erect
'Butterpat'	3–4ft × 2ft	3–9	Rich yellow, yellow-brown center, 2–3in (M–L)	As above	Needs support, long-blooming, good cut, RHS Award
'Coppelia'	2½–3ft × 2ft	3–9	Coppery-orange, brown center, 2–3in (M–L)	As above	
'Feuersiegel'	5ft × 2ft	3–9	Golden brown to red, brown center, 2–3in (M–L)	As above	RHS Award
hoopesii (syn. *Hymenoxys hoopesii*)	2–3ft × 2ft	3–9	Bright yellow or orange, yellow-brown center, 3in (M)	Gray-green, broad, lanceolate, glossy	Clump-forming, good cut
'Moerheim Beauty'	2½–4ft × 2ft	3–9	Brownish red, dark brown center, long-flowering, 2–3in (M–L)	Dark green, lanceolate	Needs support, upright, RHS Award
'Riverton Beauty'	4–5ft × 2ft	3–9	Golden yellow, maroon center, 2–3in (M–L)	As above	Upright, needs support
'Rotgold' (syn. 'Red and Gold')	3–4ft × 2ft	3–9	Shades of red and yellow, brown center, 2–3in (M–L)	As above	As above
'The Bishop'	2–3ft × 2ft	3–9	Deep golden yellow, brown center, 2–3in (M–L)	As above	Dwarf, clump-forming

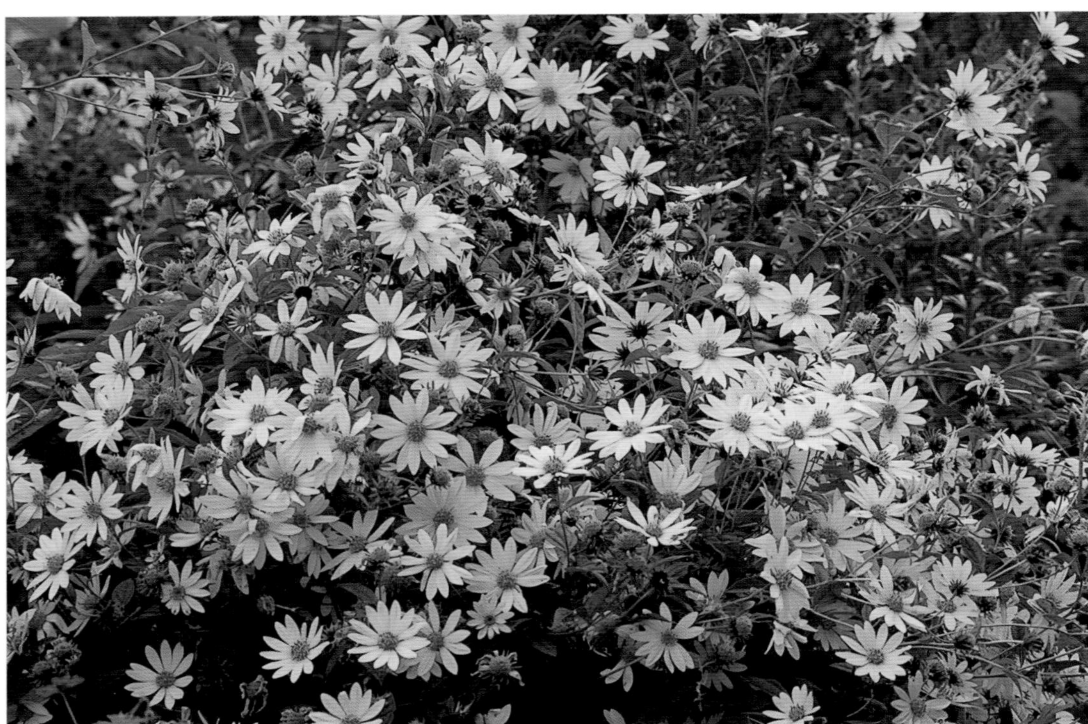

Helianthus 'Lemon Queen'.

HELIANTHUS Asteraceae

The perennial sunflowers do very well in a sunny, warm location. *Helianthus* 'Lemon Queen' makes strong dense clumps and is one of the best late, pale yellow–flowered large-scale perennials. *Helianthus giganteus* runs and can be a pest but blooms reliably. All these plants do flop; support them with friends or pea sticks (they definitely will need staking if you overhead water). Clumps will age, especially in the centers, and will need to be refreshed unless you have room for them to roam. Drought on these prairie plants can trigger both powdery mildew and botrytis, so keep them evenly moist and well fed. They make a good cut flower, but watch out for minor skin irritation from the foliage. ~ *Bob Lilly*

Scientific Name: From the Greek *helio* ("sun") and *anthos* ("flower").
Common Name: Sunflower, swamp sunflower.
Origin: North America, Central America, Peru, Chile.
Preferred Conditions: Fertile, humus-rich, moist, moisture-retentive, well-drained, neutral to alkaline soil, in an open, airy position. Some are drought tolerant.
Light: Sun.
Management: Fertilize or top-dress annually with compost or manure. Disbud side shoots for larger blooms. Plants tend to spread and will need division every two to four years to control them; the more vigorous ones may need to be shovel-pruned every spring to keep in bounds. Staking may be needed. Bait for slugs as growth emerges in spring.
Propagation: Seed (cultivars may not come true from seed); division in spring or autumn; basal or stem cuttings in spring or autumn.
Pests and Diseases: Slugs, powdery mildew (if too dry), botrytis (if too wet), rust, cutworms.
Companions: *Arundo donax*, rudbeckia, aster, solidago, miscanthus, *Cortaderia selloana*.
Notes: *Helianthus maximiliani*, *H. angustifolius*, and *H. salicifolius* all bloom extremely late for us, so in the Pacific Northwest, site them in full sun against a warm wall. In the chart, the symbol ∞ = infinite spread.

Species and Cultivars	Height/ Spread	USDA Hardiness Zone	Flowers (bloom time)	Foliage	Comments
angustifolius	5–8ft × ∞	6–9	Golden yellow, purplish center, rough hairy stems (M–L)	Mid-green, coarse, narrow, lanceolate	Swamp sunflower, likes it hot, spreads aggressively
'Capenoch Star'	3–5ft × 4ft	3–9	Pale lemon-yellow, darker yellow center, semi-double (M)	Mid-green	Good cut, self-supporting, RHS Award
giganteus 'Sheila's Sunshine'	8–10ft × 4ft+	3–9	Pastel yellow (M–L)	Mid-green, narrow, similar to *H.* 'Lemon Queen'	Giant sunflower, creeping rootstock
'Lemon Queen' (syn. 'Limelight')	4–7ft × 4ft	3–9	Soft lemon-yellow, darker yellow center, single (M–L)	Deep green	May need staking, good cut, clump-forming but will run eventually, RHS Award
'Loddon Gold' (decapetalus)	3–6ft × 3ft	3–9	Double, golden yellow (M–L)	As above	Good cut, RHS Award
maximiliani	6–10ft × 2ft	4–9	Bright yellow, golden brown center (L)	Mid-green, lanceolate, willowy	Last to bloom in the Pacific Northwest
'Monarch'	6–7ft × 3ft	5–9	Bright yellow, dark center, large, semi-double (M–L)	Mid-green, hairy, mostly basal leaves	RHS Award
salicifolius (syn. orgyalis)	6–8ft × 2½ft	6–9	Golden yellow, purple-brown center (L)	Gray-green, long, narrow, drooping, slightly hairy	Willow-leaved sunflower, needs staking, late flowering, smells like chocolate!

HELIOPSIS Asteraceae

Heliopsis is one of the more perennial of the sunflower relatives that were originally from the Americas. Long-lasting flowers are as good cut as they are in the garden. A great plant for a warm garden and will be in bloom for a long time. All are clump-forming. ~ *Bob Lilly*

Scientific Name: From the Greek *helios* ("sun") and *opsis* ("like"), a reference to the flower's resemblance to the sun.
Common Name: False sunflower.
Origin: North and South America.
Preferred Conditions: Poor to moderately fertile, humus-rich, moist, well-drained soil. Drought tolerant (especially single-flower types).
Light: Sun.
Management: Deadhead to next bud for continued bloom. Double forms may need staking in advance of a summer rain, which can make the flowers very heavy. Cut back to the ground in winter and top-dress with organic matter. Divide every two to four years to maintain vigor.
Propagation: Division in spring or seed; basal cuttings.

Heliopsis helianthoides 'Loraine Sunshine'.

Pests and Diseases: Powdery mildew, rust, aphids, snails. Most members of the daisy family are prone to severe slug damage in early spring, and heliopsis are no exception to this rule.

Companions: Helenium, aster, phlox (white), monarda, late salvias, smaller miscanthus, solidago.

Notes: These must have full sun in the Pacific Northwest.

Species and Cultivars	Height/ Spread	USDA Hardiness Zone	Flowers (bloom time)	Foliage	Comments
helianthoides	3–5ft × 2ft	4–9	Golden yellow, yellow center, single to double, 2–3in (M–L)	Mid-green, ovate to lanceolate, serrated, glossy	Clump-forming, long-blooming, good cut
h. 'Loraine Sunshine'	2½ft × 2ft	4–9	Golden yellow, 2in (M–L)	Variegated creamy-white with dark green veins	Good cut, long-blooming, comes true from seed
h. var. scabra	3–4ft × 2ft	4–9	Yellow-orange, single to double, 2–3in (M)	Mid-green, lanceolate, coarse	Bushy
h. var. scabra 'Sommersonne' (syn. 'Summer Sun')	2½–5ft × 2ft	4–9	Golden yellow, brownish center, semi-double to single, 2–3in (M–L)	Mid-green	Good cut, long-blooming
h. var. scabra 'Spitzentänzerin' (syn. 'Ballerina')	3–4ft × 2ft	4–9	Deep golden yellow, semi-double, 2–3in (M–L)	Green, glossy	Good cut, compact, RHS Award

Helleborus orientalis.

HELLEBORUS Ranunculaceae

Along with clematis, these members of the buttercup family are among the most sought-after of garden plants. In their season we often talk of nothing else. The most common, *H. niger* (Christmas rose) and *H. orientalis* (Lenten rose), are great garden plants in a semi-shady location. Most hellebores are semi-evergreen and are left standing during the winter. Elfi Rahr, a local hellebore enthusiast, routinely polices her flowers, removing any with black areas caused by botrytis and other possible fungal problems.

Helleborus niger is normally in bloom by Christmas and is a favorite pot plant (for a brief indoor show) in Germany; it's a bit more difficult to grow in heavy soils (give them a bit more sun). The best forms, with large white flowers, fading to pink, are worth finding. The Lenten rose blooms mostly in February and March in a wide color range. These have spectacular markings, from spotted to netted and picotee. It is best to buy these in flower, although we have noticed some change in flower color and appearance in the second, third, and even fourth year after planting.

Although some breeding has been focused on quick blooming from seed, this may prove to be a useless exercise. Pollinated by bumblebees and an early food source for honeybees, *H. orientalis* sets seed easily and germinates well in the garden, after a series of freeze/thaw cycles; this process can be used for growing from seed. All hellebores do best with fresh seed planted in June or July, and if left outside will germinate the following spring. As with camellias, the *H. orientalis* flowers are best not exposed to morning sun when frozen.

Helleborus foetidus seems to be short-lived, and *H. argutifolius* more long-lived. Both give us the charm of green flowers in the spring. *Helleborus foetidus* is an extremely good plant for the edge of a wood as well as hot, sunny locations. Their native environment has hotter summers than we do in the Pacific Northwest. *Helleborus argutifolius*, *H. lividus*, and *H. ×sternii* actually prefer more sun.

Hellebores are great plants for the winter garden. Bold evergreen leaves, with a wonderful leathery substance, and beautiful flowers at a time when there's not much else going on. Watch out, you may become addicted! ~ *Bob Lilly*

Helleborus orientalis and *H. foetidus* 'Narrow Leaf'.

Scientific Name: From the Greek *helein* ("to kill") and *bora* ("food").

Common Name: Hellebore, Christmas rose, Lenten rose.

Origin: Corsica, Sardinia, Greece, Turkey, central Europe, United Kingdom.

Preferred Conditions: Wide range. Well-drained, moisture-retentive, neutral to just alkaline, and humus-rich.

Light: Shade to sun.

Planting: Transplant or plant out in spring. Do not plant too deeply as this may impair flowering. Plant just below the surface, with growing tips just at the surface.

Management: Manure or compost in early winter but keep it off the crown. Top-dress the area around the crown with limestone chips to change the pH, so botrytis and other disease organisms don't overwinter.

Let hellebores that flower off the previous year's leaf stem (*H. argutifolius, H. foetidus*) flower (and set seed) before cutting their stems to the ground. New shoots will have emerged from the crown, and new stems will grow and fill out during the summer and flower the following year. Cut back the leaf stems of *H. orientalis* as the new flower stems reach three to four inches to enhance flower display and reduce carry-over of disease on old leaves; cut the leaf stems close to the crown. Remove old and damaged leaves as necessary, and in winter, just before the buds open, cut off all the old leaves. When flower stems die back after seeding, they can be cut back to the ground; this too helps to prevent and control fungal diseases.

Remove seedlings around the base of plants to keep cultivars pure and unconjested; pot them up. Hellebores resent division and reestablish slowly.

Propagation: Seed (especially *H. foetidus* and *H. argutifolius*)—do not touch stems of seedlings when potting up; division in spring.

Pests and Diseases: Snails, slugs, botrytis, aphids.

Companions: Viola, primula, ferns, hosta, polygonatum, arum, corydalis, pulmonaria, oxalis, galanthus and other spring bulbs, brunnera; *H. foetidus* and *H. argutifolius* look best on their own; plant *H. niger* in among a groundcover or mulch so the flowers stay clean.

Notes: When using hellebores as a cut flower, pierce up and down the stem with a pin and soak for several hours or overnight in the bathtub or kitchen sink (lay them in the water). Now they are ready for arranging and should last at least two weeks. All parts are poisonous.

Species and Cultivars	Height/ Spread	USDA Hardiness Zone	Flowers (bloom time)	Foliage	Comments
argutifolius (syn. corsicus)	24–49in × 24in	6–9	Apple-green pendent cups, branched clusters (E)	Bluish green above, light green reverse, toothed, veined, trifoliate, leathery	Corsican hellebore, short-lived, evergreen, self-sows, sun, RHS Award
a. 'Janet Starnes'	18–20in × 20in	6–9	Greenish white (E)	Variegated, blue-green with pink and white speckles	Evergreen, sun
a. 'Pacific Frost'	18–20in × 20in	6–9	As above	More finely mottled and speckled	As above
×ericsmithii (syn. ×nigristern)	10–14in × 18in	6–8	Green with a rose-red blush, nodding, saucer-shaped (E)	Green, glossy, etched in silver, palmate	Best foliage in sun
foetidus	18–30in × 30in+	6–9	Pale green bells, edged in maroon-purple, drooping airy clusters, long-blooming (E)	Ice-green new growth aging to dark green, leathery, lanceolate leaflets, glossy, slight unpleasant scent, may flop if soil is too rich	Stinking hellebore, evergreen, needs more alkaline soil and sun but avoid intense sun, self-sows, vigorous, RHS Award
f. 'Narrow Leaf'	18–30in × 30in	6–9	Green cups with red edge (E)	As above except has narrow green leaflets	Appeared in the NPA Borders at the Bellevue Botanical Garden
f. 'Sopron'	36in+ × 30in	6–9	Green, open clusters (E)	Metallic silvery-blue sheen	Evergreen, very large-scale and upright
f. Wester Flisk Group	10–20in × 30in	6–9	Green with red lips (E)	Dark grayish green, deeply divided, red petioles and stems	Evergreen, self-sows, may flop
lividus	15in × 18in	8–9	Creamy-green, buds tinged pink (E)	Green with creamy-silvery mottling and veins, stems and leaf reverse are pink-tinged	Tender, evergreen, RHS Award
niger	10–18in × 20in	4–8	White, faintly tinged with pink on outside, golden stamen, nodding, cup-shaped (E)	Broad, dark green, palmate, leathery, glossy, deeply divided, toothed ovate leaflets	Christmas rose, long-blooming, evergreen, slugs are a problem, RHS Award
n. Blackthorn Group	10–18in × 20in	4–8	Purplish or pink-tinged green in bud, opens white, fading to pink (E)	Grayish green, veined, purple stems	Evergreen

Species and Cultivars	Height/ Spread	USDA Hardiness Zone	Flowers (bloom time)	Foliage	Comments
n. 'Potter's Wheel'	12in × 20in	4–8	White, pink-flushed with green eye, large (E)	Green, narrowly toothed leaflets	As above
n. 'White Magic'	12in+ × 20in	4–8	White, fading to soft pink, opens nearly flat, very large (E)	Green	As above
×nigercors	18in × 18in	7–9	Greenish white, pink-flushed clusters (E)	Dark green, pedate, 3- to 5-toothed leaflets	RHS Award
odorus	12–20in × 12–20in	7–9	Yellowish green, nodding, saucer-shaped (E)	Dark green, palmate, glossy, toothed leaflets, leathery	Deciduous, clump-forming
orientalis (syn. ×hybridus)	15–24in × 18in	4–9	Variable, yellowish, creamy-green, purplish green, white, pink to maroon, some speckled or spotted with purple-maroon and subtle green flushes inside and out (E)	As above	Lenten rose, evergreen, long-blooming, long-lived
o. Ballard's Group	14–16in × 18in	4–9	Variable color range, very cup-shaped, large (E)	As above	Evergreen
o. 'Blue Lady'	20in × 18in	4–9	Deep purplish blue, up-facing (E)	As above	As above
o. double-flowered hybrids	15–24in × 18in	4–9	White to pink to darker (E)	As above	As above
o. Party Dress Group	15–24in × 18in	4–9	White through deep pink, often with spotting, pointed petals (E)	As above	Evergreen, full sun best
o. Royal Heritage Strain	18–24in × 24in	4–9	Pure white to nearly black, red, purple, and yellow, very large (E)	As above	Evergreen, vigorous
purpurascens	8–16in × 18in	5–8	Purplish maroon outside, light green inside, cup-shaped (E)	Mid to dark green, deeply cut, hairy, streaked with purple	Deciduous, summer dormant
×sternii	12–24in × 18in	7–9	Creamy-green, tinted pinkish purple, variable (E)	Gray-green with creamy veins, 3 broad elliptic leaflets or lobes on purplish pink stems	Clump-forming, evergreen
×s. Blackthorn Group	18–24in × 18in	7–9	Chartreuse with pink tints (E)	Steel-blue	Evergreen, RHS Award
×s. 'Boughton Beauty'	18–24in × 18in	7–9	Chartreuse with pink flush (E)	Gray-green, glossy	Full sun, vigorous, evergreen
thibetanus	12in × 12in	7–9	Shell-pink, pendent (E)	Apple-green, palmate, broad	Goes dormant early, deciduous
torquatus	12in × 12in+	5–8	Green and gray to nearly black with faint pink flush, pendent (E)	Mid-green, lanceolate, toothed lobes, hairy, more divided than others	Deciduous, flowers emerge before leaves
viridis subsp. viridis	12in × 12in+	7–8	Green, small, pendent (E)	Apple-green	Green hellebore, deciduous

Hemerocallis fulva 'Flore Pleno'.

HEMEROCALLIS Hemerocallidaceae

Daylilies are a perennial border staple and have introduced many gardeners into the world of herbaceous plants. There's a size, shape, and color for almost every situation, and thanks to the many amateur and professional hybridizers, the range is multiplying as I write, with reportedly more than a thousand new cultivars registered yearly.

Each flower blooms for one day, but the number of buds on each scape averages fifteen, therefore giving you two weeks of bloom. Some daylilies will produce more flower stems (scapes), extending the flowering time, and some are repeat bloomers. Flower color is pearly white, orange, yellow, red, pink, purple, melon, and brown, in varying shades for each color and in all combinations. By choosing carefully for your region, you can have daylilies in bloom from May to October. The standard bloom sequence for daylilies is as follows:

Extra Early (EE): first bloom period

Early (E): three to five weeks before peak bloom

Early Midseason (EM): one to three weeks before peak bloom

Midseason (M): peak bloom (June, July cusp)

Late Midseason (LM): one to three weeks after peak bloom

Late (L): four to six weeks after peak bloom

Very Late (VL): last bloom period

The habit is clumping, with foliage evergreen or semi-evergreen to deciduous. The leaves are arching and emerge bright green in the spring. The stout flower stems or scapes are very strong and require no staking.

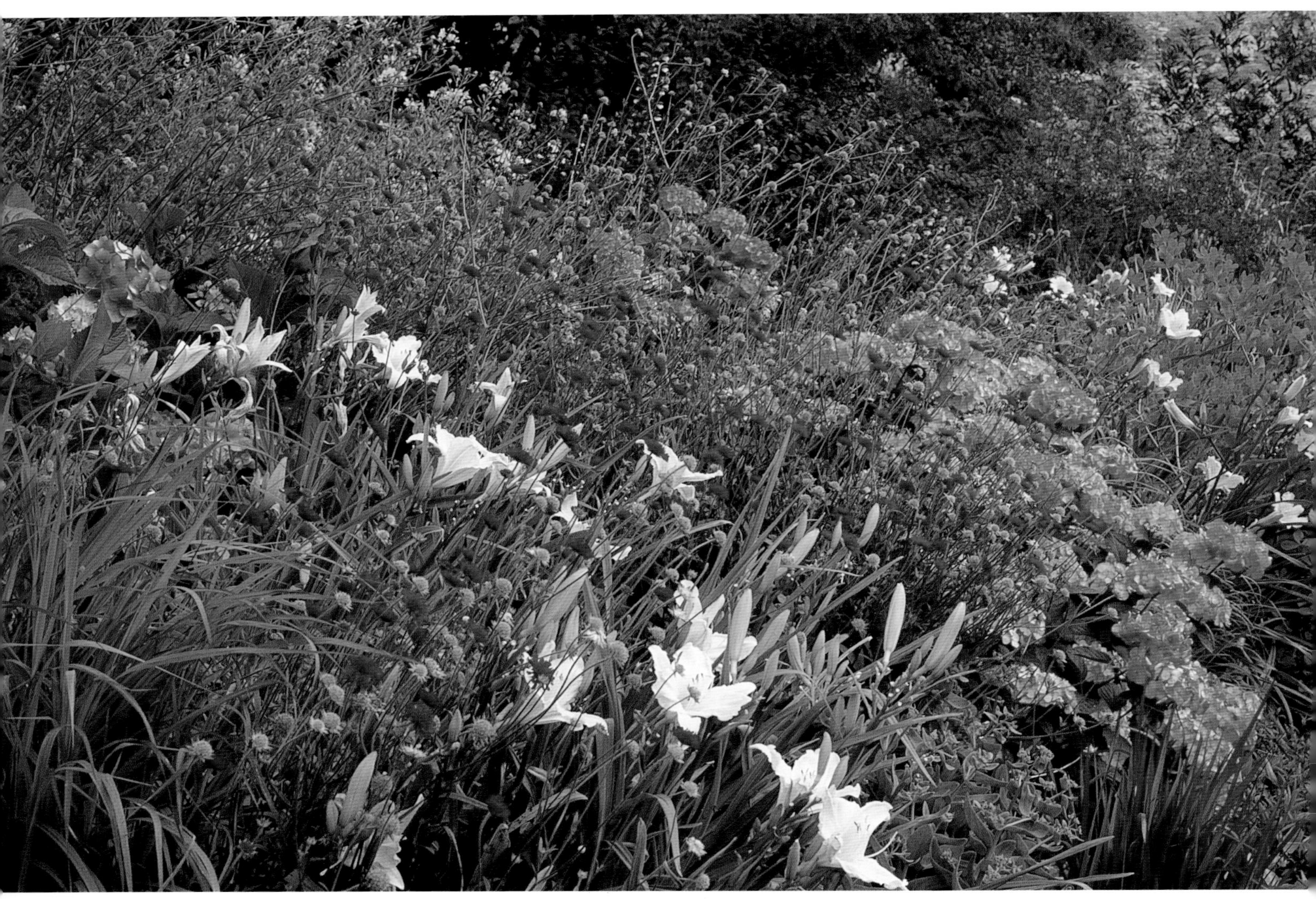

White and yellow daylilies punctuate a mixed deciduous border.

Daylilies aren't too fussy—beyond requiring a minimum of six hours of direct sun per day and adequate water to set buds. Many love the heat of the south (and don't do well in the Pacific Northwest), but their flower color is affected by heat and humidity; the pinks especially can give a variable performance. A good landscape variety will double to triple in size per year but, as with any perennial, may take a little time to settle in. Diploids, triploids, and tetraploids, whose flowers have more substance, are the focus of most breeding programs. The species and cultivars we include here have performed well for us.

The flower petals are very tasty—the smaller, the sweeter. Fresh petals are used in salads, and the buds and flowers are used in soups or sautéed in a little butter and eaten as a side dish. ~ *Susan Carter*

Scientific Name: From the Greek *hemero* ("day") and *kallos* ("beauty").
Common Name: Daylily.
Origin: Asia, China, Korea, Japan.

Preferred Conditions: Most average, fertile, well-drained soils with water as needed. Tolerates moist locations.

Light: Sun.

Planting: Spring planting, when the widest selection is available, is best.

Management: Benefits from mulching. Clear away dead foliage in spring. Deadhead spent blooms and remove spent scapes. Divide clumps when quantity and/or quality of bloom begins to decrease. Cut back in autumn when foliage collapses; can be cut back in August if they are really tired-looking but do not cut too far down: leave about six inches with a final cleanup in winter. Individual dead leaves can be removed whenever they occur. Can host many little slugs and show no damage; still, it is best to bait.

Propagation: Division in autumn or spring (anytime, really), but August is ideal.

Pests and Diseases: Spider mites, snails, slugs, aphids, rust, crown rot (not common in the Northwest).

Companions: Grasses, crocosmia, nepeta, geranium, polygonum, persicaria; the summer border.

Species and Cultivars	Height/ Spread	USDA Hardiness Zone	Flowers (bloom time)	Foliage	Comments
'Anzac'	28in × 24in	3–9	Red with yellow-green throat, 7in (M)	Green, sword-shaped	Dormant, flowers fade in strong sun
'Autumn Minaret'	66in × 36in	3–9	Gold with rusty stripe, dark rust eye, fragrant, 5in (M–VL)	Green, bladelike, arching	Dormant
'Autumn Red'	39in × 24in	3–9	Red-maroon, gold throat, fragrant, 5in (M)	As above	As above
'Baja'	26in × 24in	3–9	Red with green throat, reblooms, 6in (M)	Velvety green, sword-shaped	Semi-evergreen
'Bertie Ferris'	20in × 24in	3–9	Persimmon-orange, ruffled, 2½in (EM)	Green, sword-shaped	Dormant, night bloomer
'Bitsy'	18in × 18in	3–9	Lemon-yellow, yellow throat, reblooms, 1½in (EM–L)	Narrow, green	Semi-evergreen
'Black-Eyed Stella'	12–18in × 18in	3–9	Golden yellow with red eye, reblooms, 3⅛in (EM–L)	Green, sword-shaped	Dormant, long bloomer, winner of first All-American Daylily Award
'Bonanza'	34in × 24in	3–9	Soft orange-yellow with bronze eye, fragrant, reblooms, 4–5in (M)	Dark green, lush	Dormant
'Carlotta'	25in × 24in	3–9	Red and cherry-pink, 4½in (M)	Green, sword-shaped	Semi-evergreen
'Catherine Woodbery'	30–36in × 24in	3–9	Light pink, yellow-green throat, fragrant, 6in (M–L)	Green, arching, sword-shaped	Dormant
'Cedar Waxwing'	34in × 24in	3–9	Pink blend, yellow throat, ruffled edges, 6in (M)	Green, sword-shaped	As above
'Chicago Cattleya'	24in × 24in	3–9	Purple blend, yellow-green throat, 5¾in (M)	As above	As above
citrina	36–48in × 2in	3–9	Pale yellow, yellow throat, 4½in, fragrant (M)	Dark green	Dormant, night bloomer

Species and Cultivars	Height/ Spread	USDA Hardiness Zone	Flowers (bloom time)	Foliage	Comments
'Corky'	36in × 24in	3–9	Yellow, mahogany-brown backs, nearly black stems, 3in (M–L)	Green, arching	Dormant, clump-forming, RHS Award
'Double River Wye'	24–30in × 24in	3–9	Light yellow, yellow-green throat, double, repeat bloom, 4½in (M)	Green, sword-shaped	Dormant
'Eenie Allegro'	12in × 18in	3–9	Apricot, green throat, 2½in (M)	As above	Dwarf, dormant
'Eenie Fanfare'	12in × 18in	3–9	Red with green throat, white edges, repeat bloom, 2¾in (EM)	As above	As above
'Eenie Weenie'	10in × 18in	3–9	Yellow, green throat, repeat bloom, fragrant, 1¾in (EM)	As above	Dormant
'Frans Hals'	24in × 24in	3–9	Rust and orange bicolored, yellow throat, lemon midribs, 5in (M–L)	Dark green, straplike	As above
'Frosty Beauty'	32in × 24in	3–9	Peach-rose blend, gold throat, repeat bloom, 5½in (M)	Green, sword-shaped	As above
fulva	36–48in × 24in+	3–9	Tawny-orange, yellow throat, 5in (E)	Bright green, broad, grasslike	Dormant, spreads, very old cultivar
f. 'Flore Pleno'	30in × 24in+	3–9	Tawny-orange, with red eye, double, 5in (E)	Green, sword-shaped	Dormant
f. 'Variegated Kwanso'	30in × 12–24in	3–9	Tawny-orange, dark red eye, double, 5in (EM)	Green, narrow, irregular white stripes	Dormant, remove any green reversions
'Gentle Shepherd'	24–36in × 24in	3–9	Near white, green throat, light ruffle, 5in (EM)	Green, sword-shaped	Semi-evergreen
'Golden Chimes'	36–48in × 24in	3–9	Chrome-yellow, green throat, mahogany reverse and buds, 2in (EM)	As above	Dormant, long-blooming, RHS Award
'Grape Velvet'	24in × 24in	3–9	Grape-purple, yellow throat, fragrant, 4½in (M–L)	As above	Dormant
'Hall's Pink'	20in × 24in	3–9	Light pink, orange tinge, dark pink eye, 3–4in (M–L)	As above	As above
'Happy Returns'	18in × 24in	3–9	Light-yellow, yellow throat, repeat bloom, fragrant, 3⅛in (EE–L)	As above	As above
'Hyperion'	40in × 24in	3–9	Lemon-yellow, fragrant, repeat bloom, 5½in (EM–L)	As above	As above
'Ice Carnival'	28in × 24in	3–9	Near white, green throat, fragrant, repeat bloom, 6in (M)	As above	As above
'James Marsh'	28in × 24in	3–9	Red, lemon-lime throat, 6½in (EM)	As above	As above

Species and Cultivars	Height/ Spread	USDA Hardiness Zone	Flowers (bloom time)	Foliage	Comments
'Janice Brown'	24in × 24in	3–9	Pink with rose-pink eye and green throat, reblooms, 4¼in (EM)	As above	Semi-evergreen
'Jedi Spellbinder'	24in × 24in	3–9	Cream-yellow, 7½in (M)	As above	As above
'Joan Senior'	40in × 24in	3–9	Near white, lime-green throat, repeat bloom, fragrant, 6in (EM)	As above	Dormant, exquisite, one of the best whites
lilioasphodelus (syn. flava)	30–36in × 24in	3–9	Yellow, yellow throat, fragrant, 4in (E)	As above	Lemon daylily, dormant, RHS Award
'Little Bumble Bee'	20in × 18in	3–9	Soft yellow, chocolate eye (EM)	As above	Dormant
'Little Fred'	24in × 18in	3–9	Black-red, 3in (EM)	As above	Semi-evergreen
'Little Grapette'	12in × 18in	3–9	Grape-purple, yellow throat, repeat bloom, 2in (EM)	As above	As above
'Little Winecup'	24in × 18in	3–9	Wine-red, yellow-green throat, repeat bloom, 2in (EM)	As above	Dormant
'Lullaby Baby'	20in × 24in	3–9	Light pink, green throat, fragrant, 3½in (EM)	As above	Semi-evergreen
'Lusty Leland'	28in × 24in	3–9	Red, gold throat, 6¼in (M)	As above	Dormant
'Magic Lace'	24in × 24in	3–9	Pastel pink, green throat, 6in (EM)	As above	As above
'Mary Todd'	26in × 24in	3–9	Buff-yellow, yellow throat, ruffled, 6in (EM)	As above	Semi-evergreen
'Mini Stella'	10in × 12in	3–9	Yellow, burnt-orange eye, green throat, 1¼in (E)	As above	Dormant, compact, night bloomer
'Naomi Ruth'	30in × 24in	3–9	Apricot-pink, ruffled edges, 3½in (M)	As above	Dormant
'On Stage'	26in × 24in	3–9	Rose-pink blend, 5½in (EM)	As above	Semi-evergreen
'Pandora's Box'	20in × 24in	3–9	Cream, purple eye, green throat, fragrant, 4in (EM–L)	As above	Evergreen
'Pardon Me'	18in × 24in	3–9	Red, yellow-green throat, ruffled, repeat bloom, fragrant, 2¾in (M–L)	As above	Dormant
'Pink Damask'	36in × 24in	3–9	Warm pinkish red, green-gold throat, 5½in (M)	Green, thick, sword-shaped	Dormant, RHS Award
'Pink Embers'	20in × 24in	3–9	Salmon-pink, tangerine throat, 6in (EM)	Green, sword-shaped	Dormant
'Prairie Blue Eyes'	28in × 24in	3–9	Lavender-purple, near-blue eye, ruffled, 5¼in (M)	As above	Semi-evergreen
'Purple Waters'	36in × 24in	3–9	Purple, darker eye, repeat bloom, 4½in (EM)	Green, thick, sword-shaped	As above

Species and Cultivars	Height/ Spread	USDA Hardiness Zone	Flowers (bloom time)	Foliage	Comments
'Raspberry Pixie'	12–24in × 24in	3–9	Raspberry blend, yellow throat, fragrant, 1½in (M)	Green, sword-shaped	Evergreen, low clumping
'Red Magic'	36in × 24in	3–9	Orange-red, dark veins, yellow throat, 3in (M)	As above	Dormant
'Sammy Russell'	24–30in × 24in	3–9	Red, yellow throat (M–L)	As above	Semi-evergreen
'Siloam Amazing Grace'	24in × 24in	3–9	Bright yellow, soft green throat, ruffled, 5½in (EM)	As above	Dormant
'Siloam Button Box'	20in × 18in	3–9	Cream, maroon eye, repeat bloom, 4½in (EM)	As above	As above
'Stafford'	28in × 24in	3–9	Crimson, yellow midribs and throat (M)	Dark green, narrow	As above
'Starstruck'	24in × 24in	3–9	Yellow-green, pale green throat, fragrant, 5½in (M–L)	Green, sword-shaped	As above
'Stella de Oro'	12in × 18in	3–9	Gold-yellow, lime-green throat, fragrant, repeat bloom (EM)	As above	Dormant, dwarf, RHS Award
'Strawberry Candy'	26in × 24in	3–9	Strawberry-pink blend, rose-red eye, 4¼in (EM)	As above	Semi-evergreen
'Summer Wine'	24in × 24in	3–9	Light violet, green-yellow throat, 5½in (M)	Green, thick, sword-shaped	Dormant
'Suzie Wong'	24–30in × 24in	3–9	Light yellow, 4in (EM)	Green, sword-shaped	As above
'Tetrina's Daughter'	35in × 24in	3–9	Bright yellow, fragrant, 5in (M)	As above	Semi-evergreen, night bloomer, RHS Award
'Yellowstone'	36in × 24in	3–9	Yellow, green throat, yellow eye, 5in (M)	As above	Dormant

HEPATICA Ranunculaceae

The hepaticas, relatives of anemones, are low-growing, early-blooming plants of deciduous woodlands. The solitary cup-shaped flowers in shades of blue, pink, and white are borne on slender scapes. The leaves are kidney-shaped or lobed, and mid to dark green. *Hepatica transsilvanica* and *H. nobilis* have the most attractive foliage and are the most robust growers in our climate. A great deal of hybridization is being done in Japan. The newer double and semi-double forms are often grown as pot plants.

All hepaticas need humus-rich soil and prefer early spring sun and then shade as the season progresses; *H. transsilvanica* can handle drier soil, but they all need summer moisture. The plants are valuable additions to the late winter and early spring garden. It's worth planting a deciduous tree for them, if necessary. ~ *Ann Bucher*

Scientific Name: From the Greek *hepar* ("liver"), referring to the shape and color of the leaves.
Common Name: Liverwort.
Origin: North America, Europe, Asia.
Preferred Conditions: Humus-rich, limy, well-drained, moist soil. Doesn't like to compete with surrounding vegetation.

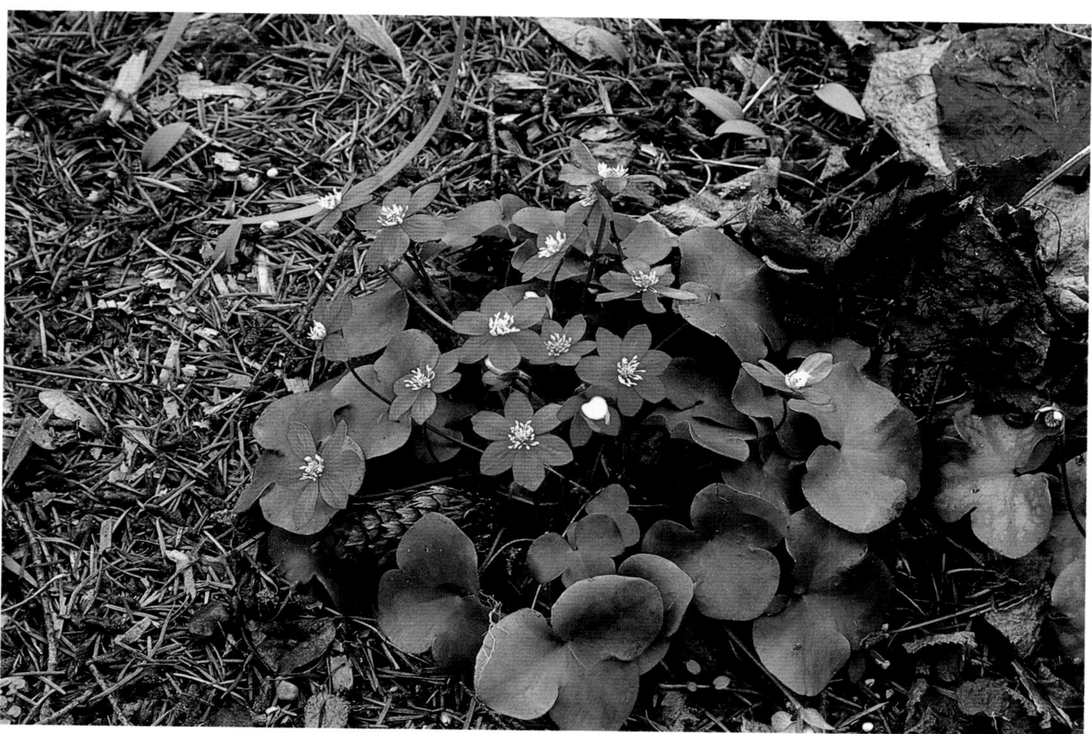

Hepatica nobilis.

Light: Part shade to shade.
Planting: Not too deep. Slow to establish. They don't transplant very well.
Management: Resents disturbance. Top-dress with leaf mold or compost in autumn or winter. Cut off old foliage in midwinter, once plants are well established, before flowers emerge, or they will be obscured. Remove dead foliage on young plants and evergreen forms; leave semi-evergreen forms alone for the first few years, then remove old foliage. Bait for slugs in early spring.
Propagation: Division in spring; seed as soon as ripe.
Pests and Diseases: Rust, snails, slugs on young plants and new growth, root weevils.
Companions: *Anemone nemorosa*, helleborus, omphalodes, trillium, primula, ferns, erythronium; the spring woodland garden.

Species and Cultivars	Height/ Spread	USDA Hardiness Zone	Flowers (bloom time)	Foliage	Comments
acutiloba	6in × 6in	4–8	Light blue-lavender, pink, or white, cup-shaped (E)	Mid-green, 3- to 7-lobed, rounded or kidney-shaped, sharp-pointed, mottled	Sharp-leaved hepatica, similar to *H. americana*, evergreen
americana	6in × 6in	4–8	As above	Mid-green, purple-tinged beneath, kidney-shaped, 3-lobed	Evergreen
nobilis (syn. triloba)	4in × 6in	4–8	Mauve to blue, white, pink, or red, bowl-shaped (E)	Dark green, purple-tinged beneath, kidney-shaped, rounded, 3-lobed	Semi-evergreen, new leaves appear after flowers
transsilvanica	5ft × 6in	4–8	Blue, white to pale pink (E)	Green, round to kidney-shaped, 3-lobed, hairy	Easiest to grow, most vigorous, takes driest soil, semi-evergreen, RHS Award

Hesperis matronalis, the rare double-flowered form.

HESPERIS Brassicaceae

Dame's rocket is an old-fashioned cottage garden plant with masses of mostly single, stocklike flowers, like those of *Matthiola incana* or lunaria, the honesty plant: four-petaled, cross-shaped flowers are characteristic of the entire family. All have fragrant flowers borne in terminal racemes or panicles; the long-blooming flowers of *H. matronalis* are particularly fragrant at night. A gangly plant, but a few are okay.

This biennial or short-lived perennial is often included in the plant list for a butterfly garden. Hesperis is sometimes considered an invasive weed; short-lived though it may be in some places, it self-sows heavily in others, especially woodland edges. Both youngsters and adults are easy to pull out, however. Plants that don't remain where originally planted bother some gardeners. Not us, not most of the time. ~ *Susan Carter*

Scientific Name: From the Greek *hespera* ("evening"), referring to its fragrance.
Common Name: Dame's rocket.
Origin: West and Central Asia, Siberia, southern and central Europe, Alps.
Preferred Conditions: Fertile, limy, moisture-retentive, well-drained, deep, loose soil. The double-flowered forms need a richer soil and are more temperamental.
Light: Sun.
Planting: Raise young plants every few years from a spring seeding, as the older ones deteriorate or the roots become woody and less productive. Alternatively, leave some self-sown seedlings in place and remove the older plants. Site them among other perennials, as they are hard to stake up.
Management: Leave seedheads on to ripen (takes a long time), or cut back for repeat bloom before they set seed. Groom youngsters in the winter.
Propagation: Seed as soon as ripe.
Pests and Diseases: Mildew, snails, slugs, cutworms.
Companions: Alchemilla, lupinus, *Lunaria rediviva*, euphorbia, tulips, tall alliums, *Digitalis purpurea*, smyrnium.

Species and Cultivars	Height/ Spread	USDA Hardiness Zone	Flowers (bloom time)	Foliage	Comments
matronalis	2–4ft × 3ft	4–9	White, pale lavender, open clusters, fragrant (E–M)	Dark green, coarse, lancelike	Self-sows
m. double-flowered	2–2½ft × 2ft	4–9	As above, double	As above	Rare, less vigorous, more difficult to grow, doesn't set seed, must be vegetatively propagated

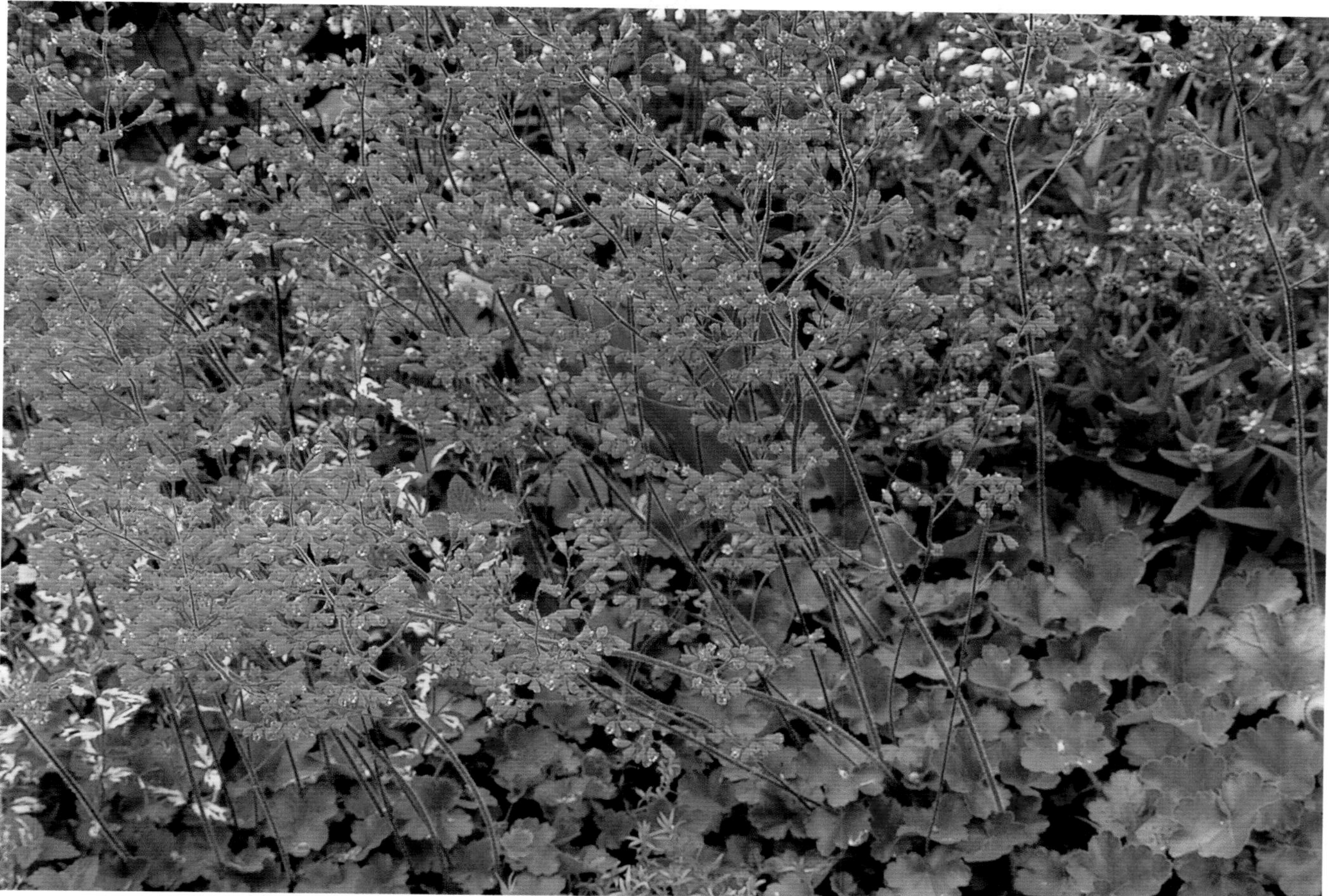

Heuchera 'Canyon Delight'.

HEUCHERA Saxifragaceae

The current interest is in the colored-leaf forms of this large genus, from the nearly perfect glossy black *H.* 'Obsidian' to the green and white mottled selections of *H. sanguinea*, 'Monet' and 'Snow Storm'. This extreme range of foliar colors makes heucheras very versatile in the garden. Both flowers and leaves appear on thin, wiry stems. Leaves are palmately lobed, two to four inches across; the small flowers are often widely spaced on the vertical stems, and vary from insignificant to moderately showy.

Heucheras can take a wide range of conditions, although deep shade will make them somewhat leggy and less floriferous. Grow your heucheras in soil that is a bit lean and don't mulch over the crown. They really resent this. Many heucheras are tissue-cultured forms; this system produces a lot of new hybrids, and many of these are brought to us courtesy of Terra Nova Nurseries. Look for the latest ('Amber Waves', 'Marmalade'), and don't expect all cultivars to be available. Some heucheras, both older and newer cultivars, are actually good cut flowers. ~ *Bob Lilly*

Scientific Name: After Johann Heinrich von Heucher, German professor of medicine.
Common Name: Alumroot, coral bells.
Origin: North America, Mexico.

Preferred Conditions: Any reasonable, well-drained, humus-rich soil except heavy, soggy ones. Prefers regular watering but tolerates summer drought once established.

Light: Sun to shade.

Management: Separate and replant the best pieces every three to four years. Some forms get a bit woody at the base and may need to be cut and rerooted in a greenhouse or cold frame. Replant the woody stems well into the soil so that only the crown is above the ground (this is not always successful, especially in heavy or wet soils). Removing the entire flowering stem on the darker leaf forms makes for a better plant. Keep removing spent flower stems as plants complete their blooming, and cut off old, ragged leaves. Groom and mulch in winter with organic material. Feed regularly for very showy plants.

Propagation: Spring division, or seed.

Pests and Diseases: Powdery mildew, rust, root weevils.

Companions: Artemisia, hemerocallis, ferns, hosta, geum, smaller geraniums, campanula, carex (especially the gold and orange forms), astilbe, rodgersia, spring bulbs, scilla, muscari, smaller iris, galanthus.

Notes: Most heucheras are evergreen in the Pacific Northwest, if a bit shabby-looking by spring, and all, unfortunately, are short-lived for us: root weevils use them as summer food, and their grubs can consume the entire root system over winter. We don't have a good root weevil control method, so replanting is often the final solution. Green-leaf forms seem a bit more resistant.

Species and Cultivars	Height/ Spread	USDA Hardiness Zone	Flowers (bloom time)	Foliage	Comments
americana	6in × 12in	4–9	Tiny, greenish, brown and white, 1–3ft scapes (E–M)	Dark green, flushed and veined coppery brown, leathery, covered with a silvery sheen, broad, ovate-cordate	Alumroot, clump-forming, very showy foliage
a. Dale's Strain	6in × 12in	4–9	Greenish white to chartreuse, small, 1½–2½ft scapes (E–M)	Dark green, marbled silver, blue, and bronze	Clump-forming
'Amethyst Myst'	10–12in × 18in	4–9	Pink, 26in scapes (E–M)	Amethyst-purple with silver sheen, glossy	
'Autumn Haze'	8–12in × 18in	4–9	Cream, rose-tinted, 1ft scapes (M)	Cinnamon with purple highlights, lobed, veined, good fall color	Dense
Bressingham Hybrids	10–12in × 15in	4–9	Mixed range of pink, red, and white, bell-shaped, 18–20in scapes (E–M)	Rich green	Very floriferous
'Can-can'	8–10in × 16in	4–9	Green and white, 12in+ scapes (M)	Plum-purple with metallic silver sheen and dark green veining, ruffled	Stays compact, RHS Award
'Canyon Delight'	8–10in × 12in	4–9	Rose to hot pink, 12in+ scapes (E)	Green, glossy	
'Canyon Pink'	8–10in × 12in	4–9	Deep pink with lighter center, 12in scapes (E)	Green, scalloped	
'Cappuccino'	8–10in × 12in	4–9	Creamy-white, 12in+ scapes (E–M)	Bronzy-brown with white splash, ruffled	

Species and Cultivars	Height/ Spread	USDA Hardiness Zone	Flowers (bloom time)	Foliage	Comments
'Cascade Dawn'	8in × 18in	4–9	White, tiny, 28–30in scapes (M)	Dark burgundy, overlaid with silver-lavender shadings, good winter color	
'Cathedral Windows'	7in × 12in	4–9	Greenish white, 26in scapes (M)	Multicolored with heavy sheen of silver-pewter variegation, glossy, veined, mahogany back	
'Checkers'	7in × 12in	4–9	White, 2–2½ft scapes (E–M)	Thick, metallic-silver patterned	
'Cherries Jubilee'	8–12in × 12in	4–9	Cherry-red, 16–24in scapes (M)	Warm chocolate-brown, ruffled	
'Chocolate Ruffles'	8–10in × 18in	4–9	Small, creamy-white, on purple 28–30in scapes (M)	Cocoa-brown, burgundy reverse, glossy, large, ruffled	Vigorous
'Chocolate Veil'	8–12in × 18in	4–9	Purple, tinged lime-green, bell-shaped, 28in scapes (M)	Chocolate-black with purple highlights, silver between veins, maroon beneath, purple stems	RHS Award
'Coral Bouquet'	5–12in × 12in	4–9	Coral, large, 20in scapes (M)	Green	
'Crimson Curls'	10–12in × 12–14in	4–9	Creamy-white on burgundy 1½–2ft scapes (E–M)	Deep burgundy-red tones on top, purplish reverse, ruffled	
cylindrica	12in × 18in	4–9	Small brownish or cream to greenish yellow, 2ft scapes (E–M)	Dark green, pale green mottling, round to ovate, toothed, hairy	Seed-grown
c. 'Greenfinch'	6–18in × 18in	4–9	Pale greenish yellow, small, tight spikes, 2–5ft scapes (E–M)	Rosettes of dark green, round, scalloped, overlaid with silvery sheen, wavy-edged	Flowers are very stiff and upright
'Ebony and Ivory'	10in × 15in	4–9	Ivory-white, 18–22in scapes (M)	Ruby base with maroon-black, ruffled	
'Eco Magnififolia'	10in × 12in	4–9	Chartreuse, insignificant, 28in scapes (E–M)	Gray-silver and purple	
'Firefly' (syn. 'Leuchtkafer')	12–18in × 12in	4–9	Dark vermilion-red, small, fragrant, 2ft scapes (E–M)	Deep green, rounded	
'Fireworks'	8in × 12in	4–9	Coral-red to light pink, 20–24in scapes (E–M)	Bronzy matte green, wine-red reverse	RHS Award
'Green Ivory'	12in × 12in	4–9	Whitish and green, 2–3ft scapes (E–M)	Cream and green	
'Green Spice'	9–12in × 15in	4–9	White, insignificant, 2ft scapes (E–M)	Emerald-green with deeper green edges, silver veining, magenta center	Good fall color
'Magic Wand'	8in × 15in	4–9	Cerise-red, double, 26–28in scapes (M)	Green	RHS Award

Species and Cultivars	Height/ Spread	USDA Hardiness Zone	Flowers (bloom time)	Foliage	Comments
micrantha	8–12in × 8–10in	4–9	Whitish or greenish to purple, 2–3ft scapes (E–M)	Gray-marbled, maplelike, 5–7 lobes, toothed, hairy	
m. var. diversifolia Bressingham Bronze = 'Absi'	12in × 10in	4–9	Creamy-white sprays, 1½–2ft scapes (E–M)	Bronzy-purple, crinkled	
m. var. diversifolia 'Palace Purple'	10in × 15in	4–9	White or creamy, bell-shaped, red anthers, 1–2ft scapes (E–M)	Mahogany-red to purple with metallic sheen, cordate, maplelike, shiny	Seed-grown, 1991 PPA Award
m. 'Martha Roderick'	6–8in × 8in	4–9	Tiny, pink, 2ft scapes (M)	Bright green	
'Mint Frost'	7–15in × 15in	4–9	Chartreuse and white, 20–28in scapes (M)	Soft green, silvery sheen, olive-green veining, turns frosty purple, veins turning silver	
'Montrose Ruby'	12in × 12in	4–9	Creamy-white, 2½–3ft scapes (M)	Deep bronze-mahogany, silver mottling	
'Northern Fire'	16–18in × 16in	4–9	Scarlet-red, 1½–2½ft scapes (E–M)	Dark green with white and silver mottling	
'Oakington Jewel'	12–15in × 15in	4–9	Coral-pink, 24–28in scapes (E–M)	Bronze mottled with metallic silvery-gray sheen, purple veins, green border, larger, lobed	
'Obsidian'	10in × 16in	4–9	Creamy-white to pink, 2ft scapes (M)	Very dark, glossy black, smooth, hold their color	The best of the newer ones
'Palace Passion'	16in × 15in	4–9	Bright rose-pink, 2–3ft scapes (M)	Mahogany-red to bronze with purple reverse	Long-blooming
'Persian Carpet'	7–12in × 12in	4–9	Pink, inconspicuous, 20–26in scapes (M)	Rose-burgundy, dark purple edges and silver highlights, dark purple veins, gray reverse	
'Petite Pearl Fairy'	2–4in × 6in	4–9	Pink, 10in scapes (M)	Mint-green base, bronze-silver marbling	Spreads slowly
'Pewter Moon'	12–15in × 15in	4–9	Pale ice-pink, large, maroon 20–24in scapes (E–M)	Coppery-pink fading to maroon with silvery sheen	One of the great modern heucheras
'Pewter Veil'	7in × 15in	4–9	Tiny, blush-white tinged purple, insignificant, 24–28in scapes (M)	Coppery-maroon aging to silver-pewter, charcoal veins	A good heuchera, clumping
'Plum Pudding'	8–12in × 12in	4–9	Off-white, insignificant, 2–3ft scapes (M)	Plum-purple with silvery veins, shiny metallic finish	Tight growth habit, excellent form
'Purple Petticoats'	7–15in × 15in	4–9	Off-white, insignificant, 2–3ft scapes (E–M)	Deep burgundy, dark purple reverse, ruffled	RHS Award
'Raspberry Regal'	8–12in × 15in	4–9	Raspberry-red, 30–40in scapes (E–M)	Blue-green marbled	Good cut, RHS Award

Species and Cultivars	Height/ Spread	USDA Hardiness Zone	Flowers (bloom time)	Foliage	Comments
'Regina'	12–14in × 12in	4–9	Light pink, 2–3ft scapes (E–M)	Dark purple-red, overlaid with silver and burgundy-bronze	RHS Award
'Ring of Fire'	8–15in × 12in	4–9	Bright cherry-red, 30in scapes (M)	Silver with purple tinge and veining, edges turn bright coral in fall	
'Ruby Mist'	8–12in × 12in	4–9	Deep pink, 2–2½ft scapes (E–M)	Dark green, light silver reverse	Compact
'Ruby Veil'	8–10in × 12in	4–9	Insignificant, ruby-red 2–2½ft scapes (M)	Deep green with slate-gray veins, zones of metallic silvery sheen with ruby shading	
sanguinea	9–12in × 15in	4–9	Pink or red, bell-shaped clusters, nodding, 15–24in scapes (E–L)	Dark green, marbled pale green, lobed, toothed, hairy, round to kidney-shaped	Coral bells, the common form in older gardens
s. 'Chatterbox'	8in × 12in	4–9	Rose-pink, bell-shaped clusters, nodding, 18in scapes (E–L)	Mid-green	
s. 'June Bride'	8–10in × 12in	4–9	White, 15–18in scapes (M)	As above	
s. 'Monet'	8in × 12in	4–9	Red-rose, 20–30in scapes (M)	Creamy-white, splashed deep green, pink fall color	Vigorous
s. 'Snow Storm'	12in × 12in	4–9	Reddish pink, 1–1½ft scapes (E–M)	Green, splashed with white and cream, edged dark green, ruffled	
s. 'Splendens'	6–8in × 12in	4–9	Bright carmine-red, 18–24in scapes (E–M)	Dark green	Very floriferous, old cultivar, seed-grown
s. 'Splish Splash'	12in × 12in	4–9	Rose-pink, 16–18in scapes (E–M)	Deep green, mottled with white, turns raspberry-red in fall	
s. 'White Cloud'	8–10in × 10in	4–9	White, fragrant, 2–2½ft scapes (M)	Green	Very floriferous
'Silver Scrolls'	10in × 12in	4–9	White, 2ft scapes (E)	Silvery with dark purple veining, purplish overlay in spring	Good, dense plant
'Silver Shadows'	6–8in × 12in	4–9	White, 26–36in scapes (M)	Dark silver tones with metallic purplish tones, veined, wavy, rosy overtones in spring	Flowers emerge in early summer
'Smokey Rose'	12in × 15in	4–9	Rose-pink to purple, 18–24in scapes (M)	Deep bronze with mahogany-silver mottling	Very good cultivar
'Stormy Seas'	8–10in × 15in	4–9	Off-white, small, 28–36in scapes (E–M)	Multicolored, bronze, silvery, and purple, ruffled	Very sun tolerant
'Velvet Night'	7–12in × 12in	4–9	Pinkish white, 26–30in scapes (M)	Dark slate-black with metallic-purple shading, red veining	

×*Heucherella* 'Kimono'.

×HEUCHERELLA Saxifragaceae

This intergeneric hybrid has the vigor of tiarella and the more showy flowers of heuchera. Plants share heuchera's problem with root weevils and are a bit messy in winter. Heucherellas are useful as groundcovers under open deciduous shrubs, where they can be allowed to run about. Many have patterned or marked foliage, and their being evergreen makes them useful in the garden. Flower stems tend to be shorter than those of their parents, with flowers packed tighter on the stems; some are quite showy. ~ *Bob Lilly*

Scientific Name: From the names of the parent genera, *Heuchera* and *Tiarella*.
Common Name: Foamy bells.
Origin: Garden origin; these are naturally occurring hybrids.
Preferred Conditions: Light, neutral to slightly acidic, fertile, moist, well-drained soil. A hot sunny location on sand in July is not advised.
Light: Sun to shade.
Management: Similar culture to heuchera and tiarella. Separate plantlets from rooted stolons. Groom in winter.
Propagation: Division in spring.
Pests and Diseases: Root weevils, slugs.

Companions: Viola, arisarum, arum, smaller bulbs, helleborus, geranium, brunnera, dicentra, hosta, polygonum; a good plant for color contrast or echo.

Notes: Watch out! These can spread quickly in some locations (good soil, regular water). Look for newer varieties—two we have yet to try are ×*Heucherella* 'Stoplight' and 'Chocolate Lace'.

Species and Cultivars	Height/ Spread	USDA Hardiness Zone	Flowers (bloom time)	Foliage	Comments
alba 'Bridget Bloom'	6–12in × 12in+	4–9	Pale pink and white, tiny, 14–20in scapes (E–L)	Mid-green with brown spots and blotches, cordate to ovate, toothed, lobed, rough and hairy	No stolons, clump-forming
a. 'Rosalie'	8–12in × 12in+	4–9	Pink fading to white, 15–24in scapes (E–M)	Dark green with prominent dark purple patch	As above
'Burnished Bronze'	8in × 12in	4–9	Pink fading to white, 1–1½ft scapes (E–M)	Burgundy-bronze, large, deeply lobed	Some repeat bloom
'Cinnamon Bear'	7in × 12in	4–9	Pink, starry, 12–20in scapes (E–M)	Cinnamon reddish brown	
'Dayglow Pink'	7in × 12in	4–9	Brilliant pink, 16–20in scapes (E–M)	Silvery-green with chocolate-brown center, deeply cut	
'Kimono'	6–9in × 12in	4–9	Soft pinkish white, 1–2ft scapes (E–M)	Silver and green with wide purple central stripe, palmate	RHS Award
'Pink Frost'	8in × 12in	4–9	Pink, 14–24in scapes (E–M)	Green, frosty, with silver sheen	Clump-forming
'Quicksilver'	8–12in × 12in	4–9	Pale pink, 15–20in scapes (E–M)	Maroon, purple, and chocolate, dark red veining, strong silver highlights	
'Silver Streak'	6–12in × 12in	4–9	Pale pink and white, tinged lavender, 20in scapes (E–M)	Maroon-purple, silver highlights	
tiarelloides	7in × 18in+	4–9	Tiny, pink bells on brownish red 12–18in scapes (E–L)	Light green, ovate to cordate	Stoloniferous, RHS Award
t. 'Crimson Cloud'	6–12in × 18in+	4–9	Pink, 14–18in scapes (E–M)	Pale green with red dots, etched in silver	Vigorous
'Viking Ship'	6in × 18in+	4–9	Pink, starry, 1–2ft scapes (E–M)	Silvery, palmate	Moderate growth

Hosta ventricosa.

HOSTA Hostaceae

Durable to dainty, hostas can find a niche in almost any garden. Most are sun tolerant in heavy, moist soils, although in some situations the pale green to gold- and white-variegated leaf forms can burn, so use care in your selection and placement. Most flower scapes tend to get ratty, so cut them off as soon as finished—the sieboldiana types can even set seed. The main trick with hostas is to bait for slugs early in the season when growth has barely begun. Any elongated pip can be munched on, causing the first leaves (those rolled on the outside of the growth pip) to be perforated or laced. A constant baiting program until summer usually keeps them looking good. Blue leaves (sieboldiana parentage) seem to be more slug resistant, dwarfs less so. There are many new forms and varieties each year; usually the leaves are sufficiently formed by 1 May, so purchase new plants then.

Hosta plantaginea and its sports and forms, with those large and quite long, fragrant flowers, do not make uniform clumps, so are best used in an open, casual woodland; these are the ones more correctly called plantain lilies. As hosta clumps mature, they become congested and less regular, with more and more overlapping leaves in odd directions. This is the time to divide: use the best divisions with the firmest and largest eyes at the edge of the clump, and divide down to three to five eyes. You can divide hostas in spring, fall, or late winter; pot up the smaller pieces for friends and the plant sales.

The best garden hostas are *H.* 'Aureomarginata' (ventricosa), *H.* 'Bressingham Blue', *H.* 'Francee', *H.* 'Frances Williams', *H.* 'Golden Tiara', *H.* 'Halcyon', *H.* 'Invincible', *H.* 'June', *H.* 'Krossa Regal', *H.* 'Minuteman', *H.* 'Patriot', *H.* 'Royal Standard', *H. sieboldiana* var. *elegans*, *H.* 'Sum and Substance', *H. tokudama* (and both its forms), and *H.* 'Wide Brim'. The undulata group, with its slightly twisted leaves, will give you a more old-fashioned look.

Hostas are edible and have been used by the Japanese and Koreans for centuries, as a pickled, fried, or steamed vegetable. Many recipes describe using the younger spring leaves in place of spinach as a steamed vegetable, while the older, more fibrous foliage is used in soups and dishes that allow for longer cooking. ~ *Bob Lilly*

Scientific Name: After Austrian physician Nicholas Tomas Host.
Common Name: Plantain lily, funkia.
Origin: China, Japan, East Asia.
Preferred Conditions: Humus-rich, moisture-retentive, well-drained soil.
Light: Shade to sun. Most gold-foliaged forms need more shade.
Management: Remove old or damaged leaves throughout the season. Cut back flower scapes in fall, to two to three inches, so you can tell where the crowns are in the winter and don't step on them. Clear away foliage as it dies back. Top-dress with organic material in winter. Hostas respond well to manure and can be mulched over the crowns. They often do not require division except for propagation. Bait for slugs.
Propagation: Seed; division of crowns in early spring before the pips begin to expand.
Pests and Diseases: Snails, slugs, rabbits, big-footed gardeners.
Companions: Ferns, bulbs, astilbe, dicentra, hemerocallis, iris, grasses, helleborus, hakonechloa, luzula, geranium, polygonatum, primula. Good alone as a container plant: police for slugs, feed them on a regular basis with a water-soluble, mixable fertilizer—they make fantastic show plants.
Notes: Can take all-morning sun and a bit more in the Pacific Northwest. American growers excel in hosta breeding; look for their new introductions (first available by mail order) every year. The chart has a (P) for those that look great in pots; AHGA = American Hosta Growers Association.

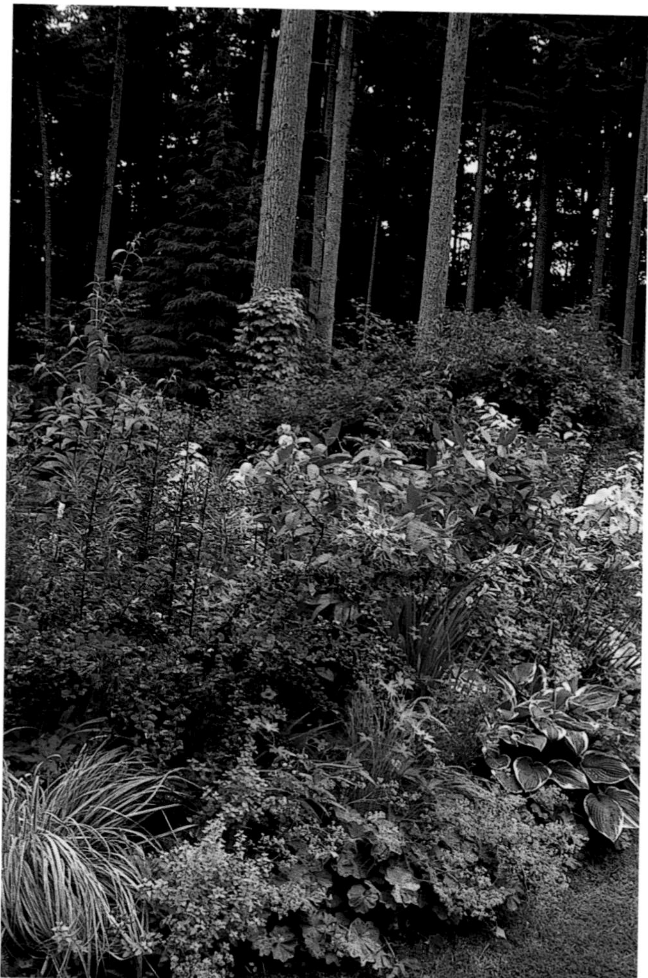

Every woodland garden benefits from a hosta or two, here paired with lady's mantle and geraniums.

Species and Cultivars	Height/ Spread	USDA Hardiness Zone	Flowers (bloom time)	Foliage	Comments
'Abba Dabba Do'	24in × 60in+	3–9	Pale lavender, 2½ft scapes (M)	Dark green, golden yellow edges that widen with age, ovate to cordate	Tolerates sun, vigorous
'Abiqua Drinking Gourd'	16–20in × 40–45in	3–9	White, lavender tinge, 2ft scapes (M)	Blue-green, frosty, very puckered, deeply cupped, round	Aptly named (P)
'Abiqua Moonbeam'	15in × 30–36in	3–9	Pale lavender, 28in scapes (M)	Bluish green, wide creamy-yellow to golden edges, round, corrugated	Vigorous (P)
'Albomarginata' (fortunei)	14–20in × 20–24in	3–9	Lavender, 30in scapes (M–L)	Green, narrow white edges, elongated, wavy, glossy reverse	Best in shade

Species and Cultivars	Height/ Spread	USDA Hardiness Zone	Flowers (bloom time)	Foliage	Comments
'Allen P. McConnell'	8–12in × 18in	3–9	Purple, 15–18in scapes (M)	Dark green, thin white edges	Compact, shade to sun, vigorous
'Antioch' (fortunei)	18–24in × 48in	3–9	Pale lavender-blue, funnel-shaped, arching stems, 3ft scapes (M)	Dark green, broadly edged in cream aging to white, ovate	Vigorous
'Aoki' (fortunei)	24in × 18in	3–9	Pale violet, 3–4ft scapes, fragrant (M–L)	Dark grayish green, cordate	
'Aphrodite' (plantaginea)	18–24in × 24–30in	3–9	Double white, fragrant, 2ft scapes (M–L)	Green, glossy, cordate	Slow to increase, divisions only, not tissue culture
'August Moon'	20–26in × 30–36in	3–9	Grayish white, frosted with lavender, 28–32in scapes (M)	Golden yellow to pale green, crinkled, round to cordate, cupped and puckered	Vigorous, needs some sun to remain yellow, can be indirect or morning sun
'Aureomarginata' (montana)	24–28in × 36in+	3–9	Pale lavender to nearly white, 3–4ft scapes (M)	Dark green, irregularly yellow edges aging to cream, narrow, tapering, wavy margins, glossy	Big plant
'Aureomarginata' (ventricosa)	18–28in × 30in	3–9	Purple, 3ft scapes (M)	Dark green center, yellow edges fading to cream, shiny, wavy, cordate	RHS Award
'Big Daddy' (sieboldiana)	24–36in × 36–60in	3–9	White, bell-shaped, 3ft scapes (E–M)	Deep gray-blue, rounded-cordate, quilted, cupped, large	Very floriferous, robust, big plant
'Birchwood Parky's Gold'	14–18in × 30in	3–9	Pale lavender, bell-shaped, 28in scapes (M)	Yellow-gold aging to yellow-green, ruffled, cordate	Sun tolerant, vigorous
'Blue Angel' (sieboldiana)	24–36in × 48–72in	3–9	White, hyacinthlike, 3–4ft scapes (E–M)	Large, bluish gray, cordate-ovate, wavy, heavily textured	Slow to establish (P), RHS Award
'Blue Boy'	6–12in × 20in	3–9	Lavender, 10–12in scapes (M)	Blue-green, frosty, small, cordate-rounded	(P)
'Blue Cadet'	12–16in × 28in	3–9	Lavender, 14in scapes (M)	Blue-green, cordate-rounded, heavily textured	Vigorous, good en masse (P)
'Blue Umbrellas' (sieboldiana)	30–36in × 48in+	3–9	Pale lavender, bell-shaped, 3ft scapes (M)	Bluish green aging to dark green, ovate-cordate, cupped, puckered, glossy	Sun tolerant, fast grower, big plant
'Blue Wedgwood' (Tardiana Group)	14–18in × 24–36in	3–9	Pale lavender, 18–24in scapes (M)	Deep gray-blue, wedge-shaped, wavy margins	Shade, neat grower, vigorous (P)
'Bressingham Blue' (syn. coerulea)	24–30in × 24–48in	3–9	White, 3ft scapes (M)	Bluish green, cupped, ribbed, puckered, large	(P)

Species and Cultivars	Height/ Spread	USDA Hardiness Zone	Flowers (bloom time)	Foliage	Comments
'Bright Lights'	12–24in × 48in	3–9	White, bell-shaped, 30in scapes (M)	Golden yellow center, wide, dark blue-green edges, cordate-rounded, puckered	Heat tolerant, vigorous
'Brim Cup'	12in × 15in	3–9	White to pale lavender, 14–18in scapes (M)	Rich green, creamy-yellow edges, puckered, cupped	
'Candy Hearts'	14–16in × 28in	3–9	Pale lavender to off-white, 20–26in scapes (M)	Blue-green, cordate, thick	Compact, good groundcover, vigorous
'Cherry Berry'	12–16in × 16in	3–9	Violet-purple, red-spotted, 30in scapes (M)	Creamy-white center, dark green edges, narrowly lanceolate	Red stems, a new direction for breeders
'Christmas Tree'	18–20in × 24–36in	3–9	Pale lavender-white, funnel-shaped, arching scapes, 20–24in (M)	Dark green, creamy-white edges, cordate-rounded, puckered	
'Color Glory' (sieboldiana)	26–30in × 40in	3–9	White, 24–26in scapes (M)	Blue-green edges, yellow center	Large plant
'Dorset Blue' (Tardiana Group)	8–10in × 12in	3–9	Lavender-white, bell-shaped, 1ft scapes (M)	Dark blue-green, ovate-cordate-rounded, cupped, puckered	Slow-growing (P)
'Elvis Lives'	16–18in × 36–60in	3–9	Lavender-purple, 2ft scapes (M)	Bluish green, wavy margins, arching, narrow	Upright
'Emerald Tiara'	12–14in × 12in	3–9	Purple and white, bell-shaped, 24–28in scapes (M)	Golden yellow center with green border, broadly lanceolate-ovate or cordate, wavy	Vigorous
'Emily Dickinson'	18in × 36in	3–9	Dark lavender, fragrant, 2ft scapes (M–L)	Mid-green, wide creamy edges, lanceolate	
'Fire and Ice'	10–14in × 15in	3–9	Pale lavender, 20in scapes (M)	White center, dark green edges, thick	Dwarf, creamy white seedpods
fortunei var. albopicta (syn. 'Aureomaculata')	18–30in × 36in	3–9	Pale lavender, trumpet-shaped, 34in scapes (M)	Bright yellow, edged in pale green, aging to solid dark green, ovate-cordate	Part shade, RHS Award
f. var. aureomarginata (syn. 'Obscura Marginata')	12–24in × 24–36in	3–9	Lavender, 2ft scapes (M)	Dark green, gold edge, prominently veined, puckered, rounded	Vigorous, RHS Award
f. var. hyacinthina	18–24in × 24in	3–9	Lavender-white to pale purple, fragrant, 1½ft scapes (M)	Bold, grayish green, edged with thin line of gray, glaucous beneath	Very common, RHS Award
'Fragrant Bouquet'	18–22in × 24–48in	3–9	Large, white, fragrant, 2–3ft scapes (M)	Apple-green, edged in white, cordate-ovate-rounded, cupped, puckered	1998 AHGA Award, vigorous

Species and Cultivars	Height/ Spread	USDA Hardiness Zone	Flowers (bloom time)	Foliage	Comments
'Francee' (fortunei)	15–22in × 36in+	3–9	Lavender, funnel-shaped, arching stems, 24–30in scapes (M)	Dark green, edged in white, cordate-ovate-rounded, cupped, puckered	Tolerates sun, vigorous, RHS Award
'Frances Williams' (sieboldiana)	36–40in × 42in+	3–9	Pale lavender-gray-white, bell-shaped, 30–60in scapes (M)	Blue-green, yellow edge, corrugated, cupped, cordate, prominently veined	May be susceptible to late frosts (P), RHS Award
'Fringe Benefit'	24–36in × 36in	3–9	Pale lavender to smoky-white, 2ft scapes (M–L)	Green, creamy edges, cordate, puckered	Very floriferous, vigorous
'Ginko Craig'	6–12in × 18in	3–9	Lavender to deep purple, funnel-shaped, 18in scapes (M)	Narrow, green with white edge, pointed	Dwarf, slow
'Gold Drop' (venusta)	6–12in × 12in	3–9	White, lavender tints, 15in scapes (M)	Chartreuse, smooth, cordate	Dwarf, shade to sun, good en masse
'Gold Edger'	8–12in × 18–24in	3–9	Pale lavender, 18in scapes (M)	Chartreuse, cordate	Prefers some sun, vigorous, use as name applies
'Golden Tiara'	12–15in × 24in	3–9	Deep lavender-purple, bell-shaped, 2ft scapes (M)	Light green, creamy-yellow edge, cordate-rounded	Vigorous, RHS Award
'Gold Standard' (fortunei)	18–24in × 30–36in	3–9	Pale lavender, funnel-shaped, 2–3½ft scapes (M)	Light greenish yellow, dark green edge, ribbed, cordate-ovate	Leaves are more gold in sun, vigorous
'Great Expectations' (sieboldiana)	20–24in × 30–36in	3–9	Grayish white, 34in scapes (M)	Dark blue-green edges, splashed creamy-yellow, large, puckered, thick, cordate	Large plant, grown for the large leaves
'Ground Master'	12in × 20in	3–9	Deep purple, funnel-shaped, 20in scapes (M)	Dark green, creamy-yellow edges, wavy, ovate to lanceolate	Prostrate, good en masse, vigorous
'Guacamole'	18–20in × 24–52in	3–9	Large, white, fragrant, 30–36in scapes (M)	Rich green, chartreuse-gold center, large	2002 AHGA, full sun, aptly named, vigorous
'Hadspen Blue' (Tardiana Group)	8–12in × 18in	3–9	Pale lavender, bell-shaped, 15in scapes (M)	Bluish green, thick, corrugated, ovate to cordate, cupped	Slow-growing (P)
'Halcyon' (Tardiana Group)	14–20in × 24–28in	3–9	Lilac-blue, bell-shaped, 18in scapes (M)	Glaucous, veined, wavy margins, thick, cordate, ribbed	The standard blue hosta, upright, best in shade (P), RHS Award
'Honeybells'	24–36in × 48in	3–9	White with lilac flush, bell-shaped, fragrant, 30–36in (M–L)	Light green, wavy margins, pointed, veined, ovate-cordate	Full sun, very common, RHS Award, vigorous
'Inniswood' (montana)	20–24in × 40–48in	3–9	Pale lavender, 30in scapes (E–M)	Bright gold, deep green edge, puckered, cordate to rounded	

Species and Cultivars	Height/ Spread	USDA Hardiness Zone	Flowers (bloom time)	Foliage	Comments
'Invincible'	10–12in × 14–18in	3–9	Pale lavender to white, arching stems, funnel-shaped, 20in scapes (M–L)	Dark green, olive edges, glossy, thick, wavy, very striking	Floriferous, sun tolerant, vigorous (P)
'Janet' (fortunei)	16in × 24in	3–9	Pale lavender, 16–18in scapes (M–L)	Bright golden yellow fading to white, green edges	(P)
'June' (Tardiana Group)	12–16in × 24–36in	3–9	Violet, bell-shaped, 16–20in scapes (M)	Blue-green edges, creamy center aging to chartreuse, cordate, smooth	An elegant plant, 2001 AHGA Award (P)
'Kifukurin'	18in × 24in	3–9	White, flushed lavender, enclosed in broad bracts, 2ft scapes (M)	Dark green, yellow-green edge, prominent veins, glossy, narrow, lanceolate-ovate or elliptic	Good en masse
'Krossa Regal'	30–36in × 40in	3–9	Pale lavender, bell-shaped, 3–4ft scapes (M)	Blue-green, frosty, veined, ovate-lanceolate, pointed, a very proper-looking hosta	Vase-shaped, early leaf color is fantastic (P), RHS Award
lancifolia	12–24in × 18–24in	3–9	Deep lilac, flushed purple, red-dotted stems, trumpet-shaped, large, 2ft scapes (M–L)	Dark green, glossy, small, pointed, veined, narrowly lanceolate	Tolerates drier and sunnier, long-blooming, RHS Award
'Little Aurora' (tokudama)	6–10in × 20in	3–9	Pale lavender, 10in scapes (M)	Golden green, thick, puckered, cupped	
'Little Sunspot' (tokudama)	6in × 12in	3–9	White, pale lavender veins, 12in scapes (M)	Golden yellow center, wide dark green edges	Dwarf, good edger
'Love Pat' (tokudama)	18–24in × 24–36in	3–9	Creamy-white to pale lavender, bell-shaped, 22–24in scapes (M)	Intensely blue, cupped, cordate to rounded, puckered, thick	Very shade tolerant, RHS Award
'Lunar Eclipse'	20in × 30–36in	3–9	White, 18–24in scapes (M)	Bright yellow, edged in white, quilted, cupped	Shade only
'Minuteman' (fortunei)	24in × 48in	3–9	Pale lavender, 2ft scapes (M)	Rich deep green, creamy white edges, cupped, glossy, heavy	One of the best newer hostas—striking in pots (P)
'Moerheim' (fortunei)	18–20in × 20in	3–9	Lavender, 32in scapes (M)	Mid-green, creamy-white edges	
montana (syn. fortunei var. gigantea)	24–30in × 36in+	3–9	Pale lavender to gray-mauve, 3–4ft scapes (M–L)	Rich green and pale green points, deeply veined, glossy, cordate-ovate, thick, large	Large plant, over time can get immense
m. 'Night Before Christmas'	12–18in × 24–30in	3–9	Pale lavender, 18–20in (M)	White center, wide dark green edges, pointed, wedge-shaped	Tolerates sun, vigorous
'Northern Exposure' (sieboldiana)	30in × 60in	3–9	White, 32–36in scapes (M)	Blue-green, broad yellow-cream edges, flat, puckered	

Species and Cultivars	Height/ Spread	USDA Hardiness Zone	Flowers (bloom time)	Foliage	Comments
'On Stage'	14in × 24in	3–9	Pale lavender, funnel-shaped, 20in scapes (M)	Light yellow, light and dark green edges, veined, puckered, center fades to cream	
'Pacific Blue Edger'	8–10in × 12in	3–9	Glaucous lavender, 20in scapes (M)	Blue-gray, corrugated, cordate, glaucous reverse	Mounding, good for the edge of paths
'Paradigm'	20in × 36in	3–9	Pale lavender, nearly white, 2ft scapes (M)	Bright golden yellow, wide bluish green edges, puckered	
'Patriot'	15–22in × 30in	3–9	Pale lavender, funnel-shaped, 26–30in (M)	Dark-green, white edges, ovate-cordate, cupped, puckered	1997 AHGA Award, vigorous (P), RHS Award
'Paul's Glory'	15–20in × 26–28in	3–9	Pale lavender, arching, bell-shaped, 2ft scapes (E–M)	Golden yellow, blue-green edges, cordate, puckered, center fades golden white	1999 AHGA Award
'Piedmont Gold'	18–20in × 24in	3–9	Whitish, 26in scapes (M)	Bright golden, wavy margins, deep veins, cordate-lanceolate	Part shade
plantaginea	20–24in × 24–30in	3–9	White, large, trumpet-shaped, fragrant, 18–24in (M–L)	Light green, yellow-veined, glossy, cordate, arching, wavy	August lily, largest flowers, spreads
p. var. japonica (syn. grandiflora)	18–24in × 36–54in	3–9	White, large, trumpetlike, fragrant, 30–36in scapes (M–L)	Bright yellowish green, glossy, narrow to cordate	Tolerates sun, RHS Award
'Regal Splendor'	30–36in × 30–36in	3–9	Pale lavender, bell-shaped, 3–4ft scapes (M)	Gray-green, yellow to white edges, frosty, arching, ovate-lanceolate	2003 AHGA Award, vase-shaped (P)
'Royal Standard'	18–24in × 38–48in	3–9	White, trumpet-shaped, large, fragrant, 3–4ft scapes (M–L)	Rich green, broad, cordate to ovate, puckered, deeply veined, wavy margins	Tolerates full sun and deep shade, vigorous, RHS Award
'Sagae'	20–30in × 36–72in	3–9	Pale purple, bell-shaped, 3–5ft scapes (M)	Green-glaucous, boldly edged creamy-yellow, veined, ovate-lanceolate-cordate	Large plant, 2000 AHGA Award, good form, vase-shaped (P), RHS Award
'Samurai' (sieboldiana)	18–24in × 36in	3–9	Pale lavender, 30–36in scapes (M)	Blue-green, yellow-edged	Part to full shade
'Shade Fanfare'	18–24in × 18–36in	3–9	Lavender, funnel-shaped, 2ft scapes (M)	Light green, creamy-white edges, wavy margins, cordate	Floriferous, RHS Award
sieboldiana	24–36in × 36–48in	3–9	White, faint lilac flush, bell-shaped, 3ft scapes (M)	Deep gray-green, very large, pointed, ribbed and quilted, white edges, cordate	Interesting seedpods

Species and Cultivars	Height/ Spread	USDA Hardiness Zone	Flowers (bloom time)	Foliage	Comments
s. var. elegans	24–36in × 36–48in	3–9	White, hint of lilac, trumpet-shaped, 40–48in scapes (M)	Deep bluish green, thick, wavy, puckered, deeply veined, rounded	The standard perfect hosta (P), RHS Award
'Snow Flakes' (sieboldiana)	8–12in × 22in	3–9	Deep violet and white, funnel-shaped, 14–20in scapes (M–L)	Grayish green, white edges, thick, flat, lanceolate, pointed	Floriferous
'So Sweet'	8–14in × 12–20in	3–9	Lavender buds open white, funnel-shaped, 14–20in scapes (M–L)	Mid-green, creamy-white edges, wavy, glossy, ovate-lanceolate	1996 AHGA Award, good en masse, sun tolerant
'Spilt Milk' (tokudama)	15in × 48in	3–9	White, 20in scapes (M)	Bluish green, white to greenish white splashes and streaks, cupped, textured, cordate	Unique look
'Stiletto'	6in × 12in	3–9	Lavender, purple stripes, fragrant, 12in scapes (M–L)	Mid-green, creamy-white edges, very narrow-lanceolate, rippled	Dwarf, erect, vigorous, good en masse
'Striptease (fortunei)	16–20in × 24in	3–9	Violet, 2ft scapes (M)	Yellow-gold, white center, wide dark green edges	2005 AHGA Award, vigorous (P)
'Sum and Substance'	24–36in × 36–72in	3–9	Pale lavender, bell-shaped, 36–38in scapes (M–L)	Chartreuse to gold-green, large, cordate, ribbed, puckered, glossy	2004 AHGA Award, best in partial sun, can get very large, RHS Award
'Sun Power'	24–30in × 36in	3–9	Pale lavender, 2–3ft scapes (M)	Bright golden yellow, cupped, twisted, veined, ruffled	Vaselike, very sun tolerant, good gold foliage
tardiflora	10in × 12in	3–9	Pale purple, darker veins, funnel-shaped, 14in scapes (L)	Dark green, lanceolate, thick, glossy, leathery, veined	Good dwarf, good en masse
'Tattoo'	10in × 18in	3–9	Pale lavender, 10in scapes (E)	Small, bright yellow, wide light green edges, each tattooed with a green maple-leaf in center	Unique look
tokudama	12–18in × 20–24in	3–9	White to pale lavender, cup-shaped, 16–24in (M)	Grayish blue, cup-shaped, yellow edges, wavy, cordate-rounded, puckered, veined	
t. f. aureonebulosa	16–18in × 24–36in	3–9	White, urn-shaped, 2ft scapes (M)	Edged blue-green, marked and striped yellowish green, yellow center, cup-shaped-round	Slow-growing, dwarf, heavy substance, slug resistant (P)
t. f. flavocircinalis	14–18in × 24–48in	3–9	White to pale lavender, 18–24in scapes (M)	Blue-green, yellow edged, puckered, ovate-cordate	Dwarf, slow grower (P)
'True Blue'	24in × 42in	3–9	Ivory-white, bell-shaped, 28in scapes (M)	Glaucous, ovate-cordate, pointed, puckered, thick, veined, cupped	Keeps color well in sun (P)

Species and Cultivars	Height/ Spread	USDA Hardiness Zone	Flowers (bloom time)	Foliage	Comments
undulata	12–24in × 42in	3–9	Rich pale lilac, arching, trumpet-shaped, 20–36in (M)	Creamy-white center, dark green edges, spirally twisted, shiny, pointed, wavy margins, lanceolate-elliptic or ovate	One of the most common hostas, increases quickly
u. var. albomarginata (syn. 'Albo-marginata')	12–24in × 24–36in	3–9	Pale lavender, trumpet-shaped, 30in scapes (M)	Dark green, broad creamy edges, glossy beneath, wavy, pointed, lanceolate	Vigorous, sun tolerant, very common
u. var. undulata (syn. 'Variegata')	12–24in × 24–36in	3–9	Pale lavender, funnel-shaped, 2ft scapes (M)	Creamy-white center, wavy green edges, twisted	RHS Award
ventricosa	20–36in × 36in	3–9	Violet, dark veins, nodding, bell-shaped, 30–36in scapes (M)	Rich dark green, broad, glossy, prominently veined, cordate-ovate, wavy margins, ribbed	Slug resistant, RHS Award
v. var. aureomaculata	18–30in × 36in	3–9	Violet-purple, bell-shaped, 45in scapes (M)	Dark green, yellow-white edges and stripes aging to deep green in summer	Slow-growing, leaf tips twist
venusta	3–7in × 10in	3–9	Lavender-violet, trumpet-shaped, 8–14in scapes (M–L)	Mid-green, glossy reverse, veined, wavy, ovate to cordate	Dwarf, good en masse, rock garden plant, RHS Award
'Wide Brim'	18–24in × 36in	3–9	Pale lavender, funnel-shaped, 2ft scapes (M)	Dark to mid-glaucous green, yellow edges tinged white, cordate, puckered, wide	Big plant, vigorous, RHS Award
'Zounds'	16–20in × 36–48in	3–9	Pale lavender-blue, funnel-shaped, 24–30in scapes (M)	Bright golden green, metallic sheen, puckered, cordate, thick, cupped	One of the best glossy-leaf types

HOUTTUYNIA Saururaceae

Dog's breath? Let's take it on faith, some common names get a bit personal. The foliage ranges in description from evil-smelling to dirty-citrus; but it's the look, not the scent, we grow this for. The cordate leaves are very attractive, and the variegated form is wildly colored. Contain this plant or grow it as a water plant in pots on the edge of a pond. Never plant it in heavy clay soil on the edge of a natural water body; you will never be able to get rid of it. Look for the double-flowered form. It grows a bit taller and seems less aggressive. Leaves are edible and used like spinach, but do we really want to get that close to dog's breath? This is actually a good plant for us, but we don't consider it fully hardy. ~ *Bob Lilly*

Scientific Name: After Dutch naturalist Maarten Houttuyn (1720–1798).
Common Name: Dog's breath.
Origin: Himalaya to Japan.
Preferred Conditions: Fertile, moisture-retentive soil. Likes it moist, even in shallow water.

Houttuynia cordata 'Chameleon'.

Light: Part shade to sun. Full sun produces best leaf color on variegated form.
Planting: Place one foot from high-water mark, if siting near water.
Management: Hard winter frosts can cut them back; otherwise keep them in check by digging around them and removing any roots that have gone beyond their assigned area. They tend to deteriorate by midsummer, particularly in times of high temperature; cut down in autumn as plant goes down. Bait for slugs in early spring as they can nearly eat them down.
Propagation: Division in April and August (why would you want to?).
Pests and Diseases: Slugs.
Companions: Persicaria, carex, other water plants, and other invasive plants. Best in that constrained spot at the base of a rockery, where they can't go far.
Notes: Be careful where you place this plant—it is invasive and can run to a nearly infinite (∞) extent.

Species and Cultivars	Height/ Spread	USDA Hardiness Zone	Flowers (bloom time)	Foliage	Comments
cordata	6in × ∞	5–9	White, insignificant, shaped like a cross, cone-shaped center (M)	Dark green edged in red, thick, cordate	
c. 'Chameleon'	6in × ∞	5–9	As above	Multicolored, yellow and red variegation over green base	Good foliage plant, stress it out for best leaf color
c. 'Flore Pleno'	6in × ∞	5–9	Double white, cone-shaped center (M)	Green, tinged with purple	Taller stems, don't allow to dry out

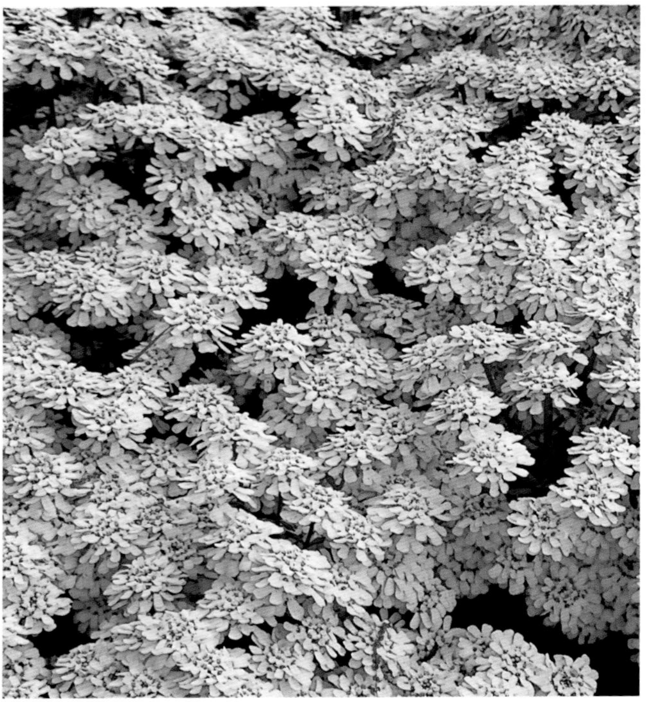

Iberis sempervirens.

IBERIS Brassicaceae

Candytuft provides us with a generous display of white flowers from late winter to early summer. Plants are compact and shrubby, with shiny, dark evergreen foliage; they are used as edgers, in rockeries, cascading over rocks and walls, or as a groundcover. *Iberis sempervirens* is a long-lasting cut flower, good for tussy mussies. ~ *Susan Carter*

Scientific Name: From the Greek *iberis* ("from Iberia").
Common Name: Perennial candytuft.
Origin: Central to southern Europe.
Preferred Conditions: Moderately fertile, alkaline, well-drained, and moist. Tolerates drought and poor soil.
Light: Sun.
Management: Shear and shape lightly after blooming to stimulate new growth and maintain compactness. Fertilize lightly after shearing. Fall trimming will result in no spring bloom.
Propagation: Best from seed; cuttings from softwood and semi-mature shoots; *I. sempervirens* cultivars must be propagated by cuttings.
Pests and Diseases: Snails, slugs.
Companions: Bergenia, osmanthus, tulips, dicentra, aquilegia, alyssum, narcissus, aubrieta, arabis.
Notes: Candytuft grows very well in our climate and seems to do fine in our more acidic soils. Follow the management instructions; they really work!

Species and Cultivars	Height/ Spread	USDA Hardiness Zone	Flowers (bloom time)	Foliage	Comments
gibraltarica	9–12in × 12in	3–9	White, fading to light pink (E–M)	Dark green	Compact, dense subshrub
'Golden Candy'	6–8in × 10in	3–9	White (E)	Golden green	Short-lived
sempervirens (syn. commuta)	8–12in × 18in+	3–9	White clusters, sometimes fades to lilac or pink (E–M)	Dark green, narrow, shiny, leathery	Candytuft, subshrub with open habit, RHS Award
s. 'Alexander's White'	10–12in × 18in+	3–9	White, dense clusters, heavy bloomer (M)	Dark green	Larger plant than type
s. 'Purity'	8–10in × 18in+	3–9	White, larger (E)	As above	Compact, long-blooming
s. 'Schneeflocke' (syn. 'Snowflake')	8–12in × 18in+	3–9	White, larger, in larger clusters (E–M)	Dark green, broader, more leathery	RHS Award
s. 'Weisser Zwerg' (syn. 'Little Gem')	6–8in × 10in	3–9	White, small (E–M)	Very dark green	Dwarf, slow-growing

Incarvillea arguta.

INCARVILLEA Bignoniaceae

Incarvillea delavayi has an exotic, somewhat tropical appearance in flower, like a supersized snapdragon of the open-mouthed type. A rosette of pinnately lobed foliage makes the base of this species; surprisingly bright pink or white tubular blooms are held above, on eighteen-inch flowering stems. A plant for sandy soil, well amended with organic matter, in full sun. A surprise every time.

Incarvillea arguta is a different cat, growing in nature in limestone cliffs on rocks in dry places. This species has many smaller, pinnate leaves and multiple flowering stems with pale pink flowers. A charmer, and a natural for the rock garden.

All forms of incarvillea resent being crowded in the garden or wet in winter (their roots rot in waterlogged soil in winter). They are heavy feeders in the summer, one cowpat per *I. delavayi*. ~ *Carrie Becker*

Species and Cultivars	Height/ Spread	USDA Hardiness Zone	Flowers (bloom time)	Foliage	Comments
arguta	3ft × 1ft	4–9	Pink and white, tubular, pendent (M)	Dark green, pinnate, with red stems	Woody base
delavayi	1–2ft × 1ft	4–9	Rose-pink to purplish with yellow and purple throat (E–M)	Mid-green, divided	Clump-forming, good cut, good seedpods, tap-rooted
d. 'Snowtop' (syn. 'Alba')	2ft × 1ft	4–9	White (M)	As above	Tap-rooted
grandiflora	6–10in × 6in	4–9	Large rose-red with yellow throat (E–M)	Dark green, deeply divided, narrow and wrinkled	As above
olgae	2–4ft × 1ft	4–9	Pale rose-pink, penstemonlike, in airy sprays (M–L)	Mid-green, narrow, deeply divided	Tap-rooted, many-stemmed, almost a subshrub

Scientific Name: After Pierre d'Incarville, French missionary and plant collector in China.
Common Name: Hardy gloxinia.
Origin: Southwest China, Central and East Asia.
Preferred Conditions: Fertile, deep, rich, well-drained, moist soil.
Light: Sun.
Planting: Plant approximately six inches deep depending on soil (deeper in light soils).
Management: This plant is tap-rooted and does not transplant well. Mulch against winter cold. Avoid damaging thick, fleshy roots—mark their position during dormancy.
Propagation: Seed in spring or autumn (generally takes three years to flower); basal cuttings in spring or early summer; division is not recommended.
Pests and Diseases: Slugs.
Companions: Rehmannia, dwarf daylilies, primula, hosta, *Geranium psilostemon, Molinia caerulea* 'Variegata'.

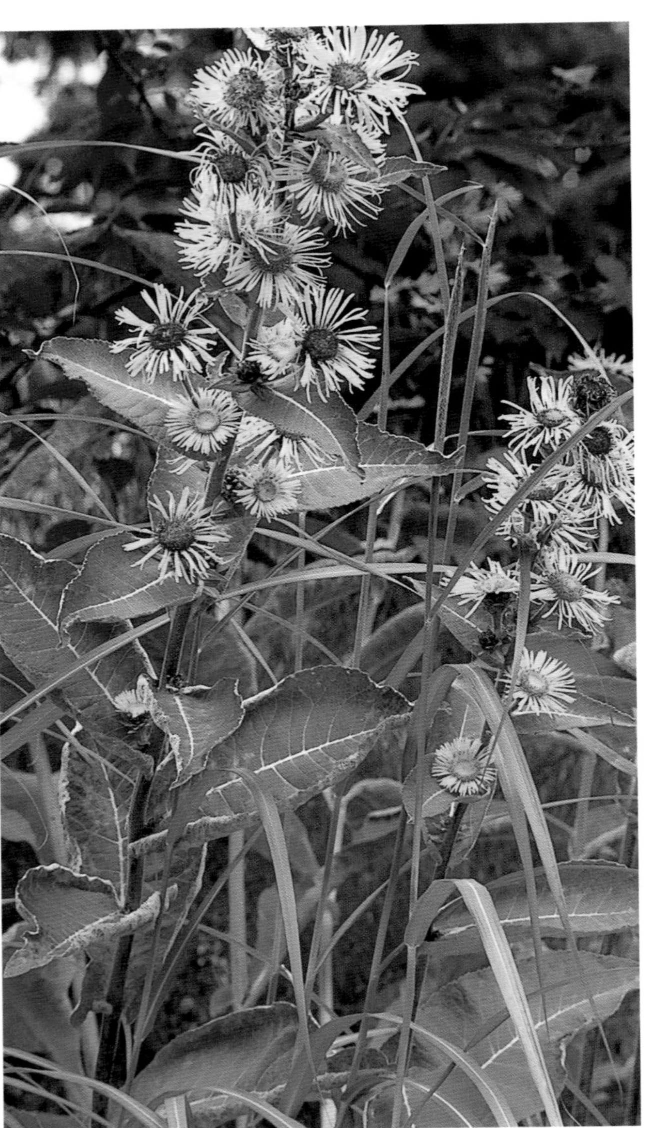

Inula helenium.

INULA Asteraceae

The threadlike, yellow ray flowers are the most novel part of this hardy perennial. Inulas like deep, rich soil and plenty of summer water; they form large clumps over time and can even seed about, which is rare in these parts for members of the daisy family. They make a good cut flower but must be handled carefully—their petals are very delicate. And watch out for *I. hookeri*—it spreads aggressively. ~ *Bob Lilly*

Scientific Name: Latin name for *Inula helenium*.
Common Name: Sunray, elecampane.
Origin: Asia, Africa.
Preferred Conditions: Any reasonable soil that is rich, deep, well-drained, moisture-retentive, and fertile.
Light: Sun. Tolerates part shade.
Planting: Larger species need lots of space.
Management: Low-maintenance plant. Cut back in fall when leaves die. Give it a heavy mulch of organic matter in winter. The taller ones may need staking. Do not let them dry out as this can trigger powdery mildew—a common syndrome with the daisy family.
Propagation: Seed in containers in cold frame in spring; division in spring.
Pests and Diseases: Powdery mildew (if too dry).
Companions: Ligularia, *Iris pseudacorus*, trollius, aconitum, *Potentilla recta* 'Sulphurea', sanguisorba, *Filipendula ulmaria, Carex elata, Miscanthus sinensis.*

Species and Cultivars	Height/ Spread	USDA Hardiness Zone	Flowers (bloom time)	Foliage	Comments
ensifolia	2–4ft × 1ft	4–8	Golden yellow, darker center, 1–2in (M–L)	Dark green, narrow, sword-shaped, hairy	Swordleaf inula, bushy, vigorous, rhizomatous
helenium	4–6ft × 3ft+	4–8	Bright yellow, 3in (M–L)	Coarse, mid-green, ridged, hairy stems with a slight gold cast	Elecampane, rhizomatous
hookeri	1½–2½ft × 2ft+	4–8	Greenish yellow, extremely narrow petals, buds covered with shaggy hairs, scented, 3in (M)	Mid-green, hairy, lanceolate to small oval	Spreads aggressively, usually needs staking, prefers shade
magnifica	6–8ft × 2½ft	4–8	Deep golden yellow, yellow center, large, 5–6in (M)	Dark green, large, broad, rough, brownish hairy stems	Needs lots of space, spreads slowly, good winter interest
orientalis (syn. glandulosa)	1½–2ft × 2ft	4–8	Yellow-orange, narrow and shaggy rays with raised central disk, 2–3in (M)	Mid-green, lanceolate, hairy	Rhizomatous, makes thick stands
royleana	1–2ft × 1½ft	4–8	Yellow-orange, darker center, narrow petals, black in bud, 3–5in (M–L)	Mid-green, white beneath, large, broad, on long stalks	Will not tolerate dry soil, clump-forming

IRIS Iridaceae

Iris is one of the larger genera of herbaceous perennials. From tiny *I. cristata* to the flamboyant Pacific Coast Hybrids, they fit into any color scheme. Like all members of the family Iridaceae,

Iris sibirica 'Silver Edge'.

A sea of Siberian irises, including *Iris sibirica* 'Chilled Wine' (background).

irises have flower parts in threes and pointed, straplike leaves. The stiff, vertical leaves of all irises are a very distinctive feature and an important element in garden design, lending drama, exclamation, and motion. Irises make a good, strong visual statement in any garden, and are a common theme in art, religion, and even flags. They have worked their way into our culture.

We have grouped irises into three main categories, beardless, bearded, and crested. The beardless *I. foetidissima* and its variegated form are particularly wonderful landscape and garden plants; leave their seedpods on for a fall and winter show of brilliant berries. Many of the Pacific Coast Hybrids, also beardless, are grown from division; others are raised from seed. Buy them in bloom if you can, but watch out for the gaudy newer ones from California breeders: they seem not to be as hardy. Every year brings new colors, color combinations, and shapes in the bearded iris category, which has a loyal following; most sales are mail order.

Slugs are always a problem for all irises; early baiting will help a great deal. ~ *Bob Lilly*

Scientific Name: After the Greek goddess of the rainbow.
Common Name: Flag.
Origin: China, Korea, Japan, Russia, Algeria, North Africa, Europe, North America, Britain.
Preferred Conditions / Light / Management:

Group 1. Beardless. Beardless irises mix easily with ordinary border plants. Plant rhizomes just below the surface in well-drained, moisture-retentive soil that has a neutral to slightly acid pH. Some will grow in standing water; others are drought tolerant. Most prefer sun but tolerate part shade. Can have a light mulch (except for *I. foetidissima*, which wants no mulch). They form dense, often circular clumps that do get very large and very old; they are best split up and divided every third or fourth year and replanted in rejuvenated soil. Note: Dig and divide the Pacific Coast Hybrids after the first fall rain, just as the new roots begin to grow, a critical time.

Group 2. Bearded. Bearded irises are difficult to use with other plants. Plant so the rhizome is only halfway in soil, which should be well-drained, fertile, and with a neutral to slightly acid pH, in sun. Do not mulch over or next to the rhizomes. Bearded irises usually have broad fans of sword-shaped leaves; most have multiple flowers per stem in a large range of colors, with prominent standards and falls and a beard of white or colored hairs in the center of each fall. Keep them moist during the active growth period but dry during dormancy. Avoid heavy or waterlogged soil and high nitrogen fertilizer. Every three to four years (or when then become congested, or begin to bloom less), dig and divide on or around 1 September; cut leaves back to four to five inches in a triangular or fanlike effect.

Group 3. Crested. The crested iris has a crest or ridge on each fall instead of a beard. They prefer sun to part shade in well-drained, moist, humus-rich soil. Can have a light mulch (except for I. japonica, which can be mulched normally). Keep moist during dormancy.

Propagation: Seed; division.

Pests and Diseases: Snails, slugs (especially *I. germanica*, *I. sibirica*, *I. japonica*, *I. unguicularis*, and *I. cristata*), crown rot, root rot.

Companions: Meconopsis, primula, hosta, aquilegia, paeonia, *Helleborus orientalis*, ligularia, camassia.

Notes: *Iris sibirica* seedpods can be left for fall interest.

Species and Cultivars	Height/ Spread	USDA Hardiness Zone	Flowers (bloom time)	Foliage	Comments
chrysographes	1½–2ft × 1ft	4–9	Dark black-purple to reddish purple, gold penciling on falls, fragrant (E–L)	Gray-green, narrow, straplike, vertical	Group 1, many cultivars, usually with “black” in the name, divide in early fall, RHS Award
cristata	4in × 6–8in	4–9	Light blue to lilac, yellow and orange crests, white throat (E)	Light bright green, arranged in fans, gracefully arched	Group 3, crested dwarf iris, many cultivars, clumps will spread to 3ft, divide in fall, RHS Award
douglasiana	1–2ft × 1½ft	7–9	Red, purple, lavender, blue, cream, or white, marked with gold, blue or purple (E–M)	Dark green, arching, stiff, glossy, red at base, ribbed, taller than the flower stems	Group 1, evergreen, vigorous, makes large colonies, divide in fall, RHS Award
ensata (syn. kaempferi)	2–4ft × 2ft	5–9	Purple to red-purple, violet, blue, or white, yellow blotches, darker veins, flat, saucerlike (E)	Bright green, narrow, erect	Group 1, Japanese iris, vigorous, will grow in water, divide in spring, RHS Award
e. ‘Cry of Rejoice’	32in × 24in	4–9	Pale blue, yellow blotches (M)	As above	Group 1, divide in spring
e. ‘Darling’	32in × 24in	4–9	Soft lilac-rose (M)	As above	As above
e. ‘Gracieuse’	2½–3ft × 2ft	4–9	White, edged in purple-lilac, purplish veining (M)	As above	As above
e. ‘Jodlesong’	32in × 24in	4–9	Purple-red (M)	As above	As above
e. ‘Variegata’	2–3ft × 1½ft	5–9	Dark purplish blue, yellow streaks on falls (E–M)	Variegated creamy-white and gray-green, fades in summer	As above, RHS Award
‘Florentina’	2ft × 1½ft	3–9	Pale grayish white, bluish sheen, yellow beard, very fragrant (E–M)	Grayish green, ribbed, spreading fans	Group 2, orris root, divide in fall, RHS Award

Species and Cultivars	Height/ Spread	USDA Hardiness Zone	Flowers (bloom time)	Foliage	Comments
foetidissima	1½–2ft × 2ft	6–9	Lilac, tinged yellow-green, veined dull purple (M)	Dark green, arching, glossy, lanceolate	Group 1, stinking iris, large seedpods with orange seeds, self-sows, evergreen, divide in spring, vigorous, RHS Award
f. var. citrina (syn. f. chinensis)	2–2½ft × 2ft	6–9	Yellow, brown veins (M)	Dark green, glossy, broad	Group 1, green seedpods, orange seeds, vigorous, evergreen, divide in spring
f. 'Variegata'	1½ft × 2ft	5–9	Rarely produced (E–M)	Variegated or striped ivory and grayish green, lanceolate	Group 1, rarely fruits, evergreen, divide in spring, RHS Award
germanica	8–24in × 18in	3–9	Almost all colors and combinations (E–M)	Glaucous, lanceolate, in a fan	Group 2, German iris, divide in fall, RHS Award
graminea	8–16in × 10–12in	5–9	Rosy-purple and violet, blue falls, fragrant (E–M)	Green, thin, upright	Group 2, grass-leaved iris, divide in fall, drought tolerant, RHS Award
'Holden Clough'	2–2½ft+ × 3ft	4–9	Buff with maroon veins (M)	Rich green, coarse, ribbed, swordlike	Group 1, divide anytime, RHS Award
japonica	1½–2½ft × 1½ft	7–9	White or pale lavender-blue, frilly (E–M)	Dark green, straplike, broad fans, glossy	Group 3, divide in spring, RHS Award
j. 'Variegata'	1ft × 1½ft	7–9	White, pale lavender tints (M)	White and green striped	As above, RHS Award
laevigata	1½–2½ft × 1½ft+	4–9	Deep bluish purple, yellow mid-stripes (M)	Mid-green, narrow, smooth	Group 1, water iris, will grow in water, divide in spring, good seedpods, RHS Award
l. 'Variegata'	1½–2½ft × 1½ft+	4–9	Paler bluish purple (M)	White and green striped	Group 1, good seedpods, divide in spring, RHS Award
Pacific Coast Hybrids (syn. California Hybrids)	8–24in × 10–18in	4–9	Large range, white, cream, yellow, bronze, rose, lilac, purple, frilled and veined, or smooth and silky (M)	Dark green, narrow, rose base	Group 1, evergreen, good seedpods, doesn't like lime, divide in fall
pallida	2–4ft × 2ft	4–9	Soft blue, yellow beard, conspicuous papery silver bud-covering, fragrant (E–M)	Gray-blue-green	Group 2, semi-evergreen, erect, divide in fall
p. 'Argentea Variegata'	2–2½ft × 2ft	4–9	Light lavender-blue, fragrant (M)	Gray-blue-green, white variegation	Group 2, divide in fall, less vigorous
p. 'Variegata' (syn. 'Aurea')	2–3ft × 2ft	4–9	Lavender-blue, fragrant (E–M)	Creamy-yellow and green striped	Group 2, stronger than above, divide in fall

Species and Cultivars	Height/ Spread	USDA Hardiness Zone	Flowers (bloom time)	Foliage	Comments
pseudacorus	3–5ft × 3ft+	4–9	Bright yellow, brown or violet markings (E)	Rich green, coarse, ribbed, swordlike, very vertical	Group 1, self-sows, French flag (fleur-de-lis), vigorous spreader (cultivars not as much), will grow in water, divide anytime, RHS Award
p. 'Alba'	3ft × 2ft+	4–9	Pale creamy-white, yellow patches, edged pale purple (E)	As above	Group 1, vigorous spreader, divide anytime
p. var. bastardii	2–4ft × 2ft+	4–9	Pale yellow (E)	As above	As above
p. 'Flore Pleno'	3–4ft × 2ft+	4–9	Double yellow (E)	As above	As above
p. 'Roy Davidson'	34in × 2ft+	4–9	Yellow, brown veins (E)	As above	As above, named for a Seattle gardener of note
p. 'Variegata'	2–4ft × 2ft+	4–9	Yellow, brown markings on falls (E)	Creamy yellow and green stripes aging to green, tends to fade out in summer	Group 1, divide anytime, RHS Award
pumila	4–8in × 6in	4–9	Blue, purple, yellow, or white, beard yellow, white, or blue, fragrant (E)	Gray-green, swordlike	Group 2, dwarf, needs lime, divide in fall
×robusta 'Gerald Darby'	2–3ft × 2ft+	4–9	Violet-blue, purple-flushed stems (E–M)	Mid-green, purple bases, striking spring growth	Group 1, good in shallow water, divide spring or fall
setosa	10–18in × 10–12in	3–9	Blue to purple, blue and violet, white center, darker veins (M)	Gray-green, red-tinted at base	Group 1, divide in fall, RHS Award
sibirica	2–4ft × 3ft	4–9	Wide range, blue-violet, darker veins, white marking, drooping falls (E)	Green, grasslike, reddish base, narrow	Group 1, Siberian iris, very adapt-able, dark brown seedpods, divide in spring, RHS Award
s. 'Baby Sister'	18–14in × 18in	3–9	Sky-blue, white signals (E)	Green, grasslike, narrow	Group 1, divide in spring
s. 'Blue King'	32–42in × 36in	3–9	Light to mid-blue (E)	As above	As above
s. 'Butter and Sugar'	2–2½ft × 2ft	4–9	White standards, ivory falls (E)	As above	Group 1, erect, divide in spring, RHS Award
s. 'Caesar's Brother'	2–3ft × 2½ft	4–9	Deep violet-blue, velvety (E)	Good rich green, narrow	Group 1, erect, divide in spring
s. 'Cambridge'	34–36in × 30in	3–9	Turquoise-blue falls, paler standards (E–M)	As above	Group 1, divide in spring, RHS Award
s. 'Chilled Wine'	2½–3ft × 2ft	4–9	Claret (E)	As above	Group 1, erect, divide in spring
s. 'Ego'	2–2½ft × 2ft	3–9	Dark purplish lavender (E)	As above	Group 1, divide in spring

Species and Cultivars	Height/ Spread	USDA Hardiness Zone	Flowers (bloom time)	Foliage	Comments
s. 'Ewen'	2½ft × 2ft	4–9	Wine-red, velvety, creamy markings (E–M)	As above	As above
s. 'Flight of Butterflies'	1½–2½ft × 1½ft	4–9	Pale violet-blue, darker blue veins, very small (E–M)	Rich green, very narrow	Group 1, slow to increase, tight clumps, divide in spring
s. 'Forrest McCord'	3ft × 2ft	3–9	Dark blue falls, gold signals, thin white margins (E)	Green, narrow, grasslike	Group 1, divide in spring
s. 'Fourfold White'	3½–4ft × 2ft	3–9	Bone-white, yellow-gold spot at base of falls (E)	Strong green, grasslike	As above
s. 'Orville Fay'	2½–3ft × 2ft	3–9	Bright mid-blue, dark veining (E–M)	As above	As above
s. 'Papillon'	3ft × 2ft	3–9	Light blue, spotted white (E–M)	As above	As above
s. 'Ruffled Velvet'	2–2½ft × 2ft	3–9	Red-purple, darker ruffled falls, black and gold center, velvety (M)	As above	As above, RHS Award
s. 'Shirley Pope'	34–36in × 2ft	3–9	Purplish red, purple veins, white signals, black buds (E–M)	Dark green, grasslike	As above, RHS Award
s. 'Showdown'	2–2½ft × 2ft	3–9	Red-purple, white signals, velvety (E–M)	Green, grasslike	Group 1, divide in spring
s. 'Silver Edge'	2–2½ft × 2ft	3–9	Sky-blue, silver edge (E–M)	As above	As above, RHS Award
s. 'Sky Wings'	2½–3ft × 2ft	3–9	Pale sky-blue, yellow sheen and markings (E–M)	As above	Group 1, divide in spring
s. 'Snow Queen'	2½–3ft × 2ft	3–9	White, yellow near center (E–M)	As above	As above
s. 'Sparkling Rose'	2½–3ft × 2ft	3–9	Soft pinkish mauve, yellow bases, purple veins (E–M)	Green, narrow, grasslike	As above
s. 'Tycoon'	2½ft × 2ft	4–9	Deep violet-blue (E–M)	As above	As above
s. 'White Swirl'	2½–3ft × 2ft	4–9	White, yellow bases, ruffled, large (E–M)	As above	As above, RHS Award
spuria	3–5ft × 3ft	4–9	Large range, violet-blue, purple, lilac, yellow, or white, some veined and edged (M)	Blue-green, narrow, swordlike, very vertical	Group 1, tolerant of heat, divide in spring
tectorum	1–1½ft × 1½ft+	4–9	Violet-blue, white beard and darker blue veins, ruffled edges (E–M)	Dark green, broad, ribbed, lanceolate, glossy	Group 2, roof iris, divide in spring semi-evergreen

Species and Cultivars	Height/ Spread	USDA Hardiness Zone	Flowers (bloom time)	Foliage	Comments
t. 'Variegata'	10–18in × 12in+	5–9	Lavender-blue (M)	Green with white stripes	Group 2, divide in spring, semi-evergreen
tenax	8–12in × 18in+	7–9	Blue, lavender-blue, dark violet, pink, white, yellow marks, fragrant (E–M)	Deep green, narrow, red-tinged bases, makes large colonies	Group 1, Pacific Coast iris, semi-evergreen, divide in fall
unguicularis	1–2ft × 2ft	7–9	Pale lavender-blue, dark violet, pink, white, yellow marks, fragrant (L–E, betw. Sept. and Apr.)	Dark green-gray, tough, grasslike	Group 1, winter iris, evergreen, untidy foliage, divide after flowering, RHS Award
versicolor	2–3ft × 1½–2ft	3–9	Violet, purple, lavender-blue, white veins, white and yellow center (E–M)	Glaucous, purple-tinged at base, narrow	Group 1, blue flag, grows in both shallow water and the border, divide in fall

JASIONE Campanulaceae

Sheep's bit is subtle and herblike, a low-growing clump of pubescent, lanceolate leaves with many erect stems. The flowers are lavender-blue in a globose head atop each stem. It is best planted in little groups and not crowded by neighbors, in rock gardens or in lower-growing combinations in the foreground. Seems to be short-lived. This stoloniferous charmer has the same flower color as *Aster* ×*frikartii*, a good color echo. They make fine if small-scale cut flowers, best shown in old-fashioned pansy vases. ~ *Carrie Becker*

Jasione laevis 'Blaulicht' with *Ballota pseudodictamnus*.

Scientific Name: Greek name for another plant.
Common Name: Sheep's bit, shepherd's scabious.
Origin: Mediterranean, Asia Minor.
Preferred Conditions: Moderately fertile, well-drained, sandy, and lime-free.
Light: Sun. Tolerates a little shade.
Management: Cut off spent flowering stems. Cut down in winter but leave basal leaves.
Propagation: Seed in cold frame as soon as ripe, or in autumn; take cuttings.
Pests and Diseases: Snails, slugs on young growth.
Companions: Santolina, nepeta, *Ajuga metallica* 'Crispa', smaller deschampsias, *Ophiopogon planiscapus* 'Nigrescens', scabiosa, *Calamintha nepeta* subsp. *nepeta*, small campanulas, *Aster ×frikartii*, *A. sedifolius*.

Species and Cultivars	Height/ Spread	USDA Hardiness Zone	Flowers (bloom time)	Foliage	Comments
laevis (syn. perennis)	12–18in × 12in	3–9	Blue-lilac, stiff collar of bracts (M)	Grayish green, slightly hairy, lanceolate	Clump-forming, stoloniferous
l. 'Blaulicht' (syn. 'Blue Light')	12–18in × 12in	3–9	Violet-blue, stiff collar of bracts (M)	As above	Clump-forming, new cultivar from Germany

JEFFERSONIA Berberidaceae

Jeffersonia diphylla is one of the great American woodland plants. There is something ethereal about both species: their two-lobed scalloped leaves narrow as they reach the almost invisible stem and seem to be floating in the air; their flowers—a striking blue in *J. dubia*, white in

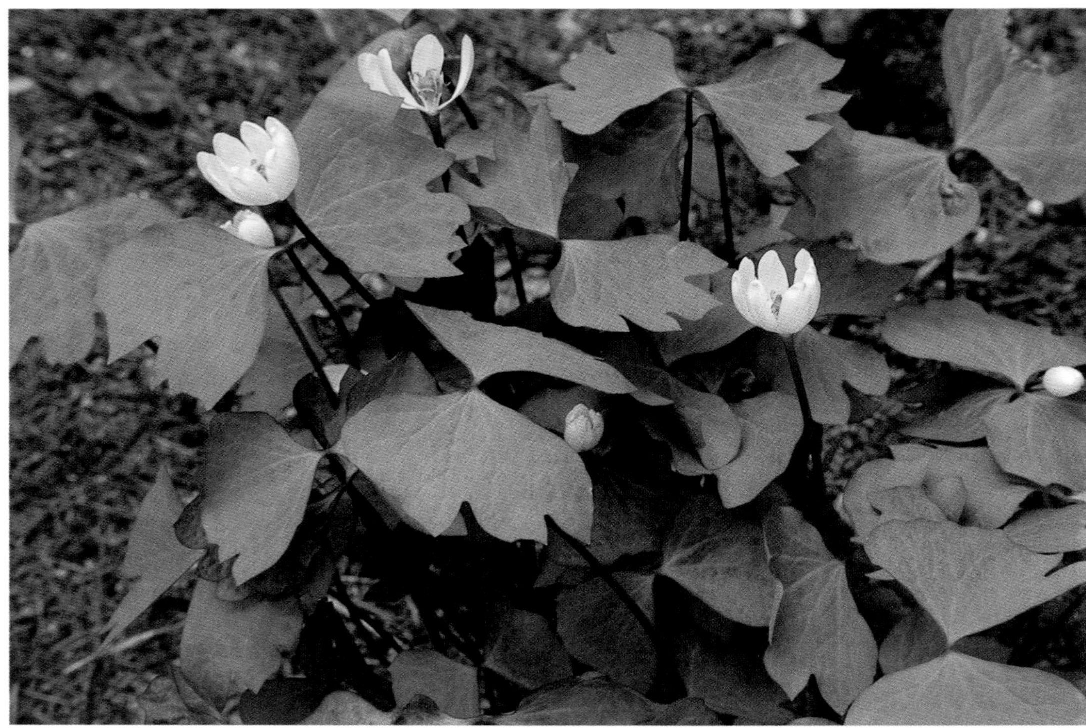

Jeffersonia diphylla.

J. diphylla—are simple, beautiful, and fleeting. They are followed by attractive small woody seedheads. Twinleafs increase very slowly, but despite their fragile appearance, I have not found them hard to grow in partially shaded, humus-rich places with no watering. ~ *Ann Bucher*

Scientific Name: After Thomas Jefferson.
Common Name: Twinleaf.
Origin: North America.
Preferred Conditions: Humus-rich, cool, moisture-retentive, loose, moist soil in a sheltered location.
Light: Part shade.
Management: Remove old foliage when plant dies back. Apply a winter organic mulch.
Propagation: Seed as soon as ripe; divide older clumps, if needed, as growth begins, or in fall.
Pests and Diseases: Slugs graze on the leaves and flowers of this woodlander at almost any time.
Companions: Shorter thalictrums, epimedium, *Anemone nemorosa*, primula, dodecatheon, erythronium.

Species and Cultivars	Height/ Spread	USDA Hardiness Zone	Flowers (bloom time)	Foliage	Comments
diphylla	6–10in × 6in	4–8	White, poppylike, single (E–M)	Gray-green, unusual kidney-shaped, scalloped margins, 2-lobed	Pear-shaped seedpods in late summer, North American native
dubia	8in × 6in	5–8	Light lavender-blue (E)	Gray-green, unusual kidney-shaped or rounded, 2-lobed	Native to NE Asia

KALIMERIS Asteraceae

These spreading plants are good as a background or filler and very suitable as a focal point in a pot. Once fully potbound, you have two years of a spectacular display, but then they must be divided, refreshed, and repotted. The variegated *K. yomena* 'Shogun' is a stunning plant but must be watched carefully for reversions to the green type, which is very invasive. With most of these variegated sports, when they revert to the parent plant, all that vigor returns with a vengeance. Kalimeris has small pale bluish daisy flowers. None is enough! ~ *Bob Lilly*

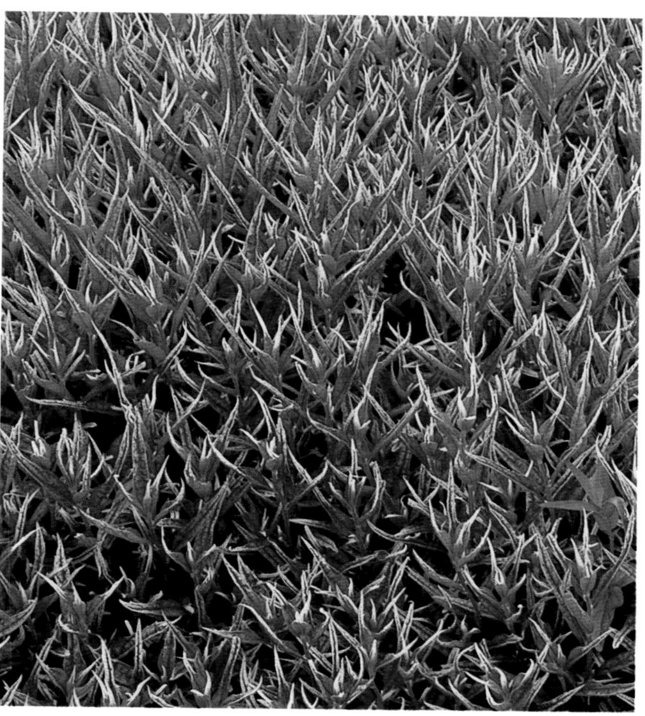

Kalimeris yomena 'Shogun'.

Scientific Name: Unknown.
Common Name: Kalimeris.
Origin: East Asia.
Preferred Conditions: Any ordinary soil, moisture-retentive. Tolerates damp soil.
Light: Sun to part shade.

Management: May need support. Cut back in fall.
Propagation: Division in spring—very easy.
Pests and Diseases: Slugs in spring.
Companions: Asters, boltonia, grasses, tall sedums, oregano, persicaria.

Species and Cultivars	Height/ Spread	USDA Hardiness Zone	Flowers (bloom time)	Foliage	Comments
incisa	2ft × 2ft+	5–8	Pale lilac-blue and white (L)	Green, jagged, on thin stems	Stoloniferous
yomena 'Shogun' (syn. 'Variegata')	2ft × 2ft+	5–8	Lavender (L)	Green and white variegated, turning more yellow late in summer	As above

KIRENGESHOMA Hydrangeaceae

With its relatively large maplelike (palmate) leaves and deep purple stems that terminate in pretty yellow bells, kirengeshoma is one of the best perennials for the fall shade border: think of it being in flower with the latest hydrangeas, the tall hardy fuchsias, the willow gentians, even the white wood aster (*Aster divaricatus*) at its feet, and perhaps the lavender fruit of a callicarpa nearby. The one thing standing between you and kirengeshoma success: this plant does not like to dry out, or to have much competition. It makes a good specimen plant: one kirengeshoma is enough. ~ *Carrie Becker*

Kirengeshoma palmata Koreana Group.

Scientific Name: From the Japanese *ki* ("yellow"), *renge* ("lotus blossom"), and *shoma* ("hat").
Common Name: Yellow waxbells, shuttlecock flower.
Origin: Japan, Korea.
Preferred Conditions: Humus-rich, cool, deep, acidic, and moist. Shelter from damaging winds and winter cold.
Light: Part shade. Tolerates sun if kept moist.
Management: Top-dress with organic material. Rarely needs division, looks best when allowed to fill in. Late flowering can be damaged by early frosts. The last seed to be collected. Cut back in fall when leaves die back. Needs to be well watered and fed. Watch for slugs on new young growth.
Propagation: Division in spring; cuttings in spring; seed in spring.
Pests and Diseases: Slugs.
Companions: *Hakonechloa macra* 'Aureola', cimicifuga, *Gentiana asclepiadea*, tall ferns, rodgersia, hydrangea, aconitum, hosta, 'Hawkshead' fuchsia, *Farfugium japonicum* 'Aureomaculatum', *Aster divaricatus*.

Species and Cultivars	Height/ Spread	USDA Hardiness Zone	Flowers (bloom time)	Foliage	Comments
palmata	2–4ft × 2ft	4–9	Pale yellow, waxy petals on purplish black stems, nodding (M–L)	Clear green, maplelike	Clump-forming, RHS Award
p. Koreana Group	4–5ft × 2ft	4–9	Lighter pale yellow, flowers more open, out- or up-facing (M)	Light green, maplelike	Clump-forming

KNAUTIA Dipsacaceae

Knautia macedonica, the only species we commonly use, has long-blooming pincushion flower heads of garnet blossoms. It looks best against a strong background or with its long wiry stems coming up through shrubby plants. This short-lived plant does seed about a bit too much if happy; the seeds fall quite quickly, even while still green. It's a good cut flower for fresh arrangements, and the bees love it. Dried seedheads are interesting in floral arrangements. ~ *Susan Carter*

Scientific Name: For German doctor and botanist Christoph Knaut.
Common Name: Macedonian scabious.
Origin: Central Europe.
Preferred Conditions: Moderately fertile, well-drained, alkaline soil. Tolerates drought once established.
Light: Sun.

Knautia macedonica.

Management: Deadheading is a pain, but cutting back older flowering stems encourages a second but smaller flush of blooms. Top-dress with organic matter in winter but not over the crown. Cut back in fall, leaving the basal growth. Can be floppy and need support.
Propagation: Seed in containers in cold frame in spring or fall; basal cuttings in spring.
Pests and Diseases: Aphids, powdery mildew.
Companions: Red-, purple-, or silver-foliaged plants; berberis, cotinus, artemisia, *Hydrangea* 'Preziosa', tall campanulas, *Miscanthus sinensis* 'Adagio', astrantia.
Notes: Wait to buy *K. macedonica* 'Melton Pastels' when plants are in flower, so you can select for color.

Species and Cultivars	Height/ Spread	USDA Hardiness Zone	Flowers (bloom time)	Foliage	Comments
macedonica	2–3ft × 1½ft	5–9	Crimson-garnet (M–L)	Dark green, deeply cut, smooth-edged	Slender, branching stems, clump-forming
m. 'Mars Midget'	1–1½ft × 1½ft	5–9	As above	Dark green, smooth-edged	Dwarf form
m. 'Melton Pastels'	1½–2½ft × 1½ft+	5–9	Mix of crimson-garnet through pinks and reds (M–L)	Dark green, deeply cut, smooth-edged	Seed-grown, variable

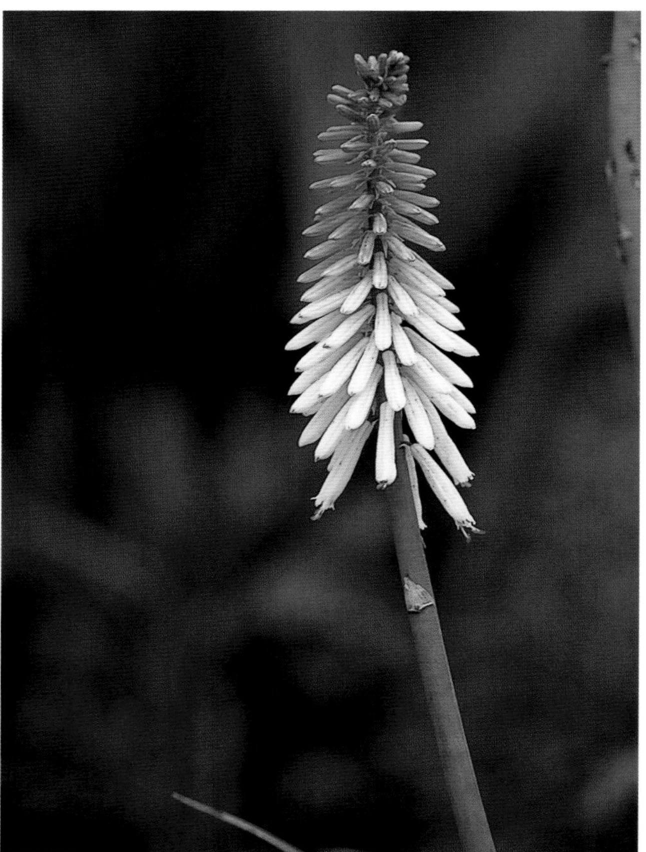
Kniphofia 'Modesta'.

KNIPHOFIA Asphodelaceae

A great background plant, our grandmothers' red hot poker now comes in colors that fit in almost any color scheme. Bees and hummingbirds love the tubular flowers, laden with pollen and nectar and hanging down to protect the store. Most are still grown from seed and sold in four-inch pots; look for the newer cultivars, from division, in one-gallon pots or larger. They'll need full sun for best performance from leaves and flowers; a less-than-ideal location leaves them looking a little weedy and long in the leaf—and more prone to flattening in a heavy summer rain. They don't like competition from more aggressive summer perennials (asters, for example) or grasses, which can shade them out. Often seen at the seashore in sandy soil, these plants actually need regular summer water. ~ *Bob Lilly*

Scientific Name: After Johann Hieronymus Kniphof.
Common Name: Poker plant, red hot poker, torch lily.
Origin: South Africa.
Preferred Conditions: Deep, well-drained (especially in winter), and moisture-retentive, but will adapt to most garden soils. Avoid windy locations. Soggy areas are fatal, but don't let them dry out.
Light: Sun.
Planting: Crown specific.

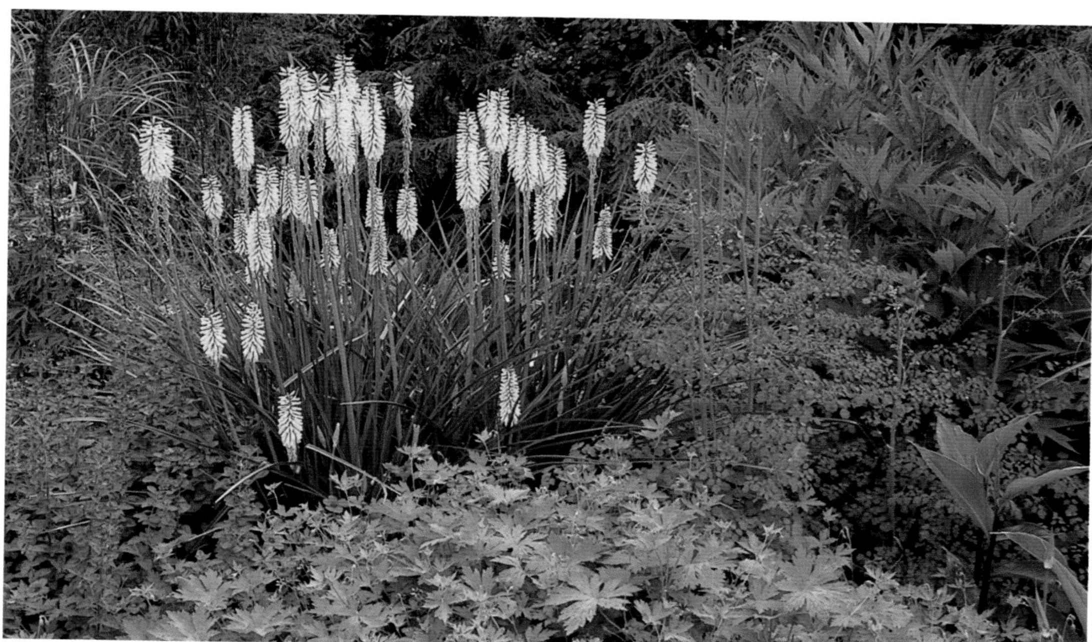

Kniphofia 'Primrose Beauty' with *Geranium* 'Ann Folkard' and *Delphinium elatum*.

Management: Most clumps will do well for up to ten years undisturbed, except for *K. caulescens*, which benefits from being split every three or four years. This does make them difficult to divide; any large clump gets quite congested, and after lifting, the roots may need to be washed before taking the clump apart. It is best to leave the leaves alone until spring, when a general tidying up can be done and damaged leaves can be removed; carefully peel them away, one by one. Cut out flower spikes as far down as possible after bloom. Watch for engulfing and overcrowding and check underneath for dead foliage and slugs on a regular basis; removing rotting leaves prevents disease from spreading throughout the crown. Mulch in autumn with leaves or straw. Surface mulch with manure in the spring to fertilize. Keep manure away from crown.

Propagation: Seed in containers in cold frame (cultivars seldom come true from seed); divide established cultivars in late spring (clean up and cut back foliage by about one-third so they are easier to handle); bulbous offsets can be planted in spring.

Pests and Diseases: Stem or crown rot, slugs, cutworms in spring—hand removal is best. If violet crown rot appears, remove the plants as soon as possible—roots and all—to the garbage, not the compost pile.

Companions: Lilies, yucca, helenium, perovskia, berberis, hemerocallis, monarda, dahlia, agapanthus, crocosmia, coreopsis, achillea; they look magnificent in large groups from a distance.

Notes: Kniphofias are evergreen perennials for us; do not hard cut back these plants in the Pacific Northwest: in our shorter and cooler season they need all those leaves for growth and health. *Kniphofia caulescens* has green seeds and is usually grown from seed.

Species and Cultivars	Height/ Spread	USDA Hardiness Zone	Flowers (bloom time)	Foliage	Comments
'Alcazar'	3–3½ft × 2ft	5–9	Salmon spires, tinged orange-red, from chartreuse buds (M)	Green, lanceolate	Good rebloomer
'Bee's Sunset'	2½–4ft × 2ft	5–9	Soft yellowish orange fading to bronze-yellow (M)	Green, narrow, toothed	RHS Award

Species and Cultivars	Height/ Spread	USDA Hardiness Zone	Flowers (bloom time)	Foliage	Comments
'Border Ballet'	2–4½ft × 2ft	5–9	Mixed cream to pink, hot coral, yellow, and orange (M–L)	Green, lanceolate	Good mix
'Bressingham Comet'	1½–2ft × 2ft	5–9	Red-tipped, orange, fading to yellow, green buds at top (M–L)	Green, narrow, grasslike	Strong plant
caulescens	2–4ft × 2½ft	5–9	Soft coral-red fading to pale greenish yellow, chubby flower heads (M–L)	Gray-green, finely toothed, purple at base, fully evergreen, remove only dead foliage	Handsome foliage, trunklike stem, do not cut back, RHS Award
'Earliest of All'	1½–4ft × 2ft	5–9	Coral-rose to orange-red upper, yellow below (E–M)	Gray-green, lanceolate	Very early
'Little Maid'	1½–2½ft × 1½ft	5–9	Pale green in bud, opening to pale yellow, aging to ivory (M–L)	Green, grasslike, short, stiff, tinted with reddish orange	Clump-forming, RHS Award
'Modesta'	2ft × 1½ft	5–9	Pink buds, open to cream and coral, pink overcast (M)	Green, more refined	Dwarf
'Percy's Pride'	3–4ft × 2ft	5–9	Large green, tinted yellow in bud, opens to creamy yellow-green (E–L)	Deep green, straplike	Vigorous, good rebloomer
'Pfitzeri'	3ft × 2ft	5–9	Bright shades of orange, red, and yellow (M–L)	Green, stiff, narrow, grasslike	Good cut, old cultivar
'Primrose Beauty'	3ft × 2ft	5–9	Pale primrose-yellow to canary-yellow as flower opens (M–L)	Green, lanceolate	Deadhead to prolong bloom through summer
rooperi (syn. 'C. M. Prichard')	4ft × 2ft	5–9	Orange-red buds, open to yellow-orange (M–L)	Dark green, lax	Last to flower, dense clumps
'Shining Sceptre'	3–4ft × 2ft	5–9	Clear golden yellow, becoming ivory (M–L)	Green, stiff, lanceolate	Vigorous
'Springtime'	3ft × 2ft	5–9	Coral-red, lower half is creamy ivory (M–L)	Green	Two-toned
'Sunningdale Yellow'	2½–3ft × 2ft	5–9	Bright yellow, light yellow below (M)	As above	RHS Award
'Toffee Nosed'	3ft × 2ft	5–9	Burnt apricot, lower half is cream (M)	Green, narrow	Long-flowering, RHS Award
triangularis	2–3ft × 2ft	5–9	Reddish orange to soft orange with flaring lobes (L)	Green, grasslike	Clump-forming, thin wiry stems
t. subsp. triangularis (syn. galpinii)	2–3ft × 1½ft	5–9	Orange, thin flowers and heads (L)	Green, narrow, grasslike	May be the hardiest
uvaria (syn. *Tritoma uvaria*)	3–5ft × 2ft	5–9	Red in bud, opens to orange, fading to yellow (M–L)	Gray-green, finely toothed, coarse, stiff, untidy, fully evergreen	Red hot poker, floppy

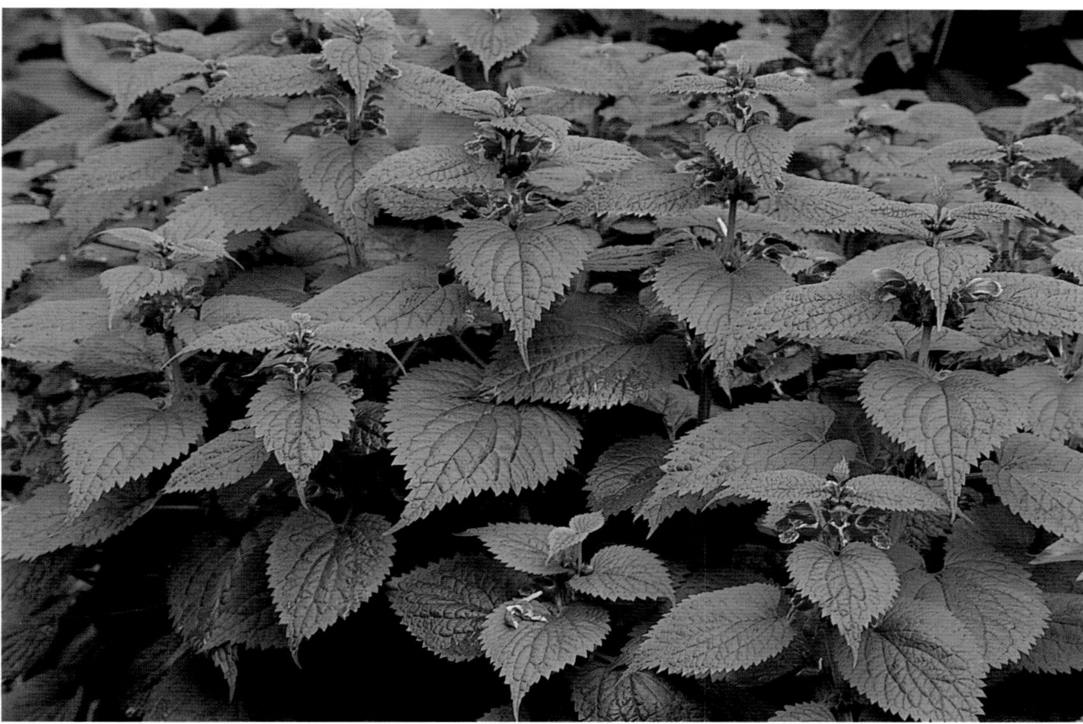

Lamium orvala.

LAMIUM Lamiaceae

Lamium, or deadnettle as it's commonly called, has long been valued as a groundcover in shady areas and may best be used en masse between taller shade plants, especially in among trees and shrubs in the less formal parts of the garden as a weed-excluding or living mulch. It's a sturdy plant and will grow almost anywhere, forming mats of green or gray-green hairy leaves, often with beautiful silvery stripes, veins, and blotches. A few have gold to chartreuse markings. The flowers are produced in whorls and vary from red, purple, and pink to yellow or white. The trailing stems will take root wherever they touch ground, but the runners are shallow and easy to remove. Be careful they don't overgrow more delicate plants.

Some forms spread more vigorously than others, to the point of being invasive. *Lamium galeobdolon* 'Hermann's Pride' is not invasive. *Lamium galeobdolon* (yellow archangel) is extremely invasive in our woods. Do not let it escape. This is also true of straight *L. album*, to which *L. a.* 'Friday' can revert—watch out! ~ *Susan Carter*

Scientific Name: The classical Latin name for this plant.
Common Name: Deadnettle, spotted deadnettle.
Origin: Europe, North Africa, western Asia.
Preferred Conditions: Well-drained, moisture-retentive, average garden loam. Tolerates poor soil. Does not like to dry out.
Light: Shade to sun.
Management: Hand-shear, using either scissors or pruners, in midsummer to encourage a dwarf, compact form and to clean up its weary growth habit. Shear off old leaves and runners in late winter before new growth starts. Cut back after the first flush of flowers to keep neat, or just mow it down (our favorite method). Dig out excess rooted rhizomes to confine the spreading.

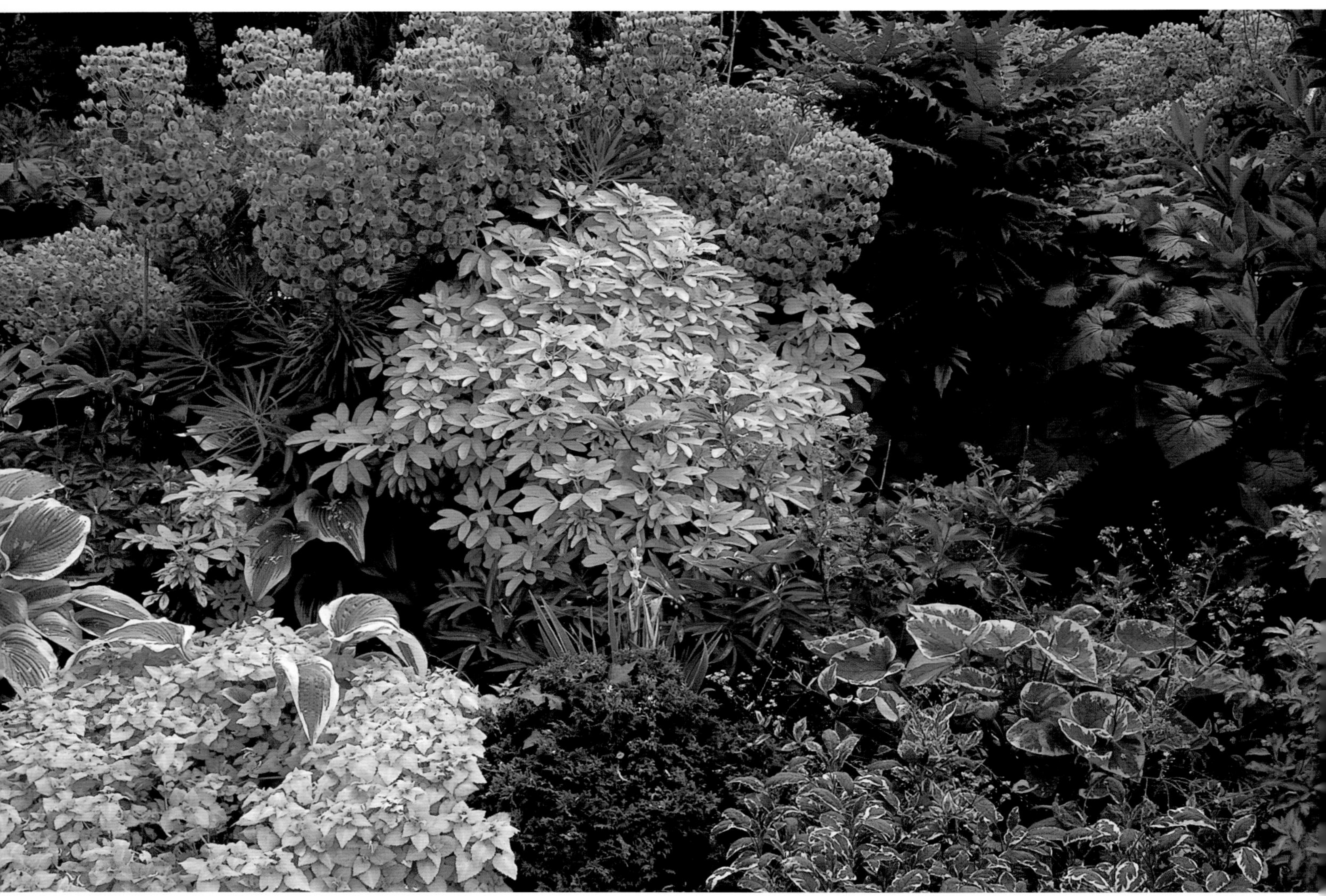

Lamium maculatum 'Aureum' lights up a border with help from *Euphorbia characias* subsp. *wulfenii*, *Choisya ternata* 'Sundance', *Brunnera macrophylla* 'Hadspen Cream', and variegated hosta and salvia. Design by Rick Kyper.

Propagation: Seed in containers; divide anytime.

Pests and Diseases: Downy mildew, powdery mildew, leaf spot, snails, slugs, crown rot (under hot and humid conditions).

Companions: Under trees and shrubs with pulmonaria, spring bulbs, dicentra, asarum, helleborus, hosta, ferns, *Iris foetidissima*, polygonatum, smilacina.

Species and Cultivars	Height/ Spread	USDA Hardiness Zone	Flowers (bloom time)	Foliage	Comments
album	1–2ft × 2ft	3–9	White in false whorls, hairy (E–M)	Gray-green, softly hairy, ovate and pointed, round-toothed margins	White deadnettle, weedy, not suitable for the border
a. 'Friday'	12–18in × 2½ft	3–9	White (E–M)	Central patch of gold surrounded by 2 shades of green	Taller than most cultivars, spreads, reverts to green
galeobdolon (syn. luteum)	1–2ft × 3ft+	3–9	Yellow in whorls, brown-spotted, hairy, 2-lipped (E–M)	Mid-green with silver markings, diamond or heart-shaped, toothed	Yellow archangel, invasive
g. 'Hermann's Pride'	10–12in × 24in	3–9	Yellow (E–M)	Silver with dark green veins	Not invasive, clumping
g. subsp. montanum 'Florentinum' (syn. 'Variegatum')	12in × 24in	3–9	As above	Silver-centered with green edges	Less invasive, sometimes reverts
maculatum	8–12in × 36in+	3–9	Reddish purple, white, or pink (E–M)	Gray-green, pointed, triangular or rounded, often mottled or zoned silver, white, or pink, scallop-edged	Spotted deadnettle, vigorous
m. 'Album'	8–12in × 36in+	3–9	White (E–M)	Mid-green, zoned white	
m. 'Aureum'	4–8in × 36in+	3–9	Light pink-mauve (E–M)	Bright yellow with paler white mid-stripes	Don't allow to dry out, shelter from direct sun, weak-growing
m. 'Beacon Silver' (syn. 'Silbergroschen')	6–10in × 36in+	3–9	Clear rose-pink (E–M)	Silver, narrowly margined green, speckled with purple blotching (caused by disease)	Mildew prone, requires shade
m. 'Beedham's White'	6–8in × 36in+	3–9	White (E–M)	Chartreuse to golden	
m. 'Chequers'	6–8in × 36in+	3–9	Deep purplish pink (E)	Dark green with silver center	Vigorous
m. 'Pink Nancy'	6–8in × 24in+	3–9	Deep pink to shell-pink (E–M)	Silver-coated edged in green	
m. 'Pink Pewter'	6–12in × 24in+	3–9	Soft pink (E–M)	Silver-gray edged in greenish gray	Semi-evergreen
m. 'Red Nancy'	4–6in × 24in+	3–9	Dark rose (E–M)	Silver, narrowly margined in green	
m. 'Roseum' (syn. 'Shell Pink')	6–10in × 36in+	3–9	Light pink (E–M)	Green, central silvery blotch, heart-shaped	Slow-growing, semi-evergreen
m. 'White Nancy'	4–8in × 36in+	3–9	White (E–L)	Silver, narrowly margined green	Tolerates sun if kept moist, invasive, RHS Award
orvala	15–24in × 18in	3–9	Pinkish purple, maroon-spotted throat, large (E–M)	Dark green, glossy, ovate-triangular, toothed	Noninvasive, clump-forming
o. 'Album'	15–18in × 18in	3–9	White, large (E–M)	As above	As above

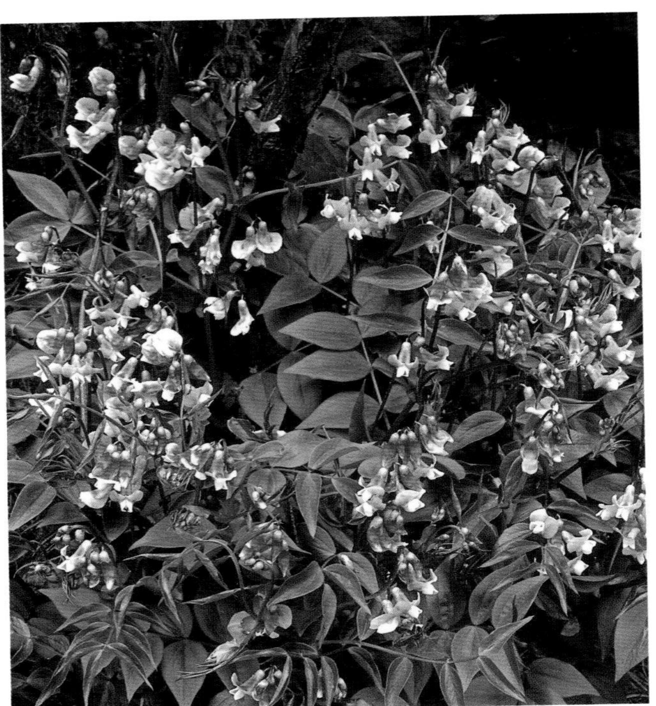

Lathyrus vernus.

LATHYRUS Papilionaceae

Lathyrus vernus is one of the most rewarding perennials. Plants do not run and can form good-sized, well-mannered clumps, with hundreds of flowers. The small mid-green leaves can get a bit ravaged by pests later in the season, but this is not a good reason not to grow them. Flower color ranges from pink through blue and almost to purple and any shade in between. Slow to establish—large plants are almost never available at retail nurseries, but seedlings are. Be sure to buy them in bloom so you know the color. ~ *Bob Lilly*

Scientific Name: The Greek word for pea.
Common Name: Spring vetchling.
Origin: Europe.
Preferred Conditions: Any soil that is moist and well-drained.
Light: Sun to part shade.
Management: They can be mulched, but watch for seedlings to pot up and give away to friends, and do not allow them to be overcome by the summer growth of neighbor perennials. Cut down in fall after first frost, when the foliage dies back.
Propagation: Seed in fall; division early spring but infrequently.
Pests and Diseases: Slugs in spring, flea beetles perforate the foliage.
Companions: Trillium, rhododendron, narcissus, aquilegia, meconopsis, euphorbia, pulmonaria, primula, chaerophyllum, 'Negrita' and 'Queen of the Night' tulips.
Notes: Seed collection is difficult. When ripe the seedpods split open and throw the seed, but, as with all peas, they must ripen on the plant. We have included one annual that can be grown into almost any shrub without causing problems.

Species and Cultivars	Height/ Spread	USDA Hardiness Zone	Flowers (bloom time)	Foliage	Comments
aureus	2ft × 1½ft	4–9	Yellow-gold (E–M)	Mid-green	Clump-forming, stiff
niger	2ft × 1½ft	4–9	Small deep violet spikes (E)	Green, lanceolate leaflets	Upright, will fall over
sativus	3–4ft × 1½ft	4–9	Cobalt to sky-blue (M)	Mid-green, pealike vine	An annual but worth growing
vernus	18in × 2ft	4–9	Reddish purple, pink, and blue (E–M)	Deep green, small, oval, pointed, semi-glossy, divided, pinnate, in pairs	Spring vetchling, noninvasive, makes a large clump, RHS Award

Leucanthemum ×superbum 'Alaska'.

LEUCANTHEMUM Asteraceae

The Shasta daisies have been popular garden plants for decades. We grew up with *L. ×superbum* 'Esther Read' as *Chrysanthemum maximum*. The new name of leucanthemum seems to have stuck for this genus. A few cultivars have been bred for seed use by the larger wholesale growers, but most do not produce seed. The taller vegetative varieties, produced by cuttings or divisions, usually have larger or more distinctive flowers. Many of these will need staking; their vigor and heavy flowers often cause them to flop over. The common field daisy *L. vulgare* is listed on some state noxious weed lists; it can colonize fields quite quickly and has shown up in our gardens as well as at plant sales. If you do grow this one, it is best to deadhead, so seed is not produced; it has very nice flowers, with a size proportional to stem length, and usually does not need staking.
~ *Bob Lilly*

Scientific Name: From the Greek *leucos* ("white") and *anthemon* ("flower").
Common Name: Shasta daisy, oxeye daisy.
Origin: Europe, temperate Asia.
Preferred Conditions: Moderately fertile, rich, and well-drained with average moisture.
Light: Sun to part shade. Shade the doubles from intense sun.
Management: Crowns can get quite congested, and division to regenerate the clumps is recommended every two or three years. Cut the first flush of flowers with long stems (and use for large bouquets), and you may get a good second flush of blooms. Deadhead *L. vulgare* to prevent self-seeding. Pinch back tall cultivars once or twice to keep compact (flowers will be smaller). Some may need staking. Cut to basal growth in autumn. Top-dress with organic matter in winter. Watch for slugs in early spring and aphids and earwigs later in the season.
Propagation: Division for all L. *×superbum* cultivars in spring or late summer; seed for *L. vulgare* and *L. v.* 'Maikönigin' (syn. 'May Queen').
Pests and Diseases: Aphids, slugs, earwigs.

Companions: Achillea, nepeta, echinacea, rudbeckia, allium, heliopsis, grasses.

Notes: As cut flowers they can smell a bit of the old gym locker—admire from a distance. Look for a new yellow cultivar from England.

Species and Cultivars	Height/ Spread	USDA Hardiness Zone	Flowers (bloom time)	Foliage	Comments
×superbum (syn. *Chrysanthemum maximum*)	3ft × 2ft	4–9	White with yellow center, 3–4in (M–L)	Dark green basal leaves, lanceolate, toothed, glossy	Shasta daisy, may need support, good cut, clump-forming
×s. 'Aglaia (syn. 'Aglaya')	1½–2ft × 2ft	4–9	White with a crested white center, frilly, double or semi-double, 3in (E–L)	Green, deeply toothed	Long-blooming, deadhead for repeat bloom, RHS Award
×s. 'Alaska'	2–3ft × 2ft	4–9	White with yellow center, single, shaggy, 4in (M)	Green, heavy	Deadhead for repeat bloom
×s. 'Cobham Gold'	1½–2½ft × 2ft	4–9	Creamy-white with yellow tints, pale yellow raised central crest, double, 2½–3in (M)	Green	Flower is a bit shaggy, not quite as yellow
×s. 'Esther Read'	1½–2½ft × 2ft+	4–9	Double white with pale yellowish center, 2½in (M–L)	Dark green, smaller	Long-blooming, short-lived
×s. 'Marconi'	2–4ft × 2ft	4–9	Double white, frilly, 4in (M–L)	Green	
×s. 'Polaris'	3ft × 3ft	4–9	Single white, 5in (M)	Green, larger	Good cut, very tall, largest flower
×s. 'Silber-prinzesschen' (syn. 'Silver Princess')	1–1½ft × 1½ft	4–9	Single white with yellow center, 2in (M–L)	Green, smaller	Dwarf, bushy, long-blooming
×s. 'Snow Lady'	10–15in × 18in	4–9	Single white with yellow center, 2in (M–L)	Green, oval-lanceolate, deeply toothed	1988 All-America Selection, dwarf, fast-growing, blooms first year from seed
×s. 'Snowcap'	1–1½ft × 1½ft	4–9	As above	Green	Dwarf, compact, long-blooming if kept deadheaded
×s. 'Summer Snowball'	2½ft × 2ft	4–9	Very double white, fluffy, no yellow center, 2½in (M–L)	Rich green	Good cut
×s. 'T. E. Killin'	2½–4ft × 2ft	4–9	Semi-double white, yellow center, 4–6in (M)	Green	Good cut, RHS Award
×s. 'Wirral Pride'	2–4ft × 2ft	4–9	Double white, crested pale yellow center, shaggy, 3in (M)	As above	Good cut
vulgare (syn. *Chrysanthemum leucanthemum*)	1–2ft × 2ft+	4–9	Single white with yellow center, 1½in (E–M)	Deep green, toothed, spoon-shaped	Tough, invasive
v. 'Maikönigin' (syn. 'May Queen')	1–2ft × 1½ft	4–9	White with yellow center, 1½–2in (E–M)	Green, toothed	The seed-grown Shasta daisy

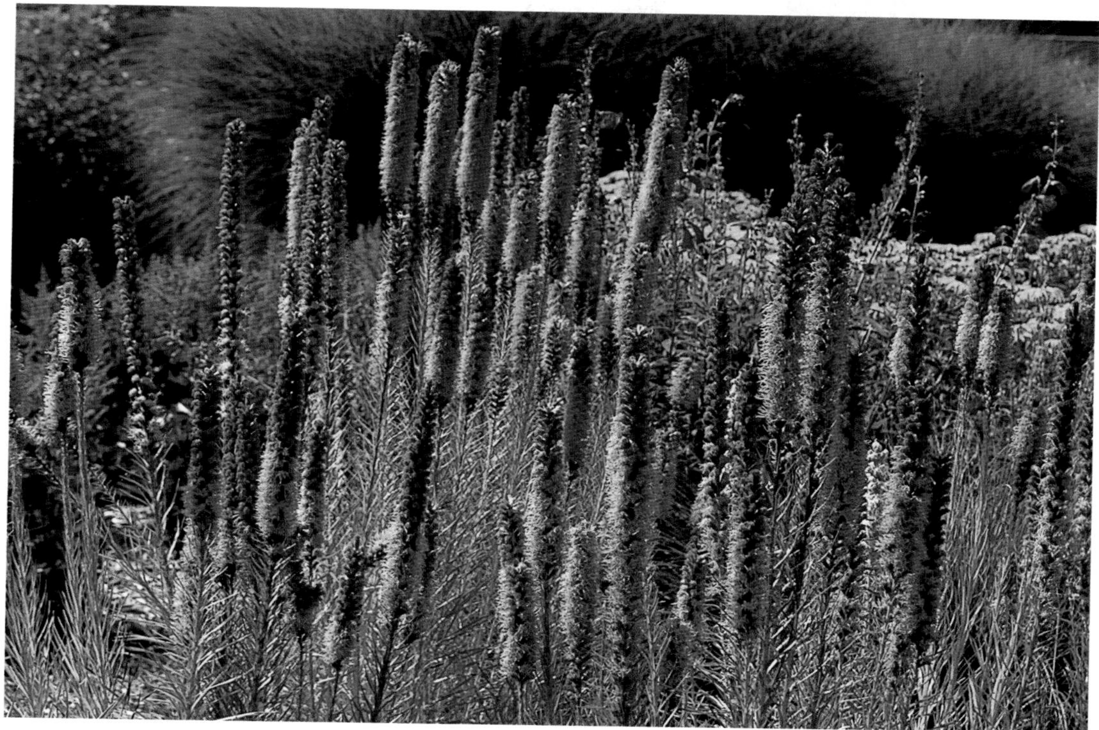

Liatris spicata 'Floristan Violett'.

LIATRIS Asteraceae

A North American native genus, *Liatris* has narrow plumes of inflorescence formed in bottle-brushlike spikes or racemes and held on stiff, upright stems, two to five feet tall. The dense clusters of florets bloom from the top down in shades of purple, pink, and white. They are long-blooming from midsummer into fall. Basal tufts of narrow, grassy leaves grow from large heavy corms. Butterflies and bees are particularly attracted to the blossoms, and birds will come looking for the fall-ripening seeds. I find gay feather easier to use in a floral arrangement than in my garden; I think if you planted large drifts of these plants it would make quite a statement. ~ *Susan Carter*

Scientific Name: Unknown.
Common Name: Gay feather, blazing star.
Origin: North America.
Preferred Conditions: Moderately fertile to poor soil, well-drained, moist (not soaking wet, especially in winter). Tolerant of most conditions.
Light: Sun.
Planting: Four to six inches deep and twelve to fifteen inches apart.
Management: Split up every four years to keep plants vigorous and prevent flower spikes' shrinking in size. Cut to ground in fall as foliage dies down. Watch for slugs on emerging growth.
Propagation: Divide corms in spring (make sure each division has an eye or bud; corms can be cut); seed in spring (will bloom the next season).
Pests and Diseases: Snails, slugs.
Companions: Phygelius, penstemon, *Dahlia* 'Fascination', rudbeckia, helenium, kniphofia, echinacea, artemisia and other gray- or silver-foliaged plants; looks best planted in groups.

Notes: In the Pacific Northwest liatris must be sited in a full-sun border. Our often misty July rain will get the flower stems soaking wet and lying on the ground; either stake or plant them among others to lean on. *Liatris spicata* can take a more moist soil than *L. pycnostachya*.

Species and Cultivars	Height/ Spread	USDA Hardiness Zone	Flowers (bloom time)	Foliage	Comments
pycnostachya	3–5ft × 1½ft	4–9	Purplish mauve, pink, sometimes white (M–L)	Dark green, narrow, grassy, hairy stems	May need support, short-lived, good cut
spicata	2–4ft × 1½ft	4–9	Purplish pink (M–L)	Dark green, narrow, grassy, hairless stems	Long-lasting, drought tolerant, good cut
s. 'Alba'	2½–4ft × 1½ft	4–9	White, fluffy (M–L)	As above	Long-lasting, drought tolerant
s. 'Floristan Violett'	2–3ft × 1½ft	4–9	Violet-purple (M–L)	As above	As above
s. 'Floristan Weiss' (syn. 'Floristan White')	3ft × 1½ft	4–9	Creamy-white, fluffy (M–L)	As above	As above
s. 'Kobold' (syn. 'Goblin')	1½–2½ft × 1½ft	4–9	Deep rosy-purple (M)	As above	Drought tolerant

LIBERTIA Iridaceae

The two libertias are alike in their thick, upright, straplike leaves and three-petaled white flowers. The difference is in the color and arrangement of the leaves. The dull green leaves of *L. formosa* are in a cluster. The bright orange leaves of *L. peregrinans* are arranged in a stiff, straight line as they spread by short rhizomes; they glow when backlit by the sun. Both have attractive seedheads, and both are somewhat tender, *L. peregrinans* particularly so (and in my experience, it does not flower as abundantly); I keep one or two in pots to overwinter with protection, and let the rest march on. ~ *Ann Bucher*

Scientific Name: After Belgian botanist Marie A. Libert.
Common Name: New Zealand satin flower.
Origin: Chile, New Zealand.
Preferred Conditions: Moderately fertile, humus-rich, well-drained, moisture-retentive. Resents drying out.
Light: Sun to part shade.
Management: Remove leaves when they become damaged or look aged. Divide and replant after several years when the clumps become congested.
Propagation: Division in spring as new roots start to grow; seed as soon as ripe.
Pests and Diseases: None.
Companions: Nepeta, sedum, bronze carex, haloragis.

Libertia formosa.

Species and Cultivars	Height/ Spread	USDA Hardiness Zone	Flowers (bloom time)	Foliage	Comments
formosa (syn. chilensis)	3ft × 2ft	8–10	White, small, stiff stems (E–M)	Mid-green, dense, sword-shaped	Evergreen, brownish seedheads
peregrinans	1½ft × 1½ft	8–10	White, starry (E–M)	Bright orange fading to pea-green	Evergreen

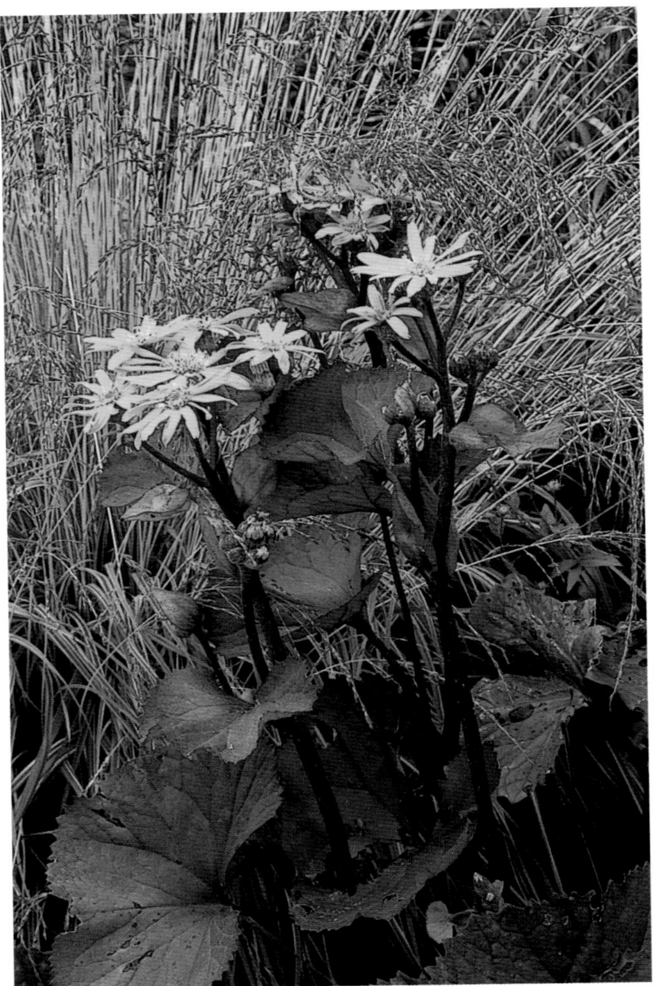

Ligularia dentata 'Othello'.

LIGULARIA Asteraceae

One of the great late-summer plants—truly, one could make an entire summer garden using solely members of the daisy family. Ligularias are bold specimen plants that form large masses of lush foliage topped by showy flowers. Planted en masse, they never fail to amaze visitors. The yellow or yellow-orange blossoms are produced in tall corymbs or racemes on erect stems. The leathery leaves, usually dark green, are rounded or kidney-shaped; some grow to two feet across. These big plants need space and plenty of water. ~ *Susan Carter*

Scientific Name: From the Latin *ligula* ("strap"), referring to the strappy ray flowers.
Common Name: Golden groundsel (*L. dentata*).
Origin: China, Japan, central and eastern Asia.
Preferred Conditions: Deep, well-cultivated, humus-rich, well-drained, moist, cool soil. Shelter from strong winds.
Light: Part shade. Too much shade will turn the purple leaves of *L. dentata* 'Desdemona' and *L. d.* 'Othello' green. Tolerates sun if grown in cool and wet conditions in heavy soil; in full sun they suffer from heat wilt but will recover in the coolness of evening.
Management: A low-maintenance plant. Will benefit from soil amendments—mulch and fertilize. Water deeply during dry spells. Can be deadheaded, but if stems are left until late winter they pull away easily, not damaging new foliage. Cut back in fall as leaves die back. This plant is a slug trap, particularly in early spring: to keep foliage looking good, bait for slugs regularly!
Propagation: Seed for the species; division in spring.
Pests and Diseases: Slugs, snails.
Companions: Grasses, ferns, large hostas, *Aruncus dioicus*, telekia, petasites, *Iris pseudacorus* as a foliage contrast, shrubby cornus, inula, rumex, *Lysimachia ciliata* 'Firecracker', *Carex elata* 'Aurea'
Notes: Perfect conditions in the Pacific Northwest would be full morning sun and light afternoon shade. Look for a new cultivar, *L. dentata* 'Britt-Marie Crawford', with even darker leaves than *L. d.* 'Desdemona'.

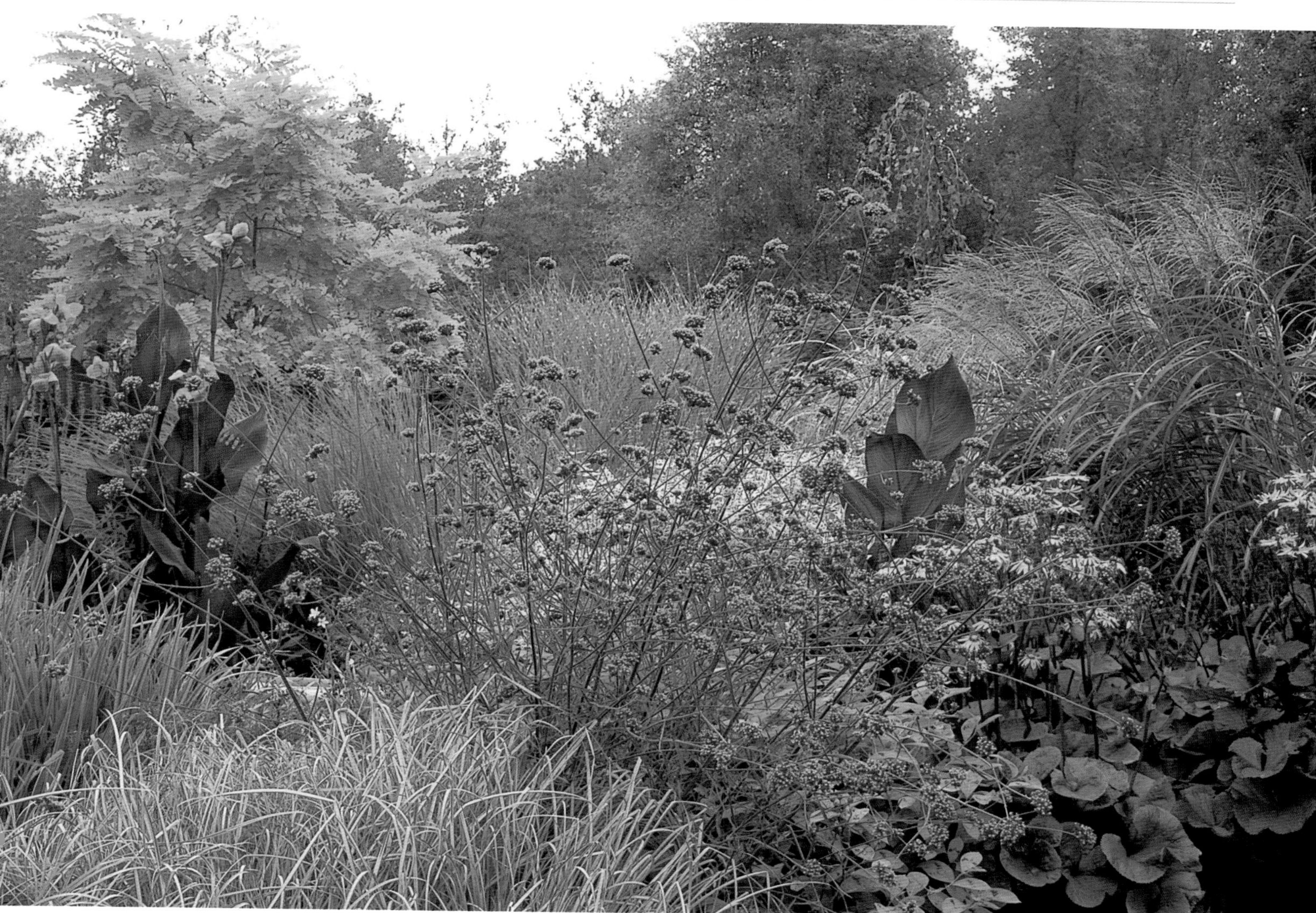

Ligularia dentata with *Verbena bonariensis*, *Canna* 'Wyoming', and *Miscanthus sinensis* 'Zebrinus'.

Species and Cultivars	Height/ Spread	USDA Hardiness Zone	Flowers (bloom time)	Foliage	Comments
dentata (syn. clivorum)	3–4ft × 3ft	3–9	Daisylike, orange-yellow, brown center, in corymbs, maroon-black stems (M–L)	Red, aging purplish dark green, purple reverse, prominent veins, kidney-shaped to rounded, leathery, 12in	Clump-forming
d. 'Desdemona'	3–4ft × 3ft	3–9	Daisylike, orange-yellow, in corymbs, dark purple stems (M–L)	Dark purplish bronze, aging to more metallic greenish purple, purple reverse and stems, leathery, 10in	More compact and refined, one of the best cultivars, RHS Award
d. 'Othello'	3–4ft × 3ft	3–9	As above	Deep purplish green above, purple-red reverse, 10in	Blooms later than *L. d.* 'Desdemona'

Species and Cultivars	Height/ Spread	USDA Hardiness Zone	Flowers (bloom time)	Foliage	Comments
'Gregynog Gold'	5–6ft × 3ft	3–9	Daisylike, vivid golden orange, brown center, in conical corymbs (M–L)	Green, cordate, toothed, wavy, veined, 14–20in	RHS Award
japonica	6ft × 3ft	3–9	Bright yellow-orange, in corymbs (M)	Green, deeply dissected, 2ft	
×palmatiloba	5–6ft × 3ft	3–9	Daisylike, yellow-orange, in racemes (M)	Green, round to cordate, jagged-edged, 2ft	A very large plant
przewalskii	4–6ft × 2ft	3–9	Yellow, small, in racemes, dark purplish black stems (M–L)	Dark green, palmately lobed, toothed, lighter reverse, 10in	Golden ray, RHS Award
sibirica	4½–5½ft × 3ft	3–9	Yellow, in racemes, black stems (M)	Dark green, rounded, wavy-edged, deeply toothed, pointed ends, 12in	
'The Rocket'	4–6ft × 2ft	3–9	Yellow, in 2ft racemes, purple-black stems (M)	Dark green with purple veins, ebony reverse, toothed and cut, rounded-cordate, leathery, 10in	Long-blooming, RHS Award
wilsoniana	5–6ft × 2ft	3–9	Golden yellow, in racemes (M–L)	Dark green, rounded-cordate, 16in	Giant groundsel, woolly seedheads

LINARIA Scrophulariaceae

Toadflax is an old cottage garden plant that looks delicate but is actually quite sturdy and very prolific. This tells us that it's short-lived, self-sowing, and long-flowering. The usually soft violet-blue flowers of *L. purpurea* are two-lipped, spurred, and resemble tiny snapdragons; all forms have an orange spot on the lip. *Linaria triornithophora* has larger flowers, purple and yellow, with longer spurs; it is more tender and difficult to grow (even though it runs) than *L. purpurea*. Both are good plants for poor soil and bad locations, often popping up in stone walls and seeding even in cracks in concrete. ~ *Susan Carter*

Scientific Name: From the Greek *linon* ("flax"), referring to the leaves, which are similar to those of linum.

Common Name: Toadflax.

Origin: Spain, Portugal, Sicily, Italy.

Preferred Conditions: A warm spot with poor to ordinary, light, well-drained, sandy, moderately fertile soil. Drought tolerant.

Light: Sun.

Management: Cut back after bloom to foliage once or twice during the growing season for repeat bloom. Plants can be moved only when very young as they form a taproot. Cut down in fall or winter once dormant, or leave crown up and just remove spent flower stems.

Linaria triornithophora.

Propagation: Division in spring; root cuttings; easy and best from seed.
Pests and Diseases: None.
Companions: Roses, stachys, allium, astrantia, pimpinella, *Papaver rhoeas*; the cottage garden.
Notes: As with many perennials that seed about into less than ideal spots, linarias can vary greatly in size.

Species and Cultivars	Height/ Spread	USDA Hardiness Zone	Flowers (bloom time)	Foliage	Comments
'Natalie'	2–3ft × 1ft	6–10	Lavender-purple (M–L)	Green with purple cast	Sterile, nearly the perfect match of flower color and foliage
purpurea	2–3ft × 1ft	5–9	Violet-blue, purple, pink, or lilac, sometimes with white (M–L)	Glaucous, narrow, in whorls	Clump-forming, self-sows
p. 'Canon Went'	2–4ft × 1ft	5–9	Pale pink (M–L)	Bluish green, narrow, in whorls	Comes mostly true from seed, self-sows
triornithophora	3ft × 1½ft	5–9	Purple and yellow with brownish purple spurs, sometimes pale pink or lavender (M–L)	Glaucous, lanceolate, in whorls	Three birds flying, coarser, short-lived in Pacific Northwest

Linum perenne.

LINUM Linaceae

The annual *L. usitatissimum* is used for flax fiber (linen), flaxseed, and linseed oil and is amazing to see in flower—a landlocked sea of intense blue. The perennial forms of flax are grown for their bright, funnel- to saucer-shaped flowers. Although white-flowered forms are available, it is the blue ones that are most enchanting. This is a perfect example of a short-lived perennial that blooms heavily in summer and will need to be replaced on a regular basis. We can usually get three good years out of them, and in some gardens they will self-sow. ~ *Bob Lilly*

Scientific Name: The Latin word for flax.
Common Name: Flax.
Origin: Central and southern Europe.
Preferred Conditions: Moderately fertile, light, well-drained, humus-rich soil. Tolerates drought. Protect from winter wet.
Light: Sun.
Management: In late summer reduce the foliage by half, including flower stalks, to prevent plant exhaustion from overblooming and extend the life of the plant (you can deadhead for the same outcome). May rebloom until fall if deadheaded regularly, or prune back by half whenever there's a lull in blooming. (The gracefulness of the plant is lost with these techniques, however.) Replant every two or three years (doesn't like to be transplanted). Cut down in fall or winter.
Propagation: Easy and best from seed in spring or autumn; difficult to divide (except for *L. narbonense*).
Pests and Diseases: Cutworms, aphids, snails, slugs, painters and weavers.
Companions: *Stachys byzantina*, liatris, *Scabiosa columbaria* subsp. *ochroleuca*, *Papaver atlanticum*; wherever a wilder look is desired.

Species and Cultivars	Height/ Spread	USDA Hardiness Zone	Flowers (bloom time)	Foliage	Comments
narbonense	1½–2ft × 1½ft	4–9	Varies from pale to rich azure-blue, small, white eye (E–M)	Glaucous, narrow, lanceolate	Clump-forming, short-lived, long-blooming
perenne (syn. sibiricum)	1–2ft × 1ft	4–9	Pale blue (E–M)	Glaucous, needlelike, lanceolate, fine-textured	Common blue flax, clump-forming, self-sows
p. 'Blau Saphir' (syn. 'Blue Sapphire')	1ft × 1ft	4–9	Sky-blue (E–M)	As above	Self-sows
p. 'Diamant'	1ft × 1ft	4–9	White (E–M)	As above	As above

LIRIOPE Convallariaceae

Lilyturf, as it's commonly called, is not actually a grass but a member of the lily of the valley family. The two species we are interested in here, *L. muscari* and *L. spicata*, have slightly different growth habits. *Liriope muscari* generally forms a clump some eighteen inches wide. *Liriope spicata* spreads rapidly by underground stems and will cover a wide area; it is therefore not suitable for an edging but is excellent for groundcover. In summer, spikes of small purple, violet, or white flowers rise from the center of the arching, straplike foliage; flowers are followed by pea-sized black berries. Plants themselves are similar in appearance and landscape use to mondo grass (ophiopogon), which has finer-textured foliage and bears its flowers within the clumps rather than above them, like liriope. ~ *Susan Carter*

Liriope muscari 'Monroe White'.

Scientific Name: After the woodland nymph Liriope, the mother of Narcissus.
Common Name: Lilyturf.
Origin: China, Japan, Korea, Vietnam, Taiwan.
Preferred Conditions: Moderately fertile, humus-rich, well-drained, moist, acid to neutral soil. Drought tolerant once established and loves summer warmth. Shelter from cold and drying winds.
Light: Shade to sun. Flowers best in sun.
Management: Liriope may become ragged with neglect after several seasons. If so, cut back to ground in spring before new growth appears, or cut off damaged leaves (those with brown tips) individually in spring. Never cut just the tips, it looks awful, and the leaves never look good again. If there's no winter damage, do not cut back.
Propagation: Division in spring; seed.
Pests and Diseases: Snails, slugs, especially on new growth.
Companions: *Aster divaricatus*, brunnera, hosta, ferns, helleborus, arum; good for edging (*L. muscari*) or massing under trees and shrubs (*L. spicata*).
Notes: Variegated forms seem to be more prone to winter cold and wind damage. In the maritime Northwest, all forms can burn in a hard winter (usually a wind burn when frozen).

Species and Cultivars	Height/ Spread	USDA Hardiness Zone	Flowers (bloom time)	Foliage	Comments
'Majestic'	1–2ft × 1½ft	6–10	Dark violet, almost purple (L)	Dark green, narrow, straplike	Vigorous
muscari (syn. graminifolia, platyphylla)	1–1½ft × 1½ft	6–10	Dark violet-blue, in whorls, looking more like round fruit, on purple-green stems (M–L)	Dark green, glossy, arching, straplike, evergreen	Glossy black berries, long-blooming, RHS Award
m. 'Big Blue'	1–1½ft × 1½ft	6–10	Dark violet-blue, larger than species (M–L)	Dark green, wider, straplike	Glossy black berries
m. 'Monroe White'	1–1½ft × 1½ft	6–10	White, last a long time with a bit of cover or protection (M–L)	Mid-green, straplike	Best in part shade
m. 'Variegata'	1–1½ft × 1½ft	6–10	Violet buds and flowers (L)	Cream, striped with green, straplike	As above
spicata	8–12in × 1½ft+	6–10	Pale violet, sometimes white (M–L)	Dark green, arching, narrow, straplike, tiny teeth, semi-evergreen	Creeping lilyturf, spreads rapidly (invasive), glossy black berries, if it looks ragged in winter, cut back in spring

Lobelia ×*speciosa* 'Dark Crusader' with artemisia.

LOBELIA Campanulaceae

The perennial lobelias are relatively new to the herbaceous border and have brought us some very intense colors on stately plants. American Indians used one species of this New World genus, *L. siphilitica*, to treat syphilis. Lobelias grow quickly but are very short-lived (especially so are the *L. cardinalis* and *L.* ×*speciosa* cultivars): heavy blooming and the formation of tight crowns at ground level (which don't form well if overgrown by other perennials) seem to be the reasons for their brief life in the garden. They are good hummingbird and butterfly plants, but some or all may tend to flop, so keep them up for the nectar lovers, eighteen inches or so, with stakes or pea sticks. If used in arrangements, the cut end of the stem must be seared with a flame. ~ *Bob Lilly*

Scientific Name: After Mathias de l'Obel, Flemish botanist and physician to James I of England.
Common Name: Cardinal flower.
Origin: North America, Mexico, Chile.
Preferred Conditions: Wide range, from marshes and wet meadows to woodlands, mountain slopes, and deserts. Humus-rich, moisture-retentive, well-drained soil. Likes it wet in the spring but not too wet. Most don't like to dry out.
Light: Part shade to sun.
Management: Divide regularly (every two years) to extend life of the plant; it rejuvenates plants enough to allow them to survive until you divide them again. Stake and tie *L. cardinalis*; its selection 'Queen Victoria' likes to be split every other year to prevent its dying out in the middle (discard any of the central older portions). Lobelias are heavy feeders and can be moved almost anytime. Cut to basal growth in fall; wait to cut back *L. tupa* until after its fall color, leaving two- to three-inch stems to protect the crown. Mulch lightly in winter but do not cover the crown. Slugs can be a very big problem on overwintering crowns, so bait early in the spring.

Propagation: Seed in spring; division in spring every two years (new basal shoots).
Pests and Diseases: Rust (on *L. siphilitica*), slugs.
Companions: Dahlia, tall ferns, aconitum, hemerocallis, grasses, *Iris sibirica* foliage; *L. laxiflora* with heuchera and cotinus.
Notes: Lobelias will not survive in flooded ground in the Northwest.

Species and Cultivars	Height/ Spread	USDA Hardiness Zone	Flowers (bloom time)	Foliage	Comments
'Brightness'	3ft × 1ft	4–9	Deep red inside, rose-red outside, velvety (M–L)	Deep green, shiny	
cardinalis	2–4ft × 1ft	3–9	Scarlet-red, reddish purple stems (M–L)	Green, narrow, lanceolate, toothed, clump-forming	Cardinal flower, North American native, constant moisture, RHS Award
c. 'Bees Flame'	2½ft × 1ft	4–9	Bright crimson, reddish purple stems (M–L)	Reddish purple	Clump-forming
c. 'Elmfeuer' (syn. fulgens 'Saint Elmo's Fire')	3ft × 1ft	5–8	Deep red (M–L)	Dark bronze-maroon, the best colored-foliage form	Clump-forming, somewhat confused in the trade
c. 'Eulalia Berridge'	1½ft × 1ft	4–8	Pink (M–L)	Dark green	Clump-forming
c. 'Queen Victoria'	3–5ft × 1ft	4–9	Scarlet-red (M–L)	Dark purplish red, lanceolate, dark purple stems	Treated as an annual by some, short-lived, RHS Award
c. 'Rose Beacon'	3ft × 1ft	4–9	Bright rose-pink (M–L)	Light green to gold	Clump-forming
'La Fresco'	2½–3ft × 1ft	4–9	Dusky plum-purple, large (M–L)	Mid-green	Tendency to fasciate
laxiflora	2ft × 3ft+	7–9	Scarlet, yellow-orange throat, stems dull to bright red (M–L)	Green, narrow, lanceolate, finely toothed	North American native, rhizomatous, semi-shrubby
l. var. angustifolia	2–3ft × 3ft+	7–9	Coral outside, yellow inside (M–L)	Mid-green, narrow, lanceolate, finely toothed	
siphilitica	2–3ft × 1ft	4–9	Light to deep blue, rarely white, purplish upper lip, lower lip white (M–L)	Bright green, coarse, toothed, lanceolate to oval	U.S. native, self-sows, tends to flop
s. 'Blue Selection'	2–3ft × 1ft	3–8	Bright blue (M)	As above	Erect
×speciosa (syn. ×gerardii)	3ft × 1ft	3–8	Reds, pinks, and purples (M–L)	Mid-green, flushed red, slightly hairy, lanceolate	Very hardy, clump-forming
×s. 'Dark Crusader'	3ft × 1ft	4–9	Dark ruby-red, maroon stems (M–L)	Burgundy-tinged green, purplish silver tint	
×s. 'Fan Orchidrosa' (syn. 'Fan Deep Rose')	18in × 9in	4–9	Deep rose, almost fluorescent pink (M–L)	Bronzy dark green	Upright, bushy habit, RHS Award

Species and Cultivars	Height/ Spread	USDA Hardiness Zone	Flowers (bloom time)	Foliage	Comments
×s. 'Fan Scharlach' (syn. 'Fan Scarlet')	18–24in × 9in	4–9	Scarlet-red, large (M–L)	As above	Bushy habit, RHS Award
×s. 'Fan Tiefrot' (syn. 'Fan Deep Red')	18–24in × 9in	4–9	Rich deep red (M–L)	As above	As above, RHS Award
×s. 'Gladys Lindley'	4ft × 1ft	4–9	Creamy-white (M–L)	Mid-green	
×s. 'Grape Knee-Hi'	24in × 10in	4–9	Rich purple (M–L)	Green	
×s. 'Kompliment Blau' (syn. 'Compliment Blue')	30in × 9in	4–9	Purplish blue (M–L)	Bright green	Clump-forming
×s. 'Kompliment Scharlach' (syn. 'Compliment Scarlet')	30–36in × 9in	4–9	Scarlet (M–L)	As above	Upright, RHS Award
×s. 'Kompliment Tiefrot' (syn. 'Compliment Deep Red')	30–36in × 9in	4–9	Deep dark red, velvety (M–L)	As above	Clump-forming
×s. 'Kompliment Violet' (syn. 'Violet Compliment')	3ft × 9in	5–9	Dark violet-pink (M–L)	As above	
×s. 'Pink Flamingo'	3ft × 1ft	4–9	Bright pink (M–L)	Light green	Upright, branching
×s. 'Purple Towers'	4–5ft × 1ft	4–9	Dark purple, velvety (M)	Mid-green	
×s. 'Ruby Slippers'	3–4ft × 1ft	4–9	Dark ruby-red, velvety (M)	Light green	Long-blooming
×s. 'Russian Princess'	3ft × 1ft	4–8	Red-purple (M–L)	Purplish green	
×s. 'Sparkle DeVine'	3–4ft × 1ft	4–9	Dark fuchsia with blue overtones (M–L)	Light green	
×s. 'Tania'	3–4ft × 1ft	4–8	Crimson-purple, velvety, large (M–L)	Burgundy-green, broad, burgundy stems	Needs lots of moisture but not too wet in winter
×s. 'Vedrariensis'	4ft × 1ft	5–9	Deep purplish violet (M–L)	Dark green turning reddish, lanceolate	
tupa	5–6ft × 3ft	8–10	Brick-red, thick and fleshy stems (M–L)	Pale green, finely toothed, felted, lanceolate	Subshrub, resents disturbance, clump-forming but sprawls
'Wildwood Splendour'	3–4ft × 1ft	4–8	Rich amethyst-purple (M–L)	Mid to dark green	

Lunaria rediviva.

LUNARIA Brassicaceae

Lunaria rediviva is a bold, early spring presence; in fact, it is blooming as most perennials are just coming into growth. It is a large plant with rough, hairy stems and broadly triangular toothed leaves. The pale lavender flowers are followed by elliptical green seedpods, which turn white and papery. Lunaria is difficult to transplant but self-sows fairly aggressively. The seedheads are interesting, especially in fall (if you cut back after flowering, you'll never know this). This is a very long-lived perennial but not as showy in seed as its annual cousin. ~ *Ann Bucher*

Scientific Name: From the Latin *luna* ("moon"), referring to the seedpods.
Common Name: Money plant, silver dollar, honesty, moonwort.
Origin: Europe, western Siberia.
Preferred Conditions: Ordinary fertile garden soil that is well-drained, moisture-retentive, and cool.
Light: Sun to part shade.
Management: To avoid seedlings and to keep the plant looking tidy, remove most flowering stems when seeds are ripe. Cut to basal growth after leaves die in autumn.
Propagation: Best from seed (leave at least one or two plants alone); the taproot makes it difficult to divide, but division can be attempted in the fall; even the seedlings don't like to be disturbed.
Pests and Diseases: Subject to a seriously disfiguring if not fatal rust disease, which seems more likely to occur on light soils; cabbage white butterfly lay eggs on leaves (remove by hand before they reduce the leaves to tatters); mildew (in dry soil).
Companions: Helleborus, primula, hosta, *Phlox stolonifera*, pulmonaria, polygonatum, spring bulbs, ferns; under tall shrubs or trees.

Species and Cultivars	Height/ Spread	USDA Hardiness Zone	Flowers (bloom time)	Foliage	Comments
rediviva	2–3ft × 3ft	6–9	Pale lilac, fragrant (E–M)	Dark green, triangular to heart-shaped, finely toothed	Clump-forming, flat elliptical seedpods, silvery and translucent

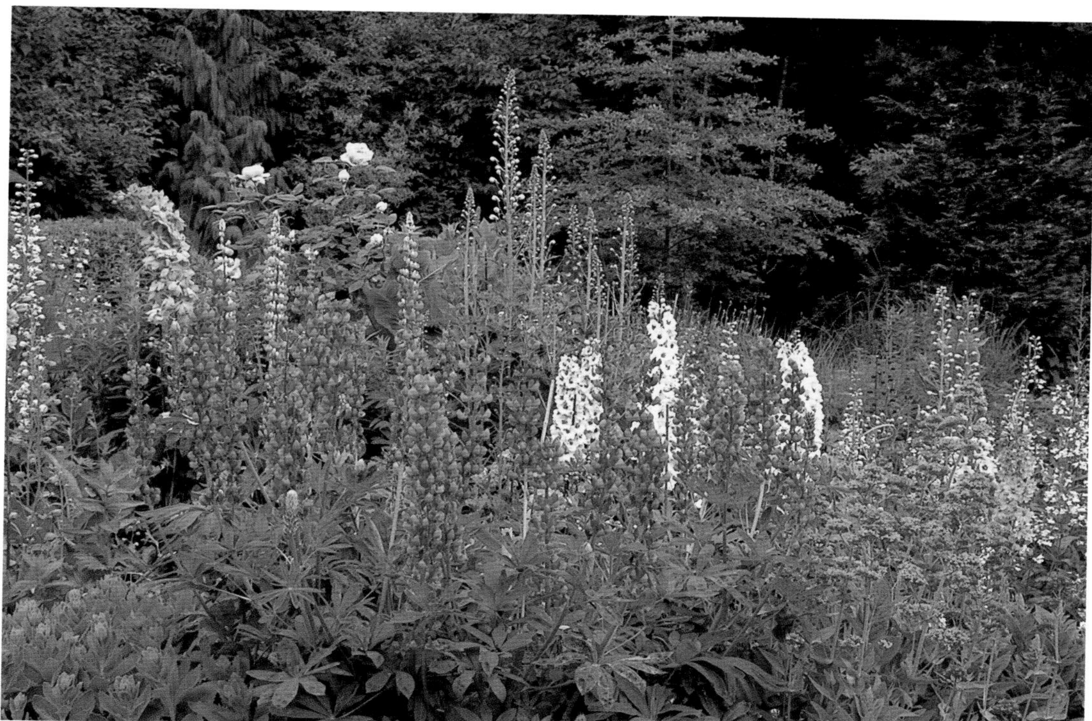

Lupinus Russell Hybrids mixed with delphiniums and *Centranthus ruber.*

LUPINUS Papilionaceae

Russell lupines were among my first perennials, but they were frustrating to grow. Even the palmate foliage and lovely flowers, in very interesting color combinations, were hardly compensation. They were prone to aphids and mildew and seemed labor intensive (not unlike delphinium) to me. The final outcome is that I no longer grow them. If I were to try lupines again, I would grow species and site them according to their natural habitat, or would grow only one or two, which would reduce the effort necessary to have them.

They are a good cut flower for fresh arrangements, with one of the oddest of floral scents—black pepper. Nitrogen fixing, as are all members of this family. All parts of the plant are poisonous.
~ *Carrie Becker*

Scientific Name: From the Latin *lupus* ("wolf").
Common Name: Lupine.
Origin: Europe, Africa, South America, North America.
Preferred Conditions: Any good fertile soil that is well-drained, lime-free to neutral, moisture-retentive, and cool.
Light: Sun to part shade.
Management: Not long-lived; replace plants regularly, every third year or so. To help prolong life, deadhead before the flower spike has even finished blooming. Cut back to side buds, to encourage a second flush of bloom. Do not disturb taproot. Do not let them dry out: give lots of water in spring and summer; water deeply during dry times; and mulch to conserve moisture. Lupines are heavy feeders! When top-dressing with manure or compost, avoid putting in contact with crown. Tall plants may need staking.
Propagation: Best from seed in situ; cuttings of young shoots in early spring; division of large clumps in early spring.

Pests and Diseases: Aphids, downy and powdery mildew, snails, slugs, rust, stem rot.
Companions: *Papaver orientale* (both in terms of contrast of shape as well as color combinations), *Alchemilla mollis, Salvia nemorosa, S. ×superba*, geranium; yellow lupine with *Sisyrinchium striatum*, anchusa.
Notes: The many cultivars are of garden origin and have been hybridized for color, height, and stature. Choose for color and grow them for the pleasure of their brief presence.

Species and Cultivars	Height/ Spread	USDA Hardiness Zone	Flowers (bloom time)	Foliage	Comments
Gallery Series	2ft × 1ft	4–9	Blue, pink, white, yellow (M)	Green	Shorter version of Russell Hybrids
latifolius subsp. parishii	2–3ft × 1ft	4–9	Blue (M)	Mid-green aging to gray	Alaskan lupine
Russell Hybrids	2½–5ft × 1½ft	4–9	Blue, purple, yellow, orange, red, pink, white, bicolors (E–M)	Deep rich green, palmately lobed	Long-blooming, bushy
Woodfield Hybrids	2–3ft × 1½ft	4–9	Cream, yellow, peach to pale pink, shades of red from light to dark (E–M)	Deep rich green, palmately lobed	Mildew not as big a problem

LYCHNIS Caryophyllaceae

Lychnis can be broken down into two groups by color of leaves and flowers. The gray-leaved, pink- to magenta-flowered species are best grown and produce the best leaf color in poorer, dry soils and full sun (except for *L. flos-cuculi*, which likes swampy soils and pond banks). They are short-lived, or should be (any plant that self-sows this freely is telling you something). I have really enjoyed growing *L. flos-jovis*, which is a much reduced and more gently colored cousin of *L. coronaria*, only one and a half feet tall, max. It is easier to combine with other plants than *L. coronaria*, does not self-sow as freely, and can just disappear from the garden after several years. Get seed and direct sow for replacement plants.

The green- to burgundy-leaved, orange- to red-flowered species want a richer soil and more water. They are even shorter lived (think annual). Actually, *L. chalcedonica* can live for several years but doesn't always. *Lychnis ×arkwrightii* and its cultivars 'Orange Gnome' and 'Vesuvius' all have larger flowers in some brightly colored version of orange and are great color additions. Even if short-lived, I'd replant them to recreate the effect. ~ *Carrie Becker*

Scientific Name: From the Greek *lychnos* ("lamp"), referring to the woolly leaves, which were used for wicks.
Common Name: Rose campion, Maltese cross, ragged robin.
Origin: Russia, southern Europe, western Asia, North America.
Preferred Conditions: Any fertile, ordinary garden soil that is well drained. Variable moisture requirements, from moist to dry.
Light: Sun.
Management: The gray-leaved forms thrive on neglect; after about year three, pull out the oldest plants in favor of the much more vigorous young plants—otherwise, the old ones linger on in a deteriorating state until death. Remove faded flowers to promote continued

Lychnis coronaria with *Geranium sanguineum*, a selection of *Erigeron glaucus*, and *Allium sphaerocephalon* (in bud), backed by *Miscanthus sinensis* 'Gracillimus'. Design by Michael Schultz.

Lychnis coronaria Oculata Group.

blooming and to prevent self-sowing. Cut flower stems out after flowering. If the plant looks ratty after blooming, cut back hard to basal foliage. *Lychnis chalcedonica* may need support; cut back to one foot after flowering. Bait for slugs.

Propagation: Division for cultivars and hybrids in spring or fall; seed—very easy; basal cuttings.

Pests and Diseases: Cutworms. And all but *L. coronaria* are very susceptible to snails and slugs; "loss of lychnis" may be entirely due to slug predation on young shoots at ground level.

Companions: Kniphofia, *Nepeta* 'Six Hills Giant', salvia, aster, centranthus, heuchera, artemisia, geranium, phygelius, miscanthus and other grasses, perovskia.

Species and Cultivars	Height/ Spread	USDA Hardiness Zone	Flowers (bloom time)	Foliage	Comments
alpina	4–6in × 6in	4–7	Purplish pink or white with frilled lobed petals (E–M)	Dark green, lanceolate, dense rosettes	Arctic campion, self-sows, mat-forming
×arkwrightii	12in × 10in	6–8	Large, orange-red (M)	Purplish bronze tinted	Short-lived, stems die back after flowering
×a. 'Orange Gnome'	8in × 8in	6–9	Shocking red-orange (M)	Deep burgundy, ovate to lanceolate	Short-lived, clump-forming
×a. 'Vesuvius'	12–18in × 10in	6–8	Scarlet-orange, star-shaped (M)	Brownish green, hairy	As above
chalcedonica	24–48in × 18in	4–8	Small, scarlet, white, or pink, star-shaped, deeply cut, in flat-topped corymb (M)	Mid-green, ovate, rough-textured, hairy, toothed	Maltese cross, Jerusalem cross, self-sows, long-lived, may need staking, keep moist, weedy, RHS Award
coronaria (syn. *Agrostemma coronaria*)	18–36in × 12–18in	4–9	Velvety magenta to deep crimson (M–L)	Silver-gray, leaves and stems, lanceolate, woolly	Rose campion, mullein pink, agrostemma, self-sows, acts more like biennial, drought tolerant, RHS Award
c. 'Alba'	18–36in × 12–18in	3–9	Single white, flush of pink (M–L)	Flannel-gray, woolly, somewhat crinkled	Self-sows, RHS Award
c. 'Angel's Blush'	18–36in × 12–18in	3–9	Soft pale pink fading to white with cerise eye (M)	Silver, woolly, somewhat crinkled	Open airy habit, self-sows
c. Oculata Group	18–36in × 12–18in	3–9	White with pink eye (M)	Silver-green, woolly	Self-sows
flos-cuculi	30in × 24in+	3–9	Deep rose-pink, sometimes white, ragged edges, in corymbs (E–M)	Mid to bluish green, narrow, lancelike	Ragged robin, cuckoo flower, clump-forming, seeds aggressively
flos-jovis	12–18in × 12–18in	3–9	Bright chalk-pink or white in corymbs (M)	Silver gray-green, leaves and stems, woolly, hairy, lance- to spoon-shaped	Flower of Jove, short-lived, self-sows, RHS Award
f. 'Nana'	8–10in × 10in	3–9	Bright chalk-pink (M)	Silver gray-green with shining silver hairs	Dwarf

Species and Cultivars	Height/ Spread	USDA Hardiness Zone	Flowers (bloom time)	Foliage	Comments
f. 'Peggy'	10–12in × 10in	3–9	Bright rose-pink with white back and edges, large (M)	Gray, felted	Compact
×haageana	12–18in × 12in	4–9	Orange, scarlet, large, on hairy, weak stems (M)	Dark reddish purple, lanceolate, hairy	Keep moist, short-lived, dies back after flowering
viscaria	12–18in × 12in	3–9	Bright pink corymbs on hairy, strong stems (E–M)	Dark green, maroon bands, shiny, sticky stems, grasslike, lanceolate	German catchfly, often evergreen
v. 'Plena'	16–18in × 12in	3–9	Double carmine-pink (E–M)	Dark green, shiny, sticky stems, grasslike, lanceolate	As above

LYSIMACHIA Primulaceae

Not all members of the genus *Lysimachia* deserve the bad rap they get from the few black sheep of the family (*L. punctata*, for example). To make matters worse, the common name loosestrife is often confused with the unrelated noxious weed *Lythrum salicaria*, purple loosestrife.

Lysimachias have a wide range of growth habits, and most share the trait of spreading fairly quickly. Some are invasive, and care with placement must be taken. *Lysimachia ephemerum* is a tall, noninvasive species with white star-shaped flowers. As do most lysimachias, it also has attractive foliage. *Lysimachia nummularia*, a short groundcover, is very easy to control: either pull it out, or manure and mulch heavily over it in the area you don't want it. *Lysimachia atropurpurea* is difficult to control, but the leaves are a great color; you can try a barrier or a constricted spot, but plants can march right through any shrub. *Lysimachia ciliata* 'Firecracker' runs further and faster in loose soil than in clay, but its purple leaves combine beautifully with many plants and are worth the effort. *Lysimachia clethroides* (gooseneck loosestrife, goose-goes-walking) also has a vigorous habit, but the gracefully arched and tapered white blossoms are just too beautiful to pass up. They are a good cut flower, too, and definitely worth finding a special spot for. ~ *Susan Carter*

Scientific Name: After Lysimachos, king of Thrace.
Common Name: Creeping Jenny, loosestrife, gooseneck loosestrife.
Origin: China, Japan, Europe, North America, Korea.
Preferred Conditions: Adaptable to most conditions, but will bloom better in rich, moisture-retentive, well-drained soil. In drier soil they are slightly better behaved and don't spread as fast.
Light: Sun to part shade.
Management: You may want to install a root barrier, or plant in pots to control spreading. You can also dig and divide every few years to reduce their territory. Most are self-supporting except *L. ciliata*, which can be very floppy. Cut back after flowering and during fall/winter cleanup.
Propagation: Division; seed for *L. ephemerum*.
Pests and Diseases: Not usually bothered by much except some slug damage in early spring.

Lysimachia punctata 'Alexander'.

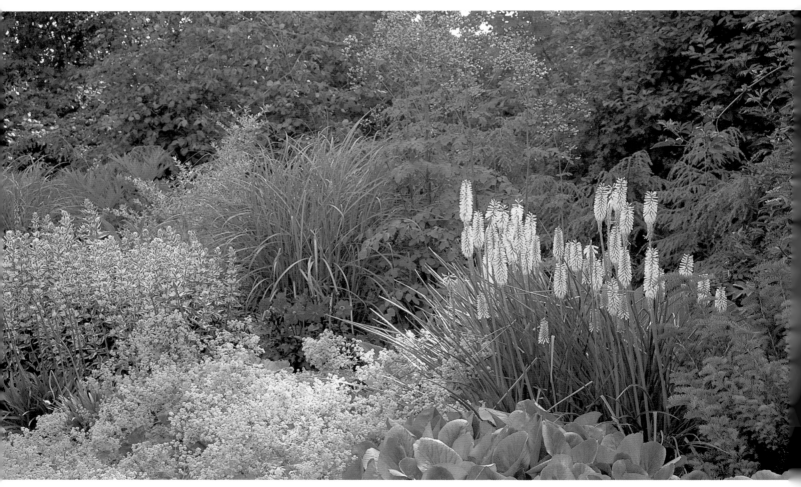

Lysimachia punctata 'Alexander' with *Dahlia* 'Bishop of Llandaff', *Thalictrum delavayi* 'Hewitt's Double', *Alchemilla mollis*, bergenia foliage, and *Kniphofia* 'Primrose Beauty'.

Companions: Heuchera, plantago, hosta, Siberian iris, *Echinacea purpurea*, rudbeckia, ligularia, anthemis, grasses.

Notes: Variegated forms of *L. punctata* revert to green quite easily; keep watch. In the chart, the symbol ∞ = infinite spread.

Species and Cultivars	Height/ Spread	USDA Hardiness Zone	Flowers (bloom time)	Foliage	Comments
atropurpurea	2–3ft × 1ft	7–9	Violet-red buds open to maroon-purple (M)	Grayish blue, narrow	Lax habit, short-lived
ciliata	3–4ft × ∞	4–9	Light yellow, orange eye, nodding (M)	Mid-green, willowlike, good autumn color, hairy leaves and stems	Fringed loosestrife, North American native, rhizomatous, invasive
c. 'Firecracker' (syn. 'Purpurea')	2½–3ft × ∞	4–9	Lemon-yellow, wide, nodding, out-facing (M)	Emerges almost black, then green	Runs but not as invasive as species, RHS Award
clethroides	2–3ft × ∞	4–9	Small, whitish, bends into gooseneck form (M–L)	Narrow, grayish green, hairless, leathery, red stems, some fall color	Clump-forming, long-blooming, RHS Award
c. 'Geisha'	2ft × 3ft+	4–9	Long (1ft) white gooseneck (M)	Green, creamy-yellow margins, jagged	Not as aggressive as species
ephemerum	3–4ft × 1½ft	6–9	White to gray-white, star-shaped, lilac center (M–L)	Grayish green, narrow, hairless, leathery	Clump-forming, not invasive, good seedheads, sun or shade
minoricensis	1ft × 1ft	6–9	White (M)	Gray-green, striking violet-veined rosettes	Short-lived
nummularia	2–4in × 3ft+	3–9	Small, bright yellow, cup-shaped (E–M)	Deep green, small, rounded, glossy	Creeping jenny, moneywort, evergreen in mild climates
n. 'Aurea'	2–4in × 3ft+	4–9	Small, bright yellow, cup-shaped (M)	Golden yellow, rounded, glossy, often reverts to green	Less invasive, evergreen, turns brown in hot sun, RHS Award
punctata	1½–3ft × 2ft+	4–8	Bright yellow whorls, star-shaped (M)	Mid-green, lancelike, coarse, softly hairy, stiff upright stems	Yellow loosestrife, invasive, long bloomer
p. 'Alexander' (syn. 'Variegata')	2–3ft × 2ft+	4–8	Golden yellow whorls (M)	Green, creamy-white variegation and margins, new growth tinged pink	Spring crowns have fantastic color
p. 'Golden Alexander'	2–3ft × 2ft+	4–8	As above	Golden variegated	Do we need another variegated thug?

Macleaya cordata.

MACLEAYA Papaveraceae

The plume poppies are stately plants that quickly achieve their full height, which can be as much as ten feet, depending on the species. They need plenty of space and can colonize a large area if not kept under control. This is relatively easy to do and certainly worth the effort. The wonderful delicately colored lobed leaves are slightly hairy and are borne on thick, erect glaucous stems; these are topped by tall plumes of tiny, coral-pink or deep buff flowers in summer. Macleaya is a good cut flower for fresh or dried arrangements, but be careful: the stems and leaf stalks produce a yellowish orange sap that can stain clothes and skin. As with all Papaveraceae (or any milky-sapped plant), singe the bottom of the flower stems when used as a cut. ~ *Susan Carter*

Scientific Name: After Alexander Macleay (1767–1848), secretary of the Linnean Society.
Common Name: Plume poppy, tree celandine.
Origin: China, Japan.
Preferred Conditions: Rich to moderately fertile, deep, well-drained soils, but will grow anywhere, really. Protect from cold and drying winds.
Light: Sun to part shade.
Planting: Best in swathes in a large, sunny area.
Management: Usually will not require staking. Cut stems to the ground in autumn. Top-dress in winter with a rich compost or manure. Dig around plants twice a year to remove spreading roots (they can run deep); do not compost, as any and every root bit will survive and continue to grow.
Propagation: Divide in late autumn; seed in containers in cold frame in spring; root cuttings; dig up runners and replant in fall.
Pests and Diseases: Slugs on new growth.
Companions: The larger, bolder grasses, *Phlomis fruticosa*, solidago, kniphofia, phygelius, phormium.

Notes: This plant works best in the garden if allowed to run about; simply remove where not needed or wanted. In the chart, the symbol ∞ = infinite spread.

Species and Cultivars	Height/ Spread	USDA Hardiness Zone	Flowers (bloom time)	Foliage	Comments
cordata	5–10ft × ∞	4–9	Creamy or buff, plumelike (M)	Large, gray-green, grayish white beneath, lobed	Rhizomatous, RHS Award
microcarpa	6–8ft × ∞	4–9	As above	Large, gray-green, grayish white beneath, deeply lobed, rounded	Rhizomatous, invasive
m. 'Kelway's Coral Plume'	5–7ft × ∞	4–9	Coral-pink, pink in bud (M)	Gray, lobed	Rhizomatous, invasive, RHS Award

MALVA Malvaceae

These cottage garden favorites, commonly called mallows, are closely related to lavatera, sidalcea, and alcea. As do their relatives, malvas offer a wealth of bloom over a long period of time, sometimes blooming themselves to death. The flowers are saucer-shaped with five petals and bloom in shades of purple, pink, blue, and white, some with beautiful veining; the leaves are also quite attractive, heart-shaped to rounded and lobed or divided, light to dark green. Plants can self-sow freely and are more than able to maintain themselves. *Malva sylvestris* (cheeses) has been around since ancient Roman times; its foliage, flowers, and seeds are still used medicinally and also to flavor foods. Although these plants are weedy, rusty, and generally short-lived, they are still worth growing. ~ *Susan Carter*

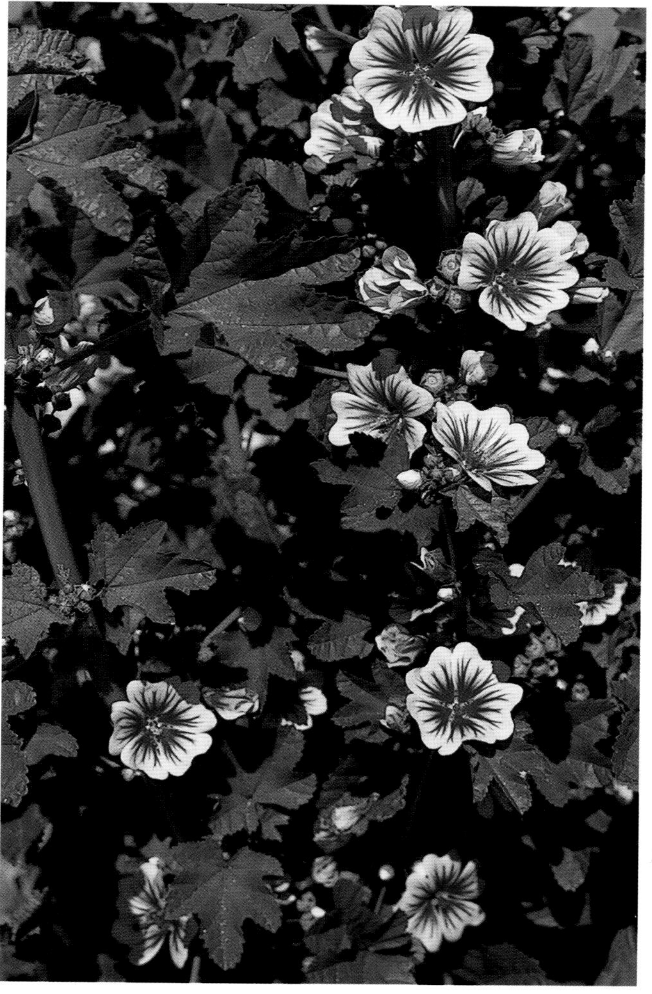

Malva sylvestris 'Zebrina'.

Scientific Name: The classical Latin name for mallow.
Common Name: Mallow.
Origin: Europe, North Africa, Turkey.
Preferred Conditions: Moderately fertile, well-drained soils. Average water requirements. Drought tolerant once established.
Light: Sun to part shade.
Management: Cut back after flowering (especially *M. moschata*) before they seed about and become pests; if you cut the flowering stems to the ground (leaving the basal leaves) when flowering is almost over, you are generally rewarded with a fresh flush of flowers in late summer. Cut back to crown in autumn.
Propagation: Seed; division in spring and basal cuttings in spring.

Pests and Diseases: Rust and fungal leaf spot. One method of rust control is to remove the first crop of leaves in spring, infected or not.

Companions: *Phlox paniculata*, boltonia, coreopsis, veronica, phlomis, veronicastrum, *Lysimachia ephemerum*.

Notes: Plants will be small if kept too dry.

Species and Cultivars	Height/ Spread	USDA Hardiness Zone	Flowers (bloom time)	Foliage	Comments
alcea	3–4ft × 1½ft	4–9	Purplish pink (M–L)	Light green, rounded, divided	Hollyhock mallow, long-blooming, self-sows, erect, bushy
a. var. fastigiata	3–4ft × 1½ft	4–9	Soft clear pink (M–L)	Light green, rounded, divided	Long-blooming, weedy, self-sows, erect, bushy
moschata	2–3ft × 2ft	4–9	Pale pink (M–L)	Mid to dark green, cordate, deeply divided, musk-scented	Musk mallow, tap-rooted, bushy
m. f. alba	2–3ft × 2ft	4–9	Pure white, fading pinkish (M–L)	Mid-green, deeply cut, lightly aromatic	White musk mallow, self-sows, bushy, RHS Award
m. rosea	2–3ft × 2ft	4–9	Satiny pink (M–L)	Mid-green, musk scented, deeply cut	Pink musk mallow
sylvestris	2–4ft × 2ft	4–9	Pinkish purple with darker purple veins (E–L)	Dark green, small, rounded, lobed, bushy	Cheeses, erect to spreading, weedy, subshrubby
s. Marina = 'Dema'	2–4ft × 2ft	4–9	Dark violet-blue, dark purple veins (M–L)	Deep green	Subshrub, dark flower
s. 'Primley Blue'	2½–3½ft × 1½ft	4–9	Pale violet-blue, purple veins, beautiful color (E–L)	Dark green, rounded, lobed	Weedy, subshrubby, more prostrate
s. 'Zebrina'	3–4ft × 2ft	4–9	Deep pink or white with purple veins (M–L)	As above	Striped mallow, self-sows, subshrubby, weedy

MARRUBIUM Lamiaceae

Members of the mint family, horehounds are grown for their interesting gray foliage, which makes them fine foils for many other plants. Wet winters are their only trial. The entire flowering plant of *M. vulgare* is considered medicinal when fresh; the flowering branches are medicinal when dried. Horehound tea is still regarded as a cure for colds in certain countries (including the United States) and is commonly used in liqueurs and aperitifs. ~ *Carrie Becker*

Scientific Name: The classical Latin name. Some say the Latin derives from the Hebrew *marrob* ("bitter juice"); it is one of the bitter herbs eaten at the feast of Passover.

Common Name: Horehound.

Origin: Europe, Italy, Sicily, Greece.

Marrubium vulgare.

Preferred Conditions: Poor to average (even sandy) soil, low water needs. Protect from cold, drying winds and excessive winter moisture.
Light: Sun.
Management: Cut back hard after flowering to retain a reasonably compact habit. May also seed about if not cut back. Take out damaged or oldest stems.
Propagation: Seed in containers in cold frame in spring—germination is erratic; softwood basal cuttings in spring or summer; division is not recommended.
Pests and Diseases: None.
Companions: Salvia, agastache, *Scabiosa ochroleuca*, anthemis, low grasses.

Species and Cultivars	Height/ Spread	USDA Hardiness Zone	Flowers (bloom time)	Foliage	Comments
cylleneum	16–18in × 18in	6–9	Creamy yellow in tight whorls, insignificant (M)	Soft sage-green, rounded, scalloped, woolly	Spreading
incanum (syn. candidissimum)	16–20in × 18in	3–10	Pale lilac, almost white in whorls, insignificant (M)	Gray-green, white felted beneath, scalloped or toothed, aromatic	Spreading, evergreen
rotundifolium	4–10in × 10in	5–10	Whitish, insignificant (M)	Pale green, spoon-shaped, felted, scalloped, cream edges	Horehound, silver-edged, mat-forming, evergreen
vulgare	18in × 18in	3–8	Small, white, insignificant (M)	Gray, silky	White horehound

Meconopsis betonicifolia.

MECONOPSIS Papaveraceae

When first gardening professionally, I had a client with lots (should have been a clue) of lovely yellow and orange poppies growing throughout their woodland garden. I carefully dug a few rooted pieces and took them home, coddled them to ensure their recovery, and in short order I was rewarded by an invasion of *M. cambrica* in my own garden. Over the intervening years, I learned to keep them deadheaded to prevent self-sowing; being quite perennial they need no replacement plants. I also saw in friends' gardens the lovely *M. cambrica* 'Frances Perry' and *M. c.* 'Muriel Brown', both of which have red flowers and do not seem to self-sow much if at all; 'Frances Perry' is single so might produce viable seed, but 'Muriel Brown' is double and reputedly sterile (propagate from basal stem cuttings).

Somewhat later, I had the good fortune to acquire *M. betonicifolia*. The lovely sky-blue flowers of the Himalayan blue poppy graced my own woodland for perhaps five years until a summer of insufficient watering killed it. Many other lovely relatives of meconopsis are monocarpic, meaning they bloom, set seed, and die; the younger the plants are when they bloom, the more likely they are to completely die away from the effort.

If the perennial forms make flowering stems the first year, remove them. As the crowns get larger, with care and time, you can let them bloom, and in the case of *M. betonicifolia*, *M. grandis*, and *M.* ×*sheldonii*, the plants will stay around for a while. Do not let them dry out in summer, and organic matter in the soil is critical. Never bury the crowns.

In the first year, leaf rosettes on the monocarpic forms (see chart) are beautiful in winter and spring, so give them some room to be seen. Also, they seem to resent other plants being too close, so don't crowd them. The beautiful creped poppy flowers will reward you in shades of pale yellow, deep red, violet, and blue, depending on which you grow. ~ *Carrie Becker*

Meconopsis cambrica 'Muriel Brown', *Tropaeolum majus* foliage, and *Rumex sanguineus* var. *sanguineus* backed by 'Atropurpurea Nana' berberis; the warm theme is continued by *Tanacetum coccineum*, *Lychnis chalcedonica*, and a good red geum. Design by Rick Kyper.

Scientific Name: From the Greek *mecon* ("poppy") and *opsis* ("like"), indicating resemblance.
Common Name: Welsh poppy, Himalayan poppy.
Origin: Himalaya, China, western Europe, Tibet, Wales.
Preferred Conditions: Moist, cool, humus-rich, deep, well-drained, and neutral to slightly acid soil. Shelter from extreme, cold, drying winds. Protect from excessive winter wet, but do not let plants dry out.
Light: Part shade to part sun.
Planting: Crowns should be level with the surface of the soil.
Management: Not the easiest plants to grow outside of the right conditions (except for *M. cambrica*, which is not as demanding and thrives in most conditions). Mulch with coarse organic material (compost would be best), along with manure (but not over the crown). Water during dry spells in the summer. *Meconopsis betonicifolia* should not be allowed

to flower the first year; it must be established, with several crowns, before flowering. *Meconopsis cambrica* requires regular deadheading to keep the self-sowing under control.

Propagation: Seed as soon as ripe (best from seed); divide after flowering (tricky).

Pests and Diseases: Snails, slugs, downy mildew, damping off of seedlings.

Companions: Pulmonaria, dicentra, hosta, helleborus, polygonatum, arisaema, geranium, heuchera; the woodland garden.

Notes: The blooms of *M. cambrica* have the fragrance of a banana popsicle.

Species and Cultivars	Height/ Spread	USDA Hardiness Zone	Flowers (bloom time)	Foliage	Comments
betonicifolia (syn. baileyi)	2–4ft × 1½ft	5–8	Varies from sky-blue to lavender-blue, yellow stamens, saucer-shaped, 3–4in (E–M)	Light bluish green with fine rust-colored hairs, toothed, cordate bases	Himalayan blue poppy
b. var. alba	2ft × 1½ft	5–8	White, yellow stamens, saucer-shaped, 3–4in (M)	As above	Weaker plant
cambrica	1–2ft × 1ft+	6–9	Bright lemon-yellow or orange, cup-shaped, tissue papery, single, 2–2½in (E–L)	Clear green, divided, hairy	Welsh poppy, deep taproot, self-sows
c. flore-pleno	2ft × 1ft	6–9	Double yellow or orange, cup-shaped, 2–2½in (M–L)	As above	Not as vigorous as the species
c. 'Frances Perry' (syn. 'Rubra')	2ft × 1ft	6–9	Deep rich orange-red, single, yellow stamens, cup-shaped, 2in (M–L)	Green, divided, hairy	Self-sows mildly if at all
c. 'Muriel Brown'	2ft × 1ft		Double red, 2in (E–L)	Clear green, divided, hairy	Sterile, sets a few seeds
grandis	3–5ft × 1½ft	5–8	Varies from rich blue to purplish red, dark yellow center and stamens, saucer-shaped, 5–6in (E–M)	Mid to dark green with reddish brown hairs, toothed	Monocarpic in dry conditions, erect, replant every 3 years
horridula	2–3ft + × 1½ft	6–8	Pale to deep blue or red, cup-shaped, 2–3in (M)	Mid gray-green, hairy, prickly, wavy edges, elliptic to lanceolate	Monocarpic, winter rosette of leaves
h. 'Slieve Donard'	3ft × 1½ft	7–8	Rich blue, pointed petals, cup-shaped, 2–3in (M)	As above	Winter rosette of leaves, vigorous, RHS Award
napaulensis	3–8ft × 2ft	8–9	Pink, red, purple, blue, yellow, white, cup-shaped, 2½–3in (E–M)	Yellow-green, red bristles, deeply cut, rosettes	Satin poppy, monocarpic, hairy seedpods, sets lots of seed
×sheldonii	3–5ft × 1½ft	7–8	Pale to rich blue, cup-shaped, 2½–4in (E–M)	Dark green rosettes, hairy, toothed, elliptic-oblong to lanceolate	More perennial than most
villosa	2ft × 1½ft	7–9	Clear yellow, dark yellow stamens, nodding, 1½–2in (E)	Green, deeply lobed, fernlike, bronze hairs on leaves and stems	Monocarpic, winter rosette of leaves, short-lived

MELISSA Lamiaceae

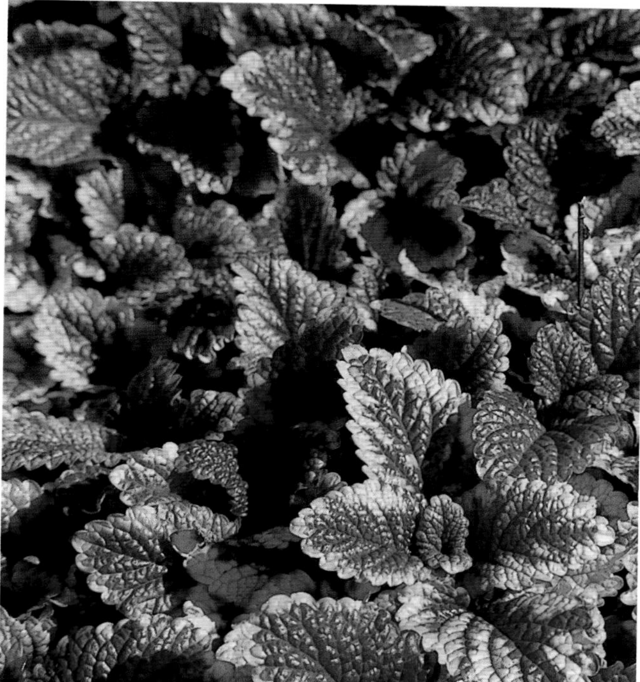

Melissa officinalis 'Aurea'.

The colored-leaf forms of lemon balm are often grown for their dramatic effect in the garden. Unfortunately, they all seed back to plain *M. officinalis*, which is often classified as an invasive or noxious weed. Don't let your variegated or golden lemon balm go to seed at all—usually by the time the plants are up to flowering height, the color has faded out. You can then cut back to the ground, and the crowns will leaf back out. This is a spring-texture and -color plant and can be totally hidden in summer by other perennials.

An old medicinal plant with many uses in the past, lemon balm is now used mostly for teas and potpourris. As with many mint family plants, this is a good plant for bees. ~ *Bob Lilly*

Scientific Name: Greek for Melissa ("bee-nymph"), daughter of King Melisseus ("bee-man"), who nursed Zeus when he was an infant (feeding him goat's milk) and taught humans the use of honey.
Common Name: Lemon balm.
Origin: Europe, Central Asia, Mediterranean.
Preferred Conditions: Easy to grow in poor to fertile, well-drained soil. Average water requirements but drought tolerant once established. Protect from excessive winter moisture.
Light: Sun to part shade. The leaves of *M. officinalis* 'Aurea' and *M. o.* 'All Gold' may scorch in hot sun, so should be grown in at least part shade (spring sun, summer shade).
Management: Cut back severely two or three times during the season to prevent self-sowing and encourage new basal growth, especially with the variegated forms. Recovers quickly from this treatment. Deadhead immediately after flowering, or before, or your garden will be full of seedlings. Don't let plants dry out in the growing season, as this will trigger the onset of powdery mildew for the rest of the summer.
Propagation: Division in spring.
Pests and Diseases: Powdery mildew (if too dry); spider mites can appear in late summer (if too dry and if not cut back after flowering).
Companions: *Carex elata*, various daisies, *Iris pseudacorus*, sanguisorba; the loosely structured cottage herb garden.
Notes: Clumps usually stay manageable; it's all those seedlings that appear. Basal growth is showiest on the colored-leaf forms.

Species and Cultivars	Height/ Spread	USDA Hardiness Zone	Flowers (bloom time)	Foliage	Comments
officinalis	2ft × 2ft	4–9	Pale yellow, turning white, insignificant (M)	Light green, veined, crinkled, ovate, toothed, lemon-scented	Bushy, vigorous
o. 'All Gold'	1½ft × 1½ft	4–9	White, tinted pale lilac, insignificant (M)	Golden yellow, veined, crinkled, ovate, toothed	Part shade helps keep the color
o. 'Aurea' (syn. 'Variegata'	1½ft × 1½ft	4–9	White, insignificant (M)	Yellow with a suffusion of bright green along main veins	Leaves on flower stems are usually green

Mertensia virginica.

MERTENSIA Boraginaceae

Mertensia is fussy by most standards but truly worth growing: there is nothing like a happy slug. *Mertensia sibirica* and *M. virginica* are companionable woodlanders; *M. maritima* and *M. simplicissima* are usually grown alone, in open, sunny locations (*M. maritima* is, oddly for a seashore plant, extremely prone to slug damage). These are spring division plants and do not establish readily; they will need a full year to look good. They have a very tight propagation window in early spring and a tendency to fail or sulk. ~ *Bob Lilly*

Scientific Name: After German botanist Franz Karl Mertens.
Common Name: Virginia bluebells, Virginia cowslip.
Origin: North America, Europe, Japan, Korea, East Asia, Russia, Siberia, Greenland.
Preferred Conditions: Rich, loamy soil for *M. sibirica* and *M. virginica*; gritty, lean soil for *M. maritima* and *M. simplicissima.*
Light: Sun for *M. maritima* and *M. simplicissima*; part shade for *M. sibirica* and *M. virginica.*
Management: Water well during the spring growth flush and keep moist during the rest of the growing season. Tall forms may need staking but are very brittle, so be careful. Cut back flowering stems in the fall and leave the basal growth.
Propagation: Division in spring (difficult even when dormant); seed in fall or when ripe; root cuttings of *M. virginica* when dormant.
Pests and Diseases: Snails, slugs, especially on new growth of *M. maritima* and *M. simplicissima.*
Companions: Trillium, dicentra, asarum, uvularia, pulmonaria, *Begonia grandis*, hosta, erythronium, primula; ferns to take over once they go dormant.
Notes: These are not the plants usually referred to as bluebells; those are bulbs (*Hyacinthoides* spp., *Scilla* spp.).

Species and Cultivars	Height/ Spread	USDA Hardiness Zone	Flowers (bloom time)	Foliage	Comments
maritima	1ft × 1ft	3–7	Pink in bud, opens light blue, bell-shaped (M)	Glaucous, spoon-shaped, fleshy	Oyster plant, spreading
sibirica (syn. pterocarpa)	2–2½ft × 1ft	3–7	Deep blue or purple-blue to white, tubular (E–M)	Glaucous, oval-round	Clump-forming, bushy
simplicissima (syn. asiatica)	1–2ft × 1ft+	6–8	Turquoise-blue-purple, pink in bud, tubular (E–M)	Very light blue, broadly ovate	Long-blooming, low, spreading
virginica (syn. pulmonarioides)	1–2ft × 2ft+	3–9	Pink in bud, opens violet-blue, nodding (E–M)	Glaucous, smooth, new shoots emerge purple	Virginia bluebells, dormant in summer, spreads a long way, RHS Award

MEUM Apiaceae

A rare plant seldom seen for sale, *M. athamanticum* is worth finding for the foliage alone. The leaves are finely divided and very similar to common fennel but have a richer, darker grass-green color. Like parsley in color (if you count white a color), meum's display of small, white flowers is a brief but noticeable event. Worth a trip to England, being sure your windowsill in London faces north, a day of washing the soil of roots, having Linda wait for the inspector, and lots of spritzing at Heathrow. ~ *Bob Lilly*

Scientific Name: Obscure. The Greek name for an herb, possibly *M. athamanticum*.
Common Name: Baldmoney, spignel.
Origin: Western and central Europe.
Preferred Conditions: Moderately fertile, moist, well-drained, lime-free soil.
Light: Sun to part shade.
Management: Undemanding. Cut back in fall once it begins looking tired. Watch for slugs in spring.
Propagation: Usually from seed as soon as ripe; divide in spring, though taproots make this difficult.
Pests and Diseases: Snails, slugs, especially on new growth.
Companions: Alchemilla, *Gentiana lutea*, aconitum, astilbe, chaerophyllum, *Brunnera macrophylla* 'Jack Frost'.

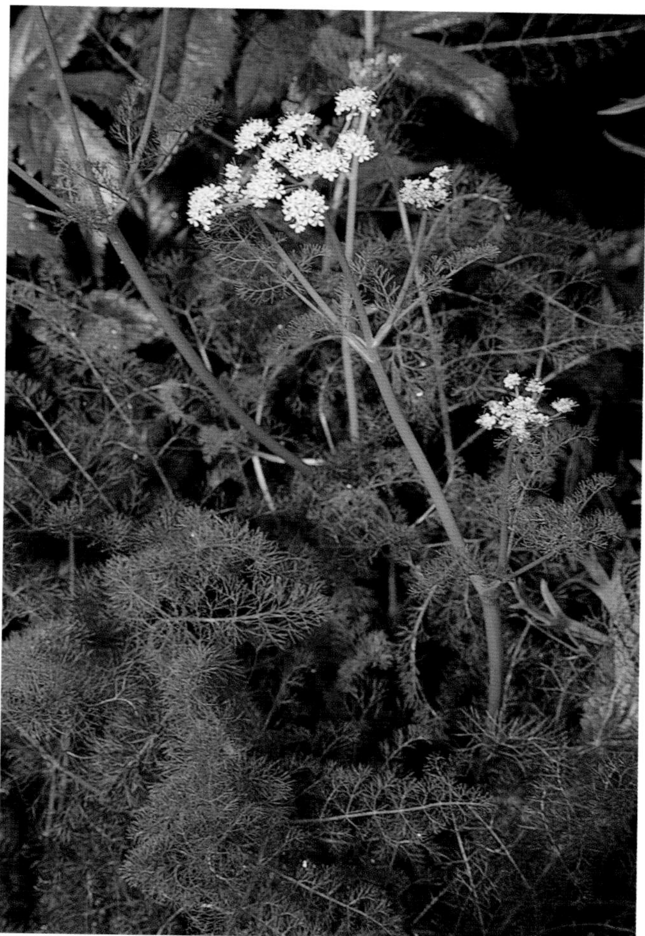

Meum athamanticum.

Species and Cultivars	Height/ Spread	USDA Hardiness Zone	Flowers (bloom time)	Foliage	Comments
athamanticum	1–2ft × 1–1½ft	5–8	Tiny, white with purple tinge, umbels (M)	Fennel-like, deep green	Darkest of all the fine-leaf foliage plants

Mimulus lewisii.

MIMULUS Scrophulariaceae

Monkey flowers grow just about anywhere as long as it's moist; some even grow in standing water. The flowers are snapdragonlike, with five lobes (the bottom two lobes are much larger); the back of the flower is tubular or funnel-shaped. Flowers occur in a variety of colors and are often spotted or blotched in contrasting colors. Mimulus, though short-lived in the garden, works very well as a container plant and is very attractive to hummingbirds. ~ *Susan Carter*

Scientific Name: From the Latin *mimus* ("mimic"), referring to the flowers, which resemble a grinning monkey's face.

Common Name: Monkey flower.

Origin: South America, South Africa, North America.

Preferred Conditions: Humus-rich, moist, and average to fertile soil. Protect from heat and drought.

Light: Sun to part shade.

Management: Water freely in the growing season and keep moist in the winter. Apply a small amount of balanced fertilizer monthly. Add organic matter to drier soils to help with moisture retention. Cut back once plants begin to look scraggly. Some may need staking with pea sticks to keep them from flopping. Mulch in winter.

Propagation: Division in spring; cuttings in early summer; usually from seed in autumn or early spring.

Pests and Diseases: Mildew, whiteflies, spider mites, aphids, slugs.
Companions: Ligularia, ajuga, *Carex elata*, *Lysimachia nummularia* 'Aurea', darmera, *Primula florindae*; small ditches, edge of small waterfall.
Notes: These are probably best classified as annuals in the Pacific Northwest.

Species and Cultivars	Height/ Spread	USDA Hardiness Zone	Flowers (bloom time)	Foliage	Comments
guttatus (syn. langsdorffii)	1–2ft × 1½ft	4–9	Bright yellow with red spots at throat (M)	Mid-green, coarsely or sometimes deeply toothed	Invasive, upright or semi-prostrate, watery stems
g. 'Richard Bish'	1–2ft × 1½ft	4–9	Bright yellow (M)	Green variegated	Invasive but short-lived
lewisii	2–2½ft × 1½ft	4–9	Deep rose-pink, yellow throat spotted with purple, sometimes white (M)	Mid-green, finely toothed	Clump-forming, tolerates drier conditions, Pacific Northwest native, RHS Award
luteus	1ft × 1–2ft	7–9	Golden yellow with large red blotches on throat (E–M)	Green	Invasive, self-sows, can be grown in water (3in deep)
ringens	2½–3ft × 2ft	4–9	Violet-blue, narrow (M)	Mid to dark green, lancelike, toothed	Upright, thrives in shallow water (6in deep), self-sows

MONARDA Lamiaceae

A member of the mint family, monarda grows wild throughout eastern North America. *Monarda didyma*, named Herb of the Year in 1996, was used by the Oswego Indians to brew a tea for both medicinal and culinary purposes, hence the common name Oswego tea. Another of its common names, bergamot, comes from its fragrant resemblance (no botanical relation) to the bergamot orange used to flavor Earl Grey tea. The striking blossoms are borne in whorls at the top of the stem in shades of scarlet, pink, violet, purple, white, or pale yellow and are usually supported by colorful leafy bracts. The foliage has a strong scent and forms dense whorls of leaves on upright stems. Monardas are long-blooming plants that are most effective if grown in large colonies. They are very attractive to hummingbirds and bees, and make a good cut flower.

Mildew is a big problem with monardas, especially if plants get too dry in the summer. The chart lists the hybrids and cultivars that demonstrate some resistance to mildew, although poorly cared for plants of any type can often show some mildew. *Monarda fistulosa* and cultivars tolerate drier conditions and are more resistant; the hybrids with zodiac names, from Piet Oudolf in Holland, are very resistant, and the hybrid 'Marshall's Delight' has high marks for both its mildew resistance and beautiful clear pink flowers. ~ *Susan Carter*

Scientific Name: After Spanish botanist and physician Nicolas Monardes (1493–1588).
Common Name: Beebalm, bergamot, horsemint, Oswego tea.
Origin: North America.
Preferred Conditions: Moderately fertile, humus-rich, well-drained, moist soil. Give plants good air circulation and protect from excessive winter wet.
Light: Sun.

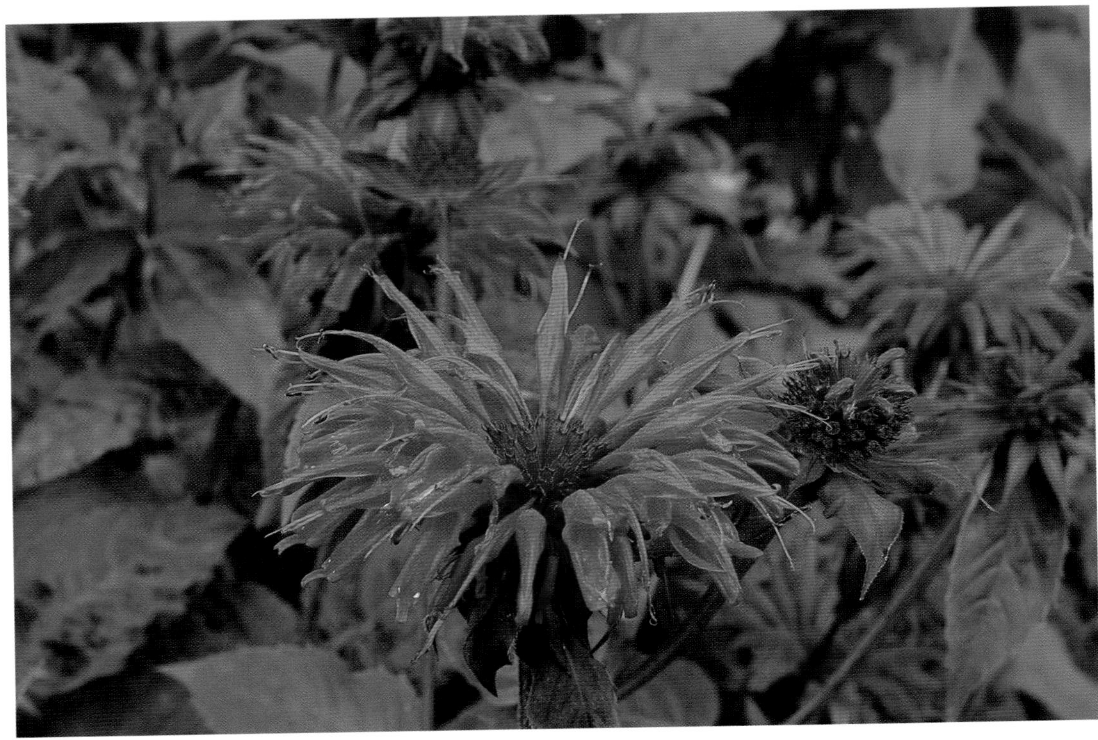

Monarda 'Gardenview Scarlet'.

Management: Divide every three to four years (may have to use a sharp-edged spade). Soil must be well fed, or plants will become less vigorous after a couple of seasons. Top-dress with manure or compost every winter. Some would benefit from pea sticks or other early staking. Deadhead as flowers fade. Don't allow plants to dry out in summer as this stresses them and can trigger mildew; plants can be cut to the ground if mildew becomes a big problem. Cut back in late fall to the crown. Bait for slugs in early spring, as they can devour all your new shoots.

Propagation: Division in spring or fall; seed; basal cuttings.

Pests and Diseases: Mildew, rust, leaf spot, snails, slugs.

Companions: Larger grasses, phlox, salvia, acanthus, achillea, penstemon, alchemilla, eupatorium. Most effective in large colonies, wild gardens (meadows), and the grass border.

Notes: A great plant to hide the compost pile (moist soil, rich in nutrients). Monardas may form a clump larger than eighteen inches across over time and will spread, but they do not root deeply so are easy to control. They do not recover well from heavy mulch.

Species and Cultivars	Height/ Spread	USDA Hardiness Zone	Flowers (bloom time)	Foliage	Comments
'Adam'	2–3ft × 1½ft	4–9	Scarlet, brown-red calyces, large (M)	Dull mid-green, lanceolate to ovate	Clump-forming
'Aquarius'	3–4ft × 1½ft	4–9	Light purplish pink with green bracts (M)	Bronze-green	Mildew resistant
'Beauty of Cobham'	3ft × 1½ft	4–9	Pale cool pink with purple-pink bracts (M–L)	Purplish green	Clump-forming, RHS Award
'Blaustrumpf' (syn. 'Blue Stocking')	2½–4ft × 1½ft	4–9	Dark violet-blue with purple bracts (M–L)	Dark green	Vigorous, mildew resistant, good cut
'Cambridge Scarlet'	2–4ft × 1½ft	4–9	Deep scarlet with purple-red calyces, large (M–L)	Grayish green, lanceolate to oval	Prefers moist, very popular, mildew resistant, RHS Award

Species and Cultivars	Height/ Spread	USDA Hardiness Zone	Flowers (bloom time)	Foliage	Comments
'Cherokee'	4ft × 1½ft	4–9	Pale lilac-pink (M–L)	Green, lanceolate to oval	Some mildew resistance
'Croftway Pink'	2–4ft × 1½ft	4–9	Clear rose-pink with pink-tinged bracts (M–L)	Mid-green, lanceolate to oval	More compact, good cut, RHS Award
'Dark Ponticum'	4ft × 1½ft	4–9	Rich purple with green bracts with purple-tinged calyces (M–L)	Dark green, lanceolate to oval	Purple stems
didyma	2–3ft × 2ft	4–9	Scarlet with reddish bracts and red calyces (M–L)	Bronze-green, hairy, toothed, ovate, aromatic	Oswego tea, beebalm, bushy, prone to mildew in dry soil, spreads rapidly
d. 'Stone's Throw Pink'	3ft × 2ft	4–9	Rose-pink (M)	Gray-green, lanceolate to oval	Mildew resistant
'Elsie's Lavender'	4ft × 1½ft	4–9	Pale lilac-purple with pink bracts, green-tinged calyces (M)	Green, lanceolate to oval	As above
'Fishes' (syn. 'Pisces')	4ft × 1½ft	4–9	Pale pink with green throat (M)	Mid-green, lanceolate to oval	As above
fistulosa	3–4ft × 1½ft	3–9	Dull lilac with pale pink bracts (M–L)	Dull grayish green, ovate, softly hairy	Wild beebalm, tolerates drier conditions
f. 'Claire Grace'	3–4ft × 1½ft	3–9	Soft lavender (M)	Ovate	Mildew resistant
'Gardenview Scarlet'	2–3ft × 1½ft	4–9	Scarlet, purple-tinged bracts, large (M)	Dark green, aromatic	Moderately mildew resistant, RHS Award
'Jacob Cline'	3–4ft × 1½ft	4–9	Deep red with dark red bracts, large (M)	Dark green	Mildew resistant
'Mahogany'	3ft × 1½ft	4–9	Deep wine-red with brownish red bracts (M–L)	Mid-green, lanceolate to oval	
'Marshall's Delight'	2½–4ft × 1½ft	4–9	Clear pink (M–L)	Light green, shiny	Mildew resistant, RHS Award
'Mohawk'	4–5ft × 1½ft	4–9	Deep mauve (M–L)	Green, lanceolate to oval	Some mildew resistance
Petite Delight = 'Acpetdel'	12–15in × 12in	4–9	Rosy-lavender, large (M–L)	Dark green, glossy, crinkled	Very mildew resistant, dwarf
'Petite Wonder'	12–15in × 1ft	4–9	Clear pink (M–L)	Dark green, lanceolate to oval	As above
'Prärienacht' (syn. 'Prairie Night')	3–4ft × 1½ft	4–9	Rich violet-purple with green, red-tinged bracts (M–L)	Dull green, lanceolate to oval	Late to bloom, more tolerant of drier conditions
punctata	2–3ft × 1ft	4–9	Pale yellow, spotted with purplish brown, pink-lavender bracts (M–L)	Softly hairy, lanceolate to oblong	Spotted beebalm, self-sows, short-lived
'Raspberry Wine'	2½–4ft × 1½ft	4–9	Raspberry-wine red (M–L)	Large, dark green	Mildew resistant

Species and Cultivars	Height/ Spread	USDA Hardiness Zone	Flowers (bloom time)	Foliage	Comments
'Sagittarius'	3–4ft × 1½ft	4–9	Pale lilac with pale green bracts, tinged red (M)	Green, lanceolate to oval	As above
'Schneewittchen' (syn. 'Snow White')	2–4ft × 1½ft	4–9	Creamy white, small (M)	Dull green, lanceolate to oval	As above
'Scorpion'	2½–3½ft × 1½ft	4–9	Purplish red with green bracts (M)	Mid-green, lanceolate to oval	Very mildew resistant
'Snow Queen'	4ft × 1½ft	4–9	White (M)	Green, lanceolate to oval	
'Squaw'	4ft × 1½ft	4–9	Clear red with blackish red bracts (M)	Bright green, long upper leaves, red veins	Mildew resistant, long-blooming, RHS Award
'Vintage Wine'	2–3ft × 1½ft	4–9	Reddish purple (M)	Green, lanceolate to oval	
'Violet Queen'	2–4ft × 1½ft	4–9	Deep violet-purple, brown calyces (M)	Grayish green, fuzzy	Mildew resistant, similar to *M.* 'Blaustrumpf', RHS Award

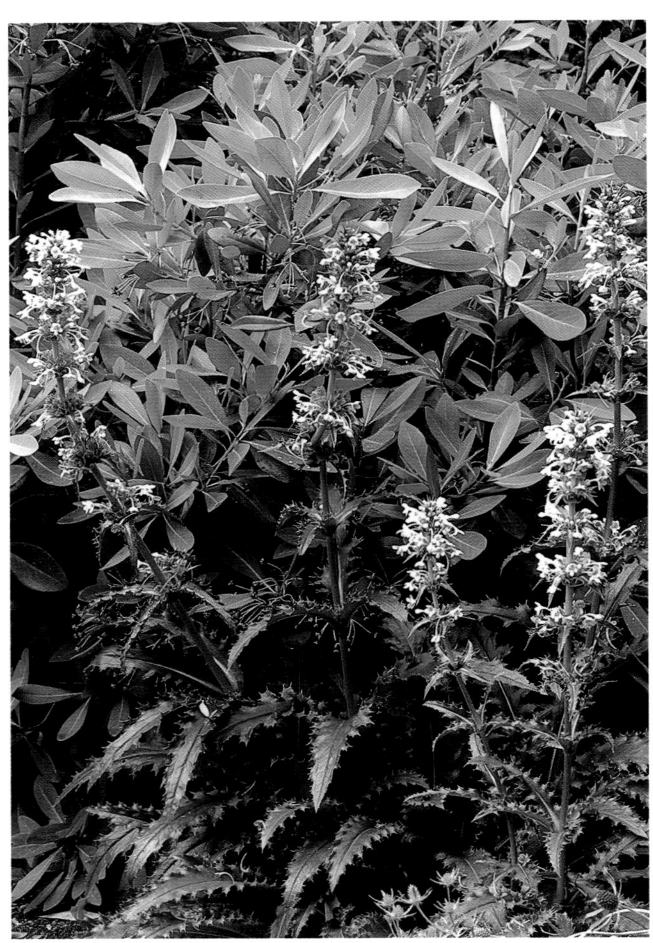

Morina longifolia.

MORINA Morinaceae

This is a wonderful semi-evergreen plant but very short-lived in the perennial border. Competition is its weak suit. Try to grow it in full sun with good drainage, or be prepared to replant. Leaves are a beautiful dark green and very elegant and formal-looking, like a refined thistle. The small white to pink flowers are borne on a tall spike and nestle in a smaller version of the base leaves. Almost always grown from seed; look for four-inch or one-gallon pots, and plant immediately. ~ *Bob Lilly*

Scientific Name: After French botanist Louis Pierre Morin (1635–1715).
Common Name: Whorlflower.
Origin: Himalayas.
Preferred Conditions: Humus-rich, poor to moderately fertile, well-drained, moisture-retentive, damp soil. Resents excessive winter wet but doesn't like to dry out. Shelter from cold and drying winds.
Light: Sun.
Management: This plant is tap-rooted and resents disturbance. Can be mistaken for thistle and weeded out, so label them clearly. Cut back in winter, but leave the basal leaves. Slugs are a menace in spring, so bait well.
Propagation: Seed as soon as ripe.

Pests and Diseases: Slugs and snails, root rot (especially in shade).
Companions: *Saxifraga stolonifera*, *Ajuga pyramidalis* 'Metallica Crispa', acaena, euphorbia, sedum.

Species and Cultivars	Height/ Spread	USDA Hardiness Zone	Flowers (bloom time)	Foliage	Comments
longifolia	2–3ft × 1ft	6–9	Waxy-white, fades to pale pink, then to dark pink (M)	Dark green, thistlelike softly prickly margins, aromatic when bruised	Whorlflower, evergreen crown, spiny seedheads

MUKDENIA Saxifragaceae

A handsome foliage plant, mukdenia is fairly low-growing and shallow-rooted; it disappears if allowed to dry out but so far has recovered for us with the first rain. The old name for the genus, *Aceriphyllum*, describes the maplelike leaves, which are palmately five- to nine-lobed and toothed; they emerge reddish, later turning a leathery dull green, and stand on six- to ten-inch petioles. Starry white flowers arranged in cymes appear in May and add to the plant's charm. Although mukdenia is rhizomatous, it is certainly not an aggressive spreader. This is a great pot plant if given adequate moisture; its leaves flow out from the center. ~ *Ann Bucher*

Scientific Name: After Mukden, the ancestral capital of the Manchu Dynasty and the old capital of Manchuria (now Shenyang).
Common Name: Mukdenia.
Origin: China, Korea.
Preferred Conditions: Leafy, moist, well-drained, cool, damp soil.

Mukdenia rossii.

Light: Part shade.

Management: Top-dress with leaf mold or other organic material during the winter. Clean up when leaves are shed.

Propagation: Seed in autumn; divide in spring.

Pests and Diseases: Snails, slugs on new growth. Like most members of the saxifrage family, this plant is a food host to adult root weevils. The grubs can damage the roots over winter, but the woody rhizomes can recover.

Companions: Helleborus, primula, smaller ferns; nice at the base of a rock wall.

Species and Cultivars	Height/ Spread	USDA Hardiness Zone	Flowers (bloom time)	Foliage	Comments
rossii	6–10in × 10in	7–9	Small white clusters (E)	Mid-green, bronze-tinted, deeply lobed, maplelike, turns bright orange in fall	Clump-forming
r. 'Crimson Fans'	6–10in × 10in	7–9	As above	Red to reddish bronze tinge all summer	As above

MYOSOTIS Boraginaceae

The flowers of *M. sylvatica* are a beautiful summer-sky blue with a bit of yellow in the middle. The drawbacks to the plant we most associate with the name forget-me-not? Its tiny, hairy leaves, and its freely self-sowing habit (forget-it-not). This is a plant that gardeners love or hate. I am in the first category, and while I do not grow as much of it as I did in my youth, I still allow some in my spring garden. It is a good companion to early narcissus and (if spring is cool) tulips. My personal management technique is to rip every bit of it out at the end of the flowering time. Since each flowering stem blooms from bottom to top, it will already have self-sown, and it will be back next year, if not before. The other colored forms are not nearly as enduring and seldom reseed: if you like the sweet little white-flowered form, you'll have to replant it every other year. Myosotis has childhood associations with the May basket as does the old bluebell, *Hyacinthoides hispanica*. Bring back the May basket, grow these flowers! ~ *Carrie Becker*

Scientific Name: From the Greek *mus* ("mouse") and *otos* ("ear"), a reference to the leaves.

Common Name: Forget-me-not.

Origin: Europe, North America, northern Asia.

Preferred Conditions: Moist, humusy, cool, and well-drained soil.

Light: Part shade to sun.

Management: Remove plants in late spring as soon as they have finished flowering, before they become prey to mildew, or cut back to the ground.

Propagation: Seed or division; seed is the preferred method.

Pests and Diseases: Snails, slugs, rust, mildew.

Myosotis alpestris 'Gold 'n' Sapphires'.

Companions: Spring-flowering bulbs, early irises, viola, dicentra, *Meconopsis cambrica*, *Galium odoratum*, erysimum; the white form pairs very nicely with *Viola* 'Bowles' Black'; try *Myosotis alpestris* 'Gold 'n' Sapphires' with tradescantias or centaureas with the same combination of blue flowers and golden leaves.

Notes: *Myosotis sylvatica* is really an annual or, generously, a biennial, but it has inhabited most perennial gardens and borders we have known.

Species and Cultivars	Height/ Spread	USDA Hardiness Zone	Flowers (bloom time)	Foliage	Comments
alpestris 'Gold 'n' Sapphires'	6–8in × 6in	4–9	Blue (E–M)	Variegated gold and green in spring with dark green ribs	Dense tufts, does not do well in prolonged drought
sylvatica	6–12in × 10in	4–9	Light blue with yellow eye (E–M)	Gray-green to dark green, hairy, sprawling stems	Behaves like a biennial, self-sows
s. 'Victoria Blue'	6–8in × 6in	4–9	Deeper blue with yellow eye (E–M)	Gray-green to dark green, hairy	Dwarf, compact, grow as an annual
s. 'Victoria Rose'	6–8in × 6in	4–9	Rose-pink (E–M)	As above	As above
s. 'White'	6–8in × 6in	4–9	White (E–M)	As above	As above

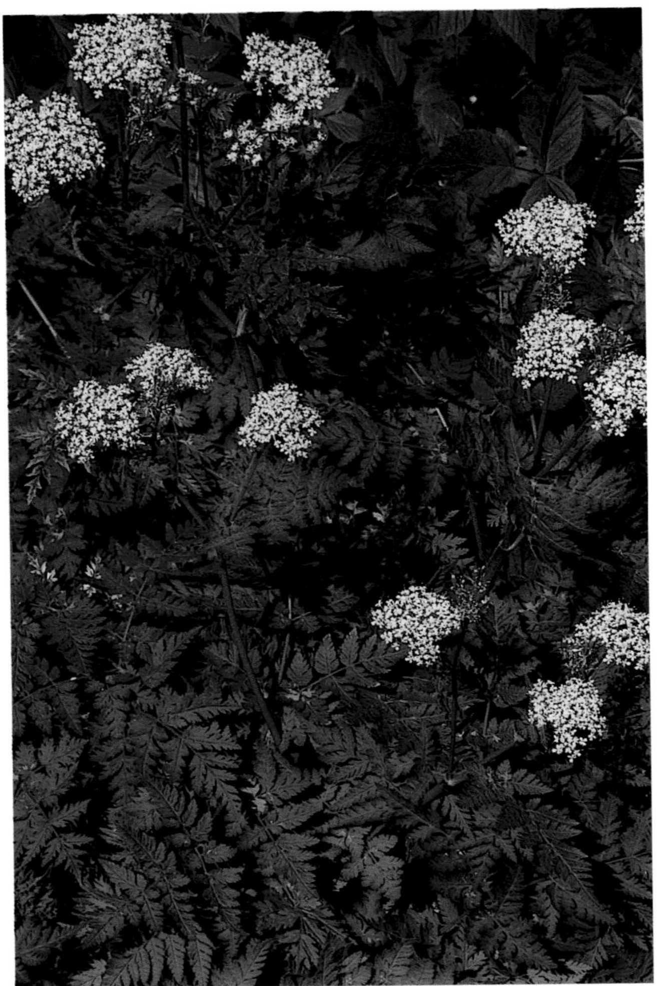

Myrrhis odorata.

MYRRHIS Apiaceae

Sweet Cicely is a bold plant with very heavily divided foliage and striking seeds. Lola Zimmerman, who began the Fall City Herbfarm, introduced me to this plant, and I have had it in the garden since the early 1970s. Thick fleshy roots give rise to bright green spring foliage and clusters of edible white flowers; try the small fresh flower heads (about the size of a quarter) in salads. Flowers are followed by apple-green seeds, which are likewise tasty when young. When ripe, the seeds stand straight up—hard, almost woody, and almost black. ~ *Bob Lilly*

Scientific Name: Thought to be named after *Commiphora myrrha*, an African and Arabian tree. Both are sometimes referred to as myrrh.

Common Name: Sweet Cicely.

Origin: Europe.

Preferred Conditions: Moderately fertile, moist, well-drained, humus-rich soil.

Light: Sun to part shade. Best in a shady location with a bit of spring sun, like in a corner under an apple tree.

Management: Doesn't like being disturbed (tap-rooted). If you must move it, dig it up and cut all the foliage down and let it regrow. This method can also be used on mature plants for a bit of size control and to refresh in midseason. Cut back to the ground after bloom, water well, and a fresh new crop of leaves will appear. A perfect plant to hold with pea sticks; plants grow so fast in spring, they cover the support quickly. Deadhead to prevent self-seeding.

Propagation: Divide in spring or fall, but division is difficult as the soil usually falls off the roots. It's best (and usually) grown from seed, in the fall; seeds need a winter on the ground to germinate.

Pests and Diseases: Not many, a bit of slug damage in spring.

Companions: Hosta, doronicum, polygonatum, smilacina.

Species and Cultivars	Height/ Spread	USDA Hardiness Zone	Flowers (bloom time)	Foliage	Comments
odorata	3ft × 3ft+	4–9	Creamy-white, small, star-shaped, in compound umbels (E–M)	Bright green, deeply cut, oblong-lanceolate, pinnate leaflets, on thick, hairy, hollow stems	Aromatic (anise), shiny, blackish seed in fall, spreads by ropy roots

NECTAROSCORDUM Alliaceae

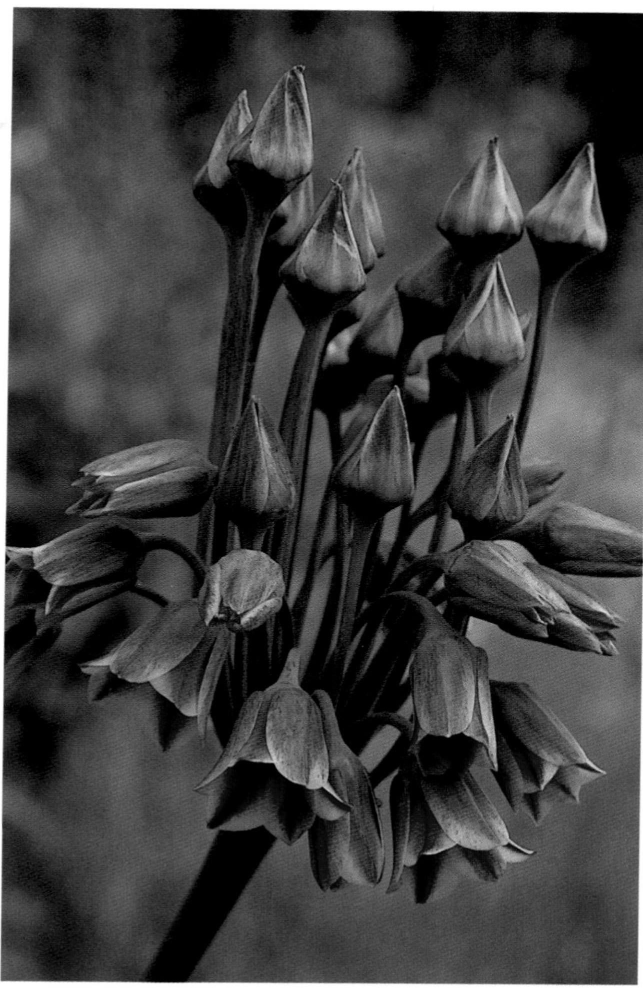

Nectaroscordum siculum.

Nectaroscordum siculum, as we now know this plant, was much easier to pronounce when it was included in the genus *Allium*. The large, bell-shaped blossoms are borne on tall stems, dangling gracefully in loose umbels. Occasionally, the stems will weaken and even start to fall over, developing a bend midway, with the flower still rising toward the sun. They do look kind of interesting leaning at these odd angles. The long-lasting cream-colored blossoms are very attractive and interesting, and they dry into decorative seedheads, making them a great addition to dried floral arrangements; but they're also great left standing in the garden. The leaves are silvery-blue, three-sided and sharply edged, twisting as they ascend. ~ *Susan Carter*

Scientific Name: From the Greek *nektar* ("nectar") and *skorodon* ("garlic").
Common Name: Nectaroscordum.
Origin: France, Italy, Sicily, Turkey.
Preferred Conditions: Well-drained, moderately fertile, light, and somewhat dry.
Light: Sun to part shade.
Management: Remove foliage when thoroughly cured. Plants prefer to be dry in their dormancy.
Propagation: Division of offsets—remove in summer and plant in fall, when planting other bulbs.
Pests and Diseases: Slugs.
Companions: Astilbe, hemerocallis, miscanthus (smaller forms), rodgersia, *Paeonia suffruticosa*, pimpinella.
Notes: This is a very long-lived bulb, and it perennializes easily here in the heavy clay of the Pacific Northwest.

Species and Cultivars	Height/ Spread	USDA Hardiness Zone	Flowers (bloom time)	Foliage	Comments
siculum (syn. *Allium siculum*)	3–4ft × 12–18in	6–10	Creamy green, lilac-pink, flushed pink markings inside, bell-shaped, nodding, in umbels (E)	Green, straplike, basal	Seedpods become erect as soon as flowers are pollinated
s. subsp. bulgaricum (syn. *Allium bulgaricum*)	3–4ft × 12–18in	6–10	Creamy green, off-white, flushed inside green and purple (E)	As above	As above

Nepeta racemosa 'Walker's Low'.

NEPETA Lamiaceae

Both catmint and catnip are in the genus *Nepeta*; some cats respond well to catmint and will crush and roll your *N. racemosa* 'Walker's Low' or *N.* 'Six Hills Giant', but they usually do not devour them. These plants need a bit more control than most summer perennials, whether by staking, pinching, or pea sticks. Alternatively, you can site them on a border edge or at the top of a wall, where a graceful flop will look good. Nepetas knit the garden or border together. All are good bee plants, and they also attract butterflies. ~ *Bob Lilly*

Scientific Name: Possibly from nepete, a similar plant of Etruscan origin.
Common Name: Catmint, catnip.
Origin: Europe, Kashmir, Asia, North Africa, Japan.
Preferred Conditions: Well-drained, average soil. *Nepeta govaniana* and *N. subsessilis* prefer moist, cool soils; *N. sibirica* likes fairly dry conditions.
Light: Sun to part shade.
Management: Provide support. In a good season most plants tend to sprawl, and in a heavy rain they will flop over. Pinching in midspring will help them stay denser, but you do lose some of the gracefulness of the plant. Cut back twice during the flowering season, to about two to four inches, to keep them compact and encourage continued bloom (especially on *N.* 'Six Hills Giant'); plants need to be grown in full sun and be several years old for this method to be really effective, and unfortunately, you need to attack them in full bloom. Water well (and treat the bee stings with meat tenderizer).
Propagation: Cuttings; division in spring; seed.
Pests and Diseases: Slugs, some cutworms.
Companions: Roses, paeonia, monarda, salvia, most grasses, santolina, echinacea, geranium, *Euphorbia wallichii*, *Allium sphaerocephalon*.

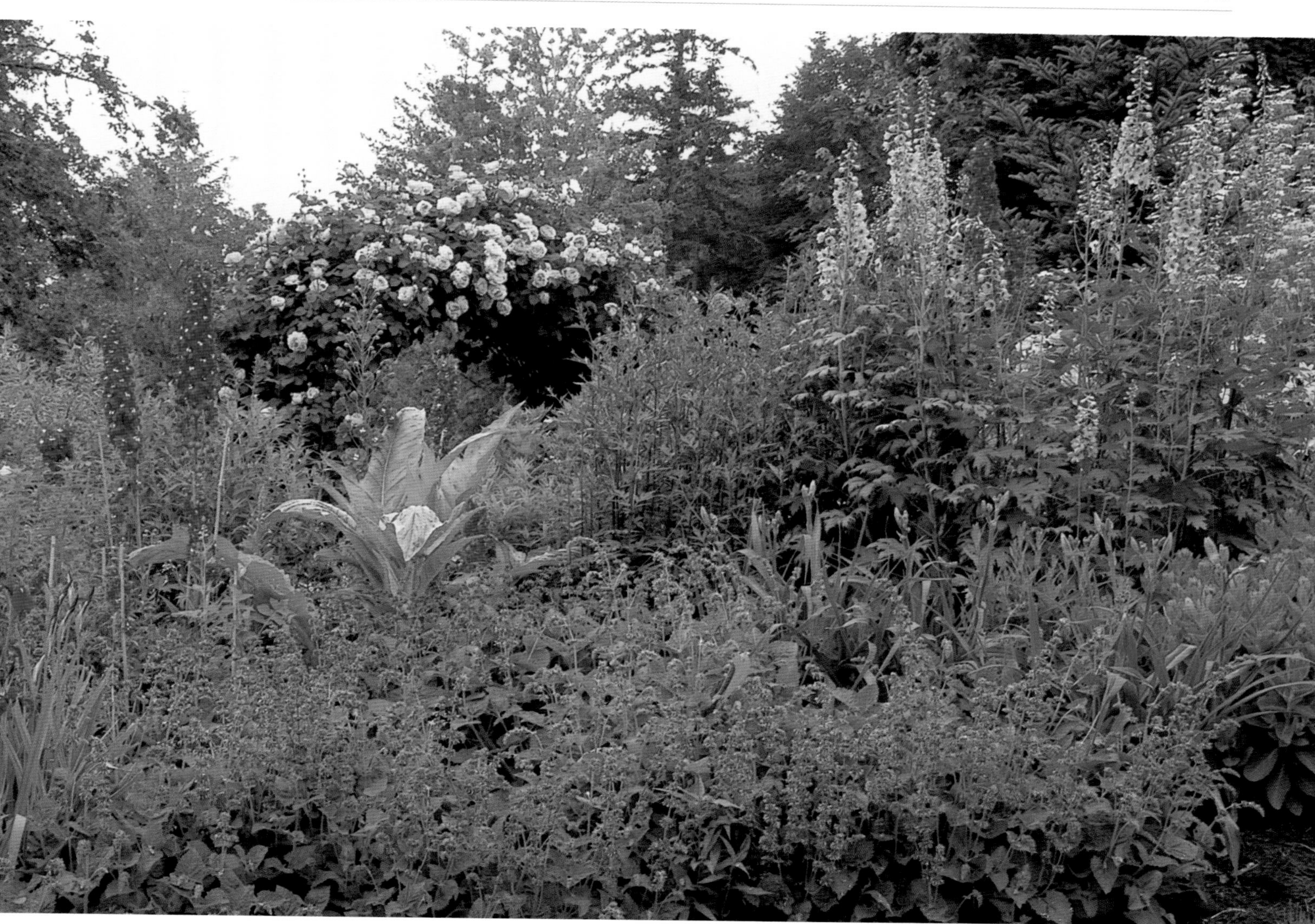

Nepeta sibirica, with well-staked delphiniums, a well-supported shrub rose, and *Cynara cardunculus* for a bit of bold foliage.

Species and Cultivars	Height/ Spread	USDA Hardiness Zone	Flowers (bloom time)	Foliage	Comments
cataria	2–3ft × 1½ft	3–8	White to violet-mauve with purple spots (M–L)	Gray-green, grayish beneath, hairy, ovate to cordate, aromatic	Catnip, erect, this one is most attractive to cats
c. 'Citriodora'	3ft × 1½ft	3–8	Dark lavender (E–L)	Grayish green, aromatic (lemon)	Erect
'Dropmore'	1ft × 1½ft	5–9	Lavender-blue, large (M–L)	Soft gray-green, toothed, aromatic	Upright, clump-forming
×faassenii	1–2ft × 1½ft	5–9	Pale lavender-blue with dark purple spots (E–L)	Gray-green, oval-lanceolate, scalloped and wrinkled, aromatic	Clump-forming, long-blooming, erect, RHS Award

Species and Cultivars	Height/ Spread	USDA Hardiness Zone	Flowers (bloom time)	Foliage	Comments
×f. 'Blue Wonder'	12–15in × 18in	5–9	Deep lavender-blue (E–M)	Gray-green, small, finely cut, aromatic	Compact, long-blooming
govaniana	2–3ft × 2ft	5–9	Pale yellow, large (M–L)	Gray-green, ovate-oblong to elliptic, pointed, scalloped, hairy	Clump-forming, okay in part shade
grandiflora 'Dawn to Dusk'	2–3ft × 2ft	5–9	Soft rose-pink with deep pink calyces	Gray-green, aromatic	Nice color change
g. 'Pool Bank'	2½–3ft × 2ft	5–9	Rich blue with purple-blue bracts (M)	Olive-green, aromatic	
nervosa	1–2ft × 1ft	5–9	Purplish blue, rarely yellow or white (M–L)	Gray-green, narrow, lanceolate, slightly toothed, veined, hairy	Bushy, erect
'Porzellan'	9–18in × 18in	5–9	Light lavender-blue (E–M)	Gray-green, narrow	
racemosa (syn. reichenbachiana, mussinii)	1ft × 1ft	4–8	Deep lavender-blue (M)	Gray-green, scalloped, hairy, aromatic	Smaller scale, RHS Award
r. 'Walker's Low'	10–18in × 18in	5–9	Lavender-blue (E–L)	Gray-green, veined, aromatic	Good edger
sibirica (syn. macrantha)	2–3ft × 1–1½ft	3–9	Blue (M)	Dark green, lanceolate-oblong, toothed, hairy, aromatic	Erect, intolerant of wet soil
s. 'Souvenir d'André Chaudron' (syn. 'Blue Beauty')	1½–3ft × 1½ft+	3–9	Deep lavender-blue, large, tubular (M)	Gray-green, oval-lanceolate, serrated, smooth, aromatic	Clump-forming and spreading, needs staking
'Six Hills Giant'	2–3ft × 2ft+	3–9	Lavender-blue in large sprays (M–L)	Gray-green, narrow, ovate, toothed, hairy, aromatic	Vigorous, more tolerant of damp soil, wide-spreading
subsessilis	1½–2ft × 1ft	3–9	Lavender-blue, large, tubular (M–L)	Dark grayish green, ovate, serrated, hairless, glossy, aromatic	Chinese catmint, clump-forming
tuberosa	2ft × 1½ft	7–8	Large violet to purple spikes with white bracts tinged purple (M–L)	Whitish gray, hairy, ovate-lanceolate, on silvery-white stems	Erect, tender, short-lived

Oenanthe javanica 'Flamingo'.

OENANTHE Apiaceae

The green form of water parsley is grown as a leafy vegetable in some parts of the world. *Oenanthe javanica* 'Flamingo' is a dense, semi-evergreen, ground-covering perennial with pink, green, and cream variegated, finely divided foliage. The flowers are small, star-shaped, and white. I don't have a lot to say about this plant except watch out—it's fast-spreading and roots wherever it touches the ground. Its hardiness is in question, but usually the spider mites get to it first. A rampant but tender plant, good in pots, as a curiosity. ~ *Susan Carter*

Scientific Name: From the Greek name for a plant smelling of wine (*oinos*).
Common Name: Water parsley (usually in reference to the green form).
Origin: Japan, Australia, Malaysia, India.
Preferred Conditions: Dense, heavy, moderately fertile, moist to wet (even boggy) soil. Shelter from cold, drying winds.
Light: Sun to part shade.
Management: If *O. javanica* 'Flamingo' reverts, remove green parts immediately! Don't let it dry out. Cut back in autumn as growth dies back to encourage new basal growth. Try to control with a barrier; it spreads on the surface. Do not plant the nonvariegated forms.
Propagation: Division in spring; stem cuttings in spring.
Pests and Diseases: Spider mites, rust, snails, slugs, aphids.
Companions: Nepeta, iris, primula.
Notes: Short-lived for us, but that may be the slugs.

Species and Cultivars	Height/ Spread	USDA Hardiness Zone	Flowers (bloom time)	Foliage	Comments
javanica 'Flamingo'	6–12in × 12in	8–11	White umbels (M)	Tri-colored, green, pink, and white, lacy	Fast-spreading

Oenothera speciosa 'Woodside White'.

OENOTHERA Onagraceae

Evening primroses bloom over a long period throughout the summer, with the individual blossoms lasting only one day. The fragrant, filmy, cup-shaped flowers of yellow, tangerine, white, pink, or deep rose fade in bright sun; the leaves are usually dark green and narrowly lanceolate with some having bronze tints and others red spots. Contrary to the common name, not all species flower at night; the sundrops (*O. fruticosa*, *O. macrocarpa*, *O. rosea*, and *O. speciosa*) open in the daytime. Some are short-lived and need to be replaced often, but most produce enough seed to keep on going. Whether by self-sowing or root, some have an invasive nature. Plants may need staking if grown in rich soil. So, with all these warnings one might well wonder, should I grow oenothera? I think it's a charming plant and definitely worth the extra effort. ~ *Susan Carter*

Scientific Name: From the Greek *onos* ("donkey") and *thera* ("hunt," possibly "to imbibe")—this is confusing and leads to odd theories.
Common Name: Evening primrose, sundrops.
Origin: North America, Mexico, South America.
Preferred Conditions: Poor to moderately fertile, well-drained to even rocky soil. *Oenothera fruticosa* prefers a more fertile soil. Tolerates drought. Will not tolerate wet feet.
Light: Sun.
Management: Deadhead aggressively to prevent self-sowing; seedpods are held close to the stems. *Oenothera speciosa* sends out runners in all directions; pull these out to control its spread. Cut back tall forms after flowering to base. Cut all back to the ground in fall.
Propagation: Seed; cutting; division in spring.
Pests and Diseases: Root rot, downy and powdery mildew, rust.
Companions: Nepeta, baptisia, grasses, salvia, allium, hardy fuchsias.

Notes: The top of the stigma is cross-shaped. Fragrance, where prominent, is noted in the chart.

Species and Cultivars	Height/ Spread	USDA Hardiness Zone	Flowers (bloom time)	Foliage	Comments
fruticosa (syn. linearis)	1–3ft × 1ft	4–9	Deep yellow, 4-petaled, saucer- to cup-shaped, red in bud, erect, fragrant (E–M)	Mid-green, bronze tints, turns red in fall, hairy, lanceolate to ovate, toothed	Sundrops, opens in daytime, red-tinged stems
f. 'Fyrverkeri' (syn. 'Fireworks')	1½ft × 1ft	4–9	Deep yellow clusters, open from red buds, fragrant (E–M)	Mid-green with purple-bronze tints	Erect, opens in daytime, RHS Award
f. subsp. glauca (syn. tetragona)	1½–2ft × 1ft	4–9	Bright yellow, reddish buds, fragrant (M)	Dark green, red-tinted when young, lanceolate, hairy	Opens in daytime, reddish stems, RHS Award
f. subsp. glauca 'Erica Robin'	1–2ft × 1ft	4–9	Bright yellow, small clusters (M)	New leaves bright yellow, suffused pink	Opens in daytime
f. subsp. glauca 'Sonnenwende'	1½–2ft × 1ft	4–9	Bright yellow, large (M)	Deep green, red-tinged	Long-blooming, opens in daytime
laciniata (syn. mexicana)	3ft × 2ft	3–7	Yellow flushed or edged in red, cup-shaped (M)	Mid-green, hairy, linear-lanceolate, toothed	Opens in evening
macrocarpa (syn. missouriensis)	6–9in × 8in	4–9	Bright golden yellow, cup-shaped, fragrant (E–L)	Dark green, trailing, hairy, lanceolate-ovate, toothed, white midribs	Vigorous, long-blooming, opens in daytime, red stems, good seedpods
odorata	2–3ft × 2ft	5–9	Pale yellow aging to pinkish red, red buds, some fragrance (M)	Glaucous, narrow, crinkled margins	Erect, opens in evening, red-tinted stems
rosea	6–20in × 12in+	5–9	Rose-pink (E–M)	Deep green, oblong-ovate, toothed, glossy	Erect, sprawling, opens in daytime
speciosa	1–2ft × 1ft+	5–9	White aging to pink, yellow center, cup-shaped (M–L)	Mid-green, oblong to lanceolate, toothed, red spots	Mexican evening primrose, invasive, open day and night
s. 'Rosea' (syn. berlandieri)	10–12in × 12in	5–8	Deep rose-pink (M–L)	Grayish green, oblong to lanceolate, toothed, red spots	Invasive, open day and night
s. 'Siskiyou'	8–12in × 1ft	5–9	Pale rose-pink, cup-shaped (M)	Green, oblong to lanceolate, red spots	Short-lived, open day and night
s. 'Woodside White'	1ft × 1ft	5–10	Creamy-white, chartreuse eye (M)	Light green	As above
versicolor 'Sunset Boulevard'	15in × 12in	8–10	Pale tangerine aging to red (M)	Dark green, lanceolate	Erect, very short-lived, opens in daytime, arching maroon stems need staking

Omphalodes cappadocica 'Starry Eyes'.

OMPHALODES Boraginaceae

Omphalodes are spring bloomers, up with the early bulbs. All are great groundcovers under deciduous shrubs; especially weed-excluding is *O. verna*—not exciting out of flower, but pretty enough leaves as a carpet under shrubs, trees, and later perennials. It's also the first to bloom, probably as much as a month before *O. cappadocica*. The flowers resemble their cousins the forget-me-nots (same family), but whereas forget-me-nots have a tendency to be rather weedy and short-lived, omphalodes have better habits, better flowers, and no nuisance factor.

Omphalodes cappadocica extends the season. A taller plant, it spreads slowly but remains a clump, and has some lovely selections: 'Lilac Mist', with pale lavender flowers, is attractive with *Primula vulgaris* 'Lilacina Plena' and silver-spotted pulmonaria foliage; 'Starry Eyes', which came from Washfield Nursery (Elizabeth Strangman) in Kent, is truly a star—deep blue flowers with thin white edges. ~ *Carrie Becker*

Scientific Name: From the Greek *omphalos* ("navel"), referring to a navel-like impression in the seeds.

Common Name: Blue-eyed Mary, navelwort.

Origin: Turkey, southeastern Europe, Asia Minor, western Caucasus.

Preferred Conditions: Moderately fertile, cool, moisture-retentive, humus-rich soil. Average water needs. Tolerates dry shade once established.

Light: Part shade. *Omphalodes cappadocica* tolerates sun with enough moisture and can have deep shade after blooming time, if necessary; *O. verna* prefers shade.

Planting: Cultivate young plants grown from seed in pots and then set them out in the following spring.

Management: Prefers not to be disturbed. Top-dress with mulch or manure. Watch for overcrowding: too much competition from overgrowing plants at ground level can make *O. cappadocica* go away. Cut back when foliage begins to deteriorate in fall.

Propagation: Seed; division in late winter or spring.

Pests and Diseases: Snails, slugs, especially on new growth.

Companions: Spring bulbs, helleborus (especially *O. verna* 'Alba'), primula, viola, brunnera, hosta, ferns, pulmonaria, dicentra.

Notes: This is a difficult plant to divide, so availability can be limited. Tissue-cultured *O. cappadocica* 'Starry Eyes' has a tendency to revert to the type. Grow the annual *O. linifolia* at least once and look at the seed! In the chart, the symbol ∞ = infinite spread.

Species and Cultivars	Height/ Spread	USDA Hardiness Zone	Flowers (bloom time)	Foliage	Comments
cappadocica	6in × 12in+	5–9	Clear blue with white throat (E)	Mid-green, cordate, veined, hairy	Navelwort, erect, evergreen, rhizomatous, RHS Award

Species and Cultivars	Height/ Spread	USDA Hardiness Zone	Flowers (bloom time)	Foliage	Comments
c. 'Alba'	6in × 12in+	5–9	White (E)	As above	As above
c. 'Lilac Mist'	8–10in × 12in	5–9	Pale lilac with white throat (E)	Green, oval, glossy	Bushy, semi-evergreen
c. 'Starry Eyes'	8–10in × 12in	3–9	Deep blue with white center, edges white (E)	Green, oval, slightly crinkled	As above
verna	6–8in × ∞	6–9	Bright blue with white throat (E)	Mid-green, cordate to ovate, hairy	Blue-eyed Mary, stoloniferous
v. 'Alba'	6–8in × ∞	6–9	White (E)	Pale green	White-eyed Mary, stoloniferous

OPHIOPOGON Convallariaceae

Commonly known as mondo grass, ophiopogon is not a true grass but a member of the lily of the valley family. Plants of this genus of evergreen perennials form small tufts of long, thin leaves and spread on short rhizomes; mass plantings are often used as groundcovers or border edging. The swollen roots are fleshy and whitish; they are widely used in China in a variety of herbal remedies. Besides the wonderful black-leafed *O. planiscapus* 'Nigrescens', there are some variegated and striped forms. Depending on the variety, the slender leaves grow from one to twelve inches long, recurving back toward the ground. In summer, small pale lilac flowers are produced on nodding stems, followed by pea-sized blue-black or green berries. ~ *Susan Carter*

Ophiopogon planiscapus 'Nigrescens'.

Scientific Name: From the Greek *ophis* ("snake") and *pogon* ("beard"); how this applies to ophiopogon is obscure.
Common Name: Mondo grass.
Origin: Japan, China, Korea.
Preferred Conditions: Slightly acidic, well-drained, humus-rich, and moisture-retentive soil with average water needs.
Light: Sun to part shade.
Management: Lightly top-dress annually with manure or compost. Used as a groundcover, they can get congested and might need to be divided. Tidy up by removing old flower spikes and dead leaves (remove only the dead leaves—this is an evergreen plant). Can scorch in a sudden hot spell during the summer. Watch for slugs in the early spring and later, oddly, on the fruits, too.
Propagation: Division or seed in spring; seed of *O. planiscapus* 'Nigrescens' will yield green plants twenty-five percent of the time.
Pests and Diseases: Snails, slugs, leaf spot.
Companions: *Lamium maculatum* 'Aureum', *L. m.* 'White Nancy', hosta, *Lysimachia nummularia* 'Aurea', *Ranunculus ficaria*, *Acorus gramineus*, dwarf shrubs and conifers, helleborus.
Notes: An invaluable foil for texture and color on the edge of the perennial border, so we included it even though it is not technically an herbaceous perennial. *Ophiopogon planiscapus* and its selection 'Nigrescens' will spread to make very large colonies. The dwarf forms would make a great grass substitute for bonsai.

Species and Cultivars	Height/ Spread	USDA Hardiness Zone	Flowers (bloom time)	Foliage	Comments
japonicus	12in × 12in	6–10	White, tinged lavender (M)	Dark green, narrow, straplike, curving	Pea-sized blue-black berries
j. 'Compactus'	2in × 4in	6–10	White, tinged lavender, rarely flowers (M)	As above	
j. 'Gyoku Ryu'	2–3in × 4in	6–10	Lavender (M)	Dark green, grasslike	Dwarf
j. 'Minor'	2in × 2in	6–10	White, tinged lavender, rarely flowers (M)	Dark green, narrow, straplike, curving	Really dwarf
j. 'Shiroshima Ryu'	6in × 6in	6–10	White-lavender (M)	Green with vertical white stripes	Vigorous
j. 'Silver Mist'	12in × 8in	6–10	White, tinged lavender, rarely flowers (M)	Dark green with narrow cream margins	Very showy
j. 'Super Dwarf'	2in × 2in	6–10	White-lilac (M)	Green, tiny, narrow	Very dwarf
j. 'Torafu'	6in × 6in	6–10	As above	Narrow, green with horizontal yellow band	Showy
planiscapus	8–10in × 12in	6–10	Pale purplish white (M)	Dark green, straplike, curving	Blue berries
p. 'Nigrescens' (syn. 'Arabicus')	6–12in × 12in+	6–10	Pink-flushed (M)	Black, straplike, emerge green	May turn green in shade, black berries

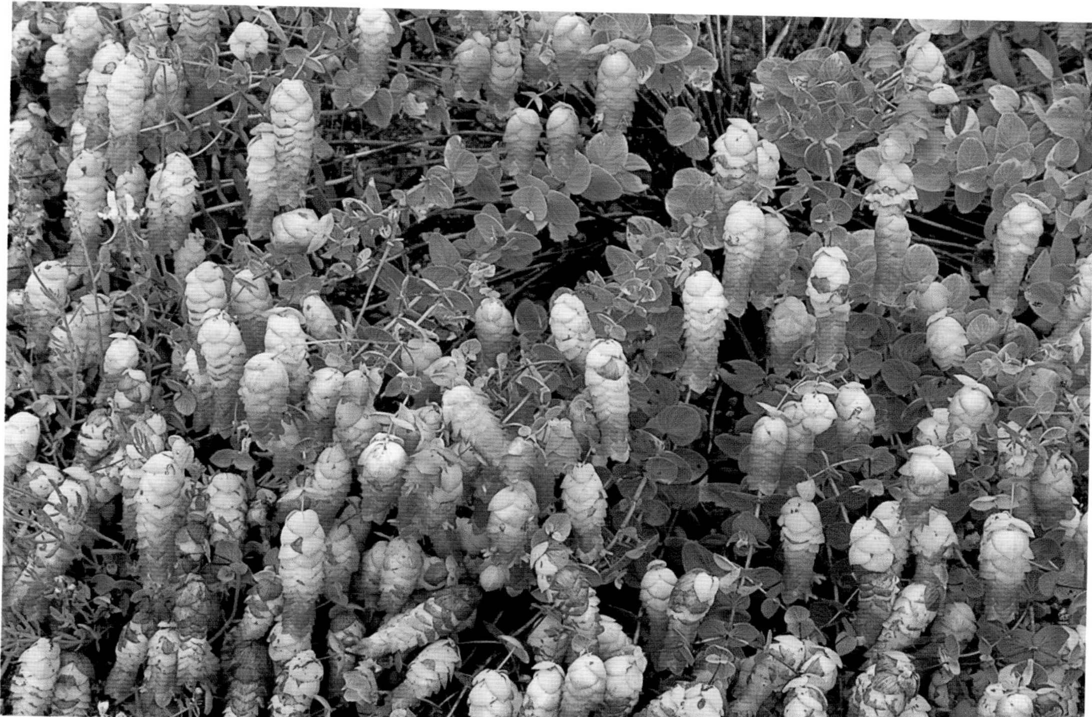

Origanum 'Barbara Tingey'.

ORIGANUM Lamiaceae

The genus *Origanum* includes oregano and marjoram. Most of us are familiar with the fine culinary properties of *O. vulgare*. Pondering them leads to salivation. Some of the ornamentals make good eatin' too, but I'd rather feast my eyes. Plants range in sizes from four inches to two and a half feet, so surely there is a plant that is an appropriate size for your garden.

The first ornamental form I remember wanting badly was *O.* 'Kent Beauty'. A friend had positioned this little plant above a cement retaining wall, where its many charms could be closely observed. The "flowers" consist of deep rose bracts with tinges of green that are stacked, hoplike, and about two inches long. Out of each bract protrudes a small pinky lavender flower of the mint persuasion, and all are perfectly accompanied by rounded gray-green leaves. Others (e.g., *O.* 'Barbara Tingey') are similar in overall appearance, and all the variations are worth seeking out and growing. Among the taller oreganos, *O. laevigatum* and its offspring 'Herrenhausen' and 'Hopleys' can be enjoyed in the mixed border, where they seed about aggressively; they are large enough to stand up to bigger companions and have lovely flowers in colored bracts that remain interesting long after the plants have bloomed. Smaller oreganos do not tolerate any competition; they are best thought of as rock garden or herb garden plants. The shorter forms grown for foliage color and the aromatic leaves, not flowers, make pretty edging plants for the border. ~ *Carrie Becker*

Scientific Name: From the classical Greek name (*origanon*) for these aromatic herbs.
Common Name: Pot marjoram (*O. onites*), oregano.
Origin: Turkey, Europe to Central Asia, Mediterranean.
Preferred Conditions: Moderately fertile, well-drained, alkaline, with average water needs. Drought tolerant when established, but not in pots.
Light: Sun.

Management: Keep *O. laevigatum* cultivars under control with a bit of early cutting back, for flower arrangements. Laevigatums can flop in a heavy summer rain, so either stake them (a pointless exercise in bad aesthetics), or plant with companions to hold them up. Do not let smaller oreganos be smothered and killed by larger plants; cut off any flowers that detract from the foliage (especially with *O. vulgare* 'Aureum'). Cut the tall forms to the crown in fall; shear the short ones lightly in spring or immediately after bloom, and only once. Remove flowering stems of taller forms to the basal growth when they are no longer attractive.

Propagation: Seed; division in spring; basal cuttings.

Pests and Diseases: Root and stem rot, aphids, spider mites.

Companions: Sedum, lavender and other gray-foliage plants, carex, geranium, short grasses, knautia, allium, *Euphorbia rigida*, *E. myrsinites*, *Erigeron karvinskianus*.

Notes: Attracts bees and butterflies. *Origanum laevigatum* cultivars do not come true from seed. All gold-foliage forms may scorch in full sun or turn green as season progresses.

Species and Cultivars	Height/ Spread	USDA Hardiness Zone	Flowers (bloom time)	Foliage	Comments
'Barbara Tingey'	4in × 8in	7–9	Pink with green bracts, aging to deep purple-pink, nodding whorls (M–L)	Bluish green, purple reverse, hairy, aromatic	Dense, clump-forming, semi-evergreen
calcaratum (syn. tournefortii)	12in × 12in	8–9	Pink with conspicuous bracts, large (M–L)	Gray-green, round to heart-shaped, fuzzy, aromatic	Less hardy, requires sharp drainage, woody base
×hybridinum (syn. pulchellum)	10–18in × 12in	5–9	Pink with pink bracts (M)	Gray-green, small, aromatic	Will flop some, good dried
'Kent Beauty'	6–8in × 10in+	5–8	Pale pink to mauve, deep rose bracts, tinged green, small, tubular, hoplike (M)	Gray-green, rounded-oval, veined, aromatic	Semi-evergreen, prostrate, pendulous habit
laevigatum	1½–2ft × 1½ft	5–9	Purplish pink, red-purple bracts (M–L)	Dark green, ovate to elliptic, hairy reverse, aromatic	Erect, wiry, red-purple stems, RHS Award
l. 'Herrenhausen'	1½–2ft × 1½ft	5–9	Dark pink, dark reddish violet bracts, dense whorls, large (M–L)	Purple-flushed, turning dark green, aromatic	Good cut fresh or dried, will flop, heavy flowering, RHS Award
l. 'Hopleys'	1½–2ft × 1½ft	5–9	Deep purplish pink flowers and bracts, hoplike (M–L)	Dark green, oval-round, smooth, aromatic	Red-purple stems, new shoots and winter growth are flushed purple
l. 'Silver Anniversary'	10in × 1½ft	5–9	Pink, dainty (M)	Creamy yellow and white, small, oval, aromatic	
libanoticum	1½ft × 1½ft	5–10	Rose-pink, pale green bracts, hoplike (M–L)	Green, roundish, aromatic	Woody base
majoricum 'White Anniversary'	2–4in × 6in	6–10	Lavender (M–L)	Gray-green with white edges, tiny, oval	
'Norton Gold'	18in × 12in	5–9	Pink (M)	Gold, rounded, aromatic	Short-lived
'Rosenkuppel'	1–1½ft × 1½ft	8–9	Dark pink, dark purple bracts (M–L)	Dark green, rounded, aromatic	Purple stems, will flop

Species and Cultivars	Height/ Spread	USDA Hardiness Zone	Flowers (bloom time)	Foliage	Comments
rotundifolium	4–8in × 8in	7–9	Pale pink, yellow-green bracts, small, whorls (M)	Gray-green, new growth tinged purple, glossy, round to cordate, aromatic	Woody base, short-lived, RHS Award
'Santa Cruz'	1–1½ft × 10in+	5–9	Dusty pink, hoplike, pale pink bracts (M)	Tints of pink, purple, and mauve aging to mid-green, aromatic	Woody base, bushy, flops badly
vulgare	1½–2½ft × 1½ft	5–9	Deep purple, pale pink, or white, purple tints, green bracts, tubular (M–L)	Dark green, rounded-ovate, hairy leaves and stems, aromatic	Oregano, bushy, vigorous, delicious, though some cultivars are even more so
v. 'Aureum'	1–1½ft × 1½ft	5–9	Pink, purple, or white (M–L)	Bright golden yellow especially in spring, rounded-ovate, aromatic	Golden oregano, bushy, not as vigorous as species, RHS Award
v. 'Aureum Crispum'	1–1½ft × 1½ft	5–9	Pink (M)	Golden, rounded-ovate, curly, aromatic	Spreads
v. 'Compactum'	6–8in × 8in	3–7	As above	Green, rounded-ovate, aromatic	Compact
v. 'Gold Tip' (syn. 'Variegatum')	6–12in × 10in	5–9	Mauve (M)	Green with bright yellow at tips, aromatic	Bushy
v. 'Thumble's Variety'	10–12in × 10in	5–9	White (M)	Golden, aromatic	As above

PAEONIA Paeoniaceae

All peonies are rewarding to grow. Handsome foliage, luscious color, amazing seed formations, a long life—all are attributes of these great plants. Most species are herbaceous, and among them they offer a wide variety of colors, shapes, and habits. For more details, I can do no better than recommend you read the descriptions written by Graham Stuart Thomas in his *Perennial Garden Plants* (1990): six pages of perfect peony prose. The largest group of peonies are the herbaceous garden selections and hybrids (see chart for a start), but mention must be made of the tree peonies: they are really shrubs, with a permanent woody structure (and so not included here), but they are as beautiful as their garden cousins.

Peonies are the queen of the herbaceous perennial garden, even to the point of some English gardens having peony borders. They are among the most expensive cut flowers and are also used in some homeopathic remedies. Herbaceous peony cultivars deserve all the care and attention you can give, especially when cutting or dividing. Beware of catalog descriptions and photographs for some of these blowsy beauties; the actual flower color may be a disappointment. It is best to see the peony in flower to judge the true color, and for the way in which the flower is held on its stalk: sometimes they droop down to the point of breaking the stem, especially when wet and heavy. Get a good one, and you will enjoy it for many years to come. ~ *Susan Buckles*

Scientific Name: From the Greek *paionia*, for Paion, physician to the gods.
Common Name: Peony.
Origin: Europe, northeastern Asia, Caucasus, Russia.

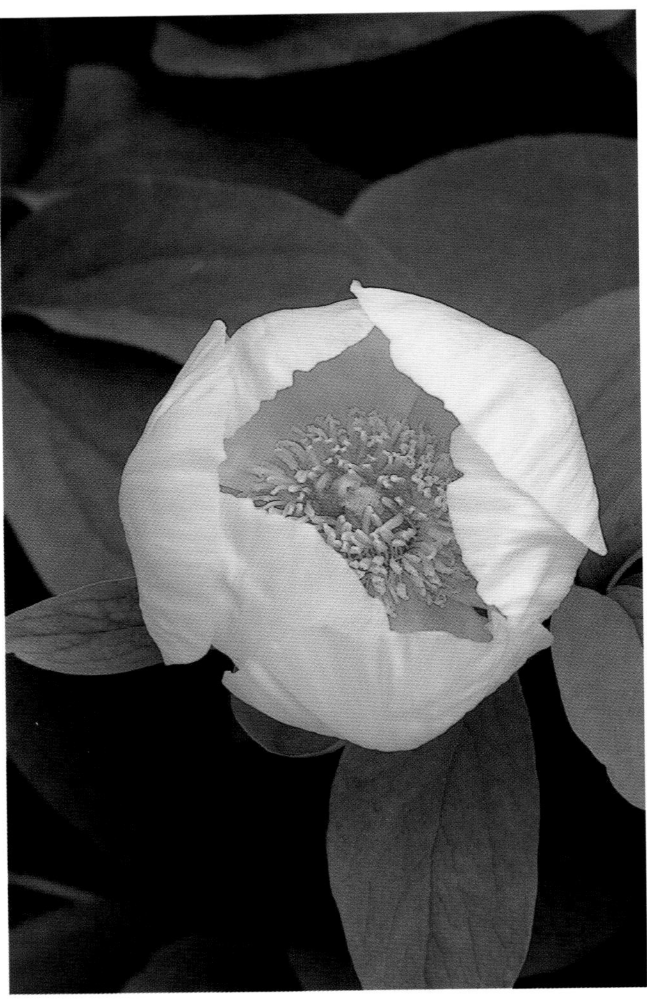

Paeonia mlokosewitschii.

Preferred Conditions: Deep, fertile, cool, humus-rich, moist, and well-drained—but tolerates average soil. Shelter from strong winds.

Light: Sun to part shade.

Planting: Don't plant too deep or too high (crown specific). The eyes should be just below the surface, and you should be able to feel the pips with your palm when dormant. They won't produce flowers if planted too deep or too high.

Management: Peonies don't like to be moved and resent root disturbance. They are hungry feeders. Manure every winter, but don't build up on top of the crown. Spread limestone chips over the crown to help prevent botrytis. Let foliage die back completely before cutting down to two to four inches. Cut back dead growth anytime it appears. Remove or deadhead flowers as soon as they fade unless you want to leave the seedpods on for decoration or seed (some do have handsome seed). Many large-flowered ones will need support, especially the doubles.

Propagation: Seed may take two or three years to germinate; division in fall.

Pests and Diseases: Botrytis, phytophthora, stem rot, verticillium wilt, slugs in early spring.

Companions: Aquilegia, *Campanula persicifolia*, digitalis, *Iris sibirica*, spring bulbs, viola, chaerophyllum, *Astrantia maxima*; the spring cottage garden.

Notes: Singles and semi-doubles are best for the Pacific Northwest. The chart includes the more commonly available cultivars; look for more unusual ones in mail-order catalogs.

Species and Cultivars	Height/ Spread	USDA Hardiness Zone	Flowers (bloom time)	Foliage	Comments
'Buckeye Belle'	1–2½ft × 2½ft	3–8	Dark red, narrow inner petals, large outer petals, semi-double, cup-shaped, 6in (E–M)	Mid-green, thick, leathery	
emodi	2–3ft × 2½ft	3–8	White, golden yellow stamens, single, cup-shaped, fragrant, 3in (E–M)	Mid-green, bronze new leaves, deeply divided, veined	Himalayan peony
'Flame'	2–3ft × 2½ft	3–8	Red, yellow stamens, single, 6in (E–M)	Dark green	
lactiflora	2½–3ft × 2½ft	3–8	White to pale pink, yellow stamens, single, cup-shaped, fragrant, 4–7in (E–M)	Dark green, divided, elliptic-lanceolate	Common garden peony, red-mottled stems

Species and Cultivars	Height/ Spread	USDA Hardiness Zone	Flowers (bloom time)	Foliage	Comments
l. 'Bowl of Beauty'	2½–3ft × 2½ft	3–8	Reddish pink, creamy-white center, cup-shaped, fragrant, 6in (M)	Mid-green	Imperial peony, RHS Award
l. 'Duchesse de Nemours'	2½–3ft × 2½–3ft	3–8	White flushed green in bud, ruffled yellowish inner petals, double, fragrant, 5–6in (E)	Deep green	RHS Award
l. 'Edulis Superba'	3–3½ft × 2½ft	3–8	Rose-red, double, fragrant, 6in (E)	As above	
l. 'Félix Crousse'	2½–3½ft × 2½ft	3–8	Deep reddish pink, darker center, ruffled silver edges, fragrant, 5–7in (M)	As above	RHS Award
l. 'Festiva Maxima'	3ft × 3ft	3–8	White, red spots, double, fragrant, 5–7in (E)	Mid-green	RHS Award
l. 'Inspecteur Lavergne'	2½–3ft × 2½ft	3–8	Red, white tips, double, 6in (M)	As above	
l. 'Kansas'	2½–3ft × 3ft	3–8	Bright red, double, fragrant, large (E–M)	As above	Does not fade in sun
l. 'Karl Rosenfield'	2½–3ft × 2½–3ft	3–8	Deep wine-red, golden stamens, double, fragrant, 6–8in (E)	Emerge reddish brown, aging to mid-green, deeply cut	Hairy stems and leaf stalks
l. 'Kelway's Glorious'	2½–3ft × 2ft	3–8	White, cream center, red edges, long petals, fragrant, 6–8in (M)	Deep green	
l. 'Lady Alexander Duff'	2½–3ft × 2ft	3–8	Pale pink to white, yellow stamens, double, fragrant, 6in (M)	As above	RHS Award
l. 'Laura Dessert'	2½–3ft × 2ft	3–8	Creamy-white, pink flushed outer petals, pale yellow stamens, double, fragrant, 6–8in (E–M)	Pale mid-green	RHS Award
l. 'Monsieur Jules Elie'	2½–3ft × 2ft	3–8	Pale rose-pink, silvery sheen, double, fragrant, 5–7in (E)	Deep green	RHS Award
l. 'Monsieur Martin Cahuzac'	2½–3ft × 2ft	3–8	Dark rose-red, velvety, silver sheen, double, 5–6in (E–M)	As above	
l. 'Peter Brand'	3ft × 2ft	3–8	Ruby-red, double, 5–7in (E–M)	Mid-green	
l. 'Sarah Bernhardt'	1½–3ft × 3ft	3–8	Pale rose-pink, silver edges, ruffled inner petals, double, fragrant, 6in (M)	As above	RHS Award

Species and Cultivars	Height/ Spread	USDA Hardiness Zone	Flowers (bloom time)	Foliage	Comments
l. 'Shirley Temple'	2½–3ft × 2½ft	3–8	Pale rose-pink, fading to buff white, double, fragrant, 7in (E–M)	Deep green	
l. 'Solange'	2½–3ft × 2½ft	3–8	Creamy-white, aging to pink, 6in (M)	As above	
l. 'Sorbet'	2–2½ft × 2ft	3–8	Light pink, yellow center, double, fragrant, 6–8in (E–M)	Green, good fall color	
l. 'White Wings'	2½–3ft × 2½ft	3–8	White, yellow center, single, fragrant, 5–6in (M)	Deep green, glossy, turns red in fall	
mascula	2–3ft × 2½ft	5–8	Deep purplish red, deep yellow stamens, cup-shaped, single, 3–5in (E)	Bluish green, paler green reverse, divided	
m. subsp. triternata (syn. daurica)	2½ft × 2ft	4–8	Magenta-red, bright yellow stamens, single, 3–5in (E)	Grayish green, bold, rounded	
mlokosewitschii	1½–2½ft × 2ft	3–8	Yellow, darker yellow stamens, cherry center, single, bowl-shaped, 6–8in (E)	Purple-tinged aging to soft gray-green, pleated, good fall color, rounded, sometimes red-edged	Molly the witch, erect, short flowering season, good seedpods, RHS Award
obovata	1½–2ft × 2½ft	5–8	White to purple-red and rose-pink, single, cup-shaped, 3–4in (E)	Deep gray-green, pale green reverse, oval to obovate	RHS Award
officinalis	2–2½ft × 2½ft	3–8	Red or rose-pink, yellow stamens, single, cup-shaped, 4–5in (E–M)	Dark green, narrow, divided, glossy, good fall color	Common peony
o. 'Rosea Plena'	2–2½ft × 2ft	3–8	Bright pink, fading with age, slightly ruffled, double, fragrant, 6in (E–M)	Dark green	RHS Award
o. 'Rubra Plena'	2–2½ft × 2ft	3–8	Deep red, double, ruffled, 6in (E–M)	As above	RHS Award
'Smouthii'	1½–2ft × 2ft	4–8	Bright red, yellow stamens, single, cup-shaped, fragrant, 3–4in (E)	Bright green, divided, fine, threadlike	Sterile
tenuifolia	1–2ft × 2ft	5–8	Deep red, yellow stamens, single, cup-shaped, 3–4in (E–M)	Deep green, paler reverse, many pointed fernlike segments	Fernleaf peony
t. 'Plena'	1½–2ft × 2ft	5–8	Dark red, double, 3–4in (E–M)	Deep green, lacy	
t. 'Rosea'	1½–2ft × 2ft	5–8	Pale pink, single, 3–4in (E–M)	As above	
veitchii	2–2½ft × 2ft	6–8	Pink, 3–4in (E–M)	Grayish green, gray reverse, lanceolate, divided	Semi-woody
'Yellow Crown'	2ft × 2ft	4–8	Bright yellow, 5–6in (E–M)	Mid-green	

Papaver orientale 'Patty's Plum'.

PAPAVER Papaveraceae

The genus *Papaver* is only one of many hardy genera in the poppy family. Of its species, *P. orientale*, albeit a bit coarse, is truly the "Queen of May." It has hairy buds and stems, very hairy leaves, and a slightly deranged habit. If you love the flowers, you will overlook a relatively short bloom time; a slow, unattractive slide to dormancy following the flowering; and the rough character already mentioned. The flowers are unlike anything else (except maybe those Kleenex flowers we made in grade school). They look like brightly colored tissue or crepe paper. The most common is an intense red-orange with black basal blotches and black anthers (like heavy eye makeup, Tammy Faye). I have grown this one and some of the deep blood-reds (*P. orientale* Goliath Group and var. *bracteatum*) to good effect with *Anchusa azurea* 'Loddon Royalist' (or other tall anchusas). They are both hairy all over and similarly deranged and bloom at exactly the same time, at about the same size. The intense cobalt-blue of the anchusa is the perfect complement to the orange of the poppies. *Nepeta* 'Six Hills Giant' would be beautiful with some of the salmon-colored forms; the nepeta's regrowth would cover the poppies after bloom time.

The only problem I have ever had with these poppies has to do with the effect of digging them up, either to move them or divide them (clumps get quite large over time in a good, sunny location). Every piece of root left behind will generate a new plant. This makes them a little difficult to move (remove, actually), as they will be in the old place as well as the new. On the other hand, it is easy to have more. ~ *Carrie Becker*

Scientific Name: The classical Latin name for a poppy.
Common Name: Poppy.
Origin: Turkey, Morocco, northern Iran, Europe, Asia.
Preferred Conditions: Well-drained, deep, moderately fertile, and not too wet. Can take some drought once established.
Light: Sun.

Planting: Avoid transplanting, as deep roots make this difficult. Plant when dormant or from containers, anytime.

Management: Stems and leaves will need cutting back to within an inch of the ground in August; a new flush of leaves will appear within several weeks. Only *P. pilosum* and *P. atlanticum* will bloom longer with deadheading. Many *P. orientale* selections will need support; short pea sticks work well.

Propagation: Best propagated by root cuttings (especially *P. orientale*); seed germinates best in cool temperatures; divide only after foliage dies down in late summer, in August or so.

Pests and Diseases: Mildew, botrytis, root rot, damping off, snails, slugs.

Companions: Aquilegia, allium, galium (tall forms), anchusa, nepeta, euphorbia, *Salvia* ×*superba*; that distant wasteland that can go scruffy in summer.

Notes: To use as a cut flower, pick with the bud just splitting open. Stand cut ends in a foot of hot water for a short time, and then add cold water, keeping them cool over night. You can also singe the bottom of cut stems with a match and put them in cool water. Arrange them the next morning.

Species and Cultivars	Height/ Spread	USDA Hardiness Zone	Flowers (bloom time)	Foliage	Comments
atlanticum	1–1½ft × 1½ft	3–9	Soft orange, saucer-shaped, hairy buds, occasionally double, frilled, 2in (E–M)	Mid-green, oblong-lanceolate, coarsely toothed, hairy	Atlas poppy, long-blooming, short-lived, self-sows, erect, green then brown seed capsules
orientale	3ft × 2–3ft	3–9	Orange with maroon blotches and dark purple stamens, frilled, 3–6in (E–M)	Mid-green, hairy, divided, coarse	Oriental poppy, clump-forming, summer dormant, bristly stems, erect
o. 'Allegro'	16–18in × 18in	3–9	Bright scarlet-orange with bold black basal splotches (E–M)	As above	Dwarf form
o. var. bracteatum	4ft × 2ft	3–9	Blood-red with elongated black spot at base, bowl-shaped (M)	As above	Great scarlet poppy, RHS Award
o. 'Brilliant'	2–3ft × 2ft	3–9	Scarlet-orange with black blotch, 4–5in (E–M)	As above	
o. 'Cedar Hill'	2–3ft × 2ft	3–9	Light pink with dark center (E–M)	As above	
o. Goliath Group	4ft × 2ft	3–9	Blood-red with black center, large (E–M)	As above	
o. Goliath Group 'Beauty of Livermere'	2–4ft × 2ft	3–9	Deep red with black marks at base, black stamens (E–M)	As above	Needs no support, comes true from seed, RHS Award
o. 'Harvest Moon'	2½ft × 2ft	3–9	Yellow-orange, unspotted, small, semi-double (E–M)	As above	

Species and Cultivars	Height/ Spread	USDA Hardiness Zone	Flowers (bloom time)	Foliage	Comments
o. 'Helen Elisabeth'	2–3ft × 2ft	3–9	Clear salmon-pink with black basal spots, crinkled (E–M)	As above	Long-lasting
o. 'Mrs. Perry'	2½–3ft × 2ft	3–9	Pale salmon-pink with black basal marks, 4in (E–M)	As above	
o. 'Patty's Plum'	2ft × 1½ft	3–9	Plum-purple with purple central blotches (E–M)	As above	Short-lived
o. 'Perry's White'	2–2½ft × 2ft	3–9	White with dark patches at base of petals (E–M)	As above	
o. 'Picotee'	2½ft × 2ft	3–9	Creamy-white, broad, frilled, orange-pink margins, black center (M)	As above	
o. 'Pinnacle'	2½ft × 2ft	3–9	Bicolored, white edged in scarlet, large, ruffled (E–M)	As above	
o. 'Prince of Orange'	2–3ft × 2ft	3–9	Scarlet-orange, large (E–M)	As above	
o. 'Prinzessin Victoria Louise'	2–3ft × 2ft	3–9	Salmon-pink with black basal blotches, 5in (E–M)	As above	
o. 'Queen Alexandra'	2–3ft × 2ft	3–9	Bright salmon-pink (E–M)	As above	
o. 'Raspberry Queen'	2–3ft × 2ft	3–9	Deep raspberry-pink with black center (M)	As above	
o. 'Salmon Glow'	2–3ft × 2ft	3–9	Rich deep salmon-pink, double (E–M)	As above	
o. 'Türkenlouis'	2–2½ft × 2ft	3–9	Fiery red-orange, fringed, dark center, unmarked (E–M)	As above	
o. 'Watermelon'	1½–2½ft × 2ft	3–9	Watermelon-red with dark blotch in center (E–M)	As above	
o. 'Wunderkind'	2½ft × 2ft	3–9	Bright pink (E)	As above	
pilosum	2–3ft × 1½ft	5–9	Bright orange (M)	Pale green, oblong, hairy	Clump-forming, stiff, upright

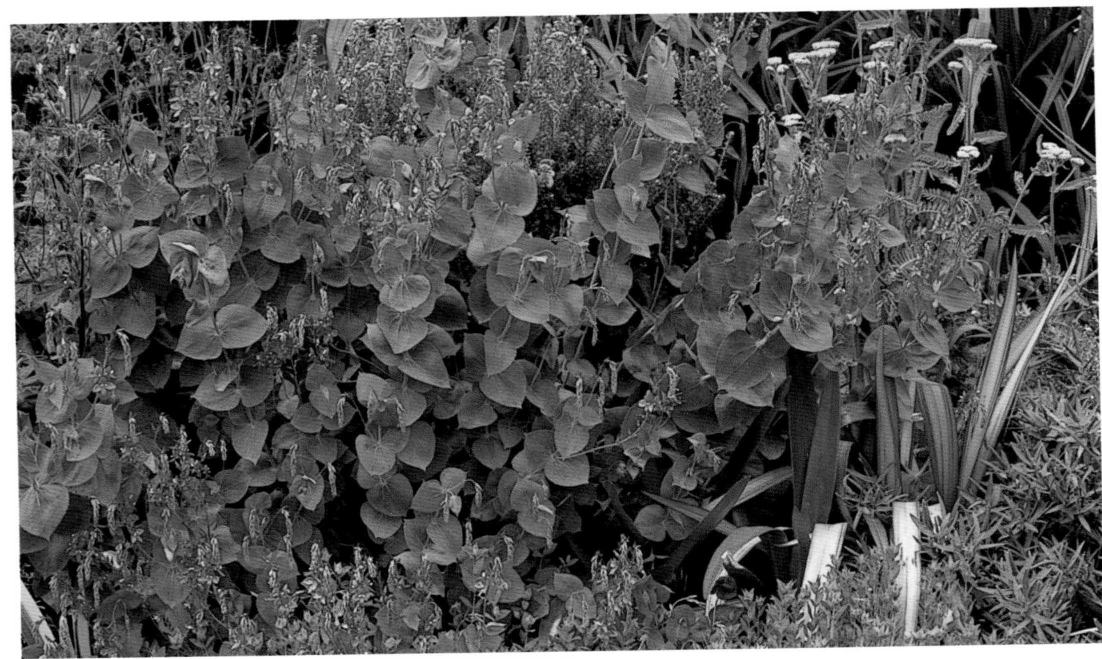

Parahebe perfoliata.

PARAHEBE Scrophulariaceae

Parahebe perfoliata has long, eventually lax stems holding fused pairs of attractive leathery blue-green leaves along their length. The leaves are perfoliate: the stem passes through or perforates them. The tips of the stems have bright violet flowers in May. It has done yeoman's service for me—encircling and holding up the usually prostrate flowers of *Helleborus argutifolius*. Plant these incredible curiosities where their lax habit can be appreciated—on a wall or small bank, or atop a rockery. In a perfect year, these make good container plants, but do not allow them to dry out. ~ *Ann Bucher*

Scientific Name: From the Greek *para* ("similar to"), hence, similar to a hebe.
Common Name: Digger's speedwell.
Origin: Australia, New Zealand.
Preferred Conditions: Light, well-drained soil in a sheltered and warm location.
Light: Sun.
Management: Cut the stems hard in early spring; cutting back old stems may promote several waves of growth and bloom. Once established, plants can be cut back to basal growth for the winter; this will also keep them tidier. You can also leave the old growth on to protect the crown over winter and remove in spring.
Propagation: Division in spring; cuttings and seedlings.
Pests and Diseases: Slugs, mildew.
Companions: Grasses, artemisia, other graylings.
Notes: Marginally hardy here but has survived six straight winters given its preferred conditions.

Species and Cultivars	Height/ Spread	USDA Hardiness Zone	Flowers (bloom time)	Foliage	Comments
perfoliata (syn. *Veronica perfoliata*)	2ft × 2ft	8–10	Violet-blue clusters (M)	Bluish green, ovate, eucalyptuslike, perfoliate	Arching stems, will sprawl but looks odd if staked, semi-evergreen, RHS Award

PARIS Trilliaceae

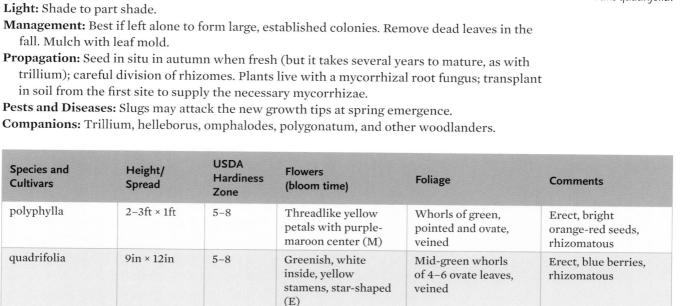

Paris quadrifolia.

Enchanting flowers for the observant gardener, green and trilliumlike. Paris typically has four leaves in a whorl that subtend the solitary flower. The leaves have noticeable netlike veining. The sepals are chartreuse to green and are held above the whorl of leaves. The threadlike petals are yellow or greenish with scarlet to blue-black berries following the flowers. Flowers and berries are poisonous in most species. When grown well, paris is long-lived and forms large colonies. Unusually, occasionally, sporadically, and infrequently, the above-ground part of this plant may not appear while the rhizome survives underground, so mark the location of your plant until you have a good clump and know exactly where it is. ~ *Carrie Becker*

Scientific Name: From the Latin *par* ("equal"), referring to the regularity of the parts.
Common Name: Herb paris.
Origin: Europe, Himalayas, Asia.
Preferred Conditions: Heavy, moist to wet, humus-laden woodland loam.
Light: Shade to part shade.
Management: Best if left alone to form large, established colonies. Remove dead leaves in the fall. Mulch with leaf mold.
Propagation: Seed in situ in autumn when fresh (but it takes several years to mature, as with trillium); careful division of rhizomes. Plants live with a mycorrhizal root fungus; transplant in soil from the first site to supply the necessary mycorrhizae.
Pests and Diseases: Slugs may attack the new growth tips at spring emergence.
Companions: Trillium, helleborus, omphalodes, polygonatum, and other woodlanders.

Species and Cultivars	Height/ Spread	USDA Hardiness Zone	Flowers (bloom time)	Foliage	Comments
polyphylla	2–3ft × 1ft	5–8	Threadlike yellow petals with purple-maroon center (M)	Whorls of green, pointed and ovate, veined	Erect, bright orange-red seeds, rhizomatous
quadrifolia	9in × 12in	5–8	Greenish, white inside, yellow stamens, star-shaped (E)	Mid-green whorls of 4–6 ovate leaves, veined	Erect, blue berries, rhizomatous
verticillata	1½ft × 1ft	5–8	Yellow (E–M)	Mid-green, ovate-lanceolate in whorls	

Patrinia villosa.

PATRINIA Valerianaceae

Patrinia is a somewhat new genus in the trade, and still relatively rare. The only form I have grown is *P. scabiosifolia* 'Nagoya', which has shiny green leaves that look like scabious leaves (note specific epithet). Its many little pale yellow flowers are held in compound cymes. Actually it looks a lot like a smaller, more refined valerian with yellow flowers. Taller than other patrinias, it is more suitable for borders (mixed or the summer yellow border) or in a naturalistic planting, as a filler. The shorter species (*P. gibbosa* and *P. triloba*) thrive in part shade in the rock garden (the north side of a large rock), and *P. villosa* extends the bloom season with its white flowers. Patrinia may be short-lived for us, but how can you resist a plant with a common name like Elvis eyes (*P. triloba*)? It just might be a hunka hunka burning love. ~ *Carrie Becker*

Scientific Name: In honor of Eugene L. M. Patrin (1724–1815), French mineralogist.
Common Name: Golden lace.
Origin: Japan, Siberia.
Preferred Conditions: Most any good garden soil that is moisture-retentive and humus-rich. *Patrinia scabiosifolia* needs a dry site.
Light: Sun to part shade.
Management: Easy to care for. Cut back in autumn as foliage dies down. Best if not engulfed by other, more vigorous plants.
Propagation: Divide in spring; seed as soon as ripe (it ripens very late); it will flower in the second year.

Pests and Diseases: Snails, slugs, especially on new growth.
Companions: Tiarella, phlox, rudbeckia, hemerocallis, helenium, geranium, heliopsis, helianthus, grasses.

Species and Cultivars	Height/ Spread	USDA Hardiness Zone	Flowers (bloom time)	Foliage	Comments
gibbosa	1–2ft × 2ft	5–9	Pale yellow with lone petal of greenish yellow (M)	Mid-green, shiny, broadly ovate, pinnately cut and jagged	Long-lasting bloom, peculiar odor
scabiosifolia	3–4ft × 2ft	5–9	Golden yellow, tiny, cup-shaped (M–L)	Mid-green, ovate to oblong, hairy, coarse, deeply divided	Golden lace, upright, needs sun
s. 'Nagoya'	3–4ft × 2ft	5–9	Golden yellow (M)	As above	More compact
triloba	1–2ft × 1ft	5–9	Yellow clusters, red-tinted stems, cup-shaped, fragrant (M)	Green, deeply cut, basal leaves mostly palmate	Clump-forming, erect
villosa	3ft+ × 2ft	5–9	White (L)	Dark green, deeply lobed	Very elegant

PELTOBOYKINIA Saxifragaceae

I grow both species of peltoboykinia for their foliage; others prize them for their pale yellowish flowers, which are diminutive (at least compared with the large, palmate leaves) but carried in cymes on a one- to two-foot stem. So they have something for everyone. They spread slowly by rhizomes. I grow *P. tellimoides* in a whisky barrel, so I can keep it fairly evenly moist. *Peltoboykinia watanabei* is in the ground, and even with supplemental moisture, its leaves crisp in late

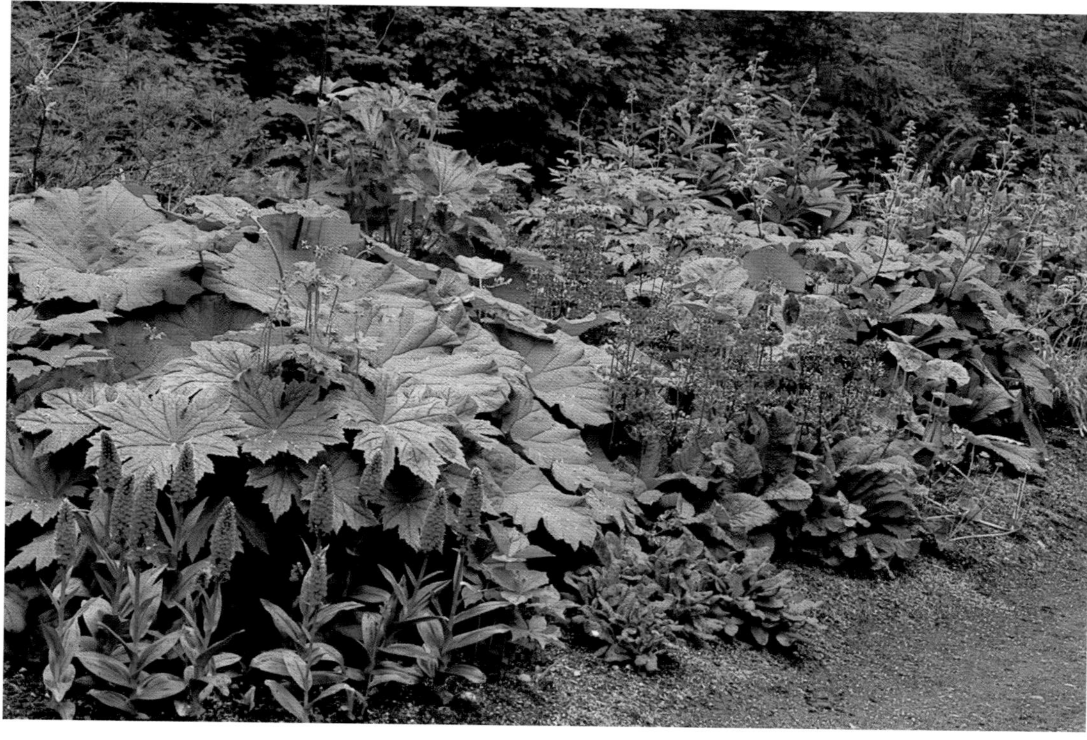

Peltoboykinia watanabei is a presence in the border even when not in flower.

summer. We have noticed the plants will be smaller in drier locations. Peltoboykinia is closely related to our native *Boykinia elata* and *B. major*. ~ *Ann Bucher*

Scientific Name: From the Greek *pelte* ("shield") and for American field botanist Samuel Boykin.
Common Name: Peltoboykinia.
Origin: Japan.
Preferred Conditions: Humus-rich, moderately fertile, moist, cool soil. Perfect alongside a bog or stream.
Light: Part shade to shade.
Planting: Plant rhizomes shallow and horizontal.
Management: Insufficient moisture will lead to premature browning of leaves as with most large-leaved shade plants. Cut back in autumn once leaves have died back (there is some fall color).
Propagation: Division in early spring; seed.
Pests and Diseases: Slugs, root weevil.
Companions: Ferns, *Primula japonica*, dactylorhiza, meconopsis, hosta, rodgersia, dicentra, polygonatum, gillenia.

Species and Cultivars	Height/ Spread	USDA Hardiness Zone	Flowers (bloom time)	Foliage	Comments
tellimoides	2½–3ft × 1½ft	5–9	Pale greenish yellow, bell-shaped (M)	Olive to mid-green, emerges red, round, peltate, palmately lobed	Clump-forming
watanabei	2–2½ft × 1½ft	5–9	Creamy-yellow (M)	Mid-green, divided, large, maplelike	As above

PENSTEMON Scrophulariaceae

Penstemons are beautiful, long-blooming, colorful additions to the mixed border and loved by bees and hummingbirds. They prefer sun but can take part shade and can grow on the sunny verge of the woodland. The woodier species and hybrids are for the dry garden or the rock garden primarily; they tend to be truly evergreen and could also serve as edging in the short or low border. The taller, more herbaceous forms, which are mostly hybrids, spread by underground roots and form fairly large colonies if given the room. Some folks like *P. digitalis* 'Husker Red', but not me; it may have dark red foliage, but it has dingy white flowers and a floppy habit, so it would not get my perennial plant of the year award (grow *Lobelia cardinalis* instead). ~ *Carrie Becker*

Scientific Name: From the Greek *pente* ("five") and *stemon* ("stamen"), referring to the five stamens.
Common Name: Beardtongue.
Origin: North America, Mexico.
Preferred Conditions / Light / Management:
Group 1. Western, the semi-woody group. Requires good drainage, full sun, and poorer soil. These resent crowding and being overgrown by others. Don't fertilize or mulch with organic material. They are not always hardy, so take cuttings.

Penstemon 'Schoenholzeri'.

Group 2. Grassland. Requires a richer, more moist soil and consorts better with other plants. Prefers good drainage and sun, but can take part shade. These tend to be semi-evergreen to herbaceous, depending on the cultivar and the winter. This group includes all the campanulatus hybrids that are semi-woody and semi-evergreen; we leave them up for winter and cut to newly emerging basal and lower stem growth in spring. Use an organic mulch, but not over the crown. Cut off spent flowers each time for nearly continuous bloom.

Both groups can be left to grow, or cut back by one-third to one-half in springtime to get vigorous new growth. If left, they will bloom earlier, but still will need a bit of shaping in the spring. If you keep your penstemons deadheaded, they will bloom from early summer until frost in most cases. Flower spikes should be cut off below the lowest blossom.

Propagation: Seed as soon as ripe; best from cuttings (especially cultivars) (cuttings and seed only for Group 1); division in spring or fall for established clumps.

Pests and Diseases: Powdery mildew, rust, leaf spot, snails, slugs, crown rot.

Companions: Heuchera, aquilegia, kniphofia, smaller euphorbias, smaller crocosmias, artemisia, eryngium, salvia, phlox.

Notes: Many are good cut flowers. *Penstemon* 'Alice Hindley', *P.* 'Sour Grapes' and *P.* 'Stapleford Gem' are mixed in the trade.

Species and Cultivars	Height/ Spread	USDA Hardiness Zone	Flowers (bloom time)	Foliage	Comments
'Alice Hindley'	3–4ft × 1½ft	7–9	Pale lilac-blue, white inside, tubular (M–L)	Glossy, mid-green	Group 2, bushy, erect, vigorous, RHS Award
'Andenken an Friedrich Hahn' (syn. 'Garnet')	2–3ft × 1½ft	7–10	Deep wine-red, tubular (M–L)	Green, narrow, shiny	Group 2, bushy, vigorous, RHS Award
'Apple Blossom'	1½–2½ft × 1½ft	6–9	Pale pink, white throat, tubular (M–L)	Green, narrow	Group 2, repeat bloomer, good cut, RHS Award

Species and Cultivars	Height/ Spread	USDA Hardiness Zone	Flowers (bloom time)	Foliage	Comments
barbatus	2–3ft × 1ft	4–9	Pink to scarlet, red-tinged, pale hairy throat, yellow beard, tubular (M–L)	Glaucous, lanceolate to linear, hairy	Group 1, semi-evergreen, long-blooming, not recommended for Pacific Northwest
b. 'Elfin Pink'	1–3ft × 1ft	3–8	Clear pink, tubular (E–M)	Lighter gray-green, glossy	Group 1, evergreen, reblooms
'Bev Jensen'	2ft × 1½ft	7–9	Rose-pink, white center, darker pink markings along throat, tubular (M–L)	Pale green, narrow	Group 2, bushy
'Blackbird'	2½–3ft × 2ft	7–9	Deep purple-maroon, tubular, reddish stems (M–L)	Green, broad	Group 2, long and heavy blooming
campanulatus	1½–2½ft × 1½ft	8–10	Pinkish purple or violet-red, bell-shaped, tubular (E–L)	Dark green, narrow, linear-lanceolate, toothed	Group 2, erect, bushy, semi-evergreen
'Crystal'	1ft × 1ft	4–9	White (M)	Bright green, glossy	Group 1, evergreen
digitalis 'Husker Red'	2–3ft × 1½ft	3–8	White with pink tints, airy, purple stems (E–M)	Maroon-red and rich bronze, toothed, ages to red-flushed green	Group 2, foxglove penstemon, vigorous! 1996 PPA Award
'Elizabeth Cozzens'	2–3ft × 1½ft	7–9	Purplish pink, magenta streaking, tubular (E)	Mid-green, lanceolate	Group 2
'Evelyn'	1½–2½ft × 2ft	7–10	Rose-pink, white throat, darker pink veins, tubular (M–L)	Narrow, green, willowy	Group 2, bushy, RHS Award
'Grape Tart'	1ft × 1½ft	6–9	Two-toned, purple and lavender (M)	New leaves orange (in sun), aging to green	Group 1
hartwegii	2–3ft × 2ft	8–10	Brilliant scarlet or dark purple-red, tubular (M–L)	Rich green, glossy, lanceolate-ovate	Group 1, bushy, RHS Award
heterophyllus 'Catherine de la Mare'	12–16in × 12in	7–9	Blue-purple, small, tubular (M–L)	Mid-green, narrow, toothed	Group 1, RHS Award
'Hidcote Pink'	2–3ft × 1½ft	7–9	Soft salmon-pink, paler throat with crimson streaks (M–L)	Mid-green, willowy, lanceloate	Group 2, long-blooming, RHS Award
hirsutus var. pygmaeus	4–6in × 6in	4–9	Lavender with white tips (M)	Dark green, toothed	Group 1, compact, evergreen
'Holly's White'	2–3ft × 1½ft	8–9	White flushed with pink, tubular (M)	Mid-green, broad	Group 2, bushy, short-lived
'Hopley's Variegated'	2–2½ft × 1½ft	7–9	Deep mauve, white throat (M–L)	Cream and green variegated and marbled, willowlike	Group 2, bushy, evergreen
'Huntington Pink'	1½–2ft × 1½ft	7–9	Soft salmon tinted bright pink, white throat (M–L)	Green, willowlike	Group 2, bushy

Species and Cultivars	Height/ Spread	USDA Hardiness Zone	Flowers (bloom time)	Foliage	Comments
'Midnight'	2–3ft × 1½ft	7–9	Deep purplish blue, large, tubular (M)	Dark green, large	Group 2, bushy, erect, strong plant
'Mother of Pearl'	2–3ft × 1½ft	7–9	Pearlish pink with white throat and red lines (M–L)	Deep green, narrow	Group 2, strong plant
'Papal Purple'	2–3ft × 1½ft	7–9	Violet-purple, white throat, spotted purple (M–L)	Green, fine	Group 2, long-blooming
pinifolius	6–8in × 8in	4–10	Scarlet, tubular (M–L)	Green, needlelike, a very small shrub	Group 1, pine leaf penstemon, spreading, long-blooming, bushy, evergreen, RHS Award
p. 'Mersea Yellow'	6–8in × 8in	4–10	Bright yellow, tubular (M–L)	Pale green, needlelike	Group 1, evergreen, seed may come true
'Prairie Dusk'	1–2ft × 1½ft	3–8	Deep rose-purple, streaked red, tubular (M)	Dark green, leathery	Group 1, erect
'Prairie Fire'	2–2½ft × 1½ft	3–9	Scarlet, tubular (M)	Deep green	As above
'Raspberry Flair'	2ft × 1½ft	7–9	Lavender-purple, white throat, streaked maroon (M–L)	Light green, narrow	Group 2, compact
'Raven'	2–3ft × 1½ft	7–9	Blackish purple and red, white and red throat, large, red-tinted stems (M–L)	Deep green	Group 2, RHS Award
'Rich Ruby'	2½–3ft × 2ft	7–9	Burgundy-red, white stamens, large (M–L)	Mid-green, broad	Group 2
'Scharlachkönigin' (syn. 'Scarlet Queen')	2ft × 1½ft	7–9	Scarlet, white throat (M)	Deep green, glossy, serrated	Group 2, bushy
'Schoenholzeri' (syn. 'Ruby')	2–3ft × 2ft	7–9	Deep scarlet with white throat, dark red stripes, tubular (M–L)	Dark green, narrow, waxy	Group 2, bushy, vigorous, RHS Award
'Sour Grapes'	2–3ft × 1½ft	7–10	Rich purple-blue, tinged green, white throat, bell-shaped, tubular (M–L)	Rich green, large, glossy	Group 2, strong plant, RHS Award
'Stapleford Gem'	2–4ft × 1½ft	7–9	Lilac-purple, white throat, purplish red line, bell-shaped, tubular (M–L)	Mid-green, glossy	Group 2, RHS Award
'Thorn'	2–3ft × 1½ft	7–9	White inside, bright red-pink tips, dark anthers (M–L)	Deep green, willowlike	Group 2, evergreen, bushy, erect, vigorous
'Wisley Pink'	2–2½ft × 1½ft	7–9	Pink with darker streaks in the throat (M–L)	Green, narrow	Group 2, very bushy

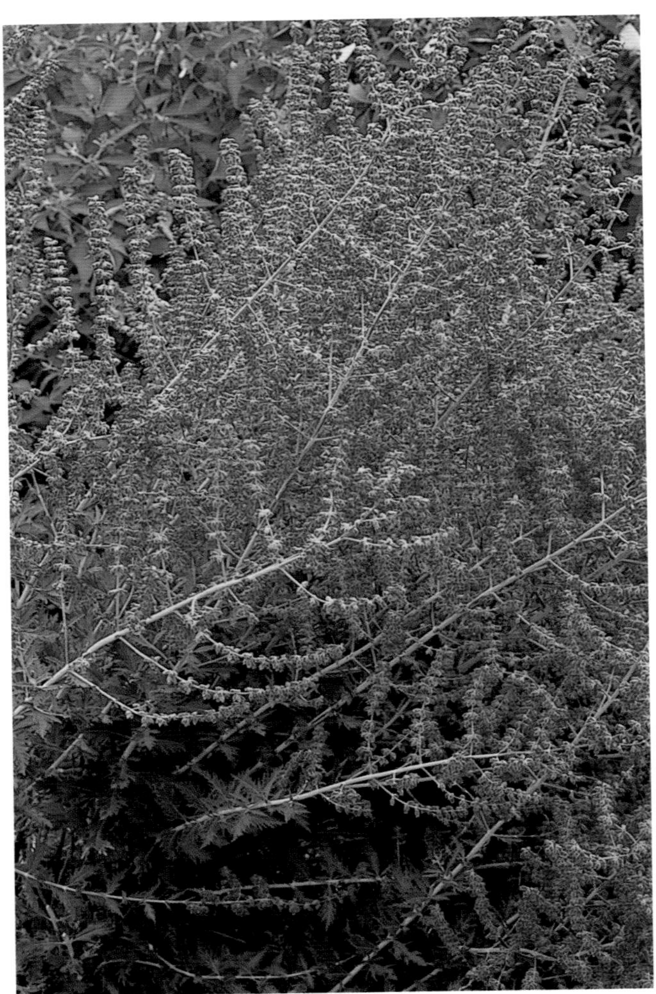

Perovskia atriplicifolia.

PEROVSKIA Lamiaceae

Russian sage is neither Russian nor a sage. *Perovskia atriplicifolia* is in the same family as sage, but so are lots of things. The cultivars of Russian sage are only slightly different, with more or less divided foliage and more or less gray foliage that has a pungent sagelike scent. When they bloom, the soft gray stems and leaves taper to a foot or more of blue flowers. If cut at this point, put in a vase in only one inch of water, and left, they'll dry to a pleasant shade of light blue. Personally, I like to leave the flower stems on the plant until spring: from fall on, they become grayer, to a gray-white, and stand as interesting "dried" stems in the garden all winter long.

Russian sages have a tendency to fall forward (or backward) into a semi-prostrate state so are well sited at tops of walls and stairways or banks, where this habit can be used to advantage. They hate competition and demand full sun for best performance. ~ *Carrie Becker*

Scientific Name: After Russian general V. A. Perovsky (1794–1857).
Common Name: Russian sage.
Origin: Afghanistan, Pakistan, Asia.
Preferred Conditions: A hot, dry location, but will grow in most any well-drained site. Poorer, drier soil would make them even happier.
Light: Sun.
Management: Cut back woody stems to about six inches every spring to encourage strong new shoots before growth begins. You can also wait until the buds begin to swell on the stems and then cut back to just above the lowest buds, to about six inches. You will need to adjust this cutting back, depending on vigor in your garden: new growth can be early in mild winters and caught by late frosts, but plants usually recover.
Propagation: Cuttings are best; division in spring, but not recommended.
Pests and Diseases: None serious.
Companions: Grasses, crocosmia, artemisia, lavandula, gaura, salvia, rudbeckia, penstemon, phlox, nepeta, echinops, echinacea; the prairie garden.
Notes: Sold as bare root shrubs in the Midwest. Probably needs more heat than we typically have here. Perovskia will sucker in loose, dry, sandy or gravelly soil once well established.

Perovskia 'Longin' with *Erysimum* 'Margaret Lockett', *Nepeta tuberosa*, *N. sibirica*, *Oenothera speciosa*, and grasses (*Stipa tenuissima*, *Miscanthus sinensis* 'Morning Light').

Species and Cultivars	Height/ Spread	USDA Hardiness Zone	Flowers (bloom time)	Foliage	Comments
atriplicifolia	3–4ft × 2ft+	4–9	Lavender-blue (M–L)	Silvery gray-green, toothed, on narrow, grayish white stems	Subshrub, will flop, 1995 PPA Award
'Blue Spire'	3–4ft × 2ft+	4–9	Deep violet-blue, tubular (M–L)	Silvery gray-green, finely dissected, grayish white stems	Upright, subshrub, rhizomatous, RHS Award
'Filigran'	3–4ft × 2ft+	4–9	Light lavender-blue (M–L)	Silver-gray, extremely finely cut, delicate, white stems	Bushier and more compact than *P. atriplicifolia*
'Longin'	2–4ft × 2ft+	4–9	Soft lavender-blue (M–L)	Silvery, not as toothed as *P. atriplicifolia*	Erect, narrow, will flop

Persicaria amplexicaulis 'Rosea' with hydrangea.

PERSICARIA Polygonaceae

The knotweeds—these are the ones we love to hate and hate to love. *Persicaria virginiana* and all its forms seed about. *Persicaria amplexicaulis* and its forms spread fast with immense woody crowns. At least they don't set seed! *Persicaria affinis* also spreads a great deal to make large mats—a good edger. Tolerant of water, these strong plants are valued for their bold look in the larger border and long flowering season. If someone could just breed a smaller form of *P. amplexicaulis* we might have the perfect border plant.

One thing to be careful with here is that there is wild name changing in this group. You can find mention of persicaria, fallopia, and polygonum all in the same sentence, and it can be hard to keep it all straight. With the amount of time taxonomists spend indoors, name changes are inevitable (see Actaea). ~ *Bob Lilly*

Scientific Name: The medieval name for knotweed, *persica* ("peach-shaped"), a reference to the leaves.
Common Name: Knotweed, fleeceflower.
Origin: Himalayas, China, India, Asia, Europe, North America.
Preferred Conditions: Moisture-retentive, well-drained soil with lots of organic material. Very adaptable. *Persicaria bistorta* tolerates dry soil but not in spring.
Light: Sun to part shade.
Management: Several are attractive in winter, so although they can be cut back in late fall, we advise waiting until spring. *Persicaria campanulata* is tender and may need some winter protection. Most are spreaders and need a certain amount of control to keep them in bounds.
Propagation: Stem cuttings; divisions in spring; seed.
Pests and Diseases: Aphids, snails, slugs.

Persicaria amplexicaulis 'Firetail' leans across the walk toward *Acanthus spinosus*, *A. s.* Spinosissimus Group, and a hardy fuchsia.

Companions: Grasses, aster, aconitum, lilium, hosta, rodgersia, monarda, filipendula, chelone, knautia, *Anemone japonica*, *Fuchsia magellanica*.

Notes: In the chart, the symbol ∞ = infinite spread.

Species and Cultivars	Height/ Spread	USDA Hardiness Zone	Flowers (bloom time)	Foliage	Comments
affinis	10–12in × 24in+	4–9	Pale pink aging to rose-red (M–L)	Green, ovate to lanceolate, turn red-copper in fall	Himalayan fleeceflower, vigorous, mat-forming
a. 'Border Jewel'	6in × 24in+	4–9	Pale pink aging to rose then red (E)	Dark black-green, glossy	Mat-forming

Species and Cultivars	Height/ Spread	USDA Hardiness Zone	Flowers (bloom time)	Foliage	Comments
a. 'Darjeeling Red'	10in × 24in+	4–9	White turning deep pink and aging to red (M–L)	Green, large, turn red in fall	All shades seen at the same time on different flowers, RHS Award
a. 'Superba' (syn. 'Dimity')	6–8in × 24in+	4–9	Pink to crimson (M–L)	Green, leathery, turn rich brown in fall	Vigorous, more drought tolerant, mat-forming, RHS Award
amplexicaulis	4–5ft × ∞	4–9	Rose-red to purple or white (M–L)	Mid-green, ovate, pointed, wavy margin, docklike	Mountain fleece, strong clumps, long-blooming, woody rootstock
a. 'Alba'	2½ft × 3ft+	4–9	White (M–L)	As above	Spreads more slowly
a. 'Atrosanguinea'	3–4ft × 3ft+	4–9	Crimson, small (M–L)	As above	Long-blooming
a. 'Firetail'	3–4ft × ∞	4–9	Crimson (M–L)	Mid-green, very bold, large	Long-blooming, RHS Award
a. 'Rosea'	2½ft × 3ft+	4–9	Soft pink (M)	As above	Spreads more slowly
a. 'Taurus'	2–3ft × ∞	4–9	Scarlet, darkest flower (M)	As above	Compact, spreads more slowly
bistorta	2–3ft × 3ft	4–9	Pale pink or white, bottlebrushlike spikes (E–L)	Mid-green, docklike, ovate, pointed, veined	Snakeweed, semi-evergreen, spreading, clump-forming
b. 'Superba'	2–3ft × 3ft	4–9	Soft mauve-pink, deepening color with age (E–M)	Dark green, docklike, wavy margins	Slowly invasive, long-blooming, erect, RHS Award
campanulata (syn. *Polygonum campanulatum*)	3–4ft × ∞	4–9	Pale pink or white, bell-shaped, deep rose buds, fragrant (M–L)	Dark gray-green, lanceolate-ovate, veined, reddish stems	Evergreen crown spreads but easy to control
microcephala 'Red Dragon'	3–4ft × 3ft	4–9	Small, white (M–L)	Tri-colored, mint-green, burgundy, with silver chevron	Not invasive but a vigorous plant with 4ft stems
polymorpha	4–6ft × 3ft	4–9	Creamy-white plumes (M–L)	Large, straplike, rough, very bold look	Not invasive, clump-forming
virginiana (syn. filiformis)	2½ft × 2½ft	4–9	Red, small, pearl-like, along red stems (M–L)	Mid-green with dark green markings, bold mahogany chevron, ovate-elliptic	Upright, clump-forming, self-sows, aggressive
v. 'Lance Corporal'	3ft × 2ft	4–9	Red, small, pearl-like along red stems (M)	Chartreuse, deep maroon chevron in center, emerges almost black, large	Clump-forming, striking in spring
v. Variegata Group 'Painter's Palette'	2–3ft × 2ft	4–9	Red (M–L)	Mid-green marbled with cream, central V-shaped maroon and red markings	Dark red seedheads, dense dome, seeds to the species

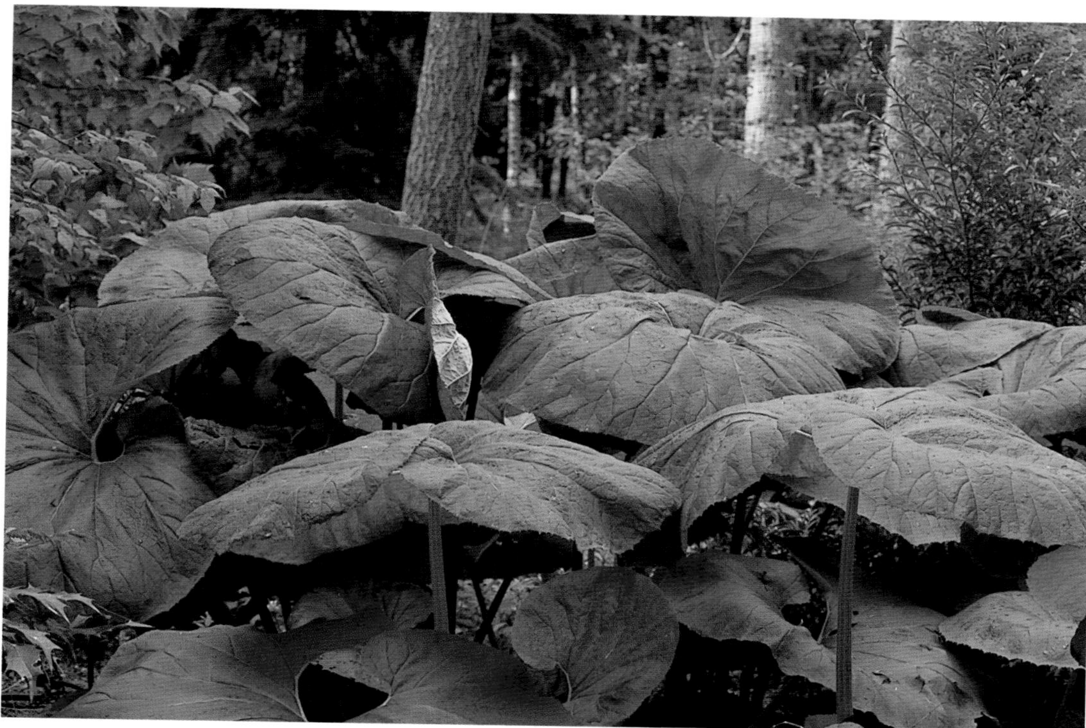

Petasites japonicus var. *giganteus.*

PETASITES Asteraceae

Petasites japonicus var. *giganteus* is very dramatic. With kidney-shaped leaves up to four feet wide on tall stems, this is a plant not to miss. My favorite planting was at Children's Hospital in Seattle, where the kids walked through a jungle of it on their way into the clinic. I have also seen it grown in a pot, where it used five gallons of water a day. If you don't have rich, mucky ground, you can still grow this plant, but beware: it is very aggressive. The early spring leaf stems are edible; the Japanese sauté them with sugar and soy sauce (George Schenk reports they tasted like mothballs in sugar and soy sauce). The flowers in dense clusters or corymbs arrive in late winter, offering food for bees at a time when it is needed. *Petasites frigidus* var. *palmatus* also has late winter flowers and that may be its only virtue; it too spreads aggressively by rhizomes, but the leaves are not as impressive, except for the golden form. ~ *Ann Bucher*

Scientific Name: From the Greek *petasos* ("hat"), referring to the large leaves.
Common Name: Sweet coltsfoot, butterbur.
Origin: China, Japan, Korea, North America, Europe.
Preferred Conditions: Deep, fertile, moist soil. Will need summer water.
Light: Part shade to shade. Tolerates sun if streamside.
Planting: Place one foot from high-water mark, if siting near water.
Management: Cut back when leaves die down. Use a heavy mulch in winter. Bait early; slugs will ruin the leaves at the drop of a hat.
Propagation: Division in fall or late winter after flowering.
Pests and Diseases: Rust, snails, slugs.

Companions: Ferns, aster, Japanese iris, *Typha angustifolia* (cattail), *Equisetum hyemale* (common horsetail), *Primula japonica* and other candelabra primroses, *Lobelia siphilitica*, *L. vedrariensis*, *L. cardinalis*, taller astilbes.
Notes: All run in rich soil to a nearly infinite (∞) size or spread.

Species and Cultivars	Height/ Spread	USDA Hardiness Zone	Flowers (bloom time)	Foliage	Comments
frigidus var. palmatus	1½ft × ∞	4–9	White (E)	Green, palmately lobed, divided and jagged edged, 1ft across	North American native, vigorous
f. var. palmatus 'Golden Palms'	1½–2ft × ∞	4–9	Pinkish (E)	Golden, palmately lobed, 1ft across	Leaves need sun for full color, just as vigorous
hybridus	2–3ft × ∞	4–9	Purple spikes (E)	Light green, heart-shaped to rounded, 2½–3ft across	Butterbur
japonicus var. giganteus	3–4ft × ∞	4–9	Tiny greenish white clusters, pale green bracts, baseball-sized buds (E)	Light green, round, wavy margins, 4ft across	Giant butterbur
j. var. giganteus 'Nishiki-buki' (syn. 'Variegatus')	3ft × ∞	4–9	Creamy-white to chartreuse clusters (E)	Green, splashed creamy-white, round to kidney-shaped, 2–3ft across	Variegation not always stable

PHLOMIS Lamiaceae

Phlomis vary in hardiness; some are subshrubs and some perennial. They all enjoy our dry Mediterranean summers and tolerate our wet winters. Their leaves are of various shapes, greenish or gray and woolly. The flower stems are very attractive even when dry—spiky calyces in dense whorls on tall, erect stems; they can be left on through winter. My experience is with *P. russeliana*, which I prize: not only is it evergreen, but it looks good in the garden all winter and may seed about. ~ *Ann Bucher*
Scientific Name: From the Greek *phlomos*, which referred to mulleins and similar plants.
Common Name: Jerusalem sage.
Origin: Europe, India, Turkey, Syria, Himalayas.
Preferred Conditions: Any fertile, well-drained, moisture-retentive soil. *Phlomis russeliana*, *P. samia*, *P. italica*, and *P. fruticosa* are drought tolerant.
Light: Sun. *Phlomis russeliana*, *P. samia*, and *P. tuberosa* can tolerate part shade.
Management: A spring bed check and evening flashlight patrols for cutworms will make for less perforated foliage the rest of the year. Cut back dead or damaged leaves as necessary. *Phlomis fruticosa* can be cut back by half after it blooms for possible rebloom. Cut back at the end of the season to the second pair of leaves or further, to control shape.
Propagation: Seed; stem cuttings; division in spring.
Pests and Diseases: Slugs, cutworms.
Companions: Grasses, nepeta, salvia, *Macleaya cordata*, helenium, *Kerria japonica* 'Picta', artemisia, olearia, carex.
Notes: We have included two evergreen shrubs (*P. italica* and *P. fruticosa*) that are invaluable to mixed herbaceous borders.

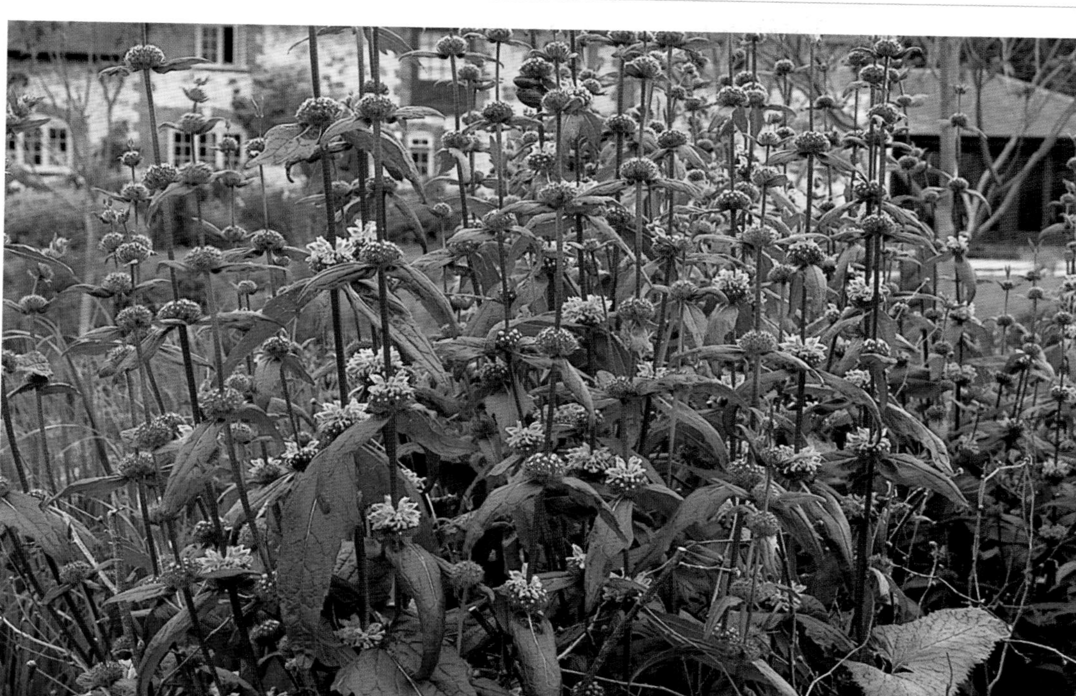

Phlomis tuberosa.

Species and Cultivars	Height/ Spread	USDA Hardiness Zone	Flowers (bloom time)	Foliage	Comments
cashmeriana	2–3ft × 2ft	7–9	Pale lilac-purple (M)	Gray-green, ovate-lanceolate, woolly	Erect
fruticosa	3–4ft × 4ft	7–9	Bright yellow (M)	Grayish green, woolly, elliptic to lanceolate, wrinkled	Jerusalem sage, shrub, new shoots white, RHS Award
italica	3–4ft × 3ft	8–10	Lilac-pink, light silver-gray stems (M)	Silvery-gray, woolly, oblong to lanceolate	Shrub, erect
russeliana	3–4ft × 2½ft+	4–9	Butter-yellow, green calyces (M)	Bright mid-green, cordate to ovate, crinkled, felted	Rhizomatous, self-sows, flops, RHS Award
samia	3ft × 2½ft+	7–10	Purplish pink (M)	Mid-green, woolly ovate-lanceolate, serrate	Greek Jerusalem sage
tuberosa	4ft × 2½ft	5–8	Pink to purple, white beard at throat, deep red stems (M)	Green, cordate-ovate, toothed, softly hairy, herbaceous	Tuberous rootstock, bushy, erect
t. 'Amazone'	4–5ft × 2½ft	4–9	Lilac-rose (M)	Dark green, coarse	As above

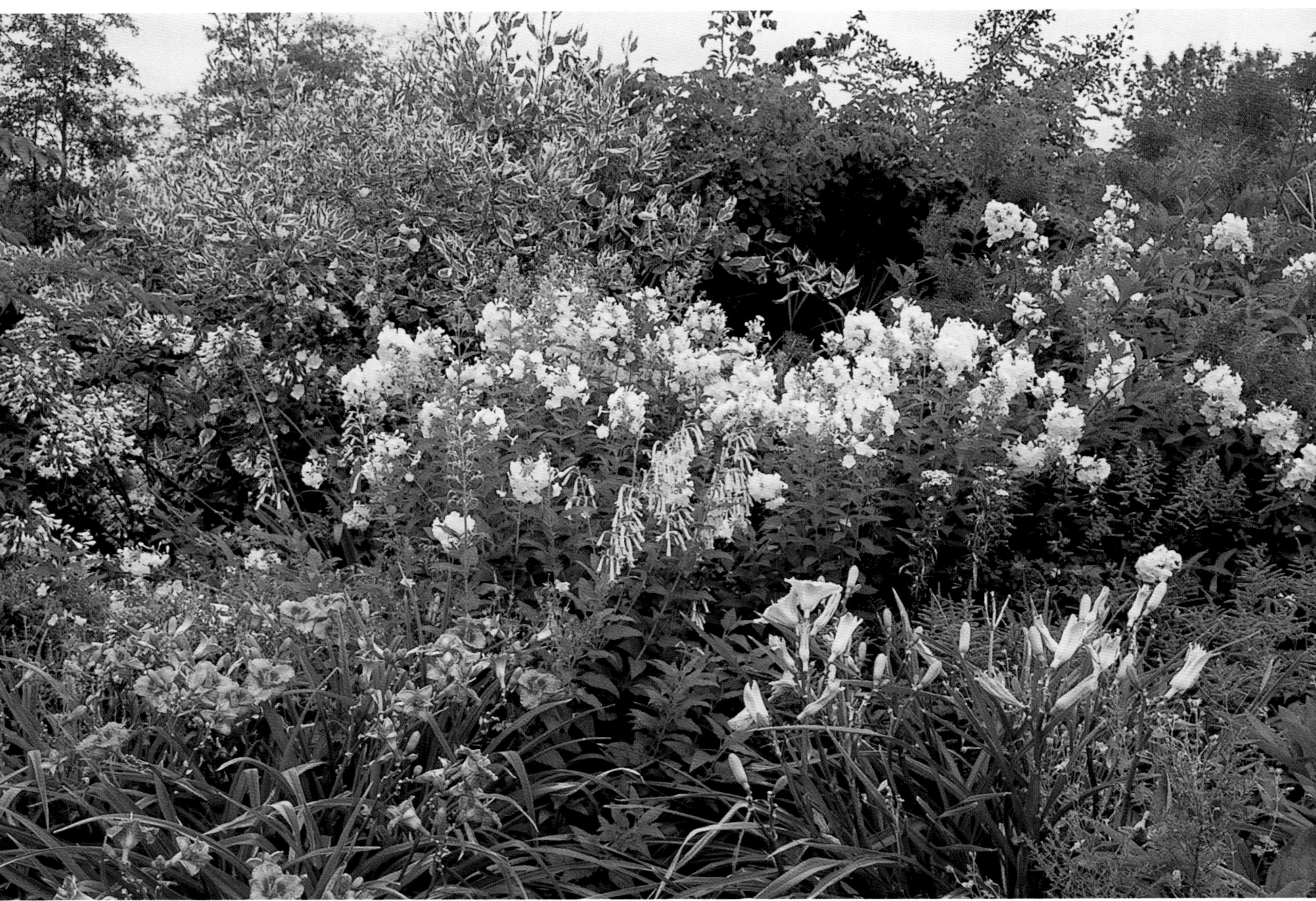

Phlox paniculata 'Mount Fuji' with *Agapanthus* 'Bressingham White', *Phygelius aequalis* 'Yellow Trumpet', and daylilies.

PHLOX Polemoniaceae

The shorter *P. divaricata* is lovely in the woodland garden; I have seen carpets of it under rhododendrons and other woodland shrubs in late spring. The erect habit of *P. paniculata* makes it a great border plant, and the many little trumpets of scent are especially nice in midsummer. All forms of *P. paniculata* have great fragrance, especially in the evening, when the moths come to sip their nectar. The white-flowered forms and variegated-leaf forms show up well in the night garden. Margery Fish said you could grow *P. paniculata* in part shade. Morning shade and afternoon sun would be best if shade is a factor in your garden. Don't forget to suck the nectar out of a few flowers yourself. ~ *Carrie Becker*

Scientific Name: From the Greek *phlox* ("flame").
Common Name: Phlox.
Origin: North America.

Preferred Conditions: Moist, well-drained, humus-rich, with good air circulation. Average water requirement, especially during dry spells.

Light: Sun to part shade.

Management: While the instructions say most tall phlox need staking, we never do this in the NPA Borders at the Bellevue Botanical Garden. We manage these plants by pinching out the tips to keep the plants more compact (if you must, pinch *P. paniculata* and *P. maculata* as early as May). Phlox do need more frequent division than many perennials, probably every three years or so (divide *P. paniculata* and *P. maculata* whenever center of clump dies out). Frequent division and additional organic matter as well as not growing them too dry all help keep mildew at bay. Avoid overhead watering for the same reason. Cut back to basal growth when stems die down or after flowering. If mildew is a problem, cut back to the ground after flowering, and water and feed with added mulch of compost or manure; new foliage should be unblemished.

You can actually delay bloom time by two weeks by simply lifting plants for half an hour or so and then replanting them. If you had six of the same variety, lift three of them and extend your bloom time by several weeks. You can also stage your show by pinching back in a particularly theatrical fashion: pinch stems at the back with a light touch, stems in front with a heavier touch, and the stems in between "just right." To have tiered plants in bloom in this manner, the pinching should all be done the same day.

Propagation: Seed; cuttings; spring division—autumn division okay with protection, *P. paniculata* is done from root cuttings (except for its variegated forms, which must be done from stem cuttings or division).

Pests and Diseases: Powdery mildew, snails, slugs, root rot, spider mites.

Companions: Eupatorium, salvia, aster, echinacea, geranium, hardy fuchsias, aconitum.

Notes: Border or garden phlox are a good cut flower but short-lived in water. More mildew-resistant forms of phlox are now appearing from the breeders.

Species and Cultivars	Height/ Spread	USDA Hardiness Zone	Flowers (bloom time)	Foliage	Comments
×arendsii 'Anja'	2ft × 1½ft	3–9	Bright reddish purple, fragrant (M)	Mid-green, lanceolate	Sun, mildew resistant, cut back hard after bloom for rebloom
×a. 'Hilda'	2ft × 1½ft	3–9	White with pink eye (E)	As above	As above
×a. 'Ping Pong'	1½–2ft × 1½ft	3–9	Light rose-pink, deep pink eye, fragrant (M–L)	As above	Mildew resistant, red stems
×a. (Spring Pearl Series) 'Miss Jill'	1½–2ft × 1½ft	3–9	White, pink eye, large (E–M)	As above	Mildew resistant
×a. (Spring Pearl Series) 'Miss Jo-Ellen'	1½–2ft × 1½ft	3–9	White with pink blush, fragrant (E–M)	As above	
×a. (Spring Pearl Series) 'Miss Karen'	1½–2ft × 1½ft	3–9	Dark rose with dark red eye (M)	As above	
×a. (Spring Pearl Series) 'Miss Margie'	1½–2ft × 1½ft	3–9	Lilac-blue (M–L)	As above	Mildew resistant

Species and Cultivars	Height/ Spread	USDA Hardiness Zone	Flowers (bloom time)	Foliage	Comments
×a. (Spring Pearl Series) 'Miss Mary'	1½–2ft × 1½ft	3–9	Clear red (M–L)	Dark green	
×a. (Spring Pearl Series) 'Miss Wilma'	1½–2ft × 1½ft	3–9	Lilac-blue fading to near white at the center (M–L)	Mid-green, lanceolate	
×a. 'Suzanne'	1–2ft × 1½ft	3–9	White with red eye (M)	As above	Sun, mildew resistant, cut back hard after bloom for rebloom
carolina 'Bill Baker'	2–4ft × 1ft	3–8	Bright pink to purple clusters, light center, fragrant, large (M–L)	Deep green, glossy, lanceolate to ovate	Carolina phlox, mildew resistant, RHS Award
c. 'Magnificence'	2–3ft × 1½ft	3–8	Pink, large, fragrant (M–L)	Dark green, glossy	Mildew resistant
c. 'Miss Lingard'	2–4ft × 1½ft	3–8	White, yellow eye, large, fragrant (E–M)	As above	Wedding phlox, mildew resistant, RHS Award
divaricata	8–15in × 12in	4–9	Light blue-lavender to violet, pink or white, fragrant (E–M)	Dark green, ovate to lanceolate to oblong	Part shade, semi-evergreen, cut back in early spring, RHS Award
d. 'Blue Perfume'	1–1½ft × 1½ft	4–9	Lilac-blue, fragrant (E–M)	As above	Semi-evergreen, cut back in early spring
d. 'Clouds of Perfume'	1ft × 1½ft	4–9	Icy blue, fragrant (E–M)	As above	As above
d. 'Dirigo Ice'	8–15in × 12in	4–9	Pale blue, fragrant (E–M)	As above	As above
d. 'Fuller's White'	8–15in × 12in	4–9	White, deeply notched petals, fragrant (E–M)	As above	Semi-evergreen, compact
d. subsp. laphamii	10–12in × 12in	4–9	Deep lavender-blue, dark violet-rose eye, fragrant (E–M)	Dark green, hairy	Semi-evergreen, cut back in early spring
d. subsp. laphamii 'Chattahoochee'	6–12in × 12in	4–9	Soft rich blue aging to purple-blue, purple-red center (E–L)	Dark green, hairy, lanceolate to linear	Lax stems, semi-evergreen, long-blooming, RHS Award
d. 'London Grove'	8–12in × 12in	4–9	Deep blue, fragrant (E–M)	Dark green, hairy, turns to burgundy in fall	Mildew resistant, semi-evergreen
d. 'Louisiana Purple'	8–12in × 12in	4–9	Dark bluish purple, darker eye, fragrant (E–M)	Dark green, hairy	Semi-evergreen
d. 'Plum Perfect'	8–12in × 12in	4–9	Light plum-purple, dark purple eye, fragrant (E–M)	As above	Shade tolerant, mildew resistant, semi-evergreen
d. 'White Perfume'	8–15in × 12in	4–9	White, fragrant (E–M)	Mid-green, hairy	Semi-evergreen, creeping
maculata	2–3ft × 1½ft	3–9	Purple and pink shades or white, conical heads, fragrant (M–L)	Green, glossy, linear to lanceolate or ovate	Wild sweet William, mildew resistant, sun, moist

Species and Cultivars	Height/ Spread	USDA Hardiness Zone	Flowers (bloom time)	Foliage	Comments
m. 'Alpha'	2–4ft × 1½ft	3–9	Lilac-pink with darker eye, fragrant (M)	Dark green, spotted stems	Mildew resistant, RHS Award
m. 'Natascha'	2–3ft × 1½ft	3–9	Bicolor, pink and white, fragrant (M–L)	Rich green, shiny	Mildew resistant
m. 'Omega'	2–3ft × 1½ft	3–9	White flushed with violet, pink eye, fragrant (M–L)	Mid-green, glossy	RHS Award
m. 'Rosalinde'	2–4ft × 1½ft	3–9	Pink, fragrant (M–L)	As above	Vigorous, long-blooming
paniculata	2–4ft × 2ft+	4–9	White to shades of pink, red, lavender, purple, and magenta, in clusters, fragrant (M–L)	Dark green, lanceolate-ovate, veined, foliage on cultivars very similar except as noted below	Prone to mildew, doesn't come true from seed, may need support, neutral pH, good air circulation
p. 'Amethyst'	2½–3ft × 2ft+	4–9	Soft lavender (M–L)	Similar to species	Mildew resistant
p. 'Blue Boy'	2–4ft × 2ft+	4–9	Bluish mauve, white eye, fragrant (M–L)	As above	Vigorous
p. 'Brigadier'	2–4ft × 2ft+	4–9	Magenta-red (M)	Dark green, lanceolate	RHS Award
p. 'Bright Eyes'	2–4ft × 2ft+	4–9	Pale pink with ruby-red eye (M–L)	Green with purple tints especially in spring	Mildew resistant, RHS Award
p. 'David'	2–4ft × 2½+	4–9	White, large, fragrant (M–L)	Green, oblong	Mildew resistant, vigorous, 2002 PPA Award
p. 'Dodo Hanbury-Forbes'	3–4ft × 2ft+	4–9	Pink with rose-red eye, large (M–L)	Similar to species	RHS Award
p. 'Duesterlohe' (syn. 'Nicky')	3–4ft × 2ft+	3–9	Dark purple, fragrant (M–L)	As above	Mildew resistant
p. 'Eva Cullum'	2–4ft × 2ft+	4–9	Clear pink with dark red eye, large, fragrant (M–L)	As above	As above
p. 'Fairest One'	2–3ft × 2ft+	4–9	Shell-pink (M–L)	As above	
p. 'Fairy's Petticoat'	3–3½ft × 2ft+	4–9	Light lilac-pink with dark red eye (M)	As above	
p. 'Franz Schubert'	2–3ft × 2ft+	4–9	Pale lilac-blue, pale margin and darker eye (M–L)	As above	Mildew resistant
p. 'Harlequin'	2½–4ft × 2ft+	4–9	Purplish pink, red eye (M–L)	White, green, and pink variegation, narrow	May revert
p. 'Juliet'	2ft × 2ft+	4–9	Pale pink, white eye (M–L)	Narrow	
p. 'Little Boy'	15in × 15in	3–9	Lilac-blue, white eye, fragrant (M)	Similar to species	Mildew resistant, long-blooming
p. 'Miss Elie'	3–3½ft × 1½ft	3–9	Bright rose (M–L)	As above	Mildew resistant
p. 'Miss Holland'	2½–3ft × 1½ft	3–9	White, red eye (M)	As above	As above

Species and Cultivars	Height/ Spread	USDA Hardiness Zone	Flowers (bloom time)	Foliage	Comments
p. 'Miss Kelly'	2½–3ft × 1½ft	3–9	Lilac, white eye (M–L)	Dark green, edged in burgundy	As above
p. 'Miss Pepper'	2–4ft × 1½ft	3–9	Pink, dark pink eye (M)	Similar to species	As above
p. 'Miss Universe'	3½ft × 1½ft	3–9	White (M)	As above	As above
p. 'Mount Fuji' (syn. 'Fujiyama')	3–4ft × 2ft+	4–9	Clear white, large (M–L)	Mid-green	Mildew resistant, needs no staking, RHS Award
p. 'Norah Leigh'	2–3ft × 2ft+	4–9	Pale lavender-pink, dark pink eye (M)	Ivory and green variegation, small patch of green in center	Mildew resistant, a good strong grower for a variegated plant
p. 'Prime Minister'	2½–3½ft × 2ft+	4–9	White, red eye (M–L)	Similar to species	Vigorous
p. 'Prince of Orange' (syn. 'Orange Perfection')	2–3ft × 2ft+	4–9	Salmon-orange, small red eye (M–L)	As above	Mildew resistant, RHS Award
p. 'Starfire'	2–3ft × 2ft+	4–9	Bright cherry-red (M–L)	Dark green with bronze	RHS Award
p. 'Tenor'	2–2½ft × 2ft+	3–9	Ruby-red (M–L)	Similar to species	
p. 'The King'	2–4ft × 2ft+	5–9	Deep purple, large (M–L)	As above	Mildew resistant, long-blooming
p. 'White Admiral'	3–4ft × 2ft+	4–9	White, fragrant (M–L)	As above	RHS Award
p. 'Windsor'	3–4ft × 2ft+	3–9	Carmine-rose, red eye (M–L)	As above	RHS Award

PHUOPSIS Rubiaceae

On first encounter *P. stylosa* is very charming, a froth of little pink flowers in small rounded heads. This easy perennial has lax stems and habit, and is usually allowed to flop about. Unfortunately, it has a rather skunky odor when brushed and can become moderately invasive. It never becomes a pest, but controlling a plant with a ripe scent can be troublesome for those with sensitive noses. The odor is more noticeable in a controlled space. If you buy it and leave it in your car, it will smell like a skunk died there when you return. Not so stinky in the garden, and it's worth noting that almost every garden in England has a clump of this plant. ~ *Bob Lilly*

Scientific Name: From the Greek *phou* (a kind of valerian) and *opsis* ("like").
Common Name: Crosswort.
Origin: Iran, Asia Minor, Caucasus.
Preferred Conditions: Any fertile, well-drained, moisture-retentive soil. Drought tolerant but protect from cold, dry winters.
Light: Sun.
Management: Clean up in fall. Cut back to original crown to control spread, and remove any rooted pieces in the process.

Phuopsis stylosa.

Propagation: Division in spring; stem cuttings; seed.
Pests and Diseases: Slugs in spring can be a problem.
Companions: A good edge-of-the-border plant, suitable as a groundcover.

Species and Cultivars	Height/ Spread	USDA Hardiness Zone	Flowers (bloom time)	Foliage	Comments
stylosa	10–12in × 18in	5–9	Rose-pink, tiny, in dense rounded heads (M–L)	Pale green, narrow, lanceolate, in whorls	Musky odor

PHYGELIUS Scrophulariaceae

These curious African plants are commonly referred to as Cape fuchsias, which of course they are not. You must look into the trumpet to see the full charm of the flower (all forms with red, orange, and pink flowers have blue pollen when they first open). The hummingbirds do this every day of the flowering season, which for us is from late May to November—an exceptionally long bloom time. They are a good cut flower, not too fussy, and great for the summer border, but they cannot be home alone: these plants need supervision. Their running nature makes them a bit sloppy; they travel out from the center, the center becomes vacant, and the outriggers are often not pinched in time and get too tall and floppy. ~ *Bob Lilly*

Scientific Name: From the Greek *phyge* ("flight") and *helios* ("sun").
Common Name: Cape fuchsia.
Origin: South Africa.

Phygelius aequalis 'Yellow Trumpet'.

Preferred Conditions: Nice, sharp, lean, well-drained soil. Protect from winter wet in cold climates.

Light: Sun. Tolerates part shade.

Management: Once they are well established (usually by the third year), cut back to the ground in spring to encourage strong shoots and new growth and to control their size. This gives a couple more years of good behavior, after which replacement is advised. Deadhead to keep plant tidy and prolong flowering; cut the old panicles just above a pair of good, strong new shoots. A well-established plant with heavy growth will respond to a bit of shaping. Remove the long underground runners (root prune) and share with your friends. Don't let them dry out during the growing season.

Propagation: Seed for species; cuttings for cultivars; division in spring.

Pests and Diseases: None except lazy gardeners.

Companions: Perovskia, carex, hemerocallis, rudbeckia, salvia, penstemon, alstroemeria, crocosmia, dahlia, *Persicaria microcephala* 'Red Dragon'.

Notes: You can see how they perform in heavy clay and poor drainage at the Bellevue Botanical Garden NPA Borders. All that manure is a bit much for them. We remove the old flower clusters just before the last flower on the tip blooms, and get reliable rebloom in a normal summer. Look for the new forms of the Croftway Series ('Purple Prince', 'Coral Princess', 'Snow Queen', 'Yellow Sovereign'); they are all more compact. In the chart, the symbol ∞ = infinite spread.

Species and Cultivars	Height/ Spread	USDA Hardiness Zone	Flowers (bloom time)	Foliage	Comments
aequalis	3ft × ∞	7–9	Soft coral-red with yellow throat, hints of green (M–L)	Dark green, ovate	A vigorous plant once established
a. Sensation = 'Sani Pass'	3–4ft × 3ft+	7–9	Red-violet (M–L)	Very dark green, leaves and stems	Slow to establish

Species and Cultivars	Height/ Spread	USDA Hardiness Zone	Flowers (bloom time)	Foliage	Comments
a. 'Trewidden Pink'	3–4ft × 3ft+	7–9	Rose-pink with deep rose inner lip, yellow throat (M–L)	Dark green	RHS Award
a. 'Yellow Trumpet'	3–8ft × ∞	7–10	Pale yellow racemes, one-sided inflorescence (M–L)	Mid-green, coarse	Vigorous, RHS Award
capensis	3–8ft × ∞	7–10	Bright red to orange, yellow throat (M–L)	Dark green, round to ovate, very dark stems	Cape fuchsia, semi-evergreen, sprawling, vigorous, RHS Award
New Sensation = 'Blaphy'	3–4ft × 3ft	7–9	Red-violet (M–L)	Very dark green, dark petioles	Slow to establish
×rectus 'African Queen'	3–4ft × ∞	7–9	Reddish orange with yellow throat (M–L)	Deep green, glossy	Extremely vigorous, RHS Award
×r. 'Devil's Tears'	3–4ft × ∞	7–9	Smoky coral, dark red buds, yellow throat (M–L)	Dark green	As above, RHS Award
×r. 'Moonraker'	3ft+ × ∞	7–9	Pale creamy yellow, arranged around the stem (M–L)	Mid-green	Extremely vigorous
×r. 'Pink Elf'	2½ft × 3ft	7–9	Pale dusky pink, deep red buds, yellow throat (M)	Dark green	More compact
×r. 'Salmon Leap'	3–4ft × 3ft+	7–9	Salmon, yellow throat, pendent toward stem (M–L)	As above	RHS Award
×r. 'Winchester Fanfare'	3–4ft × ∞	7–9	Reddish pink, yellow throat (M–L)	As above	Vigorous, open inflorescence

PHYSALIS Solanaceae

Note the drawbacks of these plants before you fall for their attractions. It doesn't take long (if conditions are right) for plants to take over their allotted space and then some. A member of the potato family, physalis has blossoms that are small, white, and starry; the light green leaves are alternate, ovate, and rather limp. Underneath it all are long, fast-growing rhizomes, so plants have to have room. But the orange lanterns look great. If you wish to try growing one, *P. alkekengi* var. *franchetii* is the best, having the largest lanterns. *Physalis peruviana* has edible, bright yellow-orange berries enclosed in a lanternlike tan calyx. The orange fruits of *P. alkekengi* are very popular for dried arrangements; cut them just as calyces get to their full color in fall and remove the leaves. ~ *Susan Buckles*

Scientific Name: From the Greek *physa* ("bladder"), referring to the bladderlike fruits.
Common Name: Chinese lantern.
Origin: Europe, Asia.
Preferred Conditions: Any fertile soil that is well drained and alkaline.
Light: Sun.

Physalis alkekengi var. *franchetii* 'Gigantea'.

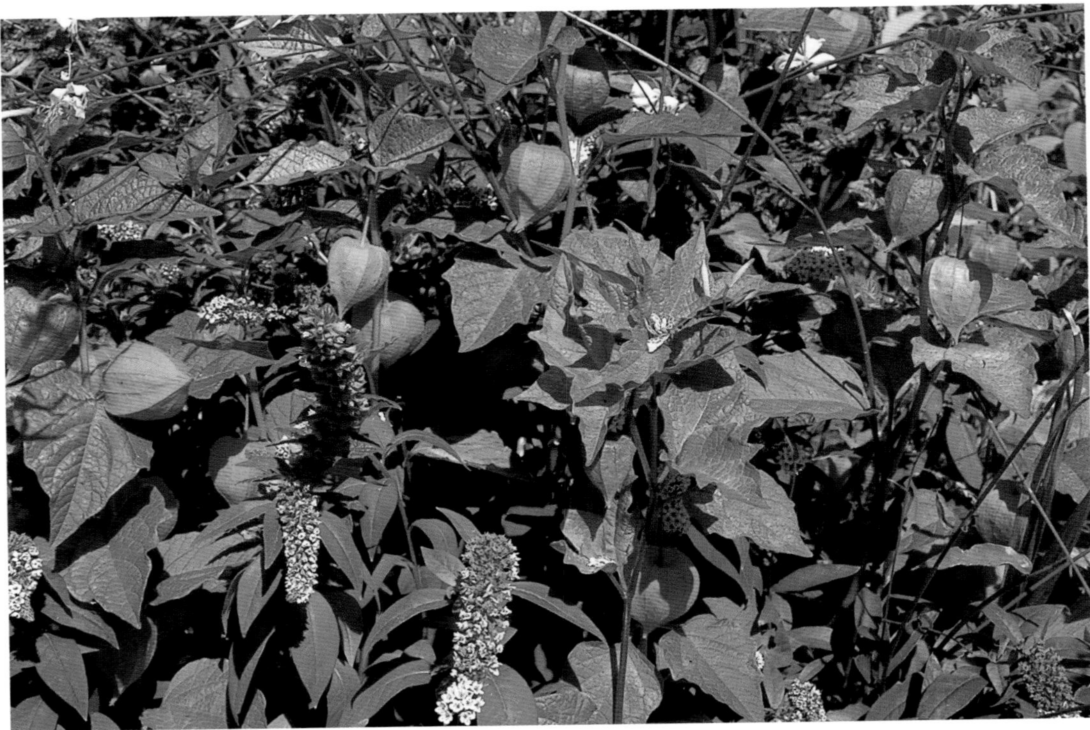

Management: They may need some twiggy support. Do not cut back after flowering, as their main attraction is the orange calyces. Clean up in winter, and bait, bait, bait! Most failure with Chinese lanterns is due to slugs eating the new shoots at or below ground level.

Propagation: Seed (germination is irregular, about fifty days); division in spring; cuttings.

Pests and Diseases: Rust, white smut, caterpillars, leaf spot.

Companions: Best grown alone in a cutting garden.

Notes: Slugs make this plant almost impossible to grow in the Pacific Northwest. The annuals *P. pruinosa* and *P. pubescens*, commonly called dwarf Cape gooseberry, husk tomato, or ground cherry, have delicious edible fruit; *P. ixocarpa*, the common tomatillo we are all familiar with, is also an annual. The leaves and stems of all the plants in the chart are skin irritants; they also should not be ingested.

Species and Cultivars	Height/ Spread	USDA Hardiness Zone	Flowers (bloom time)	Foliage	Comments
alkekengi	1–2ft × 2ft+	5–8	Creamy-white, nodding, inconspicuous (M)	Light green, triangular-ovate to diamond-shaped	Chinese lantern, bright orange-red papery calyces 2in across, RHS Award
a. var. franchetii	1½–2½ft × 2ft+	5–8	Creamy-white, inconspicuous (M)	Light green, larger than species	Larger, bright orange-red, more-pointed calyces
a. var. franchetii 'Gigantea'	1–3ft × 2½ft+	5–8	As above	As above	This may be the cut flower trade cultivar, large berries
a. var. franchetii 'Variegata'	1–2ft × 2ft+	5–8	As above	Cream and yellow-green borders	
peruviana	1–3ft × 2ft+	5–8	Greenish, starlike (M–L)	Mid-green, hairy leaves, semi-evergreen	Cape gooseberry, subshrub, the edible fruit form

PHYSOSTEGIA Lamiaceae

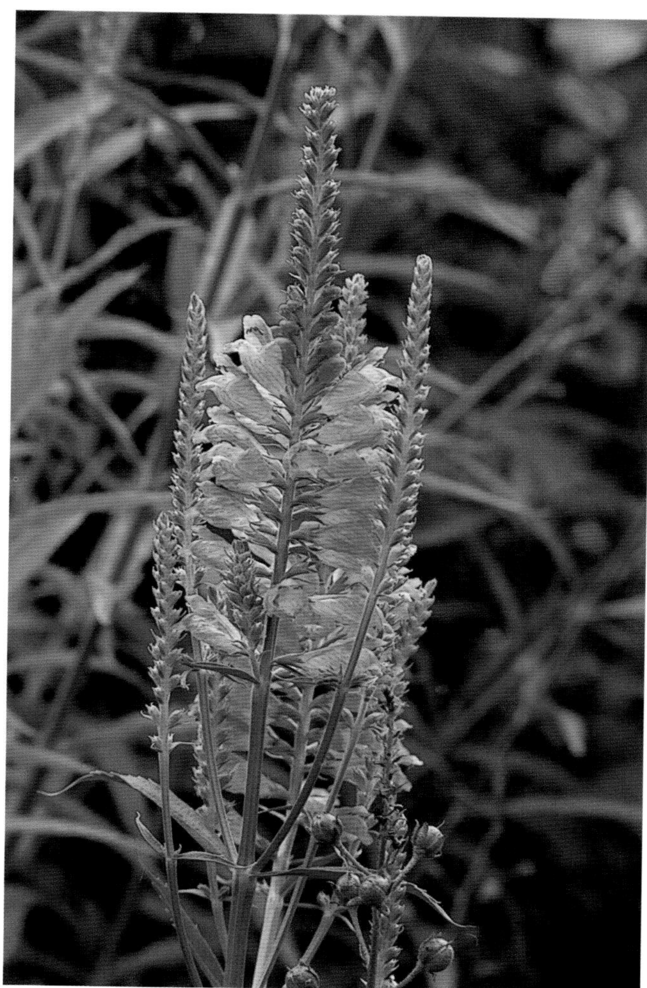
Physostegia virginiana.

The obedient plant, typical of the mint family, is not very obedient when it comes to staying where it's put in the garden. This species does move about, spreading actively by rhizomes, especially on rich, moist sites. Plant it in drier soil and fertilize sparingly, and it will be more obedient. The plant actually got its common name because if a flower is pushed aside to a new position, it will remain there obediently, as if on a hinge. This is a real bonus when using the cut flowers in arrangements, not to mention entertaining to garden visitors.

Physostegia virginiana and its cultivars have attractive flowers that appear on stiff, upright stems over a period of weeks in late summer and fall. They are tubular, two-lipped, and open from the bottom up, in shades of pink, purple, and white. Attractive green seed capsules follow the flowers; these look great in dried floral arrangements (hang them upside down to dry). The narrow, two- to six-inch-long leaves of *P. virginiana* 'Variegata' are grayish green bordered in a creamy white. This cultivar is less assertive in its rambling habit; *P. virginiana* 'Summer Snow' is also less invasive. ~ *Susan Carter*

Scientific Name: From the Greek *physa* ("bladder") and *stege* ("roof"); the fruits or seeds are covered by an inflated calyx.
Common Name: Obedient plant, false dragonhead.
Origin: North America.
Preferred Conditions: Any moist, well drained, and slightly acidic garden soil. Doesn't like it too dry or too hot, but otherwise undemanding.
Light: Sun to part shade. In too much shade, stems may be weak and flowers dull.
Management: Cutting this plant back after bloom will not produce a second flowering. Divide every two or three years to control spread. Staking may be necessary, particularly if grown in rich soil and part shade. Cut down to crown in winter.
Propagation: Seed (cultivars won't come true); cuttings; division in spring.
Pests and Diseases: Rust, snails, slugs.
Companions: Grasses, monarda, phlox, aster (especially dark-leaved forms), echinacea, *Anemone japonica*, *Cosmos bipinnatus*, *Dahlia merckii*, *D.* 'Fascination', chrysanthemum, boltonia.
Notes: If left to its own devices, *P. virginiana* will spread much further than the two feet noted in the chart.

Species and Cultivars	Height/ Spread	USDA Hardiness Zone	Flowers (bloom time)	Foliage	Comments
virginiana	2½–4ft × 2ft	4–8	Bright lilac-pink (M–L)	Dark green, narrow, toothed, lanceolate	Long-blooming, clump-forming
v. 'Alba'	1½–3ft × 2ft	4–8	Pure white (M–L)	Dark green, toothed	

Species and Cultivars	Height/ Spread	USDA Hardiness Zone	Flowers (bloom time)	Foliage	Comments
v. 'Miss Manners'	1½–2ft × 2ft	4–8	White (M–L)	Dark green, toothed, lanceolate	Clump-forming, not invasive
v. 'Rosea'	3ft × 2ft	4–8	Rose-pink (M–L)	Dark green, toothed	
v. var. speciosa 'Bouquet Rose'	2½–3ft × 2ft	4–8	Bright lilac-pink (M–L)	Dark green, coarsely toothed	Stems tend to flop
v. var. speciosa 'Variegata'	1½–3ft × 2ft	4–8	Lilac-pink, white in bud (M–L)	Grayish green, toothed, bordered in creamy white	Less invasive
v. 'Summer Snow' (syn. 'Snow Queen')	2–3ft × 2ft	4–8	Pure white, green calyces (M–L)	Mid-green	Less rampant, may need support, RHS Award
v. 'Vivid'	1–2ft × 2ft	4–8	Bright rose-pink (M–L)	Dark green	Shorter, dense inflorescence, blooms later

PHYTOLACCA Phytolaccaceae

"Poke Salad Annie, the gators got your granny, chomp, chomp, chomp." This was a popular song in the late 1960s and the only thing we knew about pokeweed until we grew it. There are only a few species in garden culture. The very tall *P. americana* and the moderately tall *P. polyandra* are what we generally find for sale. Both are herbaceous, going to ground in late fall, following frost, wind, and rain; sometimes the weather claims them earlier.

Phytolacca americana can easily grow to ten feet in a season. In bloom, tight racemes of white flowers are all over the upper half of the plant; these are followed by green fruits that, over time, turn to blue-black, with bright red-violet stems visible through the fruit clusters. This fall show brings birds, especially cedar waxwings, to the garden stage. The birds spread seed following digestion, so some monitoring of seedlings is necessary the following spring. Not a thug, but you can have too many. The other two species do roughly all these things, only shorter. ~ *Carrie Becker*

Scientific Name: From the Greek *phyton* ("plant") and the Latin *lacca*, referring to the lac insect and the dye extracted from it.
Common Name: Pokeweed.
Origin: North America, Mexico, Asia, Africa, China.
Preferred Conditions: Fertile, deep, moisture-retentive soil. Protect from autumn winds, which can damage plants that are heavy with ripened fruit.
Light: Sun to part shade.
Management: May need some support. Plants come up in the spring and go down at frost. Remove seedlings as they appear to control spread, or pot them up for new plants. Cut to the ground after fruit is eaten by birds.
Propagation: Seed; division in spring or fall.
Pests and Diseases: Slugs, early on.
Companions: Miscanthus, viburnum, hydrangea, shrub roses, dahlia, tall asters, vernonia.
Notes: Phytolacca is poisonous and must be processed (boiled in fresh water several times) before the spring greens are edible. Personally, we'd skip it.

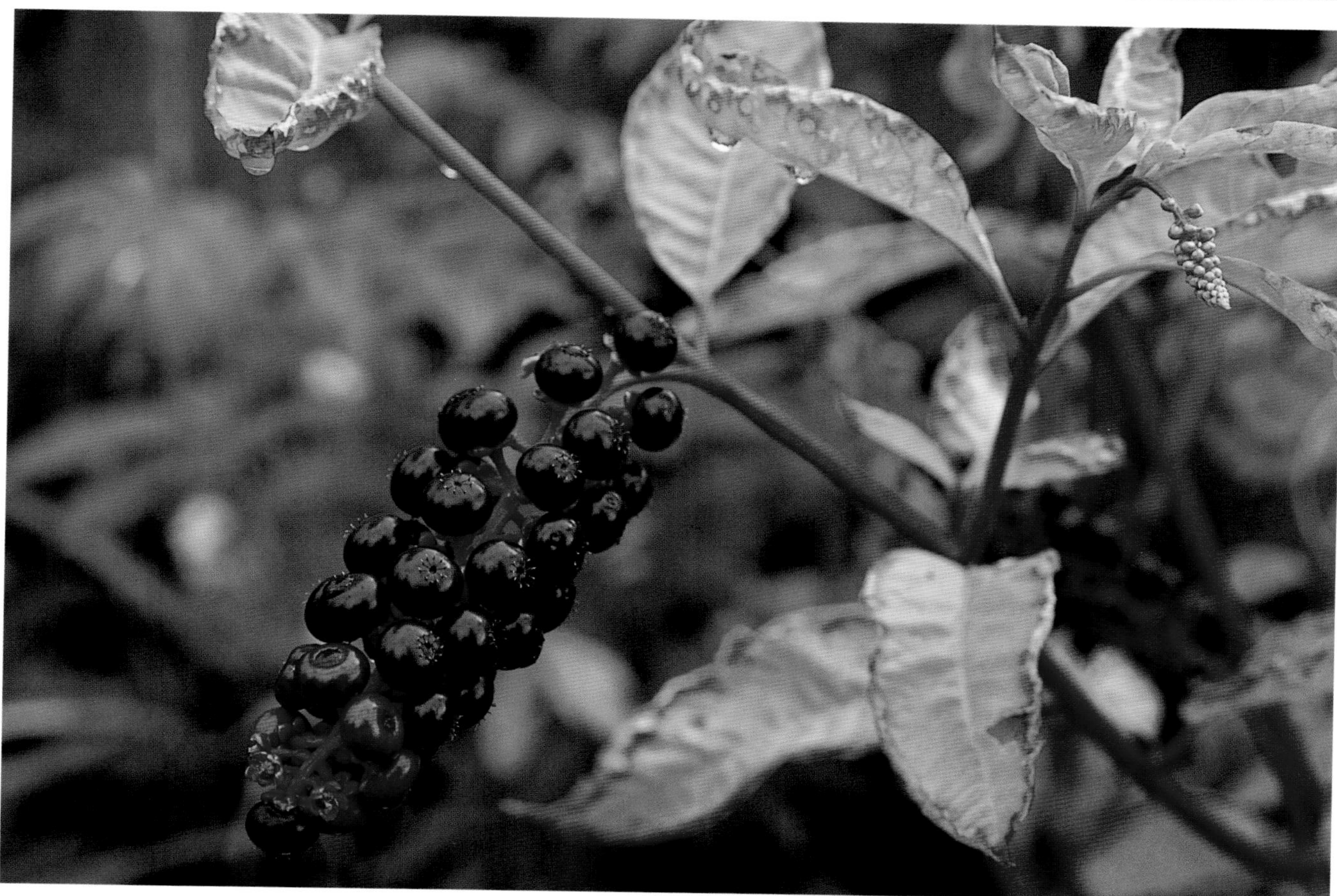

Phytolacca americana.

Species and Cultivars	Height/ Spread	USDA Hardiness Zone	Flowers (bloom time)	Foliage	Comments
acinosa	4–6ft × 3ft	4–9	White, held upright (M)	Mid-green	Upright, erect, black-purple fruit turning magenta
americana (syn. decandra)	6–10ft × 3ft	4–9	White or pinkish, drooping (M)	Mid-green, purple-tinged in autumn, lanceolate-ovate, 12in long	Erect, clump-forming, long-lived, coarse, weedy-looking, green fruit ripens to black
polyandra (syn. clavigera)	5–6ft × 2ft	6–9	Purplish pink, erect racemes (M)	Mid-green, to 12in	Fruit green then magenta then black

Pimpinella major 'Rosea'.

PIMPINELLA Apiaceae

Pimpinella major 'Rosea', a two- to four-foot plant with very divided large-toothed shiny leaves, resembles a pink Queen Anne's lace in bloom. I pictured it making a lovely bouquet among the bulbs that I plant in my upper bed. Only problem—they wanted the whole bed! I grow them and enjoy them, but now know I have to keep a sharp eye out for seedlings. Seeding seems to be more of an issue in drier, lighter soils. Theoretically, not all the seedlings will be pink-flowered, but so far mine have been. ~ *Ann Bucher*

Scientific Name: Obscure.
Common Name: Pimpinella.
Origin: North America, Caucasus, Europe.
Preferred Conditions: Average, moist, cool soil. Regular summer water but is drought tolerant (deep taproot) once established.
Light: Sun to part shade.
Planting: Avoid damage to taproots when transplanting.
Management: Resents disturbance. Clean up and cut back to crown in fall. Best to treat as short-lived (three to four years), so self-sowing is useful to keep this plant in your garden.
Propagation: Seed is best; taproot makes division difficult.
Pests and Diseases: Aphids, snails, slugs.
Companions: Grasses, *Campanula lactiflora*, *Astrantia maxima*, *Anthriscus sylvestris* 'Ravenswing', cryptotaenia, geranium, astilbe (early cultivars), delphinium, aconitum, paeonia, roses.
Notes: Best performance with its own space and not too much competition. Much better behaved on heavy soils. In fact, one wishes for more.

Species and Cultivars	Height/ Spread	USDA Hardiness Zone	Flowers (bloom time)	Foliage	Comments
major 'Rosea'	2–4ft × 1½ft	5–9	Pale pink (M)	Mid-green, pinnately divided, coarsely toothed, triangular-rounded	Will seed about over time

Pinellia cordata.

PINELLIA Araceae

These close relatives of arum and asarum are wonderful in the shade garden. They have the usual hooded spathulate flowers with long green "tails" off the usually green hoods. Clumps do get larger over time but are slow about it. They do very well in pots, particularly *P. ternata* and *P. tripartita*. ~ *Bob Lilly*

Species and Cultivars	Height/ Spread	USDA Hardiness Zone	Flowers (bloom time)	Foliage	Comments
cordata	6–8in × 4–6in	6–9	Greenish yellow spathe, curved, with hair-thin spadix, pale green (M)	Green, purple reverse, glossy, cordate, veins etched in white	Shiny black stems, bubblegum fragrance
pedatisecta	10–12in × 6in	6–9	Green to yellow-green spadix and spathe above the leaves (M)	7–11 segments, many-lobed, pedate, on a 10–12in petiole	Tuberous
ternata	8in × 6in	6–9	Pale green spathe, slightly hooded, slender green spadix, purple-tinged, at leaf level (M)	Mid-green, ovate-elliptic to oblong, 3-part	Weedy, invasive, tuberous
tripartita	10–12in × 8in	6–9	Green spathe, narrow, nodding tips, long (10in) spadix, mid-green, just below leaf level (M)	Mid-green, wider leaves, 3-part, lobed, on a 10–12in petiole	Self-sows

Scientific Name: After Giovanni Vincenzo Pinelli, who had a botanical garden in Naples.
Common Name: Sweet arum, green dragon.
Origin: China, Korea, Japan.
Preferred Conditions: Fertile, humus-rich, well-drained soil.
Light: Sun to part shade.
Management: Clean up in fall after leaves die back. Mulch for winter protection. Watch for slugs in very early spring. Do not allow it to dry out.
Propagation: Remove offsets and replant in spring.
Pests and Diseases: Slugs.
Companions: Ferns, hosta, arisaema, hakonechloa, helleborus.
Notes: They get taller for us than listed.

PLANTAGO Plantaginaceae

I never thought I would deliberately invite plantain into my garden. That was before I was introduced to *P. major* 'Rubrifolia' and its bronze-purplish leaves. If you can be diligent about cutting off the seed stalks, it's a plant worth having. It does self-sow true, so don't worry that you'd be establishing a colony of the green form, *P. major*, which you probably have already. It would be a lot safer to plant *P. major* 'Rosularis'; the entire plant is green including its interesting flower: roselike clusters of leafy bracts. ~ *Susan Carter*

Scientific Name: From the Latin *planta* ("footprint," "sole of the foot").
Common Name: Plantain.
Origin: Europe.
Preferred Conditions: Most any soil, even dry ones.
Light: Sun to part shade.

Plantago major 'Rubrifolia'.

Management: Cut off seed stalks to prevent self-sowing. Remove diseased leaves and dispose of them. Clean up in fall after leaves die back. Don't let all the seed ripen on *P. major* 'Rubrifolia'.
Propagation: Seed is usually best; division in fall or spring.
Pests and Diseases: Aphids, spider mites, rust, downy mildew, powdery mildew (especially if too dry).
Companions: Astrantia, dahlia, hemerocallis, *Ceratostigma plumbaginoides, Veronica peduncularis* 'Georgia Blue', *Lobelia laxiflora, Achillea* 'Terracotta', polemonium.
Notes: *Plantago major* 'Rosularis' always gets powdery mildew but is quite a cute little thing until the day it is suddenly covered with spots and patches.

Species and Cultivars	Height/ Spread	USDA Hardiness Zone	Flowers (bloom time)	Foliage	Comments
major 'Rosularis' (syn. 'Bowles' Variety')	8–9in × 10in	4–8	Short scapes ending in a tight rosette of leaflike green bracts (E–M)	Green, very similar to the lawn weed	Rose plantain, produces no seed, division only
m. 'Rubrifolia' (syn. 'Atropurpurea')	1ft × 1½ft	3–9	Green, flushed maroon, tiny, 4-lobed on thin spikes (E–M)	Bronze-purple above, bronze-green beneath, loose, basal rosettes, ribbed, elliptic to ovate, broad	A very tough plant, comes true from seed

PLATYCODON Campanulaceae

The flower buds of platycodon look like small, inflated balloons (hence the common name). As the bud matures, the "balloon" expands, appearing as if it will burst, and finally opens into a

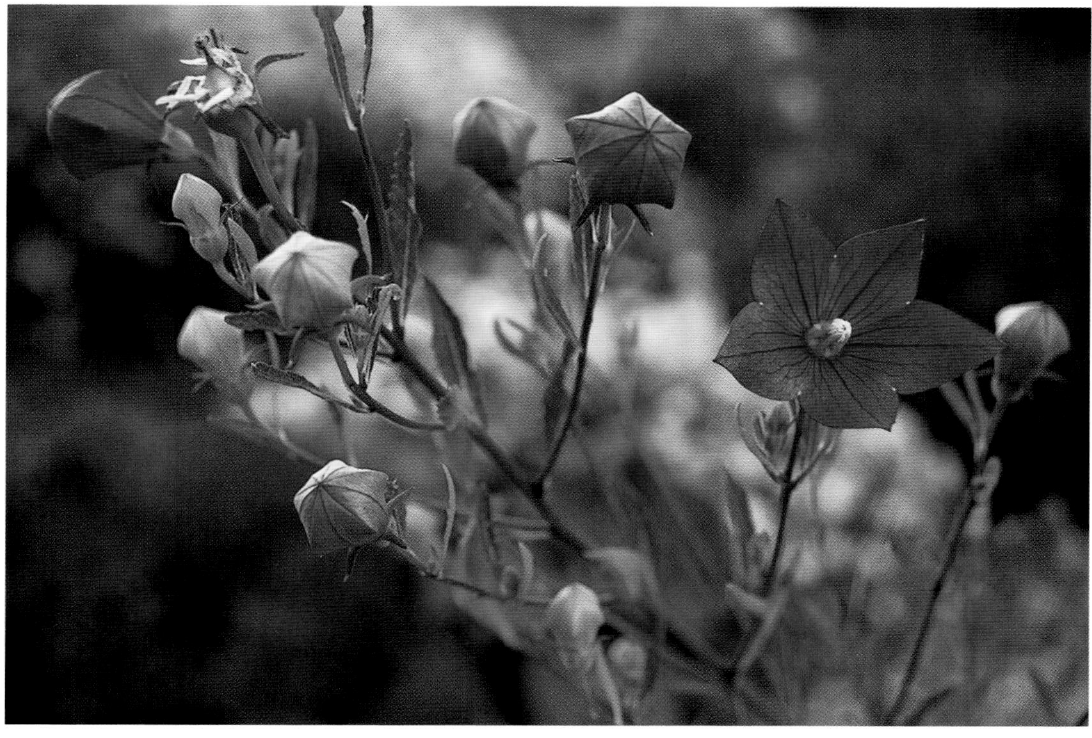

Platycodon grandiflorus.

graceful lobed flower, usually blue to purple, sometimes pink or white. The genus *Platycodon* is monotypic (one species only). *Platycodon grandiflorus* and its cultivars have flowers that are borne in clusters atop erect stems. There is a lovely double form, *P. grandiflorus* 'Hakone White'. Each flower has five pointed petals with darker veins and is two to three inches across. Plants form nice clumps of hairless stems with bluish green leaves. They are long-lived but are not fond of being crowded or overgrown by other plants. Makes an excellent, long-lasting cut flower if the base of the stem is seared with a flame before being placed into water. ~ *Susan Carter*

Scientific Name: From the Greek *platys* ("broad") and *kodon* ("bell"), referring to the shape of the corolla.
Common Name: Balloon flower.
Origin: Asia, China, Korea, Japan, Siberia.
Preferred Conditions: Deep, fertile, loamy, well-drained, moisture-retentive soil. Fleshy roots are likely to rot if soil is too damp and heavy.
Light: Sun to part shade.
Planting: Set the crown about one inch below the surface.
Management: Stems may require support. Do not cut the old stems back when the blossoms are gone (these help feed the roots); let them die away naturally, and then cut to about three inches tall to protect the crown. Clear away old foliage as it dies back in autumn or during winter cleanup. New shoots are late emerging so mark the spot, so you don't accidentally disturb or step on them. Takes two or three years to get established and resents disturbance. Do not mulch heavily over the crown.
Propagation: Seed in situ, or in containers in spring; basal cuttings; careful division in spring (roots go very deep).
Pests and Diseases: Leaf spot, snails, slugs.
Companions: Fuchsia, achillea, astrantia, nepeta, *Knautia macedonica*, campanula, veronica, *Aster ×frikartii*.
Notes: In the maritime Northwest, platycodon needs full sun and your warmest location; does well in dry soil once established.

Species and Cultivars	Height/ Spread	USDA Hardiness Zone	Flowers (bloom time)	Foliage	Comments
grandiflorus	1½–3ft × 1ft	3–8	Clusters of star-shaped bluish purple, darker veins (M)	Bluish green, ovate to lanceolate, toothed, foliage on all cultivars is very similar	Long-lived, RHS Award
g. 'Albus'	2ft × 1ft	3–8	White with blue or yellowish veins, large (M)	As above	White Chinese balloon flower
g. 'Fuji Blue'	1½–2ft × 1ft	3–8	Lavender-blue (M)	Same as species but not as large	Bred for pot culture
g. 'Fuji Pink'	1½–2ft × 1ft	3–8	Soft shell-pink (M)	As above	Best in part shade
g. 'Fuji White'	1½–2ft × 1ft	3–8	Clean white (M)	As above	
g. 'Hakone Double Blue'	1½–2ft × 1ft	3–8	Rich violet-blue, darker veins, double (M)	As above	
g. 'Hakone White'	1½–2ft × 1ft	3–8	Double white (M)	As above	A lovely form
g. 'Komachi'	9–10in × 10in	3–8	Deep purplish blue buds opens to blue (M)	As above	Flower holds the balloon shape and never fully opens

Species and Cultivars	Height/ Spread	USDA Hardiness Zone	Flowers (bloom time)	Foliage	Comments
g. 'Mariesii'	12–18in × 10in	3–8	Rich blue with deep blue buds (M)	As above	Semi-dwarf, flowers earlier than species, RHS Award
g. 'Perlmutterschale' (syn. 'Mother of Pearl', 'Shell Pink')	1½–2ft × 1ft	3–8	Pale pink (M)	As above	Long-lasting
g. 'Sentimental Blue'	6–8in × 6in	3–8	Intense blue (M)	As above	Bred for pot culture

PODOPHYLLUM Berberidaceae

All podophyllums are rhizomatous and attractive in leaf and flower. Their leaves emerge on short, eventually lengthening petioles. All leaves are peltate; some are lobed, some toothed, and some blotched between the veins; *P.* 'Kaleidoscope' is quite unreal-looking, with very dramatic patterning. The flowers, which are solitary or in clusters, are cup-shaped pink, white, or red. They arrive with the leaves, opening shortly before or shortly after the leaves unfold. Nodding green, turning red or yellow, fruit follows them, hiding under the large leaves; it's worth sneaking a peek at it. All parts of the plant are poisonous, except for the fully ripe fruit of certain species. ~ *Ann Bucher*

Scientific Name: From the Greek *podos* ("foot") and *phyllon* ("leaf").
Common Name: May apple.
Origin: Himalayas, North America, China, Taiwan, India.

Podophyllum pleianthum.

Preferred Conditions: The holy grail: humus-rich, cool, moist, deep, fertile, well-drained soil, such as might be found in undisturbed ancient woodland (*P. peltatum* tolerates drier soil).
Light: Part shade to shade.
Planting: Set rhizomes horizontally.
Management: Does not like to be disturbed. Remove old foliage and stems when plant dies back. Top-dress with organic material; the young leaves are frost tender. Protect marginally hardy species with a dry winter mulch.
Propagation: Division of rhizomes in spring once established (*P. peltatum* is especially easy to divide); seed—slow and irregular.
Pests and Diseases: Slugs, especially on emerging growth.
Companions: Ferns, hosta, epimedium, primula, geranium, *Aster divaricatus*, pulmonaria, aquilegia, asarum, hakonechloa.
Notes: Once established, *P. peltatum* is almost unstoppable and runs long distances.

Species and Cultivars	Height/ Spread	USDA Hardiness Zone	Flowers (bloom time)	Foliage	Comments
hexandrum (syn. emodi)	1–1½ft × 2ft	5–8	White or pale pink, cupped, solitary, upright, under the foliage (E–M)	Mid-green with brownish mottling, deeply lobed, rounded, 12in across	Himalayan May apple, egg-sized fleshy red edible fruit
'Kaleidoscope'	1½–3ft × 2ft	5–9	Dark burgundy-red, pendent, under the foliage (E–M)	Olive-green and burgundy over a silver-green background, peltate, 18–20in	Must be coddled when young
peltatum	1–1½ft × 2½ft+	4–9	Creamy-white to pale pink, solitary, pendent, fragrant (E)	Green, glossy, lobed and toothed, 1 round leaf, 2 half-round leaves, 12in across	May apple, East Coast native, most aggressive, 1–2in yellowish to rose edible fruit
pleianthum	1½ft × 3ft	6–8	Deep crimson to purple clusters, ill-scented (E–M)	Green, glossy, marbled, finely toothed, 18–20in across	Chinese May apple, dark red fruit, may need winter protection

POLEMONIUM Polemoniaceae

These are good plants for foliage and flower quality, although some have a tendency to flop and grow from a droopy position. There are many species, all with merit. Many are North American natives, some suited to wildflower situations, others to the mixed border; some are fragrant. Breeding has resulted in good hybrids (relatively new are *P.* 'Bressingham Purple', *P.* 'Lambrook Mauve', and *P.* 'Northern Lights'), but the species are as good as their offspring and have been growing in gardens for a long time. Graham Stuart Thomas (1990) claims they have been cultivated "since Roman days." Jacob's ladders are short-lived, but seeding must be easy if they have lasted so long in cultivation. None of the polemoniums are uncontrollably invasive; they mix well with other perennials and semi-woody plants by weaving among them, coming up through and between other, more strongly erect plants that help to support them. ~ *Susan Buckles*

Scientific Name: From *polemonion*, the Greek name of a medicinal plant.

Common Name: Jacob's ladder.

Origin: Europe, North America, Mexico, northern Asia.

Preferred Conditions: Average, fertile, cool, constantly moist, well-drained soil. Small species prefer gritty, sharply drained soil.

Light: Part shade to sun. Small species prefer sun.

Management: Divide clumps frequently (every three years) to rejuvenate the plant. Cut off mildewed parts. Cut back to basal growth after flowering and clean up in fall. Taller ones may need staking in sandy or light soils. Try pea sticks for control.

Propagation: Division; easy from seed (cultivars don't come true).

Pests and Diseases: Slugs. Another plant with drought (wilt) as a trigger for powdery mildew.

Companions: Ferns, artemisia, euphorbia, campanula, hosta, helleborus, geum, potentilla, pulmonaria, brunnera.

Notes: *Polemonium caeruleum*, *P. pauciflorum*, and all the cultivars in the chart will flop and cover a larger spread then listed.

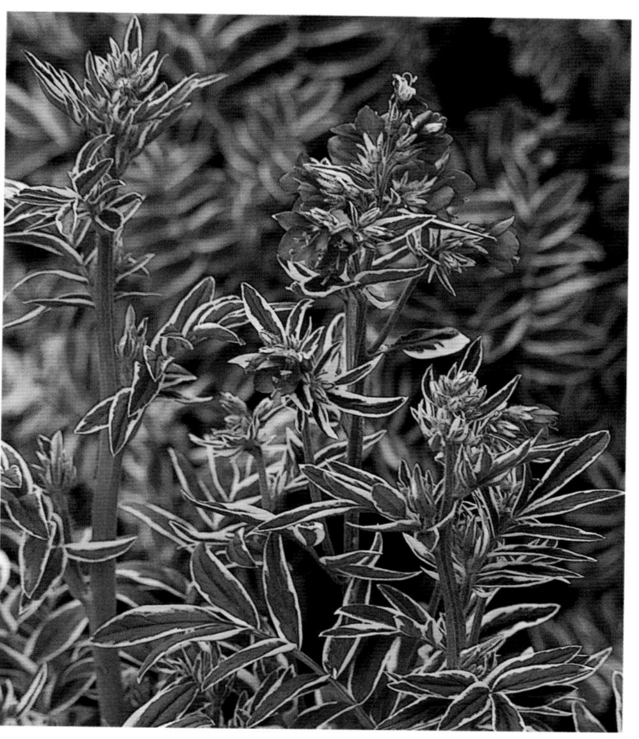

Polemonium caeruleum 'Brise d'Anjou'.

Species and Cultivars	Height/ Spread	USDA Hardiness Zone	Flowers (bloom time)	Foliage	Comments
'Bressingham Purple'	1½–2½ft × 1ft	4–8	Light violet-blue (M)	Rich dark purple in spring, green in summer, pinnate	Dark purple stems, compact, full sun for best leaf color
caeruleum	2–3ft × 1ft	4–8	Lavender-blue clusters, orange stamens, open and loose, fragrant (E–M)	Dark green, pinnate, oblong to lanceolate	Jacob's ladder, long-blooming, self-sows
c. 'Brise d'Anjou'	1½–2ft × 1ft	4–8	Violet-blue (E–M)	Dark green edged with pale cream, pinnate, showy	Flowers less profuse than species, more difficult to grow
c. subsp. caeruleum f. album	2ft × 1ft	4–8	White, fragrant (M)	Mid-green, pinnate, oblong to lanceolate	Long-blooming
carneum	1–1½ft × 10in	4–8	Pale pink, sometimes dark purple fading to lavender-blue, yellow center (E–M)	Green, hairless, coarsely divided, pinnate, elliptic to ovate	North American native, more sprawling
c. 'Apricot Delight' (syn. ambervicsii 'Apricot Beauty')	15–20in × 10in	3–9	Apricot and lilac with orange eye (E–M)	As above	Long-blooming, a lovely soft color
foliosissimum	2½–3ft × 1ft	4–8	Purplish blue, cream, or white, bright orange stamens (M)	Green, pinnate, elliptic to lanceolate, hairy stems	Long-blooming, more drought tolerant
'Lambrook Mauve'	1–1½ft × 1ft	4–8	Pale lavender-mauve, lax cymes (E–M)	Green, pinnate	Reddish stems, compact, RHS Award

Species and Cultivars	Height/ Spread	USDA Hardiness Zone	Flowers (bloom time)	Foliage	Comments
'Northern Lights'	1–1½ft × 1ft	4–8	Clear blue with a hint of purple (M)	Green	Compact
pauciflorum	12–20in × 18in	7–9	Pale yellow with red tinge, pendent (E–M)	Green, softly hairy stems	Not as cold hardy
reptans	8–10in × 12in	3–9	Pale lavender-blue, white stamens, very open (E–M)	Green, not as finely cut, 3–9 pairs of leaflets, ovate to oblong-lanceolate, new foliage has a dark cast	Greek valerian, self-sows
r. 'Blue Pearl'	10–12in × 12in	3–8	Blue, fragrant (E–M)	As above	Arching stems
yezoense 'Purple Rain'	1½–2ft × 1ft	3–8	Blue (E–M)	Green, new foliage is purple-tinged	Dark stems

POLYGONATUM Convallariaceae

Solomon's seal is a wonderful woodland plant grown both for the flowers and the foliage. If you have a spot in the shade (or part sun) this plant will win a place in your garden as well as your heart. The arching stems look very graceful holding on to leaves that vary from narrowly lanceolate-ovate to oval. This sophisticated posture continues on through the summer and into fall and the first frost, when it dies back to the ground. *Polygonatum odoratum* var. *pluriflorum* 'Variegatum', with its white-margined leaves and creamy white flowers, adds a subtle charm to the shady garden.

The flowers are either solitary or produced in clusters or pairs, hanging along the lower sides of the stems from the leaf axils. The blooms are creamy or greenish white except for *P. curvistylum* and *P. verticillatum*, which are lavender-pink. Berrylike fruits, usually blue-black or sometimes red, follow the flowers; the fall foliage color is yellow. They make an unusual and lovely cut flower if you've got a big enough stand from which to cut. ~ *Susan Carter*

Scientific Name: From the Greek *polys* ("many") and *gony* ("knee"), referring to the jointed rhizome.

Common Name: Solomon's seal.

Origin: Europe, Japan, Russia, North America, Korea.

Preferred Conditions: A cool root-run in fertile, humus-rich, moist, well-drained soil. Tolerates dry conditions once established.

Light: Shade to part sun.

Planting: Plant rhizomes very shallowly, setting them horizontally with growing tips curved upward (the side with the round leaf scar is up).

Management: Top-dress in winter with organic material. Remove foliage in fall after if has died back, and cut entire plant back when stems die back. Bait early for slugs, which can damage the emerging pips. Younger clumps are easier to divide: older clumps get extremely congested, and the rhizomes are difficult to separate; washing is the best way to work them apart. Rhizomes pieces without a prominent bud will grow but can take a year to come up. Mark your clumps so you don't step on the pips in spring.

Propagation: Seed (takes a long time to germinate); division in fall or spring; dig up rhizomes and replant.

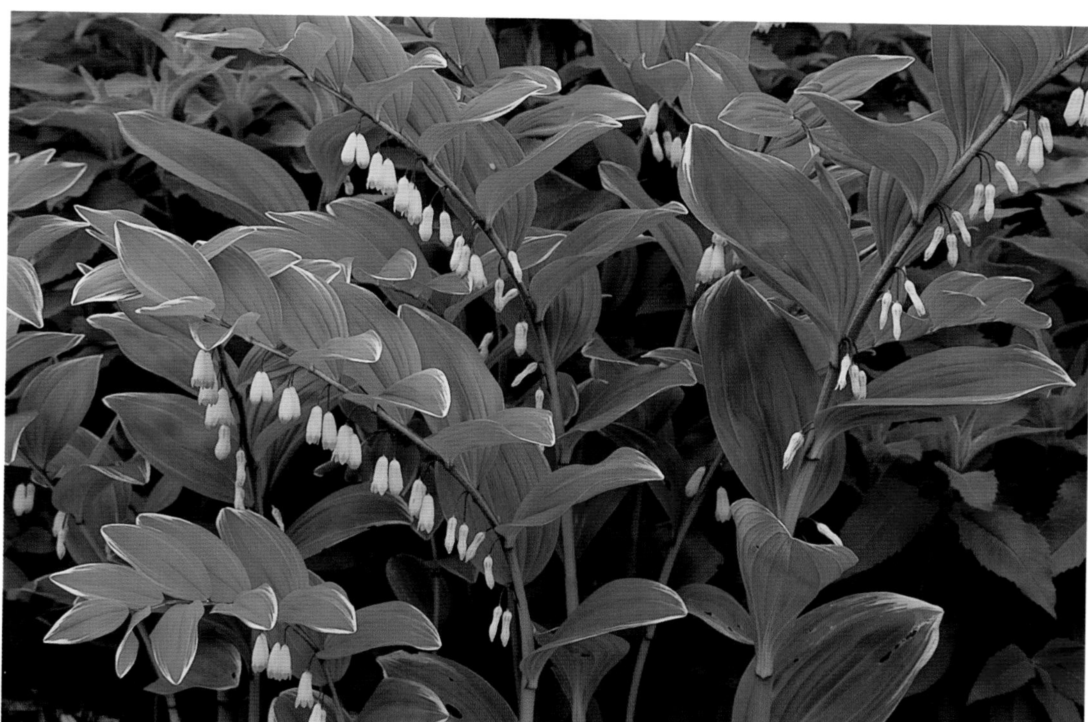

Polygonatum odoratum var. *pluriflorum* 'Variegatum'.

Pests and Diseases: Snails, slugs, sawfly larvae (especially on *P.* ×*hybridum*).

Companions: Ferns, *Galium odoratum*, hosta, *Omphalodes verna*, brunnera, helleborus, tiarella, trillium, paris, saruma, smilacina.

Notes: In the chart, the symbol ∞ = infinite spread.

Species and Cultivars	Height/ Spread	USDA Hardiness Zone	Flowers (bloom time)	Foliage	Comments
biflorum (syn. commutatum)	2–3ft × ∞	3–9	Greenish white, tubular, in pairs, fragrant (E–M)	Deep green, narrow, lanceolate, arching stems	Flowers produced in leaf axils, North American native, blue berries
b. polyploid	3–3½ft × ∞	3–9	Greenish white, tubular, in pairs (E–M)	As above	Vigorous form
curvistylum	1½ft × 2ft	5–9	Lavender-pink (M)	Green, long, narrow, in whorls	Red fruit
falcatum	2½–3ft × 2ft+	4–9	Greenish white, pendulous (E–M)	Green, pointed, oval, reddish stems	Small berries
humile	6–8in × 10in+	5–8	Greenish white, pendulous, tubular (E)	Dark green, lanceolate-ovate, hairy	Flowers produced in upper leaf axils, black fruit
×hybridum (syn. multiflorum)	2–4ft × ∞	4–9	Creamy-white, green tips, pendulous clusters (E–M)	Green, shiny, ribbed, lanceolate-ovate, arching stems	Common Solomon's seal, blue fruit, RHS Award
×h. 'Striatum'	2½–3ft × 2ft+	4–10	Cream-white, green tips, pendulous clusters (E–M)	Striped creamy-white	

Species and Cultivars	Height/ Spread	USDA Hardiness Zone	Flowers (bloom time)	Foliage	Comments
odoratum (syn. japonicum)	2–2½ft × 3ft+	4–9	Creamy-white, green tips, pendulous, fragrant (E–M)	Green, lanceolate-ovate, arching angular stems	Fragrant Solomon's seal, black fruit, spreads slowly
o. var. pluriflorum 'Variegatum' (syn. falcatum 'Variegatum')	2–2½ft × 2ft+	4–9	Cream-white, green tips, fragrant (E–M)	Green, smaller, oval, tip edged in white, reddish stems	Arching stems, blue-black fruits, spreads slowly, RHS Award
verticillatum 'Rubrum'	3ft+ × 2½ft+	5–9	Pink, small (E)	Green, long, narrow, in whorls, dark purple stems	Especially early, dense clumps, spreads slowly

POTENTILLA Rosaceae

I feel attached to these plants because my first attempts at propagation by tip cutting, on a shrub potentilla, were such a great success (my subject was the tough little semi-woody potentilla used and overused by landscapers of gas stations and road dividers). Would that all my subsequent efforts on other plants were as good. But enough of woody potentillas, let's talk about herbaceous ones. Most of the garden hybrids have strong bright colors and tough constitutions; all are good and worth searching out and growing. How can one do otherwise when William Robinson himself describes *P*. 'Gibson's Scarlet' thus: "No member of the race has flowers of so dazzling a scarlet, profuse and indispensable." That was written many years ago, and with potentilla on the rise in popularity, we now have many more cultivars as good or better from which to choose! So look for new ones, especially the doubles. ~ *Susan Buckles*

Potentilla atrosanguinea.

Scientific Name: From the Latin *potens* ("powerful"), referring to its medicinal properties.
Common Name: Cinquefoil.
Origin: Himalayas, Nepal, Europe, Kashmir, Africa.
Preferred Conditions: Not fussy, poor to average, cool, moisture-retentive soil. Tolerates some drought. May not do as well in rich soil.
Light: Sun.
Management: Cut back or remove flower stems after the first flush for repeat bloom. This also helps to keep plants more compact. Cut back to a four-inch dome of foliage in the fall cleanup, for a clean winter look. Divide every three years; these have congested crowns, so divide before too developed.
Propagation: Seed is best; very easy from cuttings; division.
Pests and Diseases: Aphids, spider mites if under stress.
Companions: Grasses, hemerocallis, iris, geranium.
Notes: Not every cinquefoil ("five leaves") has five leaflets.

Species and Cultivars	Height/ Spread	USDA Hardiness Zone	Flowers (bloom time)	Foliage	Comments
atrosanguinea	1½–2ft × 1½ft	5–9	Dark blood-red, single, velvety (M)	Silvery-gray, trifoliate, hairy reverse	Himalayan cinquefoil, evergreen sprawling
a. var. argyrophylla	1½–2ft × 1½ft	5–9	Yellow, orange center, in sprays (M)	Silvery, lobed, trifoliate, silky hairs	
'Emile'	1–1½ft × 1½ft	5–9	Mahogany-red, yellow edge, semi-double (E–M)	Green, toothed	
'Flamenco'	1–1½ft × 1½ft	5–9	Bright red with darker eye, yellow stamens (E–M)	Green	
'Gibson's Scarlet'	1–1½ft × 1½ft	5–9	Bright red, single, dark center (E–L)	As above	Lax stems, long-lived, long bloomer, RHS Award
'Melton Fire'	1½ft × 1½ft	5–9	Deep red center, creamy middle, soft red edge (M)	Green, toothed	
nepalensis	1–1½ft × 2ft	5–9	Dark red, deep pink, and purple, purple veins (E–L)	Green leaflets, hairy, obovate-oblong to oblanceolate, reddish stems	Nepal cinquefoil, short-lived, good cut, evergreen
n. 'Miss Willmott' (syn. willmottiae)	1–2ft × 2ft	5–9	Pink with deeper center (M–L)	Green, divided	Good cut, RHS Award
n. 'Ron McBreath'	1–1½ft × 1½ft	5–9	Bright red, dark center (E–M)	Green, red tints in fall	
recta	1½–2ft × 1½ft	3–9	Yellow clusters, large (M)	Gray-green, lobed, narrow, toothed, erect	Sulphur cinquefoil, seeds about, a noxious weed in many areas of North America
r. var. sulphurea	1½–2ft × 1½ft	3–9	Pale yellow (M)	Green, lobed, narrow, toothed, erect	Seed-grown, long-lived
×tonguei	6–12in × 12in	5–9	Soft apricot, deep red center (M–L)	Dark green, tinted copper, small, obovate, trailing stems	Staghorn cinquefoil, evergreen, long-lived, RHS Award
'William Rollison'	1–1½ft × 1½ft	5–9	Deep red-orange, yellow reverse, semi-double (E–L)	Mid-green	Clump-forming, RHS Award

Primula pulverulenta and *Hosta* 'Golden Tiara', with *Stachys byzantina* 'Big Ears', *Pulmonaria longifolia* 'Bertram Anderson', and *Lamium orvala*.

PRIMULA Primulaceae

Primroses, if they weren't so difficult in so many ways, would be the perfect plant. *Primula japonica*, *P. polyanthus*, and *P. auricula* are easily damaged by slugs, and *P.* 'Wanda' and similar types are additionally messed with by root weevils. Through the summer, the weevils eat the foliage and lay their eggs at the base; through the winter, their grubs merrily devour the roots. *Primula vulgaris*, the common primrose in the trade, is not reliably hardy anymore; that large flower they've been selected for seems not to be connected to perennial genes.

The polyanthus group, distinguished by flowers in small clusters on six- to eight-inch stems, can also be damaged by root weevils. The double group is experiencing a resurgence; they are all very strong plants, usually propagated by tissue culture, and moderately resistant to slugs and weevils. Members of the candelabra group can form large crowns and clumps but are somewhat short-lived; these will seed about in humus-rich soil that is damp (but not flooded) in winter and spring.

The longest-lived of the garden primroses, *P. florindae*, seems to have no pests and can actually grow in shallow running water. For more long-lived primroses, we depend on the auriculas and the Juliaes and Wandas. Our grandmothers all had *P.* 'Wanda', and we continue to hope the colors pink and white will reappear; even now there are two color forms of this deep purple-red groundcoverlike primrose. The Juliae/Wanda types are all prone to root weevil infestations. ~ *Bob Lilly*

Scientific Name: From the Latin *primus* ("first"), referring to the early flowers.
Common Name: Primrose, cowslip, oxlip.
Origin: Europe, China, Himalayas, Tibet, Japan.
Planting: Place *P. japonica*, *P. beesiana*, *P. ×bulleesiana*, and *P. bulleyana* one foot from high-water mark, if siting near water.
Preferred Conditions / Light: The primroses are complex, so we have sorted them into our own groups. You can find a primrose for almost any location, from bog to waterside to border conditions with moisture-retentive, cool, humus-rich, well-drained, neutral to slightly acid soil (except *P. auricula* must have lime and *P. florindae* likes lime), in sun to part shade (spring sun, summer shade). Most don't like winter wet (except *P. japonica* and *P. florindae*).

Group 1. Herbaceous, evergreen to semi-evergreen, depending on the winter. Flowers are of three sorts: either solitary (for example, *P. vulgaris*, *P. juliae*, *P.* 'Wanda'); in umbels on stems above the foliage (*P. polyanthus* and other polyanthus types); or doubles. Moderately fertile soil.

Group 2. Mostly deciduous. Whorls of flowers in tiers up the stems for the candelabra forms (*P. beesiana*, *P. ×bulleesiana*, *P. bulleyana*); others (*P. alpicola*, *P. denticulata*, *P. florindae*) have a single group of flowers. Peaty soil.

Group 3. Evergreen. Large flat-faced flowers; leathery foliage, often farinose (mealy). *Primula auricula* must have lime and sharp drainage (gritty soil) to do well, and its showiest forms need to be kept dry in winter; they are often grown in pots.

Management: For all groups, remove all yellowing leaves anytime. Mulch with manure or compost but not over the crown. Bait for slugs often. Control root weevils by employing the old method of constant division.
Propagation: Seed as soon as ripe; division in early fall.
Pests and Diseases: Snails, slugs, spider mites, rust, root rot, botrytis, root weevils.
Companions: The minor spring bulbs, kerria, hamamelis, rhododendron, ferns, brunnera, bergenia, corylopsis, ribes, meconopsis, hosta, myosotis, pulmonaria, trillium, omphalodes; the spring garden.
Notes: Here in Seattle several color forms of *P.* 'Wanda' have been traded around locally and are worth saving or conserving.

Species and Cultivars	Height/ Spread	USDA Hardiness Zone	Flowers (bloom time)	Foliage	Comments
'Alan Robb'	4–6in × 12in	4–9	Pale apricot, double (E–M)	Mid-green	Group 1, very floriferous, smaller flower
'Alejandra' (syn. 'Alexandra') (polyanthus)	6–8in × 12in	5–9	Scarlet-red with yellow eye (E–M)	As above	Group 1, long-blooming

Species and Cultivars	Height/ Spread	USDA Hardiness Zone	Flowers (bloom time)	Foliage	Comments
alpicola	6–12in × 12in	4–8	White, yellow, or violet umbels, white eye, root beer fragrance (E)	Mid-green rosette of elliptic leaves, toothed or scalloped	Group 2, herbaceous
'April Rose'	4–6in × 12in	4–9	Deep ruby-red, double (E)	Mid-green	Group 1
auricula	6–9in × 8–10in	3–9	Mixed yellows, reds, greens, and purples, paler contrasting eye, fragrant (E)	Gray-green rosette, fleshy, obovate to oblanceolate, toothed, wavy edges	Group 3, RHS Award
Barnhaven Hybrids (polyanthus)	4–6in × 12in	3–8	Variable (E)	Green	Group 1, specialty growers offer many colors
beesiana (candelabra)	1½–2½ft × 1½–2ft	5–8	Purplish rose to red, yellow eye, fragrant (M)	Mid-green rosette, blunt, ovate to lanceolate, toothed, red midribs	Group 2, herbaceous, summer dormant
×bulleesiana (candelabra)	1½–2½ft × 1½–2ft	5–9	Cream to rose, deep mauve to purple, and yellow (M)	Green rosette	Group 2, Bulle's primrose, herbaceous
bulleyana (candelabra)	2–2½ft × 2ft	5–8	Deep yellow to reddish or soft orange, in whorls, red buds (M)	Mid-green rosette, red midribs, long to ovate	Group 2, herbaceous, long-blooming, disappears in late fall, RHS Award
capitata	6–12in × 16in	4–8	Deep blue, drooping umbels (M)	Pale green rosette, lanceolate to oblong, toothed	Group 2, herbaceous, short-lived
c. subsp. mooreana	12in × 24in	5–9	Darker deep blue (M)	Green above, white farinose reverse	Group 2, larger, vigorous
'Cowichan' (polyanthus)	4–6in × 12in	3–8	Variable, strong colors (E)	Dark green	Group 1, from Vancouver Island, British Columbia
'Dawn Ansell'	4–6in × 10–12in	4–9	White, double (E)	Light green	Group 1, vigorous, strong
denticulata	9–18in × 18in	4–8	Variable, lilac, purple, white, red-violet, pink, yellow eye, spherical clusters (E)	Mid-green rosette, textured, spoon-shaped, toothed, leaves appear with flowers	Group 2, drumstick primula, herbaceous, RHS Award
'Dorothy' (polyanthus)	4–6in × 8–12in	4–8	Pale creamy-yellow, tubular, frilled, small, in umbels (E)	Mid-green rosette, spoon-shaped, small	Group 1, semi-evergreen, vigorous
elatior (polyanthus)	4–12in × 8–10in	4–8	Creamy-yellow, up-facing, one-sided umbel (E–M)	Mid-green rosette, ovate to oblong or elliptic, scalloped, hairy	Group 1, oxlip, semi-evergreen, RHS Award
florindae	2–3ft × 2ft	6–8	Sulphur-yellow, drooping, bell-like clusters, fragrant (M)	Mid-green, ovate to cordate, toothed, glossy	Group 2, Tibetan primrose, good cut, long-lived, herbaceous, can take wet feet

Species and Cultivars	Height/ Spread	USDA Hardiness Zone	Flowers (bloom time)	Foliage	Comments
'Francesca' (polyanthus)	4–6in × 10in	3–8	Green, yellow eye (E–M)	Light green, oval	Group 1, long-blooming, named after Francesca Darts from British Columbia
Gold-laced Group (polyanthus)	6–8in × 10in	5–8	Dark mahogany-red or red-black, narrow gold margins, gold eye (E)	Mid-green, sometimes red-tinged, oval	Group 1, semi-evergreen
'Granny Graham'	4–6in × 10in	4–9	Violet-blue, double (E)	Dark green	Group 1, reblooms in fall
'Guinevere' (polyanthus)	5–6in × 10in	6–8	Pale mauve, tinged purple (E)	Dark purplish	Group 1, RHS Award
Jack in the Green Group (polyanthus)	4–6in × 10in	3–8	Yellowish green, green calyx (E–M)	Green, same color as the calyx	Group 1, a curiosity but sweet
japonica (candelabra)	1½–2½ft × 2ft	5–9	Red-violet, pink, white, yellow eye, whorls (E–M)	Pale green rosette, crinkled, spathulate	Group 2, candelabra primrose, herbaceous, tolerates sunnier positions if moist, can take wet feet
j. 'Miller's Crimson' (candelabra)	1½–2ft × 1½–2ft	5–9	Red, yellow eye, whorls (E–M)	As above	As above, RHS Award
j. 'Postford White' (candelabra)	1½–2ft × 1½–2ft	5–9	White, yellow eye, whorls (E–M)	As above	As above, RHS Award
juliae	2–3in × 10–12in+	5–9	Red-violet, yellow eye, single, saucer-shaped (E)	Green rosette, glossy, cordate to rounded, toothed	Group 1, semi-evergreen, moist
'Ken Dearman'	4–6in × 10–12in	4–9	Coppery to salmon-orange, double (E)	Deep green	Group 1
kisoana	4–8in × 10–16in	4–9	Rose to white umbels (E)	Mid-green rosette, hairy, rounded, lobed, veined, quilted	Group 1, herbaceous, stoloniferous, sun tolerant
'Lilian Harvey'	4–6in × 12in	4–9	Magenta-pink, double (E)	Mid-green	Group 1
'Marie Crousse'	4–6in × 12–14in	4–9	Mauve-red, edged silver, double, fragrant (E)	As above	Group 1, vigorous
'Miss Indigo'	4–6in × 10–12in	4–9	Deep purplish violet, white edge, double (E)	As above	As above
polyanthus	10–18in × 12in	3–8	Variable, white, pink, red, lavender, purple, blue, orange, yellow eye, fragrant (E)	Dark green rosette, rounded, puckered, toothed, veined	Group 1, English primrose, evergreen
pulverulenta	2–3ft × 2ft	5–8	Red-violet, dark purple eye, whorls (E–M)	Deep green rosette, obovate or oblanceolate, wrinkled, toothed	Group 2, herbaceous, powdery-white (farina) all over stems, RHS Award

Species and Cultivars	Height/ Spread	USDA Hardiness Zone	Flowers (bloom time)	Foliage	Comments
'Red Velvet'	4–6in × 10–12in	4–9	Deep scarlet-red, double (E)	Green, edged in bronze	Group 1
'Roy Cope'	4–6in × 12in	4–9	Red, fading to purple-red, double (E)	Mid-green	As above
sieboldii	6–15in × 15–18in	4–9	Variable, white, mauve, pink, lavender, purple, red, lobed, clusters (E–M)	Light green rosette, hairy, wrinkled, scalloped	Group 1, Japanese primrose, herbaceous, may go dormant in summer, runs, RHS Award
'Sue Jervis'	4–6in × 12in	4–9	Pale pink, double (E)	Mid-green	Group 1
'Sunshine Susie'	4–6in × 10–12in	4–9	Bright yellow, double (E)	As above	Group 1, strong plant
'Val Horncastle'	4–6in × 10–12in	4–9	Pale sulphur-yellow, double (E)	As above	Group 1
'Velvet Moon' (polyanthus)	5–10in × 10in	6–9	Red, a deeper rich color (E)	Green, touch of maroon, veined	Group 1, reblooms
veris (polyanthus)	4–10in × 10in	4–8	Bright yellow to gold, orange, and red, darker eye, one-sided umbels, nodding, fragrant (E–M)	Mid-green rosette, ovate to ovate lanceolate, hairy reverse, wrinkled	Group 1, cowslip, long-lived, RHS Award
vialii	1–2ft × 1ft	4–9	Red-violet, fading to lilac, in a conical spike (E–M)	Green rosette, lanceolate, hairy	Group 2, orchid primrose, short-lived, RHS Award
vulgaris (syn. acaulis)	4–6in × 8–10in	4–9	Yellow, cultivars in white, red, pink, and blue, and all combinations, fragrant (E)	Mid-green, ovate to obovate to lanceolate	Group 1, common primrose, solitary flowers on stems
v. 'Lilacina Plena' (syn. 'Quaker's Bonnet')	4–6in × 10–12in	4–9	Pale lavender, double (E)	Green rosette	Group 1, vigorous
'Wanda'	4–6in × 12in+	4–8	Crimson-purple, yellow eye (E)	Dark green to purple rosette, oval, toothed	Group 1, evergreen, needs frequent division, RHS Award

Pulmonaria 'Roy Davidson'.

PULMONARIA Boraginaceae

One of the first perennials I put in my garden was *P. officinalis,* a hardworking plant, starting with its charming flowers in early spring. The funnel-shaped flowers of the many species arrive in shades of blue, pink, red, violet, or white around the same time as the hellebores, forget-me-nots, and early bulbs. Many are pink in bud and change color to blue as they open and mature. Most are long-blooming. Often their leaves are intriguingly marked and spotted, like a diseased lung, hence the awful common name, lungwort (it was thought that plants could cure the ills of the body parts they resembled). They vary in shape, too, from the long, narrow leaves of *P. longifolia* to the heart-shaped ones of *P. officinalis. Pulmonaria angustifolia,* with its blue flowers under deciduous shrubs, is the showiest form in spring; unfortunately its summer appearance ranges from ragged-looking to fully absent, especially without adequate water. Leaves tend to wilt in too much sun but should recover at night and cooler times. Pulmonarias generally retain their foliage throughout the winter, unless it's an exceptionally cold one. They are pretty care-free and self-sow in rich, moist soil, moving themselves about the garden, hybridizing among the different species and cultivars. ~ *Susan Carter*

Scientific Name: From the Latin *pulmo* ("lung").
Common Name: Lungwort, spotted dog.
Origin: Europe, Asia, Russia.
Preferred Conditions: Fertile, humus-rich, cool, well-drained, moist, acidic to alkaline. They will tolerate some dryness given fertile, humus-rich soil.
Light: Shade to sun. Shade in dry, hot conditions.
Management: Remove old or diseased leaves anytime. Mulch with organic material, for fertility and to help retain moisture. Water often during dry, hot periods to keep foliage at its best (one inch per week). Divide every three to five years.

Propagation: Division in spring at flowering time; seedlings do not come true.

Pests and Diseases: Powdery mildew (especially if too dry), snails, slugs.

Companions: Early bulbs, dicentra, hosta, astilbe, forsythia, helleborus, polygonatum, epimedium, *Ranunculus ficaria*, tiarella, hamamelis, corylopsis; pair the coral-colored forms with *Daphne odora* 'Aureomarginata', *Ribes sanguineum*, and *Tulipa* 'Toronto'.

Notes: To reduce a tendency to mildew in our gardens, we cut plants back to about two inches tall when the flowers fade, water well, and await a new flush of leaves. In the chart, the symbol ∞ = infinite spread.

Species and Cultivars	Height/ Spread	USDA Hardiness Zone	Flowers (bloom time)	Foliage	Comments
angustifolia	8–12in × ∞	3–9	Red-pink in bud, opens to deep rich blue (E)	Dark green, narrow, coarse, unspotted, 7–13in	Blue cowslip, mildew resistant, runs, deciduous, RHS Award
a. 'Blaues Meer'	10in × ∞	3–9	Bright blue to violet with a hint of pink (E)	Dark green, speckled with small silvery-white spots, 12in	Runs slowly
'Benediction'	8in × 12in+	3–9	Deep blue (E)	Dark green with light green spotting and speckling, narrow	Named for Seattle gardener Loie Benedict
'Berries and Cream'	8–12in × 12in	3–9	Coral buds, raspberry-pink and blue (E–M)	Silvery, mottled, green margins, ruffled	
'DeVroomen's Pride'	15in × 18in	3–9	Blue, fading to pink (E)	Silvery, near white, with a few green splashes and green edges	Newer cultivar
'Excalibur'	12in × 18in	3–9	Rosy-pink buds, opens violet-blue, ages to pink and blue-violet (E–M)	Silvery-white, deep green midribs and narrow edges, ovate, shiny, 10in	Long-blooming, mildew resistant
'Lewis Palmer' (syn. 'Highdown')	12in × 18in	3–9	Opens pink, ages to bright blue, violet, and pink (E)	Dark green, long, narrow, splashed and spotted greenish white	Vigorous, RHS Award
'Little Star'	8–10in × 8–10in	3–9	Cobalt-blue, large (E–M)	Green, heavily spotted silver, long, narrow	Long-blooming
longifolia	12in × 18in	3–9	Pink-violet buds, opens to clear blue (E–M)	Dark green, spotted silvery-white, narrow, pointed, 10–20in	Spotted dog
l. 'Bertram Anderson'	10–12in × 18–24in	3–9	Purple buds, opens bright blue to intense violet-blue (E)	Dark green, strongly marked with silver-white spots, narrow, 18–24in	Floppy stems
l. subsp. cevennensis	1–2ft × 2ft	3–9	Blue, fading to blue-violet, large (E–M)	Dark green, heavily spotted silvery-white, narrow, 18–24in	Mildew resistant
'Majesté'	10–12in × 12in	3–9	Pink and blue fading to pink (E)	Silver-gray, narrow green margins, long, shiny	
'Margery Fish'	12in × 18in	3–9	Bright coral-pink aging bluish purple, large (E)	Silvery-white with greenish spots, narrow	Mildew resistant, vigorous, RHS Award

Species and Cultivars	Height/ Spread	USDA Hardiness Zone	Flowers (bloom time)	Foliage	Comments
'Mawson's Blue'	9–12in × 18in	3–9	Rich blue (E)	Dark green, unspotted, long, narrow	Early to bloom
'Milchstrasse' (syn. 'Milky Way')	9–12in × 18in	3–9	Red buds, opens blue fading to reddish pink (E–M)	Bright green, densely silvered on upper surfaces with spotted margins and midribs, large, narrow	
'Mrs. Kittle'	15in × 18in	3–9	Light rose-pink turning light lavender (E)	Dark green, silvery-white spots and marbling	
officinalis	10–12in × 18in	3–9	Reddish pink buds, opens violet then blue (E)	Bright green, silvery-white spots, ovate, 4–5in	Common lungwort
o. 'Blue Mist' (syn. 'Blue Moon', 'Bowles' Blue')	14–18in × 18in	3–9	Light blue (E)	Green, lightly spotted with silver	Early bloomer
'Purple Haze'	8in × 12in	3–9	Light purplish blue (E–M)	Green, well spotted	Compact
'Roy Davidson'	12–14in × 18in	3–9	Pink buds, opens sky-blue (E)	Dark green, silver-blotched, narrow, long	Named for the U.S. plantsman, mildew resistant, long bloomer
rubra	12–16in × 18in	3–9	Bright coral-red (E)	Pale green, unspotted, velvety, elliptic, 5–7in	Vigorous, RHS Award
r. 'Barfield Pink'	12–15in × 18in	3–9	Coral-pink with white stripes (E)	Deep green, spotted, velvety	
r. 'David Ward'	12in × 24in	3–9	Coral-red to pink (E–M)	Silvery-green with pale cream margins	Flowers early, edges may burn in sun
r. 'Redstart'	12in × 18in	3–9	Coral-red (E)	Mid-green, unspotted	Vigorous
saccharata (syn. saccharata 'Picta')	9–18in × 24in	3–9	Purple-pink buds, opens red-violet or white, fading to bluish (E)	Mid to dark green, white spots, elliptic, 8–12in	Bethlehem sage
s. 'Dora Bielefeld'	10–12in × 18in	3–9	Clear bright pink (E)	Light to mid-green, silver-white spots, elliptic	Vigorous, heavy bloomer
s. 'Mrs. Moon'	10–12in × 18in	3–9	Pink buds, opens to blue-violet (E)	Dark green, silvery-white spots and marbling	Mildew prone
s. 'Pink Dawn'	10in × 18in	3–9	Rich pink, aging to violet (E)	Light to mid-green, white spots and mottling, crinkled edges	
'Sissinghurst White'	10–12in × 18in	3–9	Pale pink buds, opens white (E)	Small grayish green, silvery-white spots	Weak, RHS Award
'Smoky Blue'	12in × 12in	3–9	Pink buds, opens soft blue fading to pink (E)	Dark green, heavily spotted silver	
'Spilled Milk'	6–9in × 10in	3–9	Rose-pink, aging to blue then pink (E)	Suffused with silver, green edge, broad, ovate	Mildew resistant
'Victorian Brooch'	12–15in × 18in	3–9	Magenta-coral, deeper in throat (E–M)	Green with silver spots, long	Long-blooming

Pulsatilla vulgaris.

PULSATILLA Ranunculaceae

This one almost takes your breath away, and I'm sure a sunny meadow full of them would. In nature, pulsatilla inhabits open slopes and meadows on chalky or sandy soil at high elevations (Paradise on Mt. Rainier is six thousand feet). The early spring flowers (Pasque is the old word for Easter, hence the common name) are cup-shaped, cocooned in silky hairs, and surrounded by feathery foliage. Lavender is the usual color. The seedheads, which resemble those of clematis, are attractive and may be dried for arrangements. ~ *Ann Bucher*

Scientific Name: From the Latin *pulso* ("strike," "beat").
Common Name: Pasque flower.
Origin: Europe.
Preferred Conditions: Reasonably fertile, limy soil. Poor, rocky soil is best, if nature is the indicator. No competition.
Light: Sun.
Planting: They don't transplant well. Don't plant where other plants may overcrowd them.
Management: Best if left undisturbed. Remove dead foliage before new growth starts in the spring. Some may rot off at the neck and die when in full bloom. A top dressing of grit or crushed rock may prevent this. Cut back stems that have flowered in winter, leaving any basal growth. Do not mulch over the crowns of these plants!

Propagation: Best by seed (summer as soon as ripe); division in early winter; some forms by root cuttings in winter.

Pests and Diseases: Watch for slugs in spring, just in case.

Companions: Viola, smaller grasses (festuca), paeonia (emerging foliage), aubrieta, *Phlox subulata*, *Lychnis viscaria*, dwarf narcissus, crocus; a good rock garden plant, shows off well when backlit.

Notes: Plants have lasted years for us in sandy soil with no amendments and no competition. The lovely *P. vulgaris* var. *alba*, unfortunately, does not perform well here. It's not unusual for white-flowered forms of some perennials to be weaker than the common color of the species.

Species and Cultivars	Height/ Spread	USDA Hardiness Zone	Flowers (bloom time)	Foliage	Comments
vulgaris	8–12in × 10in	6–8	Mauve-pink and purple, nodding, saucer-shaped, emerges from veil of silky hairs, yellow center (E)	Green, fernlike	Pasque flower, large feathery seedheads, RHS Award
v. 'Alba'	10in × 10in	6–8	Creamy-white to pure white, yellow center (E)	As above	Silky seedheads last well into May, RHS Award
v. subsp. grandis 'Papageno'	12in × 10in	6–8	Variable, white-cream, bright pink, dark red, light blue to violet, fringed, semi-double (E)	As above	A newer flower form
v. var. rubra	10in × 10in	6–8	Reddish purple, yellow center (E)	As above	Many shades of red are sold as this variety

RANUNCULUS Ranunculaceae

Ranunculus are charming early ephemerals and a true sign that spring is here, but some are not suited for the border. The invasive buttercup we are constantly digging out of the grass or garden is *R. repens*; we include its double form and *R. repens* 'Buttered Popcorn' in the chart, but caution that these too are very aggressive. Most buttercups have golden yellow cup- to saucer-shaped flowers that are welcome brighteners of the garden even on a very sunny day. Leaves are mostly green basal rosettes; many are heart-shaped and glossy. Some of the buttercups are grown as much for their foliage as for their flowers. The seedlings of *R. ficaria* show a great deal of foliar variation. One, 'Brazen Hussy', with glossy dark chocolate-bronze leaves and golden yellow flowers, makes quite a statement. ~ *Susan Carter*

Scientific Name: From the Latin *rana* ("frog"), referring to the damp places that many buttercups prefer.

Common Name: Buttercup, lesser celandine.

Origin: Europe, Asia, North Africa, Caucasus.

Preferred Conditions: Well-drained, moisture-retentive, fertile. The single-flowered forms of *R. ficaria* can be quite rambunctious in moisture-retentive soil and are much better behaved in summer-dry conditions.

Ranunculus ficaria 'Green Petal'.

Light: Sun to part shade.

Planting: Newly purchased or divided plants should not be planted too deeply.

Management: *Ranunculus ficaria* goes dormant by summer and is not bothered by drought during this time; cut others back in the fall. All can be heavily mulched for the winter if necessary.

Propagation: By seed as soon as ripe or by division in spring. Named varieties should be propagated by division, as the seedlings will not be true.

Pests and Diseases: Slugs and snails are a big problem; mildew can afflict *R. aconitifolius*. The tubers of *R. ficaria* are very small, like chubby rice grains; they move around easily and can themselves become a pest, especially if moles are in your garden.

Companions: *Cornus mas*, *C. stolonifera*, *Carex elata*, ajuga, acorus, *Anthriscus sylvestris* 'Ravenswing', forsythia, early spring bulbs (narcissus, muscari), brunnera, primula, crocus; *R. ficaria* 'Brazen Hussy' looks fantastic grown with *Ophiopogon planiscapus* 'Nigrescens' and *Lysimachia nummularia* 'Aurea'.

Notes: Again, beware: they can be aggressive. Remove any rogue seedlings of *R. ficaria* in your plantings, as each cultivar grows differently, making a messy look. In the chart, the symbol ∞ = infinite spread.

Species and Cultivars	Height/ Spread	USDA Hardiness Zone	Flowers (bloom time)	Foliage	Comments
aconitifolius 'Flore Pleno'	2ft × 1½ft	5–9	Tight pompoms of double white, tinted green in the center (E–M)	Deeply cut, dark green	Fair maids of France, fair maids of Kent, difficult to grow, RHS Award
acris	1–2ft × 10in	4–8	Pale yellow (E)	Mid-green, divided, soft, 3-lobed	Tall buttercup, erect, grow in a pot

Species and Cultivars	Height/ Spread	USDA Hardiness Zone	Flowers (bloom time)	Foliage	Comments
constantino-politanus 'Plenus'	1–1½ft × 1½ft	5–9	Yellow with pale yellow-green reflexed sepals, large, glossy, double (E–M)	Deeply toothed, slightly marked with silver, 3-lobed, mid-green, basal and lower stem leaves are cordate	Clump-forming, noninvasive
ficaria	2–4in × ∞	4–8	Golden yellow, glossy, single (E)	Cordate, glossy, dark green, often with silver or bronze markings, toothed	Lesser celandine, dies back after blooming, very invasive
f. var. aurantiacus (syn. 'Cupreus')	2–4in × 12in	4–8	Coppery-orange, darker on reverse, glossy (E)	Silvery with bronze central markings, green and gray mottling, cordate	
f. 'Brambling'	2–4in × 12in	4–8	Golden yellow, single, tiny (E)	Silver-gray and green with some purple markings in a lacelike pattern	Striking foliage
f. 'Brazen Hussy'	2–4in × 12in	4–8	Golden yellow with a bronze reverse, glossy (E)	Glossy, deep chocolate-bronze	Christopher Lloyd introduction, one of the best for foliage
f. 'Collarette' (syn. 'E. A. Bowles')	2–3in × 12in	4–8	Bright yellow, single, tufted center with a collar of larger yellow petals (E)	Green with bronze central band, clumping	Petal-like stamens give it a double appearance, charming
f. 'Coppernob'	2–4in × 10in	4–8	Coppery-orange fading to yellow then to white (E)	Dark maroon, long petioles	Starlike flower, slow to establish
f. 'Double Mud'	2–3in × 10in	4–8	Creamy-white, tinted grayish purple on reverse, double (E)	Green	Slow grower
f. flore-pleno	3–5in × 12in	4–8	Double yellow with a tight green center (E)	Green in a round clump	Very vigorous to invasive, spreads by seed and tubers
f. 'Green Petal'	2–3in × 10in	4–8	Greenish, yellow-streaked, semi-double (E)	Green, cordate, marbled	Slow grower
f. 'Primrose'	2–4in × 12in	4–8	Lemon-yellow fading to cream (E)	Mottled silver	
f. 'Randall's White'	2–5in × 12in	4–8	Creamy-white with darker reverse on petals, large (E)	Green	Vigorous, a good heavy bloomer, seeds aggressively
repens 'Buttered Popcorn'	3–5in × ∞	4–8	Yellow (E)	Bright yellow-green with silvery-golden center and silvery-green edge, serrated	Invasive, variegated form of creeping buttercup
r. var. pleniflorus	1–2ft × ∞	4–8	Bright yellow with pale yellow sepals, double, glossy (E–M)	Mid-green, 3-lobed, glossy, deeply cut, hairy	Erect, fast-spreading, much larger

Rehmannia elata.

REHMANNIA Scrophulariaceae

Rehmannia elata is soft and fuzzy, tropical in look but tender in temperament. This is a plant with a long bloom season and a short life span. Its large, purplish pink to mauve, two-lipped flowers are snapdragonlike; its leaves are hairy, coarsely lobed, and ovate-oblong, forming basal rosettes. A useful plant to fill a temporary vacancy but don't plan on it as a permanent resident. ~ *Bob Lilly*

Scientific Name: After German physician John Rehmann.
Common Name: Chinese foxglove.
Origin: China.
Preferred Conditions: Nice and warm, in a woodland loamy site. Moist, well-drained, moderately fertile, humus-rich soil.
Light: Part shade. Tolerates morning sun.
Management: Cut back when leaves die back.
Propagation: Seed in late winter; root cuttings in late autumn.
Pests and Diseases: Slugs, snails.
Companions: Hardy fuchsias, helleborus, geranium, smilacina, polygonatum, *Arum italicum*.
Notes: Often treated as a biennial in the Pacific Northwest, where it is short-lived and cannot long endure the cool, wet winters.

Species and Cultivars	Height/ Spread	USDA Hardiness Zone	Flowers (bloom time)	Foliage	Comments
elata (syn. angulata)	2–3ft × 1½ft	8–10	Purplish pink to mauve, yellow and red spotted throat (E–M)	Mid-green, coarsely lobed, hairy	Clump-forming, RHS Award

RHEUM Polygonaceae

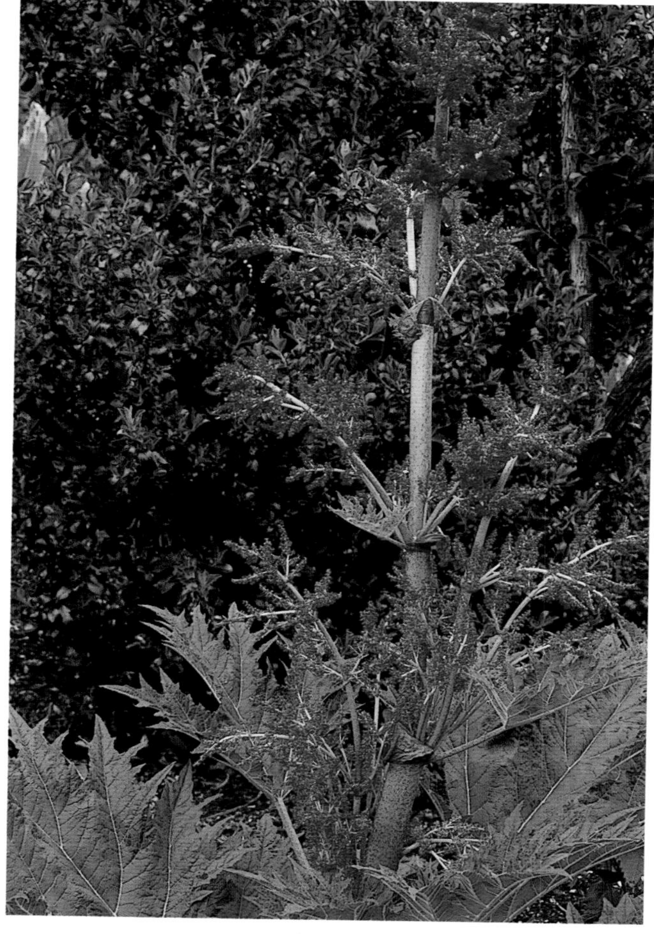

Rheum palmatum 'Atrosanguineum'.

Rhubarb forms very large leaves with long, thick (sometimes tasty) stalks. We're not concerned with the common culinary rhubarb here (*R.* ×*hybridum*); although it too has wonderful big, crinkly leaves that are showy enough for a prominent spot in the garden, it's usually grown for the delicious red-tinted leafstalks, which are used like fruit in pies and sauces.

The ornamental rheums are large plants with very interesting basal leaves, round to heart-shaped or ovate and up to three feet across; *R. palmatum* has palmately lobed leaves, with some forms deeply cut. The flower panicles are held well above the foliage; the individual flowers are star-shaped in shades of white to wine-red, and are followed by small red to brownish seeds. All rheum leaves are green with red veins, some with contrasting red tints beneath, and all are poisonous. ~ *Susan Carter*

Scientific Name: From *rheon*, the Greek name for rhubarb.
Common Name: Rhubarb.
Origin: Himalayas to China.
Preferred Conditions: Grow near water or in a moist border or woodland garden (but not with wet feet). Fertile, humus-rich, deep loam. Performs best without competition.
Light: Sun to part shade.
Management: Mulch rheums in early spring with organic matter; they are heavy feeders. Cut back in fall when stems and leaves die back.
Propagation: Seed; division in spring.
Pests and Diseases: Root rot, rust, crown rot, slugs.
Companions: Large ferns, hemerocallis, monarda, ligularia, telekia, and other large-scale perennials.

Species and Cultivars	Height/ Spread	USDA Hardiness Zone	Flowers (bloom time)	Foliage	Comments
'Ace of Hearts (syn. 'Ace of Spades')	4ft × 3ft	5–9	Pale pink to white (M)	Dark-green, red tint, cordate, veined above, purple reverse, 14in	Medium-sized plant
australe (syn. emodi)	7ft × 5ft	5–9	White to wine-red (M)	Mid-green, round to cordate, wavy margins, hairy beneath, veined, 16–30in	Himalayan rhubarb, red seeds
palmatum	6–7ft × 6ft	5–9	Creamy-white to pink or deep red (E–M)	Dark green, round to ovate, softly hairy, palmately lobed, 36in	Chinese rhubarb, dies back in midsummer
p. 'Atrosanguineum'	5–6ft × 6ft	5–9	Pink-crimson, fluffy (E–M)	Emerge from scarlet buds crimson-purple, fading to dark green above, deeply cut, 30–36in	Deep purplish red stems, RHS Award
p. var. tanguticum	5–7ft × 6ft	5–9	White, pink, or red (E–M)	Dark reddish green fading to dark green with purple tints, 24–30in	Red seeds

Rodgersia pinnata 'Elegans'.

RODGERSIA Saxifragaceae

There's no better way to rest the eye in a mixed planting than with bold foliage, and rodgersias have beautiful large leaves, textured and often bronze as they emerge, with equally arresting plumelike flowers rising above them. The numerous flowers appear on tall panicles, making this a most distinctive and desirable perennial. Besides being one of the best bold-leaved perennials, rodgersias are a good cut flower. They spread very slowly by a tight rhizome. ~ *Ann Bucher*

Scientific Name: After American Rear Admiral Rodgers (1812–1882), who led an expedition to China, where rodgersia was found.

Common Name: Rodgers' flower.

Origin: China.

Preferred Conditions: Grow near water, in a bog garden, or moist borders in cool, humus-rich soil. Resents drought and winter-wet conditions.

Light: Sun to part shade.

Management: The flower stems can be removed once they've faded, but they remain interesting for a long time. Leaves should remain on until winter cleanup. Our experience is you can grow rodgersias in less than ideal conditions: give them a good winter mulching and as much moisture as you can. They will not be as large and lush as they would be in their preferred conditions, but they are still worth growing.

Propagation: Seed (cultivars may not come true); division is easy in spring, but plants are later to emerge, so mark the spot and don't step on them.

Pests and Diseases: Slugs and root weevils, especially if grown in pots.

Companions: Ferns, *Iris ensata*, *Primula japonica*, hosta, *Helleborus orientalis*, astilbe, astrantia, trillium, *Nectaroscordum siculum*, trollius; *R. pinnata* 'Superba' makes a wonderful combination with late lilies.

Notes: Divisions take one year to settle into the garden or pot. All rodgersias spread slowly beyond the listed size.

Rodgersia pinnata and *Aruncus sylvestris* in flower with *Geranium sylvaticum*, *Campanula latiloba* 'Hidcote Amethyst', and *Tropaeolum speciosum*, scrambling through the yew hedge.

Species and Cultivars	Height/ Spread	USDA Hardiness Zone	Flowers (bloom time)	Foliage	Comments
aesculifolia	3–5ft × 3ft	5–8	Creamy-white to pink, fluffy clusters, 24in long (M)	Bronze-green, horse-chestnutlike, deeply veined, 5–7 obovate leaflets	Clump-forming, woolly red-brown stalks
henrici	3–4ft × 3ft	5–8	Rose-pink aging to red, 18in long (M)	Green with bronzy-purple tints, turning dark green, palmate	Dark red seed capsules, bright red stalks
pinnata	3–4ft × 3ft	5–8	Yellowish white to pink or red, 12–18in long (M)	Dark green, glossy, odd pinnate, crinkled, veined, 5–9 obovate pairs	Featherleaf rodgersia, reddish stalks

Species and Cultivars	Height/ Spread	USDA Hardiness Zone	Flowers (bloom time)	Foliage	Comments
p. 'Elegans'	3–4ft × 3ft	4–9	Creamy pink, 12–18in long (M)	Dark green, copper tints, glossy, palmate, 6–9 serrated leaflets	Red seedheads
p. 'Superba'	3–4ft × 3ft	4–9	Strong pink, 18in long (M)	Purplish bronze young leaves, aging to green, pinnate to palmate, 5–9 leaflets	Dark red fruit, RHS Award
podophylla	3–4ft × 3ft+	5–8	Creamy-white, 12in long (M)	Greenish bronze, palmate, jagged, 5-lobed leaflets, crinkled	RHS Award
p. 'Bronze Form'	2½–3½ft × 3ft+	5–8	Pink, 12in long (M)	Emerge bronze-maroon, age to green, coppery tints, jagged-edged leaflets	Leaves turn bronze-purple to crimson in fall
sambucifolia	2½–3ft × 3ft	4–9	White or pink, dense sprays, 18in long (M)	Dark green, pinnate, 3–9 leaflets, hairy	Elderberry rodgersia, earliest to bloom

ROMNEYA Papaveraceae

This is a lovely plant in the right spot. It has an impressive woody base, glaucous foliage, and large fragrant white flowers; the poppy flowers are solitary, six-petaled, with a bright golden yellow center and a tissue-papery texture. The trick is finding the right spot. It grows beautifully at Children's Hospital in a planting bed surrounded by a parking lot—no competition and a limit to its expansive tendencies. Romneya seems only to compete well with indifferent grasses on poor, disturbed, and emotionally crippled soil. ~ *Ann Bucher*

Scientific Name: After Irish astronomer Thomas Romney Robinson.
Common Name: Fried egg flower, Matilija poppy.
Origin: Southern California, New Mexico.
Preferred Conditions: Seems to thrive on neglect in well-drained, lean, and dry soil. Will bloom longer with more water. Shelter from cold winds.
Light: Sun.
Management: Romneyas resent transplanting or any major disturbances. Cut back to the base in winter or early spring before new growth begins. Dig around it (root pruning) once a year to remove suckering roots, but not too close to the main plant. Put a deep dry winter mulch on. Usually no staking is needed.
Propagation: Seed is difficult (requires high heat to germinate); root cuttings in fall; suckers with a bit of root in spring or fall may be the best source of new plants.
Pests and Diseases: Root fungal diseases (when roots are bruised or damaged), slugs in spring.
Companions: Grasses, solidago, artemisia, achillea, allium, boltonia, macleaya, centaurea, *Lysimachia ephemerum*, although alone seems the best! It needs all the sunshine it can get.
Notes: One of the few plants worth buying a house for. This is an aggressive spreader in the right (or wrong) location, but since they are difficult to propagate and transplant, having lots of roots to work with is helpful. In the chart, the symbol ∞ = infinite spread.

Romneya coulteri.

Species and Cultivars	Height/ Spread	USDA Hardiness Zone	Flowers (bloom time)	Foliage	Comments
coulteri	5–8ft × ∞	6–10	White, raised tuft of golden yellow stamens, silky, 5in across (M–L)	Bluish green with jagged edges	Fragrant, RHS Award
c. 'Butterfly'	5–6ft × ∞	6–10	White, round overlapping petals, 5in across (M)	As above	Branching, fragrant
c. 'White Cloud'	5–6ft × ∞	6–10	White, 6in across (M)	As above	Vigorous, fragrant, RHS Award

Roscoea cautleyoides 'Kew Beauty'.

ROSCOEA Zingiberaceae

We heard a shriek of delight from the garden visitor, followed by the explanation that she had recently returned from the Himalayas and was delighted to see roscoea here as she had seen it there. The orchidlike flowers do transport one to far pavilions, even if one has never been to the Himalayas, and the foliage sheathing the stem betrays roscoea's relationship to the exotic gingers. The plants are very late to emerge (June), so be sure to curb neighboring plants meanwhile as well as your own impulse to fill that empty space. *Roscoea alpina*, while a charming little rock garden plant, must be watched, for it spreads enthusiastically by underground runners. Many more cultivars are available in Great Britain. ~ *Ann Bucher*

Scientific Name: After William Roscoe of Liverpool, author of a book on the ginger family and founder of Liverpool's first botanic garden.
Common Name: Roscoea.
Origin: China, Himalayas.
Preferred Conditions: Moist, cool, deep, humus-rich, well-drained soil. Mild winters.
Light: Sun to part shade.
Planting: Three to four inches deep. Flowers are delicate, so it's best to locate these plants in a protected location. They tend to flop after flowering so plant among other woodlanders.
Management: Mulch in winter to protect from the cold. Watch for slugs, especially right after they emerge in May and June.
Propagation: Division in spring.
Pests and Diseases: Slugs, root weevils.
Companions: Heuchera, tiarella, tricyrtis, *Hakonechloa macra*, uvularia, cyclamen, glaucium, astrantia, primula, smaller hostas, *Polygonatum humile*.

Species and Cultivars	Height/ Spread	USDA Hardiness Zone	Flowers (bloom time)	Foliage	Comments
alpina	6–12in × 6in	6–9	Purplish pink (M)	Mid-green, lanceolate, emerge fully after flowers fade	Rock garden plant, runs
cautleyoides	12–18in × 8in	6–9	Soft yellow (M)	Gray-green to green, grasslike, appears with the flowers	RHS Award
c. 'Kew Beauty'	12–18in × 8in	6–9	Primrose-yellow, large (M)	Blue-green, swordlike	RHS Award
purpurea	12–18in × 8in	6–9	Purple-violet with white markings on each petal (M–L)	Deep green	Vigorous, vase-shaped

Rudbeckia fulgida var. *sullivantii* 'Goldsturm'.

RUDBECKIA Asteraceae

Bold, bright yellow daisy flowers in huge sweeps across the Midwest prairies—conjures up quite an image. I really do wish I could duplicate this black-eyed Susan show in my under-the-trees garden, but I can't. With that said, this North American native is gaining popularity outside of its natural habitat of moist, sun-soaked, well-drained meadow, thanks to such cultivars as *R. fulgida* var. *sullivantii* 'Goldsturm' (which is probably the best known, having won the Perennial Plant Association's Plant of the Year in 1999 and an Award of Garden Merit from the RHS).

The leaves of rudbeckias are oblong to lanceolate-ovate, dark green to gray-green, glossy or sometimes slightly hairy. The flowers are usually solitary or in cymes and made up of petal-like ray florets that radiate from a prominent central disk or cone. This disk is dark brown, black, or green and varies in size and form, some being showier than others. The flowers are held above the leaves on strong stems and offer winter interest if left on until spring. Birds will appreciate the seeds too. Most make good cut flowers. ~ *Susan Carter*

Scientific Name: After Olof Rudbeck the elder (1630–1702) and the younger (1660–1740), father-son pair of Swedish botanists.
Common Name: Coneflower, black-eyed Susan.
Origin: North America.
Preferred Conditions: Moderately fertile, moisture-retentive soil. Don't let them dry out.
Light: Sun, sun, and more sun.
Management: Remove some of the flowers to stimulate continued bloom. Deadhead the spent blooms to keep them looking good (*R. fulgida* doesn't need deadheading). Divide them every four years or so. Pinch out the tips of *R. laciniata* 'Herbstsonne' when two feet tall to curb its height. Some may need staking.
Propagation: Seed; division in spring; stem cuttings in spring.

Pests and Diseases: Snails, slugs especially on new growth, aphids, powdery mildew, rust, smut, leaf miners.

Companions: Grasses, aster, helianthus, boltonia, chrysanthemum, artemisia, *Eupatorium rugosum* 'Chocolate', solidago, ×solidaster, helenium, crocosmia, salvia, eryngium, *Dahlia* 'David Howard'.

Notes: *Rudbeckia fulgida* var. *sullivantii* 'Goldsturm' can be invasive. It's best to consider *R. laciniata* 'Herbstsonne' and *R. maxima* and *R. occidentalis* (and their varieties) to be short-lived in the Pacific Northwest. In the chart, the size listed under flowers is measured across, from tip to tip of the petals.

Species and Cultivars	Height/ Spread	USDA Hardiness Zone	Flowers (bloom time)	Foliage	Comments
fulgida	2–3ft × 2ft	3–10	Golden yellow ray florets, purplish brown disk, 3–4in (M)	Dark green, oblong to lanceolate to ovate, glossy, slightly hairy	Black-eyed Susan, vigorous, long-blooming
f. var. sullivantii 'Goldsturm'	1½–2½ft × 2ft+	3–10	Deep golden yellow, blackish brown disk, 4–5in (M–L)	Dark green, coarse, lanceolate to ovate	Erect, needs no staking, long-blooming, long-lived, vigorous, 1999 PPA Award, RHS Award
laciniata	5–6ft × 3ft	3–10	Pale yellow, greenish yellow disk, 3–6in (M–L)	Dark green, 3- to 5-lobed, toothed, veined	Cut leaf coneflower, prone to mildew, may need staking
l. 'Goldquelle' (syn. 'Golden Fountain')	2½–4ft × 2ft	3–10	Double bright yellow, green disk, 3–4in (M–L)	Mid-green, deeply cut	RHS Award
l. 'Herbstsonne' (syn. 'Autumn Sun')	5–7ft+ × 2ft+	3–10	Bright yellow, conical green disk, 4–5in (M–L)	Mid-green, oval, toothed, slightly lobed, veined, glossy	May need support, long-blooming, RHS Award
maxima	4–8ft × 2ft	4–10	Drooping yellow florets, brownish black 2in disk, 3–5in (M–L)	Glaucous, ovate to elliptic, smooth	Good foliage plant, erect
occidentalis 'Black Beauty'	3–4ft × 2ft	4–10	Tiny yellow petals, large black disk, 5in (M–L)	Green, toothed, ovate-elliptical	California coneflower
o. 'Green Wizard'	3–4ft × 2ft	3–10	Petals barely visible, dark blackish brown conical disk, 2in (M–L)	Gray-green	A curiosity
triloba	3–4ft × 3ft	4–8	Orange ray florets with black disk, 3in (M–L)	Green, 3–7 lobes, stiffly hairy	Brown-eyed-Susan, biennial, a good mixer, some seeding

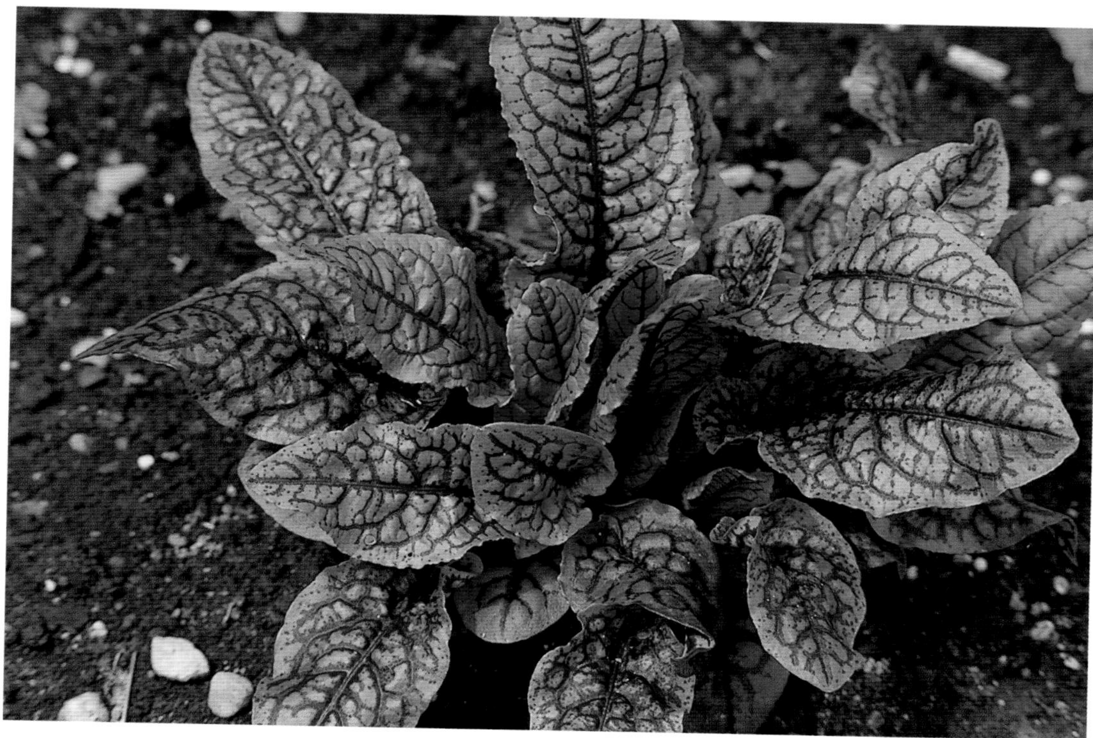

Rumex sanguineus var. *sanguineus*.

RUMEX Polygonaceae

Rumex are grown as ornamentals, primarily for their attractive leaves. The seedheads can also be attractive, but you run the risk of copious self-sowing. The stately *R. hydrolapathum* also spreads by rhizomes, but vigilance is rewarded by the sight of its large leaves and soft brownish pink flowers; its seedheads remain interesting long into the fall, a beautiful rich chestnut-brown. *Rumex sanguineus* var. *sanguineus* has bright green leaves with red veins and looks good all winter long. ~ *Ann Bucher*

Scientific Name: The classical Latin name for docks or sorrels.
Common Name: Dock, sorrel.
Origin: Europe, Asia, Africa.

Species and Cultivars	Height/ Spread	USDA Hardiness Zone	Flowers (bloom time)	Foliage	Comments
hydrolapathum	5–7ft × 2ft	6–8	Soft brownish pink aging to rusty-red (M)	Green, narrow, oblong-lanceolate, up to 3ft long, smooth, turns red in autumn	Great water dock, seeds a bit
sanguineus var. sanguineus	15in × 12in	6–8	Green aging to brown (M)	Bright green, purple-red veins, oblong-lanceolate, forms rosettes	Red-veined dock
scutatus 'Silver Shield'	1–1½ft × ∞	6–8	Greenish (M)	Silver, heart-shaped, remove any green seedlings that appear	Buckler's sorrel, edible leaves, spreads aggressively but easy to remove

Preferred Conditions: Any average, moderately fertile soil. *Rumex sanguineus* var. *sanguineus* is happiest in dry soil; *R. hydrolapathum* is at its best in wet soils (and can take even heavy soil).
Light: Sun to part shade. Sun for *R. sanguineus* var. *sanguineus*.
Management: All rumex respond positively to a manure mulch. Cut back when foliage dies down in the fall. If leaf miners are present on *R. hydrolapathum*, remove infected leaves immediately; new ones will grow.
Propagation: Seed; division in spring or fall (with protection from cold).
Pests and Diseases: Leaf miners, aphids, slugs.
Companions: Ostrich plume ferns, selinum, *Primula japonica*, telekia, *Persicaria amplexicaulis*, astilbe (tall forms), *Phalaris arundinacea* var. *picta*. In the chart, the symbol ∞ = infinite spread.

SALVIA Lamiaceae

We deal with the herbaceous perennial salvias here (for all the rest, we recommend Betsy Clebsch's monograph on salvias). Most of those we discuss will benefit from some form of support; a day of drizzle will weigh down the flowers and flop the stems down to ground level. Pea sticks work well for *S. azurea*, the taller *S. nemorosa*, *S. uliginosa*, and *S. verticillata*. To discourage their tendency to legginess, plant in full sun and use fertilizer carefully: manure mulch, unfortunately, makes them grow like crazy and too soft—they'll be snapping and flopping about even more. When using salvias as a cut flower, recut their stems underwater in the final vase. ~ *Bob Lilly*

Scientific Name: From the Latin *salvus* ("safe," "well"), referring to their medicinal qualities.
Common Name: Sage.
Origin: North America, South America, Europe, Asia, Africa.
Preferred Conditions: A spot with good air circulation and well-drained, fertile but not-too-rich soil.
Light: Sun.
Planting: Do not bury the crown.

Salvia uliginosa.

Management: Cut back the flowering stems to the crown or strong pair of new shoots in the leaf axils after flowering for a second bloom in a good summer. Generally cut to any point showing potential for branching. Do not let them dry out, as this may trigger mildew. Divide when the center of the plant starts to look sparse; in all herbaceous salvia, younger clumps bloom best, so division on a regular two- to three-year program will give you a better show. Remove spent flower stems. Cut down to basal growth in fall. Watch for slugs and snails at all times, especially on overwintering crowns.

Propagation: Division of *S. uliginosa*, *S. nemorosa*, *S.* ×*superba* in spring; the rest from seed or stem cuttings.

Pests and Diseases: Snails, slugs, whiteflies, rust, powdery mildew, stem rot, fungal leaf spot, aphids, spider mites, mealy bugs.

Companions: It's hard to generalize about companions for salvia, but here're a few: *Sisyrinchium striatum*, artemisia, hemerocallis, lavandula, helenium, papaver, scabiosa, smaller euphorbias, roses.

Notes: Salvias are probably best used as short-lived perennials; they perform best in youth. *Salvia* ×*sylvestris* 'Mainacht' and *S. nemorosa* 'Ostfriesland' are of garden origin. *Salvia nemorosa*, *S.* ×*superba*, and *S.* ×*sylvestris* are synonyms both on paper and in breeding. In the chart, the symbol ∞ = infinite spread.

Species and Cultivars	Height/ Spread	USDA Hardiness Zone	Flowers (bloom time)	Foliage	Comments
argentea	2–3ft × 2ft	5–9	White, tinged pink or yellow, inconspicuous (E–M)	Silvery-gray rosettes, woolly, ovate, oval to oblong	Silver sage, short-lived if allowed to produce seed, cut flowering stems off, RHS Award
azurea	4–5ft × 2ft	5–9	Clear blue (M–L)	Gray-green, lanceolate to oblong, toothed	Blue sage, hates winter wet, will rebloom without deadheading
a. var. grandiflora	3–4ft × 2ft	5–9	Sky-blue, larger (M–L)	Gray-green, linear to lanceolate, hairy	Prairie sage, sprawling growth habit
forsskaolii	2–3ft × 2½ft	5–9	Violet-blue, marked white and yellow (E–M)	Dark green, large, hairy, ovate, toothed	Long-blooming
guaranitica	4–5ft × 2ft	7–10	Deep indigo-blue (M–L)	Dark mid-green, rough, scented, ovate, toothed, hairy	Anise-scented sage, tender, likes it moist, may need support, long-blooming, good cut, brittle
g. 'Argentine Skies'	3–4ft × 2ft	8–10	Pale sky-blue (M–L)	As above	Tender, likes it hot, brittle
g. 'Black and Blue'	3–5ft × 2ft	7–10	Deep cobalt-blue, black calyx (M–L)	Green, cordate, fuzzy	Deep purple-black stems, brittle
g. 'Blue Enigma'	5–6ft × 2ft	5–9	Rich blue with violet-blue calyx (M–L)	Green	Brittle, RHS Award
'Indigo Spires'	3–4ft × 2ft	7–9	Deep purplish blue (M–L)	Mid-green, ovate, margins are serrated and dark	Tender, bushy, brittle
nemorosa	2–3ft × 1½ft	5–9	Violet-blue, tiny, enclosed in red-purple bracts (E–M)	Olive-green, ovate-lanceolate to oblong, crinkled	Wood sage, erect, tender in winter wet, repeat bloom

Species and Cultivars	Height/ Spread	USDA Hardiness Zone	Flowers (bloom time)	Foliage	Comments
n. 'Amethyst'	2½ft × 1½ft	5–9	Bluish violet (M)	As above	RHS Award
n. 'Lubecca'	1½–2½ft × 1½ft	5–9	Deep violet-blue, purple bracts (M–L)	Gray-green	RHS Award
n. 'Ostfriesland'	1½–2ft × 1½ft	5–9	Deep purplish blue (M)	Green	Good cut, may need support, repeat bloom, RHS Award
n. 'Pusztaflamme' (syn. 'Plumosa')	15–18in × 24in	5–9	Dusty deep rosy-purple, plumelike (M)	Deep grayish green	Good cut, leggy, RHS Award
nipponica 'Fuji Snow'	20–24in × 24in	6–9	Pale yellow (L)	Variegated with white tips	Low-spreading clumps, difficult to grow
pratensis	2–3ft × 1½ft	3–9	Violet-blue to bluish white and pure white to pink (E–M)	Rich green, low mounds, rough-textured, toothed	Meadow sage, good cut, listed on some noxious weed lists
p. 'Indigo'	1½–2½ft × 1½ft	4–9	Rich violet-blue (E–M)	As above	Good cut, RHS Award
'Purple Majesty'	2–3ft × 1½ft	8–10	Deep royal-purple, deep purple-black calyx (M–L)	Mid-yellow-green, ovate-oblong, serrated	Likes lots of heat, good cut, upright
×superba	2½–3ft × 1½ft	5–9	Violet-purple, red-purple calyx (M–L)	Mid-green, lanceolate-oblong, scalloped	Erect, RHS Award
×sylvestris	2½ft × 1½ft	5–9	Dark violet-blue (M–L)	Olive-green, oblong, wrinkled	Erect, deadhead for repeat bloom
×s. 'Blauhügel' (syn. 'Blue Hill')	1–1½ft × 1½ft	4–8	Clear blue (E–M)	Gray-green	Erect, RHS Award
×s. 'Mainacht' (syn. 'May Night')	1½–2½ft × 1½ft	5–9	Rich dark violet-blue, purplish red bracts (E–M)	Dark green	1997 PPA Award, RHS Award
×s. 'Rose Queen'	1½–2ft × 1½ft	5–9	Rose-pink (M)	Dark green, tinted gray	Floppy
×s. 'Schneehügel' (syn. 'Snow Hill')	1½–2ft × 1½ft	4–7	White (M)	Deep grayish green	Cut back for rebloom
×s. 'Viola Klose'	1½ft × 2ft	4–8	Dark violet-blue, more open spikes (E–M)	Dark green	
uliginosa	5–6ft × ∞	6–10	Sky-blue, white flecks (M–L)	Bright mid-green, lanceolate, aromatic	Bog sage, likes it moist, invasive in wet soil, flops, RHS Award
verticillata	3ft × 1½ft	5–9	Lilac-blue, small (M–L)	Green, cordate-ovate, hairy	Lilac salvia, good cut, deadhead for repeat bloom
v. 'Purple Rain'	1½–2ft × 1½ft	5–9	Dusty purple, fuzzy (M–L)	Gray-green, fuzzy, serrated	Doesn't come true from seed, good cut, deadhead for repeat bloom

Sanguinaria canadensis f. multiplex.

SANGUINARIA Papaveraceae

This woodlander, native to the east coast of North America, is a winner despite its very short bloom season. The cup-shaped white flowers arrive very early in the year. The scalloped leaves, which have five to nine lobes, are very attractive. It spreads by rhizomes, but gently. Sanguinaria is perfectly happy to go dormant if denied summer moisture. Best in a deciduous woodland, with sun in spring and no additional water. ~ *Ann Bucher*

Scientific Name: From the Latin *sanguis* ("blood"), referring to the red interior of the rhizomes.
Common Name: Bloodroot.
Origin: North America.
Preferred Conditions: Humus-rich, moderately fertile, well-drained, moist soil. Tolerates drier soil if well shaded after flowering.
Light: Shade to part shade. Tolerates sun if soil is moist.
Management: Mulch only lightly. This is a spring ephemeral and basically takes care of itself.
Propagation: Division when dormant in August (can be temperamental when divided); seed.
Pests and Diseases: Slugs in early spring as leaves emerge.
Companions: Trillium, hepatica, pulmonaria, primula, uvularia, jeffersonia, *Athyrium nipponicum* cultivars, erythronium; the spring woodland garden.
Notes: Get one or two sanguinarias, plant them, and leave them alone!

Species and Cultivars	Height/ Spread	USDA Hardiness Zone	Flowers (bloom time)	Foliage	Comments
canadensis	6in × 12in+	4–9	White, tinged pink, yellow stamens (E)	Blue-green, with grayish green reverse, lobed	Bloodroot, self-sows, summer dormant
c. f. multiplex (syn. 'Flore Pleno')	6in × 12in+	4–9	White, double, yellow stamens (E)	Grayish green, lobed	Sterile, long-blooming
c. f. multiplex 'Plena'	6in × 12in+	4–9	White, double (E)	As above	RHS Award

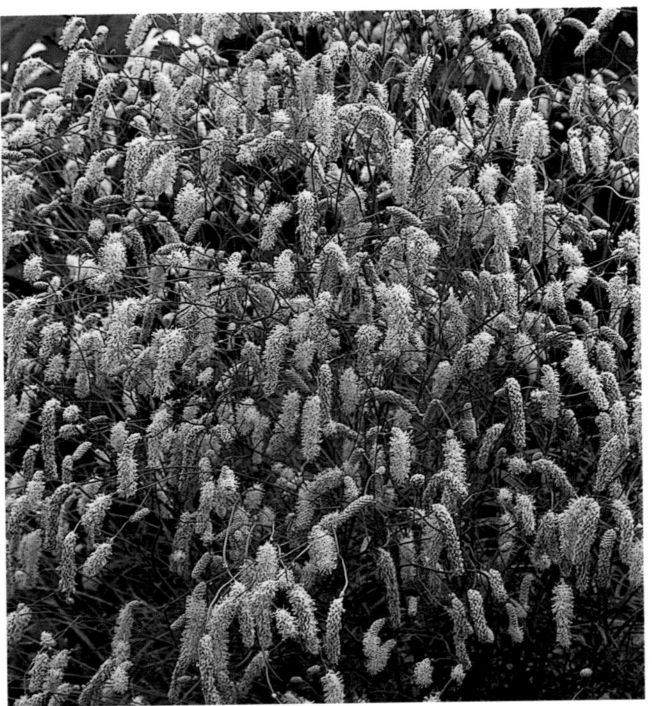

Sanguisorba tenuifolia 'Alba'.

SANGUISORBA Rosaceae

This plant offers an unusual vertical flower. Whether short and tight or longer and looser, the bottlebrushlike spikes are a change from the many rounded flower forms that are in the garden in late summer. Flowers are composed of soft prominent stamens in shades of white, pink, or red, rising above robust pinnate foliage. Plants are rhizomatous, and some self-sow. My *S. tenuifolia* is well behaved, maybe because it's in light soil (its preference would be more moisture); in late summer, tight blood-red spikes wave above its foliage. ~ *Ann Bucher*

Scientific Name: From the Latin *sanguis* ("blood") and *sorbeo* ("to absorb"); plants were used to stop bleeding.
Common Name: Burnet.
Origin: North America, Japan, Europe, Asia.
Preferred Conditions: Poor to moderately fertile, acidic, and well-drained soil. In too-rich soil, plants may be floppy.
Light: Sun. Tolerates part shade but will not bloom as well.
Planting: You may want to plant *S. officinalis* with a root barrier.
Management: Deadhead spent flowers for a longer bloom and to prevent self-sowing. Top-dress in winter with organic material. Staking may be needed.
Propagation: Seed; division in spring every three years.
Pests and Diseases: Slugs, aphids.
Companions: Grasses, astilbe, aconitum, astrantia, *Carex elata* 'Aurea', *Lysimachia nummularia* 'Aurea', *L. ephemerum*, veronicastrum, polemonium, penstemon; the autumn border.
Notes: A good cut flower.

Species and Cultivars	Height/ Spread	USDA Hardiness Zone	Flowers (bloom time)	Foliage	Comments
canadensis	4–6ft × 2ft	3–8	Green buds, open white, narrow, 6–8in long (M–L)	Bright green, oblong-lanceolate to ovate-pinnate, 7–17 leaflets, hairy	Canadian burnet, vigorous, good fall color
obtusa	2–4ft × 2ft	4–8	Light rose-pink, maturing to pale pink, 3in long (M–L)	Pale greenish gray, pinnate, 13–17 leaflets	Japanese bottle-brush, vigorous, may need support
officinalis	3–4ft × 1½ft	4–8	Red-brown to maroon, small (M–L)	Green, cordate, ovate to orbicular, pinnate, 7–25 leaflets	Salad burnet, invasive, stems have reddish tint
'Tanna'	2½ft × 1½ft	4–8	Burgundy-red, tiny (M)	Gray-green, pinnate	Vigorous
tenuifolia	4ft × 2ft	4–8	Red, 3in long (M–L)	Mid-green, large, mostly basal, pinnate, 11–15 leaflets, narrow, toothed	Erect
t. 'Alba'	3–4ft × 2ft	4–8	Greenish white (M)	Bluish green, pinnate, narrow, 11–15 leaflets	True from seed, may need support

SAPONARIA Caryophyllaceae

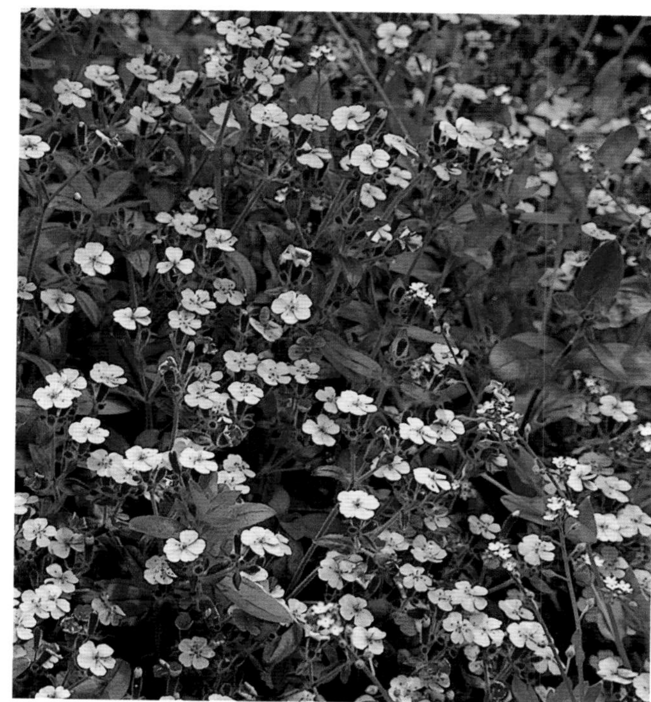

Saponaria ocymoides.

Saponaria officinalis has a long and interesting history. Because of its ability to produce a soapy lather, this species has figured in several ways for the purpose of washing and is still cultivated for that use. Woolens are washed with it in France and Syria; sheep are washed with it before shearing (it has a disinfectant quality as well); and delicate fabrics are still gently washed with saponaria during some restoration work. You might even have success applying water made soapy from the leaves and roots to a poison ivy rash. Bouncing Bet—for its ability to spread rapidly, bouncing away all around the garden—is still used as a common name. The other species are not so invasive and make attractive flowers for a wide range of situations. Of value are their drought-resistance and hardiness, and, for me personally, their cheery, optimistic outlook and charm. I find they will make a good low groundcover, and will also grow up through other plants, like Michaelmas daisies, which prevents their flopping. ~ *Susan Buckles*

Scientific Name: From the Latin *sapo* ("soap").
Common Name: Soapwort, bouncing Bet.
Origin: Asia, Europe, North America, China, Japan.
Preferred Conditions: Moderately fertile, light, humusy, well-drained, and neutral to slightly alkaline soil.
Light: Sun.
Management: Plants are a bit weedy and vigorous and can be unattractive without a lot of attention and control: staking, pinching, and fussing over. Pinch *S. officinalis* in May to encourage bushiness. Cut back stems in the fall after flowering. Top-dress with organic material.
Propagation: Division in spring; cuttings in spring.
Pests and Diseases: Snails, slugs.
Companions: Fuchsia, persicaria, chelone, aubrieta, *Anemone hupehensis* and *A.* ×*hybrida*, *Phlox subulata*, *P. paniculata* (for *S. officinalis*); the rock garden (for *S. ocymoides*).

Species and Cultivars	Height/ Spread	USDA Hardiness Zone	Flowers (bloom time)	Foliage	Comments
×lempergii 'Max Frei'	10–15in × 12in	4–8	Soft pink double (M)	Dark blue-green, lanceolate, softly hairy	Not invasive
ocymoides	8in × 18in+	4–8	Pink (E)	Bright green, ovate, hairy	Evergreen, rock garden plant, RHS Award
officinalis	2–3ft × 1ft+	3–4	Pale pink, fragrant (M–L)	Mid-green, veined, ovate, rough, leathery	Bouncing Bet, on some invasive plant lists
o. 'Alba Plena'	2–2½ft × 1ft	4–8	Double white, pink in bud (M–L)	As above	Vigorous
o. 'Rosea Plena'	2–3ft × 1ft	4–8	Double pink-mauve, scented (M–L)	As above	As above
o. 'Rubra Plena'	16–24in × 12in	4–8	Red aging to pink, double (M–L)	As above	As above

Saxifraga stolonifera.

SAXIFRAGA Saxifragaceae

Saxifraga is a large genus of low-growing, mostly mounding or mat-forming plants, many of which are alpines more suited to the rock garden. The ones we have included here are used in the border or in a woodland setting. They are grown for their lovely leaves as well as their flowers, and most are evergreen (see chart). The leaves are variable in form and are of heavy substance, either smooth or hairy, with some forming rosettes. The flowers are five-petaled, cup- or star-shaped, white or in shades of pink, and stand airily well above the foliage. Saxifrages are easy plants to grow and add a lot of interest when allowed to spread naturally into large colonies. ~ *Susan Carter*

Scientific Name: From the Latin *saxum* ("rock") and *frango* ("to break"): those growing naturally in rock crevices appear to have broken the rocks.
Common Name: Saxifrage.
Origin: Japan, China, Korea.
Preferred Conditions: Well-drained, cool, neutral to slightly acid, moisture-retentive soil, rich in loam.
Light: Part shade to sun.
Planting: Plant high so crowns don't get soggy.
Management: Cut back faded flower stems. Divide when center begins to fall apart. Clean up in the fall. Mulch to protect from early spring frost, but not over the crown.
Propagation: Division in spring for herbaceous ones, anytime for the evergreen types except in summer heat.
Pests and Diseases: Crown rot (in wet soils), root weevil grubs (over winter), aphids, snails, slugs, spider mites.
Companions: Ferns, hosta, primula, arisaema, geranium, astilbe, *Aruncus aethusifolius*, *Viola cornuta*, hakonechloa.
Notes: Look for cultivars of *S. fortunei* with striking foliage in reds, maroons, and variegated; these are all short-lived and susceptible to root weevil damage.

Species and Cultivars	Height/ Spread	USDA Hardiness Zone	Flowers (bloom time)	Foliage	Comments
cortusifolia	6in × 8in	5–9	White, tiny, cup-shaped, in sprays, spotted yellow or red (M–L)	Green, round to kidney-shaped, leathery, toothed, glossy, lobed	Deciduous or evergreen
fortunei	8in × 12in	6–8	White, blushed pink, small (L)	Green, round to kidney-shaped, usually 7 lobes	Deciduous or semi-evergreen
primuloides	4–8in × 10in	7–9	White, red spots, star-shaped (E–M)	Mid-green rosettes, reddish green reverse, spoon-shaped to rounded or ovate	Evergreen, RHS Award
stolonifera (syn. sarmentosa)	1–2ft × 2ft+	5–9	White, marked with yellow and red (M)	Rounded, veined and fleshy, marbled with pale green, scalloped and hairy	Strawberry begonia, semi-evergreen, RHS Award
umbrosa	12in × 12in+	6–9	White with red spots in center (E–M)	Green rosettes, leathery, obovate to oblong-oval	Porcelain flower, evergreen
×urbium	4–6in × 12in+	5–9	White, red center, spotted yellow and red, star-shaped (E–M)	Green, leathery, spoon-shaped to rounded-ovate, toothed	London pride, stoloniferous, slowly spreads further, evergreen, RHS Award
×u. 'Variegata'	4–6in × 12in+	5–9	As above	As above but splashed in cream	Variegated London pride, evergreen

SCABIOSA Dipsacaceae

Pincushion flower is a charming old-fashioned plant. The flower heads are composed of many small flowers (florets) with the stamens and pistils creating a pincushionlike effect. As with most flowers that form a dome, the outside florets are larger, giving a lacy effect to the pincushion. They bloom in wonderful shades of lavender, blue, pink, yellow, and white on long, wiry stems, with many in flower from spring until fall. Scabiosas are a good cut flower for fresh arrangements but last only three to five days in water (cut before central flowers open). The seedheads are oval and seem to be covered in pins; they too make an interesting cut. ~ *Susan Carter*

Scientific Name: From the Latin *scabies* ("itch"), which the rough leaves were said to cure.
Common Name: Pincushion flower.
Origin: Caucasus, Europe, Asia, Africa, Japan, Turkey.
Preferred Conditions: Easy to grow in average, light, well-drained, neutral to alkaline soil. Will be short-lived in acidic soil. Protect from excessive winter moisture.
Light: Sun.
Management: Keep crowns free of mulch. Deadhead for continuous bloom. Some of the heavier bloomers (*S.* 'Butterfly Blue', *S.* 'Pink Mist') may benefit from a forced rest in midsummer by cutting off the flowers and buds; this will encourage new vegetative growth and further blooms. Lime around plants once a year, keeping it away from the crown. Some people recommend staking, but this may just look plain awful, especially on the shorter ones. Clean up in the fall leaving the semi-evergreen basal leaves where appropriate. Watch out for slugs in spring. Divide every two to four years.

Scabiosa caucasica 'Perfecta Alba'.

Propagation: Best from seed or stem cuttings; division in spring.
Pests and Diseases: Slugs on young seedlings.
Companions: Coreopsis, hemerocallis, heliopsis, agastache, dianthus, campanula, delphinium, nepeta, calamintha, salvia, stachys; suited to the sunny border and the cottage garden.
Notes: These are short-lived perennials, known to bloom themselves almost to death even if deadheaded—something the marketers won't tell you.

Species and Cultivars	Height/ Spread	USDA Hardiness Zone	Flowers (bloom time)	Foliage	Comments
'Butterfly Blue'	1–1½ft × 1½ft	4–8	Lavender-blue, 2in (E–L)	Gray-green, deeply cut, hairy, ovate to lanceolate	Semi-evergreen, long-blooming, 2000 PPA Award
caucasica	1½–2½ft × 1½ft	4–9	Pale lavender-blue, 2½–3in (M–L)	Gray-green, smooth, lanceolate	Needs moisture during flowering season
c. var. alba	1½ft × 1½ft	5–9	White, 3in (M–L)	As above	
c. 'Clive Greaves'	2–2½ft × 1½ft	4–9	Lavender-blue, dark bracts, 3in (M–L)	Not the nicest you've ever seen	RHS Award
c. 'Fama'	1½–3ft × 1½ft	4–9	Sky-blue, 3in (M–L)	Gray-green, smooth, lanceolate	
c. House's Hybrids	1½–2ft × 1½ft	4–9	White and blue, shaggy, semi-double, 3in (M–L)	As above	
c. 'Kompliment'	12–24in × 18in	4–9	Dark lavender-blue, 3in (M–L)	As above	
c. Perfecta Series	12–24in × 18in	4–9	Lavender-blue, fringed, 2½in (M–L)	As above	Strong stems

Species and Cultivars	Height/ Spread	USDA Hardiness Zone	Flowers (bloom time)	Foliage	Comments
c. Perfecta Series 'Perfecta Alba'	12–24in × 18in	4–9	White, 3in (M–L)	As above	As above
c. 'Miss Willmott'	2–3ft × 2ft	4–9	Creamy-white, 3in (M–L)	As above	RHS Award
columbaria (syn. banatica)	1½–2½ft × 1½ft	5–8	Lavender-blue, 2in (M–L)	Gray-green, hairy, lanceolate-ovate, finely cut	Long-blooming
c. subsp. ochroleuca	2–3ft × 1½ft	5–8	Pale creamy yellow, 2in (M–L)	Gray-green, felty, obovate-lanceolate, deeply cut	Comes true from seed
lucida	8–10in × 10in	4–9	Lavender, 1½in (M–L)	Green, smooth, glossy, ovate-lanceolate, coarsely toothed	Self-sows
'Pink Mist'	1–1½ft × 1½ft	4–8	Pale lavender-pink, double, 2in (M–L)	Gray-green, deeply cut	Long-blooming, semi-evergreen

SCHIZOSTYLIS Iridaceae

I love schizostylis in the late summer and fall: spikes of open-cupped flowers with a satiny finish bloom long after almost everything else is gone. The crimson is my favorite, but there is nothing wrong with the pink or white. But I hate them in spring, when one has to deal with the masses (they really do spread quickly by short rhizomes) of unattractive light green grasslike leaves. They make a good cut flower, sometimes as late as Christmas. ~ *Ann Bucher*

Schizostylis coccinea 'Major' with canna.

Scientific Name: From the Greek *schizo* ("to divide") and *stylis* ("style"); the style is divided into three parts.
Common Name: Crimson flag, kaffir lily.
Origin: South Africa.
Preferred Conditions: Moderately fertile, well-drained, humus-rich soil. Very tolerant of most soil conditions but likes to stay moist in the summer. Shelter from cold drying winds. Lean soil yields stronger stems and less need to stake.
Light: Sun. Full, hot sun for more erect plants.
Management: Mulch with organic material. Autumn frosts damage open flowers but not the unopened buds. Groom plant by pulling out the old flowering stems and removing bad-looking leaves in a harsh winter. In spring, remove last year's flowering plants and leave the new unflowered plants; this can be done with a simple vertical yank, which reduces the size of the clump and helps to keep them in bounds. Divide every year, once established, for good flower production. Best if soil is then improved, or move plants to another, more fertile location.
Propagation: Seed; division in spring.
Pests and Diseases: Slugs, thrips, rust—all can leave plants a bit messy.
Companions: Hardy fuchsias, alstroemeria, persicaria, best on their own for cutting and late color. Hard to companion (try Craigslist).
Notes: The corms on this plant are very small and never unattached to the stems. Plants will spread beyond the one-foot noted in the chart if allowed to send their rhizomes traveling.

Species and Cultivars	Height/ Spread	USDA Hardiness Zone	Flowers (bloom time)	Foliage	Comments
coccinea	1–2ft × 1ft	6–10	Scarlet, 6-petaled cups in spikes (M–L)	Mid-green, grasslike, prominent midrib	Crimson flag, vigorous, erect
c. f. alba	1½–2ft × 1ft	6–10	White with a faint tinge of pink, small (M–L)	As above	A nice bright almost-white
c. 'Cherry Red'	2ft × 1ft	6–10	Bright red (M–L)	As above	Distinctive color
c. 'Fenland Daybreak'	1½–2ft × 1ft	6–10	Salmon-pink (L)	As above	Slightly larger flowers
c. 'Jennifer'	2ft × 1ft	6–10	Soft pink (L)	As above	RHS Award
c. 'Major' (syn. 'Gigantea', 'Grandiflora')	15–24in × 1½ft	6–10	Scarlet-red (L)	As above	Larger flowers, RHS Award
c. 'Mrs. Hegarty'	1½–2ft × 1½ft	6–10	Pale pink (M–L)	As above	Flowers all summer but mostly in the fall
c. 'Oregon Sunset'	2ft × 1½ft	6–10	Watermelon-pink (L)	As above	Slightly larger flowers
c. 'Pallida'	1–1½ft × 1ft	6–10	Pale pink almost white, large (L)	As above	Fully open, a good clear white
c. 'Snow Maiden'	1–1½ft × 1ft	6–10	Clear white (L)	As above	
c. 'Sunrise' (syn. 'Sunset')	1½–2½ft × 1ft	6–10	Salmon-pink, large (L)	As above	RHS Award
c. 'Viscountess Byng'	2ft × 1½ft	6–10	Pale pink (L)	As above	Last to bloom, vulnerable to frost damage

SCROPHULARIA Scrophulariaceae

The variegated water figwort is a striking foliage plant, more moisture-loving than aquatic. Very bold and eye-catching, it's best used as a focal point, although it's not long-lived. Its large leaves are edged in cream, crinkled and toothed, and borne on rigid upright stems; the small red flowers rise high above the foliage and are somewhat inconspicuous in comparison, but bees love them and find them quite easily. ~ *Susan Carter*

Scrophularia auriculata 'Variegata'.

Scientific Name: From the Latin *scrofulae*, a swelling of the lymph nodes, referring to the appearance of the plant's rhizomes.
Common Name: Water figwort.
Origin: Europe, North Africa, Great Britain.
Preferred Conditions: Rich, moisture-retentive soil. Shelter from wind; stems are brittle.
Light: Part shade to sun.
Management: Do not let other plants engulf it. Cut back to the crown in midsummer (or as soon as foliage and flower stems begin to look bad); a fresh new crop of leaves will emerge. Top-dress with organic matter in winter, but not over the crown.
Propagation: Cuttings; division in spring.
Pests and Diseases: Slugs, especially on early young growth.
Companions: Larger ferns, tall astilbes, *Lysimachia ciliata* 'Firecracker', *Phalaris arundinacea*, rodgersia, ligularia, hosta, *Iris pseudacorus* for its vertical foliage and similar habitat, *Persicaria amplexicaulis*.

Species and Cultivars	Height/ Spread	USDA Hardiness Zone	Flowers (bloom time)	Foliage	Comments
auriculata 'Variegata'	3–4ft × 2ft	5–9	Deep red, tiny (M)	Light green, splashed creamy-white with creamy margins, large, lanceolate	Tall, short-lived, a marginal aquatic perennial

Sedum spectabile 'Brilliant'.

SEDUM Crassulaceae

Sedums, grown for their long season of flowers as well as their distinctive fleshy foliage, contribute more than their share to the garden. The five-petaled flowers often change color throughout their life, aging finally to beautiful reddish brown seedheads that can remain a feature throughout the winter; they are star-shaped, in clusters or sprays of usually flat heads (corymbs). The fleshy leaves are also variable: opposite or alternate, whorled, and often toothed. Sedums are versatile and come in a range of shapes and sizes. Some are happiest at the front of the border or among floppier plants; others are good choices for the rock garden. We're including mostly the larger ones or border sedums here. All are hardy, undemanding plants. They make a very good cut flower and attract butterflies and bees. ~ *Susan Carter*

Scientific Name: From the Latin *sedo* ("to sit"), referring to the manner in which some species attach themselves to stones or walls.

Common Name: Stonecrop, orpine.

Origin: Europe, Russia, Korea, Japan, China, East Asia, Britain.

Preferred Conditions: Moderate to poor, well-drained soil. Sedums can become too tall in richer, heavier soils. Most are very drought tolerant but may perform better with average garden conditions. Best flower color and compact growth in full sun and lean soils. Certain cultivars, such as *S.* 'Vera Jameson' and *S.* 'Bertram Anderson', and the species *S. sieboldii* also need no competition but even so may be short-lived.

Light: Sun. Tolerates part shade, but shade may cause larger-flowered forms to be leggy and lax.

Management: Cut to the crown once the foliage begins to look bad in late fall (some turn a nice rusty brown in the winter and can be left until spring). Cut back flower stems on the spreading sedums to maintain shape. Divide larger sedums every three to four years; this will help improve the flowering. Lift with fork in spring to break feeder roots before replanting (this retards their growth, making shorter, stronger plants); or dig up, divide, and replant to the same effect. You can also pinch them back in springtime, but flower heads become smaller. For the larger *S. telephium* and *S. spectabile* forms and cultivars, neither root pruning nor pinching works very well in good soil; in lean soil, try the former (don't do the latter). The *S. spectabile* and *S. telephium* cultivars can flop in wet fall weather; try to locate them where this will work to your advantage, or try pea sticks or the techniques just noted. Bait crowns (which are evergreen) for slugs in early spring.

Propagation: Seed; division in spring; cuttings are easy in the spring and root easily.

Pests and Diseases: Snails, slugs, mealy bugs. Root weevils can damage or devour the root system over winter. The root weevil problem is much worse in pots.

Companions: Dwarf conifers, smaller grasses, asters, nepeta, penstemon, salvia, scabiosa, heuchera, carex; for the larger *S. spectabile* types, the autumn border.

Notes: In the Pacific Northwest pinching out can be a big mistake in a cool summer, as it makes ugly, runty flowers.

Species and Cultivars	Height/ Spread	USDA Hardiness Zone	Flowers (bloom time)	Foliage	Comments
'Bertram Anderson'	6–8in × 12in	5–9	Dusty-pink, purple stems (M–L)	Purple-tinted, fleshy, round to ovate	RHS Award
erythrostictum	1–1½ft × 1½ft	4–9	Greenish white clusters (M–L)	Gray-green, toothed, ovate	
e. 'Frosty Morn'	1–1½ft × 1½ft	4–9	White in warm climates, pale pink in cool climates (M–L)	Grayish green, white borders	Flops, often reverts to green
e. 'Mediovariegatum'	1–1½ft × 1½ft	4–9	Whitish, touch of pale pink (M–L)	Central creamy-yellow blotch with green margins, blotch is gold in spring	Part shade, may revert to green
'Herbstfreude' (syn. 'Autumn Joy')	1½–2ft × 2ft	3–10	Light pink to deeper pink aging to pinkish bronze then coppery (M–L)	Grayish blue-green, oblong to ovate, toothed	Good cut, RHS Award
'Ruby Glow'	8–12in × 12in	5–9	Deep ruby-red aging to russet-brown, red stems (M–L)	Gray-green, elliptic, toothed	Lax habit, large heads, RHS Award
sieboldii	6–8in × 12in	6–9	Bright rosy-pink (M–L)	Blue-green, sometimes edged purple or red, toothed, in whorls, turns coppery	October daphne, trailing
s. 'Mediovariegatum' (syn. 'Variegatum')	4–6in × 12in	6–9	Bright pink (M–L)	Blue-green, marbled with cream, red margins	RHS Award
spectabile	1–2ft × 2ft	4–9	Pale rosy-pink with prominent stamens (M–L)	Gray-green, ovate to elliptic or obovate, toothed	Showy stonecrop, large heads, RHS Award

Species and Cultivars	Height/ Spread	USDA Hardiness Zone	Flowers (bloom time)	Foliage	Comments
s. 'Brilliant'	1–2ft × 2ft	4–9	Bright pinkish rose (M–L)	Light blue-green, scalloped	Striking color, large heads, RHS Award
s. 'Carmen'	1½–2ft × 2ft	4–9	Rosy-pink (M–L)	Gray-green	Large heads
s. 'Iceberg'	1–1½ft × 2ft	4–9	White (M–L)	Apple-green	As above
s. 'Indian Chief'	15in × 2ft	4–9	Copper-red (L)	Pale green	As above
s. 'Meteor'	1–1½ft × 1½ft	4–9	Purplish red (M–L)	Gray-green	As above
s. 'Septemberglut' (syn. 'September Glow')	18–20in × 2ft	4–9	Rich pink aging to dark red (L)	As above	Very large heads
s. 'Stardust'	1–1½ft × 1½ft	3–9	Creamy-white (M–L)	As above	Large heads
telephium	1½–2ft × 2ft	4–9	Greenish white aging to reddish purple (M–L)	Gray-green, toothed, oblong-ovate	Orpine, floppy
t. 'Arthur Branch'	1½–2ft × 2ft	4–9	Reddish purple, burgundy stems (M–L)	Dark purplish black, glossy	Floppy
t. 'Matrona'	1½–2½ft × 2ft	3–9	Pale smoky-pink, shiny red stems (M–L)	Gray-bluish green, rosy-pink edges, large	Upright
t. subsp. maximum 'Atropurpureum'	1½–2ft × 2ft	3–9	Rosy-pink, small (M–L)	Purple-maroon, toothed, ovate	Chocolate-brown seedheads, open habit, RHS Award
t. subsp. maximum 'Gooseberry Fool'	1–1½ft × 2ft	5–9	Green (L)	Chalky blue-green	Great color, smaller heads. upright
t. 'Mohrchen'	1½–2ft × 2ft	3–9	Dark reddish pink (M–L)	Grayish red-purple, heavy substance	A bit more vertical
t. 'Munstead Red'	1½–2ft × 2ft	4–9	Rose-red (M–L)	Purplish green	Brown seedheads, upright
t. subsp. ruprechtii (syn. 'Eleanor Fisher')	1–1½ft × 1½ft	4–10	Pink buds open to creamy yellow (M–L)	Chalky-blue with pink tones	Good color, smaller heads, upright
t. 'Variegatum'	1ft × 1½ft	4–9	Pink with green tints (M–L)	Pale green with creamy gold variegation	May revert, remove the green shoots, upright
'Vera Jameson'	8–12in × 12in	4–9	Deep rose-pink with white accents, purple stems (M–L)	Glaucous, rosy-purple tints, toothed, rounded	RHS Award

SEMIAQUILEGIA Ranunculaceae

Semiaquilegia ecalcarata is a prolific bloomer, forming basal clumps with airy sprays of nodding flowers that rise well above the foliage. Semiaquilegia looks just like its cousin aquilegia, but its flowers are spurless. This is a charming species, sweet but short-lived. Collect and sow seed to keep it in your garden; it is worth growing! ~ *Susan Carter*

Semiaquilegia ecalcarata with a blue grass.

Scientific Name: From the Latin *semi* ("half") and *aquila* ("eagle"), referring to the form of the petals (which they don't have).

Common Name: Half columbine.

Origin: Western China.

Preferred Conditions: Easy to grow in cool, moist, moderately fertile, humus-rich, well-drained, neutral to slightly acidic soil. Provide shelter from cold, drying winds.

Light: Sun to part shade.

Management: Resents disturbance. Deadhead for rebloom, but remove only the flowering stems. Leave basal leaves until autumn. Cut back to the ground once foliage begins to look bad.

Propagation: Seed only.

Pests and Diseases: Snails, slugs, sawfly larvae.

Companions: *Ajuga pyramidalis* 'Metallica Crispa', viola, pulmonaria, primula, erythronium, *Anemone nemorosa*, *Cardamine trifolia*, *C. pratensis*.

Species and Cultivars	Height/ Spread	USDA Hardiness Zone	Flowers (bloom time)	Foliage	Comments
ecalcarata (syn. simulatrix)	8–15in × 10in	6–8	Dusky pale pink to deep violet-purple (E–M)	Gray-green, purple reverse, very finely divided	Very fine stems
e. 'Flore Pleno'	8–15in × 10in	6–8	Deep purple, double (E–M)	As above	A beautiful flower

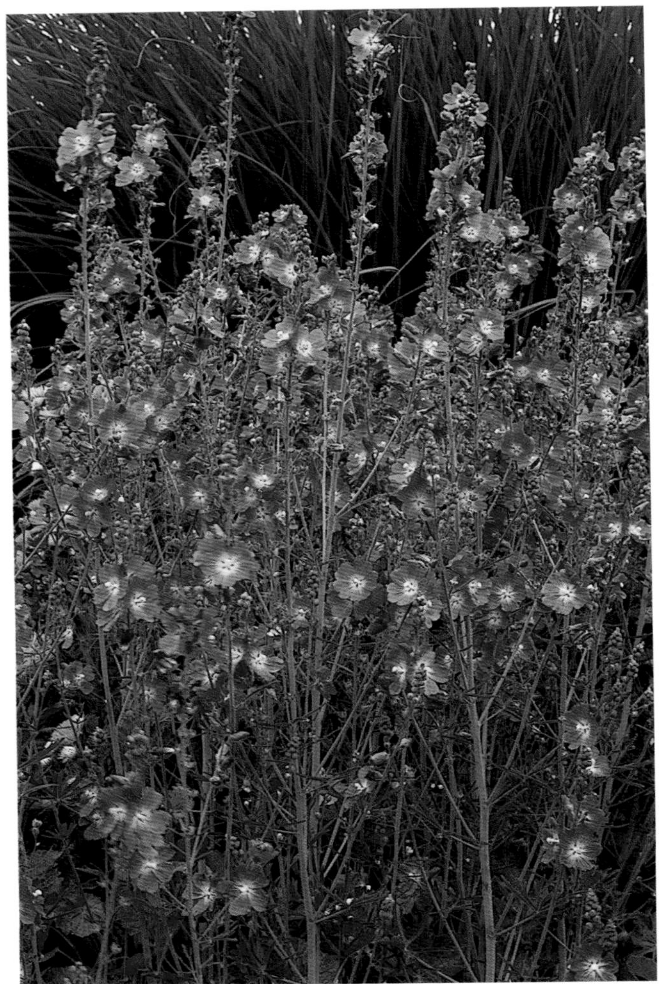

Sidalcea 'Party Girl'.

SIDALCEA Malvaceae

This North American native is an easy-care, summer-flowering perennial in shades of pink, red, and white. Plants are long-blooming with the charm of old-fashioned hollyhocks, but smaller, in both flower and height. The flowers are wide saucers of five petals, silky in texture and sometimes fringed. Prairie mallow freely self-sows (unfortunately) but is short-lived (fortunately). Named varieties do not come true from seed. ~ *Susan Carter*

Scientific Name: From *sida* and *alcea*, two Greek names for mallow, and two related genera in the family Malvaceae.

Common Name: Prairie mallow, false mallow.

Origin: North America.

Preferred Conditions: Deep, moderately fertile, humus-rich, moist, well-drained, and neutral to slightly acidic soil. Resents being waterlogged.

Light: Sun to part shade.

Management: Requires little maintenance. Cut back stems to basal growth after flowering for rebloom. Do not remove basal foliage in the fall. Some may need staking. Top-dress with organic material in the winter. Like most prairie plants, they have a deep taproot and resent transplanting.

Propagation: Best from seed; division in spring; cuttings.

Pests and Diseases: Snails, slugs. Rust can be a serious problem.

Companions: Grasses, monarda, artemisia, penstemon, centranthus, geranium, echinacea, physostegia, iron fences, picket fences, the other side of fences.

Notes: *Sidalcea candida* and *S. malviflora* are the parents of *S.* 'Elsie Heugh'. They are all used in breeding; these hollyhock relatives have more resistance to rust.

Species and Cultivars	Height/ Spread	USDA Hardiness Zone	Flowers (bloom time)	Foliage	Comments
'Brilliant'	2–2½ft × 2ft+	4–9	Carmine-red (M)	Bright green	Spreads
candida	2–3ft × 1½ft	4–9	White, small (M)	Bluish green, rounded, lobed	Rust resistant, spreads
c. 'Bianca'	2–3ft × 2ft+	4–9	Clear white (M–L)	Green, rounded, lobed, basal leaves smaller	Rust resistant, runs like crazy
'Elsie Heugh'	2½–3ft × 2ft+	4–9	Pale shell-pink, satiny, fringed (M)	Green	Self-sows, RHS Award

Species and Cultivars	Height/ Spread	USDA Hardiness Zone	Flowers (bloom time)	Foliage	Comments
malviflora	2–4ft × 2ft	4–9	Bright pink to lilac-pink, prominent reddish veins, silky (M)	Bluish green, basal clumps, round to kidney-shaped, lobed, more deeply lobed on stems	West Coast native, erect, good cut
'Party Girl'	2–3ft × 2ft+	4–9	Bright rose-pink (M–L)	Gray-green, round to kidney-shaped	Erect, clumping
'Rose Queen'	3–4ft × 2ft+	4–9	Rosy-pink, large (M)	Bluish green, basal clumps, round to kidney-shaped, lobed, more deeply lobed on stems	Strong grower

SILENE Caryophyllaceae

Silene is a large genus, closely related to *Lychnis* and with many more members suited to the rock garden than to the perennial border. *Silene dioica* (red campion) and its cultivars lend an old-fashioned cottage garden look to the foreground of the border; flowers are reddish purple to pink with five deeply divided petals, and they bloom over a long period, from late spring through summer. The small semi-evergreen *S. schafta* (moss campion) forms very neat tufts covered with large purplish rose flowers. The silenes are short-lived but are very floriferous and seem to self-sow just fine. ~ *Susan Carter*

Silene dioica 'Clifford Moor'.

Scientific Name: From the Greek *sialon* ("saliva"), referring to the sticky secretion this genus exudes from its stems, which can entrap small flies; hence the common English name catchfly for these plants.
Common Name: Campion, catchfly.
Origin: Europe, western Asia, Iran, Africa.
Preferred Conditions: Easy to grow in moderately fertile, well-drained, and neutral to slightly alkaline soil. Doesn't like to dry out.
Light: Sun to part shade.
Management: Doesn't require much maintenance other than removing the flowering stems after the blooms fade. Clean up flowering stems in winter but leave the crown alone. Bait; these are vulnerable to slugs in early spring.
Propagation: Seed; basal cuttings; division in spring.
Pests and Diseases: Snails, slugs, whiteflies, spider mites, aphids, rust.
Companions: Low-growing grasses, shorter campanulas, erigeron, *Euphorbia myrsinites*, *Dianthus deltoides*, *Iris germanica* (dwarf forms), *I. sibirica*.

Species and Cultivars	Height/ Spread	USDA Hardiness Zone	Flowers (bloom time)	Foliage	Comments
dioica	2–3ft × 1½ft	5–9	Light red-violet (E–M)	Ovate basal leaves, softly hairy	Red campion, hairy stems
d. 'Clifford Moor'	1½ft × 1ft	5–9	Pink (E–M)	Dark green edged in cream, narrow, straplike	
d. 'Flore Pleno'	1ft × 1ft	5–9	Rose-red, or pink with coral overtones, double (E)	Dark green, hairy, leafy mounds	
d. 'Graham's Delight' (syn. 'Variegata')	3ft × 1½ft	5–9	Pink, small (E–M)	Striped cream, sometimes cream margins	Seeds to *S. dioica*
d. 'Inane'	2ft × 1½ft	5–9	Bronze buds open to vivid pink (E–M)	Dark maroon basal leaves	Red stems
schafta	6–10in × 12in	5–9	Pink to purplish (M–L)	Bright green, lanceolate to ovate	Moss campion, RHS Award
uniflora 'Druett's Variegated'	8in × 10in	3–9	White (M)	Variegated white, more strikingly than *S. dioica* 'Graham's Delight'	May revert to green

SILPHIUM Asteraceae

The compass plant (*S. laciniatum*) derives its name from the behavior of its leaves, which stand upright with their edges set north-south, enabling them to better withstand the hot summer sun. *Silphium perfoliatum* (cup plant) has upper leaves that surround the stem, a classic perfoliate leaf. These members of the daisy family have flowers typical of sunflowers and are also from the American prairie. Mildew is a big problem, so don't let them dry out; this will aggravate the situation. They also have another aspect that causes gardeners quite a bit of grief—extreme vulnerability to slugs. Are there no slugs in the "Sea of Grass"? ~ *Bob Lilly*

Scientific Name: From *silphion*, the Greek term for a resinous plant.
Common Name: Compass plant, cup plant.

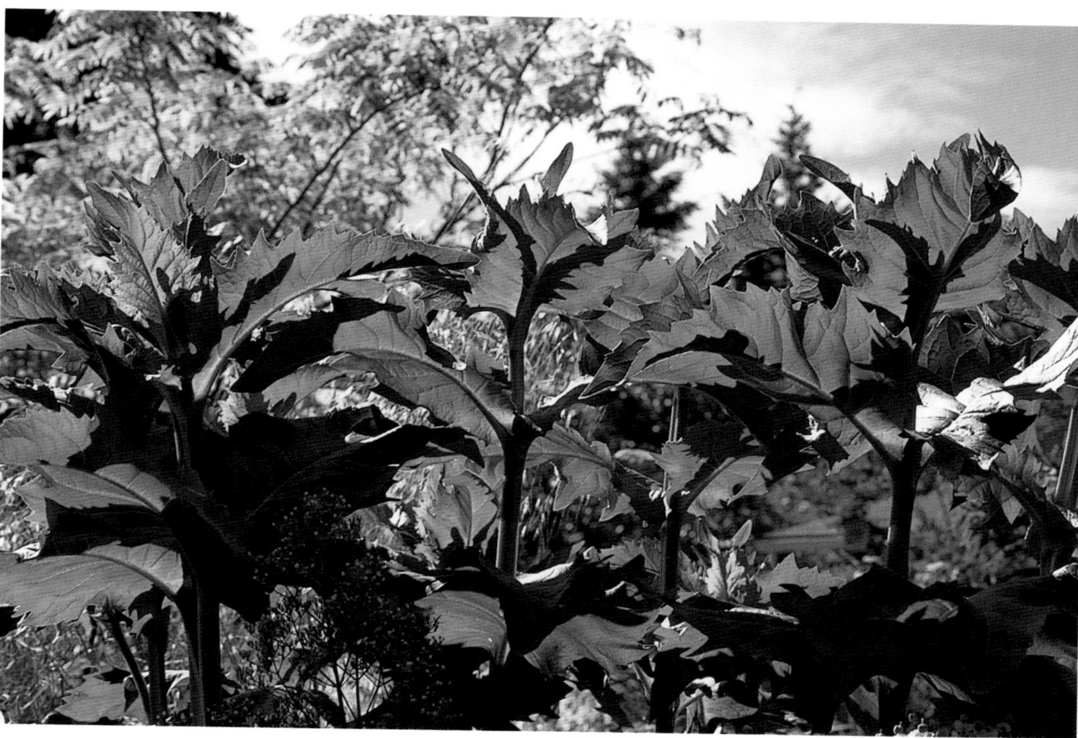

Silphium perfoliatum.

Origin: North America.
Preferred Conditions: Deep, moderately fertile, well-drained, moist, and neutral to slightly alkaline. Best in heavy soil.
Light: Sun to part shade.
Planting: Needs a location with lots of heat and summer water. In such a spot, the clumps can get quite large.
Management: Cut back in the fall when stems and foliage die back. Mulch heavily in the winter, and watch out for slugs in early spring as the plant emerges.
Propagation: Seed; division in spring.
Pests and Diseases: Snails, slugs, powdery mildew, rust.
Companions: Helianthus, echinacea, miscanthus and other grasses, liatris, American prairie plants, prairie dogs. These are plants for the back of a large-scale summer border or a yellow border—the foliage can be a bit rough-looking.

Species and Cultivars	Height/ Spread	USDA Hardiness Zone	Flowers (bloom time)	Foliage	Comments
laciniatum	7–8ft × 2ft	4–9	Small yellow ray florets, darker yellow orange disk, east-facing (M–L)	Green, fernlike, long and narrow, stiff-haired stems	Compass plant, long-lived
perfoliatum	6–8ft × 2ft	4–9	Lemon-yellow ray florets, darker disk florets (M–L)	Matte-green, triangular to ovate, perfoliate upper leaves	Cup plant, long-lived, slugs really like this one

Silybum marianum.

SILYBUM Asteraceae

Silybum marianum is now on noxious weed lists in many states—do not let it go to seed. Its extremely showy, boldly variegated leaves make it worth growing, but don't do so if you live near agricultural land. Unfortunately, the plant is a prickly beast on each lobe of each leaf, although the white and green marbled leaves compensate for this. The bad press on this plant may be traced to the fact it is happiest on the central California coast, where it is a problem for the cabbage and artichoke growers. At least it is a biennial and can't get too out of control as an ornamental in a city garden. ~ *Bob Lilly*

Scientific Name: From the Greek *silbon*, the term for a thistlelike plant.
Common Name: Blessed thistle, milk thistle.
Origin: North Africa, southwestern Europe to Afghanistan.
Preferred Conditions: Poor to moderately fertile, well-drained, neutral to slightly alkaline soil with average water conditions. Protect from excessive winter moisture and wind.
Light: Sun.
Management: Remove flowers after blooming to prevent self-sowing, or carefully remove flower stems as they form and retain the foliage effect. Watch for slugs and cutworms in early spring, as the seedlings are very tempting to them.
Propagation: Seed in situ or plant out when very young.
Pests and Diseases: Snails, slugs, caterpillars, cutworms.
Companions: Phlox, stock, hops, four o'clocks, and hollyhocks—a pox on the lot!
Notes: Milk thistle is used to make a salve for nursing mothers and will be extremely large and lush in organic-rich soil.

Species and Cultivars	Height/ Spread	USDA Hardiness Zone	Flowers (bloom time)	Foliage	Comments
marianum	4–5ft × 2–3ft	6–9	Lavender-pink (M–L)	Bright green, white streaks and marbling	Striking foliage, biennial

Sisyrinchium 'Quaint and Queer'.

SISYRINCHIUM Iridaceae

Most of the many species of sisyrinchium come from North and South America. A few are found in nurseries, seed lists, or plant sales but easiest to find is *S. idahoense* var. *bellum*. The different species require rather specific growing conditions, from moist to dry, at different times of the year; all, however, seem to need full sun. They are charming, dainty plants, worth all the attention you give them. We deal with the more easily grown members of the genus here; most grow in standard garden soil. The common name blue-eyed grass is shared by several species native to the Pacific Coast; the flowers of most of these tend to close on cloudy days, or only open in the mornings. Some will self-sow easily and given the right conditions will do quite well. Start with *S. striatum* and *S. s.* 'Aunt May': these rewarding colorful plants will tempt you to try the others.
~ *Susan Buckles*

Scientific Name: An old Greek name probably first applied to another plant. This sort of unclear notation is quite common with New World plants that were named long after their distant European cousins.

Common Name: Blue-eyed grass, yellow-eyed grass.

Origin: North America, South America.

Preferred Conditions: Most average, well-drained, moist soil. They like it warm. Protect from excessive winter moisture, or excessive winter drought.

Light: Sun.

Management: Remove old black leaves from *S. striatum* (every flower stem causes the death of the fan from which it grows). Remove flowering stems before seed sets to prevent self-sowing, should you want to (especially *S. striatum*). Leave some seedlings to replace dead plants. Divide often and replant. Clean off old foliage as necessary. Do not cut foliage tips to clean up the look of the plant; remove only entire leaves. Don't give them much fertilizer.

Propagation: Division in spring; seed; *S. striatum* 'Aunt May', which is variegated, must be from division as the seed comes up green.

Pests and Diseases: Snails, slugs, some crown rot.
Companions: Small-scale geraniums, smaller grasses, smaller campanulas, carex, armeria. With *S. striatum*—calla lilies, grasses, *Scabiosa ochroleuca*, cream-colored California poppy. The dwarfs are best all alone.
Notes: In a wet winter, all are short-lived in our heavy soils.

Species and Cultivars	Height/ Spread	USDA Hardiness Zone	Flowers (bloom time)	Foliage	Comments
'Biscutella'	10–12in × 6in	7–9	Creamy-yellow (biscuit-colored) (M)	Green, linear	An unusual and charming color, short-lived
'California Skies'	10in × 6in	7–9	Light blue, darker veins and yellow center (E–M)	Green, grasslike	
californicum	12–18in × 6–8in	8–9	Bright golden yellow, star-shaped (E–M)	Dull grayish green, sword-shaped, narrow	Yellow-eyed grass, semi-evergreen, self-sows
'E. K. Balls'	6in × 5in	7–9	Purple-blue, yellow throat, star-shaped (E–L)	Green, narrow, sword-shaped	Semi-evergreen, long-blooming, shortest cultivar
idahoense var. bellum	6–10in × 6in	4–9	Deep violet-blue, yellow throat, star-shaped (E–M)	Bluish green, narrow, linear	Blue-eyed grass, semi-evergreen, self-sows
'Marion'	10in × 6in	7–9	Purple, darker veins, rounded (E–M)	Green, grasslike	
'Mrs. Spivey'	4–6in × 6in	7–9	Pure white, small (M)	As above	
'Pole Star'	6in × 6in	7–9	Pure white, star-shaped (M)	Bluish green, linear	Semi-evergreen, short-lived
'Quaint and Queer'	10–12in × 6in	7–9	Mauve, yellow throat, star-shaped (E–M)	Green, linear	As above
striatum	18–36in × 10–12in	7–9	Pale creamy-yellow (M)	Gray-green, sword-shaped to linear	Evergreen, black seedheads, self-sows
s. 'Aunt May' (syn. 'Variegatum')	18–20in × 10–12in	7–9	Cream (M)	Gray-green, cream stripes	Propagate by division only, more tender and weaker than the species, evergreen

SMILACINA Convallariaceae

Both the smilacinas we deal with here are native to the Northwest and are tolerant of summer drought. *Smilacina racemosa* is also found on the East Coast but in a less robust form. It has smooth, alternate leaves, and its unbranched stem ends in a large panicle of small white flowers that give way to many bright red berries. The rhizomes spread slowly, but it's worth the long wait for a large clump of this plant. Lean in to enjoy the fragrant flowers. *Smilacina stellata* is a quick spreader once established, making a much less dense clump. It is not showy in bloom; the starlike flowers, rarely more than two, are at the apex of the stems. They flower later and are also followed by berries, dark red aging to black. It's a great groundcover for open shade under deciduous shrubs. ~ *Ann Bucher*

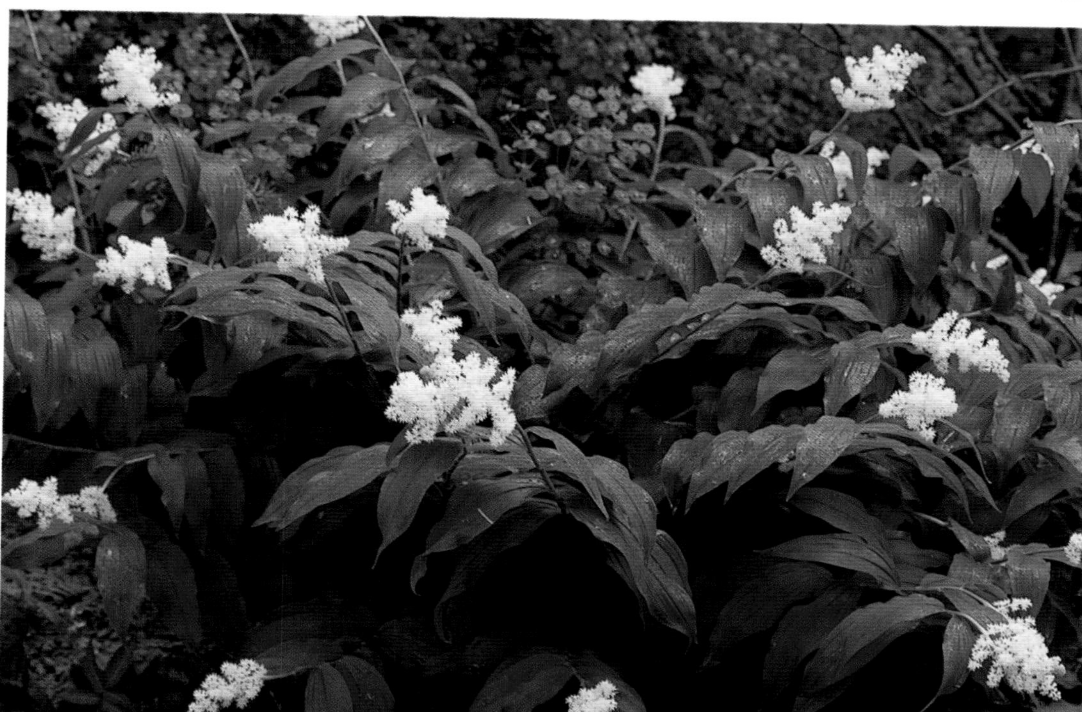

Smilacina racemosa.

Scientific Name: Diminutive of *Smilax*, a genus of greenhouse plants, which it resembles.
Common Name: False Solomon's seal, treacleberry.
Origin: North America.
Preferred Conditions: Moderately fertile, humus-rich, deep, lime-free, cool, well-drained soil. Shelter from hot sun and wind. Tolerates summer drought.
Light: Shade. Best at edge of woodland, or under trees in the mixed border.
Planting: Rhizomes should be planted shallow, with the round stem scar up. When siting in the garden, know that *S. racemosa* will always lean out toward the light, making it the perfect edge-of-the-woodland plant.
Management: Lift and split congested plants in autumn or spring. Old clumps are difficult to divide—it's easier if you wash the roots first. Top-dress the plant with organic material. Cut back foliage to the ground after the fall color (often a brilliant yellow) fades.
Propagation: Seed; division in autumn and spring.
Pests and Diseases: Snails, slugs in early spring, root weevils.
Companions: Digitalis, astilbe, paeonia, trillium, fuchsia, *Anemone nemorosa* 'Vestal', *Arum italicum*, *Dicentra formosa*, polygonatum.

Species and Cultivars	Height/ Spread	USDA Hardiness Zone	Flowers (bloom time)	Foliage	Comments
racemosa	1½–3ft × 2ft+	4–9	Creamy-white, small, fluffy, fragrant, in large panicles (E–M)	Green, glossy, parallel veins, ovate or elliptical	Bright red berries with purple spots, spreads slowly, RHS Award
stellata	1–1½ft × 2ft+	3–8	Creamy-white, small, star-shaped, in small racemes of 2 or 3 flowers (E–M)	Mid-green, lanceolate to oblanceolate	Star flower, dark red berries aging to black, can make large colonies

Solidago 'Golden Baby'.

SOLIDAGO Asteraceae

Once again, an American prairie plant that is best in full sun, with summer water and no competition. Goldenrods, as they are commonly known, should not be confused with ragweeds (*Ambrosia artemisiifolia* and *A. trifida*), the culprits responsible for all that sneezing. They do share the same sunny wild places, bloom at the same time, and are in the same family, which probably contributes to the confusion. Many of the goldenrods are invasive, but some species are more garden-worthy than others and are valued for their late-blooming golden flowers. The elongated flower heads (panicles) are borne on stiff, branching stems and make a good cut flower for fresh or dried arrangements. One of the best performers in my garden and a real favorite of mine is *S. rugosa* 'Fireworks'. *Solidago virgaurea*, the common European goldenrod, is used by herbalists for a wide range of health problems, including arthritis, allergies, and sore throats. ~ *Susan Carter*

Scientific Name: From the Latin *solida* ("to make whole," "to strengthen"), referring to its medicinal properties.
Common Name: Goldenrod.
Origin: North America, Europe.
Preferred Conditions: Any reasonably fertile, well-drained soil. Tolerates drought once established.
Light: Sun. Tolerates part shade.

Management: Deadhead to prevent self-sowing, or leave on for the birds and fall effect. Dense clumps may die back in the center over time; remove healthy young sections from the outer edge and replant, discarding the woody center. Divide every two or three years to help control the invasive forms and rejuvenate others. Some may require staking. Bait for slugs in early spring, at the same time you do your asters.

Propagation: Cuttings; division in spring.

Pests and Diseases: Powdery mildew (especially if too dry), slugs.

Companions: *Sedum ruprechtii*, helenium, kniphofia, crocosmia, achillea, aster, nepeta, salvia, ×solidaster, monarda, grasses, veronica, vernonia.

Species and Cultivars	Height/ Spread	USDA Hardiness Zone	Flowers (bloom time)	Foliage	Comments
canadensis	3–6ft × 3ft+	3–9	Bright golden yellow, large panicles (M–L)	Green, narrow, prominent veins, serrated	Canadian goldenrod, prone to mildew, vigorous, invasive
'Cloth of Gold'	1½ft × 1½ft	3–9	Deep primrose-yellow, 8in panicles (M–L)	Green, narrow	Dwarf
'Crown of Rays'	2–2½ft × 1½ft	4–9	Bright golden yellow, large, flat, 10in panicles (M–L)	Mid-green	Erect, bushy, compact
flexicaulis (syn. latifolia)	1–3ft × 2ft+	3–8	Mid-yellow, starry (M)	Green, toothed, rounded	North American native
f. 'Variegata'	2–3ft × 2ft+	3–8	Golden yellow (M)	Green, splashed or variegated yellow-gold	Vigorous, reverts
'Golden Baby' (syn. 'Goldkind')	1½–2ft × 1½ft	4–9	Golden yellow, 6–8in panicles (M–L)	Mid-green	Compact, dwarf
'Goldenmosa'	2½–3ft × 1½ft	5–9	Bright yellow, 12in panicles (M–L)	Mid-green, wrinkled	Bushy, yellow flower stems, RHS Award
'Golden Spangles'	2–3ft × 2ft	5–9	Bright yellow (M–L)	Green with gold and green splashes, toothed	
'Golden Wings'	5–6ft × 2½ft	5–9	Deep golden yellow, 10in panicles (M–L)	Mid-green	Very branched
'Queenie' (syn. 'Golden Thumb')	12in × 10in	5–9	Yellow (M–L)	Yellow-green to golden	Dwarf, bushy
rugosa	3–5ft × 2ft+	3–9	Yellow, open panicles, horizontal (M–L)	Dark green, crinkly, purple hairy stems	Rough stemmed goldenrod, vigorous
r. 'Fireworks'	2–5ft × 2ft+	4–9	Golden yellow, open 10in panicles or sprays (M–L)	Mid-green	Flowers look like exploding fireworks
sphacelata 'Golden Fleece'	15–24in × 2ft	4–9	Deep golden yellow, 10in panicles (M–L)	Mid-green, cordate to rounded and lanceolate	Dwarf goldenrod, compact, clump-forming
virgaurea	2–3ft × 2ft	3–9	Yellow (M–L)	Green, lanceolate, serrated	Common goldenrod

×*Solidaster luteus* 'Lemore'.

×SOLIDASTER Asteraceae

"Bad Love"—why do I care for this plant so much? Teeny-weeny asterlike flowers in soft panicles in late summer. That shade of pale moonlight-yellow I'm a sucker for. Thin lanceloate leaves, often covered with the gray of mildew at flowering time, below which are more leaves that are dead. I wouldn't water this one at night; oh, and it seems to be short-lived too, but I buy it again, plant it again, and then swoon when it blooms. It is a good cut flower, best grown in open ground with few competing neighbors. When well grown it's a treasure; when not, it's a dog.
~ *Carrie Becker*

Scientific Name: From the names of the parent genera, *Solidago* and *Aster*.
Common Name: Solidaster.
Origin: Garden.
Preferred Conditions: Moderately fertile, well-drained soil.
Light: Sun.
Planting: Establishes better if fed a bit of soluble fertilizer for the first few weeks.
Management: Remove spent flowers and cut to the crown in fall. Frequent division will help to keep this plant vigorous. Do not allow it to dry out. May need support with pea sticks, but this is not usually necessary.
Propagation: Division in spring; stem/basal cuttings.
Pests and Diseases: Powdery mildew is triggered by even the briefest of wilt, as with many of the Asteraceae.
Companions: Aster, sedum, salvia, solidago, rudbeckia, coreopsis, grasses, crocosmia, hemerocallis; the summer border.
Notes: This plant is offered late in the plant-buying season, so it does not make its way into many gardens. In the Pacific Northwest, give it a good warm site, with full-sun exposure, a real summer, and minimum competition.

Species and Cultivars	Height/ Spread	USDA Hardiness Zone	Flowers (bloom time)	Foliage	Comments
luteus (syn. hybridus)	2–3ft × 1ft	4–9	Pale lemon-yellow fading to creamy yellow, flat clusters, a tiny daisy (M–L)	Green, narrow-lanceolate, slightly serrated	May require staking, wiry stems
l. 'Lemore'	1½–3ft × 1ft	4–9	Soft yellow fading lighter, a tiny daisy (M–L)	Pale green, narrow, toothed	RHS Award
'Super'	3–4ft × 1½ft	4–9	Soft yellow, a tiny daisy (M–L)	Green, narrow, toothed	Cut flower cultivar

SPIGELIA Loganiaceae

Spigelia marilandica is a species for the collector who has to have one of the best plants from the great eastern forest of North America. The flowers are scarlet outside, yellow inside; when viewed from above, they look like a yellow star above a red tube. The leaves are willowlike, upright, and opposite. The roots, we trust, are pink. Extremely poisonous, extremely slow-growing, and slow to establish, this perennial needs little care. It is wonderful in a pot, all alone, so you can look right down into the flowers. Voted one of the top ten hummingbird plants in the country.~ *Bob Lilly*

Spigelia marilandica.

Scientific Name: After Flemish physician Adriaan van den Spiegel.
Common Name: Indian pink, pinkroot.
Origin: Eastern United States.
Preferred Conditions: Deep, fertile, humus-rich, well-drained, moist, slightly acidic soil.
Light: Part shade. Tolerates sun if soil is kept moist.
Management: Deadhead to prolong blooming. Cut back during the fall/winter cleanup. Divide periodically.
Propagation: Division in spring; seed in situ as soon as ripe.
Pests and Diseases: Powdery mildew.
Companions: Woodland grasses, smaller hostas, pinellia, *Fuchsia procumbens*, *Aruncus aethusifolius*, saxifraga.

Species and Cultivars	Height/ Spread	USDA Hardiness Zone	Flowers (bloom time)	Foliage	Comments
marilandica	1–2ft × 1ft	5–9	Scarlet outside, yellow inside, in clusters (M)	Mid-green	Long-blooming, slow to increase

STACHYS Lamiaceae

There are many good things to say about stachys. These plants look good with almost anything and are very popular for edging or as groundcovers (especially *S. byzantina*); but the few undesirable characteristics are important ones, and care should be taken to avoid them. Stachys seems to be the only plant with silvery felted leaves that is prone to mildew, and the dead and dying leaves can be very unsightly, requiring constant grooming. Growing stachys in full sun with well-drained soil and good air circulation will help to avoid this drawback. Some gardeners remove the flower stems on *S. byzantina* and focus only on the low-growing foliage for its silvery moonlight effect at dusk and into the evening. The flowering spikes do attract bees and butterflies but should you not want them, bring them in as cut flowers; they have a long vase life.

Stachys byzantina was an important herb during the Middle Ages, taken to ease digestive problems and as protection against witchcraft. The leaves were used to bandage wounds, especially during the Civil War. ~ *Susan Buckles*

Scientific Name: From the Greek *stachus* ("ear of grain"), referring to the spikelike form of the flowers.
Common Name: Betony, woundwort, lamb's ear.
Origin: Caucasus to Iran, Turkey, Mexico.
Preferred Conditions: Poor to average, moderately fertile, well-drained soil. Drought tolerant.
Light: Sun to part shade.
Management: Remove flower stems from *S. byzantina* if they bother you; cut back to the crown. Frost and heavy rains can make the hairy surfaces of the leaves mushy—remove these as necessary. Clean up and remove leaves (usually the ones underneath) affected by mildew. Clean the saggy mess on *S. byzantina* in fall and winter with a pair of sharp scissors, exposing new growth on the lateral stems at ground level, then bait for slugs. Divide only when necessary; every few years, use divisions to fill in gaps when plants die out in the center.

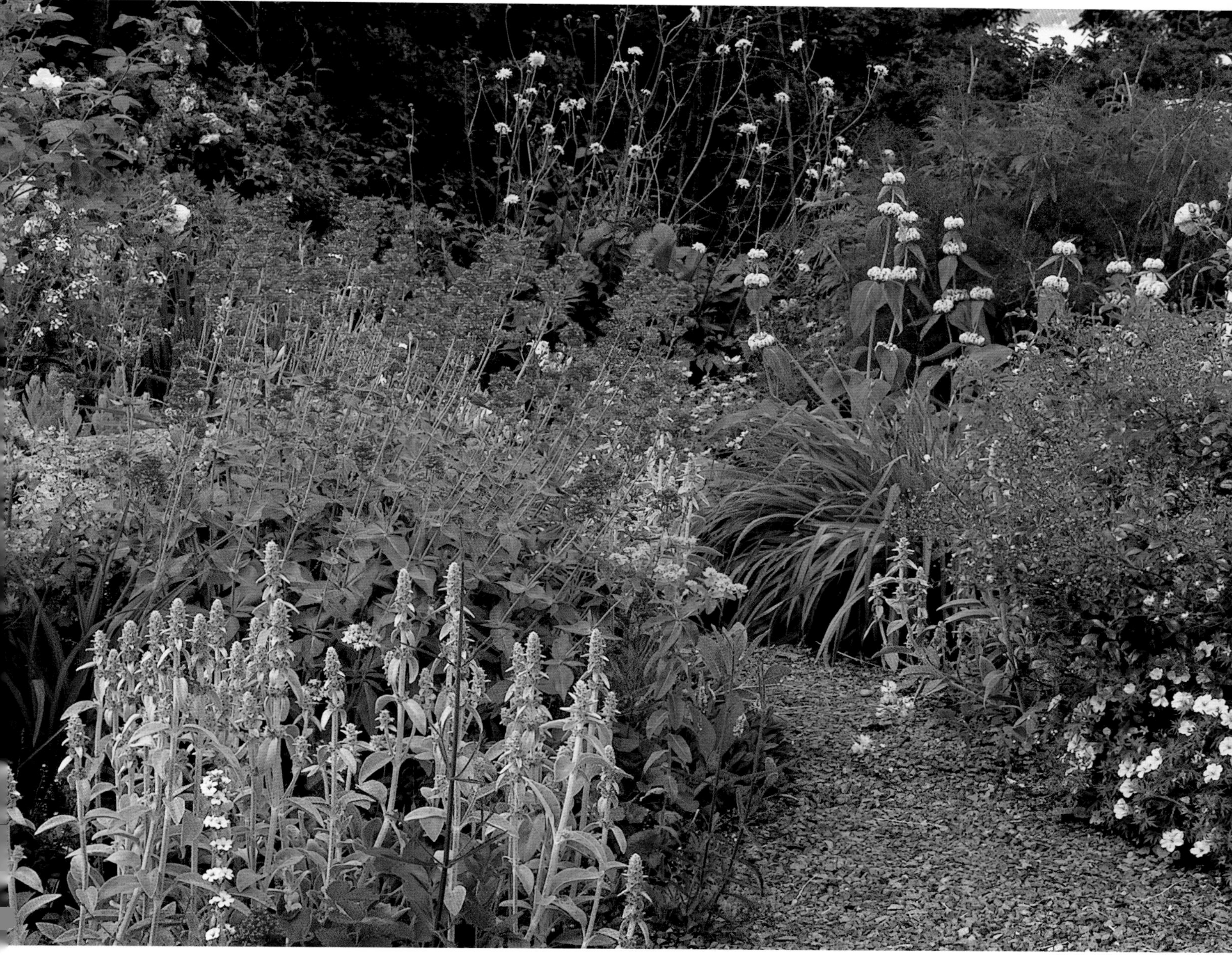

Stachys byzantina in flower with *Centranthus ruber*, a lone *Sisyrinchium striatum*, and *Phlomis fruticosa* behind.

Propagation: Division in spring or fall; seed; cuttings.
Pests and Diseases: Powdery mildew, slugs, cutworms, usually only in spring.
Companions: Salvia, roses, stokesia, dianthus, sedum, nepeta, *Molinia caerulea* 'Variegata', acaena.
Notes: Beware of *S. officinalis* (not in the chart!): it seeds itself profusely.

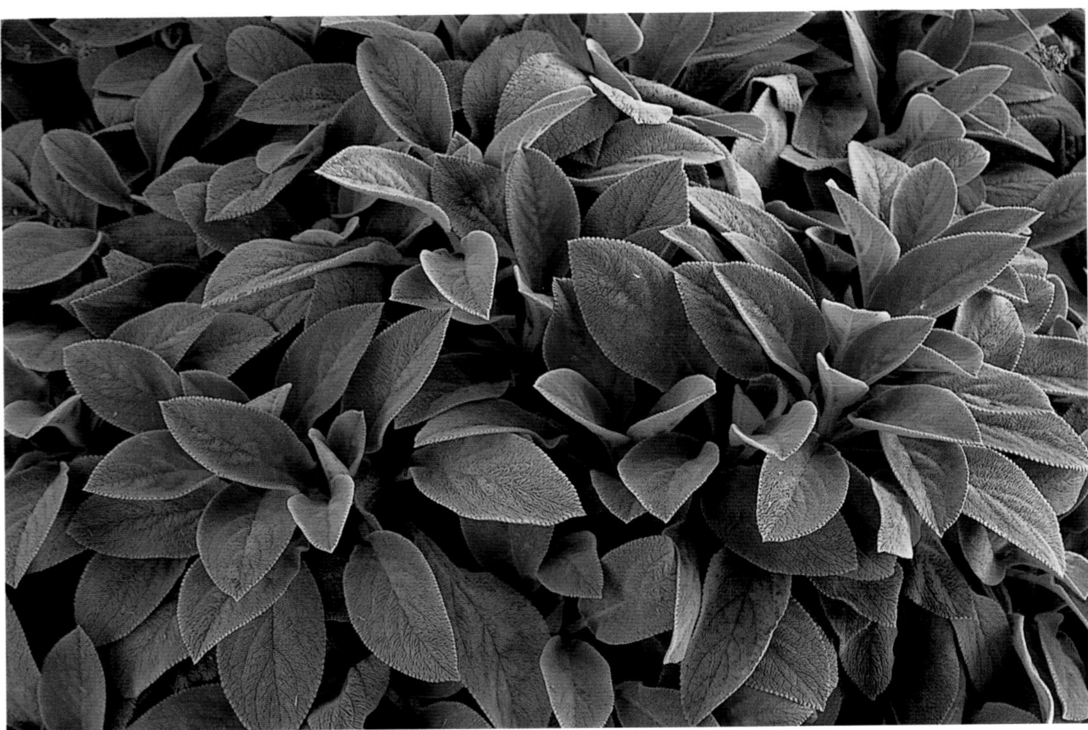

Stachys byzantina 'Big Ears'.

Species and Cultivars	Height/ Spread	USDA Hardiness Zone	Flowers (bloom time)	Foliage	Comments
albotomentosa (syn. 'Hidalgo')	15–18in × 18in	8–10	Pale salmon (cream of tomato soup) (M)	Gray-green, fragrant, felty leaves and stems	Grown from seed, a bit tender, will flop
byzantina (syn. lanata, olympica)	1–1½ft × 2ft	4–9	Pinkish purple, hairy stems, hairy calyces (M)	Silvery-whitish green, oblong-elliptic, woolly	Evergreen in mild climates, mat-forming, self-sows
b. 'Big Ears' (syn. 'Countess Helen von Stein')	1–2ft × 2ft+	4–9	Pinkish purple, rarely blooms (M)	Silvery-gray, felted, large, serrated, prominent veins	Resistant to rot, susceptible to mildew
b. 'Cotton Boll' (syn. 'Sheila McQueen')	2ft × 2ft	4–9	Pinkish purple, cottonball-like, in clusters along stems (M–L)	Silvery-white, felty, more narrow	
b. 'Primrose Heron'	1–1½ft × 1½ft	4–9	Pinkish purple, small (M)	Soft buttery yellow at first, then pale yellowish gray, aging to silvery gray, woolly	Mildew prone, doesn't spread as quickly as others
b. 'Silver Carpet'	1–1½ft × 1½ft+	4–9	Lavender-pink, rarely blooms (M)	Silvery-gray, velvety, smaller	Mildew prone, spreads
b. 'Striped Phantom' (syn. 'Variegata')	1½–2ft × 1½ft	4–9	Purplish pink, striped bracts (M)	Silvery-gray, woolly, streaked and splashed with cream and white	Reverts
coccinea	1–2ft × 1½ft	7–9	Salmon-red with purple calyces (E–L)	Gray-green, ovate to triangular, wrinkled, fragrant, toothed	Stiff, erect stems

Species and Cultivars	Height/ Spread	USDA Hardiness Zone	Flowers (bloom time)	Foliage	Comments
macrantha (syn. spicata, grandiflora)	1–2ft × 1½ft	4–8	Pale red-violet (E–L)	Dark green, ovate to cordate, wrinkled, toothed, hairy	Big betony, may need support with pea sticks
m. 'Robusta'	1½–2ft × 1½ft	4–8	Pale red-violet, large (E–M)	Rich green, large	Larger plant, RHS Award
m. 'Rosea'	1½–2ft × 1½ft	4–8	Rose-pink (E–L)	Bright green	
m. 'Superba'	1–2ft × 1½ft	5–9	Purplish pink, large (E–L)	Deep green, wrinkled, soft downy, prominent veins	Vigorous
monieri (syn. densiflora)	1–1½ft × 1ft	5–9	Deep pinkish white, shell-pink, or white (M)	Dark green, ovate-oblong and cordate, scalloped, glossy	A smaller and stiffer plant

STOKESIA Asteraceae

Stokesia, a native genus of the southeastern United States, has only one species, *S. laevis*, a plant best grown at the front of the border. It has evergreen leaves, borne in basal rosettes, and large cornflowerlike fringed ray florets; these flowers make up for any boredom the leaves may project. They are large compared to the size of the plant and make a great impact. Some of the many

Stokesia laevis 'Silver Moon'.

cultivars have deep blue flowers; others are pale blue, lavender, yellow, or silvery-white. They are long-blooming in midsummer (with some into September) and make a great cut flower.
~ *Susan Carter*

Scientific Name: After Jonathan Stokes of Edinburgh, physician and friend of Linnaeus the younger.
Common Name: Stokes' aster.
Origin: Southeastern United States.
Preferred Conditions: Any fertile soil that is well-drained, light, and acidic. Likes it moist but may rot in damp, heavy soil. Tolerates heat and drought.
Light: Sun to part shade.
Management: Deadhead to prolong the flowering. Remove spent flowering stems. Foliage can be cut back to three or four inches to make the plant tidy during the winter. Mulch in winter. May need support; a summer drizzle can weigh down the flowers. Rather than stakes or pea sticks, give them strong neighbors to lean on.
Propagation: Division for cultivars in spring; seed for species.
Pests and Diseases: Root rot and crown rot (if too wet), leaf spot, caterpillars.
Companions: Sidalcea, liatris, *Aster ×frikartii*, hemerocallis, penstemon, low grasses.
Notes: A warm location in the Pacific Northwest yields best flower production; they do not produce strong stems for us and always flop badly.

Species and Cultivars	Height/ Spread	USDA Hardiness Zone	Flowers (bloom time)	Foliage	Comments
laevis (syn. cyanea)	1–2ft × 1½ft	5–9	Blue to lilac ray florets, lighter disk flowers, 3–4in (M–L)	Mid-green, long, narrow, coarse, glossy	A more weedy look than its selections
l. 'Alba'	1ft × 1ft	5–9	White, 3–4in (M)	Mid-green, narrow, glossy	
l. 'Blue Danube'	1–1½ft × 1½ft	5–9	Deep blue, 3–4in (M–L)	As above	
l. 'Blue Star'	12–16in × 12in	5–9	Light lavender-blue, whitish center, 4in (M–L)	As above	
l. 'Klaus Jelitto'	1–1½ft × 1½ft	5–9	Pale blue, white center, 4–5in (M–L)	As above	
l. 'Mary Gregory'	1½–2ft × 1½ft	5–9	Light creamy-yellow, 2–3in (M)	Lighter green, narrow, glossy	
l. 'Purple Parasols'	1–1½ft × 1½ft	5–9	Light powder-blue aging to deep violet, 3–4in (M–L)	Mid-green, narrow, glossy	
l. 'Silver Moon'	1ft × 1ft	5–9	Silvery-white, 3–4in (M)	As above	
l. 'Wyoming'	1–2ft × 1½ft	5–9	Sky-blue, 3–4in (M)	As above	

Strobilanthes attenuata.

STROBILANTHES Acanthaceae

I am grateful to this plant. While not the most exciting thing, *S. attenuata* is attractive and survives in very difficult places. Sturdy-looking and bushy, it grows at the edge of the garden, where the hose doesn't reach and the soil is sandy. The leaves are nettlelike but stingless and have a musty odor; they're not as showy as the annual strobilanthes but still worth having. The flowers are very similar to aconitum; they begin the day a violet-blue and turn purple by midday. They are particularly welcome, as they arrive in early fall. ~ *Ann Bucher*

Scientific Name: From the Greek *strobilos* ("cone") and *anthos* ("flower"), referring to the dense inflorescence.
Common Name: Stinking nettle.
Origin: Himalayas, northern India.
Preferred Conditions: Any fertile, light, well-drained soil. Protect from wind. Drought tolerant but needs water during the growing season.
Light: Sun to part shade.
Management: Pinch to promote bushiness. Cut back after flowering in late autumn or early winter. May need a winter mulch for protection against the cold.
Propagation: Usually from seed; cuttings; division in spring.
Pests and Diseases: Root rot, spider mites.
Companions: Salvia, aster, aconitum, helianthus, dahlia, rudbeckia.

Species and Cultivars	Height/ Spread	USDA Hardiness Zone	Flowers (bloom time)	Foliage	Comments
attenuata (syn. atropurpurea)	4–5ft × 2ft+	7–9	Violet-blue aging to purple, tubular, hooded (M–L)	Dark green, opposite, ovate, hairy, with prominent veins	Blackish purple in bud, erect branching habit

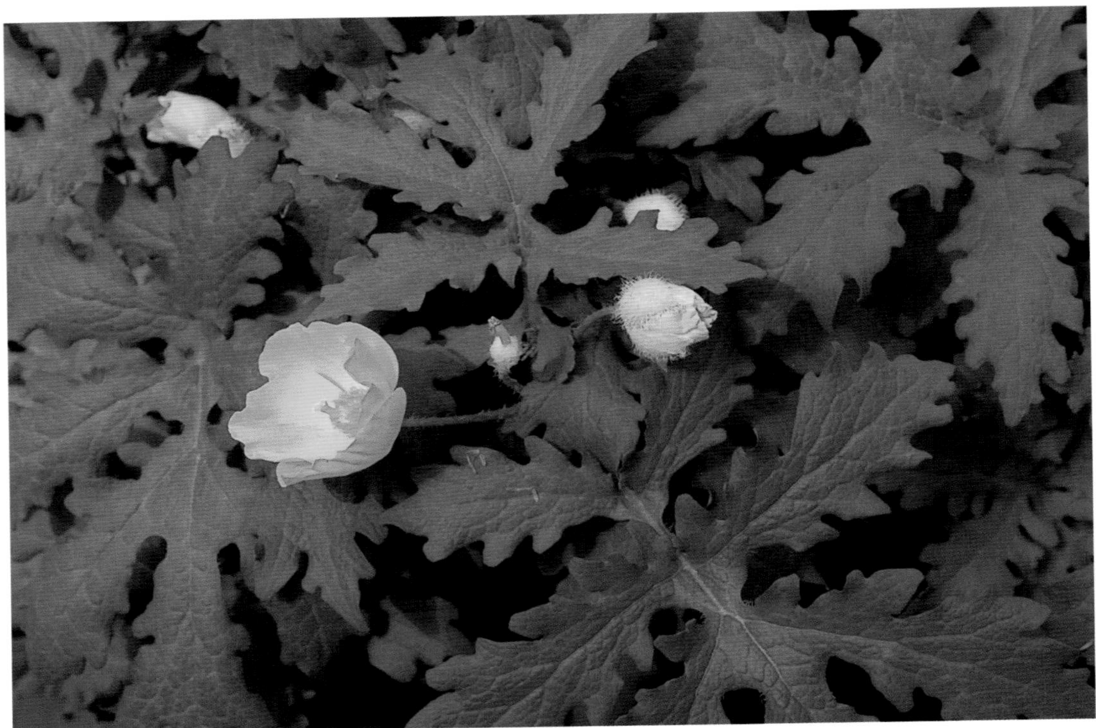

Stylophorum diphyllum.

STYLOPHORUM Papaveraceae

The celandine poppies are two wonderful perennial species with the most amazing seedpods. They are relatives of meconopsis, with similar hairy (or furry) seedpods and golden poppylike flowers. The flowers are brief and small but work well to brighten up a woodland in spring. As with many poppy family members, the sap of *S. diphyllum* is colored and was used as a dye in the Americas. Both it and *S. lasiocarpum* will seed about fairly well once established but not as aggressively as the annual celandines of the genus *Chelidonium*, with which they share flower color, orange sap, and common name. Both species are slow to settle in and go into summer looking a bit tired, so are best under shrubs, where they can be hidden by midsummer. ~ *Bob Lilly*

Scientific Name: From the Greek *stylos* ("style") and *phoros* ("bearing"), referring to the long style.
Common Name: Celandine poppy.
Origin: North America, China.
Preferred Conditions: Cool, moderately fertile, humus-rich soil. Protect from wind.
Light: Shade to part shade.
Planting: Like most poppies, they do not transplant well, so start with young plants that have not become pot-bound.
Management: Top-dress with organic material; a good mulch of compost or manure makes for large healthy plants, but this may also make them flop over a bit. Cut back when foliage dies down in autumn.
Propagation: Usually from seed; division in spring.
Pests and Diseases: Snails, slugs.
Companions: *Anemone sylvestris*, asarum, *Ribes sanguineum* 'White Icicle', hosta, *Kerria japonica* 'Picta', brunnera, pulmonaria, aconitum; good in woodland conditions.

Species and Cultivars	Height/ Spread	USDA Hardiness Zone	Flowers (bloom time)	Foliage	Comments
diphyllum	1–1½ft × 1½ft	4–8	Bright golden yellow (E–M)	Blue-green, oak-leaf shape, lobed, toothed	Nodding seedpods, U.S. native
lasiocarpum	12–20in × 18in+	4–8	Small yellow (E–M)	Pale green, ovate, toothed	Japanese celandine poppy, pale green seedpods, stick straight up

SYMPHYTUM Boraginaceae

Comfreys can be pests. Most will grow from root cuttings or cut roots left in the ground when you try to remove them or relocate them; all, even the groundcover forms, are best used in a confined space. Makes great compost, but don't put the roots in your bins. ~ *Bob Lilly*

Scientific Name: From the Greek *sympho* ("growing together") and *phyton* ("plant"), referring to its bone-healing properties.
Common Name: Comfrey, boneset.
Origin: Eurasia, Caucasus.
Preferred Conditions: Will grow most anywhere but is happiest in moderately fertile, well-drained, damp soil.
Light: Sun to shade.
Planting: Contain the roots of all comfreys with barriers or sidewalks.
Management: To keep foliage attractive, remove the flowering stems of the variegated cultivars as they form. Cut back after flowering to reduce spread and improve appearance with a

Symphytum ×uplandicum 'Axminster Gold'.

fresh crop of leaves; use the same technique as with alchemilla: cut to the ground, mulch, and then water heavily. The taller ones may need support. Top-dress with organic material in winter. Watch for slugs in spring and top-dress with plenty of organic matter (leaf mulch, compost, manure).

Propagation: Division in fall, winter, or spring; seed; cuttings (root).

Pests and Diseases: Snails, slugs. Can get a bad case of mildew on flowering stems if allowed to dry out.

Companions: Grasses, *Iris sibirica*, brunnera, astrantia, cimicifuga, campanula.

Notes: *Symphytum* ×*uplandicum* 'Axminster Gold' and 'Variegatum' are chimeras—only the crown growth point is variegated, and the roots will not produce variegated plants, so you must cut and divide the crown; nor do they spread like most other comfreys.

Species and Cultivars	Height/ Spread	USDA Hardiness Zone	Flowers (bloom time)	Foliage	Comments
'Belsay Gold'	2ft × 2ft	5–9	Blue and pink (M)	Gold aging to green, arrow-shaped, 8–10in long	Cut back in early summer for a second burst of gold foliage, spreads slowly
caucasicum	1–2ft × 2ft	3–9	Red-purple, aging to blue (E–M)	Grayish green, ovate to lanceolate, hairy, 8–10in long	Caucasian comfrey, invasive, RHS Award
'Goldsmith'	1–1½ft × 2–3ft+	3–9	Pale blue, or pink, fading to white (E–M)	Green with yellow margins, hairy, ovate to lanceolate, 6in long	May revert, spreading
'Hidcote Blue'	1–2ft × 2–3ft+	4–9	Red in bud, opens blue, fades to white (E–M)	Green, ovate to elliptic, 6in long	Spreading, invasive, takes dry shade
'Hidcote Pink' (syn. 'Roseum')	1½ft × 2–3ft+	4–9	Shades of soft pink, fading to white (E–M)	Green, hairy, ovate to elliptic, 6in long	As above
'Hidcote Variegated'	1ft × 2–3ft+	4–9	Soft blue, fades to white (E–M)	Creamy-white splashes and variegation, smooth, 6in long	Spreading
ibericum (syn. grandiflorum)	1–1½ft × 2ft	4–9	Creamy-yellow with orange-red tubes, orange in bud (E–M)	Dark green, coarse, crinkled, ovate to elliptic or lanceolate, hairy, 10–12in long	Invasive
i. 'Blaueglocken'	15in × 18in	4–9	Reddish pink in bud, opens to blue (E–M)	As above	
'Rubrum'	1–1½ft × 1½ft	4–9	Dark red-violet, nodding (M)	Dark green, hairy, ovate to lanceolate, 10in long	Upright, not as invasive
×uplandicum	3–6ft × 2ft+	3–9	Pink in bud, aging to blue (E–M)	Dark green, oblong to ovate to lanceolate, 10–12in long	Russian comfrey
×u. 'Axminster Gold'	4ft × 2ft	4–9	Pink to blue (M)	Golden yellow, 10–12in	Cut to ground for regrowth of new foliage. not invasive
×u. 'Variegatum'	1–3ft × 2ft	5–9	Pale pinkish lilac, aging to pale purple or blue (M)	Grayish green with wide bands of creamy-white margins, 10–12in long	Cut stems to ground for new basal growth and flowers, may revert, slow to spread, not invasive, RHS Award

Syneilesis aconitifolia.

SYNEILESIS Asteraceae

These perennials are worth growing, as a curiosity, for their foliage alone: the leaves look like furled umbrellas as they emerge from the ground. Unfortunately, the flowers, held above the foliage, are weedy-looking and a tremendous disappointment. Both species are very slow to increase. ~ *Bob Lilly*

Scientific Name: Obscure.
Common Name: Syneilesis.
Origin: China, Korea.
Preferred Conditions: Fertile, well-drained, slightly acidic soil.
Light: Part shade to sun.
Management: Cut back in autumn, leaving about three inches of the stem to protect the crown from being stepped on—it's the emerging shoots you want to see. Watch for slugs in early spring, as leaves are damaged easily.
Propagation: Seed as soon as ripe; division in spring.
Pests and Diseases: Slugs.
Companions: Aconitum, aquilegia, trillium, pulmonaria, heuchera.

Species and Cultivars	Height/ Spread	USDA Hardiness Zone	Flowers (bloom time)	Foliage	Comments
aconitifolia	18–36in × 10–12in	5–8	Pinkish, small (M–L)	Woolly, deeply divided, palmate	From China
palmata	30–48in × 10–12in	5–7	White, small (M–L)	White fading to gray-green, rounded, hairy, 7–9 palmate leaflets, 14–20in across	From Korea

Tanacetum parthenium 'Aureum'.

TANACETUM Asteraceae

The best tansy for us is golden feverfew, *T. parthenium* 'Aureum'; it is short-lived but will seed about. Golden feverfew is a great bonding agent in borders where gold and yellow foliage is a strong element. Never let the plain green common feverfew get established, as it can be a pest (but for some, this is a good thing). These are aromatic plants and good cut flowers. Related genera are *Chrysanthemum*, *Dendranthema*, and *Leucanthemum*. ~ *Bob Lilly*

Scientific Name: From the Greek *athanasia* ("immortality"), of uncertain application.
Common Name: Tansy, pyrethrum, feverfew.
Origin: Europe, Caucasus.
Preferred Conditions: Fertile, well-drained soil that isn't too wet or heavy. Not too fussy.
Light: Sun.
Management: Cut back hard after flowering to force a second flush of leaves and some flowers. Cut back in the fall, but leave the crowns alone. Conversely, pull out the oldest plants in favor of vigorous young seedlings. If you get a dense seeding of feverfew in your garden, be sure to thin your seedlings in midsummer and again in late winter to six to eight inches apart and leave them where you want them; you will have strong plants by the following spring.
Propagation: Seed is best in situ especially for *T. parthenium*; cuttings (cultivars); division in spring for *T. coccineum*.
Pests and Diseases: Slugs (*T. coccineum*), spider mites, aphids.
Companions: Grasses, geranium, salvia, polemonium, campanula, phlox, centaurea, *Eryngium giganteum*, verbena, stachys.
Notes: In the Pacific Northwest, *T. parthenium* and *T. p.* 'Aureum' should be treated as biennials. Some of the other named forms of *T. parthenium* are best used as annuals.

Species and Cultivars	Height/ Spread	USDA Hardiness Zone	Flowers (bloom time)	Foliage	Comments
coccineum	1½–2½ft × 1½ft	5–9	Variable pink, red or white, yellow center, single (M)	Green, finely cut, toothed, fernlike	Painted daisy, may need support, short-lived
c. 'Duro'	2–2½ft × 1½ft	5–9	Purple-red (M)	As above	
c. 'James Kelway'	1½–2½ft × 1½ft	5–9	Scarlet, yellow center, single (M)	As above	Bushy, RHS Award
c. 'Robinson's Red'	1½–2ft × 1½ft	5–9	Dark red, bright yellow center, large (M)	As above	Seed-grown
c. 'Robinson's Rose'	1½–2ft × 1–1½ft	5–9	Rose-pink, bright yellow center (M)	As above	As above
niveum	1½ft × 1ft	4–9	White, yellow eye, small (M)	Silvery-gray, lacy, divided	Snowy tansy, short-lived, fragrant
parthenium	1–3ft × 1ft	4–9	White, yellow eye, single (M–L)	Green, deeply cut	Feverfew, aromatic, short-lived, self-sows, long-blooming
p. 'Aureum'	1–2ft × 1ft	4–9	As above	Golden yellow, divided, round teeth	Short-lived
p. double white	1–2½ft × 1ft	4–9	Double white (M)	Green, deeply cut	More compact
p. 'Golden Ball'	12in × 10in	4–9	Bright golden yellow (M)	As above	As above
p. 'Plenum'	14in × 10in	4–9	Double white (M)	As above	As above
p. 'Rowallane' (syn. 'Sissinghurst White')	2ft × 1ft	4–9	Double white, large (M)	Green, deeply cut with longer petioles	A more open plant, slightly more perennial

TELEKIA Asteraceae

This bold perennial species makes a wonderful effect in summer. The leaves can be as big as those of hostas, and the graceful yellow flowers are borne on tall stems above the foliage. As an added bonus, the dried seedheads are like little rounded buzz-cuts once the seeds fall out. When grown among irises and ligularias in an area with good summer water, plants will stay lush and good-looking, even in hot weather. *Telekia speciosa* forms a heavily rooted clump quite quickly and can seed about. The youngsters are easy to remove or transplant to give to friends; established plants, with their big, ropey roots, do not like to be moved but still transplant well. ~ *Bob Lilly*

Scientific Name: After Samuel Teleki di Szek, Hungarian nobleman and botanical patron.
Common Name: Oxeye.
Origin: Southeastern Europe, Caucasus, Russia, Asia Minor.
Preferred Conditions: Deep soil and a woodland site. Shelter from strong winds, and don't let them wilt.
Light: Part shade to sun.
Management: Remove spent flowers for some rebloom. Watch for seedlings and remove as soon as possible, before they settle in. Cut back in autumn, but leave stems about three inches long to protect crown. Mulch heavily; it's a heavy feeder. Watch for slugs on young leaves and bait them along with your ligularias.

Telekia speciosa.

Propagation: Seed; division in spring.
Pests and Diseases: Slugs.
Companions: Ligularia, pulmonaria, *Carex elata*, miscanthus, *Lysimachia ciliata* 'Firecracker', *Cornus alba* 'Spaethii', *Kerria japonica* 'Picta'; well suited for naturalizing in a large space.
Notes: Used to be sold under the genus *Buphthalmum*.

Species and Cultivars	Height/ Spread	USDA Hardiness Zone	Flowers (bloom time)	Foliage	Comments
speciosa	4–6ft × 3ft+	5–9	Yellow, almost threadlike ray petals (M)	Green, ovate, toothed, large, 10–12in	A bold, wide-spreading plant

TELLIMA Saxifragaceae

These woodland plants seed about quite easily and are therefore extremely useful for covering large areas. The common name, fringe cups, describes the small cuplike flowers, fringed with frilly petals. Leaves are similar to heuchera and tiarella (hairy and five- to seven-lobed); they are evergreen, though cold weather will bronze them up a bit. As with many members of this family, root weevils are a serious problem for these plants, especially for those grown in containers; the adults damage the leaves, and the grubs will eat the roots all winter long. Be prepared to replace plants as necessary. *Tellima grandiflora* Odorata Group is a good cut flower as well as being strongly fragrant, but dissipates easily, so plant in a protected spot. ~ *Bob Lilly*

Scientific Name: An anagram of the related genus, *Mitella*.
Common Name: False alumroot, fringe cup.
Origin: North America.
Preferred Conditions: Moisture-retentive, cool, loose, humus-rich soil. Tolerates dry shade.
Light: Shade to part shade.
Management: Cut flower stems to crown and remove dying and dead leaves in the fall. Pull up any unwanted plants during the fall/winter cleanup (they are evergreen and easy to spot). You can cut most of the leaves down to the crown over winter for a neater look. With large borders, seedlings in hidden areas can be a problem: apply a heavy mulch in the spring over the seedlings to solve this.
Propagation: Seed; division in fall or spring.
Pests and Diseases: Slugs, spider mites, root weevils.
Companions: Ferns, *Aster divaricatus*, hosta, epimedium, luzula, hakonechloa, stylophorum, polygonatum, smilacina.

Tellima grandiflora Odorata Group.

Species and Cultivars	Height/ Spread	USDA Hardiness Zone	Flowers (bloom time)	Foliage	Comments
grandiflora	1½–2½ft × 1ft	4–9	Greenish white, aging to pink, tiny fringed petals (M–L)	Green, hairy, rounded, cordate	Erect
g. 'Forest Frost'	18–28in × 12in	4–9	Chartreuse, fading to pink (E–M)	Green with some bronze, silver-splashed	As above
g. Odorata Group	1½–2½ft × 1ft	4–9	Cream, aging to pink (E–M)	Green, some bronzing to the spring leaves	Very fragrant, good winter foliage
g. Rubra Group (syn. 'Purpurea')	1½–2ft × 1ft	4–9	Pale greenish, edged pink (E)	Green, aging to reddish purple in winter, scalloped	Good winter foliage

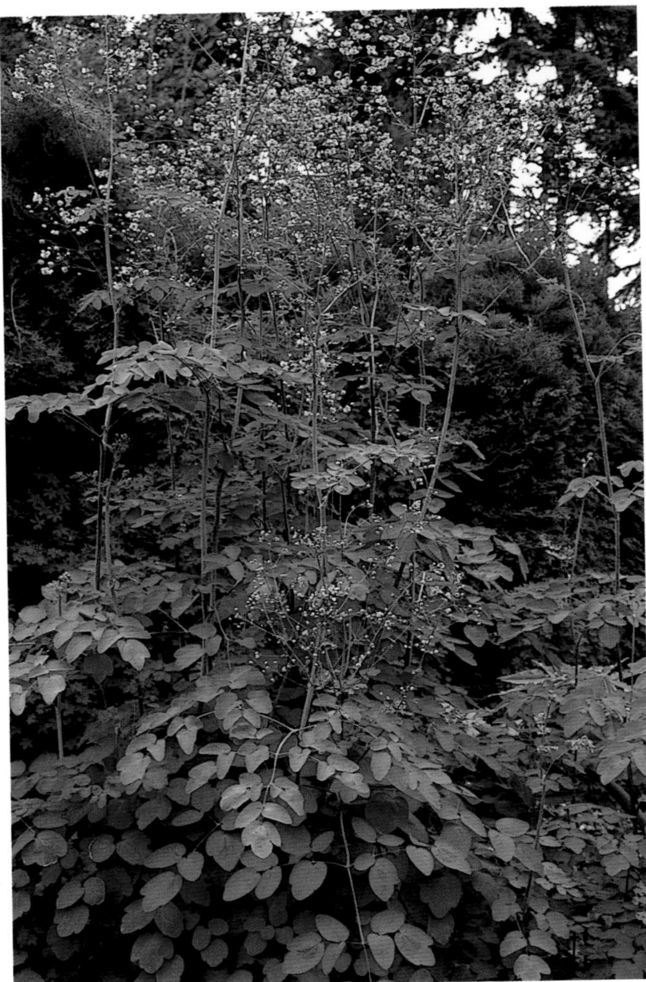

Thalictrum rochebruneanum.

THALICTRUM Ranunculaceae

Meadow rues are popular perennials valued for their fluffy flower heads and finely divided foliage, which is as attractive as the flowers. They are relatively easy to grow and care for as well as being very versatile in the garden. The delicate leaves of many are similar to columbines and range in color from bluish green on purple stems to dark or grayish green. The airy flower heads, usually in pastels, stand high above the foliage in shades of lilac, pink, yellow, white, or green. Most of the flowers have no petals but have very prominent stamens. Many are long-blooming, and some have wonderful seedheads. Thalictrums vary in height from the rock garden species *T. kiusianum*, beloved of slugs, topping out at six inches, to the taller border varieties, such as *T. delavayi* 'Hewitt's Double', which can reach six feet. The meadow rues look very delicate, and one might assume they would need extra special treatment, but their only requirements are rich organic material and plenty of water. With all these qualities, many of us find space for more than one thalictrum. ~ *Susan Carter*

Scientific Name: From the Greek *thaliktron*, a name used to describe a plant with compound leaves.

Common Name: Meadow rue.

Origin: Europe, Caucasus, Russia, Japan, China, northwestern Africa, North America.

Preferred Conditions: Adaptable. Well-drained, cool, moisture-retentive soil, rich in organic material. Drought can damage the flower tips as they grow; spring water is important.

Light: Sun to part shade. Tolerates more sun if well watered.

Management: Thalictrums don't like to be moved. Overfertilizing promotes weak growth. The taller species often need support and will stand a little straighter with the aid of pea sticks. *Thalictrum minus* is stoloniferous and may need to be kept in check. *Thalictrum lucidum* and *T. flavum* both self-sow aggressively; deadhead to help prevent this. Cut back seedheads just before they turn brown, which is when the seed is viable. Otherwise, cut dead flower stems to crown in the fall.

Propagation: Seed; division in the spring (slow to establish).

Pests and Diseases: Powdery mildew, slugs.

Companions: Roses, aconitum, astilbe, *Alchemilla mollis*, ferns, hosta, polygonatum, brunnera, smilacina, aruncus, hydrangea, *Fuchsia magellanica*.

Species and Cultivars	Height/ Spread	USDA Hardiness Zone	Flowers (bloom time)	Foliage	Comments
aquilegifolium	2–5ft × 1½ft	5–9	Purplish pink with prominent lilac or white stamens, fluffy (M)	Bluish green, similar to aquilegia, 3- to 6-lobed, purplish stems, very dark in some forms	Columbine meadow rue, long-blooming, good seedheads, clump-forming
a. var. album	4ft × 1½ft	5–9	White, white stamens (M)	Lighter grayish green, finely divided	
a. 'Thundercloud'	2–3ft+ × 1½ft	5–9	White, dark purple stamens (M–L)	Green, finely divided	RHS Award
delavayi (syn. dipterocarpum)	3–6ft × 1½ft	5–9	Rosy-lilac with creamy stamens, in open airy sprays (M–L)	Bluish green, ferny and dainty, 3-lobed	Yunnan meadow rue, may need support, prefers a deep soil, rhizomatous, RHS Award
d. 'Album'	3½ft × 1½ft	5–9	White, yellow stamens (M–L)	Mid-green	Needs more shelter, high shade, and water
d. 'Hewitt's Double'	3–6ft × 1½ft	5–9	Double lavender-lilac, long-blooming, no stamens (M)	Dark green above, paler beneath, lacy	Sterile, divide and replant every 2–3 years to maintain vigor, part shade for best bloom, RHS Award
'Elin'	6–8ft × 1½ft	5–9	Lavender, pale yellow stamens (M–L)	Silver-blue with purple-tinged stems	A big plant, stiff, upright, sturdy stems
flavum	3–5ft × 1½ft+	5–9	Pale yellow, bright yellow stamens, fragrant (M)	Bluish gray-green	Sturdy stems, rhizomatous, clump-forming
f. subsp. glaucum (syn. speciosissimum)	3–6ft × 1½ft+	5–9	Soft yellow, greenish yellow stamens (M)	Bluish green, purplish stems, finely divided	Tolerates drier soil, may need staking, spreads, aggressive self-sower
isopyroides	1–1½ft × 1ft	6–9	Greenish yellow, fluffy (M)	Steely bluish green, tiny	A texture plant
kiusianum	3–6in × 8in	5–8	Pinkish lilac (M)	Tinted purplish and bronze, toothed	Dwarf meadow rue, stoloniferous, slow spreader
lucidum (syn. angustifolium)	4–5ft × 2ft	5–8	Shiny yellow (M)	Dark green, fernlike, glossy	Clump-forming, aggressive self-sower
minus	1½ft × 1½ft	3–9	Greenish, insignificant, with prominent yellow stamens (M)	Glaucous, fernlike, divided, 3-lobed	Invasive in light soil, may need support, some people remove flowering stems and grow as a foliage plant
m. 'Adiantifolium'	2–3ft × 1½ft+	3–9	Yellow-green, tiny (M)	Slightly glaucous, fernlike, finely cut	More invasive over a long term
rochebruneanum	5–6ft × 1½ft	5–9	Reddish lilac, pale yellow stamens, in large airy panicles (M–L)	Bluish green, fernlike, large, 3-lobed, purple-black stems	Lavender mist, tall and stately

Thermopsis lanceolata.

THERMOPSIS Papilionaceae

The false lupines are great plants in the mixed border and will grow in even poor soils. Flowering is brief but charming, and the yellow flowers do attract a lot of bees. They bloom about the same time as the later narcissus, such as *N.* 'Pipit'. If you want a lupine look, grow these pest-free, low-maintenance pea family relatives. ~ *Bob Lilly*

Scientific Name: From the Greek *thermos* ("lupine") and *opsis* ("like").
Common Name: False lupine.
Origin: North America, Siberia, Asia.
Preferred Conditions: Well-drained, light, fertile, loamy soil. Tolerates drought.
Light: Sun.
Management: Resents root disturbance and is therefore difficult to transplant. Dig around the clumps once a year to control the spread (root pruning). Cut back to the ground once plant begins to fade in autumn. In our gardens, *T. lanceolata* must be staked: when in flower, it is heavy enough to lean, and then lean further, onto the ground (this doesn't hurt the plant, but it looks messy); and staking helps to highlight its wonderful nut-brown seedpods. Try peony cages or pea sticks in early spring, and let the plants grow up through the supports.
Propagation: Seed; division in fall.
Pests and Diseases: None.
Companions: Narcissus, *Brunnera macrophylla*, *Lathyrus vernus*, *Lamium orvala*, camassia, hyacinth, primula, chaerophyllum; the spring border.

Species and Cultivars	Height/ Spread	USDA Hardiness Zone	Flowers (bloom time)	Foliage	Comments
lanceolata	1–2½ft × 2ft	3–9	Primrose-yellow (E–M)	New growth blackish, fading to green, ovate-lanceolate	Dark seedpods, doesn't run, long-lived
rhombifolia var. montana	1½–2½ft × 2ft	3–9	Bright straw-yellow (E–M)	Green, silky-haired, obovate to linear-lanceolate	Mountain false lupine, rhizomatous, invasive
villosa (syn. caroliniana)	3–4ft × 2ft	3–9	Canary-yellow (E–M)	Greenish blue, silky-haired, ovate-lanceolate, 3-lobed	Carolina lupine, clump-forming

TIARELLA Saxifragaceae

These evergreen perennials are usually used as a groundcover in woodland conditions. They are exceptional when grown under deciduous shrubs that are not too dense and get some summer light under them. Most tiarellas, if given their preferred conditions, will eventually spread quite a bit by rhizomes or stolons. Some of the foamflowers are clump-forming, some run—and some sprint. Together with heuchera they are the parents of ×heucherella and have many similar characteristics. Look for patterned and marked foliage as well as deeply divided leaves. Flower stems are not as tall as those of their relatives, but they are good cut flowers. *~ Bob Lilly*

Scientific Name: From the Greek *tiara* ("small crown"), referring to the shape of the fruit.
Common Name: Foamflower.
Origin: Asia, North America.
Preferred Conditions: Humus-rich, cool, moist, well-drained soil. Doesn't do well in winter-wet or soggy ground.
Light: Part shade to shade.
Management: Remove dying or dead leaves anytime. Top-dress with leaf mold or other organic material, but not over the crowns. Tiarellas don't like having their roots disturbed (main clump).
Propagation: Seed; division in spring or fall (dig up offsets and replant).
Pests and Diseases: Slugs. Root weevils are a serious problem, especially for plant in pots.
Companions: Ferns, epimedium, pulmonaria, astilbe, helleborus, hosta, trillium, uvularia, polygonatum, spring bulbs, luzula, hakonechloa, geranium, *Aster divaricatus*.
Notes: Look for new cultivars each year (recent examples include *T.* 'Neon Lights' and *T.* 'Pink Skyrocket'). The truly spreading forms are noted in the chart.

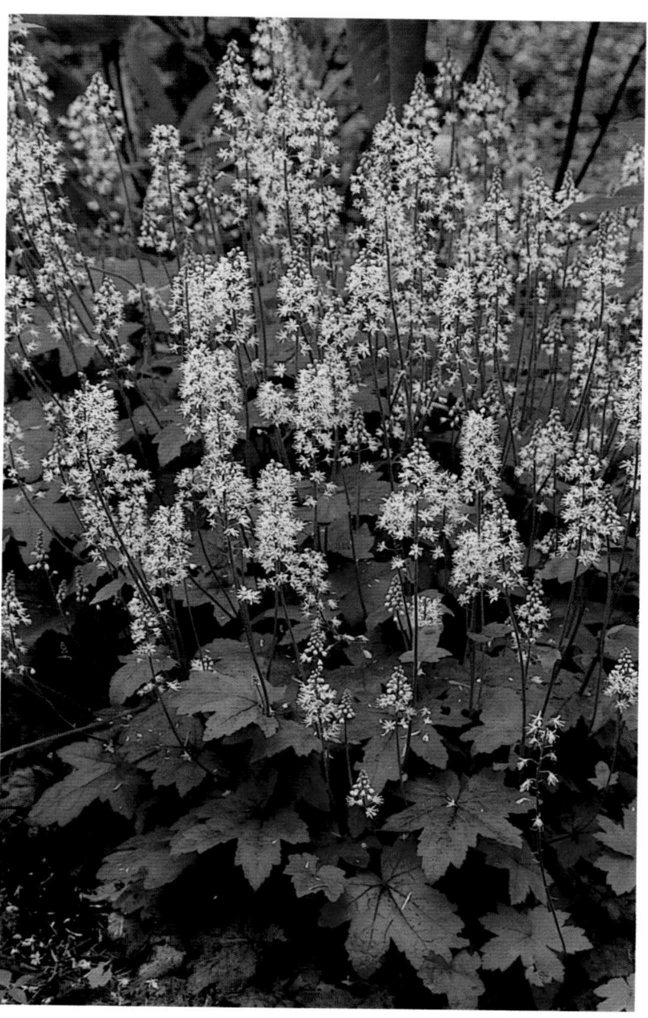

Tiarella cordifolia 'Oakleaf'.

Species and Cultivars	Height/ Spread	USDA Hardiness Zone	Flowers (bloom time)	Foliage	Comments
cordifolia	12in × 18in+	3–8	Creamy white (E–M)	Pale green, marbled bronzy-red, cordate to ovate, hairy, lobed or cut, veined	Good fall/winter color, vigorous, spreads by stolons, RHS Award
c. 'Oakleaf'	6–8in × 18in+	3–8	Pale pink aging to white (E–M)	Dark green, toothed, dissected, deep red in winter	Long-blooming, vigorous, spreads
c. 'Running Tapestry'	8–12in × 18in+	2–9	White (E–M)	Light green, red streaks, reddish brown midrib, deeply cut	Vigorous, spreads
c. 'Slick Rock'	6–8in × 18in+	3–9	Light pink, fragrant (E–M)	Dark green, deeply cut	Invasive, vigorous, spreads
'Cygnet'	16–19in × 18in+	4–9	Pink buds open whitish, fragrant (E–M)	Green, purplish red midrib, deeply cut	Spreading
'Dark Eyes'	12in × 18in+	4–8	Pale pink (E–M)	Dark green, maroon-black blotch in center, maple-shaped	Spreads
'Dunvegan'	6in × 12in	3–8	Pink-tinted (E–M)	Mid-green, dissected	Clump-forming
'Filigree Lace'	12–16in × 16in	4–9	White (E–M)	Green with dark patches at center, deeply cut	As above
'Inkblot'	6–12in × 14in	4–9	Pale pink (E–M)	Green with large black blotch	Non-running habit
'Iron Butterfly'	16in × 16in	4–9	Pink buds open white (E)	Mint-green edges, deep purplish black in center	Clump-forming
'Mint Chocolate'	8–16in × 16in	3–9	Creamy-white with pink tinge (E)	Mint-green with dark zones, deeply cut, maplelike	As above
'Ninja'	12–16in × 16in	4–9	Pinkish white with coral tints (E–M)	Green, black veins and purple-black marbling, deeply cut, lobed	As above
'Pink Bouquet'	12–16in × 12in	3–8	Pinkish, aging to white, fragrant, pink stems (E–M)	Green with red veins, deeply cut	As above
polyphylla	12–18in × 12in	5–8	Pink to reddish with white (M)	Mid-green, cordate, toothed	Clump-forming, spreads slowly by rhizomes
p. 'Filigran'	12in × 12in	5–8	Pure white, reddish stems (M)	Mid-green, cordate, toothed, more divided	Spreads slowly by rhizomes
'Skeleton Key'	10–12in × 12in	4–9	White with pink blush (M–E)	Green, purplish black mid-veins, deeply cut	Spreads
'Spring Symphony'	10in × 10in	4–9	Dark pink (E)	Green, black blotch along midribs, deeply cut	As above
'Tiger Stripe'	12–16in × 12in	5–9	Pale pink (E–M)	Chartreuse, marked with dark veins	Clump-forming
wherryi	6–16in × 12in	3–9	Pink buds open white, pink stems (E–M)	Soft green, bronzy in winter, deeply cut	Non-running, clump-forming, RHS Award

Species and Cultivars	Height/ Spread	USDA Hardiness Zone	Flowers (bloom time)	Foliage	Comments
w. 'Heronswood Mist'	10–12in × 12in	4–9	As above, fragrant	Tricolor marbling, creamy white with green and pink overtones	

TOLMIEA Saxifragaceae

Tolmiea menziesii, the best-known species in this genus, is a West Coast native woodlander, tough and invasive; thankfully, it is easy to control (easy to pull up). The flower is disappointing, but the leaves provide interest with their piggyback arrangement. This plant will fill a difficult dry shady area, although it prefers moist conditions. It is good as a green groundcover, especially around red alders. It also makes attractive filler between hedges and pavement or lawn; it even enhances the base of chain-link fences. Just keep your eye on it as it marches out, ready to cover everything in sight. As with most natives that are tolerant of our dry summers, these conditions in the garden don't always give you the best-looking groundcover. They are better with some summer water. ~ *Susan Buckles*

Scientific Name: After William Fraser Tolmie, Scottish physician and botanist.
Common Name: Piggyback plant, mother of thousands.
Origin: Western North America.
Preferred Conditions: High humidity and cool, humus-rich, moist (especially in summer), well-drained soil.

Tolmiea menziesii.

Light: Part shade to shade.
Management: Pinch back older leaves and stems to keep compact. Top-dress with leaf mold or other organic material in winter. Mulch around the crown, but do not cover the crown. Clean up dead foliage anytime.
Propagation: Cuttings; seed; division in spring; remove plantlets and plant or peg down leaves.
Pests and Diseases: Spider mites, aphids, root weevil grubs, especially in pots.
Companions: Ferns, pulmonaria, vancouveria, epimedium, polygonatum, tiarella, heuchera, ×heucherella, helleborus, luzula, hakonechloa, stylophorum, *Meconopsis cambrica*, tricyrtis.

Species and Cultivars	Height/ Spread	USDA Hardiness Zone	Flowers (bloom time)	Foliage	Comments
menziesii	12–24in × 18in	6–9	Brownish purple, fragrant (E–M)	Pale green, veined, hairy	Piggyback plant
m. 'Taff's Gold'	10–12in × 12in	6–9	Brownish purple (M)	Pale chartreuse-green, mottled cream and gold, variable throughout the seasons, hairy	RHS Award

TRADESCANTIA Commelinaceae

Known and grown since the seventeenth century, tradescantias can be classed as cottage garden plants. They are best grown in poor soil; otherwise, copious floppy foliage is the result. The drawback to this is that sandy soil encourages the plant's incredible invasiveness: a great aunt of mine grew these in standalone beds, two feet by two feet, in her lawn! They seem to grow large, thick roots overnight and to increase while you watch; they are also invasive by seed, but not so much on heavier, clay soils. A charming feature of the flowers is that the stamen stems, in many cases, are brightly colored (blue, red-violet) and topped with bright yellow pollen. The forms with dark blue flowers are particularly gorgeous; the clear yellow dots (the anthers) seem to float in the bowl formed by the three triangular petals. The flower is not large enough, however, to show well above the foliage. If you want to grow this plant be prepared to spend a lot of time maintaining it—staking, cutting back, pulling up, and discarding the excess! ~ *Susan Buckles*

Scientific Name: After John Tradescant, gardener to Charles I.
Common Name: Spiderwort.
Origin: North America.
Preferred Conditions: Moist, cool, well-drained, and not-too-fertile soil. Keep well watered during the growing season. Tolerates boggy conditions, but blooms best with good drainage and lots of heat and light.
Light: Sun. Tolerates part shade.
Management: Cut back hard after flowering, both to discourage self-sowing and to promote new foliage and rebloom. Established plants can be cut to the ground when they flop; regrowth and rebloom are usually very quick. Clean up when foliage dies back in the fall. Divide when congested, every three years or so. Remove plain green foliage from colored-leaf cultivars. Don't fertilize this plant; this may help to control excessive vegetative growth.
Propagation: Division in spring; seed (three years to bloom from seed).
Pests and Diseases: Aphids, spider mites, botrytis.
Companions: Ferns, hosta, *Iris foetidissima*, *I. sibirica*, ligularia, heuchera, brunnera, *Hemerocallis lilioasphodelus*; the summer border.

Tradescantia Andersoniana Group 'Concord Grape'.

Species and Cultivars	Height/ Spread	USDA Hardiness Zone	Flowers (bloom time)	Foliage	Comments
Andersoniana Group	1–2ft × 2ft	4–9	Shades of blue, magenta, red, pink, and white (M–L)	Mid-green, sometimes has a slight sheen	
A. 'Bilberry Ice'	12–20in × 18in	4–9	Pale lavender with deep blue center and white edge, large (M–L)	Green, purple-tinged	
A. 'Blue and Gold'	1½–2ft × 2ft	5–9	Deep blue (M–L)	Golden yellow	May scorch in sun
A. 'Blue Stone'	1½–2ft × 2ft	3–9	Blue-lavender (M–L)	Green	
A. 'Charlotte'	1–2ft × 1½ft	4–9	Pink (M–L)	As above	
A. 'Chedglow'	1½ft × 1½ft	5–9	Mauve-purple (E–M)	Bright chartreuse	
A. 'Concord Grape'	15–24in × 2ft	4–9	Purple (E–L)	Frosty bluish green	Vigorous, seedlings vary
A. 'Innocence'	1–2ft × 2ft	4–9	White, large (M–L)	Green, purple-tinged	
A. 'Iris Prichard'	1–2ft × 2ft	4–9	White, tinged violet (M–L)	As above	
A. 'Isis'	18–20in × 18in	5–9	Deep blue, violet-blue center, large (M–L)	As above	RHS Award
A. 'J. C. Weguelin'	20in × 24in	5–9	China-blue, large (M–L)	As above	Vigorous, RHS Award
A. 'Leonora'	1½ft × 1½ft	4–9	Violet-blue (M–L)	As above	
A. 'Little Doll'	12–18in × 16in	4–9	Light blue (M–L)	Green	Lots of foliage

Species and Cultivars	Height/ Spread	USDA Hardiness Zone	Flowers (bloom time)	Foliage	Comments
A. 'Osprey'	1½–2ft × 1½ft	4–9	White with blue stamens and stems (M–L)	As above	RHS Award
A. 'Pauline'	1½–2ft × 2ft	4–9	Pink-mauve (E–M)	Green, purple-tinged	
A. 'Purple Dome'	1½–2ft × 2ft	5–9	Rich purple, large (M–L)	As above	Darkest flowers
A. 'Red Grape'	15–24in × 24in	4–9	Cerise-red (M)	As above	
A. 'Rubra'	1½–2ft × 2ft	3–9	Red (M–L)	As above	
A. 'Snowcap'	1½ft × 1½ft	3–9	Pure white, large (E–M)	Green	
A. 'Sweet Kate'	1–2ft × 1½ft	4–9	Blue, large (M–L)	Bright golden yellow, may age to slightly green	May scorch in hot sun
A. 'Valour'	1½ft × 2ft	3–9	Red with purple tinge (E–M)	Green, purple-tinged	
A. 'Zwanenburg Blue'	1½–2ft × 2ft	3–9	Deep blue, large (M–L)	Green, purple veins	
'Hawaiian Punch'	1–2ft × 2ft	4–9	Magenta-pink (E–L)	Dark green	Foliage remains attractive
'Purple Profusion'	1½–2ft × 2ft	4–9	Bluish purple (M)	Dark green, purple-tinged when young	
'Red Cloud'	15–24in × 2ft	3–9	Red-violet (M–L)	As above	A bit weedy
virginiana	1½–3ft × 2ft+	4–9	Bright blue, pink, or white (E–L)	Dark green, purple veins	Common spiderwort, vigorous
v. 'Rubra'	1–1½ft × 2ft+	4–9	Rose-red (E–M)	Mid-green	Vigorous

TRICYRTIS Convallariaceae

We are so lucky to have tricyrtis. There are relatively few plants that bloom late in the season in shade, and this is a nice one. Tricyrtis flowers are orchidlike in appearance and have three petals and three sepals. They appear in the leaf axils and in terminal clusters and may be mauve, yellow, white, or purple, often with prominent spots. The leaves are perfoliate, alternate, and often glossy, sometimes subtly spotted. The stems are arching, and the leaf structure attractive. While some tricyrtis are stoloniferous, they are not strongly invasive. They are a good cut flower. I continue to try to grow white forms, but they present more of a challenge. ~ *Ann Bucher*

Scientific Name: From the Greek *tri* ("three") and *kyrtos* ("humped"), referring to the swollen bases of the petals.
Common Name: Toad lily.
Origin: Taiwan, Japan, China.
Preferred Conditions: Moist, humus-rich, moisture-retentive, well-drained, and slightly acidic soil in a sheltered location.
Light: Shade to sun.
Management: Emerging shoots can be damaged by late spring frosts, but will usually regenerate. Top-dress with organic material. Mulch and water during any hot weather. Cut down when foliage dies in fall.

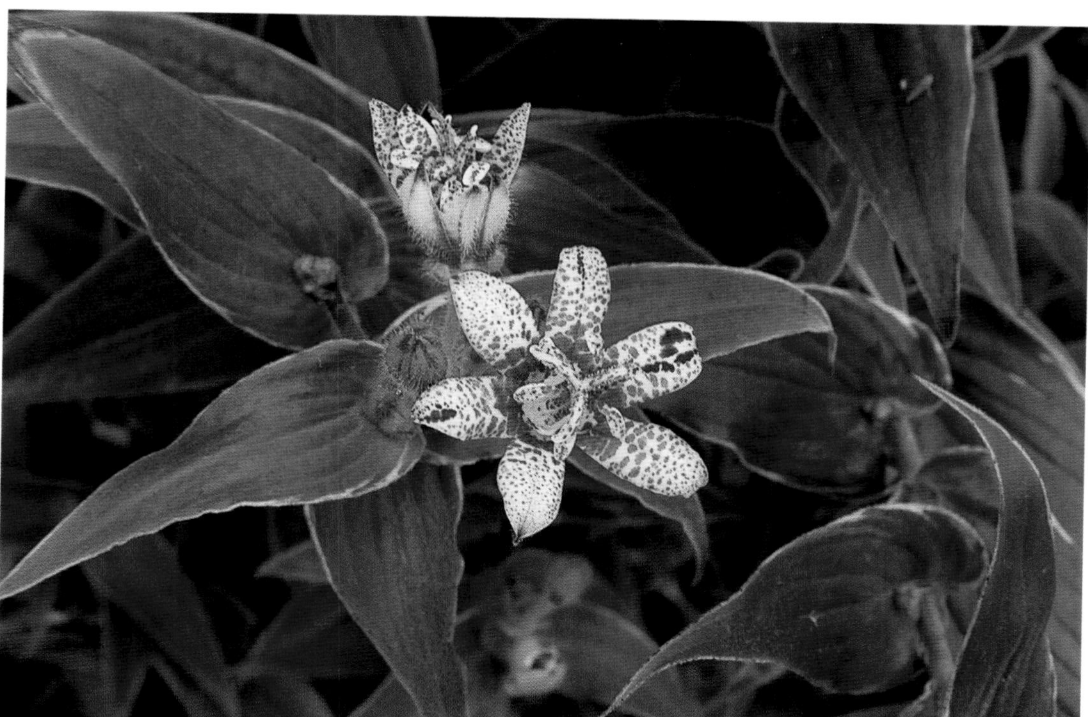

Tricyrtis hirta 'Miyazaki'.

Propagation: Seed; division in spring.

Pests and Diseases: Snails and slugs are responsible for tricyrtis failure. They can mow them down (or off) immediately at ground level in spring. You can have great roots and no tops even in pots!

Companions: Ferns, hosta, helleborus, pulmonaria, epimedium, podophyllum, polygonatum.

Species and Cultivars	Height/ Spread	USDA Hardiness Zone	Flowers (bloom time)	Foliage	Comments
formosana	2–3ft × 1½ft	5–8	White background, densely spotted purple, yellow-ringed center (M–L)	Mid-green, deeply veined and spotted dark green, glossy, lanceolate to ovate	Long-blooming, RHS Award
f. 'Amethystina'	2–3ft × 1½ft	5–8	White, spotted purple and red and flushed reddish lilac at ends, yellow throat (M–L)	Green, glossy	Long-blooming
f. 'Dark Beauty'	3ft × 1½ft	5–8	Deep lavender-purple, dark spots (L)	Dark green, lightly spotted lighter green	As above
f. 'Gates of Heaven'	1–1½ft × 1ft	5–8	Purple with darker spots (M–L)	Golden	Vigorous
f. 'Gilt Edge'	14–16in × 1ft	5–8	Rose with white spots (M–L)	Green with yellow edges	
f. 'Samurai'	2–3ft × 1½ft	5–8	White with dark purple spots (M–L)	Mid dark green with gold edges	
f. Stolonifera Group	2–3ft × 1½ft+	5–8	Cream to pale lilac with darker spots, up-facing (M–L)	Deep green, glossy, pointed, darker spots	Blooms best with lots of heat, spreads

Species and Cultivars	Height/ Spread	USDA Hardiness Zone	Flowers (bloom time)	Foliage	Comments
f. 'Variegata'	1½–2ft × 1½ft+	5–8	Lavender-purple, pink base with dark purplish red spots (M)	Glossy mid-green with yellow margins	Spreads
hirta	2–3ft × 2ft	5–8	White with purple spots, colorful stamens (M–L)	Mid-green, hairy, oval to ovate or oblong to lanceolate	Japanese toad lily
h. 'Alba'	2–3ft × 1½ft	5–8	Greenish buds, opens white with creamy center, pink stamens (L)	Mid to dark green	Weak grower
h. 'Albomarginata'	3ft × 1½ft	5–8	White, purple-spotted (L)	Variegated with white margins	
h. 'Golden Gleam'	1½ft × 1½ft	5–8	Lavender, spotted gold (L)	Chartreuse, fuzzy	Reasonably vigorous
h. 'Miyazaki'	2–3ft × 1½ft	5–8	White, spotted lilac, purple, and black, yellow eye (M–L)	Mid-green, hairy	Flowers in the leaf axils
h. 'Moonlight'	20in × 1½ft	5–8	White, purple-spotted (M–L)	Golden green	
h. 'Variegata'	15–20in × 1½ft	5–8	White, spotted purple and maroon, recurved petals (M–L)	Light green, creamy margins, hairy	
'Hototogisu'	2–2½ft × 1ft	5–8	Blue tinge with purple spots and white center (M–L)	Mid-green	Distinctive flower color, vigorous
'Kohaku'	1½ft × 1ft	5–8	White with purple spots and yellow center (M–L)	As above	Lax habit
latifolia (syn. bakeri)	2–3ft × 2ft+	6–8	Yellow with red-brown spots (M–L)	Light green, obovate to oblong to ovate, smooth	Spreads
macrantha	1–2½ft × 1½ft	8–9	Yellow, spotted red-brown, large, pendent (M–L)	Bright green, broadly ovate-oblong to oval, shining	Prefers shade, hairy arching stems
macropoda (syn. dilatata)	1½–3ft × 1½ft	5–8	White, purple spots, large (M)	Mid-green, rounded, ovate to oblong, deeply veined	
maculata	2½ft × 1½ft	5–8	Greenish, whitish, yellowish, reddish purple spots (M)	Green, oblong	
'Shimone'	2–3ft × 1½ft	5–8	Dark-maroon buds open white, splashed purple and maroon, large (M–L)	Green, glossy, deeply veined and mottled	
'Tojen'	2–3ft × 1½ft	5–8	Lavender-purple, white center and darker tips, unspotted, large (M–L)	Dark green, hairy	
'White Towers'	2–3ft × 1ft	5–8	White (M–L)	Mid-green, hairy	

Trifolium pratense 'Susan Smith'.

TRIFOLIUM Papilionaceae

Ornamental clover? Jumbo shrimp? Don't let these relatives of the clover we all know as a lawn and garden weed escape. They do not appear to seed about, but you should still be careful. The purple-leaf trifoliums in particular are a wonderful color for the edge of pots or a controlled spot in the garden. ~ *Bob Lilly*

Scientific Name: From the Latin *tri* ("three") and *folium* ("leaf"); the leaves have three leaflets.
Common Name: Clover.
Origin: Worldwide.
Preferred Conditions: Fertile, moist, well-drained soil. Moderate water needs.
Light: Sun.
Planting: Site in corners and niches, so they can't run or escape.

Species and Cultivars	Height/ Spread	USDA Hardiness Zone	Flowers (bloom time)	Foliage	Comments
pratense 'Susan Smith' (syn. 'Gold Net')	6in × 18in+	6–9	Pink on spikelike racemes (M)	Green with gold veining, obovate to elliptic leaflets	Mat-forming
repens 'Green Ice' (syn. 'Ice Cool')	4–6in × 2ft+	4–9	Cream (M)	Dark green with a frosted mint-green center and pale green patterns	As above
r. 'Purpurascens'	4–6in × 2ft+	4–9	Reddish purple (M)	Green margins, dark maroon central zone, can have 4 leaflets	As above
r. 'Purpurascens Quadrifolium'	4–6in × 2ft+	4–9	White, small (M)	Deep maroon, tinted brown, edged light green, 4 leaflets	As above

Management: Leaf color bleaches out by midsummer, at which point we recommend you cut the entire plant back and water well to encourage new growth. This management technique is extremely effective on *T. pratense* 'Susan Smith' and *T. repens* 'Green Ice'; the purple-leaf trifoliums do not respond as well. Cut back plants whenever they begin to look scraggly, or in fall/winter cleanup (water well if cut back in midsummer). Watch for slugs in early spring—why won't they eat the common white-flowered clover (*T. repens*) instead?

Propagation: Division in spring; detach rooted stems from main plant to form new plants.

Pests and Diseases: It's hard to understand how such a strong plant can have any pests, but slugs can gnaw the first flush of spring growth right to the ground, and powdery mildew and spider mites can cause a summer decline.

Companions: Foreground plants such as *Ophiopogon planiscapus* 'Nigrescens', ajuga, lysimachia.

TRILLIUM Trilliaceae

Several of the more than forty species in the genus *Trillium* are native to North America and are rewarding and easy to grow. They share similar characteristics: they are herbaceous and much valued for their appearance as an early spring flower, often under a canopy of deciduous shrubs. The leaves are equally attractive, as seen in the descriptions in the chart. The only drawback to these plants as far as I'm concerned is their very slow increase and low rate of seed production. Seedlings are slow to develop; the first year they show only a single bladelike leaf. Provide trilliums with a woodland spot that doesn't dry out in summer (when the plant is dormant), and you can enjoy these plants for many years. Never cut the leaves, and even cutting the flowers off is not recommended. ~ *Susan Buckles*

Scientific Name: From the Latin *tri* ("three"); all parts occur in threes. Trilliums used to be in the lily family, hence tri-lilium, or trillium.

Common Name: Wake robin.

Origin: North America, Asia.

Preferred Conditions: Cool, moisture-retentive, humus-rich, acidic to neutral soil. They don't like a lot of competition.

Light: Part shade to shade.

Planting: Plant in a quiet, safe location for slow success.

Management: Never cut trilliums. The buds that produce the leaves and flowers are formed on the rhizomes in late summer, when the upper growth is dormant, so provide ample water all summer to help this process. Mulch with homemade compost, leaf mold, or other organic matter in winter. Dig up when clumps are congested and carefully split them; don't break the roots, and gently separate the individual rhizomes. Cut back dead foliage in the fall/winter cleanup. Watch for slugs.

Propagation: Seed as soon as ripe (it's a lengthy process, can take five to seven years to have plants of flowering size); division in winter (will be slow to reestablish). Some good results can be had if divided in growth and kept well watered in shade.

Pests and Diseases: Snails, slugs. Rodents eat the rhizomes.

Companions: Smilacina, disporum, viola, erythronium, uvularia, primula, polygonatum, arisaema, hosta, jeffersonia, brunnera, dicentra, tiarella, pulmonaria; the woodland garden.

Notes: The rhizomes have a "scar" for each year they grow. Double flower forms are possible but still uncommon.

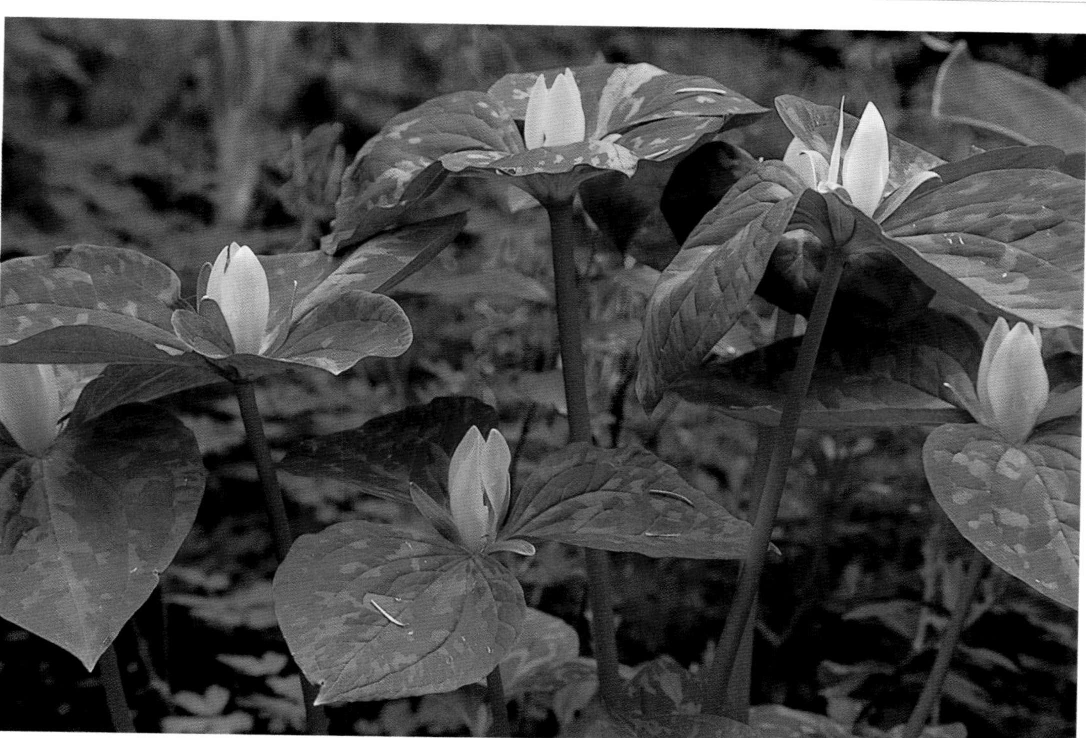

Trillium luteum.

Species and Cultivars	Height/ Spread	USDA Hardiness Zone	Flowers (bloom time)	Foliage	Comments
catesbyi (syn. stylosum)	1–1½ft × 6in	6–9	Pale to deep pink, sometimes white, nodding (E–M)	Mid-green, deeply veined, elliptic-oval-ovate	Rosy wake robin, clump-forming, red-pink stems
cernuum	1–1½ft × 10in	5–9	Pink, sometimes white, purple stamens, nodding, fragrant (E)	Mid-green, diamond-shaped, veined	Nodding trillium, clump-forming, eastern U.S. native
chloropetalum	1–1½ft × 1ft	6–9	Maroon-red, sometimes greenish white or yellow, erect, fragrant (E)	Dark green, mottled gray-cream or maroon, diamond-shaped	Red-green stems, western U.S. native
erectum	1–2ft × 1ft	4–9	Brownish purple to maroon-red, stamens white, yellow, or green, erect, recurving, out-facing (E)	Rich green, broadly ovate to diamond-shaped	Purple trillium, vigorous, oval reddish berries, RHS Award
e. f. luteum	1–1½ft × 1ft	4–9	Yellow, red tips, erect (E)	As above	Slow to increase
grandiflorum	1–2ft × 1ft	4–9	Pure white, fading to pink, yellow center, nodding (E–M)	Dark green, veined, waxy, ovate to rounded	White wake robin, eastern U.S. native, RHS Award
luteum (syn. sessile var. luteum)	6–12in × 12in	5–8	Lemon-yellow, scented, erect (E)	Mid-green, paler green marbling, elliptic to ovate	Yellow trillium, RHS Award

Species and Cultivars	Height/ Spread	USDA Hardiness Zone	Flowers (bloom time)	Foliage	Comments
ovatum	12–18in × 8–10in	5–9	White fading to pinkish or red, narrow petals, nodding, fragrant (E–M)	Mid-green, diamond-shaped to ovate and oval, prominent veins	Coast trillium, red-green stems, western U.S. native
rivale	5–6in × 6in	5–9	White or pale pink, spotted rose-red, nodding (E)	Mid-green, ovate, pointed	Brook trillium, a small plant, spreads slowly, RHS Award
sessile	10–12in × 10in	4–8	Purplish red, rarely greenish yellow, erect, no stem between flower and foliage, fragrant (E)	Marbled maroon and green fading to shades of silvery-green, elliptic to rounded	Purple berries, eastern U.S. native
vaseyi	12–18in × 10in	5–7	Red, nodding (M)	Mid-green	
viride	16–20in × 10in	5–9	Yellow-green, sometimes maroon at bases, long stamens, erect (E)	Marbled and spotted greenish and gray-green, lanceolate to round to elliptic	Wood trillium, central U.S. native

TROLLIUS Ranunculaceae

Trollius is a traditional cottage garden plant. Plants share both their flower color (creamy white to orange) and their love of moisture with other members of the buttercup family. Globeflowers are, however, much better behaved than their cousins. They slowly form clumps with deeply cut, serrated, lobed leaves. They begin blooming in early spring. The flower petals, which are often numerous, turn upward, forming the "globe." They make a good cut flower. The expensive and seductive *T.* ×*cultorum* 'Alabaster' has not lived up to my expectations. I will stick to the yellows and oranges until another white emerges, then I'll probably fall again. ~ *Ann Bucher*

Scientific Name: From the Swiss-German word for globeflower, *trollblume*.
Common Name: Globeflower.
Origin: North America, Europe, Asia.
Preferred Conditions: Fertile, humus-rich, moist, cool, and moisture-retentive. Good at watersides or moist gardens. Does not like to dry out.
Light: Sun. Tolerates part shade.
Planting: Place one foot from high-water mark, if siting near water.
Management: Some cultivars are long-blooming if deadheaded after flowering; leave basal leaves, water well, and fertilize. Clean up after growth dies back in the fall. Mulch with organic material in winter; do not mulch or manure over the crown. Divide every five years or so, when clumps thin out in the middle.
Propagation: Seed for species; division in fall or late winter.
Pests and Diseases: Powdery mildew, slugs and snails and puppy dog tails.
Companions: Ferns, *Primula japonica, P. beesiana, P. bulleyana, P.* ×*bulleesiana, P. florindae, P. poissonii*, ligularia, hosta, astilbe, *Iris sibirica*, scilla, *Carex elata* 'Aurea', *Astrantia major* 'Sunningdale Variegated', *Sanguisorba* 'Sunsplash'.

Trollius yunnanensis.

Notes: The companions for this plant are often as just listed—"shade garden" plants or plants that will do well in sun if well watered. Try globeflowers in the summer border, but don't expect them to bloom into August.

Species and Cultivars	Height/ Spread	USDA Hardiness Zone	Flowers (bloom time)	Foliage	Comments
chinensis (syn. ledebourii)	2–3ft × 1½ft	4–8	Bright yellow-orange (M)	Dark green, 5-lobed, lanceolate leaflets, divided into toothed segments	Chinese globeflower, later blooming
c. 'Golden Queen'	2–4ft × 1½ft	3–9	Bright golden orange with spiky central petals (E–M)	As above	Comes true from seed, RHS Award
×cultorum 'Alabaster'	2½ft × 1ft	3–8	Ivory-cream (E–M)	Dark green, 5-lobed, deeply divided lanceolate leaflets, toothed, glossy	Weak plant
×c. 'Cheddar'	2–3ft × 1½ft	3–9	Creamy-yellow (E–M)	As above	
×c. 'Earliest of All'	1½–3ft × 1½ft	3–9	Golden yellow (E–M)	Dark green, 5-lobed, lanceolate leaflets, divided into toothed segments	Earliest of all!
×c. 'Etna'	2–2½ft × 1½ft	4–8	Deep orange (E–M)	As above	
×c. 'Lemon Queen'	2–3ft × 1½ft	4–8	Pale lemon-yellow (E–M)	As above	Vigorous

Species and Cultivars	Height/ Spread	USDA Hardiness Zone	Flowers (bloom time)	Foliage	Comments
×c. 'Orange Princess'	2–3ft × 1½ft	4–8	Deep golden orange (E–M)	As above	RHS Award
×c. 'Prichard's Giant'	3ft × 2ft	4–8	Golden orange to yellow (E–M)	As above	
×c. 'Superbus'	2–3ft × 1½–2ft	4–8	Sulphur-yellow (E–M)	As above	RHS Award
×c. 'T. Smith'	2½ft × 18in	3–8	Lemon-yellow (E–M)	As above	
europaeus	1–2½ft × 1½ft	4–8	Soft lemon-yellow or orange (E–M)	Dark green, 5-lobed, with wedge-shaped deeply divided, toothed lobes	Common European globeflower
pumilus	8–12in × 8in	5–8	Golden orange, orange stamens, sometimes green-tinged, small, open, 5 petals (M)	Dark green speckled with white spots, 5-lobed, oblong-lanceolate leaflets, glossy, toothed, tiny, crinkled	A sweet little plant, short-lived
yunnanensis	2–2½ft × 1ft	5–8	Rich golden yellow, smaller than *T. chinensis* and *T. europaeus* (E–M)	Light green, 3- to 5-lobed, ovate to obovate leaflets, glossy, toothed	Chinese globeflower

TROPAEOLUM Tropaeolaceae

There have been problems in the classification of this genus, made difficult by the number of species involved. Most come from South America, and not all are hardy. We are left with a few very attractive species, which grow well here. The ones we deal with are climbing or trailing perennials. They are valuable for their attractive gray to gray-green foliage and varied flower colors (many share the yellow, orange, and red colors of the common annual nasturtium). None of the three or their forms are good candidates for a container; their leaves tend to turn yellow.

Tropaeolum speciosum is choice and looks wonderful against a dark green background. The flower is beautifully formed, showing a star-shaped pattern of yellow stamens in the neatly lined center of bright red petals, to be followed by blue fruit. This plant is not easy to raise from seed (low germination) or to find in the plant sales, so buy it when you see it. Young plants flower later than older ones, thus extending the flowering season. The beautiful, fiery, half-hardy *T. tuberosum* grows from tubers and flowers late in the fall. Its summer-flowering selection is *T. tuberosum* var. *lineamaculatum* 'Ken Aslet'. Both will climb on their own. I would imagine one could not have too many of these plants, as they are slow to increase. The more the merrier. ~ *Susan Buckles*

Scientific Name: From the Greek *tropaion* ("trophy").
Common Name: Perennial nasturtium.
Origin: Mexico to Chile.
Preferred Conditions: Any fertile, well-drained, moist soil. Keep moist, especially during the growing season.
Light: Sun. Prefers feet in the shade.
Planting: Plant *T. polyphyllum* deeper (ten to twelve inches) in very loose, gritty soil or almost pure sand.

Tropaeolum tuberosum var. *lineamaculatum* 'Ken Aslet'.

Management: All except *T. polyphyllum* will need support. Cut back after foliage dies down in the fall. Mulch in the winter, or store the tubers.

Propagation: Seed (may take up to four months to germinate); division in spring for *T. speciosum* (careful, it's very brittle); root cuttings; tubers.

Pests and Diseases: Snails, slugs, aphids.

Companions: *Tropaeolum speciosum* likes to climb up through bushes or hedges; it does need to be encouraged to first get up into the base, but then it will spread of its own accord. Plant *T. polyphyllum* where it can hang down from a wall, or in a rock garden, or grow it as a groundcover in a hot spot.

Notes: *Tropaeolum tuberosum* is not always hardy in the Pacific Northwest, but the tubers can be stored inside over the winter.

Species and Cultivars	Height/ Spread	USDA Hardiness Zone	Flowers (bloom time)	Foliage	Comments
polyphyllum	18ft × 2–3ft	8–10	Rich yellow, long spurs (M)	Bluish green, deeply lobed or divided	Trailing, long stems, needs good drainage, difficult to grow
speciosum	10–12ft × 2ft	8–10	Scarlet-red, long spurs, red calyx (M–L)	Rich green, palmate	Scotch flame flower, climber, blue fruit held in red calyces, RHS Award
tuberosum	6–9ft × 2ft	8–10	Orange-yellow petals, red-orange spurs and sepals (L)	Grayish green, peltate	Climber, edible tubers
t. var. lineamaculatum 'Ken Aslet'	6–9ft × 2ft	8–10	Orange-yellow petals, red-orange spurs and sepals (M–L)	As above	Climber, edible tubers, blooms earlier than species, RHS Award

Uvularia grandiflora.

UVULARIA Convallariaceae

Uvularia is a small genus. All three species have pendent, bell-shaped flowers in shades of yellow that hang from the upper leaf axils in spring. Thus suspended, they move freely with the breezes, hence the common name of the largest one, great merrybells. The leaves are ovate-lanceolate or oblong, and perfoliate in *U. grandiflora* and *U. perfoliata*. These East Coast woodland natives can form large clumps and adapt to most shady, humus-rich situations. ~ *Ann Bucher*

Scientific Name: From uvula, the fleshy lobe at the back of your soft palate.
Common Name: Bellwort, merrybells.
Origin: North America.
Preferred Conditions: Well-drained, cool, humus-rich, moist, fertile soil. Tolerates average soil as long as it doesn't dry out.
Light: Part shade to shade, especially in summer (spring sun, summer shade). Morning sun is best.
Management: Divide seldom, only as needed for propagation; this plant doesn't like to be disturbed. Cut back during fall cleanup or when fully dormant. Top-dress in winter with a leaf mold or other organic material. Watch for slugs in very early spring, bait, baiting, baited!
Propagation: Seed (will sprout the following spring); division of rhizomes in autumn (rhizomes are brittle).
Pests and Diseases: Slugs, snails, root weevils.
Companions: Trillium, polygonatum, asarum, dicentra, epimedium, hosta, tiarella, brunnera, helleborus, erythronium, pulmonaria, corydalis, *Lamium galeobdolon* 'Hermann's Pride'; the shade border.

Species and Cultivars	Height/ Spread	USDA Hardiness Zone	Flowers (bloom time)	Foliage	Comments
grandiflora	1–2½ft × 1ft	3–9	Lemon-yellow (E)	Mid-green, perfoliate, narrow on arching olive-green stems	Great merrybells, wiry, erect, RHS Award
perfoliata	1–2ft × 1ft	3–9	Paler yellow, smaller (E)	Mid-green, perfoliate	Strawbells
sessilifolia	1–1½ft × 1ft	3–9	Golden yellow, smaller (E–M)	Pale green to gray with white edge, not perfoliate	Wild oats, spreading

Valeriana phu 'Aurea'.

VALERIANA Valerianaceae

In *Gardening with Native Plants of the Pacific Northwest*, Arthur Kruckeberg said one of the nicer things about valerian: "In fruit each flower is transformed into a tiny plumed parachute perched for the flight of valerians yet to come." All the same, the only two valerians we allow in our gardens are *V. officinalis* and *V. phu* 'Aurea', and neither has much to recommend it as a flowering plant. *Valeriana officinalis,* long used as a medicinal, has tall sparsely clad stems topped by corymbs of small white to pale pink flowers in June; a quiet plant, it could be used as a filler among more vibrant companions. *Valeriana phu* 'Aurea' is grown primarily for the color of its spring foliage. It is low-growing and bright yellow-green, a great foil to other spring-flowering plants. By the time this valerian blooms on tall stems, its leaves have turned green; flowers are like those of *V. officinalis,* only white, and with the same mousey character. Graham Stuart Thomas said *V. officinalis* is known as cat's valerian because cats love it so much (cats, mice, hmm), so grow it for your whiskered friends. ~ *Carrie Becker*

Scientific Name: From the Latin *valere* ("healthy," "strong"), referring to medicinal properties; or for Valerius, a third-century Roman emperor.
Common Name: Valerian, cat's valerian.
Origin: Europe, Asia Minor.
Preferred Conditions: Any good garden soil that is moist and well-drained.
Light: Sun to part shade. *Valeriana phu* 'Aurea' keeps its gold longer in full sun.
Management: Staking may be needed. You can remove the flowers of *V. phu* 'Aurea' before they bloom. Clean up in fall, leave winter foliage.
Propagation: Division in spring; seed.
Pests and Diseases: Powdery mildew, snails, slugs.

Companions: *Milium effusum* 'Aureum', hosta. For *V. phu* 'Aurea', try pulmonaria (especially *P. angustifolia*), *Veronica peduncularis* 'Georgia Blue', and blue-flowering spring bulbs such as *Chionodoxa sardensis* or muscari.

Notes: *Valeriana officinalis* was grown for the drug valerian, still a very popular sedative.

Species and Cultivars	Height/ Spread	USDA Hardiness Zone	Flowers (bloom time)	Foliage	Comments
officinalis	3–5ft × 1ft	4–9	White to pale pink, fragrant (M)	Green, toothed, deeply lobed, aromatic	Cat's valerian, cats like this plant
phu 'Aurea'	1–1½ft × 1½ft	5–9	Small, white (M)	Bright gold aging to pale green, somewhat aromatic	Outstanding spring gold foliage

VANCOUVERIA Berberidaceae

Vancouverias are related to epimedium and have the same leaf arrangement, but smaller. The leaves are tender at the beginning of the season, gaining substance over the summer. The "inside out" flowers are white and recurved, arranged along vertical stems in a panicle.

Vancouveria hexandra is the fastest and widest reaching of the three species. It is deciduous and will make a loose groundcover in dry shade. In our experience, while it is a wide-spreader, it is not much of a threat to other plants. It just seems to move around them.

Vancouveria planipetala, in contrast, forms strong, dense evergreen clumps, preventing anything from penetrating. We have grown it right next to English ivy, and it held its own. There are two forms, one has very shiny evergreen leaves and the other has smaller matte-grayish leaves and is somewhat less evergreen. Another shade plant, this one deserves good soil. It's slow-growing in the first couple of years, becoming a moderate grower in time.

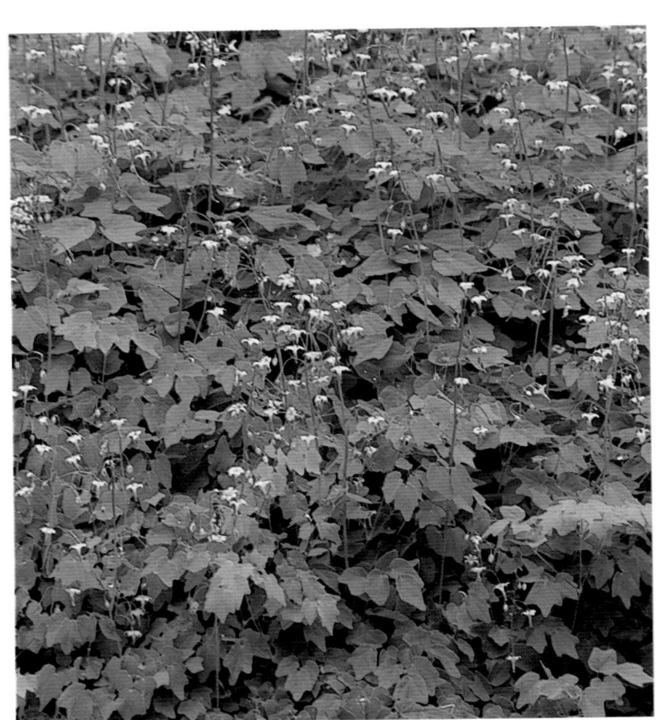

Vancouveria hexandra.

Vancouveria chrysantha, which occurs in California and Oregon, is the most tender and slowest spreader. Its evergreen leaves are much more finely divided than *V. planipetala* (closer to *V. hexandra*), and it has yellow flowers. Give it good soil and a small area.

All three plants are good groundcovers for different spaces and should be grown more widely. ~ *Ann Bucher*

Scientific Name: After Captain George Vancouver.

Common Name: Inside-out flower.

Origin: Western United States.

Preferred Conditions: Moderately fertile, moist, humus-rich, well-drained soil. A sheltered site is best.

Light: Part shade to shade. Tolerates sun with enough moisture.

Management: This is a low-maintenance plant. Cut off old leaves in January or February before new leaves begin to emerge. Top-dress in winter with leaf mold or other organic material.

Propagation: Seed; division in fall or late winter to March.

Pests and Diseases: Snails, slugs, root weevils.
Companions: Good under hydrangeas and magnolias.
Notes: This, along with *Euphorbia robbiae*, *Iris foetidissima*, epimedium, and *Geranium macrorrhizum*, is a great dry-shade groundcover. The foliage is very attractive in bouquets, but it will weaken the plant to cut it. Wait to cut until the clumps are well established. The availability of this plant is a bit tight due to its being difficult to divide (long rhizomes) and slow to increase in a pot.

Species and Cultivars	Height/ Spread	USDA Hardiness Zone	Flowers (bloom time)	Foliage	Comments
chrysantha	8–12in × 2ft+	5–8	Small, yellow (E–M)	Dark green, ternate with diamond-shaped leaflets, glossy, leathery	Evergreen, modest spreader
hexandra	1–1½ft × 3ft+	5–8	Tiny, white, pendent (E–M)	Light green, dainty, lobed, ovate, not leathery	Vancouver fern, deciduous, vigorous
planipetala	8–12in × 2ft+	5–8	White with lavender tinge, small but abundant (E–M)	Dark green, ovate-cordate, ternate, divided, wavy margins, leathery	Evergreen, rhizomatous, slower spreader

VERBASCUM Scrophulariaceae

If you are looking for big, bold plants to make a structural statement or give the back of the border interest, consider the verbascums. The biennials like *V. bombyciferum* will grow well in poor soil and with little water, but their true nature, as eight-foot monsters, will show in the garden with good soil and watering; they will seed about but are easy to control, and their big felty leaves add winter interest. All need space and a nearly full-sun location to do their best, especially the striking newer colored forms. If you grow them in a bit of shade, the flower stems will stretch, bend, and curve into the wrong shape, and flop and lay on top of other plants. The large basal leaves can be a problem because they can smother their neighbors, so try to plant them accordingly. The newer cultivars like *V.* 'Helen Johnson' and *V.* 'Jackie' are good neighbors and easier to use in a mixed border: they are smaller, and their lower basal leaves do not take up as much room. ~ *Bob Lilly*

Verbascum chaixii 'Album'.

Scientific Name: The classical Latin name, possibly a corruption of *barbascum* ("beard").
Common Name: Mullein.
Origin: West and Central Asia, Europe, North Africa.
Preferred Conditions: Lean, alkaline soil with sharp drainage. Moderate to low water needs. Tolerates drought once established.

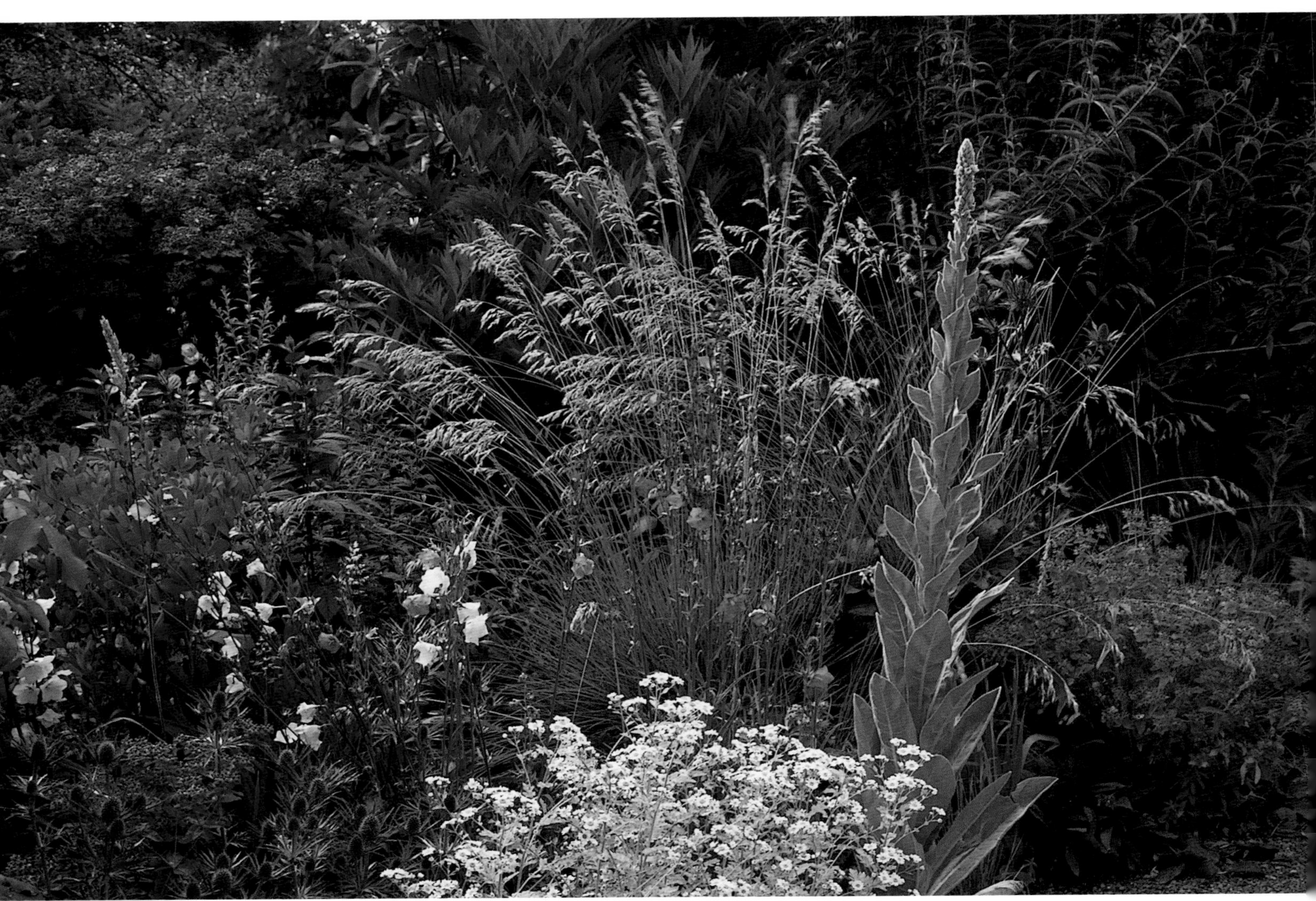

Verbascum thapsus paired with a grass (*Helictotrichon sempervirens*), *Eryngium alpinum*, *Tanacetum parthenium* 'Aureum', euphorbia, and the blues and white of *Campanula persicifolia*.

Light: Sun.

Management: Remove spent flower stems for another small flush of flowers in late summer; these will be on shorter stems. Watch for slugs in early spring and cutworms in spring and early summer. In exposed situations they may need staking.

Propagation: Seed; division in spring; root cuttings in winter (hybridizes freely, so must use cuttings to reproduce cultivars).

Pests and Diseases: Slugs, powdery mildew, cutworms (the same one that attacks digitalis and other gray-foliage plants).

Companions: Grasses, *Nepeta* 'Six Hills Giant', *Crambe cordifolia*, hemerocallis, kniphofia, dahlia, helianthus, rudbeckia; the taller ones look good as specimen plants.

Notes: These are unfortunately short-lived plants for us. The crown has a hard time making it through our wet, cold winters; give them good drainage, or a slight slope. This is especially critical with the newer types, which are vegetatively propagated (and seem to need more light as well). There has been some success in propagating cultivars from tissue culture. In the chart, the spread is the width covered by the basal leaves.

Species and Cultivars	Height/ Spread	USDA Hardiness Zone	Flowers (bloom time)	Foliage	Comments
bombyciferum	6–8ft × 2–3ft	3–9	Clear yellow, single spikes, sometimes candelabra-shaped (M–L)	Silvery-white, woolly, large basal crown	Biennial but so striking it's worth growing
b. 'Polarsommer' (syn. 'Arctic Summer')	5–6ft × 2–3ft	3–9	Sulphur-yellow (M)	Silvery-white, felty, large basal crown	Biennial
'Caribbean Crush'	2–4ft × 2ft	5–8	Mango to burnt-orange (E–M)	Felted gray	
chaixii	3–6ft × 2½ft	5–9	Pale yellow, purple stamens, purple-flushed center, purple buds (E–M)	Mid-green to gray, scalloped margins	Nettle-leaved mullein, semi-evergreen, long-blooming
c. 'Album'	3–5ft × 2½ft	5–9	White, purple stamens, purple-flushed center, purple buds (M)	Gray-green basal rosettes	Self-sows, RHS Award
Cotswold Group 'Cotswold Queen'	3–4ft × 2ft	5–9	Apricot-buff, darker yellow with purple eye, spikes (M–L)	Mid-green, wrinkled	Short-lived, semi-evergreen, RHS Award
Cotswold Group 'Gainsborough'	2–4ft × 2ft	5–9	Yellow (M)	Silvery-gray	Semi-evergreen, RHS Award
Cotswold Group 'Pink Domino'	2–4ft × 2ft	5–9	Pale pink to almost red, purple stamens (M–L)	Dark purplish green, ovate-lanceolate rosettes, wrinkled	As above, RHS Award
Cotswold Group 'White Domino'	3ft × 2ft	5–9	White (M–L)	Gray-green, wrinkled	Semi-evergreen
'Helen Johnson'	1½–3ft × 2ft	6–9	Buff-colored, unusual (M–L)	Gray, woolly	Short-lived
'Jackie'	1½–2ft × 2ft	6–9	Apricot, purple-eyed (E–M)	Grayish green, woolly	Long-blooming, short-lived
nigrum	2½–3ft × 2ft	3–8	Golden yellow or white, purple or red center, narrow spikes (M–L)	Dark green, downy	Dark mullein; propagate by seed or root cuttings
phoeniceum	2½–3ft × 1½ft	4–8	White, pink or violet to dark purple, violet filament hairs (E–M)	Dark green, slightly scalloped, hairy reverse	Biennial or short-lived, self-sows, evergreen
'Raspberry Ripple'	2½–3ft × 2ft	5–8	Purple buds open to light pink and white, dark center (M)	Green, wrinkled	Short-lived
'Southern Charm'	2–3ft × 2ft	6–9	Pastel shades of rose, cream, apricot, lavender, and pink, red eye (M)	As above	As above
'Summer Sorbet'	1½–2ft × 2ft	6–9	Dark purple buds open to lavender-purple (E–M)	As above	As above
thapsus	3½–5½ft × 2–3ft	3–9	Strong yellow (M)	Gray-green, woolly, large basal crown	Common mullein, biennial
wiedemannianum	3ft × 2ft	6–9	Indigo-blue to violet, purple stamens (M)	Dark green, silvery cobweblike hair	Biennial

Verbena bonariensis.

VERBENA Verbenaceae

Verbena is one of the basic garden plants that can bloom all summer with very little fuss. Some are considered tender perennials; others are short-lived and often treated as annuals and encouraged to self-sow. Verbenas are variable in their growth habit. Some spread, providing a mass of color that makes them a good choice for groundcovers, edging, and garden beds; others stand tall on wiry stems, waving to and fro in the wind; and then there are those that look attractive trailing out of the window box or container.

Small, funnel-shaped flowers are borne in clusters and range in color from snowy white to apricot, pink, red, blue, lavender, and purple. They all make a color statement, whether spreading on the ground or up high on wiry stems. The dark green leaves range from ovate to oblong to lanceolate; all are toothed and may be rough and hairy.

Is *V. bonariensis* an annual, biennial, or perennial? We consider it a self-sowing biennial, best as a one-year-old and allowed to seed about. Older plants are often too woody and not as graceful as the youngsters. ~ *Susan Carter*

Scientific Name: The classical Latin name of the common European vervain.
Common Name: Vervain.
Origin: South America.
Preferred Conditions: Average to moderately fertile, well-drained, moist soil. Most (especially *V. rigida*) don't like to dry out. *Verbena bonariensis* and *V. hastata* will tolerate dry conditions.
Light: Sun.
Management: Cut back all but *V. bonariensis*, especially the marginally hardy ones, after basal spring growth begins to keep them more compact and reduce overwintered problems. Deadhead to prolong bloom on all forms. You could cut *V. bonariensis* back (after the flowers are spent), but it won't prevent self-sowing as some seed is ripe while the clusters are still in bloom (*V. bonariensis* can also be a short-lived plant, so the seedlings may be wanted). Clean up and cut down to basal growth in late fall.
Propagation: Seed; division in spring; basal cuttings.
Pests and Diseases: Spider mites, whiteflies, snails, slugs, powdery mildew. The spider mite problem in the trailing forms seems to increase in the second year.

Verbena bonariensis, the perfect scrim plant, here with a grass (*Cortaderia selloana* 'Sunstripe'), *Hemerocallis* 'Autumn Minaret', and *Artemisia* 'Huntington'.

Companions: Miscanthus and other grasses, *Stachys byzantina*, coreopsis, helianthus, scabiosa, knautia.

Notes: There is a great deal of verbena breeding (*V. canadensis*, *V. peruviana*, *V. tenuisecta*) going on for summer color, but the resulting cultivars may not be hardy—time will tell.

Species and Cultivars	Height/ Spread	USDA Hardiness Zone	Flowers (bloom time)	Foliage	Comments
bonariensis (syn. patagonica)	3–6ft × 1½ft	7–10	Tiny, purple-lavender (variable), fragrant (M–L)	Dark green, oblong-lanceolate, clasping, mostly basal, wrinkled, rough, branching, wiry stems	Brazilian vervain, self-sows, may flop in rich soil, clump-forming
canadensis	6–8in × 1½ft+	6–10	Purplish pink to rose-pink (variable), clusters (M–L)	Mid-dark green, ovate-oblong-ovate, pinnately arranged, toothed, rough	Rose vervain

Species and Cultivars	Height/ Spread	USDA Hardiness Zone	Flowers (bloom time)	Foliage	Comments
hastata	3–4ft × 1½ft	4–8	Tiny violet-blue to pinkish purple, sometimes white, arranged in short candelabras (M–L)	Dark green, lanceolate, pointed, toothed, deep purple stems	Wild hyssop, clump-forming, erect
h. 'Alba'	3–4ft × 1½ft	4–8	White (M–L)	As above	As above
'Homestead Purple'	6–18in × 18in	6–10	Rich dark purple-violet (E–L)	Dark green, ovate, scalloped	Mildew resistant, trailing
peruviana	1–2in × 30in	6–10	Bright red (M)	Dark green, deeply divided	Good in hanging baskets, short-lived
rigida (syn. venosa)	1–2ft × 2ft+	7–10	Bright violet-purple, fragrant (M–L)	Dark green, oblong, toothed, rough	Upright (rigid), rhizomatous, spreads slowly, RHS Award
r. 'Polaris'	1–2ft × 2ft+	7–10	Silver-blue, almost white (M–L)	As above	Upright, rhizomatous, spreads slowly
'Silver Anne'	1ft × 1½ft	8–11	Bright pink aging to silver-white, fragrant (M–L)	Light green, ovate-oblong	Upright, tender, spreading, RHS Award

VERNONIA Asteraceae

Vernonia is a lovely perennial, like a giant aster, with a rich intense color for late summer effect way back in the border. These North American natives can be found growing wild in moist prairie

Vernonia noveboracensis.

or marsh conditions, although they are somewhat drought tolerant for us once established. The flowers of the three species are rich purple, violet-blue, or white, and age to rust-colored seed-heads. Vernonia is a good source of nectar for bees and butterflies. The leaves are narrow and dark green on tough, stiff stems (hence the common name). ~ *Susan Carter*

Scientific Name: After English botanist William Vernon.
Common Name: Ironweed.
Origin: North America.
Preferred Conditions: Rich to moderately fertile and moist soil.
Light: Sun to part shade. Give them sun to make them strong.
Management: Top-dress with organic material. Don't cut back until winter, when foliage has died back. May need staking, particularly in rich soil.
Propagation: Seed; cuttings; division in spring.
Pests and Diseases: Powdery mildew, snails, slugs (especially on the crown in spring).
Companions: Miscanthus and other tall grasses, chelone, aconitum, eupatorium, callicarpa, aster, hardy fuchsias, *Anemone ×hybrida*; good with dark purple hydrangeas in foreground.

Species and Cultivars	Height/ Spread	USDA Hardiness Zone	Flowers (bloom time)	Foliage	Comments
crinita	5–6ft × 2ft	5–9	Rich crimson-purple, in clusters (M–L)	Dark green, narrow, linear to linear-lanceolate, pointed	Clump-forming
fasciculata	3–6ft × 2ft	5–9	Violet-blue, in flat umbels (M–L)	As above	Branching stems
noveboracensis	6–8ft × 2ft	5–9	Deep violet-purple or white, in fluffy loose clusters (M–L)	Dark green, lanceolate, toothed	New York ironweed, branching stems

VERONICA Scrophulariaceae

Veronica is a large genus with a varied group of species: tall ones that supply color for the back of the border; low, bushy ones for the front of the border; and prostrate ones for groundcovers. Speedwells, as they're commonly called, are a good source of blue for the garden. The good colors don't end at blue, though, and veronicas are valued for their rich violets, purples, pinks, whites, and almost reds. The small flowers are mostly arranged on long spikes and bloom from the bottom up; some have conspicuous stamens. They are long-blooming, and the taller varieties are excellent cut flowers. The foliage also varies—broadly lanceolate or oblong to rounded, entire or toothed, green to gray—for a wide variety of effects. ~ *Susan Carter*

Scientific Name: Honors St. Veronica, patron saint of laundresses.
Common Name: Speedwell.
Origin: Europe, Asia, Caucasus, Siberia, Ukraine.
Preferred Conditions: Most any with well-drained, moist soil. Protect from winter wet, especially species with felted leaves. The gray-leaved forms need good air circulation and sharp drainage. The tall forms tend to be short-lived in soil that is too lightweight or sandy (try a heavier soil and a bit of lime). Soil that is too rich may produce leggy plants.
Light: Sun to part shade. Sun only for the gray-leaved forms.

Veronica peduncularis 'Georgia Blue'.

Management: Deadhead spent flower spikes to the first set of leaves; this will make the plant look tidier, and some may rebloom. Taller veronicas in exposed conditions may need staking. Cut to the ground in winter cleanup or when they look tired. Some are short-lived. Divide every three to four years.

Propagation: Seed; cuttings; division in spring.

Pests and Diseases: Powdery mildew, rust, leaf spot, root rot, slugs in early spring.

Companions: Miscanthus, pennisetum, molinia, hosta, primula, paeonia, carex, narcissus, *Lathyrus vernus*, *Phlox paniculata*, aconitum, aster, geranium, stachys, campanula.

Notes: In the Pacific Northwest, all the tall forms of veronica are short-lived and best as youngsters.

Species and Cultivars	Height/ Spread	USDA Hardiness Zone	Flowers (bloom time)	Foliage	Comments
allioni	3–8in × 10in	4–9	Deep violet-blue (M)	Dark green	Alpine speedwell, evergreen
austriaca subsp. teucrium	1½ft × 1ft	5–8	Bright blue, dark veins (E–M)	Gray-green, toothed, ovate to oblong, hairy	Mat-forming, semi-evergreen
a. subsp. teucrium 'Crater Lake Blue'	1ft × 1ft	3–8	Deep vivid blue, white eye (E–M)	Bright green, small, shiny	Dense, mounding habit, semi-evergreen, RHS Award
a. subsp. teucrium 'Royal Blue'	1ft × 1ft	4–9	Deep gentian-blue (M)	Dark green, small, shiny	Compact, semi-evergreen, RHS Award
chamaedrys	12–20in × 12in+	3–7	Blue, white eye, tiny (M–L)	Bright green, toothed, ovate to lanceolate	Germander speedwell, spreading

Species and Cultivars	Height/ Spread	USDA Hardiness Zone	Flowers (bloom time)	Foliage	Comments
c. 'Miffy Brute'	3–10in × 12in+	4–9	Dark blue (E–M)	Creamy-white and green, reverts easily	Spreading, pinch now and then to keep neat
gentianoides	1½–2ft × 1½ft	4–8	Pale blue with darker veination (E–M)	Broad dark green rosettes, shiny, lanceolate to oblong, ground-hugging	Gentian speedwell, evergreen, short-lived in the Pacific Northwest, RHS Award
g. 'Pallida'	1½ft × 1ft	4–9	Pale sky-blue (E–M)	Dark green, glossy	Mat-forming, good cut, short-lived
g. 'Variegata'	1½ft × 1ft	4–8	Pale blue (E–M)	Dark green splashed with creamy-white, glossy	Mat-forming, short-lived in Pacific Northwest
'Giles Van Hees'	6–8in × 8in	4–9	Bright pink (M–L)	Green, small, lanceolate	Long-blooming
'Goodness Grows"	1–1½ft × 1½ft	4–9	Rich violet-blue (E–M)	Deep green	Prostrate, semi-evergreen, long-blooming
longifolia	2–4ft × 1ft	4–8	Lavender-blue (M)	Mid-green, toothed, pointed, narrowly lanceolate to linear-lanceolate	Self-sows
l. 'Blauriesin'	2½–4ft × 1ft	3–9	Deep blue (M)	As above	Good cut, vigorous
peduncularis	4–6in × 2ft+	6–8	Deep blue, white eye (E–M)	Mid-green, ovate to lanceolate, toothed, glossy, purple-tinged	Mat-forming, spreads, evergreen, long-blooming
p. 'Georgia Blue' (syn. 'Oxford Blue')	4–6in × 2ft+	6–9	Cobalt-blue, white eye, rounded (E–M)	Dark green, purplish red tinge in new growth and in fall, glossy, small, rounded	Mat-forming, spreads, evergreen, vigorous
prostrata (syn. austriaca var. dubia, rupestris)	4–8in × 10in	4–8	Pale to deep blue (E–M)	Mid-green, small, toothed, linear-oblong to ovate	Ground-hugger, RHS Award
p. 'Heavenly Blue'	4–6in × 10in	4–9	Bright blue (E–M)	Deep green, tiny, glossy	Prostrate, vigorous
p. 'Mrs. Holt'	3–6in × 10in	5–8	Light pink, small (E–M)	Light green, tiny, oval	Mat-forming
p. 'Trehane'	3–8in × 10in	4–9	Deep sky-blue (E–M)	Bright golden yellow, may scorch in sun	Tolerates dry conditions, mat-forming
repens (syn. reptans)	2–3in × 12in+	2–9	Pale blue to white (E–M)	Dark green, small, shiny, round to ovate	Tolerates dry shade, prostrate, creeping
r. 'Sunshine'	1–2in × 12in+	7–9	Pale bluish lavender, small (E–M)	Bright golden yellow, small, rounded	Sun or shade, but don't let it dry out
'Shirley Blue'	8–10in × 12in	4–9	Vivid blue (E–M)	Grayish green, deeply toothed, oblong to lanceolate	Creeping, RHS Award
spicata	1–2ft × 1½ft	4–8	Deep blue, long purple stamens (M–L)	Grayish green, pointed, toothed, lanceolate to ovate, hairy	Spike speedwell, long-blooming, good cut, most forms upright

Species and Cultivars	Height/ Spread	USDA Hardiness Zone	Flowers (bloom time)	Foliage	Comments
s. 'Blaufuchs' (syn. 'Blue Fox')	2ft × 1½ft	4–8	Deep blue, large spikes (M)	Green	Clump-forming, upright
s. 'Heidekind'	12in × 12in	4–8	Rose-pink (M)	Gray-green, pointed, toothed, lanceolate to ovate	Long-blooming
s. 'Icicle' (syn. 'White Icicle')	1½–2ft × 1½ft	3–8	White (M–L)	Light green	Bushy growth habit, short-lived, long-blooming, upright
s. subsp. incana	10–12in × 1½ft	4–8	Blue (M)	Silvery-gray, pointed, hairy	Woolly speedwell, flops, RHS Award
s. 'Minuet'	15–18in × 1½ft	3–8	Rose-pink, dense spikes (E–M)	Silvery-gray	Clump-forming, upright
s. 'Nana Blauteppich' (syn. 'Blue Carpet')	4–6in × 1½ft	4–8	Bright blue (M)	Rich green	Clump-forming, compact
s. 'Noah Williams'	20–24in × 1½ft	4–8	White (M–L)	Creamy-white margins on glossy dark-green, toothed	Upright
s. 'Rotfuchs' (syn. 'Red Fox)	10–15in × 1½ft	3–9	Deep rosy-pink to rosy-red (M)	Green, glossy, toothed	Clump-forming, upright
'Sunny Border Blue'	1½–2ft × 1½ft	3–8	Dark violet-blue (M–L)	Green, glossy, crinkled, lanceolate	Long-blooming, 1993 PPA Award
'Waterperry Blue'	4–6in × 10in	4–8	Light lavender-blue, white eye (M)	Shiny green, turns bronzy-purple in winter	Evergreen, spreading

VERONICASTRUM Scrophulariaceae

The more I see veronicastrum, the more I appreciate it, flowering as it does here in midsummer, for six weeks or more. The inflorescences on the new cultivars are striking and more elongated than the older varieties and offer more color variations, with forms in spikes in groups at the tops of the tall stems. The stems are clothed in whorls of lanceolate leaves. A good background plant, best in groups of three or more. Veronicastrum stands on its own and needs little or no staking. It adds verticality, is easy of culture, and makes a good cut flower. ~ *Carrie Becker*

Scientific Name: From the Latin *astrum* ("like"), hence resembling veronica.
Common Name: Bowman's root, Culver's physic.
Origin: North America, Asia, Siberia.
Preferred Conditions: Any moderate soil that is humus-rich, well-drained, and moisture-retentive.
Light: Sun to part shade.
Management: Needs summer water. Rarely needs staking. Cut to the ground in winter cleanup.
Propagation: Seed; division in spring; cuttings.
Pests and Diseases: Powdery mildew.
Companions: Grasses, *Aster ×frikartii*, monarda, echinacea, *Phlox paniculata*, apricot-colored roses, polemonium.

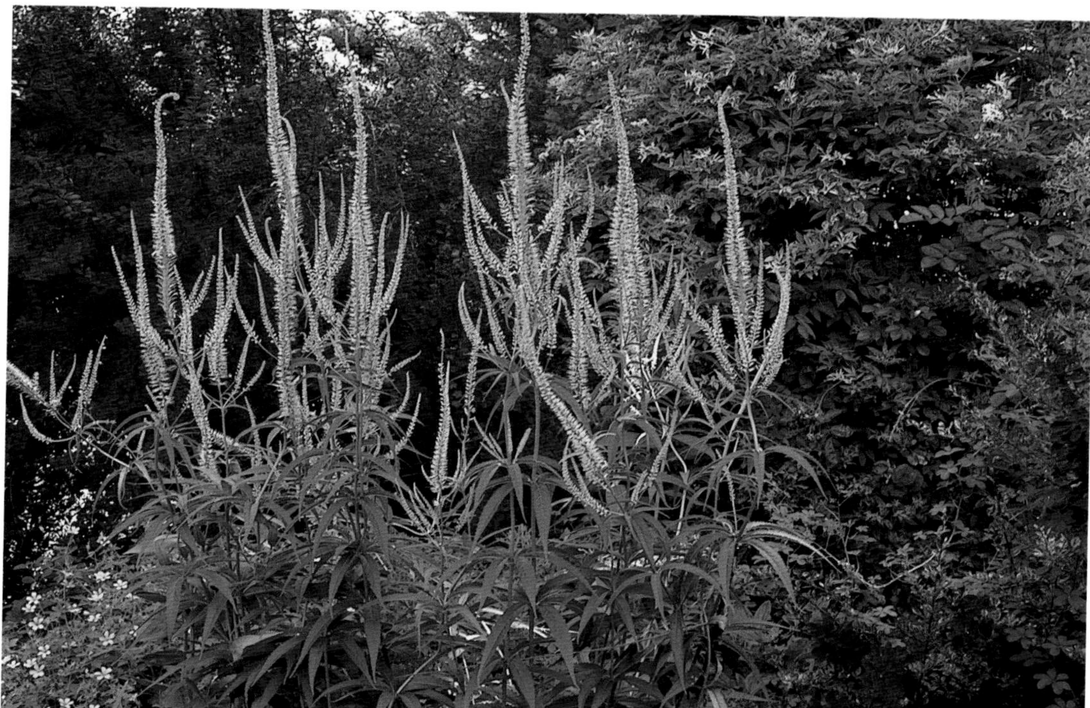

Veronicastrum virginicum.

Species and Cultivars	Height/ Spread	USDA Hardiness Zone	Flowers (bloom time)	Foliage	Comments
sibiricum	4–5ft × 1½ft	3–9	Lavender-blue (M–L)	Olive-green, lanceolate	Erect
virginicum	4–6ft × 1½ft	3–9	Pale blue, pink or white, tubular, conspicuous stamens (M–L)	Dark green, lanceolate, toothed	Erect, self-sows
v. 'Alboroseum'	4–5ft × 1½ft	3–9	White to pink, delicate (M–L)	As above	
v. 'Album'	4–6ft × 1½ft	3–9	White (M–L)	Dark grayish green	
v. 'Apollo'	3–5ft × 1½ft	3–9	Pale lilac-pink (M)	Dark green	Strong stems
v. 'Fascination'	4–6ft × 1½ft	3–9	Two-toned, pink-mauve and periwinkle-blue (M)	Dark reddish green	Erect
v. f. roseum	4–6ft × 1½ft	3–9	Pale lavender-pink (M–L)	Dark green	Sturdy stems
v. f. roseum 'Pink Glow'	3–4ft × 1½ft	3–9	Rose-pink (M–L)	As above	
v. 'Spring Dew'	3½ft × 1½ft	3–9	White (M)	As above	

Viola 'Desdemona'.

VIOLA Violaceae

There is nothing more pleasing than a well-established carpet of violets growing and flowering in the wild or in the corners of neglected gardens. These plants seem to do better when left on their own, providing the soil does not dry out, which will reduce flower production. The scent is variable and haphazard; some of the many *V. odorata* cultivars have no fragrance at all! And many more have been lost to cultivation over the years. If you must have fragrance, grow the tender Parma violets or search out the true *V. odorata*, a dark purple flower with a strong violet fragrance; *V. odorata* is most commonly found in older gardens, even in the lawn. Yes, violets can be very invasive by seed. *Viola labradorica* and *V. adunca* are most tenacious and hard to pull out, with their deep roots and smothering foliage; pretty though they are, they should not be introduced to planting beds, but under shrubs they are perfect and will survive even a dry summer. Try the invasive groundcovering *V. odorata* in poor soil and full sun in the orchard, mow as needed, and think of your grandmother. ~ *Susan Buckles*

Scientific Name: The classical Latin name for many sweet-scented flowers.
Common Name: Pansy, violet, horned violet.
Origin: North America, Africa, Europe, Asia, Caucasus.
Preferred Conditions: Best in cooler climates; they flourish in damp on a clay soil but are also very adaptable in most fertile, humus-rich, well-drained soil. Shield from the hottest time of the day.
Light: Part shade (morning sun for best flower production). Tolerates full sun if well watered.
Management: Pinch back in summer after the first bloom to encourage a second bloom and keep compact (especially the vigorous ones). The invasive groundcover types can be mowed (this treatment produces very short stems!) and will benefit from frequent division. Top-dress in winter with organic material but not over the crown. Many are short-lived, and cuttings should be taken. Early disappearance is often due to winter wet and small slugs. Bait early for slugs; they eat the flowers. Clean up as necessary.

Propagation: Seed (needs darkness to germinate); cuttings; division in spring, before, after, or during bloom (cornuta, glabella, odorata, cucullata).

Pests and Diseases: Snails, slugs, powdery mildew, spider mites, root weevils. Aphids can severely set back flower production.

Companions: Ajuga, *Lysimachia nummularia*, primula, the smaller spring bulbs, omphalodes, dicentra, *Ranunculus ficaria*, aquilegia, *Milium effusum* 'Aureum', pulmonaria, uvularia.

Notes: In the Northwest many violas are treated as an annual or short-lived perennial. Violets have a long history of commercial use (perfume, cut flowers, candied confectioneries). Work is being done on compiling an International Cultivar Registration.

Species and Cultivars	Height/ Spread	USDA Hardiness Zone	Flowers (bloom time)	Foliage	Comments
adunca	3–4in × 6in	4–8	Violet to lavender-blue, white center, fragrant (E–M)	Green, roundish to ovate, toothed	Western dog violet, spreads aggressively by seed, semi-evergreen
'Columbine' (viola)	6in × 8in	4–8	White, streaked violet-blue, slender horned spur, fragrant (E–M)	Rich green, ovate	Low, compact, long stems, semi-evergreen
cornuta	9–12in × 12in+	6–9	Rich deep violet, mauve, or white, larger, fragrant (E–M)	Rich green, small, ovate, toothed	Horned violet, evergreen, short-lived, good weaver, rhizomatous, RHS Award
c. 'Barford Blue'	8–10in × 12in	6–9	Light blue (E–M)	As above	Reblooms if cut back, evergreen
c. 'Black Magic'	8–10in × 12in	6–9	Almost black, velvety, bright yellow eye, fragrant (E–L)	As above	Long-blooming, vigorous but slower spreader, evergreen
cucullata	10in × 10in+	4–8	Violet-blue, lower petals etched in purple, darker center, fragrant (E–M)	Dark green, toothed, cordate to ovate	Marsh blue violet, herbaceous, eastern U.S. native, RHS Award
'Dancing Geisha' (violet)	6–8in × 8in	4–8	Blue, sometimes white, fragrant (E–M)	Dark green, deeply cut, streaked and marbled with pewter and white	Grown for the foliage, self-sows, clumping, semi-evergreen
'Desdemona' (viola)	6in × 8in	5–8	Pale lavender-blue, white eye, fragrant (E–M)	Green	Semi-evergreen
dissecta	4in × 6in	5–8	Rose to pale purplish or white, fragrant (E)	Dark green, toothed, dissected	Grown for the foliage as much as for the flower, herbaceous
'Etain' (viola)	6–8in × 8in	4–8	Pale lemon-yellow, violet margins, short spurs, fragrant (E–M)	Bright green, toothed, ovate	Clump-forming, evergreen, long-lived, vigorous
glabella	6in × 6in	5–8	Deep yellow, purple veins, short spurs (E)	Bright green, ovate or to rounded, cordate bases	Stream violet, herbaceous, vigorous, spreads, easy to control, U.S. native

Species and Cultivars	Height/ Spread	USDA Hardiness Zone	Flowers (bloom time)	Foliage	Comments
'Irish Molly' (viola)	6–8in × 12in	4–8	Greenish bronze, dark center (E–M)	Green, broadly ovate, deeply cut	Evergreen
'Königin Charlotte' (violet) (syn. 'Queen Charlotte')	6–8in × 18in+	4–8	Dark blue, some fragrance (E)	Green	Semi-evergreen
labradorica	3–6in × 6in	3–8	Tiny lavender-blue to deep violet (E–L)	Dark green, tinged purple, round to cordate, emerges deep purple	Leaves will retain purple if planted in sun, aggressive spreader by seed, North American native
'Lianne' (violet)	6in × 8in	5–9	Dark purple, fragrant (E–M)	Dark green, cordate	May rebloom, herbaceous
'Lorna Cawthorne' (cornuta)	6–12in × 12in+	6–9	Soft blue, small (E–L)	Rich green	Semi-evergreen
'Maggie Mott' (viola)	4–8in × 8in	7–9	Lavender-mauve to purple, large, rounded, silvery overlay, yellow eye, fragrant (E–M)	Green	Evergreen, RHS Award
'Magic'	4–8in × 8in	5–9	Light purple aging to white, prominent veining, large (E)	As above	Semi-evergreen
odorata	2–8in × 10in+	6–9	Deep violet-purple, flowers before leaves form, fragrant (E)	Dark green rosettes, toothed, cordate to rounded	Sweet violet, semi-evergreen, invasive, self-sows
o. 'Alba'	2–8in × 10in+	6–9	White (E)	Light green rosettes, toothed, cordate to rounded	As above
o. Rosea Group	2–8in × 10in	6–9	Pink (E)	As above	As above
pedata	4–8in × 8in	4–8	White or bicolor, violet to pale violet, gold center (E)	Olive-green, deeply divided, palmate	Bird's foot violet, U.S. native, semi-evergreen
pedatifida	3–5in × 6in	2–8	Deep violet-blue (E–M)	Green, palmate leaves with long narrow leaflets	Larkspur violet, clump-forming, U.S. native, semi-evergreen
'Purple Showers'	6–8in × 8in	6–8	Purple, large (E–L)	Deep green, glossy	Vigorous, long-blooming, semi-evergreen
'Rebecca' (violetta)	6–10in × 8in	4–8	White, splashed with purplish blue on margins, creamy-yellow center, fragrant (E–L)	Green	Compact, long-blooming, semi-evergreen
'Rosine'	6–8in × 8in	4–8	Rose-pink, maroon at throat, small, fragrant (E)	Mid-green, fuzzy, toothed, cordate to rounded	Not easy to establish, long-blooming, rangy

Species and Cultivars	Height/ Spread	USDA Hardiness Zone	Flowers (bloom time)	Foliage	Comments
'Royal Robe' (violet)	6–8in × 10in+	4–8	Deep violet-purple, white eye, fragrant, large (E)	Dark green, cordate to rounded, glossy	Vigorous, similar to *V. odorata*, semi-evergreen
sempervirens	5–6in × 6in	5–9	Yellow with purple center, small (E–M)	Mid-green, glossy, cordate, small	Redwood violet, western U.S. native, almost evergreen
sororia	6in × 8in	4–8	White with violet-blue veins, flat-faced (E–M)	Green, cordate to round	Woolly blue violet, self-sows, U.S. native, herbaceous
s. 'Albiflora'	6in × 8in	4–8	White (E)	As above	Herbaceous, RHS Award
s. 'Freckles'	6–8in × 8in	4–9	White, speckled pale purple-blue, large (E–M)	Light green, woolly, cordate	Self-sows, herbaceous
s. 'Priceana'	6–8in × 8in	4–8	Grayish white, darker near middle, green center, blue veins (E–M)	Light green	Confederate violet, aggressive, herbaceous
tricolor	6–12in × 4–6in	4–8	Purple, yellow, and white and variations thereof (E–L)	Green, oval, deeply toothed	Johnny-jump-up, self-sows, annual or short-lived, evergreen
'White Czar'	4–8in × 8in	4–8	White with cream throat, lower petals veined in deep purple, not fragrant (E)	Mid-green, cordate to rounded	The most common white viola, herbaceous

ZANTEDESCHIA Araceae

Calla lilies make a bold statement in the mixed border, particularly when grown en masse. The elegant shape of *Z. aethiopica*'s white flowers makes them very popular for fresh arrangements, and the very fashionable, richly colored forms, from soft pastels to the hotter shades, are available in the cut flower trade year-round for bridal bouquets. Think Diego and Frida. The "flower" or bract, which is called a spathe, surrounds a central spike, or spadix. The spadix is covered in tiny male and female flowers; the males are at the top, the females are at the bottom. The foliage is green and sometimes very glossy, arrow-shaped or lanceolate, and often spotted or mottled white. Calla lilies are not a true bulb but grow from a rhizome. A quick freeze will turn them to mush above ground; a hard freeze can damage the rhizome, and recovery will be slow or never in hard winters. They are semi-evergreen in some mild winters. ~ *Susan Carter*

Scientific Name: After Italian botanist Francesco Zantedeschi.
Common Name: Calla lily.
Origin: South Africa.
Preferred Conditions: Any well-drained soil, even heavy soil.
Light: Sun to part shade. Needs sun to flower.

Zantedeschia aethiopica 'Crowborough'.

Management: Top-dress with organic material in winter. Mulch them deeply with straw and manure. Clean up when the foliage goes to mush after a freeze. It is sometimes recommended that they be dug up after they die back in the fall and stored in a cool, dry place. Avoid damaging the rhizomes when handling.

Propagation: Division in spring; root cuttings; seed (except *Z. aethiopica* is propagated by division or root cuttings).

Pests and Diseases: Snails, slugs, aphids, botrytis.

Companions: Large-scale ferns, astilbe, aconitum, darmera, hosta, ligularia, caltha, pontederia, sagittaria; beside ponds or water gardens.

Notes: Although they are thought of as being quite tender, calla lilies survive our mild winters in the ground. They are usually purchased at flower shops in six-inch pots with lots of flower stems; these have been treated to bloom more like the dry bulbs you buy in the garden centers. Planted in the ground, they will bloom much less and flower very late in their normal bloom season.

Species and Cultivars	Height/ Spread	USDA Hardiness Zone	Flowers (bloom time)	Foliage	Comments
aethiopica	2–4ft × 2ft	8–10	White spathe, deep yellow spadix (M)	Dark green, glossy, arrow-shaped, leathery, unspotted	Calla lily, long bloomer, RHS Award
a. 'Crowborough'	2–3ft × 2ft	8–10	White spathe, yellow spadix (M)	Dark green, lanceolate, leathery	RHS Award
a. 'Green Goddess'	3–4ft × 2ft	8–10	Spathe has white base, greenish tips, yellow spadix (M)	Dull green	Large plant, a bit more tender, RHS Award
albomaculata	12–24in × 10in	8–10	Creamy-yellow or white spathe, purplish at base, yellow spadix (M)	Mid-green, arrow-shaped, spotted white	Spotted calla
'Black Magic'	2½ft × 1ft	8–10	Yellow spathe, black throat (M–L)	Green, heavily mottled white	Smaller scale
'Cameo'	2½ft × 1ft	8–10	Peachy-yellow and red spathe (M–L)	Bright green, spotted	As above
'Deep Throat'	3ft × 1ft	9–10	White spathe, pink throat (M–L)	Green, arrow-shaped	
elliottiana	18–36in × 10in	8–10	Bright yellow spathe, golden yellow spadix (E–M)	Dark green, arrow-shaped, white spots	Likes drier soil, full sun, RHS Award
'Flame'	1–2ft × 10in	9–10	Red spathe with yellow edges, yellow spadix (M–L)	Dark green, spotted	
'Mango'	2ft × 1ft	8–10	Mango-orange spathe, yellow then green at base, yellow spadix (M–L)	Green, spotted	Smaller scale
'Pink Persuasion'	2ft × 1ft	9–10	Pale pink spathe (M–L)	Rich green	
'Rubylite'	10–12in × 10in	9–10	Dark pink spathe (M–L)	Dark green, narrow	

GLOSSARY

Here are some terms we have used in this book and what we mean by them.

Basal foliage—refers to leaves growing at ground level of a plant.

Bracts—small leaves, often associated with a flower or group of flowers. Sometimes they are colorful and appear to be a part of the flower, occurring around the back or outside of the flower (as in sunflowers or astrantias).

Bulbils—a small bulb, usually one that grows in the axil of a leaf or the inflorescence (as with onions).

Burrs—rough, spiny fruit of a plant.

CBAF—cut back after flowering.

Cleanup—occurs in fall or winter after plants have gone dormant and are ready to be cut back.

Clumping—refers to the tendency of plant to expand to a finite distance; this can also refer to plants that form a rosette.

Colonize—plants with the nature to spread and take over substantial parts of a garden.

Compost—a product made of brown and green vegetable materials from the garden that are layered and aged into a brown mass resembling good soil; worth its weight in gold to gardeners. Homemade compost is always better than any you can purchase.

Corymb—a raceme with flower stems of different lengths, giving it a flat-topped appearance.

Crown—stem and leaf structures above the ground.

Crown specific—roots in the ground and stem and leaf structures above the soil level.

Cultivar—(cv.) the named cultivated variety of a plant that has been selected for specific attributes.

Curing—allowing perennial leaves to turn color in fall before removing.

Cut back—refers to cutting back the above-ground plant parts (leaves and stems).

Daisylike—frequently used to refer to members of the family Asteraceae, even those that are not called daisies, whose flowers resemble a daisy flower.

Deciduous—refers to plants whose foliage drops off at a naturally appropriate time, usually in autumn.

Dioecious—having female and male flowers on different plants.

Division—a type of propagation where a plant is either lifted from the garden and divided into viable pieces or where young growth is removed from the edge of the parent plant.

Drought tolerant—refers to plants that can tolerate low water conditions either due to climate or site. Usually these plants grow naturally in low-water areas in their native habitat.

Ephemeral—of short duration; refers to a short-season perennial, often of spring performance (e.g., *Ranunculus ficaria*).

Established plant—a plant that has lived a few years in the garden and is thriving.

Evergreen—perennials that do not go dormant and keep their leaves up throughout the year.

Fasciated—abnormally flattened or densely leafed (usually of a stem); possibly caused by a virus but not contagious; common in lilies and verbascum.

Fertile soil—soil that is rich in nutrients and organic matter.

Glabrous—without hairs, smooth.

Glaucous—a waxy gray bloom on the surface; can apply to fruits or leaves.

In situ—("in place"), sowing seeds in the garden where the plant is to grow.

Invasive—capable of spreading a lot, taking over.

Lanceolate—lance-shaped.

Layered—another means of propagation: some plants lay stems on the ground and form roots at nodes on their stems or all along the stem (depending on the plant).

Long-lived—used to describe perennials that stay in the garden more than a few years.

Mat-forming—evergreen perennials that form a large, flat, or low-growing colony.

Messy—same as ratty and scraggly, not as bad, but not acceptable to the obsessive-compulsive.

Monocarpic—flowering and fruiting once and then dying; can take more than one year to build up to this point.

Monocot—a plant whose seedlings have one cotyledon leaf; leaves have parallel veins and grasslike appearance (e.g., lilies, daylilies, crocosmia, schizostylis).

Mulching—applying some organic material to the surface of the soil.

NPA—Northwest Perennial Alliance.

Offsets—a short running stem with a new plant at its tip; also refers to plants that are in bulb or corm form that have daughter bulbs alongside or on thin rootlike stems connected to the mother bulb.

Ovate—outline of leaf is egg-shaped and wider at the base than at the tip end.

Palmate—leaf is divided at the base into separate leaflets, which arise from the end of the leaf stalk.

Panicle—a very branched inflorescence; tapers from top to bottom.

Pea sticks—branches of fine-stemmed woody plants used to support climbing peas originally; now used to describe twigs used to support perennials as well (corylus/hazel is best for the purpose).

Peltate—the petiole or stem comes to the center of each leaf; umbrellalike.

Perfoliate—stem goes through the leaves.

Pinching—whether pinching back or pinching out, the process of removing tip growth; used to control plant height, to reduce the need to stake, and to increase the number of stems and flowers in some plants; technique causes branching in response but reduces the size of the individual flowers and the flower heads in most perennials.

Pinnate—having separate paired leaflets along both sides of a leaf stalk.

Pips—ground level growth buds visible in winter during dormancy or just below the surface (e.g., paeonia, hosta, polygonatum).

PPA (Perennial Plant Association) Award—the PPA issues an annual award for the perennial of the year.

Prairie plants—plants native to the American prairie, Rockies to the Mississippi River.

Pups—offset plants; small, young plants growing alongside the parent.

Raceme—an inflorescence of indeterminate length with flowers on short stems along it.

Ratty—deeply disheveled, torn, tattered, unattractive in a serious way.

Regeneration—regrowth after a severe trauma.

Reversions—usually applied to variegated plants that have a tendency to go back (revert) to the original or green form of the plant.

Rhizomatous—spreading by rootlike underground stems, horizontal in position, producing roots below and sending up shoots.

RHS (Royal Horticultural Society) Award—the RHS bestows several kinds of awards, e.g., the Award of Garden Merit (AGM) is given to particularly fine plants after formal trials.

Root cuttings—a propagation process where plants can be successfully grown from pieces of root cut from the parent plant.

Root pruning—digging around a perennial to control the size of the plant.

Scape—the flowering stems of plants; a leafless stalk rising from the ground and carrying one or more flowers.

Scraggly—same as ratty but distorted as well; perhaps a little diseased.

Shear—the process of cutting off growth in a uniform manner all over a plant; can be used to shape, to control size, or to remove spent flowers; can be done by hand or with a shearing tool for larger plants.

Short-lived—perennials that live less than three years.

Spadix—fleshy or thickened columnar structure of minute flowers, usually enclosed in a spathe.

Spathe—a bract, often large and colored, enclosing a spadix.

Spike—a single-stemmed inflorescence of indeterminate length with stemless flowers along it.

Spreading—increases by outward expansion, sometimes indefinitely, sometimes to a specific predetermined size; by nature not invasive in habit and can be controlled or reduced in size without great effort.

Spurs—a slender, tubular projection off the back of the flower or petal of a number of flowering plants (e.g., aquilegia); frequently contains nectar.

Staking—putting in sticks or woody stems around perennials that need support to keep them from falling over on their neighbors; usually also involves tying up.

Stoloniferous—spreads by a prostrate stem that grows at or below ground level and produces new plants from buds at its tip or nodes (strawberry runners are stolons).

Stratification—refers to the process in seed germination where seed has to experience alternating periods of cold and not cold or damp conditions in order to germinate (can also be done chemically).

Thug—plants that don't play well with others; they are often invasive by seed or root and tend to take over large areas of the garden by either growing in or over their more refined neighbors; usually hard to control and harder to get rid of.

Tuberous—plants with swollen underground stems or roots that are used to store food.

Umbel—an inflorescence where all the flowering stems originate from the same place; can be flat-topped, spherical, or dome-shaped (think allium or umbrella).

COMMON NAMES

Some common names refer to the whole genus, some to very specific plants which we have noted here, and some plants have no common names.

COMMON NAME	BOTANICAL NAME
alkanet	Anchusa
alumroot	Heuchera
angel's fishing rod	Dierama
anise hyssop	*Agastache foeniculum*
artichoke, globe	*Cynara cardunculus* Scolymus Group
avens	Geum
baby's breath	Gypsophila
bachelor's buttons	Centaurea
baldmoney	Meum
balloon flower	Platycodon
baneberry	Actaea
barrenwort	Epimedium
beardtongue	Penstemon
bear's breeches	Acanthus
beebalm	Monarda
beeblossom	Gaura
bellflower	Campanula
bellwort	Uvularia
bergamot	Monarda
betony	Stachys
bishop's mitre	Epimedium
bishop's weed	Aegopodium
bittercress	Cardamine
blackberry lily	Belamcanda
bleeding heart	*Dicentra spectabilis*
blessed thistle	Silybum
bloodroot	Sanguinaria
blue plumbago	*Ceratostigma plumbaginoides*
blue star	Amsonia
blue-eyed grass	*Sisyrinchium idahoense* var. *bellum*
blue-eyed Mary	*Omphalodes verna*
boneset	Eupatorium
bouncing Bet	*Saponaria officinalis*
bowman's root	Gillenia, Veronicastrum
bridal wreath	Francoa
bugbane	Cimicifuga
bugleweed	Ajuga

COMMON NAME	BOTANICAL NAME
bugloss	Anchusa
bullslop	*Primula elatior*
burnet	Sanguisorba
butterbur	Petasites
buttercup	Ranunculus
calamint	Calamintha
calla lily	Zantedeschia
camas	Camassia
campion	Lychnis, Silene
Cape fuchsia	Phygelius
cardinal flower	*Lobelia cardinalis*
cardoon	*Cynara cardunculus*
carnation	Dianthus (especially cut flower forms)
carpet bugle	Ajuga
catchfly	Lychnis, Silene
catmint	Nepeta (except *N. cataria*)
catnip	*Nepeta cataria*
celandine poppy	Stylophorum
chalk plant	Gypsophila
chervil	Chaerophyllum
Chinese foxglove	Rehmannia
Chinese lantern	Physalis
chocolate cosmos	*Cosmos atrosanguineus*
Christmas rose	*Helleborus niger*
cinquefoil	Potentilla
clover	Trifolium
cobra lily	Arisaema
cohosh	Cimicifuga
colewort	*Crambe cordifolia*
columbine	Aquilegia

COMMON NAME	BOTANICAL NAME
comfrey	Symphytum
compass plant	Silphium
coneflower	Echinacea, Rudbeckia
coral bells	Heuchera
cornflower	Centaurea
cowslip	*Primula veris*
cranesbill	Geranium
creeping Jenny	*Lysimachia nummularia*
crimson flag	Schizostylis
crosswort	Phuopsis
cuckoo flower	Cardamine
cuckoo pint	*Arum maculatum*
Culver's physic	Veronicastrum
daisy	Aster, Chrysanthemum, Tanacetum, Leucanthemum
dame's rocket	Hesperis
daylily	Hemerocallis
deadnettle	Lamium
desert candle	Eremurus
digger's speedwell	Parahebe
dock	Rumex
dog fennel	Anthemis
dog's breath	Houttuynia
doll's eyes	Actaea
dragonhead	Dracocephalum
dropwort	Filipendula
drumstick allium	*Allium sphaerocephalon*
Dutchman's breeches	*Corydalis scouleri*
elephant ears	Bergenia
eryngo	Eryngium
evening primrose	Oenothera
fairy bells	Disporum

COMMON NAME	BOTANICAL NAME
fairy wand	Dierama
false alumroot	Tellima
false columbine	Semiaquilegia
false dragonhead	Physostegia
false indigo	Baptisia
false lupine	Thermopsis
false mallow	Sidalcea
false Solomon's seal	Smilacina
false spiraea	Astilbe, Filipendula
fennel	Foeniculum
feverfew	*Tanacetum parthenium*
figwort	Scrophularia
fireweed	Epilobium
flag	Iris
flax	Linum
fleabane	Erigeron
fleeceflower	Persicaria
flowering onions	Allium
foamflower	Tiarella
foamy bells	×Heucherella
forget-me-not	Myosotis
foxglove	Digitalis
foxtail lily	Eremurus
friar's cowl	Arisarum
fried egg flower	Romneya
fringe cups	Tellima
fumewort	Corydalis
garland lily	Hedychium
gas plant	Dictamnus
gay feather	Liatris
gentian	Gentiana
giant fennel	Ferula
giant hyssop	Agastache
giant rhubarb	Gunnera
giant scabious	*Cephalaria gigantea*
ginger lily	Hedychium
globe thistle	Echinops
globeflower	Trollius
goat's rue	Galega
goatsbeard	Aruncus
golden lace	Patrinia
goldenrod	Solidago
goldenstar	Chrysogonum
gooseneck loosestrife	*Lysimachia clethroides*
goutweed	Aegopodium
granny's bonnet	*Aquilegia vulgaris* (especially the doubles)
green dragon	Pinellia
ground elder	Aegopodium
hardy ageratum	Eupatorium
hardy begonia	Begonia
hardy Chinese orchid	Bletilla
hardy geranium	Geranium (not Pelargonium)
hardy ginger	Asarum
hardy gloxinia	Incarvillea
heliopsis	Heliopsis
hepatica	Hepatica
Himalayan poppy	Meconopsis (except *M. cambrica*)
hog fennel	Ferula
hollyhock	Alcea
honesty	Lunaria
horehound	Marrubium
horned poppy	Glaucium

COMMON NAME	BOTANICAL NAME
horsemint	*Monarda punctata*
horseradish	Armoracia
hyssop	Agastache
ice plant	Delosperma
Indian physic	Gillenia
Indian pink	Spigelia
Indian rhubarb	Darmera
Indian shot	Canna
inside-out flower	Vancouveria
ironweed	Vernonia
ivy-leaved toadflax	*Cymbalaria muralis*
Jack-in-the-pulpit	*Arisaema triphyllum*
Jacob's ladder	Polemonium
Jacob's rod	*Asphodeline lutea*
Japanese knotweed	Fallopia
Japanese sweet flag	Acorus
Jerusalem sage	*Phlomis fruticosa*
Joe-Pye weed	*Eupatorium fistulosum*
Jupiter's beard	Centranthus
Kansas gay feather	*Liatris pycnostachya*
Kenilworth ivy	*Cymbalaria muralis*
kingcup	Caltha
knotweed	Persicaria
ladybells	Adenophora
lady's mantle	Alchemilla (especially *A. mollis*)
lady's smock	*Cardamine pratensis*
lamb's ears	*Stachys byzantina*
larkspur	Delphinium
leadwort	Ceratostigma
lemon balm	Melissa
Lenten rose	*Helleborus orientalis*
leopard flower	Belamcanda
leopard's bane	Doronicum
lesser celandine	*Ranunculus ficaria*
lily of the Nile	Agapanthus
lily of the valley	Convallaria
lilyturf	Liriope
liverleaf	Hepatica
loosestrife	Lysimachia
lords and ladies	*Arum maculatum*
lungwort	Pulmonaria
lupine	Lupinus
mallow	Malva
Maltese cross	*Lychnis chalcedonica*
marguerite	Anthemis
marsh marigold	Caltha
masterwort	Astrantia
Matilija poppy	Romneya
Mayapple	*Podophyllum peltatum*
meadow rue	Thalictrum
meadowsweet	Filipendula
merrybells	Uvularia
Michaelmas daisy	*Aster novi-belgii*
milk thistle	Silybum
milkweed	Asclepias
mondo grass	Ophiopogon
money plant	*Lunaria annua*
monkey flower	Mimulus
monkshood	Aconitum
montbretia	Crocosmia
moonwort	Lunaria
morning glory	Convolvulus
mother of thousands	Tolmiea

COMMON NAME	BOTANICAL NAME
mouse plant	*Arisarum proboscideum*
mousemilk	Euphorbia
mugwort	Artemisia
mukdenia	Mukdenia
mullein	Verbascum
mum	Chrysanthemum
nasturtium	Tropaeolum
navelwort	Omphalodes
New Zealand burr	Acaena
New Zealand satin flower	Libertia
obedient plant	Physostegia
oregano	Origanum
Oswego tea	*Monarda didyma*
oxeye daisy	Buphthalmum, Leucanthemum
oxlip	*Primula elatior*
pansy	Viola
Pasque flower	*Pulsatilla vulgaris*
pearly everlasting	Anaphalis
peony	Paeonia
perennial candytuft	Iberis
Peruvian lily	Alstroemeria
pigsqueak	Bergenia
piggyback plant	Tolmiea
pinchusion flower	Scabiosa
pineapple flower	Eucomis
pinkroot	Spigelia
pinks	Dianthus
plantain	Plantago
plaintain lily	Hosta
plumbago	Ceratostigma
plume poppy	Macleaya

COMMON NAME	BOTANICAL NAME
plume thistle	Cirsium
poke	Phytolacca
poker plant	Kniphofia
pokeweed	Phytolacca
poppy	Papaver
poppy mallow	Callirhoe
pot marjoram	Origanum
prairie mallow	Sidalcea
prickly rhubarb	Gunnera
primrose	Primula
pyrethrum	*Tanacetum coccineum*
quamash	Camassia
red hot poker	Kniphofia
red valerian	Centranthus
rhubarb, ornamental	Rheum
Rodgers' flower	Rodgersia
rose campion	*Lychnis coronaria*
rue anemone	Anemonella
Russian sage	Perovskia
sage	Salvia
sea holly	Eryngium
sea pink	Armeria
seakale	*Crambe maritima*
Shasta daisy	Leucanthemum
sheep's bit	Jasione
sheepsburr	Acaena
shepherd's scabious	Jasione
shieldleaf rodgersia	*Astilboides tabularis*
shooting star	Dodecatheon
shuttlecock flower	Kirengeshoma
Siberian bugloss	Brunnera
silver dollar plant	*Lunaria annua*

COMMON NAME	BOTANICAL NAME
snakeroot	Cimicifuga
sneezeweed	Helenium
snow poppy	Eomecon
soapwort	Saponaria
Solomon's seal	Polygonatum
sorrel	Rumex
southernwood	*Artemisia abrotanum*
speedwell	Veronica
spiderwort	Tradescantia
spignel	Meum
spotted deadnettle	Lamium
spotted dog	Pulmonaria
spring vetchling	*Lathyrus vernus*
spurge	Euphorbia
star of Persia	*Allium cristophii*
stinking nettle	Strobilanthes
Stokes' aster	Stokesia
stonecrop	Sedum
strawberry	Fragaria
summer hyacinth	Galtonia
sundrops	Oenothera
sunflower	Helianthus
sunray	Inula
sweet arum	Pinellia
sweet Cicely	Myrrhis
sweet coltsfoot	Petasites
sweet flag	Acorus
tansy (silver)	*Tanacetum niveum*
thousand-flowered aster	Boltonia
thrift	Armeria
tickseed	Bidens, Coreopsis

COMMON NAME	BOTANICAL NAME
toadflax	Linaria
toad lily	Tricyrtis
tongues and lugs	Stachys
torch lily	Kniphofia
treacleberry	Smilacina
tree celandine	Macleaya
turtlehead	Chelone
twinleaf	Jeffersonia
twinspur	Diascia
umbrella plant	Darmera
valerian	Centranthus, Valeriana
vervain	*Verbena rigida*
violet	Viola
Virginia bluebells	*Mertensia virginica*
Virginia cowslip	*Mertensia virginica*
wake robin	Trillium
wallflower	Erysimum
water parsley	Oenanthe
Welsh poppy	*Meconopsis cambrica*
white horehound	*Marrubium vulgare*
whorlflower	*Morina longifolia*
wild indigo	Baptisia
willow herb	Epilobium
windflower	Anemone
windmill flower	Gaura
wolfsbane	Aconitum
wormwood	Artemisia
yarrow	Achillea
yellow asphodel	*Asphodeline lutea*
yellow waxbells	Kirengeshoma
yellow-eyed grass	*Sisyrinchium californicum*

NURSERIES AND SOURCES

MAIL-ORDER NURSERIES

Some of these nurseries can be visited; call first or check their Web site.

Aitken's Salmon Creek Garden
608 NW 119th St.
Vancouver, WA 98685
360.573.4472
www.flowerfancy.net

B&D Lilies/Snow Creek Gardens
284555 Hwy 101 S.
Port Townsend, WA 98368
360.765.7341
www.bdlilies.com

Bluestone Perennials
7211 Middle Ridge Rd.
Madison, OH 44057
800.999.9972
www.bluestoneperennials.com

Canyon Creek Nursery
3527 Dry Creek Rd.
Oroville, CA 95965
530.533.2166
www.canyoncreeknursery.com

Collector's Nursery
16804 NE 102nd Ave.
Battle Ground, WA 98604
www.collectorsnursery.com

Digging Dog
P.O. Box 471
Albion, CA 95410
707.937.1130
www.diggingdog.com

Forest Farm
990 Tetherow Rd.
Williams, OR 97544
541.846.7269
www.forestfarm.com

Geraniaceae
122 Hillcrest Ave.
Kentfield, CA 94904
415.461.4168
www.geranaceae.com

Gossler Farms Nursery
1200 Weaver Rd.
Springfield, OR 97378
541.746.3922
www.gosslerfarms.com

Jackson & Perkins Company
1 Rose Ln.
Medford, OR 97501
877.322.2300
www.jacksonandperkins.com

Joy Creek Nursery
20300 NW Watson Rd.
Scappoose, OR 97956
503.543.6933
www.joycreek.com

Klehm's Song Sparrow Farm & Nursery
13101 E. Rye Rd.
Avalon, WI 53505
800.553.3715
www.songsparrow.com

Mt. Tahoma Nursery
28111 112th Ave. E.
Graham, WA 98338
253.847.9827

Naylor Creek Nursery
2610 W. Valley Rd.
Chimacum, WA 98325
360.732.4983
www.naylorcreek.com

Niche Gardens
1111 Dawson Rd.
Chapel Hill, NC 27516
919.967.0078
www.nichegardens.com

Plant Delights Nursery
9241 Sauls Rd.
Raleigh, NC 27603
919.772.4794
www.plantdelights.com

Reath's Nursery
N 195 County Rd. 577
Vulcan, MI 49892
906.563.9777
www.reathsnursery.com

Roslyn Nursery
211 Burrs Ln.
Dix Hills, NE 11746
515.643.9347
www.roslynnursery.com

Siskiyou Rare Plant Nursery
2825 Cummings Rd.
Medford, OR 97501
541.772.6846
www.srpn.net

Wayside Gardens
1 Garden Ln.
Hodges, SC 29695
800.213.0379
www.waysidegardens.com

White Flower Farm
P.O. Box 50, Rt. 63
Litchfield, CT 06759
800.503.9624
www.whiteflowerfarm.com

RETAIL NURSERIES

Bouquet Banque Nursery & Gardens
8220 State Ave.
Marysville, WA 98270
360.659.4938

Christianson's Nursery
15806 Best Rd.
Mt. Vernon, WA 98273
360.466.3821
www.christiansonsnursery.com

Cistus Nursery
22711 NW Gillihan Rd.
Sauvie Island, OR 97231
503.621.2233
www.cistus.com

City Peoples Garden Store
2939 Madison
Seattle, WA 98112
206.324.0737

Coldsprings Garden Nursery
18013 W. Snoqualmie Valley Rd. NE
Duvall, WA 98019
www.csplants.com

Cultus Bay Nursery
7568 Cultus Bay Rd.
Clinton, WA 98236
360.579.2329

DIG Floral & Garden
19028½ Vashon Hwy. SW
Vashon, WA 98070
206.463.5096

Emerisa Gardens
555 Irwin Ln.
Santa Rosa, CA 95401
707.525.9600
www.emerisa.com

Emery's Garden
2829 164th St. SW
Lynnwood, WA 98037
425.743.4555 (call first)
www.emerysgarden.com

Fremont Gardens
4001 Leary Way NW
Seattle, WA 98107
206.781.8283
www.fremontgardens.com

Hedgerows Nursery
20165 SW Christensen Rd.
McMinnville, OR 97128
503.843.7522

Madrona Nursery
815 38th Ave.
Seattle, WA 98122
206.323.8325 (call first)

Molbak's
13625 NE 175th St.
Woodinville, WA 98072
425.483.5000
www.molbaks.com

Northwest Garden Nursery
86813 Central Rd.
Eugene, OR 97402
541.935.3915 (call first)
www.northwestgardennursery.com

Portland Nursery
5050 SE Stark
Portland, OR 97215
503.231.5050
www.portlandnursery.com

Steamboat Island Nursery
8424 Steamboat Island Rd.
Olympia, WA 98502
360.866.2516
www.olywa.net/steamboat

Sundquist Nursery, Inc.
3809 NE Sawdust Hill Rd.
Poulsbo, WA 98370
360.779.6343 (call first)

Swans Trail Gardens
7021 61st Ave. SE
Snohomish, WA 98290
425.334.4595
www.swanstrailgardens.com

Swanson's Nursery
9701 15th Ave NW
Seattle, WA 98117
206.782.2543
www.swansonsnursery.com

The Garden Spot Nursery
900 Alabama St.
Bellingham, WA 98225
www.garden-spot.com

Wells Medina Nursery
8300 NE 24th
Medina, WA 98038
425.454.1853
www.wellsmedina.com

RECOMMENDED READING

Besides the general and regional books we list here, there are many excellent monographs (books on a specific genus) that we think are worth seeking out for further depth.

Bird, Richard. *Cultivation of Hardy Perennials*. London: B. T. Batsford Ltd, 1994.

Brickell, Christopher, and Judith D. Zuk, eds. *The American Horticultural Society A–Z Encyclopedia of Garden Plants*. New York: DK Publishing, 1997.

Chatto, Beth. *Damp Garden*. Sagaponack, N.Y.: Sagapress, Inc., 1996.

——. *Dry Garden*. Sagaponack, N.Y.: Sagapress, Inc., 1996.

——. *Gravel Garden*. London: Frances Lincoln Ltd., 2000.

Coombes, Allen J. *Dictionary of Plant Names*. Portland, Ore.: Timber Press, 1994.

Hansen, Richard, and Frederich Stahl. *Perennials and Their Garden Habitats*. Portland, Ore.: Timber Press, 1993.

Harper, Pamela J. *Time-Tested Plants: Thirty Years in a Four-Season Garden*. Portland, Ore.: Timber Press, 2000.

Hickey, Michael, and Clive King. *The Cambridge Illustrated Glossary of Botanical Terms*. Cambridge: Cambridge University Press, 2000.

Hill, Susan, and Susan Narizny. *The Plant Locator, Western Region*. Portland, Ore.: Timber Press, 2004.

Jelitto, Leo, and Wilhelm Schacht. *Hardy Herbaceous Perennials*. 2 vols. Portland, Ore.: Timber Press, 1990.

Kingsbury, Noël. *The New Perennial Garden*. London: Frances Lincoln Ltd., 1996.

Liberty Hyde Bailey Hortorium of Cornell University. *Hortus Third: A Concise Dictionary of Plants Cultivated in the United States and Canada*. Indianapolis, Ind.: Wiley Publishers, 1976.

Lovejoy, Ann. *The American Mixed Border: Gardens for All Seasons*. New York: Macmillan Publishing Co., 1993.

——. *Cascadia: Inspired Gardening in the Pacific Northwest*. Seattle: Sasquatch, 1997.

——. *The Garden in Bloom: Plants and Wisdom for the Year-Round Gardener in the Pacific Northwest*. Seattle: Sasquatch, 1998.

——. *The Ann Lovejoy Handbook of Northwest Gardening*. Seattle: Sasquatch, 2003.

——. *The Border in Bloom: A Northwest Garden Through the Seasons*. Seattle: Sasquatch, 2003.

Phillips, Roger, and Martyn Rix. *Random House Book of Perennials*. 2 vols. New York: Random House, 1991.

Rice, Graham. *Reader's Digest: The Complete Book of Perennials*. Pleasantville, N.Y.: Reader's Digest Association, 1996.

Royal Horticulture Society. *RHS Plant Finder*. London: Dorling Kindersley Ltd. (updated yearly).

Stearn, William T. *Stearn's Dictionary of Plant Names for Gardeners*. Portland, Ore.: Timber Press, 1996.

Sunset Western Garden Book. Menlo Park, Calif.: Sunset Publishing Corp., 2006.

Thomas, Graham Stuart. *Perennial Garden Plants*. Portland, Ore.: Sagapress/Timber Press, 1990.

Thompson, Peter. *Creative Propagation*. 2nd ed. Portland, Ore.: Timber Press, 2005.

USDA PLANT HARDINESS ZONE MAP

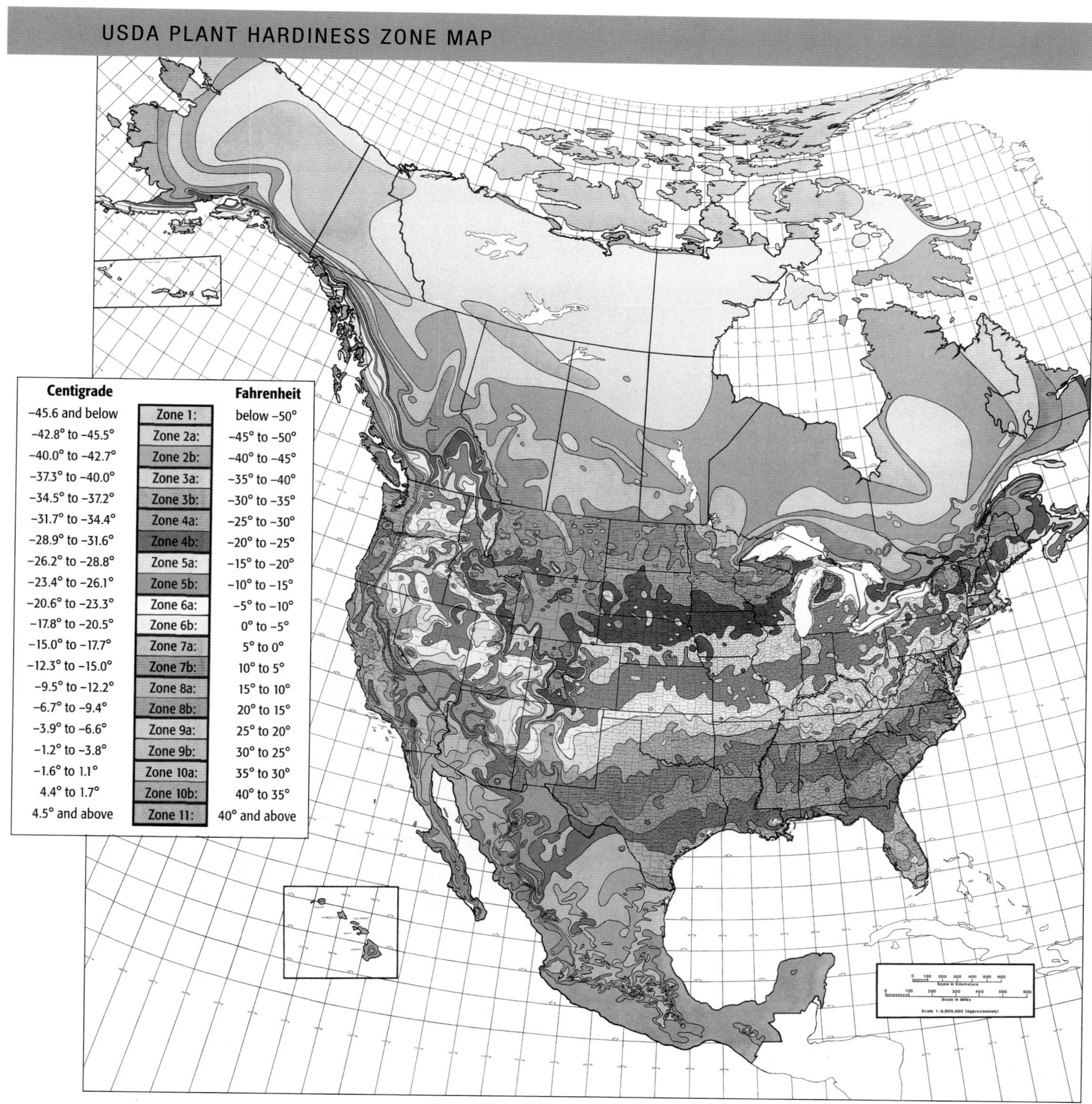

Centigrade
Fahrenheit
-45.6 and below | Zone 1: | below -50°
-42.8° to -45.5° | Zone 2a: | -45° to -50°
-40.0° to -42.7° | Zone 2b: | -40° to -45°
-37.3° to -40.0° | Zone 3a: | -35° to -40°
-34.5° to -37.2° | Zone 3b: | -30° to -35°
-31.7° to -34.4° | Zone 4a: | -25° to -30°
-28.9° to -31.6° | Zone 4b: | -20° to -25°
-26.2° to -28.8° | Zone 5a: | -15° to -20°
-23.4° to -26.1° | Zone 5b: | -10° to -15°
-20.6° to -23.3° | Zone 6a: | -5° to -10°
-17.8° to -20.5° | Zone 6b: | 0° to -5°
-15.0° to -17.7° | Zone 7a: | 5° to 0°
-12.3° to -15.0° | Zone 7b: | 10° to 5°
-9.5° to -12.2° | Zone 8a: | 15° to 10°
-6.7° to -9.4° | Zone 8b: | 20° to 15°
-3.9° to -6.6° | Zone 9a: | 25° to 20°
-1.2° to -3.8° | Zone 9b: | 30° to 25°
-1.6° to 1.1° | Zone 10a: | 35° to 30°
4.4° to 1.7° | Zone 10b: | 40° to 35°
4.5° and above | Zone 11: | 40° and above

INDEX

Synonyms are given parenthetically; photographs are indicated by **boldface** page numbers.